# Reading and Writing About Contemporary Issues

### Kathleen T. McWhorter
*Niagara County Community College*

**PEARSON**

Boston   Columbus   Indianapolis   New York   San Francisco   Upper Saddle River
Amsterdam   Cape Town   Dubai   London   Madrid   Milan   Munich   Paris   Montréal   Toronto
Delhi   Mexico City   São Paulo   Sydney   Hong Kong   Seoul   Singapore   Taipei   Tokyo

Executive Editor: Matthew Wright
Editorial Assistant: Laura Marenghi
Senior Development Editor: Gillian Cook
Senior Supplements Editor: Donna Campion
Executive Digital Producer: Stefanie Snajder
Executive Marketing Manager: Roxanne McCarley
Production Manager: Denise Phillip Grant
Project Coordination, Text Design, and Electronic
    Page Makeup: PreMediaGlobal, Inc.

Cover Designer/Manager: John Callahan
Cover Image: © Richard T. Nowitz / Corbis
Photo Researcher: Integra
Text permissions: Aptara Group
Senior Manufacturing Buyer: Dennis Para
Printer/Binder: R. R. Donnelley / Crawfordsville
Cover Printer: Lehigh-Phoenix Color Hagerstown

Credits and acknowledgments borrowed from other sources and reproduced, with permission, in this textbook
appear on the appropriate page within text and on pages 679–681.

**Library of Congress Cataloging-in-Publication Data**
McWhorter, Kathleen T.
    Reading and writing about contemporary issues / Kathleen McWhorter, Niagara County
Community College. —First edition.
        pages cm
    ISBN-13: 978-0-321-84442-2 (alk. paper)
    ISBN-10: 0-321-84442-4 (alk. paper)
    1. College readers.    2. Readers—Current events.    3. English language—Rhetoric—Problems, exercises, etc.
4.  Report writing—Problems, exercises, etc.    5. Current events—Problems, exercises, etc.    I. Title.
    PE1417.M45653 2015
    808'.0427—dc23                                                                                    2013030025

Copyright © 2015 by Pearson Education, Inc.

10 9 8 7 6 5 4 3 2 1—DOC—17 16 15 14

Student Edition ISBN-13: 978-0-321-84442-2
Student Edition ISBN-10:     0-321-84442-4
A la Carte Edition ISBN-13: 978-0-321-95961-4
A la Carte Edition ISBN-10:     0-321-95961-2

# Brief Contents

# Detailed Contents

**PART TWO    Reading and Writing About Contemporary Issues 325**

# Preface

## PURPOSE

*Reading and Writing About Contemporary Issues* offers an integrated approach to reading and writing, using a handbook for reference and instruction followed by readings for analysis and writing. The nonfiction readings are organized into units that focus on contemporary issues. Chosen to interest and motivate students, they are drawn from books, textbooks, periodicals, popular magazines, newspapers, blogs, Web sites, and Internet sources with the objective of providing stimulating readings that enable students to apply reading and critical thinking skills and respond to text through writing.

## CONTENT OVERVIEW

*Reading and Writing About Contemporary Issues* guides students in developing basic vocabulary and comprehension skills, as well as inferential and critical reading and thinking skills. Writing skills are cultivated through skill review, activities, and writing prompts that require students to write in response to the articles and essays they read. The text is organized into three parts:

- **Part One, A Handbook for Reading and Writing in College,** presents a concise introduction to reading and writing skills. Written in handbook format (1a, 1b, etc.), this part serves as a guide and reference tool for the skills students need to read and write about the readings in Part Two.
- **Part Two, Reading and Writing About Contemporary Issues,** consists of eight chapters, each containing three reading selections on a contemporary issue for reading and response.
- **Part Three, Casebook for Critical Thinking: Global Warming and Climate Change,** contains eight sources that offer a focused, in-depth examination of a single contemporary issue—global warming and climate change.

## FORMAT OF PART ONE: A HANDBOOK FOR CRITICAL THINKING AND READING IN COLLEGE

The handbook guides students in learning the reading, critical thinking, and writing skills essential for college success. It contains the following features:

- **Integrated approach to reading and writing.** Reading and writing are approached as complementary processes that are best learned together. A concise overview of both the reading and writing processes is followed by integrated coverage of topics such as strategies for strengthening vocabulary for reading and writing, reading and writing paragraphs and essays, organizing information, thinking critically, recognizing and using organizational patterns, and writing a documented paper.

- **Students approach reading and writing as thinking.** Reading and writing are approached as thinking processes involving interaction with textual material and sorting, evaluating, and responding to its organization and content. The apparatus preceding and following each reading focuses, guides, and shapes the students' thought processes and encourages thoughtful and reasoned responses.

- **Students develop a wide range of critical reading and thinking skills.** Because simply understanding what a writer says is seldom sufficient in college courses, this handbook teaches students to examine, interpret, analyze, and evaluate ideas. Students learn to make inferences, consider an author's techniques, and identify his or her biases in relation to the message presented.

- **Students learn to analyze and write arguments.** Because argumentation is an important part of both academic discourse and workplace and everyday communication, students learn to read and analyze arguments and to plan, develop, organize, write, and revise effective written arguments.

- **Students learn to write in response to what they read.** Most college reading assignments require written responses of some sort—essay exams, papers, or research projects. This text shows students how to analyze reading and writing assignments and teaches them the important skills of annotating, paraphrasing, outlining, and mapping, which enable and prepare them to write response papers.

- **Students learn to write a documented paper.** Writing a documented paper is required in many college courses. Students learn to identify trustworthy sources, extract information from them so as to avoid plagiarism, integrate information from sources into essays, and use the MLA documentation system.

- **Students can refer to Part One to get help answering questions.** The activities following each reading are parallel to the topics in Part One of the text, so if students have difficulty answering a question, they may refer to the relevant section in Part One for further explanation.

**MySkillsLab**
- **Students can test their understanding of chapter content right in MySkillsLab!** The eText/MySkillsLab *Reading and Writing About Contemporary Issues* book-specific module contains end-of-chapter assessments that flow directly into the MySkillsLab instructor Gradebook.

## FORMAT OF PART TWO: READING AND WRITING ABOUT CONTEMPORARY ISSUES

Each chapter in Part Two begins with an introduction that focuses students' attention on the issue, provides context and background information, discusses its importance and relevance to college coursework, and includes tips for reading about the issue. Each chapter contains three readings, each of which is preceded by previewing questions and followed by exercises that allow students to practice and apply the reading and writing strategies covered in Part One. Part Two concludes with a "Making Connections" section that contains Thinking Within the Issues and Thinking Across the Issues activities that encourage students to synthesize two or more readings within a given chapter and to synthesize ideas related to readings in two or more chapters.

- **Choice of Readings.** Nonfiction readings were chosen to be interesting and engaging and to serve as good models of writing. These readings are taken from a variety of sources including textbooks, books, online sites, magazines, and blogs. Issues include extreme weather, sustainability, body image, minimum wage, bilingualism, and group conformity. Three student essays are also included to provide realistic models of student writing.

- **Lexile Levels for All Readings.** Lexile® measure—the most widely used reading metric in U.S. schools—provides valuable information about a student's reading ability and the complexity of text. It helps match students with reading resources and activities that are targeted to their ability level. Lexile measures indicate the reading levels of content in MyReadingLab and the longer selections in the Annotated Instructor's Editions of all Pearson's reading books. See the Annotated Instructor's Edition of (text) and the Instructor's Manual for more details.

**MySkillsLab**

- **MySkillsLab.** Most of the exercises that follow each reading can be completed in the book specific module in MySkillsLab.

## Organization of the Apparatus

- **Source and Context.** This brief section introduces the reading, identifies its source, provokes the students' interest, and provides a framework or context for reading.
- **A Note on the Reading.** This section is intended to introduce and interest students in the reading and help them establish a purpose for reading.
- **Previewing the Reading.** Students are directed to preview the reading using the guidelines provided in Chapter One and to answer a few questions based on their preview.
- **Making Connections.** This brief section encourages students to draw connections between the topic of the reading and their own knowledge and experience.
- **Reading Tip.** A different reading tip is offered for each reading. For example, a reading tip might suggest how to highlight to strengthen comprehension or how to write annotations to enhance critical thinking.
- **Reading Selection/Vocabulary Annotation.** Most reading selections contain some vocabulary words, specific to the topic, that are essential to the meaning of the selection. Often these are words that students are unlikely to know and cannot figure out from context. These words are bolded, and their meanings are given as marginal annotations.

### Understanding and Analyzing the Reading

- **Building Vocabulary.** The first part of this section focuses on vocabulary in context, while the second is concerned with word parts. Using words from the reading selection, exercises are structured to encourage students to expand their vocabulary and strengthen their word-analysis skills.

- **Understanding the Thesis and Other Main Ideas.** This section helps students figure out the thesis of the reading and identify the main idea of selected paragraphs.

- **Identifying Details.** This section focuses on recognizing the relationship between main ideas and details, as well as distinguishing primary from secondary details. The format of questions within this section varies to expose students to a variety of thinking strategies.

- **Recognizing Methods of Organization and Transitions.** This section guides students in identifying the overall organizational pattern of the selection and in identifying signal words and phrases. Prompts serve as teaching tips or review strategies.

- **Reading and Thinking Visually.** Since textbooks and electronic media have become increasingly visual, students need to be able to read, interpret, and analyze visuals. This section guides students in responding to visuals that accompany text.

- **Figuring Out Implied Meanings.** The ability to think inferentially is expected of college students. This section guides students in making inferences based on information presented in the reading selection.

- **Thinking Critically: Analyzing the Author's Technique.** This section encourages students to examine the techniques and strategies writers use to convey their message. Skills include distinguishing fact from opinion, identifying the author's purpose, identifying tone, and analyzing figurative language.

- **Thinking Critically: Analyzing the Author's Message.** In this section students learn to analyze ideas presented by an author in terms of bias, the reliability of the data and evidence provided, and evaluation of the quantity, relevance, and timeliness of information.

### Writing in Response to the Reading

Questions in this section are intended to stimulate thought, provoke discussion, and serve as a springboard to writing about the reading.

- **Reviewing and Organizing Ideas.** Many students are proficient at literal recall of information but have difficulty condensing and organizing it into usable formats for study and review, this section offers instruction and practice in summarizing, paraphrasing, and mapping.

- **Analyzing the Issue and Argument.** These open-ended questions encourage students to think critically and formulate an oral or written response to the issues raised in the reading.

- **Writing Paragraphs and Essays.** This section contains paragraph and/or essay writing assignments that give students practice in writing in response to what they read. The writing prompts ask students to explore issues related to the chapter theme and to examine applications of the issue to their lives and the world around them.

### Activities: Exploring Issues

Appearing at the end of each chapter, this section asks students to synthesize what they have learned about the issue, extend their critical reading and thinking skills, and explore the issue further through discussion and writing.

## FORMAT OF PART THREE: CASEBOOK FOR CRITICAL THINKING: GLOBAL WARMING AND CLIMATE CHANGE

The Casebook contains eight readings from a variety of genres (online news, blogs, essays, textbooks, and infographics) that embody different perspectives on the issue of global warming and climate change, demonstrating the far-reaching social, financial, economic, and geographic implications of a single contemporary issue. The introduction provides tips for reading about the issue, synthesizing sources, and previewing. Each selection is followed by critical thinking questions and a collaborative exercise, and the "Synthesis and Integration Questions and Activities" section at the end of the Casebook encourages students to synthesize the information in the sources.

## A MODULARIZED APPROACH AND CUSTOMIZATION

*Reading Across the Disciplines* (ISBN: 0-321-96532-9), also by Kathleen McWhorter, emphasizes academic, discipline-based reading skills. It has a similar structure to *Reading and Writing About Contemporary Issues*, but chapters are organized by discipline, and Part Three contains a unique classroom simulation built around a textbook chapter excerpt. The excerpt from a interpersonal communication textbook is treated as a classroom reading assignment. Students prepare for a class lecture on the assignment, read the assignment, review the assignment, attend the lecture and participate in simulated class activities, write about the assignment, take quizzes based on the assignment, and take an exam based on the assignment.

Both books are modular in structure and can be customized to meet instructor's needs. However, instructor's may also draw chapters from both books to create a custom text with a mix of instructional topics and academic and contemporarily themed readings to accommodate student needs and interests. Additional modules written by Kathleen McWhorter (including a chapter on academic reading and writing, a casebook on the digital revolution, a biology based classroom simulation, and discipline and issue themed chapters) are also available through the Pearson Custom Library.

## TEXT-SPECIFIC ANCILLARIES

**Annotated Instructor's Edition for** *Reading and Writing About Contemporary Issues* **(ISBN 0-321-95955-8)**

The Annotated Instructor's Edition is identical to the student text but includes all the answers printed directly on the pages where questions, exercises, or activities appear.

**Instructor's Resource Manual/Test Bank for** *Reading and Writing About Contemporary Issues* **(ISBN 0-321-95948-5)**

The online Instructor's Resource Manual contains general information on how to teach an integrated course, plus a teaching tip sheet, sample pacing guide, syllabus, and other useful handouts. It includes teaching suggestions and handouts for Part One (Chapters 1-11) and provides collaborative activities that complement the readings and offers students opportunities to think critically and solve problems in a group setting for Part Two. In addition, it contains tips for teaching the Part Three Casebook and suggested writing activities and topics for each reading. The Test Bank contains a set of multiple choice, content review quizzes for Chapters 1-11 formatted for easy distribution and scoring.

**PowerPoint Presentation for** *Reading and Writing About Contemporary Issues* **(ISBN 0-321-95958-2)**

A chapter-by-chapter set of slides are available for download from the Instructor Resource Center for adopters of the text.

**Answer Key for** *Reading and Writing About Contemporary Issues* **(ISBN 0-321-95959-0)**

The Answer Key contains the solutions to the exercises in the student edition of the text. Available for download from the Instructor Resource Center.

## MYSKILLSLAB

**MySkillsLab** Efficiently blending the market-leading and proven practice from MyWritingLab and MyReadingLab into a single application and learning path, MySkillsLab offers a wealth of practice opportunity and extensive progress tracking for integrated reading-writing courses.

For more than half a decade, MySkillsLab has been the most widely used online learning application for the integrated reading-writing course across two- and four-year institutions. We have published case studies demonstrating how MySkillsLab (or, individually, MyReadingLab and MyWritingLab) consistently benefits students' mastery of key reading skills, reading comprehension, writing skills, and critical thinking.

**Reading** MySkillsLab improves students' mastery of 26 reading skills across four levels of difficulty via mastery-based skill practice, and improves students' reading levels with the Lexile® framework (www.Lexile.com) to measure both reader ability and text difficulty on the same scale and pair students with readings within their Lexile range.

**Writing** MySkillsLab offers skill remediation in grammar and punctuation, paragraph development, essay development, and research, and improves students' overall writing through automatic scoring by Pearson's proven Intelligent Essay Assessor (IEA).

**A Deeper Connection Between Print and Media:** Pearson's MySkillsLab (www.myskillslab.com) is deeply integrated into the assignments and activities in *Reading and Writing About Contemporary Issues*. Students can complete and submit various exercises and activities within the eText / MySkillsLab course and the results flow right to the Instructor Gradebook.

## ACKNOWLEDGEMENTS

I would like to express my gratitude to my reviewers for their excellent ideas, suggestions, and advice on the preparation and revision of this text:

Wes Anthony, *Cleveland Community College;* Andrea Berta, *University of Texas–El Paso;* Frances Boffo, *St. Phillip's College;* Louise Brown, *Salt Lake Community College;* Lyam Christopher, *Palm Beach State College;* Louise Clark, *Austin Community College;* Yanely Cordero, *Miami Dade, Homestead;* Cynthia Crable, *Allegany College of Maryland;* Kathy Daily, *Tulsa Community College;* Crystal Edmonds, *Robeson Community College;* Scott Empric, *Housatonic Community College;* Sally Gearhart, *Santa Rosa Junior College;* Brent Green, *Salt Lake Community College;* Elizabeth Hall, *RCC;* Caroline Helsabeck, *Forsyth Technical Community College;* Eric Hibbison, *J. Sargeant Reynolds Community College;* Suzanne Hughes, *Florida State College at Jacksonville;* Jennifer Johnson, *Vance-Granville Community College;* Patty Kunkel, *Santa Fe College;* James Landers, *Community College of Philadelphia;* Dawn Langley, *Piedmont Community College;* Joy Lester, *Forsyth Technical Community College;* Nancy Marguardt, *Gaston College;* Barbara Marshall, *Rockingham Community College;* Susan Monroe, *Housatonic Community College;* Emily Chevalier Moore, *Wake Technical Community College;* Arlene Neal, *Catawba Valley Community College;* Karen Nelson, *Craven Community College;* Mary Nielson, *Dalton State College;* Elizabeth A. O'Scanlon, *Santa Barbara Community College;* Gloria Rabun, *Caldwell Community College;* Adalia Reyna, *South Texas College;* Jason Roberts, *Salt Lake Community College;* Amy Rule, *Collin College;* Mike Sfiropoilos, *Palm Beach State College;* Susan Swan, *Glendale Community College;* Stacey Synol, *Glendale Community College;* Kelly Terzaken, *Coastal Carolina Community College;* Jeanine Williams, *The Community College of Baltimore County;* B. J. Zamora, *Cleveland Community College.*

I wish to thank Gillian Cook, my development editor, for her creative vision of the project, her helpful suggestions, her careful editing, and her overall assistance in preparing and organizing the manuscript. I also thank Eric Stano, Editor-in-Chief of Developmental Education, for his support of the project.

Finally, I owe a debt of gratitude to Kathy Tyndall, recently retired department head of the Pre-Curriculum Department at Wake Technical Community College, for consulting with me about the project.

# A Handbook for Reading and Writing in College

# 1 Active Reading Strategies

What does it take to do well in college? In answer to this question, many college students are likely to say:

- "Knowing how to study."
- "You have to like the course."
- "Hard work!"
- "Background in the subject area."
- "A good teacher!"

Students seldom mention reading and writing as essential skills. In a sense, reading and writing are the hidden factors in college success. When you think of college, you think of attending classes and labs, completing assignments, studying for and taking exams, doing research in the library or on the Internet, and writing papers. A closer look at these activities, however, reveals that reading and writing are important parts of each.

Throughout this handbook you will learn numerous ways to use reading and writing as tools for college success. You will improve your basic comprehension skills and learn to think critically about the materials you read. Thinking critically is essential to analyzing and evaluating not only college reading materials (textbooks, journal articles, research papers, and so on) but also materials that are written for a wider audience (newspapers, magazines, Web sites, and so on). You will also learn to write effective paragraphs and essays and use your skills to respond to articles, essays, and textbook excerpts that you read. Finally, you will also learn to handle high-stakes writing assignments that involve using sources to explain and support your own ideas.

## 1a    ACTIVE READING: THE KEY TO ACADEMIC SUCCESS

**LEARNING OBJECTIVE 1**
Learn to read actively

Reading involves much more than moving your eyes across lines of print, more than recognizing words, and more than reading sentences. Reading is *thinking*. It is an active process of identifying important ideas and comparing, evaluating, and applying them.

Have you ever gone to a ball game and watched the fans? Most do not sit and watch passively. Instead, they direct the plays, criticize the calls, encourage the players, and reprimand the coach. They care enough to get actively involved in the game. Just like interested fans, active readers get involved. They question, challenge, and criticize, as well as understand. Table 1-1 contrasts the active strategies of successful readers with the passive strategies of less successful readers. Not all strategies will work for everyone. Experiment to discover those that work particularly well for you.

### TABLE 1-1  ACTIVE VERSUS PASSIVE READING

| ACTIVE READERS ... | PASSIVE READERS ... |
| --- | --- |
| Tailor their reading to suit each assignment. | Read all assignments the same way. |
| Analyze the purpose of an assignment. | Read an assignment because it was assigned. |
| Adjust their speed to suit their purpose. | Read everything at the same speed. |
| Question ideas in the assignment. | Accept whatever is in print as true. |
| Compare and connect textbook material with lecture content. | Study lecture notes and the textbook separately. |
| Skim headings to find out what an assignment is about before beginning to read. | Check the length of an assignment and then begin reading. |
| Make sure they understand what they are reading as they go along. | Read until the assignment is completed. |
| Read with pencil in hand, highlighting, jotting notes, and marking key vocabulary. | Read. |
| Develop personalized strategies that are particularly effective. | Follow routine, standard methods. Read all assignments the same way. |
| Look for the relevance of the assignment to their own lives. | Fixate on memorizing terms and definitions solely to pass the exam or get a good grade. |
| Engage with the contemporary issues under discussion with an open mind. | React emotionally to reading assignments without taking the time to carefully consider the author's key points. |

*Consider each of the following reading assignments. Discuss ways to get actively involved in each assignment.*

1.  Reading two poems by Maya Angelou for an American literature class.

    _____

    _____

2.  Reading the procedures for your next chemistry lab.

    _____

3.  Reading an article in *Time* magazine, or on the *Time* magazine Web site, assigned by your political science instructor in preparation for a class discussion.

    _____

    _____

## PRE-READING STRATEGIES

## 1b    PREVIEWING BEFORE YOU READ

**LEARNING OBJECTIVE 2**
Preview before
reading

**Previewing** is a means of familiarizing yourself with the content and organization of an assignment *before* you read it. Think of previewing as getting a "sneak preview" of what a chapter or reading will be about. You can then read the material more easily and more rapidly.

### How to Preview Reading Assignments

Use the following tips to preview an entire source, such as a complete book or magazine.

- **Books, textbooks, and essay collections:** Look at the table of contents (found at the front of the book), noting the titles of chapters or essays. These will give you an overall sense of the topics covered.

- **Magazines:** Examine the table of contents, noting the sections and the articles included in the magazine. For instance, a weekly news magazine often has articles listed under categories such as Politics, Movies and Books, Business, and People.

- **Newspapers:** Flip through the paper, noting the largest (most important) headlines and the categories covered, such as local news, international news, and sports. If the newspaper has sections, flip through them to look for the materials in which you are most interested. Many newspapers feature different sections on different days, for example, a special science section on Tuesday or an entertainment section on Saturday.

- **Web sites:** Use the navigation panel (usually found at the top, bottom, left, or right of the screen) to understand how the site is organized. Click on each section and look for large headlines or any other element that stands out on the screen.

After you have previewed the full source, use the following steps to become familiar with the content and organization of a chapter, essay, or article, either print or online.

1. **Read the title and subtitle.** The title indicates the topic of the article or chapter; the subtitle suggests the specific focus of, or approach to, the topic.

2. **Check the author and source of an article or essay.** This information may provide clues about the article's content or focus. If you are reading a collection of essays, each essay may provide a **head note** before the essay. Head notes often provide concise background information about the author and the article.

3. **Read the introduction or the first paragraph.** The introduction or first paragraph serves as a lead-in, establishing the overall subject and suggesting how it will be developed.

4. **Read each boldfaced (dark black print) or colored heading.** Headings label the contents of each section and announce the major topic covered. If there are no headings, read the first sentence of each paragraph.

5. **Read the first sentence under each heading.** The first sentence often states the main point of the section. If the first sentence seems introductory, read the last sentence; often this sentence states or restates the main point.

6. **If headings are not provided, read the first sentence of several paragraphs per page.** This sentence is often the topic sentence, which states the main idea of the paragraph. By reading first sentences, you will encounter most of the key ideas in the article.

7. **Note any typographical aids and information presented in list format.** Colored print, **boldface**, and *italics* are often used to emphasize important terminology and definitions, distinguishing them from the rest of a passage. Material that is numbered 1, 2, 3; lettered a, b, c; or presented in list form is also of special importance.

8. **Read the first sentence of each item presented as a list.**

9. **Note any graphic aids.** Graphs, charts, photographs, and tables often suggest what is important. As part of your preview, read the captions of photographs and the legends on graphs, charts, and tables.

10. **Read the last paragraph or summary.** This provides a condensed view of the article or chapter, often outlining the key points.

11. **Read quickly any end-of-article or end-of-chapter material.** This material might include references, study questions, discussion questions, chapter outlines, or vocabulary lists. If study questions are included, read them through quickly because they tell you what to look for in the chapter. If a vocabulary list is included, rapidly skim through it to identify the terms you will be learning as you read.

A section of a sociology textbook chapter discussing social class is reprinted here to illustrate how previewing is done. The portions to focus on when previewing are shaded. Read only those portions. After you have finished, test how well your previewing worked by completing Exercise 1-2, "What Did You Learn from Previewing?"

### Issue: Wealth and Poverty

## Consequences of Social Class

### James Henslin

1    Does social class matter? And how! Think of each social class (whether upper-class, middle-class, working-class, or poor/underclass) as a broad subculture with distinct approaches to life, so significant that it affects our health, family life, education, religion, politics, and even our experiences with crime and the criminal justice system. Let's look at how social class affects our lives.

### Physical Health

2    The principle is simple: As you go up the social-class ladder, health increases. As you go down the ladder, health decreases (Hout 2008). Age makes no difference. Infants born to the poor are more likely to die before their first birthday, and a larger percentage of poor people in their old age—whether 75 or 95—die each year than do the elderly who are wealthy.

3    How can social class have such dramatic effects? While there are many reasons, here are three. First, social class opens and closes doors to medical care. People with good incomes or with good medical insurance are able to choose their doctors and pay for whatever treatment and medications are prescribed. The poor, in contrast, don't have the money or insurance to afford this type of medical care.

4    A second reason is lifestyle, which is shaped by social class. People in the lower classes are more likely to smoke, eat a lot of fats, be overweight, abuse drugs and alcohol, get little exercise, and practice unsafe sex (Chin et al. 2000; Dolnick 2010). This, to understate the matter, does not improve people's health.

5    There is a third reason, too. Life is hard on the poor. The persistent stresses they face cause their bodies to wear out faster (Geronimus et al. 2010). The rich find life better. They have fewer problems and more resources to deal with the ones they have. This gives them a sense of control over their lives, a source of both physical and mental health.

## Mental Health

6    Sociological research from as far back as the 1930s has found that the mental health of the lower classes is worse than that of the higher classes (Faris and Dunham 1939; Srole et al. 1978; Peltham 2009). Greater mental problems are part of the higher stress that accompanies poverty. Compared with middle- and upper-class Americans, the poor have less job security and lower wages. They are more likely to divorce, to be the victims of crime, and to have more physical illnesses. Couple these conditions with bill collectors and the threat of eviction, and you can see how they can deal severe blows to people's emotional well-being.

7    People higher up the social class ladder experience stress in daily life, of course, but their stress is generally less, and their coping resources are greater. Not only can they afford vacations, psychiatrists, and counselors, but *their class position also gives them greater control over their lives, a key to good mental health.*

## Family Life

8    Social class also makes a significant difference in our choice of spouse, our chances of getting divorced, and how we rear our children.

9    **Choice of Husband or Wife.** Members of the upper class place strong emphasis on family tradition. They stress the family's history, even a sense of purpose or destiny in life (Baltzell 1979; Aldrich 1989). Children of this class learn that their choice of husband or wife affects not just them, but the entire family, that it will have an impact on the "family line." These background expectations shrink the field of "eligible" marriage partners, making it narrower than it is for the children of any other social class. As a result, parents in this class play a strong role in their children's mate selection.

10   **Divorce.** The more difficult life of the lower social classes, especially the many tensions that come from insecure jobs and inadequate incomes, leads to higher marital friction and a greater likelihood of divorce. Consequently, children of the poor are more likely to grow up in broken homes.

11   **Child Rearing.** Lower-class parents focus more on getting their children to follow rules and obey authority, while middle-class parents focus more on developing their children's creative and leadership skills (Lareau and Weininger 1977). Sociologists have traced this difference to the parents' occupations (Kohn 1977). Lower-class parents are closely supervised at work, and they anticipate that their children will have similar jobs. Consequently, they try to teach their children to defer to authority. Middle-class parents, in contrast, enjoy greater independence at work. Anticipating similar jobs for their children, they encourage them to be more creative. Out of these contrasting orientations arise different ways of disciplining children; lower-class parents are more likely to use physical punishment, while the middle classes rely more on verbal persuasion.

## Education

12   Education increases as one goes up the social class ladder. It is not just the amount of education that changes, but also the type of education. Children of the

upper class bypass public schools. They attend exclusive private schools where they are trained to take a commanding role in society. These schools teach upper-class values and prepare their students for prestigious universities (Beeghley 2008; Stevens 2009).

13    Keenly aware that private schools can be a key to upward social mobility, some upper-middle-class parents make every effort to get their children into the prestigious preschools that feed into these exclusive prep schools. Although some preschools cost $23,000 a year, they have a waiting list (Rohwedder 2007). Not able to afford this kind of tuition, some parents hire tutors to train their 4-year-olds in test-taking skills so they can get into public kindergartens for gifted students. They even hire experts to teach these preschoolers to look like adults in the eye while they are being interviewed for these limited positions (Banjo 2010). You can see how such parental involvement and resources make it more likely that children from the more privileged classes go to college—and graduate.

### Religion

14    One area of social life that we might think would not be affected by social class is religion. ("People are just religious, or they are not. What does social class have to do with it?") However, the classes tend to cluster in different religious denominations. Episcopalians, for example, are more likely to attract the middle and upper classes, while Baptists draw heavily from the lower classes. Patterns of worship also follow class lines: The lower classes are attracted to more expressive worship services and louder music, while the middle and upper classes prefer more "subdued" worship.

### Politics

15    The rich and poor walk different political paths. The higher that people are on the social class ladder, the more likely they are to vote for Republicans (Hout 2008). In contrast, most members of the working class believe that the government should intervene in the economy to provide jobs and to make citizens financially secure. They are more likely to vote for Democrats. Although the working class is more liberal on *economic issues* (policies that increase government spending), it is more conservative on *social issues* (such as opposing the Equal Rights Amendment) (Houtman 1995; Hout 2008). People toward the bottom of the class structure are also less likely to be politically active—to campaign for candidates or even to vote (Gilbert 2003; Beeghley 2008).

This young woman is being "introduced" to society at a debutante ball in Laredo, Texas. Like you, she has learned from her parents, peers, and education, a view of where she belongs in life. How do you think her view is different from yours?

### Crime and Criminal Justice

16     If justice is supposed to be blind, it certainly is not when it comes to one's chances of being arrested (Henslin 2012). Social classes commit different types of crime. The white-collar crimes of the more privileged classes are more likely to be dealt with outside the criminal justice system, while the police and courts deal with the street crimes of the lower classes. One consequence of this class standard is that members of the lower classes are more likely to be in prison, on probation, or on parole. In addition, since those who commit street crimes tend to do so in or near their own neighborhoods, the lower classes are more likely to be robbed, burglarized, or murdered.

—adapted from Henslin, *Sociology,* pp. 261–264

## EXERCISE 1-2 . . . WHAT DID YOU LEARN FROM PREVIEWING?

*Without referring to the passage, answer each of the following true/false questions.*

_____ 1. Members of the lower classes are more likely to be in prison.

_____ 2. The higher your class, the more education you are likely to have.

_____ 3. Marital friction and divorce are more common among the upper classes than the lower classes.

_____ 4. Lower-class parents tend to encourage their children's creativity.

_____ 5. The young woman in the photograph is likely a member of the upper class.

You probably were able to answer all (or most) of the questions correctly. Previewing, then, does provide you with a great deal of information. If you were to return to the passage from the textbook and read the entire section, you would find it easier to do than if you hadn't previewed it.

## Why Previewing Is Effective

Previewing is effective for several reasons:

- **Previewing helps you make decisions about how you will approach the material.** Based on what you discover about the selection's organization and content, you can select the reading and study strategies that will be most effective.

- **Previewing puts your mind in gear and helps you start thinking about the subject.**

- **Previewing gives you a mental outline of the content.** It enables you to see how ideas are connected. And because you know where the author is headed, your reading will be easier than if you had not previewed. However, previewing is never a substitute for careful, thorough reading.

*Assume you are taking a health course. Your instructor has assigned the following excerpt, "A Blueprint for Better Nutrition," from a chapter in a health textbook titled Choosing Health. Preview, but do not read, the article using the procedure described on page 4. When you have finished, answer the questions that follow.*

**Issue: Health and Health Care**

## A Blueprint for Better Nutrition

### April Lynch, Barry Elmore, and Tanya Morgan

1    The Dietary Guidelines for Americans is a set of nine strategies for maintaining or improving your health. The following is a brief summary of each. For a complete listing of dietary guidelines, visit www.health.gov/dietaryguidelines.

### Obtain Adequate Nutrients Within Calorie Needs

2    Be careful that you don't take in more calories than you need each day. Choosing fresh fruits, vegetables, whole grains, and low-fat or fat-free dairy products will help you stay within your calorie allowance. That's because these foods are *nutrient-dense*, meaning they provide generous amounts of vitamins, minerals, fiber, and other health-producing substances but contain relatively few calories.

### Focus on Healthful Foods

3    Build meals and vegetables around four food groups: fruits, vegetables, whole grains, and low-fat or fat-free dairy products. These foods are low in saturated and *trans* fats, cholesterol, added sugars, and salt, but rich in essential nutrients as well as fiber and phytochemicals. They are also lower in calories, so choosing them will help you stay within your calorie allowance each day.

### Watch Your Intake of Fats

4    The type and amount of fat you consume can make a big difference to the health of your heart. To reduce your risk of heart disease, keep your intake of saturated and *trans* fats as low as possible. Replace these with unsaturated fats from fish, nuts, and plant oils. When selecting red meat, poultry, and dairy products, make choices that are lean, low-fat, or fat-free. Also keep your total fat intake between 20% and 35% of your total calorie intake.

### Choose Carbohydrates Wisely

5    Fresh fruits, vegetables, and whole grains promote health and reduce your risk of chronic disease. Eat more of these and less of foods containing refined carbohydrates,

## FIGURE 1-1  READ FOOD LABELS WISELY

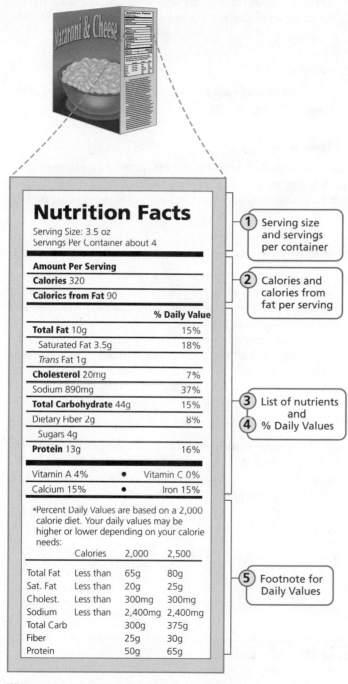

**Nutrition Facts**

Serving Size: 3.5 oz
Servings Per Container about 4

**Amount Per Serving**

**Calories** 320

**Calories from Fat** 90

|  | % Daily Value |
|---|---|
| **Total Fat** 10g | 15% |
| Saturated Fat 3.5g | 18% |
| *Trans* Fat 1g | |
| **Cholesterol** 20mg | 7% |
| Sodium 890mg | 37% |
| **Total Carbohydrate** 44g | 15% |
| Dietary Fiber 2g | 8% |
| Sugars 4g | |
| **Protein** 13g | 16% |

| | | | |
|---|---|---|---|
| Vitamin A 4% | ● | Vitamin C 0% | |
| Calcium 15% | ● | Iron 15% | |

*Percent Daily Values are based on a 2,000 calorie diet. Your daily values may be higher or lower depending on your calorie needs:

| | Calories | 2,000 | 2,500 |
|---|---|---|---|
| Total Fat | Less than | 65g | 80g |
| Sat. Fat | Less than | 20g | 25g |
| Cholest. | Less than | 300mg | 300mg |
| Sodium | Less than | 2,400mg | 2,400mg |
| Total Carb | | 300g | 375g |
| Fiber | | 25g | 30g |
| Protein | | 50g | 65g |

1. Serving size and servings per container
2. Calories and calories from fat per serving
3. List of nutrients and
4. % Daily Values
5. Footnote for Daily Values

When reading a Nutrition Facts panel, note the serving size, calories (and calories from fat), and the nutrients contained per serving.

such as pastries, white bread, white rice, crackers, and candies. Also avoid sweetened beverages, from soft drinks to flavored waters, as these contain huge amounts of simple sugars. Drink more low-fat or non-fat milk. It contains many essential nutrients. If you're not sure whether a food or beverage has added sweeteners, look for these terms on the food label: sugars (brown, invert, raw, beet, or cane), corn sweetener, corn syrup, high fructose corn syrup, fruit juice concentrates, honey, malt syrup, molasses, glucose, fructose, maltose, sucrose, lactose, and dextrose.

### Maintain Proper Levels of Sodium and Potassium

6    If you're like most Americans, you consume substantially more salt (sodium chloride) than you need. On average, as sodium intake rises, so does blood pressure, so by reducing your sodium intake, you help keep your blood pressure down. Keeping your blood pressure in the normal range, approximately 120 over 80 millimeters of mercury (120/80 mm Hg), reduces your risk of heart disease and stroke. Surprisingly, hiding the salt shaker is not the most important strategy for controlling your sodium intake. That's because most of us get far more sodium every day from the processed foods we eat. So read the Nutrition Facts panel on food labels (Figure 1-1) to check the amount of sodium in the food. Less than 140 milligrams (mg) or 5% of the Daily Value is low in salt. At the same time, make sure you're getting enough potassium, which helps blunt the effects of sodium on blood pressure. The best potassium sources are fruits

and vegetables, especially apricots, bananas, broccoli, cantaloupe, carrots, dates, mushrooms, oranges, potatoes, prunes, raisins, spinach, sweet potato, watermelon, and winter squash. Other good potassium sources are milk products, legumes, peanuts, and almonds.

### Manage Your Body Weight

7    Achieve and maintain a healthful body weight by balancing the calories you consume in foods and beverages with the calories you burn in physical activity.

### Engage in Regular Physical Activity

8    Regular physical activity improves physical fitness, promotes psychological well-being, and helps manage weight. It also reduces the risk of many chronic diseases. Adults should be moderately active for at least 30 minutes most days of the week.

### Use Alcohol Moderately or Not at All

9    Alcoholic beverages supply 7 calories per gram—that's 150 calories for a 12-ounce beer! No wonder drinking a lot of alcohol can make it hard to maintain a healthy weight. Moderate alcohol intake—defined as up to one drink per day for women and up to two drinks per day for men—is associated with mortality reduction in middle-aged and older adults. But among younger people, alcohol consumption provides little, if any, health benefit, and it is harmful for women who are or may become pregnant or are breastfeeding, anyone taking medications, people with certain medical conditions, and anyone who will be driving or using machinery.

### Be Food Safe

10    Every year about 76 million people in the U.S. experience food borne illness. Simple measures such as washing your hands and food-contact surfaces; separating raw, cooked, and ready-to-eat foods while shopping, preparing, or storing them; cooking foods to the proper temperature; and keeping cold foods cold will reduce your risk of food borne illness.

—adapted from Lynch, Elmore, and Morgan, *Choosing Health*, pp. 77–78

1. What is the overall subject of this article?

_____

2. What is the common name for sodium chloride?

_____

3. List three benefits of physical activity.

_____

_____

4. Two of the four food groups you should build meals around are whole grains and fruits. What are the other two?

_____

5. On a scale of 1 to 5 (1 = easy, 5 = very difficult), how difficult do you expect the article to be?

_____

## 1c    ACTIVATING PRIOR KNOWLEDGE

**LEARNING OBJECTIVE 3**
Activate your prior knowledge

After previewing your assignment, you should take a moment to think about what you already know about the topic. Whatever the topic, you probably know *something* about it: This is your **prior knowledge**. For example, a student was asked to read an article titled "Growing Urban Problems" for a government class. His first thought was that he knew very little about urban problems because he lived in a rural area. But when he thought of a recent trip to a nearby city, he remembered seeing the homeless people and crowded conditions. This recollection helped him remember reading about drug problems, drive-by shootings, and muggings.

Activating your prior knowledge aids your reading in three ways. First, it makes reading easier because you have already thought about the topic. Second, the material is easier to remember because you can connect the new information with what you already know. Third, topics become more interesting if you can link them to your own experiences. Here are some techniques to help you activate your background knowledge.

- **Ask questions and try to answer them.** If a chapter in your biology textbook titled "Human Diseases" contains headings such as "Infectious diseases," "Cancer," and "Vascular diseases," you might ask and try to answer such questions as the following: What kinds of infectious diseases have I seen? What causes them? What do I know about preventing cancer and other diseases?

- **Draw on your own experience.** If a chapter in your business textbook is titled "Advertising: Its Purpose and Design," you might think of several ads you have seen and analyze the images used in each, as well as the purpose of each ad.

- **Brainstorm.** Write down everything that comes to mind about the topic. Suppose you're about to read a chapter in your psychology textbook on domestic violence. You might list types of violence—child abuse, spousal abuse, and so on. You might write questions such as "What causes child abuse?" and "How can it be prevented?" Alternatively, you might list incidents of domestic violence you have heard or read about. Any of these approaches will help to make the topic interesting and relevant.

**EXERCISE 1-4    ACTIVATING PRIOR KNOWLEDGE**

*Use one of the three strategies listed above to discover what you already know about dieting and exercise.*

## DURING READING STRATEGIES

### 1d    HIGHLIGHTING AND ANNOTATING TO STRENGTHEN READING AND RECALL

**LEARNING OBJECTIVE 4**
Highlight and annotate as you read

Many students find that reading with a pen in hand is an excellent way to continue their active-reading mind-set. Two useful skills are highlighting and annotating.

### Highlighting to Identify Important Information

**Highlighting** key information in a reading helps you focus your attention, sort ideas, and create a document that helps you review the material at a later date. Consider the following passages. One is highlighted; the other is not.

> The major challenge facing single people through the ages has been building a satisfying life in a society highly geared toward marriage. Until recently, the general tendency in U.S. popular culture has been to portray singles as belonging in one of two stereotypical groups. On the one side is the "swinging single"—the partygoer who is carefree, uncommitted, sexually adventuresome, and the subject of envy by married friends. Poles apart from this image is the "lonely loser"—the unhappy, frustrated, depressed single who lives alone and survives on TV dinners, a fate few people would envy.

> The major challenge facing single people through the ages has been building a satisfying life in a society highly geared toward marriage. Until recently, the general tendency in U.S. popular culture has been to portray singles as belonging in one of two stereotypical groups. On the one side is the "swinging single"—the partygoer who is carefree, uncommitted, sexually adventuresome, and the subject of envy by married friends. Poles apart from this image is the "lonely loser"—the unhappy, frustrated, depressed single who lives alone and survives on TV dinners, a fate few people would envy.
>
> —Schwartz and Scott, *Marriages and Families*, p. 212

Which version would you prefer to study and why? You likely prefer the highlighted version, because it highlights the selection's key points and aids review.

To highlight effectively, read the selection completely through first, then go back and highlight during your second reading. Do not highlight too much or too little. If you highlight too much, you have not selected the reading's main points. If you highlight too little, you will miss key points during your review. Avoid highlighting complete sentences. Highlight only enough so that your highlighting makes sense when you read it. (For more information on highlighting, see Section 8b, p. 202.)

Highlighting is beneficial for several reasons:

- Highlighting forces you to sift through what you have read to identify important information. This sifting or sorting helps you weigh and evaluate what you read.
- Highlighting keeps you physically active while you read and improves concentration.
- Highlighting can help you discover the organization of facts and ideas as well as their connections and relationships.
- Highlighting helps you determine whether you have understood a passage you just read. If you don't know what to highlight, you don't understand it.

A word of caution. Do not assume that what is highlighted is learned. You must process the information by organizing it, expressing it in your own words, and testing yourself periodically.

## Annotating to Record Your Ideas

Active readers think as they read. They summarize, react, respond, question, judge, and evaluate ideas. Be sure to record your thoughts so you can refer to them later when studying the material, preparing for a class discussion, or searching for ideas to write about. **Annotating** is a process of making marginal notes that record your thinking. Refer to Section 7c for more information on how to annotate effectively.

### 1e   CHECKING YOUR COMPREHENSION

**LEARNING OBJECTIVE 5**
Check your comprehension

What happens when you read material you can understand easily? Does it seem that everything "clicks"? Do ideas seem to fit together and make sense? Is that "click" noticeably absent at other times?

Table 1-2 lists and compares common signals to assist you in checking your comprehension. Not all the signals appear at the same time, and not all the signals work for everyone. But becoming aware of these positive and negative signals will help you gain more control over your reading.

## TABLE 1-2  COMPREHENSION SIGNALS

| POSITIVE SIGNALS | NEGATIVE SIGNALS |
|---|---|
| You feel comfortable and have some knowledge about the topic. | The topic is unfamiliar, yet the author assumes you understand it. |
| You recognize most words or can figure them out from context. | Many words are unfamiliar. |
| You can express the main ideas in your own words. | You must reread the main ideas and use the author's language to explain them. |
| You understand why the material was assigned. | You do not know why the material was assigned and cannot explain why it is important. |
| You read at a regular, comfortable pace. | You often slow down or reread. |
| You are able to make connections among ideas. | You are unable to detect relationships; the organization is not apparent. |
| You are able to see where the author is heading. | You feel as if you are struggling to stay with the author and are unable to predict what will follow. |
| You understand what is important. | Nothing (or everything) seems important. |
| You read calmly and try to assess the author's points without becoming too emotionally involved. | When you encounter a controversial topic, you close your mind to alternative viewpoints or opinions. |

## EXERCISE 1-5   CHECKING YOUR COMPREHENSION

*Read the article titled "Consequences of Social Class" that appears on page 6. Be alert for positive and negative comprehension signals as you read. After reading the article, answer the following questions.*

1. On a scale of 1 to 5 (1 = very poor, 5 = excellent), how would you rate your overall comprehension?_____

2. What positive signals did you sense? List them below.

_____

_____

_____

3. What negative signals did you experience, if any? List them below.

_____

_____

_____

4. In which sections was your comprehension strongest? List the paragraph numbers. _____

5. Did you feel at any time that you had lost, or were about to lose, comprehension? If so, go back to that part now. What made it difficult to read?

_____

_____

_____

## POST-READING STRATEGIES

## 1f    STRENGTHENING YOUR COMPREHENSION

**LEARNING OBJECTIVE 6**
Strengthen your
comprehension

When you have finished reading, don't just close the book. Stop and assess how well you understood what you read. Test yourself. Take a heading and turn it into a question. Cover up the text following it and see if you can answer your questions. For example, for a heading "Effects of Head Trauma," convert it to the question "What are the effects of head trauma?" and then answer your question mentally or in writing. Then check your answer by looking that text itself. This self-testing process will also help you remember more of what you read because you are reviewing what you just read.

If you are not satisfied with your self-test, or if you experienced some or all of the negative signals mentioned in Table 1-2, be sure to take action to strengthen your comprehension. Chapter 4 presents basic comprehension strategies for reading paragraphs, including identifying main ideas, details, and signal words. Chapter 7 discusses how to read textbooks, essays, and longer works. Using context clues to figure out words you don't know is covered in Chapter 3. Be sure to consult these chapters. Here are some immediate things you can do when you realize you need to strengthen your comprehension.

### Tips for Strengthening Your Comprehension

1. **Analyze the time and place in which you are reading.** If you've been reading or studying for several hours, mental fatigue may be the source of the problem. If you are reading in a place with distractions or interruptions, you might not be able to concentrate on what you're reading.

2. **Rephrase each paragraph in your own words.** You might need to approach complicated material sentence by sentence, expressing each sentence in your own words.

3. **Read aloud sentences or sections that are particularly difficult.** Reading out loud sometimes makes complicated material easier to understand.

4. **Reread difficult or complicated sections.** At times, several readings are appropriate and necessary.

5. **Slow down your reading rate.** On occasion, simply reading more slowly and carefully will provide you with the needed boost in comprehension.

6. **Write questions next to headings.** Refer to your questions frequently and jot down or underline answers in the reading selection.

7. **Write a brief outline of major points.** This will help you see the overall organization and progression of ideas. (For more on outlining, see Section 8e, p. 210.)

8. **Determine whether you lack prior knowledge.** Comprehension is difficult, and at times impossible, if you lack essential information that the writer assumes you have. Suppose you are reading a political science textbook in which the author describes implications of the balance of power in the Third World. If you do not understand the concept of balance of power, your comprehension will break down. When you lack background information, take immediate steps to correct the problem:

   - Consult other sections of your text, using the glossary and index.

   - Obtain a more basic text that reviews fundamental principles and concepts.

   - Consult reference materials (encyclopedias, subject or biographical dictionaries, reliable Web sources).

   - Ask your instructor to recommend additional sources, guidebooks, or review texts.

## 1g    AN INTRODUCTION TO CONTEMPORARY ISSUES

**LEARNING OBJECTIVE 7**
Understand the definition of a contemporary issue

**Contemporary issues** are those controversial topics that are relevant to individuals, groups, and societies today. These issues can be very polarizing, with radically different viewpoints being put forth in written materials, as well as in speeches and commentaries on TV and radio. Consider the controversial issue of illegal or undocumented immigration in the United States, which occurs when people move to the United States without permission from the U.S. government. When reading about this topic, you may find all of the following assertions or arguments:

- All illegal immigrants should be deported immediately.

- Undocumented immigrants should be given the opportunity to earn citizenship.

- The children of illegal immigrants should not be granted automatic U.S. citizenship.

- States should be in charge of immigration policy, not the federal U.S. government.

- Undocumented immigrants should be allowed to stay in the United States if they have jobs that allow them to support themselves.

Because emotions can run very high when contemporary issues are being discussed, it is essential to think critically when engaging in these discussions. This means that you need to think critically all the time, because many college courses deal with these issues. Instructors often ask you to analyze viewpoints and read studies that either support or contradict statements made about a particular issue.

In many cases, a person's opinions about contemporary issues are influenced by family background, political beliefs, upbringing, religion, and a host of other complicated factors. To help you think deeply and critically about many of the issues facing society today, Part Two of this text book offers 24 readings about some of the most hotly debated issues of the day. These issues include the following topics:

- the environment
- society
- self-identity, which includes such categories as race and ethnicity
- relationships and changes in family life and family structure
- science and ethics
- the advantages and disadvantages of technology, including privacy issues
- government and politics

In addition, throughout Part One, many of the excerpts you will read in order to learn comprehension and critical-reading skills are based on contemporary issues. Look for a heading next to each excerpt to understand which issue is being discussed. For example, the heading "Issue: Health and Health Care" appears next to the reading on page 11. Chapter 10 of this handbook provides more detailed coverage of analyzing issues and arguments.

Sometimes contemporary issues are framed in terms of a pro/con argument. The **pros** are the reasons or opinions supporting a particular viewpoint. The **cons** are the reasons or opinions opposing that same viewpoint. To gain experience reading a pro/con selection, complete Exercise 1-7.

## EXERCISE 1-7     READING A PRO/CON ARGUMENT

*Read the following excerpt from a social problems textbook; then answer the questions that follow. You may need to do some additional research to answer these questions.*

**Issue: Gun Control**

## Gun Control

The issue of gun control is extremely controversial. Many people feel that it is their personal right to protect themselves with a weapon, whereas others believe that guns are the source of crime. As you know, the United States is the leader in murder rates in the industrialized world, and guns provide an effective and efficient way to kill another person. What do you think—should we have stricter gun control? That is, should the United States place tighter restrictions on those who can purchase and carry guns?

| Pro | Con |
| --- | --- |
| • There is no obvious constitutional right allowing individuals to carry guns. The U.S. Constitution guarantees states' rights of militia, which is a significantly outdated clause. | • The Constitution grants "the right of the people" to bear arms, not merely militia. |
| • Crime has not decreased in states with concealed weapons laws. | • People who are armed can defend themselves from crime. As the saying goes, "If guns are outlawed, only the outlaws will have guns." |
| • Other similar countries with strict gun controls have lower homicide rates. | • It would be nearly impossible to confiscate all the guns in the country if personal firearms were made illegal. |
| • Most gun homicides occur among family members during heated disputes. | • Guns themselves aren't responsible for violence; if they were seized, those who used them hostilely would simply find other weapons. |

—adapted from Carl, *Think Social Problems*, p. 189

1. What specific question does the author ask before providing the list of pros and cons?

   _____

2. The pro/con list refers to "militia." What is a militia, and what is its purpose?

   _____

   _____

3. What is a "concealed weapons law"?

_____

_____

4. Someone says to you, "Guns don't kill people. People kill people." Would this person more likely be in favor of gun control or against gun control?

_____

5. Does the author of the selection support gun control? Oppose gun control? Or is he neutral on the topic?

_____

_____

## SUMMARY OF LEARNING OBJECTIVES

**MySkillsLab**
Complete the mastery test for this chapter in **MySkillsLab.**

| | |
|---|---|
| **1 Learn to read actively.** *What is active reading?* | **Active reading** is the process of identifying important ideas in a reading selection and comparing, evaluating, and applying them. **Active readers** determine the purpose of a reading assignment and then adjust their speed to suit the purpose. |
| **2 Preview before reading.** *How do you preview effectively?* | **Previewing** is a means of familiarizing yourself with the content and organization of an assignment *before* you read it. Effective previewing involves using the title and subtitle, headings, the introductory and concluding paragraphs, key sentences, and typographical aids to get a "sneak preview" of what a reading selection will be about. |
| **3 Activate your prior knowledge.** *Why is activating prior knowledge important?* | Your **prior knowledge** is what you already know about the topic you are reading about. Activating—connecting to—prior knowledge, makes reading easier because you have already thought about the topic. It helps with recall, as you can connect the new information to what you already know, and it makes topics become more interesting because you have linked them to your own experiences. |
| **4 Highlight and annotate as you read.** *Why is marking text helpful?* | **Marking text** is helpful because it forces you to sift through what you have read to identify and evaluate important information; keeps you physically active while you read and improves concentration; enables you to discover the organization of facts and ideas as well as their connections and relationships; and helps you determine whether you have understood a passage you just read. **Highlighting** helps focus your attention, sort ideas, and make review easier and faster. To highlight effectively, read the selection first, then go back and highlight key points. **Annotating** is a process of recording your thinking about the ideas you encounter by making marginal notes and marking text. |

| 5 Check your comprehension. *How do you check your comprehension?* | **Active readers use comprehension signals** (*such as the level of the vocabulary and their ability to make connections among ideas*) while they read to determine how well they understand the material. If they experience a low level of comprehension, they adjust their reading strategy. (See Table 1-2 on p. 16.) |
| 6 Strengthen your comprehension. *How do you strengthen your comprehension?* | To **strengthen comprehension**, use self-testing to make sure you understood what you just read. Also, be sure your reading area is free of distractions. Rephrase paragraphs and ideas in your own words, and reread complicated sections. Decrease your reading rate or read sentences aloud. Create questions and outlines to engage with the reading. Assess your background knowledge and consult other sources if necessary. |
| 7 Understand the definition of contemporary "issue" *How do you define "contemporary issue"?* | **Contemporary issues** are those controversial topics that are relevant to individuals, groups, and societies today. These issues can be very polarizing, with radically different viewpoints being put forth in written materials, as well as in speeches and commentaries on TV and radio, by their proponents. |

# 2 The Writing Process

Like any other skill (such as playing basketball, accounting, or cooking), reading and writing require both instruction and practice. In Chapter 1, we provided an overview of the active reading process. In this chapter, we discuss the writing process. Reading and writing go hand in hand: Readers read what writers have written, and writers write for readers.

Writing involves much more than sitting down at your computer and starting to type. It involves reading about others' ideas, generating and organizing your own ideas, and expressing your ideas in sentence, paragraph, or essay form. Writing is a *process*; it involves prewriting, drafting, revising, and editing and proofreading your work. Following the sample student essay in this chapter (beginning on page 30) will give you a good sense of what writing involves. The final version of this essay appears in Chapter 12, page 356.

## 2a   UNDERSTANDING THE WRITING PROCESS

**LEARNING OBJECTIVE 1**
Understand the writing process

Writing, like many other skills, is not a single-step process. Think of the game of football, for instance. Football players spend a great deal of time planning and developing offensive and defensive strategies, trying out new plays, improving existing plays, training, and practicing. Writing involves similar planning and preparation. It also involves testing ideas and working out the best way to express them. Writers often explore how their ideas might "play out" in several ways before settling upon one plan of action.

Writing should always be an expression of your own ideas. Be sure that you do not use ideas or wording of other authors without giving them credit through a source citation in your essay or paragraph. Using the ideas of others without giving proper acknowledgment is known as **plagiarism**, and it can result in academic penalties such as failing grades or even academic dismissal. For a more detailed explanation of plagiarism, see Chapter 11, page 308.

All writing involves four basic steps, as outlined in Table 2-1.

**TABLE 2-1  STEPS IN THE WRITING PROCESS**

| STEP IN THE WRITING PROCESS | DESCRIPTION |
| --- | --- |
| 1. Prewriting | Finding ideas to write about and discovering ways to arrange your ideas logically. |
| 2. Drafting | Expressing your ideas in sentence, paragraph, or essay form. |
| 3. Revising | Rethinking your ideas and finding ways to make your writing clearer, more complete, and more interesting. Revising involves changing, adding, deleting, and rearranging your ideas and words to improve your writing. |
| 4. Editing/Proofreading | Checking for errors in spelling, punctuation, capitalization, and grammar. |

## 2b   USING TECHNOLOGY FOR WRITING

**LEARNING OBJECTIVE 2**
Use technology effectively

Technology has much to offer writers for each step in the writing process. Technology can help you produce a well-written correct paragraph or essay, save you time, and allow you spend more of your time on the creative task of writing and less on the mechanical details of presenting your work in a readable, visually appealing form.

## Using Technology to Generate Ideas

The methods for prewriting suggested later in this chapter (Section 2d, page 29) can be done on the computer, often more easily than on paper. You might try dimming your computer screen so you are not distracted by what you are typing and don't become concerned with correctness or typing errors. And, after you have finished, you can easily move and rearrange usable ideas.

You might also use social media such as Facebook or blogs to generate ideas and share them with others. Think of your page as a type of journal in which you record and exchange ideas. Your posts may feel conversational, but they will work in helping you share and explore ideas and responses. Because you can post different types of media, you might include photos and videos that stimulate your thinking, spur your creativity, and help you generate ideas. Be sure to check your privacy settings so access is restricted, and never post anything on the site that you wouldn't want everyone to see.

## Using Technology for Drafting and Revising

Drafting on your computer is faster and more efficient than on paper. When drafting on a computer, be sure to do the following:

- **Format your paper before you begin,** considering font, spacing, margins, page numbering, and so forth. Check to be sure you are using a format preferred by your instructor or specified by MLA or APA style (see Chapter 11).
- **Name and store each document so you can easily retrieve it.**
- **Copy each draft and create a new file for it.** Date each draft, as you may want to go back to an earlier draft to include things from it.
- **Save your work frequently** and every time you leave your computer so you do not lose material.
- **Share your work with peers.** Many course management systems such as Blackboard make it easy to share your work with your classmates for peer review. Check with your instructor or the computer lab for more information.

The following box contains tips that will help you use the features in your word processing program for editing and proofreading.

### WORD PROCESSING FEATURES FOR WRITERS

- **Use a spell-checker to identify misspellings and typing mistakes.** However, do **not** rely on the program to catch all the errors. The checker will not flag words that you have misused (*to*, instead of *two*, for example). It may also suggest incorrect alternatives, so be sure to evaluate each suggested alternative.
- **Use a grammar and style checker** to help you identify incorrect grammar or punctuation, repeated words, and awkward or wordy sentences. Do **not** rely on the checker to spot all your errors, and realize that the checker may flag things that are correct.
- **Use the Find command to locate and correct common problems or errors,** such as words you commonly misspell, overused words, or wordy phrases.

## PREWRITING STRATEGIES

## 2c   PREWRITING: THINKING ABOUT AUDIENCE, PURPOSE, TONE, AND POINT OF VIEW

**LEARNING OBJECTIVE 3**
Consider your audience, purpose, tone, and point of view

Prewriting is an important first step in the writing process. Many students mistakenly believe they can just sit down at a computer and start writing a paragraph or essay. Writing requires thinking, planning, and organizing. Although these strategies take time, they pay off in the long run by saving you time later on and enabling you to produce a more effective piece of writing.

### Considering Your Audience

Considering your audience is essential to good writing. When you write, ask yourself: Who will be reading what I write? How should I express myself so that my readers will understand what I write?

What is appropriate for one audience may be inappropriate for another. For example, if you were writing about social issues that affect life in your city, you would write one way to a close friend and another way to a member of the city council. When writing for a friend, you might use casual, informal language. When writing for the city council, you would use more formal language. Study the following emails. What differences do you notice?

### E-mail to a Friend

| From: | Moreno, Jasmine |
|---|---|
| Sent: | Friday, 15 February 2013 2:38 PM |
| To: | Delgado, Marie |
| Subject: | I'm going insane!!!!!!!!!!!! |

You asked how I am—I am going insane about graffiti all over the neighbourhood. My landlord tries his best—he just painted the side of my building last week, and this morning when I left, there it was again—filled with tags from the local gangs. And not only that, the taggers painted some really nasty stuff that I don't want my kids to see. The landlord tried putting up a fence, they climb over it. He tried putting up a camera, they broke it. It's like it's a game for them. Well I am fed up with it and I am going to do something about it. Do you think a neighbourhood watch would work?? Any other ideas?

### E-mail to a Member of the City Council

| From: | Moreno, Jasmine |
|---|---|
| Sent: | Friday, 15 February 2013 4:45 PM |
| To: | Cervantes, Isabella |
| Subject: | Neighborhood Graffiti |

Dear Councillor Cervantes,

I think you would agree that we are experiencing a serious problem with graffiti in the third ward, where I live with my family. I have heard you speak about these problems, and I am wondering if I can help in any way. I agree with you: Tagging shows a lack of respect for people and property, and I don't want my children to think tagging is acceptable. I am willing to start a neighborhood watch to try to discourage taggers, and I am also open to any suggestions you may have about how to tackle this problem.

Yours sincerely,

Jasmine Moreno

While the e-mail to the friend is casual, the note to the councilwoman is businesslike. The writer included details and described her feelings when telling her friend about the graffiti problem, but she focused on finding a solution to the problem in her note to the city councilwoman.

Writers make many decisions based on the audience they have in mind. As you write, consider the following:

- How many and what kinds of details are necessary?
- What format is appropriate (paragraph, essay, e-mail, etc.)?
- What kinds of words should you use (simple, technical, emotional, etc.)?
- What tone should you use (friendly, knowledgeable, formal, etc.)?

Here are four key questions you can ask to assess and write for your audience:

- Who is your audience, and what is your relationship with your audience?
- How is your audience likely to respond to your message?
- What does your audience already know about your topic?
- What does your audience need to know to understand your point?

## Writing for a Purpose

When you call a friend on the phone, you have a reason for calling, even if it is just to stay in touch. When you ask a question in class, you have a purpose for asking. When you describe to a friend an incident you were involved in, you are relating the story to make a point or share an experience. These examples demonstrate that you use spoken communication to achieve specific purposes.

Good writing must also achieve your *intended purpose*. If you write a paragraph on how to change a flat tire, your reader should be able to change a flat tire after reading the paragraph. Likewise, if your purpose is to describe the sun rising over a misty mountaintop, your reader should be able to visualize the scene. If your purpose is to argue that the legal age for drinking alcohol should be 25, your reader should be able to follow your reasoning, even if he or she is not won over to your view.

---

### EXERCISE 2-1   WRITING A PARAGRAPH

*Think of a public event you recently attended, such as a concert or film showing. Complete two of the following activities. Make sure you adjust your writing to suit each audience.*

1. Write a paragraph describing the event to a friend.
2. Write a paragraph describing the event to your English instructor.
3. Write a paragraph describing the event as the movie or music critic for your local newspaper.

## Considering Your Tone

**Tone** refers to how you "sound" or come across to your reader. You might sound angry, or sympathetic, or excited, for instance. Tone reveals your attitudes or feelings toward the subject you are writing about. Be sure to choose a tone that is appropriate for your audience and your purpose. If your audience is a serious group of people, for example, your tone should appeal to serious-minded people. A tone that is sarcastic or cynical might not appeal to them, so you probably do not want to "sound" angry when trying to convince your readers to agree with you; a serious, thoughtful tone might be more effective. For more about tone, see Chapter 9.

## Considering Point of View

Your **point of view** is the perspective from which you are writing. Writing in the first person (*I, me*) allows the writer to speak as him- or herself directly to the reader. Writing in the second person (*you*), is more formal, but addresses the reader directly. The third person (*he, she, they, James*, etc.) is the most formal and is most commonly used in academic writing. In choosing a point of view, consider both your audience and your purpose. What point of view will accomplish your purpose and suit your audience?

## 2d    PREWRITING: GENERATING IDEAS

**LEARNING OBJECTIVE 4**
Use prewriting to generate ideas for your writing

Before you can write about a topic, you must generate ideas to write about. Three techniques are helpful in collecting ideas: *freewriting, brainstorming*, and *diagramming*.

### Freewriting

**Freewriting** is writing nonstop about a topic for a specified period of time. In freewriting, you write whatever comes into your mind without worrying about punctuation, spelling, and grammatical correctness. After you have finished, you go back through your writing and pick out ideas that you might be able to use.

Here is a sample freewrite on the topic of climate change:

It's so hard to sort out the facts about climate change. On the one hand it seems like the weather has been crazy. I'm 22 years old and I never remember summers being so hot when I was a kid. And the humidity is so bad too, it seems like summer now starts in April and goes straight through to December. We've had hurricanes, tornadoes, and unbelievable rainfall, plus high winds that have brought trees

crashing down. And I keep reading that climate change is responsible for this
extreme weather. But on the other hand I know that a lot of people don't believe
that climate change is really happening. From what I can figure out, they think
"climate change" is not really happening and that all the talk of "global warming"
is greatly exaggerated. It's so hard to know who to believe, everyone seems to
have an agenda and it seems like nobody reports the facts. Even when facts and
figures are reported, can I really trust them? Because as soon as they come out,
people start disputing them.

## Brainstorming

**Brainstorming** involves making a list of everything you can think of that is
associated with your topic. When you brainstorm, try to stretch your imagi-
nation and think of everything related to your topic: facts, ideas, examples,
questions, and feelings. When you have finished, read through what you have
written and highlight usable ideas.

Imagine that you have been asked to write an essay about "identity" and
how you see yourself. Here is the brainstorming list that one student, Santiago
Quintana Garcia, wrote about his identity.

Identity—Mexican? White? Very arbitrary and flimsy

Easily deconstructed when seen from the edges

Not wrong to subscribe to a certain identity

Everyone has their in-betweens, not all race and nationality

Mexican stereotype: I don't look Mexican. I'm foreign in my own country/race

White: Not quite. I <u>am</u> Mexican after all.

Creates a struggle between the ideal and the reality, from this comes synthesis,
movement

Feelings of not belonging as a teenager. No comfort objects. No cushion to fall
back to easily, BUT growth and awareness.

I am Mexican. I still subscribe but with a lot more awareness of how that label is not
representative and exhaustive. It is necessary; practical.

Living in between = energy, movement, growth.

## Diagramming

Drawing diagrams or drawings is a useful way to generate ideas. Begin by drawing a 2-inch oval in the middle of a page. Write your topic in that oval. Think of the oval as a tree trunk. Next, draw lines radiating out from the trunk, as branches would. Write an idea related to your topic at the end of each branch. When you have finished, highlight the ideas you find most useful.

Here is a sample branching diagram on the topic of labor unions:

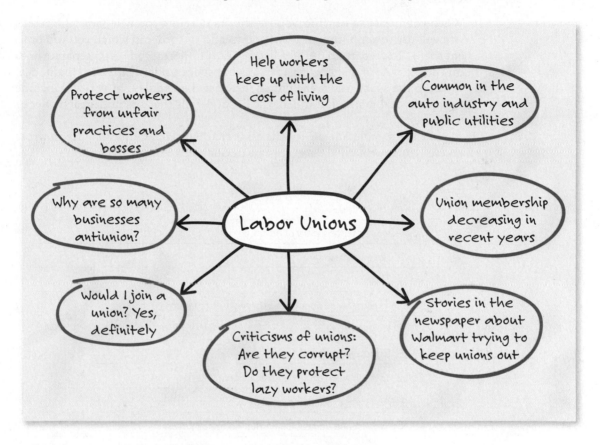

EXERCISE 2-2   THE WRITING PROCESS: GENERATING IDEAS

*Select two of the following topics. Then generate ideas using two different idea-generation techniques.*

1. Identity theft
2. Texting while driving
3. Doping in sports
4. Government spying
5. Social impacts of Twitter

## 2e    PREWRITING: ORGANIZING IDEAS

Two common methods of organizing ideas are outlining and idea mapping. Understanding each will help you decide how to arrange the ideas that you have identified as useful.

### Outlining

When you create an **outline**, you list the main points you will cover, the details you will use to support your main points, and the order in which you will present them. To prepare an outline, list the most important ideas on separate lines on the left side of a sheet of paper, leaving space underneath each main idea. Then, in the space under each main idea, list the details that you will include to explain that main idea. Indent the list of details that fits under each of your main ideas.

Here is a sample outline for the essay that Santiago Quintana Garcia wrote about identity. His final essay appears in Chapter 12, page 328.

I.  Living in two worlds

   A.  Never completely part of either world

      1.  Complicated

      2.  Interesting

   B.  Living in between encourages growth and maturity

      1.  Nothing to hold on to

      2.  Effects of culture

   C.  Living in between offers a vantage point

      1.  Analyze opinions and habits

      2.  See virtues and faults through different eyes

   D.  Live where outsider meets insider

### Idea Mapping

An **idea map** shows how you will organize the content of your writing. It shows how ideas are connected and can help you identify which ideas are not relevant to your topic. Here is a sample idea map drawn for the topic of protecting your identity.

To protect your identity, take several precautions when making purchases or posting online.

Choose unique passwords that use a combination of numbers and letters.

Do not share your passwords or access codes with anyone.

Carefully examine e-mail to be sure you are not responding to scams.

Protect all your credit card and banking information.

Never give information to anyone who has called you. Get their phone number and call them back. Be sure you are taking with a legitimate representative of the company.

---

**EXERCISE 2-3   THE WRITING PROCESS: USING OUTLINING OR MAPPING**

*Prepare an outline or idea map for one of the topics you chose in Exercise 2-2.*

---

## DRAFTING STRATEGIES

### 2f    DRAFTING AND REVISING PARAGRAPHS

**LEARNING OBJECTIVE 6**
Write an effective paragraph

A **paragraph** is a group of sentences, usually at least three or four, that express one main idea. Paragraphs may stand alone to express one thought, or they may be combined into essays or longer readings. Paragraphs are one of the basic building blocks of writing.

### The Structure of a Paragraph

A paragraph's one main idea is often expressed in a single sentence called the **topic sentence**. The other sentences in the paragraph, which explain or support the main idea, are called **supporting details**. (These terms are explained in more detail in Chapter 4.) You can visualize a paragraph as shown below:

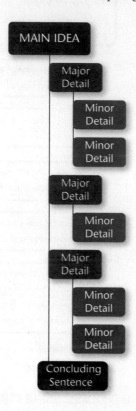

Here is a sample paragraph; its idea map follows.

> Turkey continues to find itself strategically positioned between diverse, often contradictory geopolitical forces. Many pro-Westerners within Turkey, for example, are committed to joining the European Union (EU). To do so, the country has embarked on an active agenda of reforms designed to demonstrate its commitment to democracy. Press freedoms and multiparty elections have been permitted, the role of the military downplayed, and minority groups (particularly the Kurds) have gained greater recognition from the central government. At the same time, anti-Western Islamist political elements have been on the rise, linked to a growing number of terrorist bombings in the country since 2003. Moderate Turks are hoping that its road to the EU will not be interrupted with the violence, but Islamists and ultra-nationalists are suspicious of the EU pledge to move the country in a radically different direction. Turkey also has continuing tensions with nearby Greece and Cyprus, two countries that are both in the EU.
>
> —Rowntree et al., *Diversity Amid Globalization,* p. 326

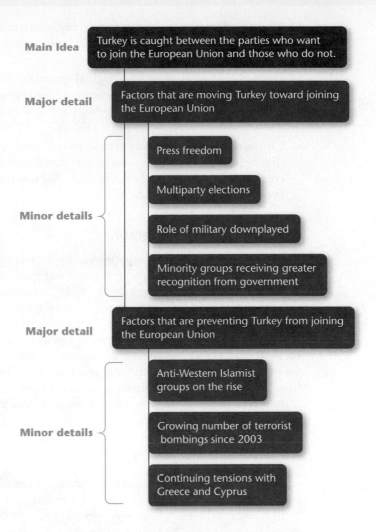

**Main Idea:** Turkey is caught between the parties who want to join the European Union and those who do not.

**Major detail:** Factors that are moving Turkey toward joining the European Union

**Minor details:**
- Press freedom
- Multiparty elections
- Role of military downplayed
- Minority groups receiving greater recognition from government

**Major detail:** Factors that are preventing Turkey from joining the European Union

**Minor details:**
- Anti-Western Islamist groups on the rise
- Growing number of terrorist bombings since 2003
- Continuing tensions with Greece and Cyprus

## Tips for Writing Effective Paragraphs

You can write an effective paragraph if you follow the organization shown in the diagram above. Use the following suggestions to make sure your paragraph is clear and understandable.

1. **Choose a manageable topic.** Your topic should be broad enough to allow you to add interesting and relevant details, but specific enough to allow you to adequately cover it in approximately five to ten sentences.

2. **Write a clear topic sentence.** Your topic sentence should state the main point of your paragraph. Often it works well to place your topic sentence first in the paragraph and then go on to explain and support it in the remaining sentences. Avoid announcing your topic ("This paragraph is about ...").

3. **Choose details to support your topic sentence.** Each sentence in your paragraph should explain or support your topic sentence. Be sure to include enough details to fully explain it.

4. **Organize your details in a logical manner.** Make your paragraph easy to understand by arranging your details using one of the patterns described in Chapter 6: *illustration, process, definition, classification, cause and effect,* and *comparison and contrast.*

5. **Connect your ideas using transitions.** Transitions are words and phrases that help your reader move from one detail to the next and understand the connections between and among them. See Chapters 4 (p. 100) and 5 (p. 117) for lists of useful transition words.

## Tips for Revising Paragraphs

**Revision** involves examining your ideas by rereading all the sentences you have written and making changes to them. Your goal is to examine your ideas to make sure you have explained them clearly and correctly. It is usually best to let your paragraph sit for a while before you revise it. Turn to page 43 to see how Santiago revised several draft paragraphs within his essay.

If you have trouble knowing what to revise, try drawing an idea map of your ideas. Construct a map similar to the one shown on page 37. A map will help you see exactly how much support you have for your topic sentence, how your ideas fit together, and whether a detail is off-topic. Here is a sample paragraph, followed by an idea map a student drew to identify where she strayed off her topic.

### Sample Student Paragraph

The disposal of toxic waste has caused serious health hazards. Love Canal is one of the toxic dump sites that have caused serious health problems. This dump site in particular was used by a large number of nearby industries. The canal was named after a man named Love. Love Canal, in my opinion, was an eye-opener on the subject of toxic dump sites. It took about ten years to clean the dump site up to a livable condition. Many people living near Love Canal developed cancers. There were many miscarriages and birth defects. This dump site might have caused irreversible damage to our environment, so I am glad it has been cleaned up.

The following idea map shows the topic sentence of the paragraph and, underneath it, the supporting details that directly relate to the topic sentence. All the unrelated details are in a list to the right of the map. Note that the concluding sentence is also included in the map, since it is an important part of the paragraph.

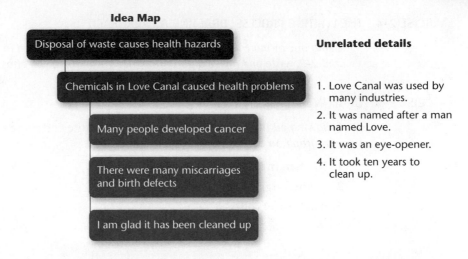

**Idea Map**

Disposal of waste causes health hazards

Chemicals in Love Canal caused health problems

Many people developed cancer

There were many miscarriages and birth defects

I am glad it has been cleaned up

**Unrelated details**

1. Love Canal was used by many industries.
2. It was named after a man named Love.
3. It was an eye-opener.
4. It took ten years to clean up.

In this paragraph, the author began by supporting her topic sentence with the example of Love Canal. However, she began to drift when she explained how Love Canal was named. To revise this paragraph, the author could include more detailed information about Love Canal health hazards or examples of other disposal sites and their health hazards.

You can use an idea map to spot where you begin to drift away from your topic. You might also ask a classmate to read and comment on your paragraph. For suggestions on finding grammatical errors in your paragraph, see Section 2j on proofreading later in this chapter (page 45).

Below is a Revision Checklist that you can use to make sure you have done a careful and thorough revision.

---

## PARAGRAPH REVISION CHECKLIST

### Paragraph Development

1. Is the topic manageable (neither too broad nor too narrow)?
2. Is the paragraph written with the reader in mind?
3. Does the topic sentence identify the topic?
4. Does the topic sentence make a point about the topic?
5. Does each sentence support the topic sentence?
6. Is there sufficient detail?
7. Is there a sentence at the end that brings the paragraph to a close?

### Sentence Development

8. Are there any sentence fragments, run-on sentences, or comma splices?
9. Are ideas combined to produce more effective sentences?
10. Are adjectives and adverbs used to make the sentences vivid and interesting?
11. Are relative clauses and prepositional phrases used to add detail?
12. Are pronouns used correctly and consistently?

EXERCISE 2-4   THE WRITING PROCESS: DRAFTING A PARAGRAPH

*Using one or more of the ideas you generated and organized in Exercises 2-2 and 2-3, write and revise a paragraph about the topic you chose.*

EXERCISE 2-5   DRAFTING A PARAGRAPH

*Following all the steps of the writing process, write and revise a well-developed paragraph on one of the following topics.*

1. Women in the military
2. Animal rights
3. The cost of college

## 2g    UNDERSTANDING THE STRUCTURE OF ESSAYS

**LEARNING OBJECTIVE 7**
Understand the structure of an effective essay

An **essay** is a group of paragraphs about one subject. It contains one key idea about the subject. This key idea is called the **thesis statement**. Each paragraph in the essay supports or explains some aspect of the thesis statement.

An essay follows a logical and direct plan. It introduces an idea (the thesis statement), explains it, and draws a conclusion. Therefore, an essay usually has at least three paragraphs:

1. Introductory paragraph
2. Body (one or more paragraphs)
3. Concluding paragraph

### The Introductory Paragraph

Your introductory paragraph should accomplish three goals:

- It should establish the topic of the essay.
- It should present your essay's thesis statement in a manner that is appropriate for your intended audience.
- It should stimulate your audience's interest. That is, it should make readers want to read your essay.

### The Body

The body of your essay should accomplish three goals:

- It should provide information that supports and explains your thesis statement.
- It should present each main supporting point in a separate paragraph.
- It should contain enough detailed information to make the main point of each paragraph (that is, the topic sentence) understandable and believable.

## The Concluding Paragraph

Your concluding paragraph should accomplish two goals:

- It should reemphasize but not restate your thesis statement.
- It should draw your essay to a close.

The following idea map shows the ideal organization of an essay:

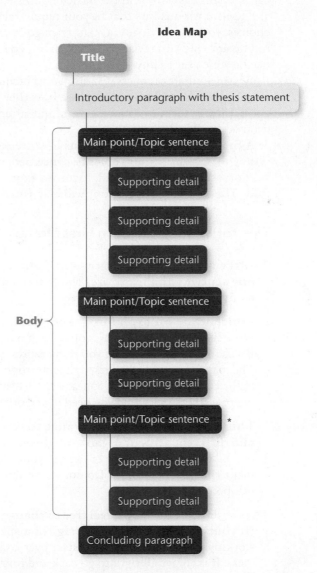

**Idea Map**

Title

Introductory paragraph with thesis statement

Main point/Topic sentence

Supporting detail

Supporting detail

Supporting detail

Main point/Topic sentence

Supporting detail

Supporting detail

Main point/Topic sentence    *

Supporting detail

Supporting detail

Concluding paragraph

Body

\* Number of main points may vary. Each main point should contain a sufficient number of details.

## 2h    WRITING THE FIRST DRAFT OF AN ESSAY

**LEARNING OBJECTIVE 8**
Write a first draft of
your essay

Once you have used prewriting to develop and organize your ideas, you are ready to write a first draft of the essay. **Drafting** is a way of trying out ideas to see if and how they work.

To understand what drafting involves, consider the following comparison. Suppose you need to buy a car. You have decided that you can afford a used car and you have in mind the basic features you need. You visit a used car lot and look at various cars that fit your requirements. After narrowing down your choices, you test drive several cars, then go home to think about how each one might suit you. You revisit the used car lot, go for another test drive, and finally decide which car to buy.

Writing a draft of an essay is similar to buying a car. You have to try out different ideas through prewriting, see how they work together as you organize them, express them in different ways, and, after writing several drafts, settle on what you will include.

A first draft expresses your ideas in sentence form. Work from your list of ideas (see Section 2d), and don't be concerned with grammar, spelling, or punctuation at this point. Instead, focus on expressing and developing each idea fully. The following suggestions will help you write effective first drafts.

### Tips for Writing Effective First Drafts

1. **After you have thought carefully about the ideas on your list, write one sentence that expresses the thesis statement (main point) of your essay.**

2. **Concentrate on explaining your thesis statement, using ideas from your list.** Devote one paragraph to each main idea that supports your thesis. Focus first on the ideas that you think express your main point particularly well. The main point of each paragraph is the topic sentence. It usually appears first in the paragraph, but it can appear anywhere in the paragraph. Later in the writing process, you may find you need to add other ideas from your list.

3. **Think of a first draft as a chance to experiment with different ideas and different ways of organizing them.** While you are drafting, if you think of a better way to organize or express your ideas, or if you think of new ideas, make changes. Be flexible. Do not worry about getting your wording exact at this point.

4. **As your draft develops, feel free to change your focus or even your topic (if your instructor has not assigned a specific topic).** If your draft is not working out, don't hesitate to start over completely. Go back to generating ideas. It is always all right to go back and forth among the steps in the writing process. Many writers make a number of "false starts" before they produce a first draft that satisfies them.

5. **Don't expect immediate success.** When you finish your first draft, you should feel that you have the beginnings of a paper you will be happy with. Now ask yourself if you have a sense of the direction your paper will take. Do you have a thesis statement for your essay? Do the paragraphs each explain or support your thesis? Does each paragraph have sufficient supporting details? Is the organization logical? If you can answer "yes" to these questions, you have something good to work with and revise.

The following first draft evolved from Santiago's brainstorming list on page 30 and outline on page 32. The highlighting indicates the main points he developed as he wrote.

## First Draft of Santiago's Essay

1    There are around twenty million people living in Mexico City, and this number is constantly increasing. Mexico is where I was born and grew up, before I moved to Beloit, Wisconsin to attend Beloit College. The town of Beloit has roughly thirty thousand people. This means that about seven hundred towns the size of Beloit would fit inside Mexico City. In Mexico City, I was no more than a speck of dust in a dirty room. In Beloit, if I go have breakfast in one of three downtown cafés, I can be sure that there will be at least one person I know, probably around five or more. *Beloit and Mexico City are two completely different worlds that I have come to call home.*

2    I am Mexican. I probably have beautiful cinnamon skin, hair black as night and falling straight like a waterfall to frame two glowing brown eyes. Many people think this is what a "true Mexican" looks like. Drawing a line between what is a true Mexican and what isn't based on looks is not a simple task. I myself think it is impossible. This stereotype has played a role in my life both in Mexico and Beloit. I have white skin, the only blue eyes in my family of brown eyes, and curly light brown hair. When I go to the market to buy vegetables for the week, people don't bother to ask my name. They call me *güerito*, blonde. I get asked if I am from the United States or from another country. I was never completely a part of the nation I was born and grew up in. In Beloit though, people are fascinated by my cultural background and ask about my customs and daily life back home. Inevitably, at some point in the conversation they tell me that I don't look Mexican. I live between two worlds; being racially "foreign" in Mexico, and being culturally "foreign" in Beloit.

3    Living a life in between two worlds, never completely a part of any, is a very complicated and extremely interesting place to be. Living in-between

encourages growth and maturity. On one hand, in my teenage years, when I desperately wanted to feel I was a part of something, there wasn't anything to take refuge in and feel strongly about. On the other, though, this made me see the effects of the culture I grew up with on my way of thinking. Standing in this middle ground was a vantage point where I could analyze the opinions I held and the habits I developed and see the virtues and faults through different eyes. The hardiest weeds live where the pavement meets the prairie. I live where outsider meets insider.

4    I became used to being in the middle. I discovered that most questions can have more than one answer, or no answer at all. I realized that people are a lot more complex than I thought, and you really can't stick a label to them that won't become old and fall off. I had thought that people who fit snugly into the stereotype would never experience being an outsider. But I soon found out otherwise. Some had to choose between going to the cinema with their friends and going to church with their family. Some loved playing soccer in the mornings, and then go ballroom dancing in the afternoon. Everyone had their own experience of being in-between two places they sometimes love and sometimes hate.

5    It is the places in-between where the most potential for growth lives. Everyone has their own place where they feel like outsiders, or not completely insiders. Realizing that this is where you are standing, and that it is perfectly fine to have one foot inside and one foot outside, will let the unique reveal itself through you. Being in-between can be difficult, but it is there that the most unexpected and wonderful things happen.

## EXERCISE 2-6    THE WRITING PROCESS: WRITING THE FIRST DRAFT OF AN ESSAY

*Choosing one of the topics you did not use in Exercise 2-2, generate ideas about it using freewriting, brainstorming, or branching. Then create an outline or idea map to organize the ideas that best support your topic, and write a short essay.*

## REVISION STRATEGIES

### 2i    REVISING THE FIRST DRAFT OF AN ESSAY

**LEARNING OBJECTIVE 9**
Revise a draft

Think again about the process of buying a car. At first you may think you have considered everything you need and are ready to make a decision. Then, a while later, you think of other features that would be good to have in your car; in fact, these features are at least as important as the ones you have already thought of. Now you have to rethink your requirements and perhaps reorganize your thoughts about what features are most important to you. You might eliminate some features, add others, and reconsider the importance of others.

A similar thing often happens as you revise your first draft. When you finish a first draft, you are more or less satisfied with it. Then you reread it later and see you have more work to do. When you revise, you have to rethink your entire paper, reexamining every part and idea.

Revising is more than changing a word or rearranging a few sentences, and it is not concerned with correcting punctuation, spelling, or grammar. (You make these proofreading changes later, after you are satisfied that you have presented your ideas in the best way. See Section 2i.) Revision is your chance to make significant improvements to your first draft. It might mean changing, adding, deleting, or rearranging whole sections of your essay.

Here is an excerpt from a later draft of Santiago Quintana Garcia's essay. In this revised draft of the third and fourth paragraphs, you can see how Santiago expands his ideas, adding words and details (underlined), and deleting others. You can read his final essay in Chapter 12, page 328.

## Santiago's Revision of Paragraphs 3 and 4

3    Living a life in-between two worlds, never completely a part of any, is a very complicated and extremely interesting place to be. Living in-between encourages growth and maturity. As a teenager, I struggled with feelings of not belonging and wanting to be a part of a group. I did not play soccer, or the guitar, and suffered from bullying. The impact this had in my life was emotionally wrecking. Often when people find themselves in similar situations, they turn to familiar things for comfort. Things like a group they belong to, like a culture, or a race, or a religious group. This was not accessible to me in the same way as it was to others. ~~On one hand, in my teenage years, when I desperately wanted to feel I was part of something, there wasn't anything to take refuge in and feel strongly about.~~ On the other hand, though, standing on no man's land let this made me observe ~~see~~ the effects of the culture I grew up with on my way of thinking, and has greatly influenced my area of focus in my college studies. Standing in this middle ground was a vantage point from which I could analyze the opinions I held and the habits I developed and see my virtues and faults through different eyes. The hardiest weeds live where the pavement meets the prairie. I live where outsider meets insider.

4    ~~I became used to being in the middle. I discovered that most questions can~~
~~have more than one answer, or no answer at all. I realized that people are a lot~~
~~more complex that I thought, and you really can't stick a label to them that~~
~~won't become old and fall off.~~ What happens in this middle ground is that
concepts such as gender, race, nationality and other identities seem held up by
pins. They are extremely volatile and impermanent; constantly changing and
molding. This knowledge is present with me every time I say "I am Mexican" or
"I am white." I had thought that people who fit snugly into a stereotype would
never experience being an outsider. But I soon found out otherwise.

## Essay Revision Checklist

Use these suggestions to revise an essay effectively.

1. **Reread the sentence that expresses your main point, the thesis statement of your essay.** It must be clear, direct, and complete. Experiment with ways to improve it.

2. **Make sure each paragraph supports your thesis statement.** Do all the paragraphs relate directly to the thesis? If not, cross out or rewrite those that do not clarify their connection to the main point.

3. **Make sure your essay has a beginning and an end.** An essay should have introductory and concluding paragraphs.

4. **Replace words that are vague or unclear with more specific or more descriptive words.**

5. **Seek advice.** If you are unsure about how to revise, visit your writing instructor during office hours and ask for advice, or try peer review (discussed below).

6. **When you have finished revising, you should feel satisfied with what you have said and with the way you have said it.** If you do not feel satisfied, revise your draft again.

   Once you are satisfied, you are ready to edit and proofread.

## The Revision Process: Peer Review

**Peer review** entails asking one or more of your classmates to read and comment on your writing. It is an excellent way to discover what is good in your draft and what needs improvement. Here are some suggestions for making peer review as valuable as possible.

## When You Are the Writer ...

1. Prepare your draft in readable form. Double-space your work and print it on standard 8.5″ × 11″ paper.

2. When you receive your peers' comments, weigh them carefully. Keep an open mind, but do not feel that you must accept every suggestion.

3. If you have questions or are uncertain about your peers' advice, talk with your instructor.

## When You Are the Reviewer ...

1. Read the draft through at least once before making any suggestions.

2. Use the revision checklist on page 44 as a guide.

3. As you read, keep the writer's intended audience in mind (see Section 2c, p. 26). The draft should be appropriate for that audience.

4. Offer positive comments first. Say what the writer did well.

5. Be specific in your review and offer suggestions for improvement.

6. Be supportive; put yourself in the place of the person whose work you are reviewing. Phrase your feedback in the way you would want to hear it!

---

**EXERCISE 2-7    THE WRITING PROCESS: REVISING A DRAFT**

*Revise the first draft you wrote for Exercise 2-6.*

---

**EXERCISE 2-8    USING PEER REVIEW**

*Pair with a classmate for this exercise. Read and evaluate each other's drafts written for Exercises 2-6, using the peer review guidelines provided in this section.*

---

## 2j    EDITING AND PROOFREADING YOUR WORK

**LEARNING OBJECTIVE 10**
**Proofread for correctness**

**Editing** and **proofreading** require a final reading of your paper to check for errors. In this final polishing of your work, the focus is on correctness, so don't proofread until you have completed your drafting and revising. When you are ready to edit and proofread, you should check your writing for errors in

- sentences (run-ons or fragments)
- grammar
- spelling
- punctuation
- capitalization

## Editing and Proofreading Checklist

The following tips will help you as you edit and proofread.

1. **Review your paper once for each type of error.** First, read it for run-on sentences or fragments. Take a short break, and then read it four more times, each time paying attention to one of the following: *grammar, spelling, punctuation*, and *capitalization*. Don't do this when you are tired; you might miss some mistakes or introduce new ones.

2. **To find spelling errors and identify fragments, read your paper from the last sentence to the first sentence and from last word to first word.** By reading this way, you will not get distracted by the flow of ideas, so you can focus on finding spelling errors. Also use the spell-checker on your computer, but be sure to proofread for the types of errors it cannot catch: missing words, errors that are themselves words (such as *of* for *or*), and homonyms (for example, using *it's* for *its*).

3. **Read each sentence, slowly and deliberately.** This technique will help you catch endings that you have left off verbs or missing plurals.

4. **Check for errors one final time after you print out your paper.** Ask a classmate or friend to read your paper to catch any mistakes you missed.

Here is a paragraph that shows the errors that a student corrected during editing and proofreading. Notice that errors in grammar, spelling, and punctuation were corrected.

> The Robert Burns, said that the dog is man's best friend. To a large extent, this statement may be more true/truer than we thinks. What makes dogs so special to humans is they're/their unending loyalty and their unconditional love. Dogs have been known to cross the entire United states to return home. They/Never make fun of you or criticize you, Or/They throw fits, and they are alswways happey to see you. Dogs never lye/lie to you, never betray your confidences, and never stays angry with you for more than five minutes. The/World would be a better place if only people could be more like dogs.

To view Santiago Quintana Garcia's final, proofread essay, see Reading Selection 3, "The Space In-Between," on page 328.

### EXERCISE 2-9   WRITING IN PROCESS: EDITING AND PROOFREADING

*Prepare a final version of your essay by editing and proofreading the revised draft you created in Exercise 2-6.*

## SUMMARY OF LEARNING OBJECTIVES

**MySkillsLab**
Complete the mastery test for this chapter **in MySkillsLab.**

**1  Understand the writing process.**
*What is the writing process?*

The **writing process** consists of *four basic steps*: prewriting to generate ideas and organize ideas, writing a first draft, revising, and editing and proofreading.

**2  Use technology effectively.**
*What are drawbacks of using technology?*

**Computers** are useful at each stage of the writing process. They save you time, but be sure not to rely solely on their features to produce error free text.

**3  Consider your audience, purpose, tone, and point of view.**
*What should you consider before you write?*

To consider your **audience**, ask yourself who will be reading what you write. To consider your **purpose**, think about what you are trying to achieve through your writing. Choose a **point of view** and **tone** appropriate to your audience and purpose.

**4  Use prewriting to generate ideas for your writing.**
*What are prewriting techniques?*

Three techniques for generating ideas are **freewriting** (writing non-stop about a topic for a specified period without worrying about punctuation, spelling, and grammatical correctness), **brainstorming** (making a list of everything you can think of that is associated with your topic), and **diagramming** (writing your topic in a circle and drawing lines out from it to connect to related ideas).

**5  Use prewriting to organize your ideas.**
*How can you organize ideas?*

Two common methods of organizing ideas are **outlining** (listing main points and details in the order in which you will present them) and idea **mapping** (creating a drawing that shows the content and organization of your writing).

**6  Write an effective paragraph.**
*What constitutes an effective paragraph?*

A **paragraph** is a group of sentences, usually at least three or four, that express one main idea. An **effective paragraph** contains a topic sentence that clearly states the main idea and logically organized supporting details that explain and illustrate it. Transitional words and phrases are use to connect ideas within and between paragraphs. Paragraphs may stand alone or be combined into essays or longer works.

**7  Understand the structure of an effective essay.**
*How do you structure an essay?*

An **essay** is a group of at least three paragraphs about one subject. Essays should include an introductory paragraph, a body, and a concluding paragraph. (See the idea map for essays on page 39.)

**8  Write a first draft of your essay.**
*What is involved in drafting?*

**Drafting** is a way of trying out ideas to see if and how they work. Begin by writing one sentence expressing your main point, your thesis statement, then focus on explaining that sentence. A first draft is ideal for experimenting with different ideas and different ways of organizing them.

**9  Revise a draft.**
*What is revision?*

**Revision** allows you to make significant improvements to your draft by changing, adding, deleting, or rearranging words, parts, and ideas.

**10  Proofread for correctness.**
*How do you edit and proofread?*

**Edit** and **proofread** by checking for errors in sentences, grammar, spelling, punctuation, and capitalization. Read your paper once for each type of error, read your paper from the end to the beginning, read aloud, and check for errors again after you print your paper.

# 3 Vocabulary for Readers and Writers

## LEARNING OBJECTIVES

**1** Use a dictionary and a thesaurus

**2** Use context clues

**3** Use affixes: prefixes, roots, and suffixes

**4** Use language effectively

Your vocabulary can be one of your strongest assets or one of your greatest liabilities. It defines and describes you by revealing a great deal about your level of education and your experience. Your vocabulary contributes to that all-important first impression people form when they meet you. A strong vocabulary provides both immediate academic benefits and long-term career effects, increasing your comprehension and critical-thinking skills. This chapter helps you to strengthen your vocabulary and use language effectively when you write.

## 3a USING A DICTIONARY AND A THESAURUS

**LEARNING OBJECTIVE 1**
Use a dictionary and a thesaurus

To read and write effectively, you need resources to help you find the meanings of unfamiliar words as you read and to locate exact and precise words that convey your intended meaning when you write.

### Using a Dictionary

There are several types of dictionaries, each with its own purpose and use:

1. **Online dictionaries** are readily available. Two of the most widely used are *Merriam-Webster* (http://www.m-w.com) and *American Heritage* (http://www.ahdictionary.com/). Both of these sites feature an audio component that allows you to hear how a word is pronounced. Online dictionaries have several important advantages over print dictionaries.

   - **Audio component.** Some online dictionaries such as *Merriam-Webster Online* and *The American Heritage Dictionary of the English Language* feature an audio component that allows you to hear how words are pronounced.

- **Multiple dictionary entries.** Some sites, such as Dictionary.com, display entries from several dictionaries for each word you look up.

- **Misspellings.** If you aren't sure of how a word is spelled or if you mistype it, several possible words and their meanings will be provided.

2. A **pocket or paperback dictionary** is an inexpensive, easy-to-carry, shortened version of a standard desk dictionary. It is small enough to carry to classes and costs around $7.

3. A **desk dictionary** is a more complete and extensive dictionary. Although a pocket dictionary is convenient, it is also limited in use. A pocket edition lists about 50,000 to 60,000 words; a standard desk edition lists up to 150,000 words. Also, the desk edition provides much more complete information about each word. Several standard dictionaries are available in both desk and paperback editions. These include:

   *The Random House Dictionary of the English Language*

   *Merriam-Webster's Collegiate Dictionary*

   *The American Heritage Dictionary of the English Language*

4. An **unabridged dictionary** can be found in the reference section of the library or online. An unabridged edition provides the most complete information on each word in the English language.

## EXERCISE 3–1 . . . USING A DICTIONARY

*Use a dictionary to answer each of the following questions. Write your answer in the space provided.*

1. What does the abbreviation *e.g.* stand for? _____

2. How is the word *deleterious* pronounced? (Record its phonetic spelling.)

   _____

3. From what languages is the word *delicatessen* taken?

   _____

4. Locate one restricted meaning for the word *configuration*.

   _____

   _____

5. What is the history of the word *mascot*?

   _____

   _____

   _____

   _____

6. What is the plural spelling of *addendum*? _____

7. What type of punctuation is a virgule?

_____

8. List a few words that contain the following sound: ī.

_____

9. Who or what is a Semite?

_____

10. Can the word *phrase* be used other than as a noun? If so, how?

_____

A dictionary lists all the common meanings of a word, but usually you are looking for only one definition. Meanings in an entry are grouped and numbered consecutively according to part of speech. If you are able to identify the part of speech of the word you are looking up, you can skip over all parts of the entry that do not pertain to that part of speech. If you cannot identify the part of speech of a word you are looking up, begin with the first meaning listed. Generally, the most common meaning appears first, and more specialized meanings appear toward the end of the entry. When you find a meaning that could fit into the sentence you are working with, replace the word with its definition and then read the entire sentence. If the definition makes sense in the sentence, you can be fairly certain that you have selected the appropriate meaning.

## EXERCISE 3-2 . . . FINDING MEANINGS

*Write an appropriate meaning for the underlined word in each of the following sentences. Use the dictionary to help you find the meaning that makes sense in the sentence.*

1. He <u>affected</u> a French accent.

_____

2. The <u>amphibian</u> took us to our destination in less than an hour.

_____

3. The plane stalled on the <u>apron</u>.

_____

4. We <u>circumvented</u> the problem by calculating in metric.

_____

5. Many consumers have become <u>embroiled</u> in the debate over the rising inflation rate.

_____

## Using a Thesaurus

A **thesaurus**, or dictionary of synonyms, is a valuable reference for locating a precise, accurate, or descriptive word to fit a particular situation. A thesaurus lists synonyms for words and phrases, and you can choose from the list the word that most closely suggests the meaning you want to convey. The easiest way to do this is to test out, or substitute, various choices in your sentence to see which one is most appropriate; check a dictionary if you are not sure of a word's exact meaning. Here's an example:

> The young man was **sad** about losing his girlfriend.
> Sad: *bitter, dejected, despondent, gloomy, heartbroken, pensive, melancholy, wistful*

Try substituting several of the synonyms listed above for the word *sad* and see how doing so changes the tone and meaning of the sentence.

Many students misuse thesauruses by choosing words that do not fit the context of their writing. *Be sure to use words only when you are familiar with all their shades of meaning.* Remember, a misused word is often a more serious error than a wordy or imprecise expression.

The most widely used print thesaurus is *Roget's Thesaurus*; it is readily available in an inexpensive paperback edition. Online thesauruses are available at the sites below; you can also pick a thesaurus from search choices.

- Roget's Thesaurus    http://www.bartleby.com/62/
- Merriam-Webster    http://merriam-webster.com/

### EXERCISE 3-3 . . . USING A THESAURUS

*Replace the underlined word or phrase in each sentence with a more descriptive word or phrase. Use a thesaurus to choose your replacement.*

1. When Sara learned that her sister had committed a crime, she was mad. _____

2. Compared with earlier chapters, the last two chapters in my chemistry text are hard. _____

3. The instructor spent the entire class talking about the causes of inflation and deflation. _____

4. The main character in the film was a thin, talkative British soldier.

   _____

5. We went to see a great film that won the Academy Award for best picture. _____

## 3b    USING CONTEXT CLUES

LEARNING OBJECTIVE 2
Use context clues
Read the following brief paragraph in which some words are missing. Try to figure out the missing words and write them in the blanks.

> Rate refers to the _____ at which you read. If you read too _____, your comprehension may suffer. If you read too _____, you are not likely to complete your assignments on time.

Did you insert the word *speed* in the first blank, *fast* in the second blank, and *slowly* in the third blank? Most likely you correctly identified all three missing words. You could tell from the sentence which word to put in. The words around the missing words—the sentence **context**—provided clues as to which word would fit and make sense; such clues are called **context clues**.

While you probably won't find missing words on a printed page, you will often find words whose meaning you do not know. Context clues can help you figure out the meanings of unfamiliar words.

### Examples

> A **neurosis**, such as short-term depression, mild anxiety, or hypochondria, can make it difficult for a person to live a fully healthy life.

From the sentence, you can tell that *neurosis* means "a relatively mild mental illness." Here's another example:

> The couple finally **secured** a reservation at the wildly popular new ski lodge.

You can figure out that *secured* means "got" or "succeeding in getting" a reservation.

There are four types of context clues to look for: (1) definition, (2) example, (3) contrast, and (4) logic of the passage. Study the chart below to learn how to use each type.

### TYPES OF CONTEXT CLUES

| CONTEXT CLUE | HOW TO FIND MEANING | EXAMPLE |
|---|---|---|
| Definition | 1. Look for words that announce that meanings will follow (*is, are, refers to, means*). | Broad, flat noodles that are served with sauce or butter are called **fettuccine.** |
|  | 2. Look for parentheses, dashes, or commas that set apart synonyms or brief definitions. | Psychologists often wonder whether **stereotypes**—the assumptions we make about what people are like—might be self-fulfilling. |

| CONTEXT CLUE | HOW TO FIND MEANING | EXAMPLE |
|---|---|---|
| Example | Figure out what the examples have in common. (For example, both peas and beans are vegetables and grow in pods.) | Most **condiments**, such as pepper, mustard, and ketchup, are used to improve the flavor of foods. |
| Contrast | Look for a word or phrase that is the opposite of a word whose meaning you don't know. | Before their classes in manners, the children were disorderly; after graduation, they acted with more **decorum**. |
| Logic of the Passage | Use the rest of the sentence to help you. Pretend the word is a blank line and fill in the blank with a word that makes sense. | On hot, humid afternoons, I often feel **languid**. |

## EXERCISE 3-4 . . . USING DEFINITION CLUES

*Read the following excerpt and use definition clues to help you determine the meaning of each boldfaced word or phrase.*

### Issue: Cultural Similarities and Differences

Within every culture, there is an overall sense of what is beautiful and what is not beautiful, what represents good taste as opposed to tastelessness or even obscenity. Such considerations are matters of **aesthetics**. Global marketers must understand the importance of visual aesthetics embodied in the color or shape of a product, label, or package. Aesthetic elements that are attractive, appealing, and in good taste in one country may be perceived differently in another. In some cases, a **standardized color** can be used in all countries; an example is the distinctive yellow color on Caterpillar's earth-moving equipment and its licensed outdoor gear.

Music is an aesthetic component of all cultures and is accepted as a form of artistic expression and a source of entertainment. In one sense, music represents a **transculture** that is not identified with any particular nation. However, sociologists have noted that national identity derives in part from a country's **indigenous**, or native, music; a unique musical style can represent the uniqueness of the culture and the community.

—adapted from Keegan and Green, *Global Marketing*, p. 104

1. aesthetics _____

_____

2. standardized color _____

_____

3. transculture _____

_____

4. indigenous _____

---

### EXERCISE 3-5 . . . USING EXAMPLE CLUES

*Read the following excerpt and use definition and example clues to help you determine the meaning of each boldfaced word.*

#### Issue: Terrorism

**Terrorism** is the systematic use of violence by a group in order to **intimidate** a population or **coerce** a government into granting its demands. Terrorists attempt to achieve their **objectives** through organized acts that spread fear and anxiety among the population, such as bombing, kidnapping, hijacking, taking of hostages, and **assassination**. They consider violence necessary as a means of bringing widespread publicity to goals and **grievances** that are not being addressed through peaceful means. Belief in their cause is so strong that terrorists do not hesitate to strike despite knowing they will probably die in the act.

Distinguishing terrorism from other acts of political violence can be difficult. For example, if a Palestinian suicide bomber kills several dozen Israeli teenagers in a Jerusalem restaurant, is that an act of terrorism or wartime **retaliation** against Israeli government policies and army actions? Competing arguments are made: Israel's **sympathizers** denounce the act as a terrorist threat to the country's existence, whereas **advocates** of the Palestinian cause argue that long-standing injustices and Israeli army attacks on Palestinian civilians provoked the act.

—Rubenstein, *Contemporary Human Geography*, p. 190

1. terrorism _____

_____

2. intimidate _____

3. coerce _____

4. objectives _____

5. assassination _____

6. grievances _____

7. retaliation _____

8. sympathizers _____

9. advocates _____

## EXERCISE 3-6 . . . USING CONTRAST CLUES

*Read the following excerpt and use contrast clues to help you determine the meaning of each boldfaced word. Consult a dictionary, if necessary.*

### Issue: "Dirty" Political Campaigns

The Whigs chose General William Henry Harrison to run against President Martin Van Buren in 1840, using a **specious** but effective argument: General Harrison is a plain man of the people who lives in a log cabin. Contrast him with the suave Van Buren, **luxuriating** amid "the Regal Splendor of the President's Palace." Harrison drinks ordinary hard cider with his hog meat and grits, while Van Buren **eschews** plain food in favor of expensive foreign wines and fancy French cuisine. The general's furniture is **unpretentious** and sturdy; the president dines off gold plates and treads on carpets that cost the people $5 a yard. In a country where all are equal, the people will reject an **aristocrat** like Van Buren and put their trust in General Harrison, a simple, brave, honest, public-spirited common man. (In fact, Harrison came from a distinguished family, was well educated and financially comfortable, and certainly did not live in a log cabin.)

—adapted from Carnes and Garraty, *The American Nation*, p. 267

1. specious _____

2. luxuriating _____

3. eschews _____

4. unpretentious _____

5. aristocrat _____

## EXERCISE 3-7 . . . USING LOGIC OF THE PASSAGE CLUES

*Read the following excerpt and use the logic of the passage clues to help you select the correct meaning of each boldfaced word or phrase.*

### Issue: Cultural Similarities and Differences

In 2005, while writing a children's book on the life of the **prophet** Mohammed, Danish author Klare Bluitgen searched unsuccessfully for an **illustrator**. The problem: Many of the world's Muslims believe that it is **blasphemy** to **depict** images of the prophet. Denmark's conservative *Jyllands-Posten* newspaper picked up the story; concerned that this was a case of **self-censorship**, the paper's cultural editor challenged dozens of well-known illustrators to "draw Mohammed in the way they see him." In September 2005, *Jyllands-Posten* printed submissions from 12 illustrators **in conjunction with** articles on freedom of speech; one of the images depicted Mohammed with a bomb in his turban.

—Keegan and Green, *Global Marketing*, p. 105

1. prophet _____

2. illustrator _____

3. blasphemy _____

4. depict _____

5. self-censorship _____

6. in conjunction with _____

---

## 3c    LEARNING AFFIXES: PREFIXES, ROOTS, AND SUFFIXES

**LEARNING OBJECTIVE 3**
Use affixes: prefixes, roots, and suffixes

Suppose you come across the following sentence in a human anatomy textbook:

> Trichromatic plates are used frequently in the text to illustrate the position of body organs.

If you did not know the meaning of *trichromatic*, how could you determine it? There are no context clues in the sentence. One solution is to look up the word in a dictionary. An easier and faster way is to break the word into parts and analyze the meaning of each part. Many words in the English language are made up of affixes called **prefixes, roots,** and **suffixes**. These affixes have specific meanings that, when added together, can help you determine the meaning of the word as a whole.

The word *trichromatic* can be divided into three parts: its prefix, root, and suffix.

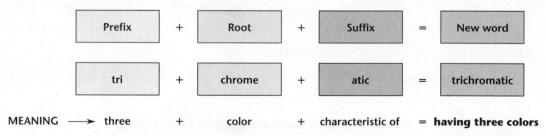

MEANING ──▶ three + color + characteristic of = **having three colors**

You can see from this analysis that *trichromatic* means "having three colors." Here are two other examples of words that you can figure out by using prefixes, roots, and suffixes:

> The student found the philosophy textbook completely **incomprehensible.**
>
> **in-** = not
>
> **comprehend** = understand
>
> **-ible** = able to do something
>
> **incomprehensible** = not able to be understood

> I wanted to run the marathon, but after suffering from the flu for two weeks, I was a **nonstarter.**
>
> **non-** = not
>
> **start** = begin
>
> **-er** = one who does something
>
> **nonstarter** = someone who fails to take part in (or begin) a race

The first step in using the prefix–root–suffix method is to become familiar with the most commonly used affixes. The prefixes and roots listed in Tables 3-1 and 3-2 (pages 58 and 60) will give you a good start in determining the meanings of thousands of words without having to look them up in the dictionary. Before you begin to use affixes to figure out new words, there are a few things you need to know:

1. **In most cases, a word is built upon at least one root.**
2. **Words can have more than one prefix, root, or suffix.**
   a. Words can be made up of two or more roots (*geo/logy*).
   b. Some words have two prefixes (*in/sub/ordination*).
   c. Some words have two suffixes (*beauti/ful/ly*).
3. **Words do not always have a prefix and a suffix.**
   a. Some words have neither a prefix nor a suffix (*read*).
   b. Others have a suffix but no prefix (*read/ing*).
   c. Others have a prefix but no suffix (*pre/read*).
4. **The spelling of roots may change as they are combined with suffixes.** Some common variations are included in Table 3-2 (page 60).
5. **Different prefixes, roots, or suffixes may have the same meaning.** For example, the prefixes *bi-, di-,* and *duo-* all mean "two." The prefixes *un-, in-,* and *non-* all mean "not."
6. **Some roots, prefixes, and suffixes have different meanings in different words.** The meaning is based on whether the word part comes from Latin or Greek. For example, the biological term for mankind is *homo sapiens*. Here, *homo* means "man." In the word *homogenous*, which means "all of the same kind," *homo* means "same." Other words that use the Greek meaning of homo are *homogenize* (to make uniform or similar) and *homonym* (two words that sound the same).
7. **Sometimes you may identify a group of letters as a prefix or root but find that it does not carry the meaning of that prefix or root.** For example, the letters *mis* in the word *missile* are part of the root and are not the prefix *mis-,* which means "wrong; bad."

## Prefixes

**Prefixes** appear at the beginning of many English words. They alter the meaning of the root to which they are connected. For example, if you add the prefix *re-* to the word *read,* the word *reread* is formed, meaning "to read again."

If *pre-* is added to the word *reading,* the word *pre-reading* is formed, meaning "before reading." If the prefix *post-* is added, the word *post-reading* is formed, meaning "after reading." Table 3-1 lists common prefixes grouped according to meaning.

## TABLE 3.1  COMMON PREFIXES

| PREFIX | MEANING | SAMPLE WORD | MEANING OF SAMPLE WORD |
|---|---|---|---|
| *Prefixes referring to amount or number* | | | |
| mono-/uni- | one | monocle/unicycle | eyeglass for one eye/one wheel vehicle |
| bi-/di-/duo- | two | bimonthly/diandrous/ duet | twice a month/flower with two stamens/two singers |
| tri- | three | triangle | a figure with three sides and three angles |
| quad- | four | quadrant | any of four parts into which something is divided |
| quint-/pent- | five | quintet/pentagon | a group of five/five-sides figure |
| deci- | ten | decimal | based on the number ten |
| centi- | hundred | centigrade | divided into 100 degrees, as a thermometer scale |
| milli- | thousand | milligram | one thousandth of a gram |
| micro- | small | microscope | an instrument used to see a magnified image of a small object |
| multi-/poly- | many | multipurpose/ polygon | having several purposes/figure with three or more sides |
| semi- | half | semicircle | half of a circle |
| equi | equal | equidistant | at equal distances |
| *Prefixes meaning "not" (negative)* | | | |
| a- | not | asymmetrical | not identical on both sides of a central line |
| anti- | against | antiwar | against war |
| contra- | against, opposite | contradict | deny by stating the opposite |
| dis- | apart, away, not | disagree | have a different opinion |
| in-/il-/ir-/im- | not | incorrect/illogical/ impossible | wrong/not having sound reasoning/not possible |
| mis- | wrongly | misunderstand | fail to understand correctly |

## TABLE 3.1 COMMON PREFIXES  (*Continued*)

| PREFIX | MEANING | SAMPLE WORD | MEANING OF SAMPLE WORD |
|---|---|---|---|
| non- | not | nonfiction | writing that is factual, not fiction |
| pseudo- | false | pseudoscientific | a system of theories of methods mistakenly regarded as scientific |
| un- | not | unpopular | not popular |
| *Prefixes giving direction, location, or placement* | | | |
| ab- | away | absent | away or missing from place |
| ad- | toward | adhesive | able to stick to surface |
| ante-/pre- | before | antecedent/ premarital | something that came before/before marriage |
| circum-/peri- | around | circumference/ perimeter | the distance around something/ border of an area |
| com-/col-/con- | with, together | compile/collide/ convene | put together/come into violent contact/come together |
| de- | away, from | depart | leave, go away from |
| dia- | through | diameter | a straight line passing through the center of a circle |
| ex-/extra- | from, out of, former | ex-wife/ extramarital | former wife/occurring outside marriage |
| hyper- | over, excessive | hyperactive | unusually or abnormally active |
| inter- | between | interpersonal | existing or occurring between people |
| intro-/intra- | within, into, in | introvert/intramural | turn or direct inwards/involving only students within the same school |
| post- | after | posttest | a test given after completion of a program of course |
| re- | back, again | review | go over or inspect again |
| retro- | backward | retrospect | a survey or review of the past |
| sub- | under, below | submarine | a ship designed to operate under water |
| super- | above, extra | supercharge | increase or boost the power of something |
| tele- | far | telescope | an instrument for making distant objects appear nearer |
| trans- | across, over | transcontinental | extending across a continent |

## EXERCISE 3-8 . . . USING PREFIXES

*Read the following excerpt and choose the correct prefix from the box below to fill in the blank next to each boldfaced word part. One prefix will not be used.*

| multi | uni | in |
|-------|-----|-----|
| eu | bi | dis |

### Issue: Mental Health Disorders

Major depression is sometimes referred to as a (1) _____ **polar** disorder because the emotional problems exist at only one end, or "pole," of the emotional range. When a person suffers from severe mood swings that go all the way from depression to manic episodes (excessive excitement, energy, and elation), that person is said to suffer from a (2) _____ **polar** disorder, meaning that emotions cycle between the two poles of possible emotions. Unlike mild or moderate mood (3) _____ **orders**, there is usually no external cause for the extreme ups and downs of the bipolar person. The depressive phases of a bipolar person are (4) _____ **distinguishable** from major depression but give way to manic episodes that may last from a few weeks to a few months. In these manic episodes, the person is extremely happy or (5) _____ **phoric** without any real cause to be so happy.

—Ciccarelli and White, *Psychology*, p. 547

## Roots

**Roots** carry the basic or core meaning of a word. Hundreds of root words are used to build words in the English language. Some of the most common and most useful are listed in Table 3-2. Knowing the meanings of these roots will help you unlock the meanings of many words. For example, if you know that the root *dic/dict* means "tell or say," then you have a clue to the meanings of such words as *dictate* (to speak for someone to write down), *diction* (wording or manner of speaking), and *dictionary* (book that explains word meanings).

### TABLE 3.2 COMMON ROOTS

| COMMON ROOT | MEANING | SAMPLE WORD | MEANING OF SAMPLE WORD |
|-------------|---------|-------------|------------------------|
| aster/astro | star | astronaut | a person trained to travel in space |
| aud/audit | hear | audible | able to be heard |
| bene | good, well | benefit | an advantage gained from something |
| bio | life | biology | the scientific study of living organisms |
| cap | take, seize | captive | a person who has been taken prisoner |

## TABLE 3.2  COMMON ROOTS

| COMMON ROOT | MEANING | SAMPLE WORD | MEANING OF SAMPLE WORD |
|---|---|---|---|
| chron/chrono | time | chronology | the order in which events occur |
| cog | to learn | cognitive | relating to mental processes |
| corp | body | corpse | dead body |
| cred | believe | incredible | difficult/impossible to believe |
| dict/dic | tell, say | predict | declare something will happen in the future |
| duc/duct | lead | introduce | bring in or present for the first time |
| fact/fac | make, do | factory | a building where goods are manufactured |
| geo | earth | geophysics | the physics of the earth |
| graph | write | telegraph | a system for sending messages to a distant place |
| log/logo/logy | study, thought | psychology | the scientific study of the human mind |
| mit/miss | send | permit/dismiss | allow or make possible/send away |
| mort/mor | die, death | immortal | everlasting, not subject to death |
| path | feeling | sympathy | sharing the feelings of another |
| phon | sound, voice | telephone | a divice used to transmit voices |
| photo | light | photosensitive | responding to light |
| port | carry | transport | carry from one place to another |
| scop | seeing | microscope | an instrument that magnifies small objects |
| scrib/script | write | inscription | a written note |
| sen/sent | feel | insensitive | lacking concern for others' feelings |
| spec/spic/spect | look, see | retrospect | a survey or review of the past |
| tend/tens/tent | stretch or strain | tension | mental or emotional strain |
| terr/terre | land, earth | territory | a geographic area, a tract of land |
| theo | god | theology | the study of the nature of God and religious belief |
| ven/vent | come | convention | a meeting or formal assembly |
| vert/vers | turn | invert | put upside down or in the opposite position |
| vis/vid | see | invisible/video | not able to be seen/related to televised images |
| voc | call | vocation | a person's occupation or calling |

## EXERCISE 3-9 . . . USING ROOTS

*Read the following excerpt and choose the correct root from the box below to fill in the blank next to each boldfaced word part. One root will not be used.*

| | | |
|---|---|---|
| osteo | phys | mort |
| vasc | cardio | dic |

### Issue: Health and Fitness

(1) _____ **respiratory** fitness reflects the heart and lungs' ability to perform exercise using large-muscle groups at moderate to high intensity for prolonged periods. Because it requires the blood vessels of the (2) **cardio** _____ **ular** system as well as respiratory systems to supply oxygen to the body during sustained physical activity, it is a good (3) **in** _____ **ator** of overall health. Low levels of fitness are associated with increased risk of premature death and disease.

A common affliction among older adults is (4) _____ **porosis**, a disease characterized by low bone mass and deterioration of bone tissue, which increase facture risk. Bone, like other human tissues, responds to the demands placed on it. Women (and men) have much to gain by remaining (5) _____ **ically** active as they age—bone mass levels are significantly higher among active than among sedentary women. Regular weight-bearing exercise, when combined with a healthy diet containing adequate calcium, helps keeps bones healthy.

—adapted from Donatelle, *Health*, pp. 329–330

### Suffixes

**Suffixes** are word endings that often change the word's tense and/or part of speech. For example, adding the suffix *-y* to the noun *cloud* forms the adjective *cloudy*. Accompanying the change in part of speech is a shift in meaning (*cloudy* means "resembling clouds; overcast with clouds; dimmed or dulled as if by clouds").

### Examples

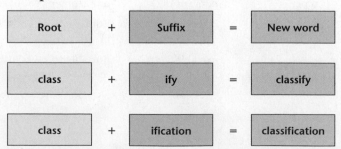

| Root | + | Suffix | = | New word |
|---|---|---|---|---|
| class | + | ify | = | classify |
| class | + | ification | = | classification |

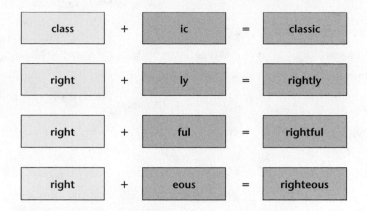

Often, several different words can be formed from a single root word with different suffixes. If you know the meaning of the root word and the ways in which different suffixes affect the meaning of the root word, you will be able to figure out a word's meaning when a suffix is added.

A list of common suffixes and their meanings appears in Table 3-3.

## TABLE 3.3  COMMON SUFFIXES

| SUFFIX | MEANING | SAMPLE WORD | MEANING OF SAMPLE WORD |
|---|---|---|---|
| *Suffixes that refer to a state, condition, or quality* | | | |
| -able | capable of | touchable | capable of being touched |
| -ance | characterized by | assistance | the action of helping |
| -ation | action or process | confrontation | an act of confronting or meeting face to face |
| -ence | state or condition | reference | an act or instance of referring or mentioning |
| -ible | capable of | tangible | capable of being felt, having substance |
| -ion | action or process | discussion | examining topic in speech or writing |
| -ity | state or quality | superiority | the quality or condition of being higher in rank or status |
| -ive | performing action | permissive | characterized by freedom of behavior |
| -ment | action or process | amazement | a state of overwhelming surprise or astonishment |
| -ness | state, quality, condition | kindness | the quality of being kind |

**TABLE 3.3  COMMON SUFFIXES**    (*Continued*)

| SUFFIX | MEANING | SAMPLE WORD | MEANING OF SAMPLE WORD |
|---|---|---|---|
| -ous | possessing, full of | jealous | envious or resentful of another |
| -ty | condition, quality characterized by | loyalty | the state of being loyal or faithful |
| -y | | creamy | resembling or containing cream |
| *Suffixes that mean "one who"* | | | |
| -an | | Italian | one who is from Italy |
| -ant | | participant | one who participates |
| -ee | | referee | one who enforces the rules of a game or sport |
| -eer | | engineer | one who is trained in engineering |
| -ent | | resident | one who lives in a place |
| -er | | teacher | one who teaches |
| -ist | | activist | one who takes action to promote or advocate a cause |
| -or | | advisor | one who advises |
| *Suffixes that mean "pertaining to or referring to"* | | | |
| -al | | autumnal | occurring in or pertaining to autumn |
| -ship | | friendship | the state of being friends |
| -hood | | brotherhood | the relationship between brothers |
| -ward | | homeward | leading towards home |

You can expand your vocabulary by learning the variations in meaning that occur when suffixes are added to words you already know. When you find a word whose meaning you do not know, look for the root. Then, using context, figure out what the word means with the suffix added. Occasionally you may find that the spelling of the root word has changed. For instance, a final *e* may be dropped, a final consonant may be doubled, or a final *y* may be changed to *i*. Consider the possibility of such changes when trying to identify the root word.

**Examples**

The article was a **compilation** of facts.

**root + suffix**

compil(e) + -ation = something that has been compiled, or put together into an orderly form

I was concerned with the **morality** of my decision.

**root + suffix**

moral + -ity = pertaining to moral matters

Our college is one of the most **prestigious** in the state.

**root + suffix**

prestig(e) + -ous = having prestige or distinction

## EXERCISE 3-10 . . . USING SUFFIXES

*Read the following excerpt. For each pair of words in parentheses, underline the word that correctly completes the sentence.*

### Issue: Business Ethics

Oil companies aren't usually known for their (environmentalism / environmentally) responsible reputations. Global energy giant BP, however, has made an effort to market an image that is Earth-friendly. For the most part, this strategy has (worked / working)—leading many to overlook the facts (suggesting / suggestion) that BP's claims are exaggerated or even completely false.

For the past several years, BP has (commitment / committed) environmental offenses almost (annually / annual). In 2000, the company was convicted of a felony for failing to report that its subcontractor was dumping (hazardously / hazardous) waste in Alaska. In 2005, BP allegedly ignored knowledge that its Texas City refinery was unsafe in a cost-cutting effort that led to an (explosive / explosion), 15 deaths, and even more injuries. The following year, BP's negligence at its Prudhoe Bay oil field (caused / causes) a 200,000-gallon oil spill and violation of the Clean Water Act. Then, in 2007, BP lobbied Indiana regulators for an (exemption / exemptive) allowing it to increase its daily release of ammonia and sludge into Lake Michigan.

—adapted from Ebert and Griffin, *Business Essentials,* p. 21

## 3d    USING LANGUAGE EFFECTIVELY

**LEARNING OBJECTIVE 4**
Use language effectively

Words have incredible power. On the positive side, words can inspire, comfort, and educate. At the other end of the spectrum, words can inflame, annoy, or deceive. Good writers understand that word choices greatly influence the reader, and they choose the words that will help them achieve their goals. Careful readers understand the nuances of words and pay attention to how writers use them. This section describes numerous language features important to both readers and writers.

## Denotation and Connotation

To understand the nuances (shades of meaning) of words, it is important to understand the difference between denotation and connotation. Which of the following would you like to be a part of: a *crowd, mob, gang, audience, congregation,* or *class*? Each of these words has the same basic meaning: "an assembled group of people." But each has a different *shade* of meaning. *Crowd* suggests a large, disorganized group. *Audience,* on the other hand, suggests a quiet, controlled group. Try to figure out the meanings suggested by each of the other words in the list.

This example shows that words have two levels of meanings—a literal meaning and an additional shade of meaning. A word's **denotation** is the meaning stated in the dictionary—its literal meaning. A word's **connotation** is the set of additional implied meanings, or nuances, that a word may take on. Often the connotation carries either a positive or negative association. The words *mob* and *gang* have a negative connotation because they imply a disorderly, disorganized group. *Congregation, audience,* and *class* have a positive connotation because they suggest an orderly, organized group.

Here are a few more examples. Would you prefer to be described as *slim* or *skinny*? As *intelligent* or *brainy*? As *heavy* or *fat*? As *frugal* or *cheap*? Notice that the words in each pair have a similar literal meaning, but that each word has a different connotation.

Depending on the words they choose, writers can suggest favorable or unfavorable impressions of the person, object, or event they are describing. For example, through the writer's choice of words, the two sentences below create two entirely different impressions. As you read them, notice the boldfaced words and their positive or negative connotations.

### Examples

> The *unruly* crowd *forced* its way through the restraint barriers and *ruthlessly attacked* the rock star.
>
> The *enthusiastic* group of fans *burst* through the fence and *rushed* toward the rock star.

Connotations can help writers paint a picture to influence the reader's opinion. Thus a writer who wishes to be kind to an overweight politician might describe him as *pleasingly plump* (which carries an almost pleasant connotation) or even *quite overweight* (which is a statement of fact that remains mostly neutral). However, a writer who wishes to be negative about the same politician might describe him as *morbidly obese.*

When reading, pay attention to the writer's choice of words and their connotations. Ask yourself: What words does the writer use, and how do they affect me?

## EXERCISE 3–11 . . . USING CONNOTATIVE LANGUAGE

*For each of the following pairs of word or phrases, write two sentences. One sentence should use the word with the more positive connotation; the second should use the word with the less positive connotation.*

1. request          demand
2. overlook         neglect
3. ridicule         tease
4. display          expose
5. garment          gown
6. gaudy            showy
7. artificial       fake
8. cheap            cost effective
9. choosy           picky
10. seize           take

## EXERCISE 3–12 . . . USING CONNOTATIVE LANGUAGE

*For each of the following sentences, underline the word in parentheses that has the more appropriate connotative meaning. Consult a dictionary, if necessary.*

1. The new superintendent spoke (extensively / enormously) about the issues facing the school system.
2. The day after we hiked ten miles, my legs felt extremely (rigid /stiff).
3. Carlos thought he could be more (productive / fruitful) if he had a home office.
4. The (stubborn /persistent) ringing of my cell phone finally woke me up.
5. The investment seemed too (perilous /risky), so we decided against it.

## Synonyms and Antonyms

**Synonyms** are words with similar meanings: **antonyms** are words with opposite meanings. Both categories of words are useful to expand and diversify your reading and writing vocabulary. When writing, you may want to find a synonym, a word with a more exact, descriptive, or specific meaning than the one that comes to mind. For example, you might want to explain how a person walks. There are many words that mean *walk*, although each may have a different connotation: *strut, meander, stroll, hike, saunter,* and *march*. A thesaurus can help you choose the word with the exact meaning you intend.

**Antonyms** are useful when making a contrast or explaining differences. You might be describing two different types of communication styles of friends. One style is decisive. Finding antonyms for the word *decisive* may help you describe differing styles. Antonyms include *faltering, wavering,* or *hesitant.*

## Slang

Most of what you read in textbooks, magazines, newspapers, and a variety of online sources is written in Standard Written English. This means it is written using a set of conventions and rules that make language clear, correct, and easy to understand by anyone who reads it. **Slang** is an informal, nonstandard form of expression used by a particular group. It is used by people who want to give themselves a unique identity, and it can be a useful in some social situations, in informal writing, and in some forms of creative writing. It is *not* appropriate to use in academic writing, so be sure to avoid using it in papers, essays, and exams.

| | |
|---|---|
| **Slang** | She and her mom are *so tight*. |
| **Standard Written English** | She and her mom *have a close relationship*. |

| | |
|---|---|
| **Slang** | On Saturday I plan to *chill* by the pool. |
| **Standard Written English** | On Saturday I plan to *relax* by the pool. |

## Colloquial Language

**Colloquial language** refers to casual, everyday spoken language. Be sure to avoid it in most formal writing assignments. Words that fall into this category are labeled *informal* or *colloquial* in a dictionary.

| | |
|---|---|
| **Colloquial** | I almost *flunked bio* last sem. |
| **Standard Written English** | I almost *failed* biology last semester. |

| | |
|---|---|
| **Colloquial** | Janice *go* to the store. |
| **Standard Written English** | Janice *goes* to the store. |

## Idioms

An **idiom** is a phrase with a meaning different from the phrase's individual words. Sometimes you can figure out an idiom's meaning from context within the sentence or paragraph, but more commonly you must simply know the idiom to understand it.

**Examples**

> The $10,000 he embezzled was just the *tip of the iceberg* (a small, observable part of something much larger).
>
> While the company's sales are excellent, its *bottom line* (total profit) is awful. ("Bottom line" refers to the last line of a financial statement, showing the company's overall profit or loss.)
>
> The only *sure-fire* (guaranteed to work) method of losing weight is diet and exercise.
>
> We have *buried our head in the sand* (denied reality) about our nation's deficit for far too long.

As you read, be on the lookout for phrases that use common words but do not make sense no matter how many times you reread them. When you find such a phrase, you have likely encountered an idiom. (It is estimated that English has almost 25,000 idiomatic expressions.)

## EXERCISE 3-13 . . . UNDERSTANDING IDIOMS

*For each sentence, write the meaning of the idiomatic expression in boldface.*

1. The kidnapping of the twins from Utah in 1985 has turned into a **cold case**.

   _____

2. Jake decided to **zero in on** his goal of becoming a firefighter.

   _____

3. I am trying to make an appointment with my academic advisor, but she's been hard to **pin down**.

   _____

4. The mystery novels of P.D. James **blur the line** between popular fiction and literature.

   _____

5. Milton **saw red** when someone rear-ended his car. _____

## Analogies

**Analogies** are abbreviated statements that express similarities between two pairs of items. You will find them on a variety of entrance and competency tests and exams. They are tests of both your thinking skills and your word knowledge. Analogies are often written in the following format:

> black : white :: dark : light

This can be read in either of two ways:

1. Black is to white as dark is light.
2. White has the same relationship to black as light does to dark. (White is the opposite of black and light is the opposite of dark.)

In analogies the relationship between the words or phrases is critically important. Analogies become test items when one of the four items is left blank, and you are asked to supply or select the missing item.

> Celery : vegetable :: orange:_____
> video : watch :: audio :_____

A variety of relationships are expressed in analogies. These include

- Opposites     yes: no :: stop : start
- Whole/part     year : month :: week : day
- Synonyms     moist: damp :: happy : glad
- Categories     dessert : cake :: meat : beef
- Similarities     lemon : orange :: broccoli : cabbage
- Association or action     train : conductor :: airplane : pilot
- Knowledge     Picasso : painter :: Shakespeare : writer

## EXERCISE 3-14 . . . WORKING WITH ANALOGIES

*Complete each of the following analogies by supplying a word or phrase that completes it.*

1. sculptor: statue :: musician : _____

2. Allah : Islam :: God : _____

3. fresh : rancid :: unique : _____

4. hasten : speed up :: outdated : _____

5. old age : geriatrics :: infancy : _____

## Technical and Academic Language

Have you noticed that each sport and hobby has its own language—a specialized set of words and phrases with very specific meanings? Baseball players and fans talk about slides, home runs, errors, and runs batted in, for example. Each academic discipline also has its own language. For each course you take, you will encounter an extensive set of words and terms that have a particular, specialized meaning in that subject area. In this reading and writing course, you will learn terms such as *topic sentence, supporting details, idea map,* and *transitions.*

One of the first tasks you will face in a new college course is to learn its specialized language. This is particularly true of introductory courses in which a new discipline or field of study is explained.

It is important to learn to understand the language of a course when reading and to use the language of a course when speaking and writing.

A sample of the words introduced in economics and chemistry are given below. Some of the terms are common, everyday words that take on a specialized meaning; others are technical terms used only in that subject area.

| New Terms: Economics Text | New Terms: Chemistry Text |
| --- | --- |
| capital | matter |
| ownership | element |
| opportunity cost | halogen |
| distribution | isotope |

Recognition of academic and technical terminology is only the first step in learning the language of a course. More important is the development of a systematic way of identifying, marking, recording, and learning these terms. Because new terminology is introduced in both class lectures and course textbooks, be sure to develop a procedure for handling the specialized terms in each. You might highlight them, annotate, or create a vocabulary log using computer file or notebook, for example.

## SUMMARY OF LEARNING OBJECTIVES

**MySkillsLab**
Complete the mastery test for this chapter **in MySkillsLab.**

**1 Use a dictionary and a thesaurus.**
*How can you build vocabulary?*

To **build vocabulary**, you can use online, pocket, desk, and unabridged dictionaries to locate the meanings of unfamiliar words. A *thesaurus*, a dictionary of synonyms, is also useful for selecting the most accurate and precise word to fit a particular situation.

**2 Use context clues.**
*What are context clues?*

**Context clues** help readers figure out the meaning of unfamiliar words. Context clues fall into four categories: (1) *definition clues*, (2) *example clues*, (3) *contrast clues*, and (4) *logic of the passage clues*.

**3 Use affixes: prefixes, roots, and suffixes.**
*How can word parts unlock meaning?*

Many words are composed of some combination of prefix, root, and suffix. The **prefix** precedes the main part of the word; the **root** is the key part of the word that carries its core meaning; and the **suffix** appears at the end of the word. Knowing the meanings of key prefixes, roots, and suffixes will help you unlock the meaning of many unfamiliar words.

**4 Use language effectively.**
*How can you use language effectively?*

Good writers understand that word choices greatly influence the reader, and they choose the words that will help them achieve their goals. Careful readers understand the nuances of words and pay attention to how writers use them. **Knowing about the following types of language will help you read and write more effectively.** The *denotative meaning* of a word is its stated dictionary meaning; a word's *connotation* is a set of implied meanings a word may take on. *Synonyms* are words of similar meaning; *antonyms* are word of opposite meaning. *Slang* refers to non-standard or everyday informal language used by a particular group. *Colloquial language* refers to casual, everyday spoken language. An *idiom* is a phrase with a meaning different from the phrase's individual words. *Analogies* are abbreviated statements that express a relationship between two pairs of items. *Technical and academic language* refers to specialized use of terms in particular academic disciplines.

# 4 Reading Paragraphs: Main Ideas, Supporting Details, and Transitions

## LEARNING OBJECTIVES

1 Understand the structure of a paragraph
2 Find stated main ideas
3 Recognize supporting details
4 Find implied main ideas
5 Recognize transitional words and phrases

Most articles, essays, and textbook chapters contain numerous ideas expressed in paragraph form. As you read, your job is to sort out the important ideas from those that are less important. As you write, you are expected to express your ideas clearly and correctly in paragraph form. In this chapter, you will learn to identify main ideas and supporting details, find implied main ideas, and recognize how signal words link ideas together. In the next chapter, you will focus on writing paragraphs.

## 4a   WHAT IS A PARAGRAPH?

**LEARNING OBJECTIVE 1**
Understand the structure of a paragraph

A **paragraph** is a group of related sentences that develop a main thought, or idea, about a single topic. The structure of a paragraph is not complex. There are usually four basic elements: (1) a topic, (2) a main idea, or topic sentence, (3) supporting details, and (4) transitions.

A **topic** is the one thing a paragraph is about. The **topic sentence** expresses an idea about that topic. The topic sentence states the main point or controlling idea. The sentences that explain this main point are called **supporting details**. Words and phrases that connect and show relationships between and among ideas are called **transitions**. Stand-alone paragraphs (those not part of an essay) often include a concluding sentence that wraps up the paragraph and brings it to a close. These elements help you know what to look for and ensure that you will understand and remember what you read.

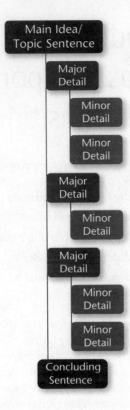

Now, read the following paragraph, noticing how all the details relate to one point, explaining the topic sentence.

### Issue: Color Psychology

Topic sentence

> There is some evidence that colors affect people physiologically. For example, when subjects are exposed to red light, respiratory movements increase; exposure to blue decreases respiratory movements. Similarly, eye blinks increase in frequency when eyes are exposed to red light and decrease when exposed to blue. After changing a school's walls from orange and white to blue, the blood pressure of the students decreased while their academic performance improved. This seems consistent with the intuitive feelings about blue being more soothing and red being more arousing.
>
> —adapted from DeVito, *Human Communication*, p. 182

In this paragraph, the topic sentence identifies the topic as *color* and states that *colors affect people physiologically*. The remaining sentences provide further information about the effects of color. Since this paragraph first appeared in a textbook chapter, it does not have a concluding sentence. Below is a map of the paragraph on color.

**Idea Map**

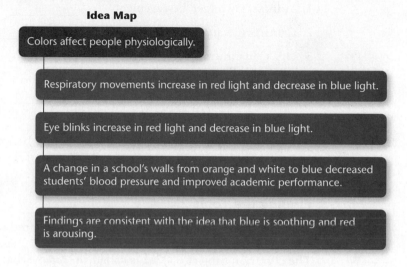

Colors affect people physiologically.

Respiratory movements increase in red light and decrease in blue light.

Eye blinks increase in red light and decrease in blue light.

A change in a school's walls from orange and white to blue decreased students' blood pressure and improved academic performance.

Findings are consistent with the idea that blue is soothing and red is arousing.

## 4b    FINDING STATED MAIN IDEAS

**LEARNING OBJECTIVE 2**
Find stated main ideas

In most paragraphs the main idea is expressed in a single sentence called the **topic sentence**. Occasionally, you will find a paragraph in which the main idea is not expressed in any single sentence. The main idea is **implied**; that is, it is suggested but not directly stated in the paragraph. (For more on implied main ideas, see Section 4d, p. 89.)

### Distinguishing Between General and Specific Ideas

A **general idea** applies to a large number of individual items. The term *television programs* is general because it refers to a large collection of shows—soap operas, sports specials, sitcoms, and so on. A **specific idea** or term is more detailed or particular. It refers to an individual item. The term *reality TV*, for example, is more specific than the word *program*. The title *The Real Housewives of Atlanta* is even more specific.

### Examples

| | | | |
|---|---|---|---|
| *General:* | Continents | *General:* | U.S. Presidents |
| *Specific:* | Asia | *Specific:* | John F. Kennedy |
| | Africa | | Barack Obama |
| | Australia | | Thomas Jefferson |

## EXERCISE 4-1 . . . IDENTIFYING GENERAL IDEAS

*For each list of items, write a word or phrase that best describes that grouping.*

1. sadness, joy, anger, bereavement _____

2. Capricorn, Aquarius, Taurus, Libra _____

3. U.S. Constitution, Bill of Rights, Federalist Papers, First Amendment
   _____

4. Mars, Saturn, Jupiter, Mercury _____

Now that you are familiar with the difference between general and specific, you will be able to use these concepts in the rest of the chapter.

## Finding the Topic

We have defined a paragraph as a group of related ideas. The sentences are related to one another, and all are about the same person, place, thing, or idea. The common subject or idea is called the *topic*—what the entire paragraph is about. As you read the following paragraph, you will see that its topic is unemployment and inflation.

### Issue: The Economy

Unemployment and inflation are the economic problems that are most often discussed in the media and during political campaigns. For many people, the state of the economy can be summarized in just two measures: the unemployment rate and the inflation rate. In the 1960s, Arthur Okun, who was chairman of the Council of Economic Advisors during President Lyndon Johnson's administration, coined the term *misery index*, which adds together the inflation rate and the unemployment rate to give a rough measure of the state of the economy. Although unemployment and inflation are important problems in the short run, the long-run success of an economy is best judged by its ability to generate high levels of real GDP (gross domestic product) per person.

—adapted from Hubbard and O'Brien, *Essentials of Economics*, p. 408

Each sentence of this paragraph discusses or describes unemployment and inflation. To identify the topic of a paragraph, then, ask yourself: *"What or whom is the paragraph about?"*

## EXERCISE 4-2 . . . IDENTIFYING THE TOPIC

*After reading each of the following selections, select the choice that best represents the topic of the selection.*

### Issue: Prejudice and Stereotypes

_____ 1.    Everyone is familiar with the legacy of racial prejudice in the United States. Arguments over the legitimacy of slavery are 150 years in the past and it has been decades since public schools were integrated, yet racial prejudice remains a major concern among all demographic groups in this country. The emphasis on race has also increased our awareness of other forms of stereotyping. For example, psychologists have researched stereotypes and prejudice related to weight and body size, sexual orientation, and religious affiliation. Racial, ethnic, and other outgroup stereotypes are pervasive and, unfortunately, seem to thrive in times of hardship. For example, during economic slumps, an outgroup (a collection of people who are perceived as different) is often targeted for taking jobs from the in group or for draining resources from the local economy.

—adapted from Krause and Corts, *Psychological Science*, p. 569

a.  racial prejudice and forms of stereotyping

b.  U.S. history

c.  in groups and out groups

d.  the results of economic hardship

### Issue: Personal Relationships

_____ 2.    According to Bella DePaulo and Wendy Morris, one of the major disadvantages of not being married is that single adults are the targets of *singlism*, the negative stereotypes and discrimination faced by singles. Their research found that single people were viewed more negatively than married people. Compared to married or coupled people, who are often described in very positive terms, singles are assumed to be immature, maladjusted, and self-centered. Loneliness, lack of companionship, being excluded from couples' events, or feeling uncomfortable in social settings involving mostly couples, not having children, and social disapproval of their lifestyle are among the other frequently reported disadvantages of being single. Another disadvantage of living alone is more gender-specific. Women living alone confront safety issues in deciding where to live, what mode of transportation to use, and which leisure activities to attend.

—Schwartz and Scott, *Marriages and Families,* p. 211

a.  singlism

b.  gender-specific perceptions

c.  disadvantages of being single

d.  societal perceptions of married people

### Issue: Environmental Conservation

_____ 3.    Our planet is called the "Blue Marble," and for good reason: Over 70% of Earth's surface is covered with water. Solar energy and gravity drive the hydrologic cycle, moving water between the oceans, the atmosphere, and the land. Precipitation that falls on land may evaporate back into the atmosphere, percolate down into aquifers in the ground, or flow back to the sea in one of the thousands of streams and rivers that course across every continent. Lakes and inland seas store water and slow its movement. Wetlands store and filter water. Human use of water affects every part of Earth's hydrologic cycle, including the distribution of water in streams, lakes, and groundwater and the kinds and amounts of chemicals and sediments that water carries.

—Christensen, *The Environment and You*, p. 336

a. Earth

b. precipitation

c. water

d. lakes and rivers

## Stated Main Ideas

The **main idea** of a paragraph is what the author wants you to know about the topic. It is the broadest, most important idea that the writer develops throughout the paragraph. The entire paragraph explains, develops, and supports this main idea. A question that will guide you in finding the main idea is *"What key point is the author making about the topic?"* In the paragraph about unemployment and inflation on page 76, the writer's main idea is that unemployment and inflation are two important measures of the economy's overall health. Often, but not always, one sentence expresses the main idea. This sentence is called the **topic sentence**.

## Finding the Topic Sentence

To find the topic sentence, search for the one general sentence that explains what the writer wants you to know about the topic; the remaining sentences of the paragraph will provide details about or explain the topic sentence.

In the following paragraph, the topic is practical learning in the United States. Read the paragraph to find out what the writer wants you to know about this topic. Look for the one sentence that states this.

### Issue: Education

In the United States, the educational system stresses the value of *practical learning*, knowledge that prepares people for their future jobs. This is in line with what the educational philosopher John Dewey (1859–1952) called *progressive education*, having the schools make learning relevant to people's lives. Students seek out subjects of study that they believe will give them an advantage when they are ready to compete in the job market. For example, as concerns about international terrorism have risen in recent years, so have the number of students choosing to study geography, international conflict, and Middle Eastern history and culture.

—Macionis, *Society*, p. 376

The paragraph opens with a statement and then proceeds to explain it with supporting evidence. The first sentence is the topic sentence, and it states the paragraph's main point: *The U.S. educational system stresses practical learning.*

## TIPS FOR LOCATING TOPIC SENTENCES

1. **Identify the topic.** Figure out the general subject of the entire paragraph. In the preceding sample paragraph, "practical learning" is the topic.
2. **Locate the most general sentence (the topic sentence).** This sentence must be broad enough to include all of the other ideas in the paragraph. The topic sentence in the sample paragraph ("In the United States, the educational system stresses the value of *practical learning*, knowledge that prepares people for their future jobs.") covers all of the other details in the paragraph.

## Common Positions for the Topic Sentence

The topic sentence can be located anywhere in the paragraph. However, there are several positions where it is most likely to be found.

**Topic Sentence First.**   Most often the topic sentence is placed first in the paragraph. In this type of paragraph, the writer first states his or her main point and then explains it.

### Issue: Popular Psychology

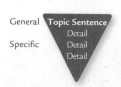

General

Specific

Color influences perceptions and behaviors. People's acceptance of a product, for example, is largely determined by its packaging—especially its color. In one study the very same coffee taken from a yellow can was described as weak, from a dark brown can as too strong, from a red can as rich, and from a blue can as mild. Even your acceptance of a person may depend on the color he or she wears. Consider, for example, the comments of one color expert: "If you have to pick the wardrobe for your defense lawyer heading into court and choose anything but blue, you deserve to lose the case." Black is so powerful it could work against the lawyer with the jury. Brown lacks sufficient authority. Green would probably elicit a negative response.

—DeVito, *Human Communication*, pp. 127–128

Here the writer first states that color influences perceptions and behaviors. The rest of the paragraph presents evidence and examples to support the topic sentence.

**Topic Sentence Last.**    The second most likely place for a topic sentence to appear is last in the paragraph. When using this arrangement, a writer leads up to the main point and then directly states it at the end.

### Issue: Parents and Children

> To spank or not to spank has been a controversial issue for many years now. Child development experts have typically advised parents to use other methods of disciplining their children, citing the possibility of encouraging child abuse as well as the role played by spanking in the modeling of aggression. Now the results of a new study suggest there is a significantly increased risk of higher levels of aggression at age 5 when spanking is used at age 3. While older studies have found similar results, the study by Dr. Catherine Taylor and her colleagues differs from those earlier studies in that possible maternal risk factors such as neglect, the mother's use of drugs, and maternal psychological problems were measured and controlled. The Taylor study found that when mothers stated that they spanked their 3-year-olds more than twice in the previous month, those same children at 5 years of age were much more likely to be aggressive. <u>The conclusion seems to be that sparing the rod may spare the child (and those around the child) from an unpleasant personality trait.</u>
>
> —adapted from Ciccarelli and White, *Psychology*, p. 191

In this paragraph, the author ponders the relationship between spanking and aggression and concludes with the paragraph's main point: that children who are spanked are more likely to become aggressive.

**Topic Sentence in the Middle.**    If it is placed neither first nor last, then the topic sentence appears somewhere in the middle of the paragraph. In this arrangement, the sentences before the topic sentence lead up to or introduce the main idea. Those that follow the main idea explain or describe it.

### Issue: Wildlife Conservation

> In colonial days, huge flocks of snowy egrets inhabited the coastal wetlands and marshes of the southeastern United States. In the 1800s, when fashion dictated fancy hats adorned with feathers, egrets and other birds were hunted for their plumage. By the late 1800s, egrets were almost extinct. In 1886, the newly formed National Audubon Society began a press campaign to shame "feather wearers" and end the practice. The campaign caught on, and gradually, attitudes changed; new laws followed. <u>Government policies that protect animals from overharvesting are essential to keep species from the brink of extinction.</u> Even when cultural standards change due to the efforts of individual

> groups (such as the National Audubon Society), laws and policy measures must follow to ensure that endangered populations remain protected. Since the 1800s, several important laws have been passed to protect a wide variety of species.
>
> —Wright and Boorse, *Environmental Science*, p. 150

In this paragraph, the writers first give an example of a species that became almost extinct until action was taken to prevent it. Then they state their main point: Government regulation is necessary to protect species from extinction. The remainder of the paragraph explains that laws must follow cultural change and states that several laws have been passed that do protect species.

**Topic Sentence First and Last.**   Occasionally the main idea is stated at the beginning of a paragraph and again at the end, or elsewhere in the paragraph. Writers may use this organization to emphasize an important idea or to explain an idea that needs clarification. At other times, the first and last sentences together express the paragraph's main idea.

### Issue: Government and Politics

> A key instrument of a state's [country's] power against its enemies is its security forces, which include official groups such as the regular military and the secret police, as well as unofficial armed groups. In some countries, such as Libya, Syria, and Yemen, the secret police have a record of using violence against anti-government demonstrators. In Columbia, paramilitary forces, which are not officially part of the Columbian military, have been held responsible for 70 to 80% of political murders in recent years. Another form of state power is judicial systems and prison systems, which punish those whose behaviors displease the state.
>
> —adapted from Danzinger, *Understanding the Political World,* p. 320

The first and last sentences together explain the key forms of a country's powers against the people it perceives as its enemies.

---

### EXERCISE 4-3 . . . FINDING TOPIC SENTENCES

*Underline the topic sentence of each of the following paragraphs.*

### Paragraph 1

**Issue: Poverty**

Sociologists have several different ways of defining poverty. *Transitional poverty* is a temporary state that occurs when someone loses a job for a short time. *Marginal poverty* occurs when a person lacks stable employment (for example, if your job is lifeguarding at a pool during the summer season, you might experience marginal poverty when the season ends). The next, more serious level, *residual poverty*, is chronic and multigenerational. A person who experiences *absolute poverty* is so poor that he or she doesn't have resources to survive. *Relative poverty* is a state that occurs when we compare ourselves with those around us.

—adapted from Carl, *Think Sociology*, p. 122

### Paragraph 2

### Issue: Medical Liability and the Law

In the past, exposure to liability made many doctors, nurses, and other medical professionals reluctant to stop and render aid to victims in emergency situations, such as highway accidents. Almost all states have enacted a Good Samaritan law that relieves medical professionals from liability for injury caused by their ordinary negligence in each set of circumstances. Good Samaritan laws protect medical professionals only from liability for their *ordinary negligence*, not for injuries caused by their gross negligence or reckless or intentional conduct. Many Good Samaritan laws have protected licensed doctors and nurses and laypersons who have been certified in CPR. Good Samaritan statutes generally do not protect laypersons who are not trained in CPR—that is, they are liable for injuries caused by their ordinary negligence in rendering aid.

—Goldman and Cheeseman, *Paralegal Professional*, p. 459

### Paragraph 3

### Issue: Fashion

One of the best ways to analyze your wardrobe is to determine which items you already own. This requires a thorough closet cleaning, purging items that no longer fit, are out of fashion, are not appropriate for your career or leisure time, or have not been worn in a year. Trying on everything gives you the opportunity to categorize clothing into piles labeled: keepers, "iffy," resells, and purge. After this exercise, organize the garments that remain by category and color, starting with neutrals and moving to brights in this order: shirts/tops, bottoms, jackets/coats/sweaters, and for women dresses. Put out-of-season in another storage area. After wearing, always replace garments in their original location.

—adapted from Marshall, Jackson, and Stanley, *Individuality in Clothing Selection and Personal Appearance*, p. 293

### Paragraph 4

### Issue: Electronic Communication and Social Media

With so many people participating in social networking sites and keeping personal blogs, it's increasingly common for a single disgruntled customer to wage war online against a company for poor service or faulty products. Unhappy customers have taken to the Web to complain about broken computers or poor customer service. Individuals may post negative reviews of products on blogs, upload angry videos outlining complaints on YouTube, or join public discussion forums where they can voice their opinion about the good and the bad. In the same way that companies celebrate the viral spread of good news, they must also be on guard for online backlash that can damage a reputation.

—adapted from Ebert and Griffin, *Business Essentials*, p. 161

### Paragraph 5

#### Issue: Cultural Similarities and Differences

In Japan, it's called *kuroi kiri* (black mist); in Germany, it's *schmiergeld* (grease money), whereas Mexicans refer to *la mordida* (the bite), the French say *pot-de-vin* (jug of wine), and Italians speak of the *bustarella* (little envelope). They're all talking about *bakshseesh*, the Middle Eastern term for a "tip" to grease the wheels of a transaction. Giving "gifts" in exchange for getting business is common and acceptable in many countries, even though this may be frowned on elsewhere.

—adapted from Solomon, *Consumer Behavior*, p. 21

---

## EXERCISE 4-4 . . . FINDING MAIN IDEAS

*After reading the following passage, answer the questions that follow.*

### What Makes Eating So Enjoyable?

Topic:

_____

_____

1    As much fun as it is to eat, you're not just taking in food for fun. Food satisfies a genuine physical need. Eating food and drinking fluids often begins with the sensation of either **hunger** or **thirst**. The amount of food that we eat and the timing of our meals are driven by physical needs. **Appetite** is another powerful drive, but it is often unreliable. Appetite is influenced by our food preferences and the psychological stimulation to eat. In other words, you can become interested in food, pursue food, and experience the desire to eat too much food without actually needing nourishment or being hungry.

### We Develop a Taste for Certain Foods

Topic:

_____

_____

2    Everyone enjoys eating food that tastes delicious, but what exactly *is* taste? There are five basic categories of taste: sweet, salty, sour, bitter, and savory ("umami"). Most taste buds are located on the tongue, but additional taste buds are found in the throat and elsewhere in the mouth. Food scientists estimate that each of us has at least 10,000 taste buds.

Topic:

_____

_____

3    Even though we each have our own favorite foods, we share some taste traits. In general, we all have an innate preference for sweet, salty, and fatty foods. There is a scientific explanation for these preferences. Sugar seems to elicit universal pleasure (even among infants), and the brain seeks pleasure.[1] Salt provides two important **electrolytes** (sodium and chloride) that are essential to your body and can stimulate the appetite. Your liking of both sugar and salt makes carbohydrate-rich foods appealing to you. Foods rich in carbohydrates provide the fuel that your body needs daily. High-fat foods not only have rich textures and aromas that round out the flavors of food, but also provide essential nutrients that are critical to your health.[2] Thus while we tend to enjoy rich sauces, gravies, and salad dressings, we are, at the same time, meeting our nutritional needs.

Topic:

_____

_____

4    Sometimes, our food preferences and our nutritional needs conflict. We may eat too much because the food is so pleasurable. When there is a reason to change our food habits, such as a need to lose weight or reduce salt or fat intake, we realize how challenging it can be to control our food choices.

Topic: _____  5

How does the brain recognize taste? When food is consumed, portions of the food are dissolved in saliva. These fluids then make contact with the tongue's surface. The taste (gustatory) cells send a message to the brain. The brain then translates the nerve impulses into taste sensations that you recognize.

### Aromas and Flavors Enhance the Pleasure of Eating

Topic: _____  6

The sensing structures in the nose are also important to the ability to taste foods. The average person is capable of distinguishing 2,000 to 4,000 aromas.[3] We detect food aroma through the nose when we smell foods and, as we eat, when food odors enter the mouth and migrate to the back of the throat and into the nasal cavities.[4] The average person has about 10 million to 20 million olfactory cells (odor cells) in the nasal cavity. Therefore, both your mouth and your nose contribute to the tasting of foods. This explains why you lose interest in eating when you have a cold or other forms of nasal congestion. Food loses some of its appeal when you can't smell it.

Topic: _____  7

Both the taste and the aroma of a food contribute to its *flavor*. The term flavor also refers to the complete food experience. For example, when you eat a candy bar, you sense a sweet taste, but the flavor is chocolate.

Topic: _____  8

The presence of fat tends to enhance the flavor of foods. When the fat content increases, the intensity of the flavor also increases, as many aromatic compounds are soluble in fat. Increased fat content causes the flavor of food to last longer compared with flavor compounds dissolved in water. Flavors dissolved in water are quickly detected, but also quickly dissipated.[5] This explains why most people prefer premium ice cream over frozen popsicles. It also explains why several low-fat foods have an acceptable flavor, but they are not as delicious as their high-fat counterparts.

—Blake, *Nutrition and You*, pp. 66–67

1. Identify the topic of each paragraph and write it on the line provided.
2. Underline the topic sentence of each paragraph.
3. Did you find any paragraphs that did not have topic sentences? If so, which were they? _____

---

## 4c    RECOGNIZING SUPPORTING DETAILS

**LEARNING OBJECTIVE 3**
Recognize supporting details

**Supporting details** are those facts and ideas that prove or explain the main idea of a paragraph. While all the details in a paragraph support the main idea, not all details are equally important. As you read, try to identify and pay attention to the most important details. Pay less attention to details of lesser importance. The key details directly explain the main idea. Other details may provide additional information, offer an example, or further explain one of the key details.

Figure A below shows how details relate to the main idea and how details range in degree of importance. In the diagram, more important details are placed toward the left; less important details are closer to the right.

Read the following paragraph and study Figure B.

## Issue: Health and Wellness

The skin of the human body has several functions. First, it serves as a protective covering. In doing so, it accounts for 17% of the body weight. Skin also protects the organs within the body from damage or harm. The skin serves as a regulator of body functions. It controls body temperature and water loss. Finally, the skin serves as a receiver. It is sensitive to touch and temperature.

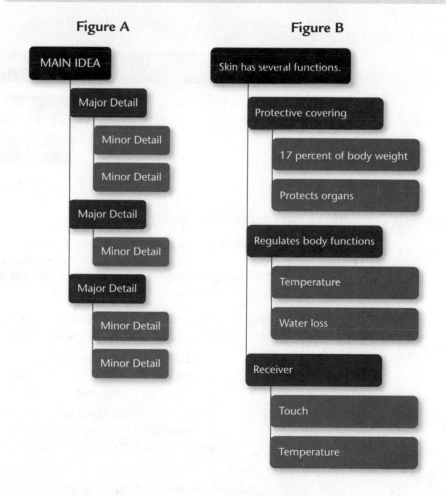

From this diagram you can see that the details stating the three functions of skin are the key details. Other details, such as "protects the organs," provide further information and are less important.

Read the following paragraph and try to pick out the more important details.

## Issue: Cultural Similarities and Differences

Many cultures have different rules for men and women engaging in conflict. Asian cultures are more strongly prohibitive of women's conflict strategies. Asian women are expected to be exceptionally polite; this is even more important when women are in conflict with men and when the conflict is public. In the United States, there is a verbalized equality; men and women have equal rights when it comes to permissible conflict strategies. In reality, there are many who expect women to be more polite, to pursue conflict in a non-argumentative way, while men are expected to argue forcefully and logically.

This paragraph could be diagrammed as follows (key details only):

Many cultures have different rules for men and women engaging in conflict.

Rules in Asian cultures

Rules in the United States

## EXERCISE 4–5 . . . RECOGNIZING SUPPORTING DETAILS

*Each of the following topic sentences states the main idea of a paragraph. After each topic sentence are five sentences containing details that may or may not support the topic sentence. Read each sentence and put an "S" beside those that contain details that support the topic sentence.*

1. **Topic Sentence:** A monopoly is a company that controls the sale of a certain good and therefore is able to set high prices.

   _____ a. The automobile industry is a good example of an oligopoly, because none of the large companies (such as Ford, Toyota, and Honda) controls the industry.

   _____ b. Markets for agricultural products like cotton and wheat are considered very competitive, and farmers are often unable to set high prices for their goods.

   _____ c. Many critics have accused monopolies of unfair pricing.

   _____ d. The DeBeers Company, which mines diamonds in Africa and elsewhere, holds a monopoly in the world market for diamonds.

   _____ e. Some common examples of monopolies are public utility companies and the sports franchises in major U.S. cities.

2. **Topic Sentence:** *Mens rea,* a term that refers to a person's criminal intent when committing a crime, or his or her state of mind, can be evaluated in several ways.

_____ a. Confessions by criminals are direct evidence of their criminal intent.

_____ b. Circumstantial evidence can be used to suggest mental intent.

_____ c. *Actus rea* is the set of a person's actions that make up a crime.

_____ d. People who commit crimes are often repeat offenders.

_____ e. Expert witnesses may offer an opinion about a person's criminal intent.

3. **Topic Sentence:** Food irradiation is a process in which food is treated with radiation to kill bacteria.

_____ a. Many consumers are concerned about the increasing number of genetically modified foods.

_____ b. The radioactive rays pass through the food without damaging it or changing it.

_____ c. One form of irradiation uses electricity as the energy source for irradiation.

_____ d. Irradiation increases the shelf life of food because it kills all bacteria present in the food.

_____ e. *E. coli,* salmonella, and listeria cause many illnesses each year.

4. **Topic Sentence:** The television and film industries promote unhealthy body images for both women and men.

_____ a. Many Hollywood films feature unacceptable levels of violence.

_____ b. Many TV and film stars have undergone extensive plastic surgery that makes them look not quite human.

_____ c. Movies and television programs portray the ideal female body type as slender and curvaceous.

_____ d. Television relies on advertisements to fund its programming.

_____ e. Many teenage boys are injecting themselves with illegal steroids to achieve muscular bodies like those they see on television and in the movies.

## EXERCISE 4-6 . . . RECOGNIZING SUPPORTING DETAILS

*Underline only the most important details in each of the following paragraphs.*

### Paragraph 1

#### Issue: Drugs and Addiction

*Physiological dependence*, the adaptive state that occurs with regular addictive behavior and results in withdrawal syndrome, is only one indicator of addiction. Chemicals are responsible for the most profound addictions because they cause cellular changes to which the body adapts so well that it eventually requires the chemical to function normally. Psychological dynamics, though, also play an important role. Psychological and physiological dependence are intertwined and nearly impossible to separate; all forms of addiction probably reflect dysfunction of certain biochemical systems in the brain.

—Donatelle, *My Health*, p. 122

### Paragraph 2

#### Issue: Crime and Communities

There are four different dimensions of an arrest: legal, behavioral, subjective, and official. In legal terms, an arrest is made when someone lawfully deprives another person of liberty; in other words, that person is not free to go. The actual word *arrest* need not be uttered, but the other person must be brought under the control of the arresting individual. The behavioral element in arrests is often nothing more than the phrase "You're under arrest." However, that statement is usually backed up by a tight grip on the arm or collar, or the drawing of an officer's handgun, or the use of handcuffs. The subjective dimension of arrest refers to whenever people believe they are not free to leave; to all intents and purposes, they are under arrest. In any case, the arrest lasts only as long as the person is in custody, which might be a matter of a few minutes or many hours. Many people are briefly detained on the street and then released. Official arrests are those detentions that the police record in an administrative record. When a suspect is "booked" at the police station, a record is made of the arrest.

—Barlow, *Criminal Justice in America*, p. 238

### Paragraph 3

#### Issue: Health and Appearance

The use of cosmetics has a long and interesting history, but past usage doesn't even come close to the amounts and varieties of cosmetics used by people in the modern industrial world. Each year, we spend billions of dollars on everything from hair sprays to nail polishes, from mouthwashes to foot powders. Combined sales of the world's 100 largest cosmetics companies were more than $125 billion in 2008.

What is a cosmetic? The U.S. Food, Drug, and Cosmetic Act of 1938 defined cosmetics as "articles intended to be rubbed, poured, sprinkled, or sprayed on, introduced into, or otherwise applied to the human body or any part thereof, for cleansing, beautifying, promoting attractiveness or altering the appearance." Soap, although obviously used for cleansing, is specifically excluded from coverage by the law. Also excluded are substances that affect the body's structure or functions. Antiperspirants, products that reduce perspiration, are legally classified as drugs, as are antidandruff shampoos.

—Hill, McCreary, and Kolb, *Chemistry for Changing Times*, p. 663

### EXERCISE 4-7 . . . RECOGNIZING SUPPORTING DETAILS

*Reread the article "Consequences of Social Class" on page 6 and underline the most important supporting details in each paragraph.*

## 4d    UNDERSTANDING IMPLIED MAIN IDEAS

**LEARNING OBJECTIVE 4**
Find implied main ideas

Study the cartoon below. What main point is it making? Although the cartoonist's message is not directly stated, you were able to figure it out by looking at the details in the cartoon. Just as you figured out the cartoonist's main point, you often have to figure out the implied main ideas of speakers and writers. When an idea is **implied**, it is suggested but not stated outright. Suppose your favorite shirt is missing from your closet and you know that your roommate often borrows your clothes. You might say to your roommate, "If my blue plaid shirt is back in my closet by noon, I'll forget it was missing." This statement does not directly accuse your roommate of borrowing the shirt, but your message is clear—Return my shirt! Your statement implies or suggests to your roommate that he has borrowed the shirt and should return it.

**Roadkill**

## EXERCISE 4–8 . . . UNDERSTANDING IMPLIED MAIN IDEAS

*For each of the following statements, select the choice that best explains what the writer is implying or suggesting.*

_____ 1. You know what I like in a book? A master detective going up against a master criminal, good suspense, and plot twists that keep me guessing.

    a.  I like romance novels.

    b.  I like mystery novels.

    c.  I prefer to read nonfiction.

    d.  I am a big fan of poetry.

_____ 2. This semester, Dino is taking courses in biochemistry, human anatomy and physiology, medical lab procedures, and medical research.

    a.  Dino is a senior.

    b.  Dino is studying to become a doctor.

    c.  Dino spends all his time studying.

    d.  Dino has no interest in the social sciences or liberal arts.

_____ 3. The steak was overcooked and tough, the mashed potatoes were cold, the green beans were withered, and the chocolate pie was mushy.

    a.  The dinner was tasty.

    b.  The dinner was nutritious.

    c.  The dinner was prepared poorly.

    d.  The dinner was served carelessly.

## Inferring Implied Main Ideas

When trying to figure out the implied main idea in a paragraph, it is important to remember the distinction between general and specific ideas (see page 75). You know that a *general* idea applies to many items or ideas, while a *specific* idea refers to a particular item. The word *color*, for instance, is general because it refers to many other specific colors—purple, yellow, red, and so forth. The word *shoe* is general because it can apply to many types, such as running shoes, high heels, loafers, and slippers.

You also know that the main idea of a paragraph is not only its most important point but also its most *general* idea. *Specific* details back up or support the main idea. Although most paragraphs have a topic sentence, some do not. Instead, they contain only details or specifics that, taken together, point to the main idea. The main idea, then, is implied but not directly stated. In such paragraphs you must **infer**, or reason out, the main idea. **Inference** is a process of adding up the details and deciding what they mean together or what main idea they all support or explain.

What general idea do the following specific sentences suggest?

> The plumber made appointments he did not keep.
>
> The plumber exaggerated the extent of the needed repairs in order to overcharge his customers.
>
> The plumber did not return phone calls when people complained about his work.

You probably determined that the plumber is inconsiderate, incompetent, and unethical.

What larger, more general idea do the specific details and the accompanying photograph point to?

> The wind began to howl at over 90 mph.
>
> A dark gray funnel cloud was visible in the sky.
>
> Severe storms had been predicted by the weather service.

Together these three details and the photograph suggest that a tornado has devastated the area.

## EXERCISE 4-9 . . . WRITING GENERAL IDEAS

*For each item, read the specific details. Then select the word or phrase from the box below that best completes the general idea in the sentence that follows. Make sure that each general idea fits all of its specific details. Not all words or phrases in the box will be used.*

| | | |
|---|---|---|
| advertisers | contributes | dangerous effects |
| process | factors | techniques |

1. a. Celebrity endorsements catch consumers' attention.

   b. Emphasizing the negative consequences of not purchasing a particular product employs fear as a motive for buying it.

   c. "Sex sells" is a common motto among those who write commercials.

   **General idea:** _____ use a variety of appeals to sell products.

2. a. Children who are abused are more likely to be abusers when they become parents.

   b. Abused children often suffer from low self-esteem.

   c. Those who have been abused as children often find it difficult to develop healthy romantic relationships.

   **General idea:** Child abuse has _____.

3. a. Many immigrants come to the United States because they cannot make enough money to feed their families in their home country.

   b. Immigrants often come to the United States in order to be closer to their families.

   c. Sometimes immigrants are forced to flee their home countries due to warfare or persecution.

   **General idea:** A number of different _____ contribute to people leaving their country in search of a better life.

## How to Find Implied Main Ideas in Paragraphs

When a writer leaves his or her main idea unstated, it is up to you to look at the details in the paragraph and figure out the writer's main point. The details, when taken together, will all point to a general and more important idea. Use the following steps as a guide to find implied main ideas:

1. **Find the topic.** The *topic* is the general subject of the entire paragraph. Ask yourself: "What *one thing* is the author discussing throughout the paragraph?"

2. **Figure out the most important idea the writer wants you to know about that topic.** Look at each detail and decide what larger idea is being explained.

3. **Express the main idea in your own words.** Make sure that the main idea is a reasonable one. Ask yourself: "Does it apply to all of the details in the paragraph?"

Here is a sample passage; identify the main idea.

### Issue: Health and Appearance

The Romans, with their great public baths, probably did not use any sort of soap. They covered their bodies with oil, worked up a sweat in a steam bath, and then wiped off the oil. A dip in a pool of fresh water completed the "cleansing."

During the Middle Ages, bodily cleanliness was prized in some cultures, but not in others. For example, twelfth-century Paris, with a population of about 100,000, had many public bathhouses. In contrast, the Renaissance, a revival of learning and art that lasted from the fourteenth to the seventeenth centuries, was not noted for cleanliness. Queen Elizabeth I of England (1533–1603) bathed once a month, a habit that caused many to think her overly fastidious. A common remedy for unpleasant body odor back then was the liberal use of perfume.

And today? With soap, detergent, body wash, shampoo, conditioner, deodorant, antiperspirant, aftershave, cologne, and perfume, we may add more during and after a shower than we remove in the shower.

—adapted from Hill et al., *Chemistry for Changing Times*, p. 644

The topic of this passage is *personal cleanliness.* The author's main point is that standards for bodily cleanliness have fluctuated over human history. You can figure out the writers' main idea even though no single sentence states this directly. You can visualize this paragraph as follows:

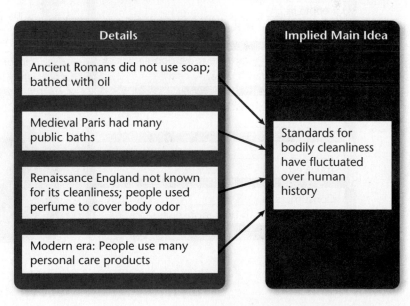

EXERCISE 4-10 . . . FINDING IMPLIED MAIN IDEAS

*After reading each of the paragraphs, complete the diagram that follows by filling in the missing information.*

**Paragraph A**

**Issue: Health and Diet**

The average American consumer eats 21 pounds of snack foods in a year, but people in the West Central part of the country consume the most (24 pounds per person) whereas those in the Pacific and Southeast regions eat "only" 19 pounds per person. Pretzels are the most popular snack in the mid-Atlantic area, pork rinds are most likely to be eaten in the South, and multigrain chips turn up as a favorite in the West. Not surprisingly, the Hispanic influence in the Southwest has influenced snacking preferences—consumers in that part of the United States eat about 50 percent more tortilla chips than do people elsewhere.

—adapted from Solomon, *Consumer Behavior,* p. 184

Topic _____

Details

The average consumer eats _____ of snack food in a year.

People in _____ part of the country consume the most.

People in _____ regions consume the least.

_____ are the most popular snack in the mid-Atlantic area.

Pork rinds are most likely to be eaten in _____ .

_____ are the favorite in the West.

Consumers in _____ eat more tortilla chips than do people elsewhere.

Implied Main Idea

_____ differ in their preferences for

_____

according to where they live.

## Paragraph B

### Issue: Alternative Medicine

By now, most people know that the herb echinacea may help conquer the common cold. Herbal remedies that are less well known include flaxseed, for treating constipation, and fennel, for soothing an upset stomach. In addition, the herb chamomile may be brewed into a hot cup of tea for a good night's sleep.

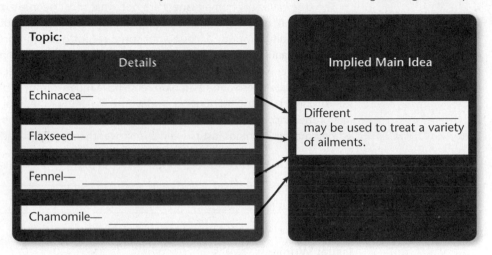

Topic: _____

Details

Echinacea— _____

Flaxseed— _____

Fennel— _____

Chamomile— _____

Implied Main Idea

Different _____ may be used to treat a variety of ailments.

## Paragraph C

### Issue: Personal Relationships

Men's friendships are often built around shared activities—attending a ball game, playing cards, working on a project at the office. Women's friendships, on the other hand, are built more around a sharing of feelings, support, and "personalism." One study found that similarity in status, in willingness to protect one's friend in uncomfortable situations, in academic major, and even in proficiency in playing Password were significantly related to the relationship closeness of male–male friends but not of female–female or female–male friends.

—DeVito, *Messages*, p. 290

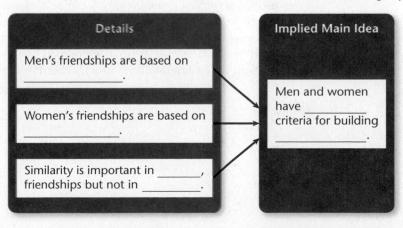

Details

Men's friendships are based on _____.

Women's friendships are based on _____.

Similarity is important in _____, friendships but not in _____.

Implied Main Idea

Men and women have _____ criteria for building _____.

EXERCISE 4-11 . . . FINDING IMPLIED MAIN IDEAS

*Write a sentence that states the main idea for each of the following paragraphs.*

### Paragraph 1

### Issue: Homelessness

The true causes of homelessness are not what most people expect. Deinstitutionalization of mentally ill people, released from hospitals without adequate care and community support, accounts for some recent gains in homelessness. The exodus of manufacturing firms, chronic unemployment, and decline in real wages in many American cities have pushed many others into the streets. At the same time, real estate speculation and high rents have made it impossible for large segments of the poor to find housing. Today, the majority of the poor pay more than half of their incomes for housing, and many single moms pay almost three-fourths of their meager earnings just to keep a roof over their family's heads.

—adapted from Thompson and Hickey, *Society in Focus*, p. 216

*Main idea:* _____

_____

### Paragraph 2

### Issue: Women's Issues

In 1985, an anonymous group of women that called themselves the Guerrilla Girls began hanging posters in New York City. They listed the specific galleries who represented less than 1 woman out of every 10 men [artists]. Another poster asked: "How Many Women Had One-Person Exhibitions at NYC Museums Last Year?" The answer:

Guggenheim  0
Metropolitan  0
Modern  1
Whitney  1

One of the Guerrilla Girls' most daring posters was distributed in 1989. It asked, "When racism & sexism are no longer fashionable, what will your art collection be worth?" It listed 67 women artists and pointed out that a collection of works by all of them would be worth less than the art auction value of any *one* painting by a famous male artist. Its suggestion that the value of the male artists' work might be drastically inflated struck a chord with many.

—adapted from Sayre, *Discovering the Humanities*, pp. 490–491

*Main idea:* _____

_____

### Paragraph 3

**Issue: Health and Wellness**

Have you ever noticed that you feel better after a belly laugh or a good cry? Humans have long recognized that smiling, laughing, singing, dancing, and other actions can elevate our moods, relieve stress, make us feel good, and help us improve our relationships. Crying can have similar positive physiological effects. Several recent articles have indicated that laughter and joy may increase endorphin levels, increase oxygen levels in the blood, decrease stress levels, relieve pain, enhance productivity, and reduce risks of chronic disease; however, the long-term effects on immune functioning and protective effects for chronic diseases is only just starting to be understood.

—Donatelle, *Health*, pp. 92–93

*Main idea:* _____

_____

---

### EXERCISE 4–12 . . . FINDING IMPLIED MAIN IDEAS

*After reading each of the following paragraphs, select the choice that best answers each of the questions that follow.*

### Paragraph A

**Issue: Social Networking and Privacy**

When registering for online services under a screen name, it can be tempting to think your identity is a secret to other users. Many people will say or do things on the Internet that they would never do in real life because they believe that they are acting anonymously. However, most blogs, e-mail and instant messenger services, and social networking sites are tied to your real identity in some way. While your identity may be superficially concealed by a screen name, it often takes little more than a quick Google search to uncover your name, address, and other personal and possibly sensitive information.

—Ebert and Griffin, *Business Essentials*, p. 188

_____ 1. What is the topic?
   a. online identity
   b. screen names
   c. online services
   d. Google searches

_____ 2. What is the writer saying about the topic?

    a. Google searches offer clues to your identity.

    b. People write things on the Internet they would never say face-to-face.

    c. Your identity is not secret on the Internet.

    d. Screen names help conceal your identity.

### Paragraph B

### Issue: Business Ethics

"Frugal engineering." "Indovation." "Reverse innovation." These are some of the terms that GE, Procter & Gamble, Siemens, and Unilever are using to describe efforts to penetrate more deeply into emerging markets. As growth in mature markets slows, executives and managers at many global companies are realizing that the ability to serve the needs of the world's poorest consumers will be a critical source of competitive advantage in the decades to come. Procter & Gamble CEO Robert McDonald has set a strategic goal of introducing 800 million new consumers to the company's brands by 2015. This will require a better understanding of what daily life is like in, say, hundreds of thousands of rural villages in Africa, South America, and China.

Consider, for example, that two-thirds of the world's population—more than 4 billion people—live on less than $2 per day. This segment is sometimes referred to as the "bottom of the pyramid" and includes an estimated 1.5 billion people who live "off the grid"; that is, they have no access to electricity to provide light or to charge their cell phones. Often, a villager must walk several miles to hire a taxi for the trip to the nearest city with electricity. Such trips are costly in terms of both time and money.

—Keegan and Green, *Global Marketing*, p. 192

_____ 3. What is the topic?

    a. global branding and income inequality

    b. life off the grid

    c. marketing strategies aimed at the poor

    d. supply and demand in developing countries

_____ 4. What main idea is the writer implying?

    a. The poor people of the world do not have access to transportation.

    b. Companies are looking for ways to make money by selling their products to the world's poor people.

    c. Procter & Gamble is the world leader in supplying inexpensive products to developing nations.

    d. Cell phones offer developing nations many opportunities for increasing the standard of living.

_____ 5. Which one of the following conclusions does not logically follow from the passage?

   a. Reverse innovation is aimed at getting more products into the hands of wealthy consumers.

   b. "Emerging markets" are home to huge numbers of poor people.

   c. The majority of the world's people live on less than $2 per day.

   d. In the world's developing countries, many residents of the countryside are poor.

## Paragraph C

### Issue: Family

In all societies, people have ways of organizing their relationships with other people, especially their primary relationships with kin. As children, our earliest and most influential interactions are with our parents, siblings, and other relatives. We rely on our families for all of our survival needs. Our families feed us, clothe us, and provide our shelter. They also help us adjust to the world around us, teaching us the behavior and attitudes that our culture expects, and they provide emotional support in both good times and bad.

Many of our relatives continue as important economic and emotional supports throughout our lives. Even as adults, we can turn to our kin in networks of reciprocity, asking for aid in times of need. In turn, we may be asked to respond to their requests when they are in need. We may align ourselves with our relatives when they are engaged in disputes with others. We may expect loyalty from our kin when we are in conflict with neighbors or other community members. During personal or family crises, we may expect emotional support from our relatives. Together we celebrate happy occasions such as births and marriages, and we mourn the deaths of our kin.

—Bonvillain, *Cultural Anthropology*, pp. 186–187

_____ 6. What is the topic?

   a. parents

   b. siblings

   c. family

   d. culture

_____ 7. What is the writer saying about the topic?

   a. Family is more important in some societies than in others.

   b. Regardless of culture, family is one of the most important and constant influences in our lives.

   c. Most people see their family members as their "safety net" in times of difficulty.

   d. It is impossible to define the terms *kinship* and *family* with any accuracy.

## EXERCISE 4-13 . . . FINDING STATED AND IMPLIED MAIN IDEAS

*Turn to the article titled "Consequences of Social Class" on page 6.
Using your own paper, number the lines from 1 to 16, to correspond to
the 16 paragraphs in the article. For each paragraph number, if the main
idea is stated, record the sentence number in which it appears (1, 2, etc.).
If the main idea is unstated and implied, write a sentence that expresses the
main idea.*

## 4e    RECOGNIZING TRANSITIONS

**LEARNING OBJECTIVE 5**
Recognize
transitional words
and phrases

**Transitions** are linking words or phrases used to lead the reader from one idea
to another. If you get in the habit of recognizing transitions, you will see that
they often guide you through a paragraph, helping you to read it more easily.
When writing, be sure to use these words to help your reader follow your train
of thought and to see connections between and among your ideas. In the following paragraph, notice how the underlined transitions lead you from one
important detail to the next.

### Example

Kevin works as a forensic scientist. When he examines a crime scene, he follows
a certain procedure. First of all, he puts on special gear to avoid contaminating the
crime scene. For example, he wears gloves (so that he doesn't leave fingerprints)
and a special hat (so that he does not leave hair samples). Next, he prepares his
camera and other forensic equipment, such as plastic bags and glass slides. Then,
he presses "record" on his tape recorder so that he can describe the crime scene
as he examines it. Finally, he goes over the crime scene one square foot at a time,
very slowly, so that he does not miss any evidence.

Not all paragraphs contain such obvious transitions, and not all transitions serve as such clear markers of major details. Often, however, transitions
are used to alert you to what will come next in the paragraph. If you see the
phrase *for instance* at the beginning of a sentence, then you know that an
example will follow. When you see the phrase *on the other hand*, you can predict that a different, opposing idea will follow. Table 4-1 lists some of the
most common signal words used within a paragraph and indicates what they
tell you.

## TABLE 4-1  COMMON TRANSITIONS

| TYPES OF TRANSITIONS | EXAMPLES | WHAT THEY TELL THE READER |
|---|---|---|
| Time or Sequence | *first, later, next, finally* | The author is arranging ideas in the order in which they happened. |
| Example | *for example, for instance, to illustrate, such as* | An example will follow. |
| Enumeration or Listing | *first, second, third, last, another, next* | The author is marking or identifying each major point (sometimes these may be used to suggest order of importance). |
| Continuation | *also, in addition, and, further, another* | The author is continuing with the same idea and is going to provide additional information. |
| Contrast | *on the other hand, in contrast, however* | The author is switching to a different, opposite, or contrasting idea than previously discussed. |
| Comparison | *like, likewise, similarly* | The writer will show how the previous idea is similar to what follows. |
| Cause and Effect | *because, thus, therefore, since, consequently* | The writer will show a connection between two or more things, how one thing caused another, or how something happened as a result of something else. |

## EXERCISE 4-14 . . . RECOGNIZING TRANSITIONS

*Select the signal word or phrase from the box below that best completes each of the following sentences. Two of the signal words in the box may be used more than once.*

| | | | |
|---|---|---|---|
| on the other hand | for example | because | in addition |
| similarly | after | next | however |
| also | | | |

1. Typically, those suffering from post-traumatic stress disorder (PTSD) are soldiers after combat. Civilians who witnessed or lived through events such as the World Trade Center destruction can _____ experience PTSD.

2. Columbus was determined to find an oceanic passage to China _____ finding a direct route would mean increased trading and huge profits.

3. In the event of a heart attack, it is first important to identify the symptoms. _____, call 911 or drive the victim to the nearest hospital.

4. In the 1920s, courtship between men and women changed dramatically. _____, instead of visiting the woman's home with her parents present, men began to invite women out on dates.

5. Direct exposure to sunlight is dangerous because the sun's ultraviolet rays can lead to skin cancer. _____, tanning booths emit ultraviolet rays and are as dangerous as, if not more dangerous than, exposure to sunlight.

6. Lie detector tests are often used by law enforcement to help determine guilt or innocence. _____, because these tests often have an accuracy rate of only 60 to 80 percent, the results are not admissible in court.

7. The temporal lobes of the brain process sound and comprehend language. _____, the temporal lobes are responsible for storing visual memories.

8. The theory of multiple intelligences holds that there are many different kinds of intelligence, or abilities. _____, musical ability, control of bodily movements (athletics), spatial understanding, and observational abilities are all classified as different types of intelligence.

9. During World War II, Japanese Americans were held in relocation camps. _____ the war was over, the United States paid reparations and issued an apology to those who were wrongfully detained.

10. Many believe that the United States should adopt a flat tax in which every person pays the same tax rate. _____, it is unlikely that the tax code will be overhauled any time soon.

## EXERCISE 4–15 . . . RECOGNIZING TRANSITIONS

*Each of the following beginnings of paragraphs uses a transitional word or phrase to tell the reader what will follow. Read each, paying particular attention to the underlined word or phrase. Then, in the space provided, specifically describe what you would expect to find immediately after the transitional word or phrase.*

1. Proximity should not be the only factor to consider in choosing a doctor or health-care provider. Many other factors should be considered. *For instance, . . .*

   _____

   _____

2. There are a number of things you can do to manage your stress level. *First, . . .*

   _____

   _____

3. Many banks have privacy policies. *However, . . .*

   _____

   _____

4. One advantage of taking online courses is all the time you will save by not having to travel to and from campus. *Another . . .*

   _____

   _____

5. To select the classes you will take next term, first consult with your faculty advisor about the courses you are required to take. *Next . . .*

   _____

   _____

### EXERCISE 4-16 . . . IDENTIFYING TRANSITIONAL WORDS AND THEIR FUNCTION

*For each paragraph in the article "Consequences of Social Class" on page 6, highlight each transitional word and indicate what each tells the reader.*

## SUMMARY OF LEARNING OBJECTIVES

**MySkillsLab**
Complete the mastery test for this chapter **in MySkillsLab.**

**1 Understand the structure of a paragraph.**
*What are the elements of a paragraph?*

A **paragraph** is a group of sentences about a single topic. A paragraph has three essential parts:
- Topic: the subject of the paragraph
- Main Idea: the most important idea expressed about the topic
- Details: the information that explains or supports the main idea

**2 Find stated main ideas.**
*What are main ideas?*

A **main idea** expresses a single idea about the topic of a paragraph. Main ideas are often expressed directly in a topic sentence. The **topic sentence** is the most general sentence in the paragraph. The topic sentence often appears first in a paragraph, but it may also appear in the middle or at the end of the paragraph. Sometimes it appears both at the beginning and at the end of the paragraph.

**3 Recognize supporting details.**
*What are supporting details?*

**Supporting details** are facts and ideas that prove or explain a paragraph's main idea. Not all details are equally important.

**4 Find implied main ideas.**
*How do you find implied main ideas?*

When a main idea is **implied**, it is not stated outright. To identify an implied main idea, look at the details in the paragraph and figure out the writer's main point. The details, when taken together, will point to a general and more important idea. This is the implied main idea.

**5 Recognize transitional words and phrases.**
*What are transitions?*

**Transitional words or phrases** lead the reader from one idea to another. They are often used to alert the reader to what is coming next.

# 5 Writing and Revising Paragraphs: Main Ideas, Supporting Details, and Transitions

## LEARNING OBJECTIVES

**1** Write effective topic sentences

**2** Select and organize details to support topic sentences

**3** Use transitional words and phrases to connect details

**4** Use specific language

**5** Revise paragraphs

A **paragraph** is a group of related sentences. The sentences are all about one thing, called the **topic.** A paragraph expresses a single idea about that topic. This idea is called the **main idea.** All the other sentences in the paragraph support this main idea. These sentences are called **supporting details.** Not all details in a paragraph are equally important. Ideas are connected using **transitional words.**

## 5a    WRITE EFFECTIVE TOPIC SENTENCES

**LEARNING OBJECTIVE 1**
Write effective topic sentences

As a writer, it is important to develop clear and concise topic sentences that help your readers understand your main ideas and guide them through your paragraphs.

### The Function of Topic Sentences

A good topic sentence does two things:

- It makes clear what the paragraph is about—the topic.
- It expresses a view or makes a point about the topic.

In the following examples, the topic is in boldface and the point about the topic is in italics.

1. **The first week of college** *is a frustrating experience.*
2. **State-operated lotteries** *are growing in popularity.*
3. **Time management** *is a vital skill in college and on the job.*

### EXERCISE 5-1 . . . EXPRESSING VIEWPOINTS ABOUT A TOPIC

*Working with a classmate, create two topic sentences that offer differing or opposing points of view about each of the following topics.*

1. Shopping malls

   _____

   _____

2. Fast-food restaurants

   _____

   _____

   _____

3. Monday mornings

   _____

   _____

   _____

4. Violence on television

   _____

   _____

   _____

5. College professors

   _____

   _____

   _____

## Narrowing Your Focus

To write a good paragraph, you need to narrow your focus to a manageable topic. Your topic must be general enough to allow you to add interesting details that will engage your reader. It must also be specific or narrow enough that you can cover it adequately in a few sentences. If your topic is too general, you'll end up with a few unrelated details that do not add up to a specific point. If your topic is too narrow, you will not have enough to say.

Suppose you have decided to write a paragraph about sports. You write the following topic sentence:

> Sports are a favorite activity for many people.

This topic is much too broad to cover in one paragraph. Think of all the different aspects you could write about. Which sports would you consider? Would you write about both playing sports and watching them? Would you write about both professional and amateur sports? Would you write about the reasons people enjoy sports? The topic sentence must be more specific:

> My whole family likes to watch professional football on Sunday afternoons.

Here you have limited your topic to a specific sport (football), a specific time (Sunday afternoon), and some specific fans (your family).

Here are other examples of sentences that are too general. Each has been revised to be more specific.

| **Too General** | My parents have greatly influenced my life. |
| **Revised** | My parents helped me make the decision to attend college. |

| **Too General** | Sex education is worthwhile. |
| **Revised** | Sex-education courses in high school allow students to discuss sex openly. |

If your topic is *too* specific (narrow), you will not have enough details to use in the paragraph, or you may end up including details that do not relate directly to the topic. Suppose you decide to write a paragraph about the Internet and come up with this topic sentence:

> The Internet allows me to stay in touch with friends in other parts of the country.

What else would your paragraph say? You might name some specific friends and where they are, but this list wouldn't be very interesting. This topic sentence is too specific. It might work as a detail, but not as a main idea. To correct the problem, ask, "What else does the Internet allow me to do?" You might say that it allows you to stay in touch with friends by e-mail, that it makes doing research for college papers easier, and that the World Wide Web has information on careers and even specific job openings. Here is a possible revised topic sentence:

> The Internet is an important part of my personal, college, and work life.

Here are a few other examples of topic sentences that are too narrow, along with revisions for each one:

| | |
|---|---|
| **Too Narrow** | Only 36 percent of Americans voted in the last election. |
| **Revised** | Many Americans do not exercise their right to vote. |

| | |
|---|---|
| **Too Narrow** | Markel Carpet Company offers child-care leave to both men and women. |
| **Revised** | The child-care leave policy at Markel Carpet Company is very flexible. |

| | |
|---|---|
| **Too Narrow** | A yearly subscription to *Appalachian Voice* costs $25. |
| **Revised** | *Appalachian Voice*, a magazine devoted to environmental issues, is a bargain, considering the information it provides. |

How can you tell if your topic sentence is too general or too specific? Try brainstorming or branching to generate ideas. If you find you can develop the topic in many different directions, or if you have trouble choosing details from a wide range of choices, your topic is probably too general. If you cannot think of anything to explain or support it, your topic sentence is too specific.

## EXERCISE 5-2 . . . EVALUATING TOPIC SENTENCES

*Evaluate the following topic sentences. Label each* G *for too general or* S *for too specific. Then rewrite each to create an effective topic sentence.*

_____ 1. Learning a new sport is challenging.

_____

_____ 2. Dinner for two at my favorite Italian restaurant costs $25.

_____

_____ 3. The new day-care center opens earlier than most.

_____

_____ 4. Many rules of etiquette have changed over the past 25 years.

_____

_____ 5. Passive cigarette smoke makes me feel sick.

_____

## TIPS FOR WRITING EFFECTIVE TOPIC SENTENCES

Use the following suggestions to write clear topic sentences:

1. **Your topic sentence should state the main point of your paragraph.** Be sure your topic sentence has two parts. It should identify your topic and express a view toward it.

2. **Be sure to choose a manageable topic.** It should be neither too general nor too specific.

3. **Make sure your topic sentence is a complete thought.** Be sure your topic sentence is not a fragment or run-on sentence.

4. **Place your topic sentence first in the paragraph.** Topic sentences often appear in other places in paragraphs, as described earlier, or their controlling idea is implied, not stated. For now, it will be easier for you to put yours at the beginning. That way, as you write, you can make sure you stick to your point, and your readers will immediately be alerted to that point.

5. **Avoid announcing your topic.** Sentences that sound like announcements are usually unnecessary. Avoid such sentences as "This paragraph will discuss how to change a flat tire," or "I will explain why I object to legalized abortion." Instead, directly state your main point: "Changing a flat tire involves many steps," or "I object to abortion on religious grounds."

Not all expert or professional writers follow all of these suggestions. Sometimes, a writer may use one-sentence paragraphs or include topic sentences that are fragments to achieve a special effect. You will find these paragraphs in news and magazine articles and other sources. Although professional writers can use these variations effectively, you probably should not experiment with them too early. It is best while you are polishing your skills to use a more standard style of writing.

### EXERCISE 5-3 . . . EVALUATING TOPIC SENTENCES

*Evaluate each of the following topic sentences and mark them as follows:*

E = effective    G = too general    A = announcement    N = not complete thought
S = too specific

_____    1. This paper will discuss the life and politics of Simón Bolívar.

_____    2. Japanese culture is fascinating to study because its family traditions are so different from American traditions.

_____    3. The admission test for the police academy includes vocabulary questions.

_____    4. The discovery of penicillin was a great step in the advancement of modern medicine.

_____    5. I will talk about the reasons for the popularity of reality television shows.

_____ 6. A habit leading to weight gain.

_____ 7. Each year Americans are the victims of more than 1 million auto thefts.

_____ 8. The White House has many famous rooms and an exciting history.

_____ 9. There are three factors to consider when buying a flat screen TV.

_____ 10. Iraq has a long and interesting history.

## EXERCISE 5-4 ... REVISING TOPIC SENTENCES

*Analyze the following topic sentences. If a sentence is too general or too specific, or if it makes a direct announcement or is not a complete thought, revise it to make it more effective.*

1. World hunger is a crime.

   Revised: _____

2. E-mail is used by a great many people.

   Revised: _____

3. I will point out the many ways energy can be saved in the home.

   Revised: _____

4. Because Congress is very important in the United States.

   Revised: _____

5. In 2010, over 10,000 people died in alcohol-impaired driving crashes.

   Revised: _____

## 5b    SELECT AND ORGANIZE DETAILS TO SUPPORT YOUR TOPIC SENTENCE

**LEARNING OBJECTIVE 2**
Select and organize details to support the topic sentence

A paragraph must have **unity**; that is, it must identify and explain a single idea. It must also have **coherence,** meaning that all the sentences make sense together. The following section will show you how to achieve both unity and coherence.

The details you choose to support your topic sentence must be both relevant and sufficient. Relevant means that the details directly explain and support your topic sentence. For example, if you were to write a paragraph for your employer explaining why you deserve a raise, it would not be relevant to mention that you plan to use the money to go to Florida next spring. A vacation has nothing to do with—is not relevant to—your job performance.

Sufficient means that you must provide enough information to make your topic sentence understandable and convincing. In your paragraph explaining why you deserve a raise, it would probably not be sufficient to say that you are always on time. You would need to provide more information about your job performance: for example, that you always volunteer to work holidays, that you've offered good suggestions for displaying new products, and that several customers have written letters praising your work.

In addition to choosing relevant and sufficient details, be sure to select a variety of details, use specific words, and organize your paragraph effectively.

## Selecting Relevant Details

**Relevant details** directly support your topic sentence. They help clarify and strengthen your ideas, whereas irrelevant details make your ideas unclear and confusing. Here is the first draft of a paragraph written by a student named Alex to explain why he decided to attend college. Can you locate the detail that is not relevant?

> [1]I decided to attend college to further my education and achieve my goals in life. [2]I am attempting to build a future for myself. [3]When I get married and have kids, I want to be able to offer them the same opportunities my parents gave me. [4]I want to have a comfortable style of living and a good job. [5]As for my wife, I don't want her to work because I believe a married woman should not work. [6]I believe college is the way to begin a successful life.

Sentence 5 does not belong in the paragraph. The fact that Alex does not want his wife to work is not a reason for attending college. Use the following simple test to be sure each detail you include belongs in your paragraph.

### Test for Relevant Details

1. **Read your topic sentence in combination with each of the other sentences in your paragraph.** For example,

   - read the topic sentence + the last sentence.
   - read the topic sentence + the second-to-last sentence.
   - read topic the sentence + the third-to-last sentence.

2. **For each pair of sentences, ask yourself, "Do these two ideas fit together?"** If your answer is "No," then you have found a detail that is not relevant to your topic. Delete it from your paragraph.

   Another student wrote the following paragraph on the subject of the legal drinking age. As you read it, cross out the details that are not relevant.

> [1]The legal drinking age should be raised to 25. [2]Anyone who drinks should be old enough to determine whether or not it is safe to drive after drinking. [3]Bartenders and others who serve drinks should also have to be 25. [4]In general, teenagers and young adults are not responsible enough to limit how much they drink. [5]The party atmosphere enjoyed by so many young people encourages crazy acts, so we should limit who can drink. [6]Younger people think drinking is a game, but it is a dangerous game that affects the lives of others.

Which sentence did you delete? Why did you delete it? The third sentence does not belong in the paragraph because the age of those who bartend or serve drinks is not relevant to the topic. Sentence 5, about partying, should also be eliminated or explained because the connection between partying and drinking is not clear.

## EXERCISE 5-5 . . . IDENTIFYING RELEVANT DETAILS

*Place a check mark by those statements that provide relevant supporting details.*

1. Sales representatives need good interpersonal skills.
   _____ a. They need to be good listeners.
   _____ b. They should like helping people.
   _____ c. They should know their products well.

2. Water can exist in three forms, which vary with temperature.
   _____ a. At a high temperature, water becomes steam; it is a gas.
   _____ b. Drinking water often contains mineral traces.
   _____ c. At cold temperatures, water becomes ice, a solid state.

3. Outlining is one of the easiest ways to organize facts.
   _____ a. Formal outlines use Roman numerals and letters and Arabic numerals to show different levels of importance.
   _____ b. Outlining emphasizes the relationships among facts.
   _____ c. Outlines make it easier to focus on important points.

## Including Sufficient Detail

Including sufficient detail means that your paragraph contains an adequate amount of specific information for your readers to understand your main idea. Your supporting details must thoroughly and clearly explain why you believe your topic sentence is true. Be sure that your details are specific; do not provide summaries or unsupported statements of opinion.

Let's look at a paragraph a student wrote on the topic of billboard advertising.

> There is a national movement to oppose billboard advertising. Many people don't like billboards and are taking action to change what products are advertised on them and which companies use them. Community activists are destroying billboard advertisements at an increasing rate. As a result of their actions, numerous changes have been made.

This paragraph is filled with general statements. It does not explain who dislikes billboards or why they dislike them. It does not say what products are advertised or name the companies that make them. No detail is given about how the billboards are destroyed, and the resulting changes are not described. There is not sufficient support for the topic sentence. Here is the revised version:

Among residents of inner-city neighborhoods, a national movement is growing to oppose billboard advertising. Residents oppose billboards that glamorize alcohol and target people of color as its consumers. Community activists have organized and are taking action. They carry paint, rollers, shovels, and brooms to an offending billboard. Within a few minutes the billboard is painted over, covering the damaging advertisement. Results have been dramatic. Many liquor companies have reduced their inner-city billboard advertising. In place of these ads, some billboard companies have placed public-service announcements and ads to improve community health.

If you have trouble thinking of enough details to include in a paragraph, try brainstorming or one of the other techniques for generating ideas described in Chapter 2. Write your topic sentence at the top of a sheet of paper. Then list everything that comes to mind about that topic. Include examples, events, incidents, facts, and reasons. You will be surprised at how many useful details you think of. When you finish, read over your list and cross out details that are not relevant. (If you still don't have enough, your topic may be too specific. See pages 106–108.) The section "Arranging Details Logically" on page 114 will help you decide in what order you will write about the details on your list.

### Types of Supporting Details

There are many types of details that you can use to explain or support a topic sentence. The most common types of supporting details are (1) examples, (2) facts or statistics, (3) reasons, (5) descriptions, and (5) steps or procedures. It is advisable to vary the types of details you use, and to choose those appropriate to your topic.

### EXERCISE 5-6 . . . WRITING SUPPORTING DETAILS

*Working with a classmate, for each topic sentence write at least three different types of details that could be used to support it. Label each detail as* example, fact or statistic, reason, description, *or* steps or procedure.

1. People make inferences about you based on the way you dress.

2. Many retailers with traditional stores have decided to market their products through Web sites as well.

3. Many Americans are obsessed with losing weight.

4. Historical and cultural attractions can be found in a variety of shapes, sizes, and locations throughout the world.

5. Using a search engine is an effective, though not perfect, method of searching the Internet.

## Arranging Details Logically

Nan had an assignment to write a paragraph about travel. She drafted the paragraph and then revised it. As you read each version, pay particular attention to the order in which she arranged the details.

### First Draft

This summer I had the opportunity to travel extensively. Over Labor Day weekend I backpacked with a group of friends in the Allegheny Mountains. When spring semester was over, I visited my seven cousins in Florida. My friends and I went to New York City over the Fourth of July to see fireworks and explore the city. During June I worked as a wildlife-preservation volunteer in a Colorado state park. On July 15 I celebrated my twenty-fifth birthday by visiting my parents in Syracuse.

### Revision

This summer I had the opportunity to travel extensively in the United States. When the spring semester ended, I went to my cousins' home in Florida to relax. When I returned, I worked during the month of June as a wildlife-preservation volunteer in a Colorado state park. Then my friends and I went to New York City to see the fireworks and look around the city over the Fourth of July weekend. On July 15th, I celebrated my twenty-fifth birthday by visiting my parents in Syracuse. Finally, over Labor Day weekend, my friends and I backpacked in the Allegheny Mountains.

Did you find Nan's revision easier to read? In the first draft, Nan recorded details as she thought of them. There is no logical arrangement to them. In the second version, she arranged the details in the order in which they happened. Nan chose this arrangement because it fit her details logically.

The three common methods for arranging details are as follows:

1. Time sequence
2. Spatial arrangement
3. Least/most arrangement

### Time Sequence

Time sequence means the order in which things happen. For example, if you were to write about a particularly bad day, you could describe the day in the order in which everything went wrong. You might begin with waking up in the morning and end with going to bed that night. If you were describing a busy or an exciting weekend, you might begin with what you did on Friday night and end with the last activity on Sunday. Here is an example of a time sequence paragraph:

When Su-ling gets ready to study at home, she follows a set routine. First of all, she tries to find a quiet place, far away from her kid sisters. This place might be her bedroom or the porch, or the basement, depending on the noise levels in her household. Next, she finds a snack to eat while she is studying, perhaps potato chips or a candy bar. If she is on a diet, she tries to find some healthy fruit. Finally, Su-ling tackles the most difficult assignment first because she knows her level of concentration is higher at the beginning of study sessions.

## Spatial Arrangement

Suppose you are asked to describe the room in which you are sitting. You want your reader, who has never been in the room, to visualize it. You need to describe, in an orderly way, where items are positioned. You could describe the room from left to right, from ceiling to floor, or from door to window. In other situations, your choices might include front to back, inside to outside, near to far, east to west, and so on. This method of presentation is called spatial arrangement. How are the details arranged in the following paragraph?

Keith's antique car was gloriously decorated for the Fourth of July parade. Red, white, and blue streamers hung in front from the headlights and bumper. The hood was covered with small American flags. The windshield had gold stars pasted on it, arranged to form an outline of our state. On the sides, the doors displayed red plastic-tape stripes. The convertible top was down, and Mary sat on the trunk dressed up like the Statue of Liberty. In the rear, a neon sign blinked "God Bless America." His car was not only a show-stopper but the highlight of the parade.

The details are arranged from front to back in the sample paragraph. The topic you are writing about will often determine the arrangement you choose. In writing about a town, you might choose to begin with the center and then move to each surrounding area. In describing a building, you might go from bottom to top.

### EXERCISE 5-7 . . . USING SPATIAL ARRANGEMENT

*Indicate which spatial arrangement you would use to describe the following topics. Then write a paragraph on one of the topics.*

1. A local market or favorite store

2. A photograph you value

3. A prized possession

4. A building in which you work

5. Your campus cafeteria, bookstore, or lounge

### Least/Most Arrangement

Another method of arranging details is to present them in order from least to most or most to least, according to some quality or characteristic. For example, you might arrange details from least to most *expensive*, least to most *serious*, or least to most *important*. The writer of the following paragraph uses a least-to-most arrangement.

> The entry level job in many industries today is administrative assistant. Just because it's a lower-level job, don't think it's an easy job. A good administrative assistant must have good computer skills. If you aren't proficient on a computer you won't be able to handle your supervisor's correspondence and other paperwork. Even more important, an administrative assistant must be well organized. Every little task—from answering the phone to setting up meetings to making travel arrangements—lands on the administrative assistant's desk. If you can't juggle lots of loose ends, this is not the job for you. Most important of all, though, an administrative assistant needs a sense of humor. On the busiest days, when the office is in total chaos, the only way to keep your sanity—and your temper—is to take a deep breath, smile, and say "When all this is over, I'm going to have a well-earned nervous breakdown!"

Notice that this writer wrote about a basic requirement for the job—computer skills—and then worked up to the most important requirement.

You can also arrange details from most to least. This structure allows you to present your strongest point first. Many writers use this method to construct a case or an argument. For example, if you were writing a business letter requesting a refund for damaged mail-order merchandise, you would want to begin with the most serious damage and put the minor complaints at the end, as follows:

> I am returning these boots, which I just received in the mail, because they are damaged. The heel is half off on the left shoe and there is a deep scratch across the toe. The right shoe has black streaks on the sides, and the buckle is tarnished. I trust you will refund my money promptly.

## 5c    USE TRANSITIONAL WORDS AND PHRASES TO CONNECT DETAILS

**LEARNING OBJECTIVE 3**
Use transitional words and phrases to connect details

**Transitional words and phrases** allow readers to move easily from one detail to another; they show how details relate to one another. You might think of them as words that guide and signal. They guide the reader through the paragraph and signal what is to follow. As you read the following paragraph, notice the transitional words and phrases (highlighted in color) that this student used.

> I have so many things to do when I get home today. First, I have to take my dog, Othello, for a walk. Next, I should do my homework for history and study the chapter on franchises for business. After that I should do some laundry, since my drawers are empty. Then my brother is coming over to fix the tailpipe on my car. Afterward, we will probably order a pizza for a speedy dinner.

Table 5-1 shows some commonly used transitional words and phrases for each method of arranging details discussed on pages 114–116. To understand how they work, review the sample paragraph for each of these arrangements. Underline each transitional word or phrase.

### TABLE 5-1   FREQUENTLY USED TRANSITIONAL WORDS AND PHRASES

| ARRANGEMENT | TRANSITIONAL WORDS AND PHRASES |
|---|---|
| Time Sequence | *first, next, during, eventually, finally, later, meanwhile, soon, when, then, suddenly, currently, after, afterward, before, now, until* |
| Spatial | *above, below, behind, in front of, beside, next to, inside, outside, to the west (north, etc.) of, beneath, nearby, on the other side of* |
| Least/Most Important | *most, above all, especially, even more* |

## 5d    USE SPECIFIC LANGUAGE

**LEARNING OBJECTIVE 4**
Use specific language

When you are writing a paragraph, use specific words to give your reader as much information as possible. You can think of words the way an artist thinks of colors on a palette. Vague words are brown and muddy; specific words are brightly colored and lively. Try to paint pictures for your reader with specific, vivid words. Here are a few examples of vague words along with more specific words or phrases for the same idea:

| | |
|---|---|
| **Vague** | fun |
| **Specific** | thrilling, relaxing, enjoyable, pleasurable |
| **Vague** | dark |
| **Specific** | hidden in gray-green shadows |
| **Vague** | experienced |
| **Specific** | five years in the job |
| **Vague** | tree |
| **Specific** | red maple |

## Ways to Develop Details

The following suggestions will help you develop your details using specific language:

1. **Use specific verbs.** Choose verbs (action words) that help your reader picture the action.

| | |
|---|---|
| **Vague** | The woman left the restaurant. |
| **Specific** | The woman stormed out of the restaurant. |

2. **Give exact names.** Include the names of people, places, objects, and brands.

| | |
|---|---|
| **Vague** | A man was eating outside. |
| **Specific** | Anthony Hargeaves lounged on the deck of his yacht *Penelope*, spearing Heinz dill pickles out of a jar. |

3. **Use adjectives before nouns to convey details.**

| | |
|---|---|
| **Vague** | Juanita had a dog on a leash. |
| **Specific** | A short, bushy-tailed dog strained at the end of the leash in Juanita's hand. |

4. **Use words that appeal to the senses.** Choose words that suggest touch, taste, smell, sound, and sight.

| | |
|---|---|
| **Vague** | The florist shop was lovely. |
| **Specific** | Brilliant red, pink, and yellow roses filled the florist shop with their heady fragrance. |

To summarize, use words that help your readers create mental pictures.

| | |
|---|---|
| **Vague** | Al was handsome. |
| **Specific** | Al had a slim frame, curly brown hair, deep brown almond-shaped eyes, and perfectly straight, gleaming white teeth. |

EXERCISE 5-8 . . . USING SPECIFIC WORDS

*Rewrite these vague sentences, using specific words.*

1. The hair stylist used a gel on my hair.
2. Dress properly for an interview.
3. I found an interesting Web site on the Internet.
4. The job fair was well attended.
5. I'm going to barbecue something for dinner.

EXERCISE 5-9 . . . WRITING A PARAGRAPH

*Using the process described in this chapter, write a paragraph on one of the following topics or a topic assigned by your instructor.*

1. Genetically engineered foods are (are not) a solution to food shortages.
2. My hometown (city) has (has not) changed in the past five years.
3. Religion is (is not) important in my life.
4. Terminally ill people should (should not) have the right to end their lives.
5. The government does (does not) do a good job of preparing for natural disasters.

## 5e   HOW AND WHEN TO REVISE

**LEARNING OBJECTIVE 5**
Revise paragraphs

It is usually best after writing a draft to wait a day before beginning to revise it. You will have a fresh outlook on your topic and will find that it is easier to see what you need to change, add, or delete. Even after giving yourself some distance from your work, it may be difficult to know how to improve your own writing. Simply rereading may not help you discover flaws, weaknesses, or needed changes. The remainder of this section offers guidelines to follow and questions to ask to help you spot problems. It also shows you how to use a revision map and includes a revision checklist to guide your revision.

### Revising Ineffective Topic Sentences

To revise a paragraph, begin by examining your topic sentence; once you are satisfied with it, you can determine whether you have provided adequate details to support it.

As your topic sentence is the sentence around which your paragraph is built, it has to be strong and effective. The most common problems with topic sentences include the following:

- The topic sentence lacks a point of view.
- The topic sentence is too broad.
- The topic sentence is too narrow.

For suggestions on how to revise ineffective topic sentences, see Tips for Writing Effective Topic Sentences on page 109.

## Revising Paragraphs to Add Supporting Details

The details in a paragraph should give your reader sufficient information to make your topic sentence believable. Paragraphs that lack necessary details are called *underdeveloped paragraphs*. **Underdeveloped paragraphs** lack supporting sentences to prove or explain the point made in the topic sentence. As you read the following student paragraph, keep the topic sentence in mind and consider whether the rest of the sentences support it.

### Sample Student Paragraph

> I am a very impatient person, and my impatience interferes with how easily I can get through a day. If I ask for something, I want it immediately. If I'm going somewhere and I'm ready and somebody else isn't, I get very upset. I hate driving behind someone who drives slowly when I cannot pass. I think that annoys me the most, and it never happens unless I am in a hurry. If I were less impatient, I would probably feel more relaxed and less pressured.

This paragraph begins with a topic sentence that is focused (it is neither too broad nor too narrow) and that includes a point of view. It promises to explain how the writer's impatience makes it difficult for him to get through a day. However, the rest of the paragraph does not fulfill this promise. Instead, the writer gives two very general examples of his impatience: (1) wanting something and (2) waiting for someone. The third example, driving behind a slow driver, is a little more specific, but it is not developed well. The last sentence suggests, but does not explain, that the writer's impatience makes him feel tense and pressured.

Taking into account the need for more supporting detail, the author revised his paragraph as follows:

### Revised Paragraph

> I am a very impatient person, and my impatience interferes with how easily I can get through a day. For example, when I decide to buy something, such as a new phone, I *have* to have it right away—that day. I usually drop everything and run to the store. Of course, I shortchange myself on studying, and that hurts my grades. My impatience hurts me, too, when I'm waiting for someone, which I hate to do. If my friend Alex and I agree to meet at noon to work on his car, I get annoyed if he's even five minutes late. Then I usually end up saying something nasty or sarcastic like "What a surprise,

> you're actually here!" which I regret later. Perhaps I am most impatient when I'm behind the steering wheel. If I get behind a slow driver, I get annoyed and start honking and beeping my horn. I know this might upset the other driver, and afterward I feel guilty. I've tried talking to myself to calm down; sometimes it works, so I hope I'm overcoming this bad trait.

Did you notice that the writer became much more specific in the revised version? He gave an example of something he wanted—a phone—and he described his actions and their consequences. The example of waiting for someone was provided by the incident involving his friend Alex. Finally, the writer explained the driving example in more detail and stated its consequences. With the extra details and supporting examples, the paragraph is more interesting and effective.

The following suggestions will help you revise an underdeveloped paragraph:

### Ways to Revise Underdeveloped Paragraphs

- **Analyze your paragraph sentence by sentence.** If a sentence does not add new, specific information to your paragraph, delete it or add to it so that it becomes relevant.
- **Think of specific situations, facts, or examples that illustrate or support your topic.** Often you can make a general sentence more specific.
- **Brainstorm, freewrite, or branch.** To come up with additional details or examples to use in your paragraph, try some prewriting techniques. If necessary, start fresh with a new approach and new set of ideas.
- **Reexamine your topic sentence.** If you are having trouble generating details, your topic sentence may be the problem. Consider changing the approach.

| | |
|---|---|
| **Example** | Rainy days make me feel depressed. |
| **Revised** | Rainy days, although depressing, give me a chance to catch up on household chores. |

- **Consider changing your topic.** If a paragraph remains troublesome, look for a new topic and start over.

### EXERCISE 5-10 . . . REVISING A PARAGRAPH

*The following paragraph is poorly developed. What suggestions would you make to the writer to improve the paragraph? Write them in the space provided. Be specific. Which sentences are weak? How could each be improved?*

I am attending college to improve myself. By attending college, I am getting an education to improve the skills that I'll need for a good career in broadcasting. Then, after a successful career, I'll be able to get the things that I need to be happy in my life. People will also respect me more.

_____
_____
_____
_____

## EXERCISE 5-11 . . . EVALUATING A PARAGRAPH

*Evaluate the following paragraph by answering the questions that follow it.*

One of the best ways to keep people happy and occupied is to entertain them. Every day people are being entertained, whether it is by a friend for a split second or by a Broadway play for several hours. Entertainment is probably one of the nation's biggest businesses. Entertainment has come a long way from the past; it has gone from plays in the park to films in eight-screen movie theaters.

1. Evaluate the topic sentence. What is wrong with it? How could it be revised?

   _____

   _____

2. Write a more effective topic sentence about entertainment.

   _____

   _____

3. Evaluate the supporting details. What is wrong with them?

   _____

   _____

4. What should the writer do to develop her paragraph?

   _____

   _____

5. Use the topic sentence you wrote in item 2 above to develop a paragraph about entertainment.

## Asking Questions and Using Idea Maps to Spot Revision Problems

Some students find revision a troublesome step because it is difficult for them to see what is wrong with their own work. After working hard on a first draft, it is tempting to think that you have done a great job and nothing more is needed. Other times, you may think you have explained and supported an idea clearly when actually you have not. In other words, you may be blind to your own paper's weaknesses. Almost all writing, however, needs and benefits from revision. Two ways to revise effectively are to use idea maps and ask questions.

An **idea map** can help you spot weaknesses in your writing by showing how each of your ideas fits with and relates to all of the other ideas in a paragraph or essay. An idea map reduces your ideas to a skeleton form that allows you to see and analyze them more easily. You can use an idea map to (1) discover problems in a paragraph and (2) guide your revision.

In addition to using idea maps, here are four questions to ask that will help you identify weaknesses in your writing:

- Does the paragraph stray from the topic?
- Does every detail belong?
- Are the details arranged and developed logically?
- Is the paragraph repetitious?

Here are some suggestions for ways to revise your paragraphs to correct each of the weaknesses you identify using an idea map or by asking the questions above.

## Does the Paragraph Stray from the Topic?

When you are writing a first draft of a paragraph, it is easy to drift away from the topic. As you write, one idea triggers another and that idea another, and eventually you end up with ideas that have little or nothing to do with your original topic, as in the following first-draft student paragraph.

### Sample Student Paragraph

#### A Checklist for Leaving Home on Time

If you are not a naturally well-organized person, you may need to compensate by being super organized in the morning so you can you leave on time. A detailed checklist can help you achieve the seemingly impossible goal of leaving home exactly when you are supposed to. It is especially difficult to leave on time if you are tired or feeling lazy. When making such a checklist, most people find it helpful to make plans for the previous evening. Check if you have clean clothes for the next day or need to do a load of laundry. Are materials for school or work neatly assembled, or is there a landslide of papers covering your desk? Do you need to pack lunch? You get the picture. In your checklist, include tasks to complete the night before as well as a precise sequence of morning tasks with realistic estimates of the time required for each task. If you have children, help them to make checklists to keep track of homework assignments. Child development experts stress the importance of predictable structure in children's lives. If you live with a friend or spouse, make sure to divide all the chores in an equitable way. Often one person tends to be neater than the other, so you may need to make compromises, but having an explicit agreement can help prevent resentment and conflicts at home.

The idea map below of the sample paragraph shows the topic sentence and, underneath it, the supporting details that directly relate to it. All the unrelated details are in a list to the right of the map.

### Idea Map for A Checklist for Leaving Home on Time

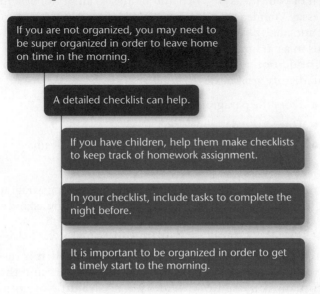

**Unrelated Details**

1. It is especially difficult to leave on time if you are tired or feeling lazy.
2. Child development experts stress the importance of predictable structure.
3. If you live with a friend or spouse, make sure to divide chores equitably.
4. Explicit agreements about household responsibilities and a willingness to compromise help prevent resentment and conflict.

In this paragraph the author began by supporting her topic sentence with examples of what needs to be included in a checklist to help with leaving home on time in the mornings. However, she began to drift when she started talking about how to negotiate about chores with a spouse or roommate. To revise this paragraph, the author could delete irrelevant details and include more information about the tasks that need to be completed in the morning.

You can use an idea map to spot where you begin to drift away from your topic. To do this, take the last idea in the map and compare it with your topic sentence. Does the last idea directly support your topic sentence? If not, you may have drifted from your topic. Check the second-to-last detail, going through the same comparison process. Working backward, you'll see where you started to drift. This is the point at which to begin revising.

### What to Do If You Stray Off Topic

Use the following suggestions to revise your paragraph if it strays from your topic:

- **Locate the last sentence that does relate to your topic, and begin your revision there.** What could you say next that *would* relate to the topic?
- **Consider expanding your existing ideas.** If, after two or three details, you have strayed from your topic, consider expanding the details you have, rather than searching for additional details.

- **Reread your brainstorming, freewriting, or branching to find more details.** Look for additional ideas that support your topic. Do more brainstorming, if necessary.
- **Consider changing your topic.** Drifting from your topic is not always a loss. Sometimes by drifting you discover a more interesting topic than your original one. If you decide to change topics, revise your entire paragraph. Begin by rewriting your topic sentence.

## EXERCISE 5-12 . . . DRAWING AN IDEA MAP

*Read the following first-draft paragraph. Then draw an idea map that includes the topic sentence, only those details that support the topic sentence, and the concluding sentence. List the unrelated details to the side of the map. Identify where the writer began to stray from the topic, and make specific suggestions for revising this paragraph.*

Junk food lacks nutrition and is high in calories. Junk food can be anything from candy and potato chips to ice cream and desserts. All of these are high in calories. But they are so tasty that they are addictive. Once a person is addicted to junk food, it is very hard to break the addiction. To break the habit, one must give up any form of sugar. And I have not gone back to my old lifestyle in over two weeks. So it is possible to break an addiction, but I still have the craving.

### Does Every Detail Belong?

Every detail in a paragraph must directly support the topic sentence or one of the other details. Unrelated information should not be included, a mistake one student made in the following first-draft paragraph.

### Sample Student Paragraph

In a world where stress is an everyday occurrence, many people relieve stress through entertainment. There are many ways to entertain ourselves and relieve stress. Many people watch movies to take their minds off day-to-day problems. However, going to the movies costs a lot of money. Due to the cost, some people rent or stream movies. Playing sports is another stress reliever. Exercise always helps to give people a positive attitude and keeps them in shape. Racquetball really keeps you in shape because it is such a fast game. A third form of entertainment is going out with friends. With friends, people can talk about their problems and feel better about them. But some friends always talk and never listen, and such conversation creates stress instead of relieving it. So if you are under stress, be sure to reserve some time for entertainment.

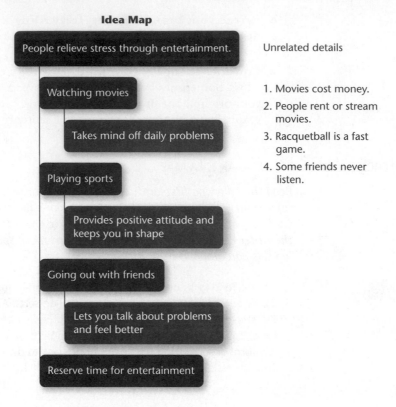

**Idea Map**

People relieve stress through entertainment.

Watching movies

Takes mind off daily problems

Playing sports

Provides positive attitude and keeps you in shape

Going out with friends

Lets you talk about problems and feel better

Reserve time for entertainment

Unrelated details

1. Movies cost money.
2. People rent or stream movies.
3. Racquetball is a fast game.
4. Some friends never listen.

To revise the paragraph, the student drew an idea map. He asked himself whether each detail he listed directly explained the topic sentence or one of the other details. If he was not sure of the answer, he asked whether deleting the detail in question would make the paragraph lose meaning or become confusing. Through doing this, he realized that the details about the high cost of movies and the low-cost alternatives of renting or streaming them do not directly explain how or why movies are entertaining; the racquetball detail does not explain how exercise relieves stress; and the detail about friends not listening does not explain how talking to friends is helpful in reducing stress.

The following suggestions will help you use supporting details more effectively:

### Make Sure Every Detail Belongs

- **Add explanations to make the connections between your ideas clearer.** Often a detail may not seem to relate to the topic because you have not explained *how* it relates. For example, health-care insurance may seem to have little to do with the prevention of breast cancer deaths until you explain that mammograms, which are paid for by some health-care plans, can detect very small cancers, allowing for early treatment and the prevention of some deaths.

- **Add transitions.** Transitions make it clearer to your reader how one detail relates to another.
- **Add new details.** If you've deleted several nonessential details, your paragraph may be too sketchy. Return to the prewriting step to generate more details you can include.

### EXERCISE 5-13 . . . IDENTIFYING UNRELATED DETAILS

*Read the following paragraph and draw an idea map of it. Underline any unrelated details and list them to the side of your map. Compare your results with those of a classmate and then decide what steps the writer should take to revise this paragraph.*

Your credit rating is a valuable thing that you should protect and watch over. A credit rating is a record of your loans, credit card charges, and repayment history. If you pay a bill late or miss a payment, that information becomes part of your credit rating. It is, therefore, important to pay bills promptly. Some people just don't keep track of dates; some don't even know what date it is today. Errors can occur in your credit rating. Someone else's mistakes can be put on your record, for example. Why these credit-rating companies can't take more time and become more accurate is beyond my understanding. It is worthwhile to get a copy of your credit report and check it for errors. Time spent caring for your credit rating will be time well spent.

### Are the Details Arranged and Developed Logically?

Details in a paragraph should follow some logical order. As you write a first draft, you are often more concerned with expressing your ideas than with presenting them in the correct order. As you revise, however, you should make sure you have followed a logical arrangement. Common arrangements include time sequence, spatial order, and arranging details from least to most according to a particular quality or characteristic (see pages 114–116). Additional methods for organizing ideas are summarized below and discussed in detail in Chapter 6.

### Methods of Organizing Using Patterns

| METHOD | DESCRIPTION |
| --- | --- |
| Process | Arranges steps in order in which they are completed |
| Definition | Explains a term by giving its general class and specific characteristics |
| Illustration | Explains by giving situations that illustrate a general idea or statement |
| Classification | Explains a topic by identifying categories or parts |
| Cause and effect | Explains why something happened or what happened as a result of a particular action |
| Comparison and contrast | Explains an idea by comparing or contrasting it with another, usually more familiar, idea |

Your ideas need a logical arrangement to make them easy to follow. Poor organization creates misunderstanding and confusion. Here is a poorly organized sample student paragraph.

### Sample Student Paragraph

When I was pregnant with my son, I wondered if life would ever be normal again. There were the nights I couldn't sleep because of all the kicking and the baby moving up to my lungs so I couldn't breathe. That was when I really had it! Each month I got bigger and bigger, and after a while I was so big I couldn't bend over or see my feet. Then there was the morning sickness. I don't know why they call it that because you're sick all the time for the first two months. Then there were all those doctor visits during which she told me, "Not for another week or two." Of course, when I realized my clothes didn't fit, I broke down and cried. But all of a sudden everything started up, and I was at the hospital delivering the baby two weeks early, and it's like it happened so fast and it was all over, and I had the most beautiful baby in my arms and I knew it was worth all that pain and suffering.

**Idea Map**

An idea map lets you see when a paragraph is poorly organized or when an idea is out of order. This student's map showed that her paragraph did not present the events of her pregnancy in the most logical arrangement: time sequence. She therefore reorganized the events in the order in which they happened throughout her pregnancy.

### Arranging and Developing Details Logically

The following suggestions will help you revise your paragraph if it lacks organization:

- **Review the methods of arranging and developing details and of organizing and presenting material in this chapter** (see Chapter 6 for more information). Will one of those arrangements work? If so, number the ideas in your idea map according to the arrangement you choose. Then begin revising your paragraph.

   If you find one or more details out of logical order in your paragraph, do the following:

   - **Number the details in your idea map to indicate the correct order, and revise your paragraph accordingly.**
   - **Reread your revised paragraph and draw another idea map.**
   - **Look to see if you've omitted necessary details.** After you have placed your details in a logical order, you are more likely to recognize gaps.

- **Look at your topic sentence again.** If you are working with a revised arrangement of supporting details, you may need to revise your topic sentence to reflect that arrangement.

- **Check whether additional details are needed.** Suppose, for example, you are writing about an exciting experience, and you decide to use the time-sequence arrangement. Once you make that decision, you may need to add details to enable your reader to understand exactly how the experience happened.

- **Add transitions.** Transitions help make your organization obvious and easy to follow.

---

### EXERCISE 5-14 . . . EVALUATING ARRANGEMENT OF IDEAS

*Read the following student paragraph, and evaluate the arrangement of ideas. What revisions would you suggest?*

The minimum wage is not an easily resolved problem; it has both advantages and disadvantages. Its primary advantage is that it does guarantee workers a minimum wage. It prevents the economic abuse of workers. Employers cannot take advantage of workers by paying them less than the minimum. Its primary disadvantage is that the minimum wage is not sufficient for older workers with families to support. For younger workers, such as teenagers, however, this minimum is fine. It provides them with spending money and some economic freedom from their parents. Another disadvantage is that as long as people, such as a teenagers, are willing to work for the minimum, employers don't need to pay a higher wage. Thus, the minimum wage prevents experienced workers from getting more money. But the minimum wage does help our economy by requiring a certain level of income per worker.

### Is the Paragraph Repetitious?

In a first draft, you may express the same idea more than once, each time in a slightly different way. Repetitive statements may help you stay on track, as they keep you writing and help you generate new ideas. However, it is important to eliminate repetition at the revision stage; it detracts from the clarity of your writing. An idea map will bring repetition to your attention quickly because it makes it easy to spot two or more very similar items.

As you read the following first-draft student paragraph, see if you can spot the repetitive statements. Then notice how the idea map below it clearly identifies the repetition.

### Sample Student Paragraph

Chemical waste dumping is an environmental concern that must be dealt with, not ignored. The big companies care nothing about the environment. They would just as soon dump waste in our backyards as not. This has finally become a big issue and is being dealt with by forcing the companies to clean up their own messes. It is incredible that large companies have the nerve to dump just about anywhere. The penalty should be steep. When the companies are caught, they should be forced to clean up their messes.

**Idea Map**

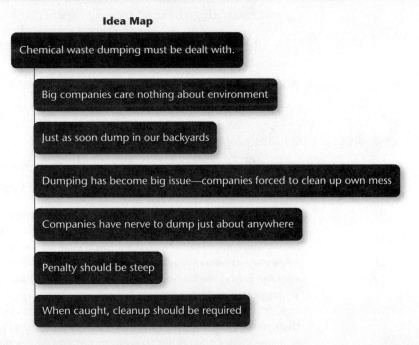

Chemical waste dumping must be dealt with.

Big companies care nothing about environment

Just as soon dump in our backyards

Dumping has become big issue—companies forced to clean up own mess

Companies have nerve to dump just about anywhere

Penalty should be steep

When caught, cleanup should be required

The idea map shows that points 1, 2, and 5 say nearly the same thing—that big companies don't care about the environment and dump waste nearly anywhere. To revise, the writer first needs to eliminate the repetitious statements. Then she needs to generate more ideas that support her topic sentence and explain why or how chemical waste dumping must be dealt with.

## How to Avoid Repetition

The following suggestions will help you revise a paragraph with repetitive ideas:

- **Try to combine ideas.** Select the best elements and wording of each idea and use them to produce a revised sentence. Add more detail if needed.

- **Review places where you make deletions.** When you delete a repetitious statement, check to see whether the sentence before and the sentence after the deletion connect. Often a transition will be needed to help the paragraph flow easily.

- **Decide whether additional details are needed.** Often we write repetitious statements when we don't know what else to say. Thus, repetition often signals lack of development. Refer to page 121 for specific suggestions on revising underdeveloped paragraphs.

- **Watch for statements that are only slightly more general or specific than one another.** For example, although the first sentence below is general and the second is more specific, they repeat the same idea.

> Ringing telephones can be distracting. The telephone that rang constantly throughout the evening distracted me.

To make the second sentence a specific example of the idea in the first sentence, rather than just a repetition of it, the writer would need to add specific details about how the telephone ringing throughout the evening was a distraction.

> The telephone that rang continuously in my neighbor's apartment yesterday woke my baby and made it impossible to get her back to sleep.

### EXERCISE 5-15 . . . IDENTIFYING AND REVISING REPETITIVE STATEMENTS

*Read the following paragraph and delete all repetitive statements. Make suggestions for revision.*

Children misbehaving is an annoying problem in our society. I used to work as a waiter at Denny's, and I have seen many incidences in which parents allow their children to misbehave. I have seen many situations that you would just not believe. Once I served a table at which the parents allowed their four-year-old to make his toy spider crawl up and down my pants as I tried to serve the food. The parents just laughed. Children have grown up being rewarded for their actions, regardless of whether they are good or bad. Whether the child does something the parents approve of or whether it is something they disapprove of, they react in similar ways. This is why a lot of toddlers and children continue to misbehave. Being rewarded will cause the child to act in the same way to get the same reward.

## Revision Checklist

Refer to the following revision checklist to help you revise paragraphs.

### REVISION CHECKLIST

#### Paragraph Development

1. Is the topic manageable (neither too broad nor too narrow)?
2. Is the paragraph written with the reader in mind?
3. Does the topic sentence identify the topic?
4. Does the topic sentence make a point about the topic?
5. Does each sentence support the topic sentence?
6. Is there sufficient detail?
7. Are the details arranged and developed logically?
8. Is the paragraph repetitious?
9. Is there a sentence at the end that brings the paragraph to a close?

#### Sentence Development

10. Are there any sentence fragments, run-on sentences, or comma splices?
11. Are ideas combined to produce more effective sentences?
12. Are adjectives and adverbs used to make the sentences vivid and interesting?
13. Are relative clauses and prepositional phrases used to add detail?
14. Are pronouns used correctly and consistently?

### EXERCISE 5-16 . . . REVISING A PARAGRAPH

*Review the paragraph you wrote for Exercise 5-9. Use the Revision Checklist to guide your revision.*

## SUMMARY OF LEARNING OBJECTIVES

**MySkillsLab**
Complete the mastery test for this chapter **in MySkillsLab.**

**1  Write effective topic sentences.**
*What is an effective topic sentence?*

An **effective topic sentence** identifies the topic and expresses a view or makes a point about the topic. Choose a manageable topic and be sure the sentence expresses a complete thought.

**2  Select and organize details to support the topic sentence.**
*How do you choose and use details to support a topic sentence?*

Use **relevant details** that directly explain and support the topic sentence. Use **sufficient details** to make your topic sentence understandable and convincing. Use a **variety of details** to develop the topic sentence: examples, facts or statistics, reasons, descriptions, and steps or procedures. **Organize details logically** based on the topic of the paragraph using time sequence, spatial, or least/most arrangements.

**3  Use transitional words and phrases to connect details.**
*What are transitional words and phrases, and how do you use them?*

**Transitional words and phrases** allow readers to move easily from one detail to another; they guide the reader through the paragraph, signal what is to follow, and show how details relate to one another. Transitional words and phrases are used to indicate when events happened (*first, last, now, then,* etc.) where things appear in space (*above, beside, behind, below,* etc.), and how important events, people, or items are. See Table 5-1 (page 117) for a list of common transitional words.

**4  Use specific language.**
*What is specific language, and how do you use it?*

**Vague words** provide limited information while **specific words** convey exact details. Use specific words to give your reader as much information as possible. Try to paint pictures for your reader with specific, vivid words: choose active verbs, give exact names, use adjectives to describe, and use words that appeal to the senses.

**5  Revise paragraphs.**
*What is involved in revising a paragraph?*

**Revise paragraphs** by evaluating your topic sentence, adding supporting details, and using a revision map. A **map** will help you discover whether you have *strayed from your topic,* and help you be sure that *every detail belongs,* that the *details are arranged and developed logically,* and that you have *avoided repetition.* Use the Revision Checklist on page 132 to help you revise.

# 6 Reading and Writing Organizational Patterns

## LEARNING OBJECTIVES

**1** Read and write illustration

**2** Read and write process

**3** Read and write definition

**4** Read and write classification

**5** Read and write cause and effect

**6** Read and write comparison and contrast

**7** Read and write mixed patterns

Most college students take courses in several different disciplines each semester. They may study psychology, anatomy and physiology, mathematics, and English composition all in one semester. In the course of one day, they may read a poem, solve math problems, study early developments in psychology, and learn about controversial issues in politics and government.

What few students realize is that biologists and psychologists, for example, think about and approach their subject matter in similar ways. Both carefully define terms, examine causes and effects, study similarities and differences, explain processes, and illustrate ideas. They may study different subject matter and use different language, but their approaches to their studies are basically the same. Researchers, textbook authors, your professors, and professional writers use standard approaches, or **organizational patterns,** to express their ideas. In English composition, they are sometimes called the **rhetorical modes** or simply **modes**.

To learn what patterns of organization are and why they are useful for reading and writing, consider the following lists.

Lists A and B each contain five facts. Which would be easier to learn?

List A

1. Cheeseburgers contain more calories than hamburgers.
2. Christmas cactus plants bloom once a year.
3. Many herbs have medicinal uses.
4. Many ethnic groups live in Toronto.
5. Fiction books are arranged alphabetically by author.

List B

1. Effective advertising has several characteristics.
2. An ad must be unique.
3. An ad must be believable.
4. An ad must make a lasting impression.
5. An ad must substantiate a claim.

Most likely, you chose list B. There is no connection between the facts in list A; the facts in list B, however, are related. The first sentence makes a general statement, and each remaining sentence gives a particular characteristic of effective advertising. Together they fit into a *pattern*.

The details of a paragraph, paragraphs within an essay, events within a short story, or sections within a textbook often fit a pattern. If you can recognize the pattern, you will find it easier to understand and remember the content. You will be able to comprehend the work as a unified whole rather than independent pieces of information.

Patterns are useful when you write, as well. They provide a framework within which to organize and develop your ideas and help you present them in a clear, logical manner. Sections of this chapter are devoted to reading and writing each of the following patterns: *illustration, process, definition, classification, cause and effect,* and *comparison and contrast.* Each of these patterns can work alone or with other patterns.

Organizational patterns can work for you in several ways:

- Patterns help you anticipate the author's thought development and thus focus your reading.
- Patterns help you remember and recall what you read.
- Patterns are useful in your own writing; they help you organize and express your ideas in a coherent, comprehensible form.

Each section of this chapter describes how to read and write using a common pattern and provides examples of its use.

## 6a    READING AND WRITING ILLUSTRATION

**LEARNING OBJECTIVE 1**
Read and write
illustration

**Illustration** uses examples—specific instances or situations—to explain a general idea or statement. Peaches and plums are examples of fruit. Presidents' Day and Veterans Day are examples of national holidays. Here are two general statements with specific examples that illustrate them.

| GENERAL STATEMENT | EXAMPLES |
|---|---|
| I had an exhausting day. | • I had two exams.<br>• I worked four hours.<br>• I swam 20 laps in the pool.<br>• I did three loads of laundry. |
| Research studies demonstrate that reading aloud to children improves their reading skills. | • Whitehurst (2011) found that reading picture books to children improved their vocabulary.<br>• Crain-Thompson and Dale (2012) reported that reading aloud to language-delayed children improved their reading ability. |

In each case, the examples make the general statement clear, understandable, and believable by giving specific illustrations or supporting details. Example paragraphs consist of examples that support the topic sentence.

## Reading Illustration Paragraphs

The **illustration pattern** uses specific instances or detailed situations or examples to explain an idea or concept. One of the clearest ways to explain something is to give an example. This is especially true when a subject is unfamiliar. Suppose, for instance, that your younger brother asks you to explain what anthropology is. You might give him examples of the topics you study such as apes and early humans and the development of modern humans. Through examples, your brother would get a fairly good idea of what anthropology is all about.

When organizing a paragraph, a writer often states the main idea first and then follows it with one or more examples. In a longer piece of writing, a separate paragraph may be used for each example. Notice how the illustration pattern is developed in the following paragraph:

### Issue: Popular Physics

Static electricity is all around us. We see it in lightning. We receive electric shocks when we walk on a nylon rug on a dry day and then touch something (or someone). We can see sparks fly from a cat's fur when we pet it in the dark. We can rub a balloon on a sweater and make the balloon stick to the wall or the ceiling. Our clothes cling together when we take them from the dryer.

—Newell, *Chemistry*, p. 11

Here the writer explains static electricity through the use of everyday examples. You could visualize the paragraph as follows:

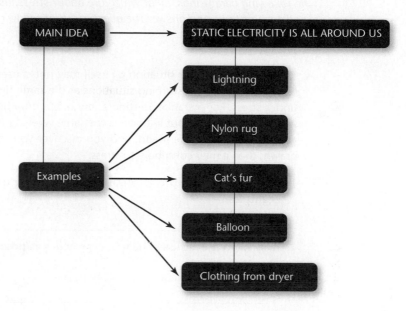

Writers often use transition words—*for example, for instance,* or *such as*—to signal the reader that an example is to follow. By using examples and transitions, the writer explains why Shadow is Charlie's best friend.

> Charlie agrees with the old saying that "a dog is a man's best friend." When he comes home from work, for instance, his dog Shadow is always happy to see him. He wags his tail, licks Charlie's hand, and leaps joyously around the room. Shadow is also good company for him. The dog is always there, for example, when Charlie is sick or lonely or just needs a pal to take for a walk. Many pets, such as cats and parakeets, provide companionship for their owners. But Charlie would put his dog Shadow at the top of any "best friend" list.

## COMMON ILLUSTRATION TRANSITIONS

| | | | |
|---|---|---|---|
| for example | for instance | such as | in particular |
| to illustrate | an example is | also | when |

**EXERCISE 6-1 . . . ANALYZING THE ILLUSTRATION PATTERN**

*The following paragraphs, all of which are about stress, use the example pattern. Read each of them and answer the questions that follow.*

### Issue: Stress

A.    Any single event or situation by itself may not cause stress. But, if you experience several mildly disturbing situations at the same time, you may find yourself under stress. For instance, getting a low grade on a biology lab report by itself may not be stressful, but if it occurs the same week during which your car "dies," you argue with a close friend, and you discover your checking account is overdrawn, then it may contribute to stress.

1. What transition word or phrase does the writer use to introduce the examples?

_____

2. List the four examples the writer provides as possible causes of stress.

a. _____

b. _____

c. _____

d. _____

B.    Every time you make a major change in your life, you are susceptible to stress. Major changes include a new job or career, marriage, divorce, the birth of a child, or the death of someone close. Beginning college is a major life change. Try not to create multiple simultaneous life changes, which multiply the potential for stress.

3. Does the topic sentence occur first, second, or last?

_____

4. The writer gives six examples of major changes. List them briefly.

a. _____       d. _____

b. _____       e. _____

c. _____       f. _____

C.    Because you probably depend on your job to pay part or all of your college expenses, your job is important to you and you feel pressure to perform well in order to keep it. Some jobs are more stressful than others. Those, for example, in which you work under constant time pressure tend to be stressful. Jobs that must be performed in loud, noisy, crowded, or unpleasant conditions—a hot kitchen, a noisy machine shop—with co-workers who don't do their share can be stressful. Consider changing jobs if you are working in very stressful conditions.

5. Does the topic sentence occur first, second, or last?

_____

6. What transition does the writer use to introduce the first type of job?

_____

7. To help you understand "jobs that must be performed in loud, noisy, crowded, or unpleasant conditions," the writer provides three examples. List these examples in the diagram below.

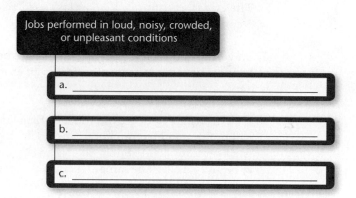

Jobs performed in loud, noisy, crowded, or unpleasant conditions

a. _____

b. _____

c. _____

## Writing Illustration Paragraphs

Writing paragraphs using examples involves writing a clear topic sentence, selecting appropriate and sufficient examples, arranging your details, and using transitions. When writing illustration paragraphs, be sure to use the third person in most situations (see discussion of point of view in Chapter 2, page 26).

### Write Your Topic Sentence

You must create a topic sentence before you can generate examples to support it. Consider what you want to say about your topic and what your main point or fresh insight is. From this main idea, compose a first draft of a topic sentence. Be sure it states your topic and the point you want to make about it. (See Chapter 5, page 106, if necessary, for a review of developing your point.) You will probably want to revise your topic sentence once you've written the paragraph, but for now, use it as the basis for gathering examples.

### Select Appropriate and Sufficient Examples

Use brainstorming to create a list of as many examples as you can think of to support your topic sentence. Suppose your topic is dog training. Your tentative topic sentence is "You must be firm and consistent when training dogs;

otherwise, they will not respond to your commands." You might produce the following list of examples:

> My sister's dog jumps on people; sometimes she disciplines him and sometimes she doesn't.
>
> Every time I want my dog to heel, I give the same command and use a firm tone of voice.
>
> If my dog does not obey the command to sit, I repeat it, this time saying it firmly while pushing down on his back.
>
> The dog trainer at obedience class used a set of hand signals to give commands to his dogs.

Then you would review your list and select between two and four examples to support your topic sentence. Here is an example of a paragraph you might write:

> When training dogs, you must be firm and consistent; otherwise, they will not respond to your commands. The dog trainer at my obedience class has a perfectly trained dog. She uses a set of hand signals to give commands to her dog, Belle. The same signal always means the same thing, it is always enforced, and Belle has learned to obey each command. On the other hand, my sister's dog is a good example of what not to do. Her dog Maggie jumps on people; sometimes she disciplines Maggie, and sometimes she doesn't. When she asks Maggie to sit, sometimes she insists Maggie obey; other times she gets discouraged and gives up. Consequently, the dog has not learned to stop jumping on people or to obey the command to sit.

**Idea Map**

| | |
|---|---|
| **Topic sentence** | Dog training must be firm and consistent; otherwise dogs will not obey. |
| **Example** | Belle |
| **Example** | Maggie |

In the example paragraph, you probably noticed that some of the brainstormed examples were used; others were not. New examples were also added. Use the following guidelines in selecting details to include:

### Guidelines for Selecting and Using Details

- **Each example should illustrate the idea stated in your topic sentence.** Do not choose examples that are complicated or have too many parts; your readers may not be able to see the connection to your topic sentence clearly.

- **Each example should be as specific and vivid as possible, accurately describing an incident or situation.** Suppose your topic sentence is "Celebrities are not reliable sources of information about a product because they are getting paid to praise it." Rather than follow it with a general statement like "Many sports stars are paid to appear in TV commercials," name specific athletes and products or sponsors: "Tom Brady, star quarterback for the Patriots, endorses UGG Boots and Under Armour; LeBron James, basketball superstar, endorses Nike products."

- **Choose examples that your readers are familiar with and understand.** If you choose an example that is out of the realm of your readers' experience, the example will not help them understand your main point.

- **Choose a sufficient number of examples to make your point understandable.** The number you need depends on the complexity of the topic and your reader's familiarity with it. One example may be sufficient if it is well developed and the reader has some background knowledge about the topic. However, the more difficult and unfamiliar the topic, the more examples you will need. For instance, if you are writing about how poor service at a restaurant can be viewed as an exercise in patience, two examples may be sufficient; describing your long wait and your rude waiter could make your point powerfully. But if you are writing about test anxiety as a symptom of poor study habits, you probably would need several examples, such as the need to organize one's time, set realistic goals, practice relaxation techniques, and work on self-esteem.

- **Vary your examples.** If you are giving several examples, choose a wide range from different times, places, people, and so on.

- **Choose typical examples.** Avoid outrageous or exaggerated examples that do not accurately represent the situation.

- **Draw the connection for your reader between your example and your main point.** The following is a presentation by a social worker during a closed staff meeting at Carroll County Mental Health Services:

> We are continuing to see the after effects of last spring's tornado on our clients. In some cases, we have had to make referrals to meet our clients' needs. Several children have suffered PTSD (post traumatic stress disorder). Natoya Johns, for example, has nightmares and panic attacks. Natoya and the other children have been referred to Dr. Browntree at the Children's Clinic. We are also seeing increased occurrences of domestic violence that seem to be due to economic problems caused by the tornado. The worst case was Betsy Coster, who came to her counseling session with broken ribs, a black eye, and bruises. Betsy was referred to Safe Harbor, where she will receive legal and medical assistance while in protected housing. Several cases of substance abuse appeared to be aggravated by the stress of the situation. We put four clients in touch with AA, and Ken Lacoutez was referred to City Hospital for the inpatient program.
>
> (*Note:* Names have been changed to protect client privacy.)

### Arrange Your Details

Once you have selected examples to include, arrange your ideas in a logical sequence. Here are a few possibilities:

- **Arrange the examples chronologically.** If some examples are old and others more recent, you might begin with the older examples and then move to the more current ones.

- **Arrange the examples from most to least familiar.** If some examples are more detailed or technical, and therefore likely to be unfamiliar to your reader, place them after more familiar examples.

- **Arrange the examples from least to most important.** You may want to begin with less convincing examples and finish with the strongest, most convincing example, thereby leaving your reader with a strong final impression.

- **Arrange the examples in the order suggested by the topic sentence.** In the earlier sample paragraph about dog training, being firm and consistent is mentioned first in the topic sentence, so an example of firm and consistent training is given first.

### Use Transitions

Transition words and phrases are needed in illustration paragraphs, both to signal to your reader that you are offering an example and to signal that you are moving from one example to another (see page 137 for a list of commonly used illustration transitions). Notice in the following paragraph how the transition words connect the examples and make them easier to follow:

#### Issue: Institutional heterosexism

Institutional heterosexism is easy to identify. For example, the ban on gay marriage in many states and the fact that at this time only a handful of states allow gay marriage are good examples of institutional heterosexism. Other examples include the ban on homosexual bishops and priests, the United States military's prohibiting openly gay people from serving in the armed forces [since repealed], and the many laws that prohibit adoption of children by gay people. In some cultures, homosexual relations are illegal (for instance in India, Malaysia, Pakistan, and Singapore); penalties range from a misdemeanor conviction in Liberia, to life in jail in Singapore, to death in Pakistan.

—DeVito, *Human Communication*, p. 106

---

**EXERCISE 6-2 . . . WRITING AN ILLUSTRATION PARAGRAPH**

*Select one of the topics listed below and write a paragraph that follows the guidelines given above.*

1. Slang language

2. Daily hassles or aggravations

3. The needs of infants or young children

4. Overcommercialization of holidays

5. Growing use of blogs

6b     **READING AND WRITING PROCESS**

**LEARNING OBJECTIVE 2**
Read and write
process

The term *process* refers to the order in which something occurs or the order in which it is done. When textbook authors explain how to do something or how something works, they use the **process** pattern, presenting ideas in sequence. *Chronological order* is a variation of process that writers use to describe events in the order in which they happened. For example, a historian may discuss the sequence of events preceding the Iraq war. Another variation is *narration*, in which writers tell a story, describing events in the order in which they occurred to create a narrative. While this section focuses on process, you can use many of the same guidelines for reading and writing chronological order and narration as well.

When writing process paragraphs, it is sometimes acceptable to write in the second person (you), but it is not acceptable to use the second person when writing in other patterns.

### Reading Process Paragraphs

Disciplines and careers that focus on procedures, steps, or stages use the process pattern. In many cases, the steps must happen in a specific order; in some cases, certain steps may happen at the same time or in no particular order. Using bulleted and numbered lists allows writers to provide clear, step-by-step explanations of processes. They also use transitions to guide the reader from one step to the next.

### COMMON PROCESS TRANSITIONS

| | | | | | |
|---|---|---|---|---|---|
| after | as soon as | finally | in addition | meanwhile | then |
| also | before | first | last | next | until |
| another | during | following | later | second | when |

Note that the following selection uses numbered points to walk the reader through the process of performing mouth-to-mask ventilation in the correct, step-by-step manner. Notice that all of the steps are parallel: They begin with verbs.

### Issue: Emergency Care

Mouth-to-mask ventilation is performed using a pocket face mask, which is made of soft, collapsible material and can be carried in your pocket, jacket, or purse. Many emergency medical technicians (EMT's) purchase their own pocket face masks for workplace or auto first aid kits.

To provide mouth-to-mask ventilation, follow these steps:

1. Position yourself at the patient's head and open the airway. It may be necessary to clear the airway of obstructions. If appropriate, insert an oropharyngeal airway to help keep the patient's airway open.

2. Connect oxygen to the inlet on the mask and run at 16 liters per minute. If oxygen is not immediately available, do not delay mouth-to-mask ventilations.

3. Position the mask on the patient's face so that the apex (top of the triangle) is over the bridge of the nose and the base is between the lower lip and prominence of the chin. (Center the ventilation port on the patient's mouth.)

4. Hold the mask firmly in place while maintaining head tilt.

5. Take a breath and exhale into the mask port or one-way valve at the top of the mask port. Each ventilation should be delivered over 1 second in adults, infants, and children and be of just enough volume to make the chest rise. Full expansion of the chest is undesirable; the ventilation should cease as soon as you notice the chest moving.

6. Remove your mouth from the port and allow for passive exhalation. Continue as you would for mouth-to-mouth ventilations or CPR.

—adapted from Limmer and O'Keefe, *Emergency Care*, pp. 211–212

You can visualize the process pattern as follows:

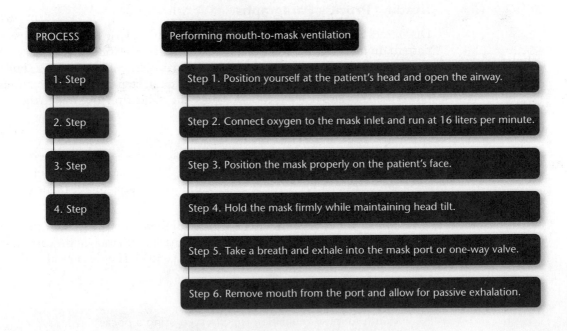

PROCESS    Performing mouth-to-mask ventilation

1. Step    Step 1. Position yourself at the patient's head and open the airway.

2. Step    Step 2. Connect oxygen to the mask inlet and run at 16 liters per minute.

3. Step    Step 3. Position the mask properly on the patient's face.

4. Step    Step 4. Hold the mask firmly while maintaining head tilt.

Step 5. Take a breath and exhale into the mask port or one-way valve.

Step 6. Remove mouth from the port and allow for passive exhalation.

## EXERCISE 6-3 . . . USING PROCESS

*Read the following selection and answer the questions that follow.*

### A. Issue: Organ Donation

The young motorcyclist was a good candidate for organ donation because he died from a brain injury. People who die from cardiac death can be tissue donors, but the lack of oxygen experienced during cardiac death causes organs to deteriorate, making such people less suitable organ donors. Since many more people will die of cardiac death than brain injury, tissues can be banked for future use, but there is a shortage of organs for use in transplant operations.

If the family agrees, the young man will be kept on a ventilator so that his organs continue to be nourished with oxygen and blood until the organs can be surgically removed. While the organs are being removed, medical personnel will attempt to find the best recipient. To select the recipient, a search of a computerized database is performed. Starting at the top of the list, medical staff will narrow down possible recipients, based in part on how long the recipient has been waiting. People at the top of the waiting list for a given organ tend to be very ill and will die if a transplant does not become available in a matter of days or weeks. These people are often hospitalized or waiting at home or in hotels near the hospital, hoping to receive a call telling them that an organ has become available. Recipients must be located close to the hospital since donor organs cannot be preserved indefinitely; they must be transplanted as soon a possible. Lungs, for instance, can be preserved for around 6 hours before the transplant operation must begin.

Organs donors and recipients must have the same blood type so that the recipient's immune system does not react against the organ. Likewise, donors and recipients are matched for the presence of certain markers on the surface of their tissues. When it has been determined that blood and marker types of donor and recipient are a close enough match, a transplant may occur. The most commonly transplanted organs are the liver, kidney, heart, and lungs. Around 10% of people on waiting lists for replacement organs will die before one becomes available.

If you would like to be an organ donor, discuss your plans with your family. Even if you carry a signed organ donor card and indicate your preference to be a donor on your driver's license, your family will need to agree to donate your tissues and organs. If you should suffer an accidental death, like the young motorcyclist, your family will be forced to make many difficult decisions quickly. Having a discussion about organ donation now will relieve them of the burden of trying to make this decision for you.

—Belk and Maier, *Biology*, pp. 435–436

1. Which processes does this passage explain?

   _____

   _____

2. Highlight each topic sentence.

3. What is the best way to ensure that someone who needs your organs receives them after you die?

   _____

   _____

4. How many steps are involved in the process? List them on your own paper.

5. Highlight each of the transition words used in the passage, both those suggesting process and others, as well.

## Writing Process Paragraphs

There are two types of process paragraphs—a "how-to" paragraph and a "how-it-works" paragraph.

- **"How-to" paragraphs explain how something is done.** For example, they may explain how to change a flat tire, aid a choking victim, or locate a reference source in the library.
- **"How-it-works" paragraphs explain how something operates or happens.** For example, they may explain the operation of a pump, how the human body regulates temperature, or how children acquire speech.

Here are examples of both types of paragraphs. The first explains how to wash your hands in a medical environment. The second describes how hibernation works. Be sure to study the idea map for each.

### "How-to" Paragraph

Washing your hands may seem a simple task, but in a medical environment it is your first defense against the spread of disease and infection, and must be done properly. Begin by removing all jewelry. Turn on the water using a paper towel, thus avoiding contact with contaminated faucets. Next, wet your hands under running water and squirt a dollop of liquid soap in the palm of your hand. Lather the soap, and work it over your hands for two minutes. Use a circular motion, since it creates friction that removes dirt and organisms. Keep your hands pointed downward, so water will not run onto your arms, creating further contamination. Use a brush to clean under your fingernails. Then rinse your hands, reapply soap, scrub for one minute, and rinse again thoroughly. Dry your hands using a paper towel. Finally, use a new dry paper towel to turn off the faucet, protecting your hands from contamination.

**Idea Map**

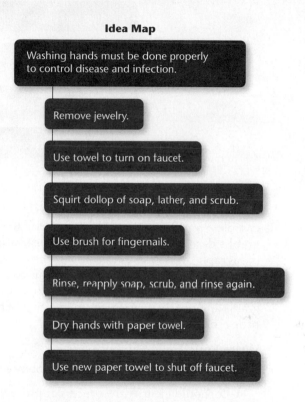

## "How-It-Works" Paragraph

Hibernation is a biological process that occurs most frequently in small animals. The process enables animals to adjust to a diminishing food supply. When the outdoor temperature drops, the animal's internal thermostat senses the change. Then bodily changes begin to occur. First, the animal's heartbeat slows, and oxygen intake is reduced by slowed breathing. Metabolism is then reduced. Food intake becomes minimal. Finally, the animal falls into a sleeplike state during which it relies on stored body fat to support life functions.

**Idea Map**

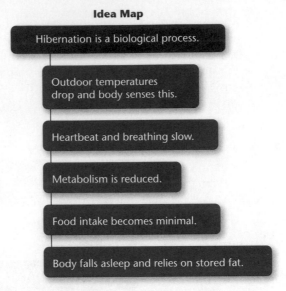

Hibernation is a biological process.

Outdoor temperatures drop and body senses this.

Heartbeat and breathing slow.

Metabolism is reduced.

Food intake becomes minimal.

Body falls asleep and relies on stored fat.

### Select a Topic and Generate Ideas

Before you can describe a process, you must be very familiar with it and have a complete understanding of how it works. Both how-to and how-it-works paragraphs describe steps that occur in a specified order. Begin developing your paragraph by listing these steps in the order in which they must occur. It is helpful to visualize the process. For how-to paragraphs, imagine yourself actually performing the task. For complicated how-it-works descriptions, draw diagrams and use them as guides in identifying the steps and putting them in the proper order.

### Write Your Topic Sentence

For a process paragraph, your topic sentence should accomplish two things:

- It should identify the process or procedure.
- It should explain to your reader why familiarity with the process is useful or important (*why* he or she should learn about the process). Your topic sentence should state a goal, offer a reason, or indicate what can be accomplished by using the process.

Here are a few examples of topic sentences that contain both of these important elements.

> Reading maps, a vital skill if you are orienteering, is a simple process, except for the final refolding.
>
> Because leisure reading encourages a positive attitude toward reading in general, every parent should know how to select worthwhile children's books.
>
> To locate books in the library, you must know how to use the computerized catalog.

### EXERCISE 6–4 . . . REVISING TOPIC SENTENCES

*Working with a classmate, revise these topic sentences to make clear why the reader should learn the process.*

1. Making pizza at home involves five steps.
2. Making a sales presentation requires good listening and speaking skills.
3. Most people can easily learn to perform the Heimlich Manoeuvre on choking victims.
4. The dental hygienist shows patients how to use dental floss.
5. Here's how to use Tumblr.

## Develop and Sequence Your Ideas

Because your readers may be unfamiliar with your topic, try to include helpful information that will enable them to understand (for how-it-works paragraphs) and follow or complete the process (for how-to paragraphs). Consider including the following:

- **Definitions.** Explain terms that may be unfamiliar. For example, explain the term *bindings* when writing about skiing.
- **Needed equipment.** For how-to paragraphs, tell your readers what tools or supplies they will need to complete the process. For a how-to paragraph on making chili, list the ingredients, for example.
- **Pitfalls and problems.** Alert your reader about potential problems and places where confusion or error may occur. Warn your chili-making readers to add chili peppers gradually and to taste along the way so the chili doesn't get too spicy.

Use the following tips to develop an effective process paragraph:

### DEVELOPING A PROCESS PARAGRAPH

1. **Place your topic sentence first.** This position provides your reader with a purpose for reading.
2. **Present the steps in a process in the order in which they happen.**
3. **Include only essential, necessary steps.** Avoid comments, opinions, or unnecessary information because they may confuse your reader.
4. **Assume that your reader is unfamiliar with your topic** (unless you know otherwise). Be sure to define unfamiliar terms and describe clearly any technical or specialized tools, procedures, or objects.
5. **Use a consistent point of view.** Use either the first person (*I*) or the second person (*you*) throughout. Don't switch between them. (Note: Process is the *only* pattern in which it is acceptable to use the second person.)

### Use Transitions

Transition words are particularly important in process paragraphs because they lead your reader from one step to the next. Specifically, they signal to your reader that the next step is about to begin (see page 143 for a list of common process transitions). In the following paragraph, notice how each of the highlighted transition words announces that a new step is to follow:

> Do you want to teach your children something about their background, help develop their language skills, *and* have fun at the same time? Make a family album together! First, gather the necessary supplies: family photos, sheets of colored construction paper, yarn, and glue. Next, fold four sheets of paper in half; this will give you an eight-page album. Unfold the pages and lay them flat, one on top of the other. After you've evened them up, punch holes at the top and bottom of the fold, making sure you get through all four sheets. Next, thread the yarn through the holes. Now tie the yarn securely and crease the paper along the fold. Finally, glue a photo to each page. After the glue has dried, have your child write the names of the people in the pictures on each page and decorate the cover. Remember to talk to your children about the people you are including in your album. Not only will they learn about their extended family, but they also will have great memories of doing this creative project with you.

### EXERCISE 6–5 . . . WRITING A PROCESS PARAGRAPH

*Think of a process or procedure you are familiar with, or select one from the following list. Using the guidelines presented in this section, write a process paragraph on the topic.*

1. How to find a worthwhile part-time job

2. How to waste time

3. How to learn to like _____

4. How the NFL football draft works

5. How to win at _____

6. How to make a marriage or relationship work

7. How to protect your right to privacy

8. How to improve your skill at _____

9. How to make your boss want to promote you

10. How to stop a bad habit.

## 6c  READING AND WRITING DEFINITION

**LEARNING OBJECTIVE 3**
Read and write
definition

Each academic discipline, field of study, and business has its own specialized vocabulary. Consequently, **definition**—providing explanations of the meaning of terms or concepts—is a commonly used pattern throughout most introductory-level college texts. Definition is also used in general-interest magazines to help readers become familiar with new ideas and concepts; for example, if *Time* publishes an article about *gerrymandering* (the process of changing boundaries of voting districts to favor a particular candidate or political party), you can expect the author to define the term early in the article.

### Reading Definition Paragraphs

Suppose you are asked to define the word *actuary* for someone unfamiliar with the term. First, you would probably say that an actuary is a person who works with numbers. Then you might distinguish an actuary from other people who work with numbers by saying that an actuary compiles and works with statistics. Finally, you might mention that many actuaries work with insurance companies to help them understand risks and calculate insurance premiums.

Although you may have presented it informally, your definition would have followed the standard, classic pattern. The first part of your definition tells what general class or group the term belongs to (people who work with numbers). The second part tells what distinguishes the term from other items in the same class or category (such as accountants). The third part includes further explanation, characteristics, examples, or applications.

See how the term squatter settlement is defined in the following paragraph, and notice how the term and the general class are presented. The remainder of the paragraph presents the distinguishing characteristics of squatter settlements. Sometimes writers use typographical aids, such as *italics*, **boldface**, or color to emphasize the term being defined. Here is an example.

#### Issue: Squatter Settlements

Overurbanization, or the too-rapid growth of cities, often results in **squatter settlements**, illegal developments of makeshift housing on land neither owned nor rented by their inhabitants. Such settlements are often built on steep hillsides or even on river floodplains that expose the occupants to the dangers of landslide and floods. Squatter settlements also are often found in the open space of public parks or along roadways, where they are regularly destroyed by government authorities, usually to be quickly rebuilt by migrants who have no other alternatives.

—Rowntree et al., *Diversity Amid Globalization*, p. 26

You can visualize the definition pattern as follows:

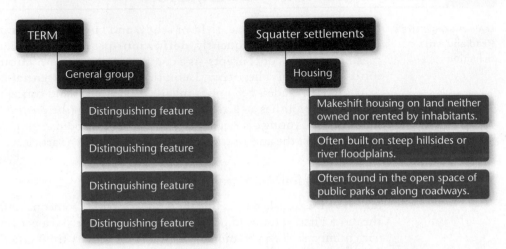

Writers often provide transitions that signal the organizational pattern being used. These transitions may occur within single sentences or as connections between sentences. (Transition words are italicized in the box below.)

## COMMON DEFINITION TRANSITIONS

Genetics *is* . . .
Bureaucracy *means* . . .
Patronage *refers to* . . .
Aggression *can be defined* as . . .
Deficit is *another term* that . . .
Balance of power *also means* . . .

### EXERCISE 6-6 . . . USING DEFINITION

*Read each of the following paragraphs and answer the questions that follow.*

### A. Issue: Globalization and Cultural Diversity

A **pidgin** is a language that blends elements of at least two parent languages and that emerges when two different cultures with different languages come in contact and must communicate. All speakers of pidgin have their own native language(s) but learn to speak pidgin as a second, rudimentary language. Pidgins are typically limited to specific functional domains, such as trade and basic social interactions. Many pidgins of the Western Hemisphere were the result of the Atlantic slave trade and plantation slavery. Owners needed to communicate with their slaves, and slaves from various parts of Africa needed to communicate with each other. Pidgins are common throughout the South Pacific.

A pidgin often evolves into a **creole**, which is a language descended from a pidgin and which subsequently has its own native speakers, a richer vocabulary than a pidgin has, and a more developed grammar. Throughout the Western Hemisphere, many localized creoles have developed in areas such as Louisiana, the Caribbean, Ecuador, and Suriname. Though a living reminder of the heritage of slavery, Creole languages and associated literature and music are also evidence of resilience and creativity in the African diaspora.

—Miller, *Cultural Anthropology in a Globalizing World,* pp. 195–196

1. What terms are being defined?

_____

2. Explain the meaning of the terms in your own words.

_____

_____

_____

3. Where will you find pidgin and creole languages spoken?

_____

_____

### B. Issue: Health and Wellness

Stress can be associated with most daily activities. Generally, positive stress—stress that presents the opportunity for personal growth and satisfaction—is termed **eustress**. Getting married, successfully kayaking Class II rapids, beginning a career, and developing new friends may all give rise to eustress. **Distress**, or negative stress, is caused by events that result in debilitative stress and strain, such as financial problems, the death of a loved one, academic difficulties, and the breakup of a relationship. Prolonged distress can have negative effects on health.

—Donatelle, *Health,* p. 68

4. What terms are being defined, and what are the definitions?

_____

_____

_____

5. List at least three activities that the author provides to help readers understand the definition of each term.

_____

_____

_____

## Writing Definition Paragraphs

Developing a definition paragraph involves writing a topic sentence and adding explanatory details. Be sure to write using the third person *(he, they, Samantha)*.

### Write Your Topic Sentence

The topic sentence of a definition paragraph should accomplish two things:

1. **It should identify the term you are explaining.**
2. **It should place the term in a general group.** It may also provide one or more distinguishing characteristics.

In the topic sentence below, the term being defined is *psychiatry*, the general group is "a branch of medicine," and its distinguishing feature is that it "deals with mental and emotional disorders."

> Psychiatry is a branch of medicine that deals with mental and emotional disorders.

### Add Explanatory Details

Your topic sentence will usually *not* be sufficient to give your reader a complete understanding of the term you are defining. You will need to explain it further in one or more of the following ways:

1. **Give examples.** Examples can make a definition more vivid and interesting to your reader.
2. **Break the term into subcategories.** Breaking your subject down into subcategories helps to organize your definition. For example, you might explain the term *discrimination* by listing some of its types: racial, gender, and age.
3. **Explain what the term is not.** To bring the meaning of a term into focus for your reader, it is sometimes helpful to give counterexamples, or to discuss in what ways the term means something different from what one might expect. Notice that student Ted Sawchuck does this in the following paragraph on sushi.

> Sushi is a Japanese food consisting of small cakes of cooked rice wrapped in seaweed. While it is commonly thought of as raw fish on rice, it is actually any preparation of vinegared rice. Sushi can also take the form of conical hand rolls and the more popular sushi roll. The roll is topped or stuffed with slices of raw or cooked fish, egg, or vegetables. Slices of raw fish served by themselves are commonly mistaken for sushi but are properly referred to as *sashimi*.

4. **Trace the term's meaning over time.** If the term has changed or expanded in meaning over time, it may be useful to trace this development as a way of explaining the term's current meaning.

5. **Compare an unfamiliar term with one that is familiar to your readers.** If you are writing about rugby, you might compare it to football, a more familiar sport. Be sure to make the connection clear to your readers by pointing out characteristics that the two sports share.

### Organize Your Paragraph

You should logically arrange the distinguishing characteristics of a term. You might arrange them from most to least familiar or from more to less obvious, for example. Be sure to use strong transition words and phrases to help your readers follow your presentation of ideas, guiding them from one distinguishing characteristic to another. Useful transition words and phrases are shown on page 152.

---

### EXERCISE 6-7 . . . WRITING A DEFINITION PARAGRAPH

*Write a paragraph that defines one of the following terms. Be sure to include a group and distinguishing characteristics.*

1. Skype
2. Horror
3. Hip-hop
4. Gender identity
5. Break dancing

---

## 6d    READING AND WRITING CLASSIFICATION

**LEARNING OBJECTIVE 4**
Read and write classification

**Classification** explains a subject by identifying and describing its types or categories. For instance, a good way to discuss medical personnel is to arrange them into categories: doctors, nurse practitioners, physician's assistants, nurses, technicians, and nurse's aides. If you wanted to explain who makes up your college faculty, you could classify the faculty members by the disciplines they teach (or, alternatively, by age, level of skill, or some other factor).

### Reading Classification Paragraphs

Textbook writers often use the classification pattern to explain an unfamiliar or complicated topic by dividing it into more easily understood parts. These parts are selected on the basis of common characteristics. For example, a psychology textbook writer might explain human needs by classifying them into two categories, primary and secondary. Or in a chemistry textbook, various compounds may be grouped or classified according to common characteristics, such as the presence of hydrogen or oxygen.

The following paragraph explains horticulture. As you read, try to identify the categories into which the topic of horticulture is divided.

Horticulture, the study and cultivation of garden plants, is a large industry. Recently it has become a popular area of study. The horticulture field consists of four major divisions. First, there is pomology, the science and practice of growing and handling fruit trees. Then there is olericulture, which is concerned with growing and storing vegetables. A third field, floriculture, is the science of growing, storing, and designing flowering plants. The last category, ornamental and landscape horticulture, is concerned with using grasses, plants, and shrubs in landscaping.

This paragraph approaches the topic of horticulture by describing its four areas or fields of study. You could diagram the paragraph as follows:

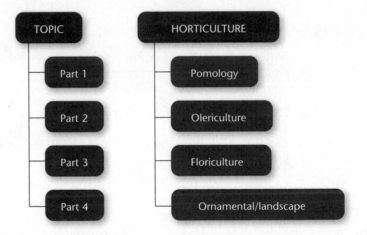

When reading textbook material that uses the classification pattern, be sure you understand *how* and *why* the topic was divided as it was. This technique will help you remember the most important parts of the topic.

Here is another example of the classification pattern:

A newspaper is published primarily to present current news and information. For large city newspapers, more than 2,000 people may be involved in the distribution of this information. The staff of a large city paper, headed by a publisher, is organized into departments: editorial, business, and mechanical. The editorial department, headed by an editor-in-chief, is responsible for the collection of news and preparation of written copy. The business department, headed by a business manager, handles circulation, sales, and advertising. The mechanical department is run by a production manager. This department deals with the actual production of the paper, including typesetting, layout, and printing.

You could diagram this paragraph as follows:

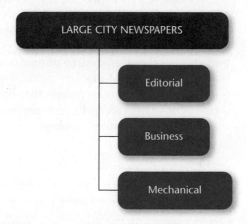

Paragraphs and passages that are organized using classification frequently use transition words and phrases to guide the reader, as shown in the following box.

## COMMON CLASSIFICATION TRANSITIONS

| | | |
|---|---|---|
| another | different stages of | last |
| another kind | finally | one |
| classified as | first | second |
| comprises | include | types of |
| different groups that | is composed of | varieties of |

## EXERCISE 6-8 . . . ANALYZING CLASSIFICATION PARAGRAPHS

*Read each of the following paragraphs. Then identify the topic and the parts into which each topic is divided.*

1.  We can separate the members of the plant kingdom into a mere four types. These are the *bryophytes*, which include mosses; the *seedless vascular plants*, which include ferns; the *gymnosperms*, which include coniferous ("cone-bearing") trees; and the *angiosperms*, a vast division of flowering plants—by far the most dominant on Earth today—that includes not only flowers such as orchids, but also oak trees, rice, and cactus.

—adapted from Krogh, *Biology*, p. 429

Topic: _____

Parts: _____

2.  The name of the cancer is derived from the type of tissue in which it develops. Carcinoma (carc = cancer; omo = tumor) refers to a malignant tumor consisting of epithelial cells. A tumor that develops from a gland is called an adenosarcoma (adeno = gland). Sarcoma is a general term for any cancer arising from connective tissue. Osteogenic sarcomas (osteo = bone; genic = origin), the most frequent type of childhood cancer, destroy normal bone tissue and eventually spread to other areas of the body. Myelomas (myelos = marrow) are malignant tumors, occurring in middle-aged and older people, that interfere with the blood-cell-producing function of bone marrow and cause anemia. Chondrosarcomas (chondro = cartilage) are cancerous growths of cartilage.

—Tortora, *Introduction to the Human Body*, p. 56

Topic: _____

Parts: _____

_____

3.  The amount of space that people prefer varies from one culture to another. North Americans use four different "distance zones." *Intimate distance* extends to about 18 inches from our bodies. We reserve this space for comforting, protecting, hugging, intimate touching, and love-making. *Personal distance* extends from 18 inches to 4 feet. We reserve it for friends and acquaintances and ordinary conversations. *Social distance*, extending out from us about 4 to 12 feet, marks impersonal or formal relationships. We use this zone for such things as job interviews. *Public distance*, extending beyond 12 feet, marks even more formal relationships. It is used to separate dignitaries and public speakers from the general public.

—adapted from Henslin, *Sociology*, pp. 109, 111

Topic: _____

Parts: _____

## Writing Classification Paragraphs

Developing a **classification paragraph** involves deciding on a basis of classification for the subject you are discussing, writing a topic sentence, and explaining each subgroup.

### Decide on What Basis to Classify Information

To write a paper using classification, you must first decide on a basis for breaking your subject into subgroups. Suppose you are given an assignment to write about some aspect of campus life. You decide to classify the campus services into groups. You could classify them by benefit, location, or type of facility, depending on what you wanted the focus of your writing to be.

The best way to plan your classification paragraph is to find a good general topic and then brainstorm different ways to break it into subgroups or categories.

## EXERCISE 6-9 . . . USING BRAINSTORMING

*For three of the following topics, brainstorm to discover different ways you might classify them. Compare your work with that of a classmate and select the two or three most effective classifications.*

| | | | |
|---|---|---|---|
| 1. Crimes | 4. Books | 7. Music | 10. TV shows |
| 2. Movies | 5. Cars | 8. Jobs | 11. Social media |
| 3. Web sites | 6. Dances | 9. Phones | 12. Politicians |

Most topics can be classified in a number of different ways. Stores can be classified by types of merchandise, prices, size, or customer service provided, for example. Use the following tips for choosing an appropriate basis of classification:

### Tips for Choosing an Appropriate Basis for Classification

- **Consider your audience.** Choose a basis of classification that will interest them. Classifying stores by size may not be as interesting as classifying them by merchandise, for example.
- **Choose a basis that is uncomplicated.** If you choose a basis that is complicated or lengthy, your topic may be difficult to write about. Categorizing stores by prices may be unwieldy, since there are thousands of products sold at various prices.
- **Choose a basis with which you are familiar.** While it is possible to classify stores by the types of customer service they provide, you may have to do some research or learn more about available services in order to write about them.

## EXERCISE 6-10 . . . USING BRAINSTORMING

*Choose one of the following topics. Brainstorm a list of possible ways to classify the topic.*

1. Professional athletes or their fans

2. Bad drivers

3. Diets

4. Cell phone users

5. Friends

### Write Your Topic Sentence

Once you have chosen a way to classify a topic and have identified the sub-groups you will use, you are ready to write a topic sentence. Your topic sentence should accomplish two things:

1. It should identify your topic.
2. It should indicate how you will classify items within your topic.

The topic sentence may also mention the number of subgroups you will use. Here are a few examples:

> Three relatively new types of family structures are single-parent families, blended families, and families without children.
>
> Since working as a waiter, I've discovered that there are three main types of customer complaints.

### EXERCISE 6-11 . . . WRITING A TOPIC SENTENCE

*For one of the topics in Exercise 6-10, write a topic sentence that identifies the topic and explains your method of classification.*

### Explain Each Subgroup

The details in your paragraph should explain and provide further information about each subgroup. Depending on your topic and/or your audience, it may be necessary to define each subgroup. If possible, provide an equal amount of detail for each subgroup. If you define or offer an example for one subgroup, you should do the same for each of the others.

### Organize Your Paragraph

The order in which you present your categories depends on your topic. Possible ways to organize the categories include from familiar to unfamiliar, from oldest to newest, or from simpler to more complex. Be sure to use transitions to signal your readers that you are moving from one category to another (see page 157 for a list of commonly used classification transitions).

### EXERCISE 6-12 . . . WRITING A CLASSIFICATION PARAGRAPH

*For the topic sentence you wrote in Exercise 6-11, write a classification paragraph. Be sure to identify and explain each group. Use transitions as needed.*

---

### 6e    READING AND WRITING CAUSE AND EFFECT

**LEARNING OBJECTIVE 5**
Read and write
cause and effect

The **cause and effect** pattern expresses a relationship between two or more actions, events, or occurrences that are connected in time. The relationship differs, however, from chronological order. In the cause and effect pattern, one event leads to another by *causing* it. Information organized with the cause and effect pattern may

- explain causes, sources, reasons, motives, and actions
- explain the effect, result, or consequence of a particular action
- explain both causes and effects

## Reading Cause and Effect Paragraphs

Cause and effect is clearly illustrated by the following paragraph, which gives the sources of fashions or the reasons why fashions occur.

### Issue: Fashions

> Why do fashions occur in the first place? One reason is that some cultures, like that of the United States, *value change:* What is new is good. And so, in many modern societies, clothing styles change yearly, while people in traditional societies may wear the same style for generations. A second reason is that many industries *promote* quick changes in fashion to increase sales. A third reason is that fashions usually *trickle down from the top.* A new style may occasionally originate from lower-status groups, as blue jeans did. But most fashions come from upper-class people, who like to adopt some style or artifact as a badge of their status. They cannot monopolize most status symbols for long, however. Their style is adopted by the middle class and may be copied or modified for use by lower-status groups, offering many people the prestige of possessing a high-status symbol.
>
> —Thio, *Sociology,* p. 409

You can visualize the cause and effect pattern as follows:

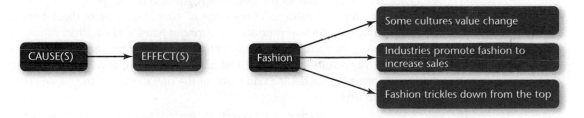

The cause and effect pattern is used extensively in many academic fields. All disciplines that ask the question "Why?" employ the cause and effect thought pattern. It is widely used in careers in the sciences, technologies, and social sciences.

Many statements expressing cause and effect relationships appear in direct order, with the cause stated first and the effect stated second: "When demand for a product increases, prices rise." However, reverse order is sometimes used, as in the following statement: "Prices rise when a product's demand increases."

The cause and effect pattern is not limited to an expression of a simple one-cause, one-effect relationship. There may be multiple causes, or multiple effects, or both multiple causes and multiple effects. For example, both slippery road conditions and your failure to buy snow tires (causes) may contribute to your car sliding into the ditch or into another car (effects).

In other instances, a chain of causes or effects may occur. For instance, failing to set your alarm clock may force you to miss your 8:00 A.M. class, which in turn may cause you not to submit your term paper on time, which may result in a penalty grade. This is sequence is known as a causal chain. The following box lists transitional words used in cause and effect writing.

## COMMON CAUSE AND EFFECT TRANSITIONS

| For Causes | For Causes | For Effects | For Effects |
|------------|------------|-------------|-------------|
| because | as a result | for this reason | therefore |
| because of | consequently | one cause is | thus |
| cause is | hence | one reason is | |
| due to | one result is | since | |
| for | results in | stems from | |

## EXERCISE 6–13 . . . USING CAUSE AND EFFECT

*Read each of the following selections and answer the questions that follow.*

### A. Issue: Health and Fitness

Physical activity is one of the best things you can do for yourself. It benefits every aspect of your health, at every stage of your life. Some of these benefits are purely physical, such as producing a stronger heart and healthier lungs. But physical activity can also put you in a better mood and help you manage stress. Physical activity results in a lower risk of premature death, and as you age it will help postpone physical decline and many of the diseases that can reduce quality of life in your later years.

—adapted from Lynch, Elmore, and Morgan, *Choosing Health,* p. 92

1. What are the purely physical effects of exercise?

   _____

   _____

2. What are the nonphysical effects of exercise?

   _____

3. Underline the transition words used in the paragraph.

## B. Issue: Health and Wellness

It's the end of the term and you have finished the last of several papers. After hours of nonstop typing, your hands are numb and you feel an intense, burning pain that makes the thought of typing one more word almost unbearable. If this happens, you may be suffering from one of several **repetitive motion disorders** (RMDs), sometimes called *overuse syndrome, cumulative trauma disorders,* or *repetitive stress injuries.* These refer to a family of painful soft tissue injuries that begin with inflammation and gradually become disabling.

Repetitive motion disorders include carpal tunnel syndrome, bursitis, tendonitis, and ganglion cysts, among others. Twisting of the arm or wrist, overexertion, and incorrect posture or position are usually contributors. The areas most likely to be affected are the hands, wrists, elbows, and shoulders, but the neck, back, hips, knees, feet, ankles, and legs can be affected, too. Usually, RMDs are associated with repeating the same task in an occupational setting and gradually irritating the area in question. However, certain sports (tennis, golf, and others), gripping the wheel while driving, keyboarding or texting, and a number of newer technology-driven activities can also result in RMDs.

—Donatelle, *Access to Health,* pp. 646–647

4. What is the cause of RMDs? _____

5. What do students often do that can cause RMDs? _____

6. Underline the transition words used in the passage.

## Writing Cause and Effect Paragraphs

Writing a cause and effect paragraph involves writing a clear topic sentence that indicates whether you are talking about causes, effects, or both; organizing supporting details; and using transitional words.

### Write Your Topic Sentence

To write effective topic sentences for cause and effect paragraphs, do the following:

1. **Clarify the cause and effect relationship.** Before you write, carefully identify the causes and the effects. If you are uncertain, divide a sheet of paper into two columns. Label one column "Causes" and the other "Effects." Brainstorm about your topic, placing your ideas in the appropriate column.

2. **Decide whether to emphasize causes or effects.** In a single paragraph, it is best to focus on either causes or effects—not both. For example, suppose you are writing about students who drop out of college. You need to decide whether to discuss why they drop out (causes) or what happens to students

who drop out (effects). Your topic sentence should indicate whether you are going to emphasize causes or effects. (In essays, you may consider both causes and effects.)

3. **Determine whether the events are related or independent.** Analyze the causes or effects to discover whether they occurred as part of a chain reaction or whether they are not related to one another. Your topic sentence should suggest the type of relationship about which you are writing. If you are writing about a chain of events, your topic sentence should reflect this—for example, "A series of events led up to my sister's decision to drop out of college." If the causes or effects are not related to one another, then your sentence should indicate that—for example, "Students drop out of college for a number of different reasons."

Now read the following paragraph that a sales representative wrote to her regional manager to explain why she had failed to meet a monthly quota. Then study the diagram that accompanies it. Notice that the topic sentence makes it clear that she is focusing on the causes (circumstances) that led to her failure to make her sales quota for the month.

> In the past, I have always met or exceeded my monthly sales quota at Thompson's Office Furniture. This January I was $20,000 short, due to a set of unusual and uncontrollable circumstances in my territory. The month began with a severe snowstorm that closed most businesses in the area for most of the first week. Travel continued to be a problem the remainder of the week, and many purchasing agents did not report to work. Once they were back at their desks, they were not eager to meet with sales reps; instead, they wanted to catch up on their backlog of paperwork. Later that month, an ice storm resulted in power losses, again closing most plants for almost two days. Finally, some of our clients took extended weekends over the Martin Luther King holiday. Overall, my client contact days were reduced by more than 26%, yet my sales were only 16% below the quota.

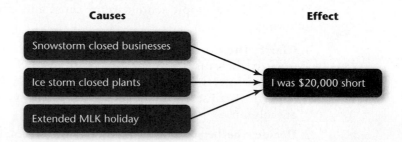

## EXERCISE 6-14 . . . WRITING TOPIC SENTENCES

*Select one of the topics below, and write a topic sentence for a paragraph that will explain either its causes or effects.*

1. Spending too much time on a computer

2. Texting while driving

3. The popularity of vampire films

4. Rising cost of attending college

5. Eating locally grown food

### Provide Supporting Details

Providing supporting details for cause and effect paragraphs requires careful thought and planning. Details must be relevant, sufficient, and effectively organized.

***Provide Relevant and Sufficient Details***    Each cause or effect you describe must be relevant to the situation introduced in your topic sentence. Suppose you are writing a paragraph explaining why you are attending college. Each sentence must explain this topic. You should not include ideas about how college is different from what you expected. If you discover you have more ideas about how college is different from what you expected than you do about your reasons for attending college, you need to revise your topic sentence in order to refocus your paragraph.

Each cause or reason requires explanation, particularly if it is *not* obvious. For example, it is not sufficient to write, "One reason I decided to attend college was to advance my position in life." This sentence needs further explanation. For example, you could discuss the types of advancement (financial, job security, job satisfaction) you hope to attain. Jot down a list of the causes or reasons you plan to include. This process may help you think of additional causes and will give you a chance to consider how to explain or support each one. You might decide to eliminate one or to combine several. Here is one student's list of reasons for attending college.

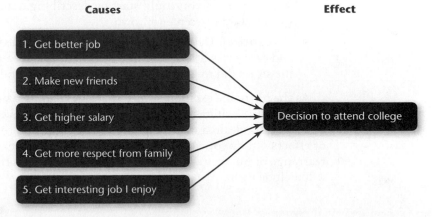

By listing his reasons, this student realized that the first one—to get a better job—was too general and was covered more specifically later in the list, so he eliminated it. He also realized that "get higher salary" and "get interesting job" could be combined. He then wrote the following paragraph:

There are three main reasons I decided to attend Ambrose Community College. First, and most important to me, I want to get a high-paying, interesting job that I will enjoy. Right now, the only jobs I can get pay minimum wage, and as a result, I'm working in a fast-food restaurant. This kind of job doesn't make me proud of myself, and I get bored with routine tasks. Second, my parents have always wanted me to have a better job than they do, and I know my father will not respect me until I do. A college degree would make them proud of me. A third reason for attending college is to make new friends. It is hard to meet people, and everyone in my neighborhood seems stuck in a rut. I want to meet other people who are interested in improving themselves like I am.

**Organize Your Details**    There are several ways to arrange the details in a cause and effect paragraph. The method you choose depends on your purpose, as well as your topic. Suppose you are writing a paragraph about the effects of a hurricane on a coastal town. Several different arrangements of details are possible:

- **Chronological.** Using chronological order, you would arrange your details in the order in which situations or events happened. It is particularly useful when it is important to note the order in which events occurred. For example, the order in which the hurricane damage occurred might become the order for your details.

- **Order of importance.** Using order of importance, you would arrange your details from least to most important or from most to least important. In describing the effects of the hurricane, you could discuss the most severe damage first and then describe lesser damage. Alternatively, you could build up from the least to the most important damage for dramatic effect.

- **Spatial.** Using spatial arrangement of your details, you would arrange your details by physical or geographical position. In describing the hurricane damage, you could start by describing damage to the beach and work toward the center of town.

- **Categorical.** Using categories, you would divide your topic into parts and categories to describe hurricane damage, recounting details of what the storm did to businesses, roads, city services, and homes.

As the hurricane example shows, there are many ways to organize cause and effect details. Each has a different emphasis and achieves a different purpose. Once you decide on a method of organization, return to your preliminary list of effects. Study your list again, make changes, eliminate, or combine. Then rearrange or number the items on your list to indicate the order in which you will include them.

### Use Transitions

To blend your details smoothly, use transition words and phrases. The student paragraph on page 166 is a good example of how transitional words and phrases are used. Notice how these transition words function as markers and help you to locate each separate reason. Some common transition words for the cause and effect pattern are listed on page 162.

---

### EXERCISE 6-15 . . . WRITING A CAUSE AND EFFECT PARAGRAPH

*Choose one of the following topic sentences and develop a paragraph using it. Organize your paragraph by using one of the methods described above.*

1. Exercise has several positive (or negative) effects on the body.

2. Professional athletes deserve (or do not deserve) the high salaries they are paid.

3. There are several reasons why parents should reserve time each day to spend with their children.

4. Many students work two or even three part-time jobs; the results are often disastrous.

---

## 6f     READING AND WRITING COMPARISON AND CONTRAST

**LEARNING OBJECTIVE 6**
Read and write comparison and contrast

The **comparison organizational pattern** emphasizes or discusses similarities between or among ideas, theories, concepts, or events. The **contrast pattern** emphasizes differences. When a speaker or writer is concerned with both similarities and differences, a combination pattern called **comparison and contrast** is used. You can visualize these three variations of the pattern as follows:

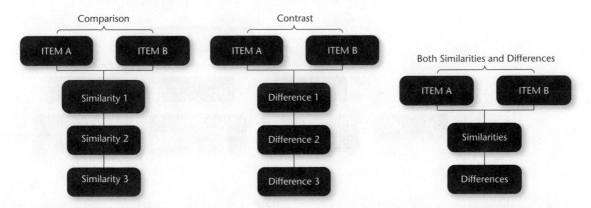

## Reading Comparison and Contrast Paragraphs

The comparison and contrast pattern is widely used in the social sciences, which study different groups, societies, cultures, and behaviors. Literature courses may require comparisons among poets, among several literary works, or among stylistic features. A business course may examine various management styles, compare organizational structures, or contrast retailing plans.

A contrast is shown in the following selection, which outlines the differences among felonies, misdemeanors, and violations.

### Issue: Criminal Law

The sources of local criminal laws are city or county charters, municipal or county ordinances or violations, common law, and decisions of municipal judges interpreting codes and common law. Nearly all local laws are misdemeanors, or violations. Serious criminal conduct is called a **felony,** and less-serious criminal conduct is called a **misdemeanor.** The difference between a felony and a misdemeanor is usually defined by the amount of time in prison or jail that the offender can receive as punishment for violation of a statute. Felonies commonly are crimes for which an offender can receive a punishment of 1 year or more in a state prison, whereas misdemeanors are crimes for which an offender can receive a punishment of 1 year or less in a state prison or county jail.

Violations, a relatively new classification of prohibited behaviors, commonly regulate traffic offenses. A violation is less than a misdemeanor and might carry the punishment of only a fine or suspension of privilege, such as losing one's driver's license temporarily. Many states have redefined misdemeanor traffic offenses as violations. The advantage of this is that violations free up the resources of the criminal courts for more-serious cases and allow for speedier processing of cases through the system.

—Fagin, *CJ2012*, p. 43

A map of this passage might look like this:

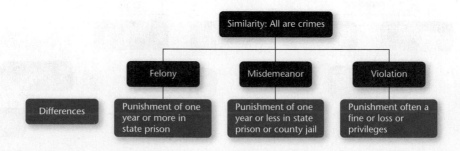

Depending on whether the speaker or writer is concerned with similarities, differences, or both similarities and differences, the pattern might be organized in different ways. Suppose a professor of American literature asks you to compare the work of two English poets, William Wordsworth and John Keats. Each of the following assignments is possible:

1. **Compare and then contrast the two.** That is, first discuss how Wordsworth's poetry and Keats's poetry are similar, and then discuss how they are different.
2. **Discuss by author.** Discuss the characteristics of Wordsworth's poetry, then discuss the characteristics of Keats's poetry, and then summarize their similarities and differences.
3. **Discuss by characteristic.** First discuss the two poets' use of metaphor, next discuss their use of rhyme, and then discuss their common themes.

### COMMON COMPARISON TRANSITIONS

*Similarities between* Frost and Whitman . . .

Frost is *as* powerful *as* . . .
*Like* Frost, Whitman . . .
*Both* Frost and Whitman . . .
Frost *resembles* Whitman in that . . .

Other transition words of comparison are *in a like manner, similarly, similar to, likewise, correspondingly,* and *in the same way.*

### COMMON CONTRAST TRANSITIONS

*Unlike* Whitman, Frost . . .
*Less* wordy *than* Whitman . . .
*Contrasted with* Whitman, Frost . . .
Frost *differs from* . . .

Other transition words of contrast are in *contrast, however, on the other hand, as opposed to,* and *whereas.*

### EXERCISE 6-16 . . . USING COMPARISON AND CONTRAST

*Read each of the following selections and answer the questions that follow.*

#### A. Issue: Business Structures

**Supermarkets** are the most frequently visited type of retail store. Today, however, they are facing slow sales growth because of slower population growth and an increase in competition from discounters (Walmart, Costco, Dollar General) on the one hand and specialty food stores (Whole Foods Market, Trader Joe's, Sprouts) on the other. Supermarkets also have been hit hard by the rapid growth of out-of-home eating over the past two decades. In fact, supermarkets' share of the groceries and food market plunged from 66 percent in 2002 to less than 62 percent in 2009. Meanwhile, during the same time period, supercenters boosted their market share from 16.6 percent to 20.6 percent.

**Superstores** are much larger than regular supermarkets and offer a large assortment of routinely purchased food products, nonfood items, and services. Walmart, Target, Meijer, and other discount retailers offer *supercenters*, very large combination food and discount stores. While a traditional grocery store brings in about $486,000 a week in sales, a supercenter brings in about $1.6 million a week. Walmart, which opened its first supercenter in 1988, has almost 3,000 supercenters in North America and is opening new ones at a rate of about 140 per year.

—Armstrong and Kotler, *Marketing,* pp. 327–328

1. What three types of stores are discussed?

_____

2. Does this passage mainly use comparison, contrast, or both?

_____

3. Explain how the three types of stores are similar and different.

_____

_____

_____

_____

4. What type of store is Trader Joe's?

_____

5. Underline the transition words in the paragraph, regardless of the type of organizational pattern they signal.

## B. Issue: Environmental Issues and Conservation

Local and regional variation in temperatures produces weather and climate. **Climate** refers to atmospheric conditions such as temperature, humidity, and rainfall that exist over large regions and relatively long periods of time. In contrast, **weather** refers to short-term variations in local atmospheric conditions. When we say that Los Angeles will experience a cool, foggy morning and hot afternoon, we're talking about weather. When we say that Southern California has mild, moist winters and hot, dry summers, we are describing the climate of this region.

—Christensen, *The Environment and You,* p. 86

6. What two things are being compared or contrasted?

_____

7. Which two factors are used to define the difference between weather and climate?

_____

8. Which transition phrase signals the paragraph's primary organizational pattern?

_____

9. Which term would be used to describe a snowstorm that occurred in Chicago in November 2013?

_____

10. Which term would be used to describe the high level of heat but relatively low level of humidity found in Arizona and New Mexico?

_____

## Writing Comparison and Contrast Paragraphs

Writing a comparison and contrast paragraph involves identifying similarities and differences between two items, writing a topic sentence that indicates the item you will be comparing and contrasting and your point, organizing your paragraph, developing your points, and using transition words.

### Identify Similarities and Differences

If you have two items to compare or contrast, the first step is to figure out how they are similar and how they are different. Be sure to select subjects that are neither too similar nor too different. If they are, you will have either too little or too much to say. Follow this effective two-step approach:

1. Brainstorm to produce a two-column list of characteristics.
2. Match up the items and identify points of comparison and contrast.

***Brainstorm to Identify Points of Comparison and Contrast***    Let's say you want to write about two friends—Maria and Vanessa. Here is how to identify their similarities and differences and develop points of comparison and contrast to write about:

1. **Brainstorm and list the characteristics of each person.**
2. **Match up items that share the same point of comparison or contrast**—age, personality type, marital status—as shown below.
3. **If you list an item in a certain category for one person but not for the other, think of a corresponding detail that will balance the lists.**

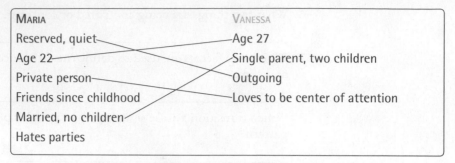

4. **Identify points of comparison and contrast** by reorganizing the lists so that the items you **matched up appear next to each other.** In a new column to the left of your lists, write the term that describes or categorizes each set of items in the lists. These general categories are your "points of comparison/contrast," the characteristics you will use to examine your two subjects. As you reorganize, you may find it easier to group several items together. For example, you might group some details about Maria and Vanessa together under the category of personality.

| Points of Comparison/ Contrast | Maria | |
|---|---|---|
| Personality | Quiet, reserved, private person | Outgoing, loves to be center of attention |
| Marital status | Married, no children | Single parent, two children |
| Length of friendship | Friends since childhood | Met at work last year |
| Shared activities | Go shopping | Play softball together, go to parties |

This two-step process can work in reverse order as well. You can decide points of comparison/contrast first and then brainstorm characteristics for each point. For example, suppose you are comparing and contrasting two restaurants. Points of comparison/contrast might be location, price, speed of service, menu variety, and quality of food.

5. **Study your list and decide whether to write about similarities or differences, or both.** It is usually easier to concentrate on one or the other. If you see similarities as more significant, you might need to omit or de-emphasize differences—and vice versa if you decide to write about differences.

## EXERCISE 6-17 . . . SELECTING A TOPIC AND LISTING POINTS OF COMPARISON/CONTRAST

*List at least three points of comparison/contrast for each of the following topics. Then choose one topic and make a three-column list on a separate sheet of paper.*

1. Two films you have seen recently

   Points of comparison/contrast: _____

2. Two jobs you have held

   Points of comparison/contrast: _____

3. Baseball and football players

   Points of comparison/contrast: _____

### Write Your Topic Sentence

Your topic sentence should do two things:

- It should identify the two subjects that you will compare or contrast.
- It should state whether you will focus on similarities, differences, or both.

Suppose you are comparing two world religions—Judaism and Hinduism. Obviously, you could not cover every aspect of these religions in a single paragraph. Instead, you could limit your comparison to their size, place of worship, or the type of divine being(s) worshipped, as in the following examples.

Judaism is one of the smallest of the world's religions; Hinduism is one of the largest.

Neither Judaism nor Hinduism limits worship to a single location, although both hold services in temples.

Unlike Hinduism, Judaism teaches belief in only one god.

Be sure to avoid topic sentences that announce what you plan to do such as "I'll compare network news and local news and show why I prefer local news."

### Organize Your Paragraph

Once you have identified similarities and differences and drafted a topic sentence, you are ready to organize your paragraph. There are two ways you can organize a comparison or contrast paragraph:

- Subject by subject
- Point by point

***Subject-by-Subject Organization***    In the **subject-by-subject** method, you write first about one of your subjects, covering it completely, and then about the other. Ideally, you cover the same points of comparison and contrast for both, and in the same order so your paragraph or essay is easy to follow. If you are discussing only similarities or only differences, organize your points within each topic, using a most-to-least or least-to-most arrangement. If you are discussing both similarities and differences, you might discuss points of similarity first and then points of difference, or vice versa. Here is a sample paragraph using the subject-by-subject method and a map showing its organization:

> Two excellent teachers, Professor Meyer and Professor Rodriguez, present a study in contrasting teaching styles. Professor Meyer is extremely organized. He conducts every class the same way. He reviews the assignment, lectures on the new chapter, and explains the next assignment. He gives essay exams and they are always based on important lecture topics. Because the topics are predictable, you know you are not wasting your time when you study. Professor Meyer's grading depends half on class participation and half on the essay exams. Professor Rodriguez, on the other hand, has an easygoing style. Each class is different and emphasizes whatever she thinks will help us better understand the material. Her classes are fun because you never know what to expect. Professor Rodriguez gives both multiple-choice and essay exams. These are difficult to study for because they are unpredictable. Our final grade is based entirely on the exams, so each exam requires a lot of studying beforehand. Although each professor teaches very differently, I am figuring out how to learn from each particular style.

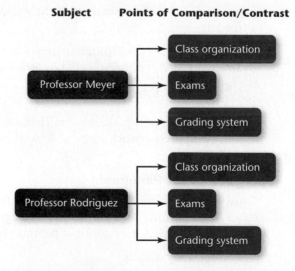

## Point-by-Point Organization

In the **point-by-point** method of organization, you discuss both of your subjects together for each point of comparison and contrast. When using this organization, maintain consistency by discussing the same subject first for each point. If your paragraph focuses only on similarities or only on differences, arrange your points in a least-to-most or most-to-least pattern. You could move from the simplest to the most complex similarity, or from the most obvious to least obvious difference, for example. Here is a sample paragraph using the point-by-point method and a map showing its organization:

> Professor Meyer and Professor Rodriguez demonstrate very different teaching styles in how they operate their classes, how they give exams, and how they grade us. Professor Meyer's classes are highly organized; we work through the lesson every day in the same order. Professor Rodriguez uses an opposite approach. She creates a lesson to fit the material, which enables us to learn the most. Their exams differ too. Professor Meyer gives standard, predictable essay exams that are based on his lectures. Professor Rodriguez gives both multiple-choice and essay exams, so we never know what to expect. In addition, each professor grades differently. Professor Meyer counts class participation as half of our grade, so if you talk in class and do reasonably well on the exams, you will probably pass the course. Professor Rodriguez, on the other hand, counts the exams 100 percent, so you *have* to do well on them to pass the course. Each professor has a unique, enjoyable teaching style, and I am learning a great deal from each.

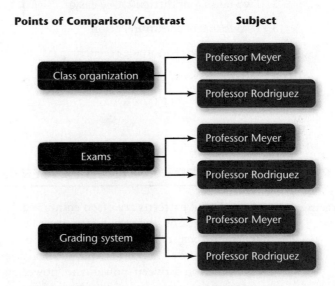

## Develop Your Points of Comparison and Contrast

As you discuss each point, don't feel as if you must compare or contrast in every sentence. Your paragraph should not just list similarities and/or differences. For every point, provide explanation, descriptive details, and examples. Try to maintain a balance in your treatment of each subject and each point of comparison and contrast. Give equal attention to each point and each subject. If you give an example for one subject, try to do so for the other as well.

### Use Transitions

Transition words are particularly important in comparison and contrast writing. Because you are discussing two subjects and covering similar points for each, your readers can easily become confused, so use the list of transition words and phrases on page 169.

Note that each method of organization uses different transitions in different places. If you choose a subject-by-subject organization, you'll need the strongest transition in the middle of the paragraph, when you switch from one subject to another. You will also need a transition each time you move from one point to another while still on the same subject.

If you choose point-by-point organization, use transitions as you move from one subject to the other. On each point, your reader needs to know quickly whether the two subjects are similar or different.

---

### EXERCISE 6-18 . . . WRITING A COMPARISON AND CONTRAST PARAGRAPH

*Choose one of the following topics. Using the guidelines presented in the section, write a comparison/contrast paragraph.*

1. Two courses you are taking

2. Two tasks (one difficult, one easy)

3. Two forms of communication

4. Two decisions you made recently

5. Two businesses

6. Two types of entertainment

---

### 6g   READING AND WRITING MIXED PATTERNS

**LEARNING OBJECTIVE 7**
Read and write
mixed patterns

Organizational patterns are often combined. In describing a process, a writer may also give reasons why each step must be followed in the prescribed order. An instructor may define a concept by comparing it with something similar or familiar. Suppose a chapter in your political science textbook opens by stating, "The distinction between 'power' and 'power potential' is an important one in considering the balance of power." You might expect a definition pattern (where the two terms are defined), but you also might anticipate that the chapter would discuss the difference between the two terms (contrast pattern). The longer the reading selection, the more likely it combines multiple patterns of organization.

### Reading Mixed Pattern Paragraphs

In the following paragraph, notice how the author combines two patterns: definition and contrast.

| | |
|---|---|
| Definition #1→ | A city's central business district, or CBD, grows around the city's most accessible point, and it typically contains a dense concentration of offices and stores. CBDs grow with the needs of the community; they expand and contract organically as the |
| Contrast→ | city grows and changes. In contrast, a master-planned community is a residential suburban development. In master-planned developments, houses are designed to |
| Definition #2→ | look alike and "match," and the community also offers private recreational facilities (such as tennis courts and swimming pools) for its residents. Often, the community is gated to prevent nonresidents from entering. Weston is a master-planned community that covers 10,000 acres in Florida. In Weston, almost all aspects of the community are controlled and regulated. Shrubs are planted to shield residents from having to look at the interstate highway. Road signs have a uniform style, each in a stylish frame. Weston offers different areas to cater to different incomes and lifestyles. The houses in the Tequesta Point section come with Roman bathtubs, while an even wealthier section provides larger plots of land for people who own horses. |

Look back over the examples provided in this chapter and notice that many of them combine more than one organizational pattern. The discussion of organ donation on page 145 for example, combines process and case and effect. The discussion of criminal law on page 168 combines comparison and contrast with definition.

## EXERCISE 6-19 . . . USING MIXED PATTERNS

*For each of the following topic sentences, anticipate what organizational pattern(s) the paragraph is likely to exhibit. Record your prediction in the space provided.*

1. Many people wonder how to tell the difference between the flu and the common cold.

   Pattern: _____

2. Narcissistic personality disorder—in which the sufferer is excessively occupied with himself or herself—usually results from a number of factors working together.

   Pattern: _____

3. GDP, or gross domestic product, is the total value of goods and services produced in a country during a given year.

   Pattern: _____

4. To migrate to the United States legally, an immigrant must follow a strict set of rules.

   Pattern: _____

5. A poor diet and lack of exercise are the leading causes of obesity in the world today.

   Pattern: _____

6. Many of the contestants on *American Idol* share a number of characteristics. They are all fairly young, they are all amateurs, they all cultivate a certain image, and they all believe they are talented.

Pattern: _____

## Writing Mixed Pattern Paragraphs

Individual patterns of organization provide a clear method for organizing and presenting your thoughts. Each of these patterns allows you to focus on one important aspect of the topic. As you think about combining patterns, your paragraph should always have one primary pattern. The main pattern provides the framework for the paragraph. Additional patterns can be used to add further details and information but should not distract your reader from the main pattern.

**Choose a Primary Pattern of Organization for Your Paragraph**    There are will five main factors to consider when choosing a primary pattern of organization:

- The assignment
- Your purpose
- Your audience
- The complexity of your topic
- The course for which you are writing

**The Assignment**    In some cases, your instructor will ask you to choose a topic and write about it. However, instructors often provide specific writing assignments or writing prompts. Analyzing the assignment will help you determine the primary pattern of organization. Look in the assignment for key words and phrases that offer clues. Suppose, for example, you receive the following assignment in your hotel and restaurant management class:

Choose one of the following beverages and write an essay describing how it is made: espresso, beer, or soda.

The assignment makes it clear that process is required. The key phrase "how it is made" is your clue. The key word *describing* also appears in the assignment, so be sure to include some description. Suppose you choose to write about soda. Your key goal, then, is to organize your essay to focus on the *process* of soda making. Your essay might also include examples of specific types of soda (cola, ginger ale, club soda) or a narrative about John Pemberton, who created Coca-Cola.

**Your Purpose**    When an instructor gives you a specific writing assignment, your purpose for writing is quite clear: to answer the question that has been raised. You simply need to follow the directions, write a good essay, and collect a good grade! However, when you must choose your own topic, you need to determine your purpose for writing. You can clarify your purpose by asking yourself the following questions:

- What am I trying to accomplish?
- What do I want my readers to understand?

**Your Audience**    All good writing takes the audience into account. To help determine the primary pattern of organization for your essay, ask yourself the following questions:

- How much do my readers know about the topic?
- What can I assume about my readers' backgrounds and experiences?
- Who is most likely to read what I've written?

**The Complexity of Your Topic**    Some topics are simply more complex or more multifaceted than others. Consider the following topics:

- The range of human emotions
- The three branches of the U.S. government: executive, legislative, judicial
- Your bedroom

Which of these topics is the simplest? Which is the most complicated? Most likely you would agree that your bedroom is the simplest topic, and the range of human emotions is the most complicated. For an essay about your bedroom, you could write effectively using one of the less complicated patterns, such as *description* or *example*, because your bedroom is most likely a fairly small room with limited contents: a bed, a television, a bookshelf, a closet. However, for an essay on the much more complicated topic of human emotions, you will want to choose a pattern that allows for greater depth of analysis, such as *comparison and contrast* (How do conscious feelings differ from subconscious feelings?), *classification* (What are the different kinds of emotions?), or *cause and effect* (What causes depression? What are the effects of depression?).

---

### EXERCISE 6-20 . . . CHOOSING MULTIPLE PATTERNS OF ORGANIZATION

*Choose a primary pattern of organization for each of the following writing assignments. Indicate what other patterns you might use and why.*

1. Mystery novels are a popular genre and people read them for a variety of reasons. Define mystery novels and give reasons for their popularity.

_____

_____

2. Those who don't travel on airplanes are often unprepared for the demands of air travel. What steps can an inexperienced traveler take to ensure a comfortable airline flight?

_____

_____

3. Two of the most famous American poets are Emily Dickinson and T.S. Eliot. How did each poet approach the writing of poetry? In what ways are the poems of Dickinson and Eliot similar? In what ways are they different?

_____

_____

_____

### EXERCISE 6-21 . . . WRITING A MIXED PATTERN PARAGRAPH

*Analyze the following writing assignment and answer the questions that follow.*

Your psychology instructor asked the class to read a chapter titled " Health and Stress" and gave the following writing assignment:  Choose several stress producing incidents from your life, briefly describe each, and explain what coping strategies you used.  From what you learned in the chapter, define and describe other coping mechanisms that might have been more effective for each incident.

1. Describe your intended audience.

2. What is your purpose for writing?

3. Brainstorm a list of ideas your readers might find helpful or illuminating.

4. Determine a primary pattern of organization for the assignment. Which secondary patterns will you use?

5. Write the paragraph, and then share it with a classmate. Revise and finalize.

## SUMMARY OF LEARNING OBJECTIVES

**MySkillsLab**
Complete the mastery test for this chapter **in MySkillsLab.**

**1 Read and write illustration.**

*How do you read and write illustration?*

**Illustration** uses examples—specific instances or situations—to explain a general idea or statement. **As you read**, look for transitions—*for example, for instance,* or *such as*—that signal examples are to follow. **As you write**, use vivid, accurate, examples that are typical and familiar for readers, drawing connections between them and your main point, and organizing them logically.

**2 Read and write process.**

*How do you read and write process?*

**Process** focuses on the procedures, steps, or stages by which actions are accomplished and is used to explain how things work and how to perform specific actions. **As you read**, look for numbered or bulleted lists and transitions that indicate a process is being described. **As you write**, identify the process you are describing and why it is important, provide necessary definitions, identify required equipment, provide only the essential steps in a logical order, and note possible problems.

**3 Read and write definition.**

*How do you read and write definition?*

In the **definition pattern**, a key word, phrase, or concept is defined and explained. **As you read**, ask what is being defined and what makes it different from other items or ideas. **As you write**, place the term in a general group, break it into categories, explain it with examples, trace its meaning over time, explain what it is not, and compare it with a familiar term.

**4 Read and write classification.**

*How do you read and write classification?*

The **classification pattern** explains a topic by dividing it into parts or categories. **As you read**, be sure you understand *how* and *why* the topic was divided as it was. **As you write**, decide on a basis for breaking your topic into subgroups, or categories, that is uncomplicated and with which you are familiar, and consider your audience.

**5 Read and write cause and effect.**

*How do you read and write cause and effect?*

The **cause and effect pattern** expresses a relationship between two or more actions, events, or occurrences that are connected in time. One event leads to another by causing it. There may be multiple causes and/or effects. **As you read**, look for explanations of why events occurred and their effects and cause and effect transition words. **As you write**, identify the relationship you are discussing, decide on your emphasis (causes or effects), and determine whether causes and/or effects are related or independent. Provide explanations of your reasons.

**6 Read and write comparison and contrast.**

*How do you read and write comparison and contrast?*

The **comparison pattern** emphasizes or discusses similarities among ideas, theories, concepts, or events. The **contrast pattern** emphasizes differences. Both patterns can be used together, creating the comparison and contrast pattern. **As you read**, identify whether the writer is comparing or contrasting items or doing both, and look for transitions that indicate which pattern is being used. **As you write**, identify the subjects you will compare and/or contrast; decide on what bases you will compare or contrast them; and determine your purpose for writing about them.

**7 Read and write mixed patterns.**

*How do you read and write mixed patterns?*

**Organizational patterns are often combined** in paragraphs, essays, and longer readings. **As you read**, look for indications (transitions, formatting, type of topic) to identify the overall pattern of a piece of writing and the additional pattern used to support it. **As you write**, use a primary pattern as a framework for your paragraph, using additional patterns to provide further details and information.

# 7 Reading College Level Sources

## LEARNING OBJECTIVES

**1** Read textbooks

**2** Read essays

**3** Read longer works

**4** Read visuals

**5** Think critically about source materials

## 7a    READING TEXTBOOKS

**LEARNING OBJECTIVE 1**
Read textbooks

In most college courses, textbooks are the primary source of reading material. In general, students are expected to read assignments before class. Each textbook reading will present key terms and information that you will explore in more depth in classroom lectures and discussions. Students who do not read assignments before class put themselves at a disadvantage. They are always playing catch-up.

Textbooks are almost always written by college teachers. Because of their experience in the classroom, they know what you are likely to need help understanding. They know when you need, for example, a diagram to help you visualize a concept. Consequently, they build valuable learning aids into each chapter.

### Guidelines for Getting the Most Out of Textbooks

Use the following guidelines to get the most from your textbooks.

1. **Use the textbook's pedagogical aids to help you learn.** Textbooks provide many features designed to help you learn and remember the content. Some common textbook features include the following:

   - **Learning objectives.** These appear at the beginning of the chapter and outline specific learning goals, clearly stating what you should know (or what you should be able to do) when you have finished reading the chapter. After you've completed the assignment, review the learning objectives.

If you cannot accomplish all of the goals, reread the relevant parts of the chapter until you can.

- **Headings.** Each chapter in a textbook provides headings that serve as an outline of the chapter. Before you begin reading, preview all the headings, formulating guide questions as you go along. (You may have noticed that this handbook is divided into numbered sections, or headings, to help you find what you need quickly.)

- **Opening stories or examples.** Many textbook chapters begin with a story that introduces the subject matter in a way designed to capture students' attention and interest. For example, a chapter on abnormal psychology may provide a case study about a person suffering from multiple-personality disorder.

- **Marginal vocabulary and definitions.** Each academic discipline has its own special vocabulary. (For instance, in common English, *affect* is a verb that means "to have an effect on." But in psychology, *affect* is pronounced differently and is a synonym for the display of emotions.) To learn the chapter material, you must learn and memorize many new words and definitions. Key terms often appear in **boldface** or *italics* and may be repeated in the margin with definitions.

- **Visual aids.** Visual aids are designed to work with the text, so examine the visual aids—tables, diagrams, infographics, photos, or any other type— when the text tells you to. Moving back and forth between the text and the visual aids helps you learn the material. Don't rush through the visual aids; many of them summarize important information or processes. For more on reading and interpreting visual aids, see Section 7e.

- **Boxes.** Some textbooks include boxes set off from the main text. Boxes often feature discussions of interesting or relevant topics related to chapter content, and they usually highlight key or controversial issues in the discipline.

- **End-of-chapter material.** Most textbook chapters end with a summary of key points (sometimes tied to the chapter's learning objectives), a vocabulary list, and exercises or problems. If your instructor assigns exercises from the end of the chapter, read them *before* you start the chapter. Doing so will tell you what to look for as you read.

- **Answers or solutions.** Some, but not all, textbooks include an answer section at the end of the book. Use the answer section judiciously to check your work *after* you have completed it. Do not use the answer key as a shortcut; doing so will not help you prepare for exams!

- **Glossary and index.** A *glossary* lists all the key vocabulary in the book (along with definitions) in alphabetical order. An *index* is an alphabetical listing of all the topics, terms, people, and places in the textbook. A page reference is included with each item, allowing you to find the discussion quickly and easily.

2. **Pay close attention to the examples.** Many students find that they learn concepts and ideas best by way of examples. If your textbook does not provide an example of an important concept, ask your instructor for one.

3. **Be patient, and reward yourself when you have reached key milestones in the assignment.** It is unlikely that you will find every discipline and every reading assignment equally interesting. Try to keep an open mind, if only because you know you will be tested on the material later. Take occasional breaks from reading (a 10-minute break after an hour of reading is a good guideline), and reward yourself with a snack, short walk, or something else that motivates you to complete the assignment with a high level of comprehension.

4. **Look for relevance to your own life.** When you actively think about how a textbook discussion relates to your own life, it is much easier to learn new concepts. For instance, a business textbook might discuss the fact that some expensive brand names have generic equivalents that are a fraction of the price. How might these concepts help you the next time you need to buy aspirin or orange juice?

5. **Use additional print-based or online resources.** Many textbooks offer a printed study guide or workbook to help you work through the textbook, which can be an excellent investment, especially in more challenging courses. In many disciplines, there are online labs that provide additional practice opportunities; check your textbook to find out what is available.

6. **Read with a highlighter or pen in hand.** Highlighting (see Section 8b) can be a particularly helpful way of marking key points in the textbook. Annotating (see Section 8c) is also a useful study aid. Many studies have proven that students learn better when they write, annotate, and take notes as they read.

---

### EXERCISE 7–1 . . . READING COLLEGE TEXTBOOKS

*Using a textbook from one of your other courses, make a list of the learning aids it contains. Then briefly indicate how you can use each to study.*

---

## 7b    READING ESSAYS

**LEARNING OBJECTIVE 2**
Read essays

Unlike many textbook readings, an *essay* presents information on a specific topic from the writer's point of view. While textbooks are often neutral presentations of facts, essays are often quite personal and reflect writers' perspectives. An essay can be as short as a few paragraphs or as long as 20 pages (sometimes longer, depending on the topic). Here are some specific suggestions for reading essays using "All Guts, No Glory" by Molly Ginty that appears in Chapter 12. (see page 353) as an example:

## Guidelines for Reading Essays

1. **Closely examine the title and subtitle.** The title of an essay often announces its topic and may reveal the author's point of view about it, although sometimes the meaning of the title may not become clear until you finish reading it. For example, the title "All Guts, No Glory" might suggest the topic relates to war, but it is not until you start to read it that you realize it is about the unacknowledged role of women soldiers in combat situations and how this affects their careers.

2. **Read the headnote.** Many essays, especially those in college textbooks and anthologies (collections of writing), provide background information about the essay, the author, or the topic in a headnote preceding the essay. The contents of headnotes vary widely: some provide context for the essay; others talk about the writer and his or her qualifications, point to key aspects of the essay, or provide a list of questions for the reader to consider while reading. For example, the headnote to "All Guts, No Glory" provides information about the author and the magazine the article originally appeared in.

3. **Carefully read the introduction to the essay.** The essay's opening paragraph or paragraphs often provide background information to grab the reader's attention and/or announce the topic and the writer's point of view. Some introductory paragraphs carefully define words, ideas, and issues; be sure you understand these definitions before you read the entire essay. The opening paragraphs of "All Guts, No Glory" read as follows:

> Captain Dawn Halfaker saw a flash of light and heard an explosion—then suffered shrapnel wounds, a 12-day coma, and the amputation of her right arm.
>
> Sergeant Rebekah Havrilla collected the remains of a suicide bomber and his victims from a room where blood ran down the walls—then endured years of nightmares.
>
> Private First Class Lori Piestewa was ambushed by insurgents, who killed three of the passengers in her Humvee—then was taken captive and died of her head wounds.
>
> —Ginty, "All Guts, No Glory," *Ms. magazine*

Notice that the introductory paragraphs provide background information and are designed to grab a reader's attention.

4. **Find the thesis statement.** The **thesis** is the main point of an entire reading selection. In many essays, writers place their thesis in a single **thesis sentence** or **thesis statement** in the first or second paragraph. However, the thesis statement may sometimes appear in the middle of or at the end of the essay instead. Test your understanding of the thesis statement by rewriting it in your own words. (In "All Guts, No Glory," the thesis appears at the end of the fourth paragraph: "But the Department of Defense (DOD) policy belies the reality of the conflicts in Iraq and Afghanistan, and its willful avoidance of the truth denies military women safety training, health care, and career advancement."

Sometimes, a writer will imply or suggest a thesis statement rather than state it directly. When you cannot find a clear thesis statement, ask yourself: "What is the one main point the author is making?" Your answer is the implied thesis statement.

5. **Within the essay, identify main ideas (topic sentences), supporting details, and other evidence used by the author to support his or her thesis statement.** Keep track of the essay's main ideas, as well as its major supporting details (review Section 4c if necessary). Supporting details fall into many categories: *personal experiences and observations, examples, descriptions, statistics, facts, anecdotes (stories that illustrate a point), expert opinions,* and *quotations from recognized authorities.* Highlight main ideas as you read, then review your highlighting as soon as you've completed the reading assignment. (For specific highlighting guidelines, see Section 8b, p. 202).

6. **Closely read the essay's concluding paragraph.** An essay's final paragraph or paragraphs frequently revisit the author's thesis. They may also offer possible solutions, ideas for further thought or discussion, additional sources of information, or ways to get involved in the cause. This is the closing paragraph of "All Guts, No Glory":

> According to the iCasualties website, 136 servicewomen have died in Iraq and Afghanistan since 2001, and by the DOD's own admission, 60 percent of these deaths have stemmed from "hostile attacks." "The loss of life in battle can be the ultimate act of bravery," says retired Air Force pilot Brigadier General Wilma Vaught, president of the Women in Military Service for America Memorial Foundation in Arlington, Virginia. "There's nothing more frustrating than hearing it said that this sacrifice isn't happening, that somehow the loss of a servicewoman's life in battle isn't as noble or heroic or as meaningful."
>
> —Ginty, "All Guts, No Glory," *Ms. magazine*

7. **Respond to the essay by writing.** Writing about a reading helps you better engage with and understand the essay. See Chapter 8 for specific writing techniques, such as outlining, summarizing, and drawing a graphic organizer.

## EXERCISE 7-2 . . . READING AN ESSAY

*Read the following essay and answer the questions that follow.*

**Issue: Pet Ownership**

## Innocent Until Proven a Pet "Owner"

### Bruce Watson

1      There's a new puppy in our house and we're treating her like a queen. At dawn's early whimper, we let Lucca right outside. We feed her on demand. When she chews

a book or breaks a priceless vase, we say, "Atta girl, Lucca!" We're not just being kind, we're being cautious. We can't afford another lawsuit; animal law is a burgeoning field.

2    Courses in animal law are now taught at major law schools. Lawyers with clients named Ginger and Snuggums are stepping to the bar, and every dog is having his day in court. Cats, too, not to mention a dolphin named Rainbow who, with the help of an animal lawyer, sued her aquarium. Only last year, the U.S. Court of Appeals in Washington, D.C., granted a lonely chimp named Barney the right to share a cage. One animal law professor has even proposed that lawyers sue on behalf of gorillas, asserting that "they should be declared 'persons' under the Constitution."[1] We the people, and primates . . .

3    Some see animal law as animal rights run amok, but our other dog, Rosie, begs to differ. A white mutt easily muddied by a romp outside, Rosie may look meek and tame, but she's in the forefront—forepaw, perhaps—of animal law. Back when other pets were just howling about their rights, Rosie was getting even.

4    Two years ago, Rosie filed suit against my wife and me. Her suit charged: "1) that defendants fed plaintiff inedible chunks of stale fodder laughingly called 'dog food;' 2) that defendants regularly pet plaintiff on the head resulting in a crippling loss of self-esteem; and 3) that plaintiff's so-called 'owners' treated plaintiff as if she were not a sentient being but a lowly dog, i.e., mere property."

5    Go ahead and make all the usual lawyer jokes. We laughed, too, until we found out that Rosie was seeking $4 billion in punitive and $8 billion in actual damages. Her lawyer vowed to take the case all the way to the Supreme Court. To avoid having our pet ownership set a major animal law precedent, we tried to settle out of court.

6    First we offered Rosie steaks. Her lawyer wouldn't even talk to our lawyer about them. Then we tried doggie pillows and whole bags of bones, but those only made it worse. Soon she and our other pets—Mittens the cat, Beauty the hermit crab, and Gertrude Stein, our goldfish—became co-plaintiffs. Their suit charged us with attempted poisoning with tick powder, wrongful imprisonment, and overfeeding. When we tried to reason with their lawyer, he took the moral high ground. "Are we to be a nation of laws," he asked, "or a nation of men who think it's cute to make their pets do stupid tricks on Letterman?"

7    When the suit came to trial last month, Rosie was the first witness. She looked so noble as she barked to tell the truth, the whole truth, and nothing but. Then her lawyer began priming her with questions. And hunks of raw meat.

8    "Rosie, where were you on the night of October 27, 1991? The night your so-called 'owners' brought you home?"

9    "Arf!"

10    "In your dog house, I thought so. And did the plaintiffs feed you those inhumane doggie crumbles?"

[1]Glaberson, William, "Legal Pioneers Seek to Raise the Lowly Status of Animals," *New York Times*, Aug. 18, 1999, p. 1.

11    "Arf!"

12    "Objection!" our lawyer chimed in. "Counsel is obviously leading the witness! Look at that meat in his hand!"

13    "Objection overruled!"

14    It was then that I noticed the jury. Seated in the jury box were three collies, two Siamese cats, two goldfish, a hermit crab, and four gerbils. We didn't stand a chance. On our lawyer's advice, we plea bargained. We agreed not to treat our pets like lowly animals, and our menagerie agreed to seek no monetary damages. My wife and I were sentenced to 100 hours of community service in a pet shop and two years probation. If we humiliate Rosie or Mittens by petting them, if we don't feed Gertrude Stein the best goldfish flakes, if we don't get Beauty a new shell every year, we'll be behind bars before you can say "my dog has fleas."

15    On second thought, they're not fleas. They're sophisticated *siphonoptera*, hosted by our gracious canine, the honorable Rosie, esq. Try suing us over that, you little cur.

1. What does the title reveal about the essay?

_____

2. Highlight the sentence that expresses the thesis statement.

3. What background information does the introductory paragraph provide?

_____

_____

4. Reread the conclusion. What does it accomplish?

_____

5. What point does the author make about dogs through his use of humor.

_____

_____

_____

6. What do you think the author's attitude toward dogs really is, despite his humorous complaints about them?

_____

_____

## 7c    READING LONGER WORKS

**LEARNING OBJECTIVE 3**
**Read longer works**

Most college textbooks are designed to be read one chapter at a time; students rarely sit down and read a textbook straight through. Many essays and articles are also fairly short, allowing you to finish them in one or two sittings. However, in your college studies and beyond, you will often be asked to read longer works.

For example, you might take an ethics course in which you study various viewpoints about contemporary issues. Your textbook includes chapters on various topics such as decriminalization of drug possession, amnesty for illegal/undocumented immigrants, business ethics, and animal rights. For the class on animal rights, your instructor may require you to read not only the textbook but also opinion essays, articles from scholarly journals, and even sections from complete books on the topic in order to obtain a more in-depth understanding of the topic.

## Guidelines for Reading Longer Works

The following are some suggestions for reading longer works:

1. **Preview the selection using the guidelines in Section 1b (p. 4)**. This will give you an overview of the book as well as a framework on which to build your knowledge. Identify portions that pertain to the particular topic or issue that you are concerned with.

2. **Read relevant portions, starting at the beginning of the book and reading through to the end.** College textbooks are often written in a *modular* fashion that keeps all related subject matter together in one chapter. In contrast, books on a single topic gradually build the reader's knowledge base, so you must read earlier chapters before you will be able to understand later chapters.

3. **Write summary notes at the end of each section or chapter.** Each time you complete a chapter, jot down its two or three main points. By the time you have finished reading the book, you will have a summary of the entire work to use for review, study, and discussion.

4. **Plan to read in concentrated periods.** Most readers benefit from reading books or longer works in a concentrated period—over the course of a week rather than a month. So, even though you may have a month to finish the assignment, it's better to plan to read a good chunk of it each night for a week. This is particularly helpful when you are reading novels. Reading in a concentrated period will help you remember key details about character, plot, and sequence of events. If you put down a novel and come back to it two weeks later, you may find that you remember very little of what you've read!

5. **Divide the reading task into manageable chunks.** Suppose you have two weeks to read six chapters from Paul Waldau's *Animal Rights: What Everyone Needs to Know*. You might plan to read three chapters a week. Schedule your time so that you can concentrate on a solid, identifiable chunk of the assignment with each reading. In the case of Waldau's book, each chapter is a manageable chunk.

### EXERCISE 7-3 . . . THINKING CRITICALLY ABOUT LONGER WORKS

*Complete the following matching exercise about animal-rights books. Use the books' titles and your inference skills to complete the exercise.*

_____ 1. *Animal Rights: Current Debates and New Directions*

a. Likely to emphasize the pain that humans cause animals

_____ 2. *Animal Rights: What Everyone Needs to Know*

b. Likely to be a good introductory book for people who do not know much about the issues involved in animal rights

_____ 3. *Dominion: The Power of Man, the Suffering of Animals, and the Call to Mercy*

c. Likely to present multiple viewpoints and perspectives on the animal-rights controversy

_____ 4. *Animal Liberation: The Definitive Classic of the Animal Movement*

d. Likely a book that has been widely read and serves as a "manifesto" of the animal-rights movement

## 7d    READING AND INTERPRETING VISUALS

**LEARNING OBJECTIVE 4**
**Read visuals**

Many textbooks and other reading materials include graphics and photographs. All **visual aids** share one goal: to illustrate concepts and help you understand them better. As a reader, your key goal is to extract important information from them. Visual aids work best when you read them *in addition to* the text, not *instead of* the text. As a writer, you need to be able to use, interpret, and condense information from visual aids as you make text-to-text and text-to-world connections.

Keep in mind that the author chose the visual aid for a specific purpose. To fully understand it, be sure you can explain its purpose.

### A General Approach to Reading Graphics

You will encounter many types of **graphics** in your reading materials. These include

- maps
- charts
- graphs
- diagrams

### Guidelines for Reading Graphics

Here is a step-by-step approach to reading any type of graphic effectively. As you read, apply each step to Figure 7-1.

1. **Make connections between written text and graphics.** Look for the reference in the text. The author will usually refer you to each specific graphic. When you see the reference, finish reading the sentence, then look at the graphic. In some cases, you will need to go back and forth between the text

and the graphic, making text-to-text connections, especially if the graphic has multiple parts. Here is the original reference to Figure 7-1:

> I'm going to reveal how you can make an extra $1,357 per month between the ages of 25 and 75. Is this hard to do? Actually, it is simple for some, and impossible for others. As Figure 7-1 shows, all you have to do is be born a male.

2. **Read the title and caption.** The title will identify the subject, and the **caption** will provide important information. In some cases, the caption will specify the graphic's key takeaway point. The title of Figure 7-1 makes the graph's subject clear: the differences between men's salaries and women's salaries. The caption summarizes one of the graphic's important points.

3. **Examine how the graphic is organized and labeled.** Read all headings, labels, and notes. Labels tell you what topics or categories are being discussed. Sometimes a label is turned sideways, like the words "Earnings per year" in Figure 7-1. Note that the title has a note (found at the bottom of the graphic) that provides information on how to read the graphic. The category "College Graduates" (at the bottom right of the figure) also has a note providing more specific information.

## FIGURE 7-1  THE GENDER PAY GAP, BY EDUCATION[1]

The gender pay gap—that is, the difference in average salary between men and women doing the same job—shows up at all levels of education.

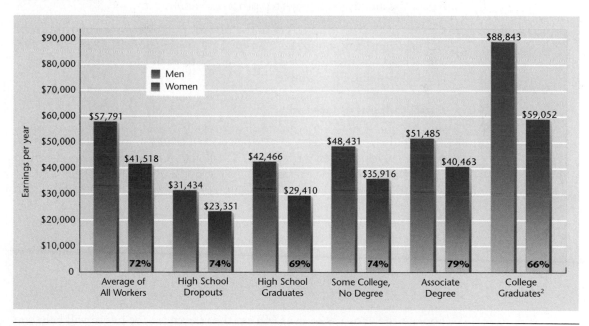

[1]Full-time workers in all fields. The percentages at the bottom of each red bar indicate the women's average percentage of men's incomes.

[2]Bachelor's and all higher degrees, including professional degrees.

—Henslin, *Sociology: A Down-to-Earth Approach*, p. 317. By the author. Based on the *Statistical Abstract of the United States* 2009: Table 681.

4. **Look at the legend.** The **legend** is the guide to the graphic's colors, terms, and other important information. In Figure 7-1, the legend appears toward the upper left and shows blue for men and red for women.

5. **Analyze the graphic.** Based on what you see, determine the graphic's key purpose. For example, is its purpose to show change over time, describe a process, present statistics? The purpose of Figure 7-1 is clear: It compares men's and women's salaries for a number of categories based on education level.

6. **Study the data to identify trends or patterns.** If the graphic includes numbers, look for unusual statistics or unexplained variations. What conclusions can you draw from the data?

7. **Write a brief annotation (note to yourself).** In the margin, jot a brief note summarizing the graphic's trend, pattern, or key point. Writing will help cement the idea in your mind. A summary note of Figure 7-1 might read, "Both male and female college graduates earn higher salaries than anyone else, but regardless of education level, men always earn more than women."

## Reading and Analyzing Photographs

An old saying goes, "A picture is worth a thousand words." Photographs can help writers achieve many different goals. For example, writers can use photos to spark interest, provide perspective, or offer examples. Let's look at the photo in Figure 7-2 and use a step-by-step process to analyze it.

1. **First read the text that refers to the photo.** Photos are not a substitute for the reading. They should be examined *along with* the text. For this reason, many readings include specific references to each photo, usually directly after a key point. For example,

### Issue: Cultural Relativism

To counter our own tendency to use our own culture as the standard by which we judge other cultures, we can practice cultural relativism; that is, we can try to understand a culture on its own terms. With our own culture so deeply embedded within us, however, practicing cultural relativism can challenge our orientations to life. For example, most U.S. citizens appear to have strong feelings against raising bulls for the purpose of stabbing them to death in front of crowds that shout "Olé!" According to cultural relativism, however, bullfighting must be viewed from the perspective of the culture in which it takes place—*its* history, *its* folklore, *its* ideas of bravery, and *its* ideas of sex roles (Figure 7-2).

—Henslin, *Sociology*, p. 39

Look at the photo as soon as you see the reference. The photo will help you visualize the concept under discussion, making it easier to remember.

## FIGURE 7-2  THE BULLFIGHT: CULTURAL EXPERIENCE OR ANIMAL CRUELTY?

Many Americans perceive bullfighting as a cruel activity that should be illegal everywhere. To most Spaniards, bullfighting is a sport that pits matador and bull in a unifying image of power, courage, and glory. *Cultural relativism* requires that we suspend our own perspectives in order to grasp the perspectives of others, something easier said than done.

—Henslin, *Sociology*, p. 39

2. **Read the photo's title and/or caption.** The caption is usually placed above, below, or to the side of the photo and explains how the photo fits into the discussion.

3. **Ask: What is my first overall impression? Why has the author included this photo?** Because photos can be so powerful, they are often chosen to elicit a strong reaction. Analyze your response to the photo. For example, Figure 7-2 is quite violent; note the blood on the bull's shoulders. What purpose is the author trying to achieve by including this photo?

4. **Examine the details.** Look closely at the picture, examining both the foreground and the background. Details can provide clues regarding the date and location of the photograph. For example, people's hairstyles and clothing often give hints to the year or decade. Landmarks and buildings help point to location. In Figure 7-2, you can see that bullfighting takes place in front of an audience. What point is the author making about the audience's cultural experiences and beliefs regarding bullfighting?

5. **Look for connections to society or your life.** Ask yourself how the photo relates to what you are reading or to your own experiences. For example, what

are your own thoughts about bullfighting? Do you know anyone who feels differently? What are the sources of your disagreement?

## EXERCISE 7–4 . . . ANALYZING A PHOTOGRAPH

*Flip through one of your textbooks and choose a photo of interest to you. Analyze it according to the five-step process outlined above.*

---

## 7e    THINKING CRITICALLY ABOUT SOURCE MATERIALS

**LEARNING OBJECTIVE 5**
Think critically about source materials

A recent study noted that college students tend to focus on the first page of results generated by a Google search. Many mistakenly believe that the first page of "hits" on a Google search contains the "best" links, but the best, most valuable information may be found on, for example, the tenth page of results. Google allows paid advertisers to buy placement for their links on the first page of results, and various companies offer what they call "search engine optimization" that will make a business's Web site one of the first to appear on the Google results page.

The lesson here is simple: Just as you think critically about materials you are reading, you should think critically about the **sources** of these materials. Who wrote the material, and why? Is it trustworthy? For example, do you think you can expect *High Times*, a magazine devoted to legalizing marijuana usage, to present fair evidence regarding the effects of smoking marijuana? Can you trust the Web site of the National Rifle Association (NRA), which is strictly opposed to gun control, to offer full information about the impacts of guns on American society? Most likely you cannot. These sources are one-sided and biased. Although the NRA's Web site uses the .org extension to indicate that it is a nonprofit organization, the association is an advocacy group with a strong agenda. You cannot expect its Web site to be impartial regarding a controversial issue like gun control.

To evaluate source materials, consider their content, accuracy and reliability, authority, timeliness, and objectivity.

### Evaluating Content

When evaluating a source's content, examine its appropriateness, its level of technical detail, and its completeness.

- **Appropriateness.** To be worthwhile, the source should contain the information you need. It should answer one or more of the questions you need answered. If the source does not answer your questions in detail, check other sources for more information. Some Web sites will provide additional links to more detailed sites with more complete information.

Many books will provide a list of references at the end; these references may contain the information you're searching for.

- **Level of technical detail.** A usable source should contain the level of technical detail that suits your purpose. Some sources may provide information that is too sketchy or incomplete; others assume a level of background knowledge or technical sophistication that you may lack. For example, if you are writing a short, introductory-level paper on ecological threats to marine animals, information on the Scripps Institution of Oceanography Web site may be too technical and contain more information than you need. Unless you already have some background knowledge in that field, you may want to search for a different Web site.

- **Completeness.** Determine whether the source provides complete information on the topic. Does it address all aspects of the topic that you feel it should? For example, if a book about important nineteenth-century American poets does not mention Emily Dickinson, then it is incomplete. If you discover a source that is incomplete (and many are), search for sources that provide a more thorough treatment of the topic.

## Evaluating Accuracy and Reliability

When using a source to research or write an academic paper, be sure that it contains accurate and reliable information. The source itself will also provide clues about the accuracy of the information it contains, so ask the following questions:

1. **Is the source professionally edited and presented? Has it been published by a professional organization or reputable publisher?** Check the copyright page to see whether the source has been professionally edited and published, or whether it has been "self-published" by someone with few credentials. Errors such as misspellings, grammatical mistakes, a messy or cluttered layout, unclear graphics, and a lot of typographical errors usually signal an unreliable source.

2. **Is the information presented in the source verifiable?** Compare the information you find with the information in other sources (periodicals, books, Web sites) on the same topic. If you find a discrepancy, conduct further research to determine which sources are trustworthy and which are not.

3. **Does the source provide a list of works cited?** In all serious research, the sources of information and the techniques used to collect and analyze data are fully documented. If the source does not contain a References or Works Cited section, you should question its accuracy and reliability.

4. **Is the information complete or in summary form?** If it is a summary, use the Works Cited or References section to locate the original source. Original information is less likely to contain errors.

5. **Could the information be a spoof or parody?** Some publications and Web sites that appear serious are actually spoofs, hoaxes, or satires designed to poke

fun at topics and issues. An example is *The Onion* newspaper and its Web site. *The Onion* appears to offer legitimate information but actually provides political and social commentary through made-up stories.

## Evaluating Authority

Before using information from a source, use the following questions to evaluate the authority of the person or group presenting the information.

1. **Who is the publisher or sponsor?** Is the publisher or sponsor a university press, a respected publisher, a private individual, an institution, a corporation, a government agency, or a nonprofit organization? Identifying the publisher or sponsor is often the key to evaluating the source's authority and expertise. For example, a Web site sponsored by Nike is designed to promote its athletic products, while a site sponsored by a university library is designed to help students learn to use its resources. A book published by the Sierra Club (a well-respected environmental organization) will likely provide authoritative, but biased, information about environmental issues. Material published by the U.S. government either in print form (for example, *The Statistical Abstract of the United States*) or on the Web (any URL ending in .gov) is highly authoritative and reliable. In general, if the author, business, publisher, or sponsoring agency is not identified, the source lacks authority and reliability.

2. **Who wrote the material?** Is the author's name provided, and are his or her professional credentials listed? If the author's name is not given, the source lacks authority. If the author's name is given, is the author an expert in his or her field? If not, the information may not be trustworthy.

3. **Is the author's contact information provided?** Often, authors provide an e-mail address or other address at which they can be reached. If no contact information is provided, the source may not be reliable.

When working with Web sites, it is sometimes useful to trace a particular Web page back to its source by trying to locate its home page.

## Evaluating Timeliness

Many books that represented the most current thinking or research in an area when they were published can become dated or even obsolete as new information is uncovered. Such books may be useful for historical information, but in most areas—whether business disciplines, the sciences, or the latest in medical advances—you will generally want to consult recently published materials.

The same holds true for Web sites. Although the Web often provides up-to-the-minute information, not all Web sites are current. Evaluate a Web site's timeliness by checking

- the date on which the materials were posted to the Web site.
- the date when the site was last revised or updated.
- the date when the links were last checked.

## Evaluating Objectivity

Reliable sources fall into two categories:

1. Sources that treat the subject in a fair, unbiased manner (see Chapter 9, Section 9f, p. 237, for more about bias)
2. Sources that support a particular viewpoint

A source with a specific viewpoint is not necessarily unreliable. In fact, many people who write about contemporary issues strongly argue in favor of or against a particular policy, practice, or government action. Such sources often cite supporting studies or examples, and they are often written by educated authorities and experts whose experiences can be trusted. You can use these sources as a way of opening up your mind to alternative viewpoints, but in the end you must evaluate the competing viewpoints and decide your own opinions.

Still, you must carefully evaluate each source's objectivity. An **objective** source is not influenced by personal prejudices or emotions; instead, it seeks to present all the facts in an even, unbiased way.

### Guidelines for Assessing Source Objectivity

To assess a source's objectivity, ask yourself the following questions:

1. **What is the author's goal?** Is it to present information objectively or to persuade you to accept a particular point of view or to take a specific action? If it is not to present balanced information, you can justifiably question the author's objectivity.

2. **Are opinions clearly identified?** An author is free to express opinions, but these should be clearly identified as such. Look for words and phrases that identify ideas as opinions. (See Chapter 9, Section 9b, p. 228, for a list of these words and phrases.) If a source presents opinions as facts or does not distinguish between facts and opinions, the source is most likely unreliable.

3. **Is the source a mask for advertising?** Be cautious of sources that present information to persuade you to purchase a product or service. If a magazine, newspaper, letter, or Web site resembles an infomercial you might see on television, be just as suspicious of it as you would be of an infomercial.

---

### EXERCISE 7-5 . . . EVALUATING ONLINE MATERIALS

*Conduct a Google search on a contemporary issue that you find interesting. Choose two Web sites to examine. Evaluate the content, accuracy, reliability, authority, timeliness, and objectivity of each.*

## SUMMARY OF LEARNING OBJECTIVES

MySkillsLab
Complete the mastery test for this chapter in MySkillsLab.

**1    Read textbooks.**
*How do you read text-books effectively?*

To **read a textbook selection**, use the textbook's pedagogical aids (learning objectives, headings, marginal terms, etc.) to help you learn. Pay close attention to the examples, and be patient as you make your way through the assignment. Look for relevance to your own life and use additional print-based or online resources if necessary to improve your comprehension. Read with a highlighter or pen in hand.

**2    Read essays.**
*How do you read essays effectively?*

An **essay** presents information on a specific topic from the writer's point of view. To **read an essay**, first examine the title and subtitle. Read the headnote (if one is provided) as well as the introduction to the essay. Find the thesis statement and identify main ideas, supporting details, and other evidence used to support the thesis statement. Closely read the essay's concluding paragraph, and respond to the essay by writing.

**3    Read longer works.**
*What strategies help in reading longer texts?*

To **read a longer work**, first preview it. Start at the beginning of the book and read through to the end. Write summary notes at the end of each chapter. Plan to read in concentrated periods, and divide the reading task into manageable chunks.

**4    Read visuals.**
*How do you read visuals effectively?*

To **read visuals effectively**, make connections between the text and the accompanying graphic (or graphics), examine the title, caption and legend, study its organization, determine its purpose, identify trends and patterns, and write annotations. When analyzing photographs, read the accompanying text, study the title and/or caption, consider your first impression, examine the details, and connect what you see to society or your own life.

**5    Think critically about source materials.**
*How do you think critically about source materials?*

To **think critically** about source materials, first evaluate their content. Then consider their accuracy and reliability, as well as the author's authority, the timeliness of the source, and the objectivity of the content.

# Organizing Information and Writing in Response to Reading

## LEARNING OBJECTIVES

**1** Analyze the reading and writing task

**2** Highlight effectively

**3** Use annotation to record your thinking

**4** Paraphrase ideas

**5** Outline text

**6** Draw maps and graphic organizers to show relationships among ideas

**7** Summarize text

**8** Write a response paper

Have you ever wondered how you will learn all the facts and ideas from your instructors, textbooks, and other source materials? How will you keep track of the multiple opinions on various aspects of contemporary issues? Reading and learning a large amount of information is a two-step process. First, you must reduce the amount to be learned by deciding what is most important, less important, and unimportant to learn. Then you must organize the information to make it more meaningful and easier to learn. This chapter describes how to analyze your reading and writing tasks and offers three strategies for reducing the information to be learned—*highlighting*, *annotating*, and *paraphrasing*. It also offers three means of organizing information—*outlining*, *mapping*, and *summarizing*—and concludes with tips for writing in response to what you've read.

## 8a PREPARING TO READ AND WRITE: ANALYZE THE TASK

**LEARNING OBJECTIVE 1**
Analyze the reading and writing task

In most college assignments, reading is only the first step in the learning process. You will likely participate in class discussions, take exams, and write papers in response to what you read. To get the most from your reading, you must analyze the assignment before you begin. Here are some tips for doing so.

## Tips for Getting the Most Out of Reading Assignments

1. **Determine what you must do after you have finished the reading.** If you must answer a series of questions at the end of a chapter, read those questions before you begin to find clues for what to look for as you read. If you must write a paper or a journal entry in response to the reading, use annotation (Section 8c, p. 205) and paraphrasing (Section 8d, p. 207) to help you keep track of ideas as you read.

2. **Read the assignment several times before you begin.** Express in your own words what the assignment requires. If you have a choice of assignments, it is worth taking a few minutes to think about your choices so that you choose the assignment that you will find most worthwhile.

3. **Plan a reading strategy.** Decide what level and type of information you need to learn (facts, reasons, dates and places, etc.), and then decide what you will do during reading (highlight, write guide questions) and after reading (review sections, answer guide questions).

4. **Look for key words in the assignment.** Many assignments have two specific parts: *limiting words* and *topic*. Consider the following example:

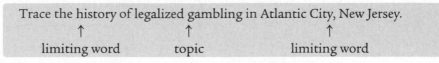

Trace the history of legalized gambling in Atlantic City, New Jersey.

    ↑                ↑                   ↑

limiting word       topic        limiting word

Here, the topic, *legalized gambling*, is clearly defined, and it is limited in two ways: (1) you are concerned only with its history—not its status today, or its effects; and (2) you are concerned only with the city of Atlantic City, New Jersey, not with any other gambling venues, such as Las Vegas. Also notice the word *trace*. It suggests that you must track something through time in chronological order. Table 8-1 summarizes some common words found in assignments. Note that these words often correspond to the patterns of organization you studied in Chapter 6. Understanding these words will also be very useful when you are taking essay exams.

EXERCISE 8-1 . . . ANALYZING ASSIGNMENTS

*Read each of the following assignments. Discuss the meaning of the first word of each assignment and how it affects your preparation for reading. Be aware that each assignment may contain more than one part.*

1. Discuss the long-term effects of the trend toward a smaller, more self-contained family structure.

2. List four factors that influence memory or recall ability, and explain how each can be used to make study more efficient.

3. Trace the development of monopolies in the late nineteenth and early twentieth centuries in the United States.

4. Describe the events leading up to the U.S. invasion of Iraq.

5. Evaluate the evidence that concludes day care has serious negative effects on infants, toddlers, and young children.

## TABLE 8-1  COMMON WORDS FOUND IN ASSIGNMENTS

| WORD | INFORMATION TO INCLUDE | EXAMPLE |
|---|---|---|
| Argue | Make the case for a particular idea or course of action, providing convincing, reliable, valid evidence that supports your argument. | Argue that the United States should decrease its deficit by stopping foreign aid to all other countries. |
| Compare | Show how items are similar and include details or examples. | Compare the causes of air pollution with those of water pollution. |
| Contrast | Show how the items are different; include details and examples. | Contrast the health-care system in the United States with that in Canada. |
| Criticize | Make judgments about quality of worth; include both positive and negative aspects, explaining or giving reasons for your judgments. | Criticize the current environmental controls in place to combat carbon emissions. |
| Define | Give an accurate meaning of the term with enough detail to show that you really understand it. | Define welfare as the term is used in the United States. |
| Describe | Tell how something happened, including how, who, where, and why. | Describe the effects of social media on today's adolescents. |
| Diagram | Make a drawing and label its parts. | Diagram the stamen and pistil of the lily. |
| Discuss | Consider important characteristics and main points. | Discuss the effectiveness of drug rehabilitation programs. |
| Enumerate | List or discuss one by one. | Enumerate the reasons for U.S. involvement in Afghanistan and Iraq. |
| Evaluate | React to the topic in a logical way. Discuss the merits, strengths, weaknesses, advantages, or limitations of the topic, explaining your reasons. | Evaluate the strategies our society has used to treat mental illness. |
| Justify | Give reasons that support an action, event, or policy. | Justify the decision to place economic sanctions on Iran. |
| Prove | Give reasons or evidence, or establish that a concept or theory is correct, logical, or valid. | Prove that ice is a better cooling agent than air when both are at the same temperature. |
| State | Explain using examples that demonstrate or clarify a point or idea. | State Boyle's Law and illustrate its use. |
| Summarize | Briefly cover the major points; use complete sentences and organize your ideas into paragraphs. | Summarize the arguments for and against offering sex education in public schools. |
| Trace | Describe the development or progress of a particular trend, event, or process in chronological order. | Trace the history of the U.S. stock exchange. |

## 8b    HIGHLIGHTING

LEARNING OBJECTIVE 2
Highlight effectively

**Highlighting** forces you to decide what is important and distinguish key information from less important material. Sorting ideas this way improves both comprehension and recall. To decide what to highlight, you must think about and evaluate the relative importance of each idea you encounter. To highlight effectively, use these guidelines:

### Guidelines for Effective Highlighting

1. **Analyze the assignment.** Preview the assignment and define what type of learning is required. Doing so will help you determine how much and what type of information you need to highlight.

2. **Assess your familiarity with the subject.** Depending on your background knowledge, you may need to highlight only a little or a great deal. Do not waste time highlighting what you already know.

3. **Read first, then highlight.** Finish a paragraph or self-contained section before you highlight. As you read, look for words and phrases that signal organizational patterns (see Chapter 6). Each idea may seem important when you first encounter it, but you must see how it compares with other ideas before you can judge its relative importance.

4. **Use headings as a guide.** Headings are labels that indicate the overall topic of a section. They indicate what is important to highlight.

5. **Highlight only main ideas and key supporting details.** Avoid highlighting examples and secondary details.

6. **Avoid highlighting complete sentences.** Highlight only enough so that your highlighting makes sense when you reread it. In the following selection, note that only key words and phrases are highlighted. Now read only the highlighted words. Can you grasp the key idea of the passage?

**Issue: Immigrant families**

Like multiracial families, immigrant families face myriad challenges although they differ in nature. Fathers often find that the vocational and educational skills they worked so hard to achieve in their nation of origin are not transferable to the United States; former professionals may find themselves performing unskilled labor, earning incomes too meager to adequately support a family. Financial need may require the wife, who probably did not work in the nation of origin, to find a job to supplement the family income. In the new work setting she may find that gender roles in the United States allow more freedom to women and that she has new legal rights. She may begin to challenge the gender roles of her nation of origin, leading to marital strife. Men may begin to feel a loss of power and self-esteem while the wife gains more power and authority.

—Stuppes and Wells, *The Social Work Experience*, p. 148

7. **Move quickly through the document as you highlight.** If you have understood a paragraph or section, then your highlighting should be fast and efficient.

8. **Develop a consistent system of highlighting.** Decide how you will mark main ideas, how you will distinguish main ideas from details, and how you will highlight new terminology. You can also use brackets, asterisks, and circles or different ink colors or combinations of pens and pencils to distinguish various types of information. (See also Section 8c on annotating.)

9. **Use the 15–25 percent rule of thumb.** Although the amount you will highlight will vary from source to source, try to highlight no more than 15 to 25 percent of any given page. If you exceed this amount, you are likely not sorting ideas as efficiently as possible. Remember: The more you highlight, the smaller your time-saving dividends when you review.

---

**EXERCISE 8-2 . . . HIGHLIGHTING**

*Read the following pairs of passages, which have been highlighted in two different ways. Look at each highlighted version, and then write your answers to the questions that follow in the spaces provided.*

### Issue: Social Media

### Example A

**Social media marketing** refers to the use of blogs, linked social networks (Facebook, Twitter), and online communities (sports and celebrity fans, brand communities) to build relationships with customers. For example, for the launch of its 2010 GTI Hatchback, Volkswagen created a racing game using iPhones and iPod Touch to win a car. Players could send messages on Twitter and post videos of their games on YouTube.

Marketers use these new social media tools to promote brands, engage customers, and create brand relationships—and most of these efforts are free or cheap compared to other forms of marketing communication. They are not only a point of connection—a digital touchpoint—but they also open up a "social web," a network of people connected through the social media site. Social media sites open up a new environment of conversation-based marketing communication, creating opportunities for entirely different forms of nearly instantaneous customer connections. It's word-of-mouth advertising on steroids.

—Moriarty, Mitchell, and Wells, *Advertising & IMC*, p. 405

### Example B

**Social media marketing** refers to the use of blogs, linked social networks (Facebook, Twitter), and online communities (sports and celebrity fans, brand communities) to build relationships with customers. For example, for the launch of its 2010 GTI Hatchback, Volkswagen created a racing game using iPhones and iPod Touch to win a car. Players could send messages on Twitter and post videos of their games on YouTube.

Marketers use these new social media tools to promote brands, engage customers, and create brand relationships—and most of these efforts are free or cheap compared to other forms of marketing communication. They are not only a point of connection—a digital touchpoint—but they also open up a "social web," a network of people connected through the social media site. Social media sites open up a new environment of conversation-based marketing communication, creating opportunities for entirely different forms of nearly instantaneous customer connections. It's word-of-mouth advertising on steroids.

—Moriarty, Mitchell, and Wells, *Advertising & IMC*, p. 405

1. Is Example A or Example B the better example of effective highlighting? _

2. Why isn't the highlighting in the other example effective?

_____

_____

### Issue: The Economy

### Example C

In the more than 100 years that Ford Motor Company has been in business, its experiences have often mirrored those of the U.S. economy. So, it was no surprise that in the spring of 2009, with the U.S. economy suffering from its worst downturn since the 1930s, sales of Ford cars and trucks plummeted. In May 2009, Ford's sales were down 20 percent from a year earlier. Still, Ford was doing better than General Motors and Chrysler, Ford's two great American rivals, which had both declared bankruptcy. Those firms survived largely because the federal government invested more than $62 billion in them. While Ford suffered heavy losses, it did not require direct government aid.

—Hubbard and O'Brien, *Essentials of Economics*, p. 381

### Example D

In the more than 100 years that Ford Motor Company has been in business, its experiences have often mirrored those of the U.S. economy. So, it was no surprise that in the spring of 2009, with the U.S. economy suffering from its worst downturn since the 1930s, sales of Ford cars and trucks plummeted. In May 2009, Ford's sales were down 20 percent from a year earlier. Still, Ford was doing better than General Motors and Chrysler, Ford's two great American rivals, which had both declared bankruptcy. Those firms survived largely because the federal government invested more than $62 billion in them. While Ford suffered heavy losses, it did not require direct government aid.

—Hubbard and O'Brien, *Essentials of Economics*, p. 381

3. Is Example C or Example D the better example of effective highlighting? _

4. Why isn't the highlighting in the other example effective?

_____

_____

_____

*Highlight an essay provided by your instructor, or choose one from Part Two of this text book or from another class you are taking. Use the techniques discussed above.*

## 8c   ANNOTATING

**LEARNING OBJECTIVE 3**
Use annotation to record your thinking

In many situations, highlighting (see Section 8b) is not a sufficient means of identifying what to learn. It does not give you any opportunity to comment on or react to the material. **Annotating** text as you read is an interactive process that allows you to keep track of your comprehension as well as react and respond to the ideas of the writer. You might underline important ideas, number supporting details, write comments to the author, indicate important information with an asterisk, or write questions that you want to follow up on later.

Figure 8-1 suggests various types of annotation that you can use and provides examples of each in relation to a political science textbook chapter. However, you should feel free to develop your own system of annotations, symbols, and abbreviations. Annotating is a very personal process; you should annotate using whatever system helps you study best.

Here is an example of the annotations one student made on an excerpt from a reading on how the media treat images of men and women differently.

### Issue: Media Gender Images

*All media?*

<u>Media</u> images of men and women also differ in other subtle ways. In any visual representation of a person—such as a photograph, drawing, or painting—you can measure the relative prominence of the face by calculating the percentage of the vertical dimension occupied by the model's head. When Dane Archer and his colleagues inspected 1,750 photographs from *Time*, *Newsweek*, and other magazines, they found what they called "face-ism," a bias toward greater facial prominence in pictures of men than of women. This phenomenon is so prevalent that it appeared in analyses of 3,500 <u>photographs</u> from different countries, classic portraits painted in the seventeenth century, and the amateur drawings of college students.

*Who selected them? Were they selected randomly?*

*Aren't men's faces larger?*

<u>Why is the face more prominent in pictures of men than of women?</u> One possible interpretation is that face-ism reflects historical conceptions of the sexes. The face and head symbolize the mind and *intellect*—which are traditionally associated with men. With respect to women, more importance is attached to the heart, emotions, or perhaps just the body. Indeed, when people evaluate models from photographs, <u>those pictured with high facial prominence are seen as smarter and more assertive, active, and ambitious</u>—regardless of their <u>gender</u>. Another interpretation is that facial prominence signals power and *dominance*.

*Stereotyping -------->*

*Stereotyping -------->*
*Why?*

—Brehm, Kassin, and Fein, *Social Psychology*, p. 189.

### FIGURE 8-1 SAMPLE MARGINAL ANNOTATIONS

| TYPES OF ANNOTATION | EXAMPLE |
|---|---|
| Circling unknown words | ... redressing the apparent asymmetry of their relationship |
| Marking definitions | To say that the balance of power favors one party over another is to introduce a disequilibrium |
| Making examples | ... concessions may include negative sanctions, trade agreements ... |
| Numbering lists of ideas, causes, reasons, or events | components of power include self-image, population, natural resources, and geography |
| Placing asterisks next to important passages | Power comes from three primary sources ... |
| Putting question marks next to confusing passages | war prevention occurs through institutionalization of mediation ... |
| Making notes to yourself | power is the ability of an actor on the international stage to ... |
| Marking possible test items | There are several key features in the relationship ... |
| Drawing arrows to show relationships | ... natural resources ..., ... control of industrial manufacture capacity |
| Writing comments, noting disagreements and similarities | war prevention through balance of power is ... |
| Marking summary statements | the greater the degree of conflict, the more intricate will be ... |

### EXERCISE 8-4 . . . ANNOTATING

*Review Figure 8-1 and then annotate the reading you highlighted for Exercise 8-3.*

## 8d  PARAPHRASING

LEARNING OBJECTIVE 4
Paraphrase ideas

A **paraphrase** is a restatement of a reading selection's ideas in *your own words* that retains the author's meaning. We use paraphrasing frequently in everyday speech. For example, when you relay a message from one person to another you convey the meaning but generally do not use the person's exact wording.

A paraphrase can be used to make a reading selection more concise. For this reason, it is an effective learning and review strategy. It is particularly useful for portions of a text for which exact, detailed comprehension is required. For example, you might paraphrase the steps in solving a math problem, the process by which a blood transfusion is administered, or the levels of jurisdiction of the Supreme Court.

In addition, paraphrasing is a useful way to be certain you understand difficult or complicated material. If you can express the author's ideas in your own words, you can be certain you understand them. If you find yourself at a loss for words—except for those of the author—you will know your understanding is incomplete. Paraphrasing is also a useful strategy when working with material that is stylistically complex, poorly written, or overly formal, awkward, or biased. Figure 8-2 is a paraphrase of a paragraph from the preceding example.

### FIGURE 8-2  A SAMPLE PARAPHRASE

| PARAGRAPH | PARAPHRASE |
|---|---|
| Why is the face more prominent in pictures of men than of women? One possible interpretation is that face-ism reflects historical conceptions of the sexes. The face and head symbolize the mind and *intellect*—which are traditionally associated with men. With respect to women, more importance is attached to the heart, emotions, or perhaps just the body. Indeed, when people evaluate models from photographs, those pictured with high facial prominence are seen as smarter and more assertive, active, and ambitious—regardless of their gender). Another interpretation is that facial prominence signals power and *dominance*. | In photographs, men's faces are shown more obviously than women. One explanation is that the face and head stand for the mind and intellect and that, in the past, has been more often connected with men than women. The body, heart, and emotions are more often associated with women. When people study photographs, they regard both males and females whose images take up a large portion of the page to be more intelligent than those that take less. Another explanation is that larger facial size suggests power and control. |

Use the following suggestions to paraphrase effectively.

### Tips for Effective Paraphrasing

1. Read slowly and carefully.
2. Read the selection through in its entirety before writing anything.

3. As you read, pay attention to exact meanings and relationships among ideas.

4. Paraphrase sentence by sentence.

5. Read each sentence and express the key idea in your own words. Reread the original sentence; then look away and write your own sentence. Finally, reread the original and add anything you missed.

6. Don't try to paraphrase word by word. Instead, work with ideas.

7. For words or phrases you are unsure of or words you feel uncomfortable with, check a dictionary to locate a more familiar meaning.

8. You may combine several original sentences into a more concise paraphrase.

9. Do not plagiarize; your paraphrase should use your own words as much as possible, and you should include source information or an in-text citation (see Chapter 11) to avoid plagiarism.

## EXERCISE 8-5 . . . PARAPHRASING

*Read each paragraph and the paraphrases following them. Then answer the questions about the paraphrases.*

### Paragraph A

**Issue: Alternative Medicine**

Leaves of the coca plant have for centuries been a key part of the health system of the Andean region of South America. Coca is important in rituals, in masking hunger pains, and in combating the cold. In terms of health, Andean people use coca to treat gastrointestinal problems, sprains, swellings, and colds. The leaf may be chewed or combined with herbs or roots and water to make a *maté (mah-tay)*, a medicinal beverage. Trained herbalists have specialized knowledge about preparing *matés*. One *maté*, for example, is for treating asthma. The patient drinks the beverage, made of ground root and coca leaves, three to four times a day until cured.

—Miller, *Cultural Anthropology*, p. 166

### Paraphrase 1

A *maté* is a medicinal drink made from coca. Coca is an important plant in South America. It has a wide variety of uses, both ritualistic and medicinal.

### Paraphrase 2

The coca plant is an important part of health care in the Andes Mountains of South America. The leaves of this plant are used not only in rituals but also to hide hunger pangs and to fight the common cold. It is also used to help digestive problems as well as swollen or twisted joints. Sometimes the patient chews the coca leaf, and sometimes the patient drinks a coca-based medicinal beverage called a *maté*. People who are trained in herbs and their effects generally also have knowledge about how to prepare *matés* to cure such problems as asthma (Miller 166).

### Paraphrase 3

The coca plant is found only in the Andes of South America, where people use it not only for rituals but also for its medicinal properties. A *maté* is a medicinal drink made from coca leaves, and it is used primarily to treat asthma, though it can also help lessen the pain of twisted or swollen joints (Miller 166).

1. Which is the best paraphrase of Paragraph A? ____

2. Why are the other paraphrases not as good?

_____

_____

_____

_____

_____

## Paragraph B

### Issue: Family Trends

Today, the dominant family form in the United States is the child-free family, where a couple resides together and there are no children present in the household. With the aging of the baby boomer cohort, this family type is expected to increase over time. If current trends continue, nearly three out of four U.S. households will be childless in another decade or so.

—Thompson and Hickey, *Society in Focus*, p. 383

### Paraphrase 1

A child-free family is one where two adults live together and have no children. It is the dominant family form (Thompson and Hickey 383).

### Paraphrase 2

The child-free family is dominant in the United States. Baby boomers are having fewer children. Three out of four homes do not have children in them (Thompson and Hickey 383).

### Paraphrase 3

The child-free family is dominant in the United States. As baby boomers get older, there will be even more of these families. If this trend continues, three-quarters of all U.S. homes will be childless ten years from now (Thompson and Hickey 383).

3. Which is the best paraphrase of Paragraph B? ____

4. Why are the other paraphrases not as good?

_____

_____

## 8e   OUTLINING

LEARNING OBJECTIVE 5
Outline text

**Outlining** is a writing strategy that can assist you in organizing information and pulling ideas together. It is also an effective way to pull together information from two or more sources—your textbook and class lectures, for example. Finally, outlining is a way to assess your comprehension and strengthen your recall. Use the following tips to write an effective outline.

### Tips for Writing an Effective Outline

1. **Read an entire section and then jot down notes.** Do not try to outline while you are reading the material for the first time.

2. **As you read, be alert for organizational patterns** (see Chapter 6). These patterns will help you organize your notes.

3. **Record all the most important ideas in the briefest possible form.**

4. **Think of your outline as a list of the selection's main ideas and supporting details.** Organize your outline to show how the ideas are related or to reflect the organization of the selection.

5. **Write in your own words; do not copy sentences or parts of sentences from the selection.** Use words and short phrases to summarize ideas. Do not write in complete sentences.

6. **Keep entries parallel.** Each entry in your outline should use the same grammatical form. Express all of your ideas in words, or all of them in phrases, or all in full sentences.

7. **Use an indentation system to separate main ideas and details.** As a general rule, the more important the idea, the closer it is placed to the left margin. Ideas of lesser importance are indented and appear closer to the center of the page. Your outline should follow the format pictured here:

### Outline Format

```
TOPIC
Main Idea
    Supporting detail
        fact
        fact
    Supporting detail
Main Idea
    Supporting detail
    Supporting detail
        fact
        fact
```

Now study the following sample outline. It is based on a portion (the first seven paragraphs) of the textbook excerpt "Consequences of Social Class" on page 6 of Chapter 1.

I. Consequences of Social Class
  A. Physical Health
    1. Higher social class = better health; lower social class = worse health
    2. Three main reasons
      a. access to medical care
      b. lifestyle: diet, drugs, alcohol, exercise, sexual practices
      c. persistent stresses faced by poor (not faced by rich)
  B. Mental Health
    1. Higher social class = better mental health; lower social class = worse mental health
      a. poor: more stress, less job security, lower wages, more likely to divorce, be victims of crime
      b. higher social class: lower stress, better coping skills, afford vacations and doctors

## EXERCISE 8-6 . . . OUTLINING

*Read the following passage and complete the outline.*

### Issue: Business Issues and Practices

**Behavior segmentation** focuses on whether people buy and use a product, as well as how often and how much they use or consume. Consumers can be categorized in terms of **usage rates**: heavy, medium, light, or nonusers. Consumers can also be segmented according to **user status**: potential users, nonusers, ex-users, regulars, first-timers, or users of competitors' products. Marketers sometimes refer to the **80/20 rule** when assessing usage rates. This rule (also known as the *law of disproportionality* or *Pareto's Law*) suggests that 80 percent of a company's revenues or profits are accounted for by 20 percent of a firm's products or customers. Nine country markets generate about 80 percent of McDonald's revenues. This situation presents McDonald's executive with strategy alternatives: Should the company pursue growth in the handful of countries where it is already well known and popular? Or, should it focus on expansion and growth opportunities in the scores of countries that, as yet, contribute little to revenues and profits?

—Keegan and Green, *Global Marketing*, pp. 202, 204

## Behavior Segmentation

**A.** User status: _____

    1. potential users

    2. _____

    3. ex-users

    4. _____

    5. _____

    6. users of competitive products

**B.** _____ : how much or how often people use or consume the product

    1. _____

    2. medium

    3. _____

    4. non-users

**C.** 80/20 rule

    1. also known as _____ or _____

    2. _____% of customers or products account for _____% of revenue or profit

    3. McDonald's strategy

        a. _____

        b. option 1: pursue growth where the company is already well known and popular

        c. option 2: _____

                _____

## 8f    USING GRAPHIC ORGANIZERS TO SHOW RELATIONSHIPS

**LEARNING OBJECTIVE 6**
Draw maps and graphic organizers to show relationships among ideas

**Graphic organizers** allow you to organize text material visually. **Mapping** involves drawing a diagram to describe how a topic and its related ideas are connected and is a visual means of organizing, consolidating, and learning information. This section discusses four types of maps: *conceptual maps, process diagrams, time lines,* and *part and function diagrams.*

### Conceptual Maps

A **conceptual map** is a diagram that presents ideas spatially rather than in list form. It is a "picture" of how ideas are related. Use the following steps to construct a conceptual map.

**Steps for Constructing a Conceptual Map**

1. **Identify the topic and write it in the center of the page.**
2. **Identify ideas, aspects, parts, and definitions that are related to the topic.** Draw each one on a line radiating from the topic.
3. **As you discover details that further explain an idea already recorded, draw new lines branching from the idea and add the details to them.**

A conceptual map of this handbook is shown in Figure 8-3. This figure shows only the major topics included in the handbook. Maps can be much more detailed and include more information than the one shown.

**FIGURE 8-3  A CONCEPTUAL MAP OF THIS HANDBOOK**

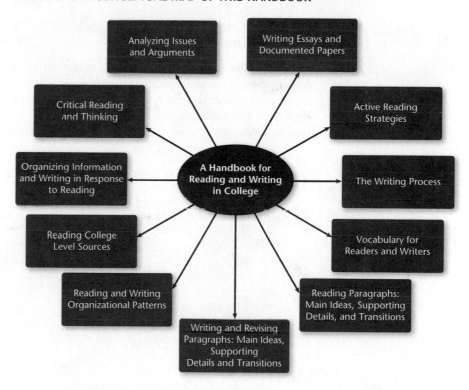

---

EXERCISE 8-7 . . . DRAWING A CONCEPTUAL MAP

*Create a conceptual map of the following paragraph about social institutions.*

**Issue: Social Institutions**

Society cannot survive without social institutions. A **social institution** is a set of widely shared beliefs, norms, and procedures necessary for meeting the basic needs of society. The most important institutions are family, education, religion, economy, and politics. They have stood the test of time, serving society well. The family institution leads countless people to produce and raise children to ensure that they can eventually take over from the older generation the task of keeping society going. The educational institution teaches the young to become effective contributors to the welfare—such as the order, stability, or prosperity—of society. The religious institution fulfills spiritual needs, making earthly lives seem more meaningful and therefore more bearable or satisfying. The economic institution provides food, clothing, shelter, employment, banking, and other goods and services that we need to live. The political institution makes and enforces laws to prevent criminals and other similar forces from destabilizing society.

—Thio, *Sociology,* pp. 35–36

## Process Diagrams

In the technologies and the natural sciences, as well as in many other courses and careers, *processes* are an important part of the course content or job. Process diagrams visually describe the steps, variables, or parts of a process, making learning easier. For example, the diagram in Figure 8-4 visually describes the steps that businesses follow in selecting a brand name for a new product.

**FIGURE 8-4  A PROCESS DIAGRAM: SELECTING A BRAND NAME FOR A NEW PRODUCT**

**Process: Selecting a Brand Name for a New Product**

Identify objectives → Brainstorm possible names → Evaluate and select better names → Field test on consumers → Select brand name

## Time Lines

When you are reading a selection focused on sequence or chronological order, a time line is a helpful way to organize the information. Time lines are especially useful in history courses. To map a sequence of events, draw a single line and mark it off in year intervals, just as a ruler is marked off in inches. Then write events next to the correct year. The time line shown in Figure 8-5 shows an effective way to organize historical events.

### FIGURE 8-5  SAMPLE TIME LINE

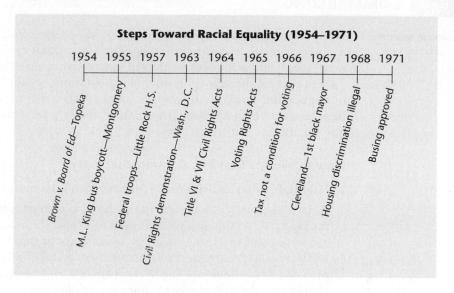

### Part and Function Diagrams

In college courses that deal with the use and description or classification of physical objects, labeled drawings are an important learning tool. In a human anatomy and physiology course, for example, the easiest way to learn the parts and functions of the brain is to draw it. To study it, you would sketch the brain and test your recall of each part and its function. Figure 8-6 shows a part and function diagram of the human ear.

### FIGURE 8-6  A PART/FUNCTION DIAGRAM

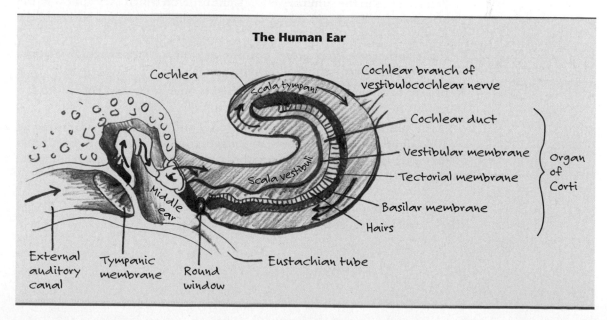

## 8g    SUMMARIZING

LEARNING OBJECTIVE 7
Summarize text

Like outlining, summarizing is an excellent way to learn from your reading and to increase recall. A **summary** is a brief statement that condenses an author's main ideas into sentences written in your own words. A summary contains only the gist of the text, with limited explanation, background information, or supporting detail. Be sure you understand the material and have identified the writer's major points before using the following suggestions to write a summary:

### How to Write a Concise, Accurate Summary

1. **Highlight or write brief notes on (annotate) the material.**

2. **Write one sentence that states the author's overall concern or most important idea.** To do this, ask yourself what one topic the material is about. Then ask what point the author is trying to make about that topic. This sentence will be the topic sentence of your summary. (You may find that the author has provided this sentence for you in the form of a thesis sentence. **But you must rewrite that thesis sentence in your own words.**)

3. **Throughout the summary, be sure to paraphrase, using your own words rather than the author's.**

4. **Review the major supporting information that the author provides to explain the major idea or thesis.**

5. **The amount of detail you include, if any, depends on your purpose for writing the summary.** For example, a summary of a television documentary for a research paper might be more detailed than a summary of the same program you write to jog your memory for a class discussion.

6. **Present ideas in the summary in the same order in which they appear in the original material.** Begin your summary by noting the title and author of the original material.

7. **If the author presents a clear opinion or expresses a particular attitude toward the subject, include it in your summary.**

8. **Be sure to acknowledge any sources used in your summary.** For more information on giving credit to sources, see Chapter 11, p. 315.

9. **If the summary is for your own use only and will not be submitted as an assignment, do not worry about sentence structure.** Some students prefer to write summaries using words and phrases rather than complete sentences.

Figure 8-7 is a sample summary of the article "Consequences of Social Class," which appears on page 6 of Chapter 1.

FIGURE 8-7  A SAMPLE SUMMARY

> According to James Henslin in his book *Sociology*, social class plays an important role in most aspects of a person's life. In terms of both physical and mental health, people of the higher social classes are healthier than those of the lower classes. In terms of family life, social class affects the choice of spouse, with upper-class parents playing a larger role in maintaining the sense of family and helping choose their children's mates. Divorce is more common among the lower classes, who are more likely than the middle and upper classes to orient their children toward following the rules. The upper classes are more educated than the lower classes, and people of different classes are even drawn to different religious denominations. Politically, the upper classes tend to vote Republican, the lower classes Democrat. Members of the lower classes are more likely to be arrested and imprisoned, while the white-collar crimes committed by the upper classes don't often land the criminals in jail (261–264).

### EXERCISE 8-8 . . . SUMMARIZING

*Write a summary of four paragraphs of a reading assigned by your instructor.*

## 8h  WRITING A RESPONSE PAPER

**LEARNING OBJECTIVE 8**
Write a response paper

At first, reading and writing may seem like very different, even opposite, processes. A writer starts with a blank page or computer screen and creates and develops ideas, while a reader starts with a full page and reads someone else's ideas. Although reading and writing may seem very different, they are actually parts of the same communication process. Because reading and writing work together, improving one set of skills often improves the other.

Some instructors assign a response to a reading, which requires you to read the selection, analyze it, and then write about it. The response may be somewhat informal (for example, adding an entry in your writing journal or posting a response to an electronic bulletin board), or it may be more formal (for example, a standard essay that should be drafted, revised, and proofread before being handed in).

Before responding to any reading, make sure you understand the response assignment. If you are unclear about your instructor's expectations or the specifics of the assignment, ask for clarification. For example, you may want to ask:

- How long should this response be?
- Do you want my opinion on the topic, a summary of the author's ideas, or both?
- Would it be acceptable to include a map or graphic organizer as part of my response?

### Writing an Informal Response

In an informal response, you simply write and respond without worrying about grammar, punctuation, and the other requirements of a formal paper. Suppose you have been assigned a reading titled "Adoption by Single People: Bad for the Parent, Bad for the Child." Your instructor asks you to write a journal entry responding to the reading. Here are some ways you might respond:

## How to Write an Informal Response

- **Write about your opinion on the topic.** Do you think single people should be allowed to adopt? Why or why not? It is acceptable to write about your emotional response to the topic in your journal. (In more formal response assignments, emotion is discouraged and convincing evidence and examples are encouraged.)

- **Talk about your personal experiences with the subject.** Do you know any single people who have adopted children? What have their experiences been? Would they agree or disagree with the author, and why?

- **Speculate why the author is so opposed to single people adopting children.** Is he basing his conclusions on his own experiences or on good, solid research?

- **Think about alternate scenarios.** Is a child better left in an orphanage than adopted by an unmarried person? Suppose you were an orphan. Would you rather be adopted by an unmarried person or left in a foster home or orphanage?

Here is a sample journal entry by a student writing in response to "Adoption by Single People: Bad for the Parent, Bad for the Child":

I can see the writer's point even if I don't agree with it. Of course we all want to have both a mother and a father. I think that's true whether you're male or female—you always want both. But that's just not always possible, and I personally would rather be adopted by a loving unmarried woman, or man, than have to live in a group home or be out there in the world fending for myself. People who want to adopt have a lot of love in their hearts, otherwise why would they want someone else's child? I don't think it should matter if the person is unmarried, but I do think it's important that the person have the financial means to support the kid they adopt.

## EXERCISE 8-9 . . . WRITING AN INFORMAL RESPONSE

*Write an informal response (in the form of a journal entry) to "A Blueprint for Better Nutrition" on pages 10–13 of Chapter 1.*

## Writing a Formal Response

In a formal response, you may decide to include a brief summary, but you should focus on analyzing and evaluating the reading selection. Do not discuss all of your reactions, however. Rather, select one key idea, one question the reading raises, or one issue it tackles. Then respond to that one idea, question, or issue.

For example, suppose your instructor asks you to read an article titled "Facebook: Many Friends, Few Relationships," which argues that Facebook encourages surface friendships at the expense of deeper, more lasting relationships. Your instructor asks you to write a formal one-page response paper about the article, allowing you to choose your own topic. In writing your response, you might take one of the following approaches:

- Discuss your own experiences with Facebook, as a way of confirming or refuting the author's main points.
- Evaluate the author's claim, evidence, and overall argument, either agreeing or disagreeing with her conclusions.
- Discuss some interesting aspects of Facebook that the author has not considered.
- List and discuss the author's assumptions or omissions.

Before you sit down to write, devise critical questions about the reading. Use the suggestions in Chapter 9 of this handbook to identify the author's opinions, her purpose for writing, her tone, her use of figurative language, her possible bias, and the reliability, relevance, and timeliness of her examples. Examining these aspects of the reading will likely generate many ideas to which you can choose to respond. (Of course, you will have to narrow your list and choose just one topic to write about.)

Because you will likely be graded or otherwise evaluated on your formal response, be sure to use good writing practices before you submit your formal response paper. Ask a classmate to read your first draft and offer ideas for improvement. Revise your paper to ensure it reads clearly and presents valid arguments and evidence. Before turning it in, proofread it for grammar, spelling, and punctuation.

### EXERCISE 8-10 . . . WRITING A FORMAL RESPONSE

*Write a one-page formal response to a reading from the text assigned by your instructor.*

---

| **SUMMARY OF LEARNING OBJECTIVES** | **MySkillsLab**<br>Complete the mastery test for this chapter **in MySkillsLab.** |
|---|---|
| **1 Analyze the reading and writing task.**<br>*How do you analyze a reading-writing task?* | To **analyze** the reading and writing task, first determine what you must do after you have finished the reading. Reread the assignment several times before you begin, looking for key words that will help you define your task. |
| **2 Highlight effectively.**<br>*How do you highlight effectively?* | To **highlight** effectively, analyze the assignment, assess your familiarity with the topic, read first before highlighting, use headings as a guide, highlight main ideas and key details, avoid highlighting complete sentences, work quickly, use a highlighting system, and apply the 15-25 percent rule. |

**3  Use annotation to record your thinking.**
*How do you annotate?*

**Annotating** text as you read is an interactive process that allows you to keep track of your comprehension as well as react and respond to the ideas of the writer. You might underline important ideas, number supporting details, write comments to the author, indicate important information with an asterisk, or write questions that you want to follow up on later. Develop your own system and symbols.

**4  Paraphrase ideas.**
*How do you paraphrase?*

To **paraphrase** a reading selection, rewrite the selection, keeping the author's meaning but using your own words. Paraphrase sentence by sentence, but work with ideas rather than individual words. Paraphrasing can help you make a reading selection more concise (by combining several original sentences into one paraphrased sentence) and can help you check your understanding. Be sure that you credit the source that you are paraphrasing.

**5  Outline text.**
*How do you outline?*

**Outlining** is a listing strategy that helps you organize information and pull ideas together. To outline a reading selection, read the entire reading selection and jot down notes, being alert for organizational patterns. Record the most important ideas and supporting details in the briefest possible form. Use your own words, and use an indentation system to separate main ideas from details. For an outline format, see page 210.

**6  Draw maps and graphic organizers to show relationships among ideas.**
*How can you use graphic organizers?*

**Drawing maps and graphic organizers** allows you to organize text material visually, drawing a diagram to show how a topic and its related ideas are connected. Four common types of maps/graphic organizers are conceptual maps, process diagrams, time lines, and part and function diagrams, which allow you to see connections between ideas, steps in a process, the order in which events occurred, and the structure and function of items.

**7  Summarize text.**
*How do you summarize?*

A **text summary** reviews the key points of what you have read. It condenses the author's ideas into sentences written in your own words and contains only the gist of the text, with limited explanation, background information, or supporting detail. To write a summary, first highlight or annotate the material. Then write one sentence that states the author's overall concern or most important idea. Throughout the summary, use your own words rather than the author's. Include the amount of detail required by the assignment, and present ideas in the same order in which they appear in the original. If the author presents a clear opinion or expresses a particular attitude toward the subject, include it in your summary. Be sure to indicate clearly the source of the material you are summarizing.

**8  Write a response paper.**
*How do you write informal and formal response papers?*

Written responses to a reading may be either formal or informal. To write an **informal response** (for example, a journal entry) you might write about your opinion on the topic, discuss your personal experience, speculate about the author's purpose, or think about other aspects of the topic. To write a **formal response** (for example, an essay) select one key idea, one question raised by the reading, or one issue discussed in the reading. Then respond to that one idea, question, or issue in a piece of writing that you edit, improve, and proofread before you submit it to your instructor.

# 9 Critical Reading and Thinking

## LEARNING OBJECTIVES

1 Make inferences and draw conclusions
2 Distinguish fact from opinion
3 Identify the author's purpose
4 Evaluate tone
5 Interpret figurative language
6 Identify bias
7 Evaluate data and evidence

## 9a  MAKING ACCURATE INFERENCES AND DRAWING CONCLUSIONS

**LEARNING OBJECTIVE 1**
Make inferences and draw conclusions

Look at the photograph below, which appeared in a psychology textbook. What do you think is happening here? What are the feelings of the participants?

To answer these questions, you had to use information you could get from the photo and make decisions based on it. The facial expressions, body language, clothing, and musical instruments presented in this photo provide clues. This reasoning process is called "**making an inference**." You also had to use your prior knowledge about concerts, performers, musicians, and so forth. When you use both your prior knowledge and information from a text or image, you "**draw a conclusion**."

**Inferences** and **conclusions** are reasoned guesses about what you don't know made on the basis of what you do know. They are common in our everyday lives. When you get on a highway and see a long, slow-moving line of traffic, you might predict that there is an accident or roadwork ahead. When you see a puddle of water under the kitchen sink, you can infer that you have a plumbing problem. The inferences you make may not always be correct, even though you base them on the available information. The water under the sink might have been the result of a spill. The traffic you encountered on the highway might be normal for that time of day, but you didn't know it because you aren't normally on the road at that time. An inference is only the best guess you can make in a situation, given the information you have.

## How to Make Accurate Inferences and Conclusions

When you read the material associated with your college courses, you need to make inferences and draw conclusions frequently. Writers do not always present their ideas directly. Instead, they often leave it to you—the reader—to add up and think beyond the facts they present, and to use your prior knowledge about the topic. You are expected to reason out the meaning an author intended (but did not say) on the basis of what he or she did say.

Each inference and conclusion you make depends on the situation, the facts provided, and your own knowledge and experience. Here are a few guidelines to help you see beyond the factual level and make accurate inferences from your reading materials.

### Understand the Literal Meaning

Be sure you have a firm grasp of the literal meaning. You must understand the stated ideas and facts before you can move to higher levels of thinking, which include inference making and drawing conclusions. You should recognize the topic, main idea, key details, and organizational pattern of each paragraph you have read.

### Notice Details

As you are reading, pay particular attention to details that are unusual or stand out. Often, such details will offer you clues to help you make inferences. Ask yourself:

- What is unusual or striking about this piece of information?
- Why is it included here?

Read the following excerpt, which is taken from an essay about a young Polish immigrant to the United Kingdom, and mark any details that seem unusual or striking.

**Issue: Immigration**

### An Immigration Plan Gone Awry

Due to her own hardship, Katja was not thrilled when her younger brother called her from Warsaw and said that he was going to join her in the United Kingdom (U.K.). Katja warned him that opportunities were scarce in London for a Polish immigrant. "Don't worry," he said in an effort to soothe her anxiety. "I already have a job in a factory." An advertisement in a Warsaw paper had promised good pay for Polish workers in Birmingham. A broker's fee of $500 and airfare were required, so her brother borrowed the money from their mother. He made the trip with a dozen other young Polish men.

The "broker" picked the young men up at Heathrow [airport] and piled them in a van. They drove directly to Birmingham, and at nightfall the broker dropped the whole crew off at a ramshackle house inside the city. He ordered them to be ready to be picked up in the morning for their first day of work. A bit dazed by the pace, they stretched out on the floor to sleep.

Their rest was brief. In the wee hours of the night, the broker returned with a gang of 10 or so thugs armed with cricket [similar to baseball] bats. They beat the young Polish boys to a pulp and robbed them of all their valuables. Katja's brother took some heavy kicks to the ribs and head, then stumbled out of the house. Once outside, he saw two police cars parked across the street. The officers in the cars obviously chose to ignore the mayhem playing out in front of their eyes. Katja's brother knew better than try to convince them otherwise; the police in Poland would act no differently. Who knows, maybe they were part of the broker's scam. Or maybe they just didn't care about a bunch of poor Polish immigrants "invading" their town.

—Batstone, "Katja's Story," from *Sojourner's*

Did you mark details such as the $500 broker's fee, the promise of a well-paying job despite scarce job opportunities for Polish immigrants, and the terrible sleeping conditions?

## Add Up the Facts

Consider all of the facts taken together. To do this, ask yourself the following questions:

- What is the writer trying to suggest with this set of facts?
- What do all these facts and ideas seem to point toward or add up to?
- Why did the author include these facts and details?

Making an inference is somewhat like assembling a complicated jigsaw puzzle; you try to make all the pieces fit together to form a recognizable picture. Answering these questions requires you to add together all the individual pieces of information, which will help you arrive at an inference.

When you add up the facts in the article "An Immigration Plan Gone Awry," you realize that Katja's brother is the victim of a scam.

### Be Alert to Clues

Writers often provide you with numerous hints that can point you toward accurate inferences. An awareness of word choices, details included (and omitted), ideas emphasized, and direct commentary can help you determine a writer's attitude toward the topic at hand. In "An Immigration Plan Gone Awry," the "ramshackle" house, the men "piled" into a van, and the immigrants sleeping on the floor are all clues that something is amiss.

### Consider the Author's Purpose

Also study the author's purpose for writing. What does he or she hope to accomplish? In "An Immigration Plan Gone Awry" the writer is critical of immigrant brokers and of the police.

### Verify Your Inference

Once you have made an inference, check to make sure that it is accurate. Look back at the stated facts to be sure you have sufficient evidence to support the inference. Also be certain you have not overlooked other equally plausible or more plausible inferences that could be drawn from the same set of facts.

---

**EXERCISE 9-1 . . . MAKING INFERENCES AND DRAWING CONCLUSIONS**

*Study the cartoon below and place a check mark in front of each statement that is a reasonable inference or conclusion that can be made from the cartoon.*

*"We get it, Tom—you're management now."*

_____ 1. The cartoonist thinks workers are physically abused.

_____ 2. The cartoonist is critical of those in management.

_____ 3. Many conflicts exist between workers and supervisors.

_____ 4. The cartoonist believes that people change when they become managers.

_____ 5. The cartoonist is a labor relations specialist.

## EXERCISE 9-2 . . . MAKING INFERENCES AND DRAWING CONCLUSIONS

*Read each of the following statements. Place a check mark in front of each sentence that follows that is a reasonable inference or conclusion that can be made from the statement.*

1.  Many job applicants have found that their postings on Facebook or their tweets on Twitter have had negative effects on their job interviews.

    _____ a.  Job recruiters look up candidates' online histories.

    _____ b.  Young people should be careful about what they post online.

    _____ c.  The majority of people over age 23 now have Facebook accounts.

    _____ d.  Tweeting has become an accepted method of staying in touch with friends.

2.  Reality TV may look spontaneous and unscripted, but reality TV shows are carefully edited before they are televised.

    _____ a.  In truth, reality TV is not particularly realistic.

    _____ b.  The directors and producers of reality TV may distort facts and events.

    _____ c.  Reality TV shows are cheaper to produce because there is no need for writers to write the dialogue.

    _____ d.  Most people now prefer to watch reality TV rather than sitcoms or dramas.

3.  The goal of health care reform in the United States is to ensure that as many people as possible have medical insurance and decent medical care, as in Canada and Europe.

    _____ a.  The cost of medical care is likely to decrease.

    _____ b.  Under the old medical care system, many people in the United States had no access to medical care.

    _____ c.  As a result of health care reform, there is likely to be a shortage of doctors.

    _____ d.  Canada and Europe currently do a better job of providing health care to their citizens than the United States does.

## EXERCISE 9-3 . . . MAKING INFERENCES AND DRAWING CONCLUSIONS

*Read each of the following passages. Determine whether the statements following each passage are true or false. Place a T next to each true statement and an F next to each false statement.*

### A. Issue: Literacy

On the surface, development statistics show impressive gains in education among developing countries. By the early twenty-first century, more than 80 percent of children were enrolled in primary school, and five out of six of the world's adults were literate, according to the United Nations Development Report in 2008. Yet the same report notes that only slightly over one-half of children attend school in sub-Saharan Africa and in many developing countries few children even graduate from primary school. Illiteracy rates in most middle-income nations are much lower, typically less than 20 percent. However, millions of rural and urban children receive no education whatsoever.

—adapted from Thompson and Hickey, *Society in Focus*, p. 239

_____ 1. In middle-income nations, urban children are more likely to be denied an education than rural children.

_____ 2. Today, the great majority of the world's population is literate.

_____ 3. Literacy rates are generally higher in middle-income nations than they are in developing nations.

_____ 4. More than half the children in sub-Saharan Africa will graduate from primary school.

_____ 5. The United Nations Development Report describes social trends in developing (poor) nations.

### B. Issue: Family and Family Trends

Many of you have probably grown up on tales of men running from marriage, going to great lengths to avoid being "trapped." This folklore actually runs counter to the reality of women's and men's lives. In reality, men seem to prefer marriage to being single. For example, when asked if they would marry the same person again, they respond in the affirmative twice as often as their wives. In addition, most divorced and widowed men remarry, and the rate of marriage for these men at every age level is higher than the rate for single men. Furthermore, when compared with single men, married men live longer, have better mental and physical health, are less depressed, have a lower rate of suicide, are less likely to be incarcerated for a crime, earn higher incomes, and are more likely to define themselves as happy.

—Schwartz and Scott, *Marriages and Families*, p. 255

_____ 6. Marriage has a number of beneficial effects on men.

_____ 7. Marriage is more beneficial to men than to women.

_____ 8. Married men are less likely to be in jail than married women are.

_____ 9. More men than women are happy in their current marriage.

_____ 10. A man who has been married is not likely to marry again.

## EXERCISE 9-4 . . . MAKING INFERENCES AND DRAWING CONLUSIONS

*Read the following passage and the statements that follow. Place a check mark next to the statements that are reasonable inferences or conclusions.*

### Issue: Police Techniques

August Vollmer was the chief of police of Berkeley, California, from 1905 to 1932. Vollmer's vision of policing was quite different from most of his contemporaries. He believed the police should be a "dedicated body of educated persons comprising a distinctive corporate entity with a prescribed code of behavior." He was critical of his contemporaries and they of him. San Francisco police administrator Charley Dullea, who later became president of the International Association of Chiefs of Police, refused to drive through Berkeley in protest against Vollmer. Fellow California police chiefs may have felt their opposition to Vollmer was justified, given his vocal and strong criticism of other California police departments. For example, Vollmer publicly referred to San Francisco cops as "morons," and in an interview with a newspaper reporter, he called Los Angeles cops "low grade mental defectives."

Because of his emphasis on education, professionalism, and administrative reform, Vollmer often is seen as the counterpart of London's Sir Robert Peel and is sometimes called the "father of modern American policing." Vollmer was decades ahead of his contemporaries, but he was not able to implement significant change in policing during his lifetime. It remained for Vollmer's students to implement change. For example, O.W. Wilson, who became chief of police of Chicago, promoted college education for police officers and wrote a book on police administration that reflected many of Vollmer's philosophies. It was adopted widely by police executives and used as a college textbook well into the 1960s.

Vollmer is credited with a number of innovations. He was an early adopter of the automobile for patrol and the use of radios in police cars. He recruited college-educated police officers. He developed and implemented a 3-year training curriculum for police officers, including classes in physics, chemistry, biology, physiology, anatomy, psychology, psychiatry, anthropology, and criminology. He developed a system of signal boxes for hailing police officers. He adopted the use of typewriters to fill out police reports and records, and officers received training in typing. He surveyed other police departments to gather information about their practices. Many of his initiatives have become common practice within contemporary police departments.

—Fagin, *Criminal Justice,* pp. 245–246

_____ 1. Vollmer did not have a college degree.

_____ 2. Most police officers of Vollmer's time had a limited education.

_____ 3. Vollmer believed police should be held accountable for their actions.

_____ 4. Sir Robert Peel dramatically changed policing procedures in England.

_____ 5. Vollmer received support from most police officers on the street.

_____ 6. Vollmer would support recent technological advances in policing.

_____ 7. Police departments of Vollmer's time were run with a careful eye toward accuracy and fairness.

_____ 8. Vollmer outlawed billy clubs.

## 9b    FACT AND OPINION

LEARNING OBJECTIVE 2
Distinguish fact
from opinion

When working with any source, readers and writers should try to determine whether the material is factual or an expression of opinion. **Facts** are statements that are true and can be verified. **Opinions** are statements that express feelings, attitudes, or beliefs and are neither true nor false. Following are examples of each:

### Facts

1. Canada, the United States, and Mexico are all members of the North American Free Trade Agreement.
2. Facebook has become the world's most popular social networking site.

### Opinions

1. Employers should be banned from spying on employees and reading their e-mail.
2. All immigration into the United States must be halted for a ten-year period.

Facts, when verified or taken from a reputable source, can be accepted and regarded as reliable information. Opinions, on the other hand, are not reliable sources of information and should be questioned and carefully evaluated. Look for evidence that supports the opinion and indicates that it is reasonable. For example, opinion 2 is written to sound like a fact, but look closely. Would everyone agree with this statement? Can it be disputed?

Some writers signal the reader when they are presenting an opinion. Watch for the following words and phrases:

| | | |
|---|---|---|
| according to | it is believed that | presumably |
| apparently | it is likely that | seemingly |
| in my opinion | one explanation is | this suggests |
| in my view | possibly | |

In the following excerpt from a business textbook, notice how the author uses qualifying words and phrases (underlined), as well as direct quotations from social critics, to indicate opinions on the topic "Are advertising and marketing necessary?"

### Issue: Advertising and Ethics

#### Are Advertising and Marketing Necessary?

More than 50 years ago, the social critic Vance Packard wrote, "Large-scale efforts are being made, often with impressive success, to channel our unthinking habits, our purchasing decisions, and our thought processes by the use of insights gleaned from psychiatry and the social sciences." The economist John Kenneth Galbraith <u>charged</u> that radio and television are important tools to accomplish this manipulation of the masses. Because consumers don't need to be literate to use these media, repetitive and compelling communications can reach almost everyone. This criticism may be even more relevant to online communications, where a simple click delivers a world of information to us.

<u>Many feel that</u> marketers arbitrarily link products to desirable social attributes, fostering a materialistic society in which we are measured by what we own. <u>One influential critic even argued</u> that the problem is that we are not materialistic enough—that is, we do not sufficiently value goods for the utilitarian functions they deliver but instead focus on the irrational value of goods for what they symbolize. <u>According to this view</u>, for example, "Beer would be enough for us, without the additional promise that in drinking it we show ourselves to be manly, young at heart, or neighborly. A washing machine would be a useful machine to wash clothes rather than an indication that we are forward-looking or an object of envy to our neighbors."

—Solomon, *Consumer Behavior*, p. 23

Other authors do just the opposite; they try to make opinions sound like facts, or they mix fact and opinion without making clear distinctions. This is particularly true in the case of **expert opinion**, which is the opinion of a recognized authority on a topic. Political commentators on Sunday news programs (sometimes called "pundits") represent expert opinion on politics, for example. Textbook authors, too, often offer expert opinion, as in the following statement from an American government text.

Ours is a complex system of justice. Sitting at the pinnacle of the judicial system is the Supreme Court, but its importance is often exaggerated.

—Lineberry et al., *Government in America*, p. 540

The author of this statement has reviewed the available evidence and is providing his expert opinion regarding what the evidence indicates about the Supreme Court. The reader is free to disagree and offer evidence to support an opposing view.

### EXERCISE 9-5 . . . DISTINGUISHING FACT AND OPINION

*Read each of the following statements and identify whether it is fact (F), opinion (O), or expert opinion (EO).*

_____ 1. Toyota is the world's largest automaker.

_____ 2. Apple Computers, already one of the world's most successful companies, will continue to be successful because of its history of innovation and product design.

_____ 3. Americans spend approximately $40 billion per year on diet aids, diet books, and diet foods.

_____ 4. The best way to read a book is on the Kindle Fire.

_____ 5. A capital good, as defined by economists, is a good bought by businesses to increase their productive resources.

_____ 6. The U.S. government is comprised of three branches: executive, legislative, and judicial.

_____ 7. Anthropologists believe that some native communities in the Americas practiced human sacrifice.

_____ 8. According to Dr. Elaine Feldman, a psychologist who specializes in anxiety management, deep breathing can greatly help people reduce their stress levels.

_____ 9. The finest novels in English history were written by Jane Austen.

_____ 10. The hammer and sickle are found on Russia's national flag.

## EXERCISE 9-6 . . . DISTINGUISHING FACT AND OPINION

_Each of the following paragraphs contains both facts and opinions. Read each paragraph and label each sentence as fact (F), opinion (O), or expert opinion (EO)._

### A. Issue: Slavery and Freedom

[1]Harriet Tubman was born a slave in Maryland in 1820 and escaped to Philadelphia in 1849. [2]Her own escape presumably required tremendous courage, but that was just the beginning. [3]Through her work on the Underground Railroad, Harriet Tubman led more than 300 slaves to freedom. [4]During the Civil War, Tubman continued her efforts toward the abolition of slavery by working as a nurse and a spy for the Union forces. [5]Today, Americans of all races consider Harriet Tubman one of the most heroic figures in our country's history.

_Sentences:_ 1. _____  2. _____  3. _____  4. _____  5. _____

### B. Issue: Drugs and Addiction

[1]Those big stogies that we see celebrities and government figures smoking are nothing more than tobacco fillers wrapped in more tobacco. [2]Since 1993, cigar sales in the United States have increased dramatically, up nearly 124 percent between 1993 and 2007. [3]The fad, especially popular among young men and women, is fueled in part by the willingness of celebrities to be photographed puffing on a cigar. [4]It's also fueled by the fact that cigars cost much less than cigarettes in most states. [5]Also, among some women, cigar smoking symbolizes being slightly outrageous and liberated. [6]According to a recent national survey, about 11 percent of Americans aged 18 to 25 had smoked a cigar in the past month.

—Donatelle, _Access to Health_, p. 386

_Sentences:_ 1. _____  2. _____  3. _____  4. _____  5. _____  6. _____

### C. Issue: Cultural Similarities and Differences

[1]Some sociologists believe that if any nation deserves the "pro-family" label, it is Sweden. [2]In the past century, the Swedish state, in cooperation with labor, industry, and the feminist and other social movements, has provided money and services to support family life and the employment of women. [3]And, to a lesser degree, it has sought to eliminate gender inequality and laws and customs that reinforce women's secondary place in society. [4]As a result, wrote sociologist Joan Acker, "Swedish women enjoy public programs and economic guarantees that have made Sweden a model for women in other countries."

—adapted from Thompson and Hickey, *Society in Focus,* p. 383

*Sentences: 1.* _____   *2.* _____   *3.* _____   *4.* _____

---

## 9c  AUTHOR'S PURPOSE

**LEARNING OBJECTIVE 3**
Identify the author's purpose

Writers have many different reasons or purposes for writing. Read the following statements and try to decide why each was written:

### Examples

1. In 2011, about 17.5 million people traveled through the Chunnel, the tunnel that connects France and England. This averages to about 48,000 people per day.

2. *New Vegetable Sticks in Sensible Portions.* Finally, a snack made from real vegetables with no added sugar or fats. We lightly sauté the vegetables so that they're crispy and crunchy, and then we package them in 100-calorie packets. Buy a box this week.

3. I don't like when people repeat themselves. I also do not like when they are redundant or repetitive, or when they repeat themselves.

4. To prevent yourself from being attacked by mosquitoes or ticks on a hike, be sure to use an insect repellent made with Deet.

Statement 1 was written to give information, 2 to persuade you to buy vegetable sticks, 3 to amuse you and make a comment on human behavior, 4 to give advice.

In each of the examples, the writer's purpose is fairly clear, as it is in most textbooks (to present information), newspaper articles (to communicate local, national, or world events), and reference books (to compile facts). However, in many other types of writing—especially materials concerning controversial contemporary issues—writers have varied, sometimes less obvious, purposes. In these cases, the writer's purpose must be inferred.

Often a writer's purpose is to express an opinion directly or indirectly. The writer may also want to encourage the reader to think about a particular issue or problem. Writers achieve their purposes by manipulating and controlling what they say and how they say it.

## EXERCISE 9-7 . . . IDENTIFYING THE AUTHOR'S PURPOSE

*Read each of the following statements. Then find the author's purpose for each statement in the box below and write it in the space provided.*

| to persuade | to entertain | to inform |
|---|---|---|
| to advise | to criticize | |

_____ 1. When choosing your courses for next year, try to find a balance between required courses and electives that you will enjoy.

_____ 2. I don't want to belong to any club that will accept me as a member. (Groucho Marx)

_____ 3. Travelers to Saudi Arabia should be aware that non-Muslims are not permitted in the cities of Mecca and Medina.

_____ 4. Now is the time to support gun-control legislation, before more innocent lives are lost to illegal firearms.

_____ 5. The mayor's plan to limit the sizes of sugary soft drinks to a maximum of 16 ounces is simply ridiculous. It is an example of intrusive government at its worst.

## 9d    TONE

**LEARNING OBJECTIVE 4**
Evaluate tone

The tone of a speaker's voice helps you interpret what he or she is saying. If the following sentence were spoken, the speaker's voice would tell you how to interpret it: "Would you mind closing the door?" In print you cannot tell whether the speaker is polite, insistent, or angry.

Just as a speaker's tone of voice tells how the speaker feels, a writer conveys a tone, or feeling, through his or her writing. **Tone** refers to the attitude or feeling a writer expresses about his or her subject. The tone of the article "Consequences of Social Class" (page 6) is informative. The author presents facts, research, and other evidence to support his thesis.

A writer may adopt a sentimental tone, an angry tone, a humorous tone, a sympathetic tone, an instructive tone, a persuasive tone, and so forth. Here are some examples of different tones. How does each make you feel?

- **Instructive**

When purchasing a used car, let the buyer beware. Get a CarFax report that shows the vehicle's history, and ask the seller for a copy of the maintenance records, which will tell you how closely the owner has followed the recommended maintenance schedule.

- **Sympathetic**

Each year, millions of women have miscarriages. My heart goes out to these strong women, who often suffer in silence.

- **Persuasive**

For just 40 cents a day, you can sponsor a poor child in a developing country. Yes, you can make a difference in a child's life for only $12 per month. The question is: How can you afford *not* to contribute?

- **Humorous**

There are two kinds of people in the world: Italians, and those who wish they were Italian.

- **Nostalgic**

Oh, how I long for the simplicity of the 1980s: before everyone was glued to their computers or cell phones every minute of the day; before cable television offered hundreds of channels I cannot possibly watch; before everyone decided to become a singer, celebrity, or reality TV star.

In the first example, the writer offers advice in a straightforward, informative style. In the second, the writer wants you to feel sympathy for women who have miscarried; she encourages this sympathy by describing that these women "often suffer in silence." In the third example, the writer tries to convince the reader to donate to a worthy cause. In the fourth example, the writer charms with a witty observation, and in the fifth example, the writer fondly reminisces about a simpler time before technology played such a prominent role in society.

To identify an author's tone, pay particular attention to descriptive language and connotations (see Section 3d). Ask yourself: "How does the author feel about the subject, and how are these feelings revealed?" It is sometimes difficult to find the right word to describe the author's tone. Table 9-1 on page 234 lists words that are often used to describe tone. Use this list to help you identify tone. If any of these words are unfamiliar, check their meanings in a dictionary.

## TABLE 9-1 WORDS FREQUENTLY USED TO DESCRIBE TONE

| | | | | |
|---|---|---|---|---|
| amused | condemning | formal | loving | playful |
| angry | condescending | frustrated | malicious | reverent |
| arrogant | cynical | hateful | mocking | righteous |
| assertive | depressing | impassioned | nostalgic | sarcastic |
| bitter | detached | indignant | objective | serious |
| caustic | disapproving | indirect | optimistic | sympathetic |
| celebratory | distressed | informative | outraged | vindictive |
| cheerful | excited | intimate | pathetic | worried |
| comic | flippant | irreverent | persuasive | |
| compassionate | forgiving | joyful | pessimistic | |

## EXERCISE 9-8 . . . RECOGNIZING TONE

*Read each of the following statements. Then choose a word from the box that describes the statement's tone, and write it in the space provided. Only some of the tone words are used.*

| | | | |
|---|---|---|---|
| optimistic | angry | admiring | cynical/bitter |
| excited | humorous | nostalgic | disapproving |
| formal | informative | sarcastic | |

_____ 1. Cecelia lets her young children stay awake until all hours of the night. Doesn't she realize that growing children need sleep and a predictable schedule?

_____ 2. The ostrich is the world's largest bird, the capybara is the world's largest rodent, and the tarantula is the world's largest spider.

_____ 3. Sir Walter Scott was not only a gifted novelist; he was also a kind, generous man who was widely respected and loved.

_____ 4. Every time I see figs, I think about the fig tree in my grandfather's garden.

_____ 5. I avoid clichés like the plague, and I eschew obfuscation.

_____ 6. What selfless civil servants politicians are! While everyone else struggles in a difficult economy, they vote themselves large pay raises and extended vacations.

_____ 7. The success of a newly launched news magazine, *The Week*, is proof that print magazines can survive and flourish in the Internet era.

_____ 8. Every time a woman asks me what I do for a living, I wonder if she is trying to figure out how much money I make.

_____ 9. Finally, after years of waiting, I am taking a cruise to Alaska!

_____ 10. Mr. and Mrs. Dane LeFever request the honor of your presence at the wedding celebration of their daughter, Sandra Anne, on Wednesday, December 5. Kindly RSVP at your earliest convenience.

## EXERCISE 9-9 . . . RECOGNIZING TONE

_Read each of the following statements, paying particular attention to the tone. Then write a sentence that describes the tone. Prove your point by listing some of the words that reveal the author's feelings._

1. No one says that wind power is risk-free. There are dangers involved in all methods of producing energy. It is true that wind turbines can harm or kill birds. But science and experience have shown us that wind power can be generated cleanly and efficiently. Wind power is at least as safe, or safer than, many other means of generating power.

   _____

   _____

2. The state of our schools is shocking. Their hallways are littered with paper and other garbage. Their restrooms are dirty and unsafe for children. The playgrounds are frequented by drug dealers and other unsavory people. Don't we pay school taxes to give our children a safe place to learn and grow?

   _____

   _____

3. I am a tired homeowner. I am tired of mowing the lawn. I'm sick of raking leaves. I'm thoroughly worn out by cleaning and dusting. I am exhausted by leaky faucets, unpainted rooms, and messy basements.

   _____

   _____

4. Cross-country skis have heel plates of different shapes and materials. They may be made of metal, plastic, or rubber. Be sure that they are tacked on the ski right where the heel of your boot will fall. They will keep snow from collecting under your foot and offer some stability.

   _____

   _____

## 9e    FIGURATIVE LANGUAGE

**LEARNING OBJECTIVE 5**
Interpret figurative
language

**Figurative language** is a way of describing something that makes sense on an imaginative level but not on a literal or factual level. Many common expressions are figurative:

> It was raining cats and dogs.
>
> His head is as hard as a rock.
>
> I was so nervous, I was sweating like a pig.

In each of these expressions, two unlike objects are compared on the basis of some quality they have in common. This is similar, for example, to Hamlet's statement "I will speak daggers to her, but use none." Here the poet (William Shakespeare) is comparing the features of daggers (sharp, pointed, dangerous, harmful) with something that can be used like daggers—words.

Figurative language is striking, often surprising, sometimes shocking. These reactions are created by the dissimilarity of the two objects being compared. To find the similarity and understand the figurative expression, focus on connotative (the feelings and emotions that a word suggests) rather than literal meanings. For example, in reading the lines

> "Life's but a walking shadow, a poor player
>
> That struts and frets his hour upon the stage
>
> And then is heard no more."
>
> —Shakespeare, *Macbeth*, Act V, Scene V

from Shakespeare's play *Macbeth*. Here the playwright is comparing an entire life to an actor's brief appearance in a play, implying life is very short and for all an individual's sense of importance he or she dies leaving no trace.

**Figurative expressions**, sometimes called **figures of speech**, communicate and emphasize relationships that cannot be communicated through literal meaning. For example, Jonathan Swift's statement, "She wears her clothes as if they were thrown on by a pitchfork," creates a stronger image and conveys a more meaningful description than the statement "She dressed sloppily."

The three most common types of figurative expressions are similes, metaphors, and personification. **Similes** make a comparison explicit by using the word *like* or *as*. **Metaphors** directly equate two objects without using the word *like* or *as*. **Personification** is a technique in which human characteristics are given to objects or ideas. For instance, to say "My old computer moans and groans each morning when I turn it on" gives the computer human characteristics of moaning and groaning.

- **Similes**

> She dressed like a rag doll.
>
> Sam was as happy as a clam.

- **Metaphors**

> Jane wears her heart on her sleeve.
> My life is a junkyard of broken dreams.

- **Personification**

> The earthquake has swallowed all my future plans.
> Nature abhors a peaceful man.

## EXERCISE 9-10 . . . USING FIGURATIVE LANGUAGE

*Study the figurative expression in each of the following statements. Then, in the space provided, explain the meaning of each.*

1. Hope is like a feather, ready to blow away.

   _____

   _____

2. Once Alma realized she had made an embarrassing error, the blush spread across her face like spilled paint.

   _____

   _____

   _____

3. A powerboat, or any other sports vehicle, devours money.

   _____

4. Sally's skin was like a smooth, highly polished apple.

   _____

5. Upon hearing the news, I took shears and shredded my dreams.

   _____

   _____

## 9f   BIAS

**LEARNING OBJECTIVE 6**
Identify bias

**Bias** refers to an author's partiality, inclination toward a particular viewpoint, or prejudice. A writer is *biased* if he or she takes one side of a controversial issue and does not recognize opposing viewpoints. Perhaps the best example of bias can be found in advertising. A magazine advertisement for a new car, for instance, describes only positive, marketable features—the ad does not recognize the car's limitations or faults.

Sometimes writers are direct and forthright in expressing their bias; other times a writer's bias might be hidden and discovered only through careful analysis. Read the following comparison of organic farming and conventional farming. The authors express a favorable attitude toward organic farming and a negative one toward conventional farming while also recognizing the reality that a sudden change to the type of farming they support would have serious consequences. Notice, in particular, the underlined words and phrases.

### Issue: Environmental Issues

### Organic Farming vs. Conventional Farming

Organic farming is carried out without the use of <u>synthetic</u> fertilizers or pesticides. Organic farmers (and gardeners) use manure from farm animals for fertilizer, and they rotate other crops with legumes to <u>restore</u> nitrogen to the soil. They control insects by planting a variety of crops, alternating the use of fields. (A corn pest has a hard time surviving during the year that its home field is planted in soybeans.) Organic farming is also <u>less energy intensive</u>. According to a study by the Center for the Biology of Natural Systems at Washington University, <u>comparable conventional farms used 2.3 times as much energy</u> as organic farms. Production on organic farms was 10% lower, but <u>costs were comparably</u> lower. Organic farms require 12% more labor than conventional ones. Human labor is <u>a renewable resource</u>, though, whereas petroleum is not. Compared with conventional methods, organic farming uses <u>less energy</u> and leads to <u>healthier soils</u>.

In addition to organic practices, sustainable agriculture involves buying <u>local products</u> and using <u>local services</u> when possible, thus <u>avoiding the cost of transportation</u> while getting <u>fresher goods</u> and <u>strengthening the economy</u> of the local community. Sustainable agriculture <u>promotes independent farmers and ranchers</u> producing <u>good food</u> and making a <u>good living</u> while <u>protecting the environment</u>.

Conventional agriculture can result in severe <u>soil erosion</u> and is the source of considerable <u>water pollution</u>. No doubt we should practice organic farming to the limits of our ability to do so. But we should not <u>delude</u> ourselves. Abrupt banning of synthetic fertilizers and pesticides would likely lead to a drastic drop in food production.

—Hill, McCreary, and Kolb, *Chemistry for Changing Times*, p. 634

### Ways to Identify Bias

To identify bias, use the following suggestions:

1. **Analyze connotative meanings.** Do you encounter a large number of positive or negative terms in the reading selection?
2. **Notice descriptive language.** What impression is created?
3. **Analyze the tone.** The author's tone often provides important clues.
4. **Look for opposing viewpoints.**

### EXERCISE 9-11 . . . DETECTING BIAS

*Read each of the following statements and place a check mark in front of each one that reveals bias.*

_____ 1. Killing innocent animals so that wealthy women can wear fur coats is a crime against life.

_____ 2. Organic chemistry studies substances that contain carbon, the element essential to life.

_____ 3. While most Americans identify themselves as either Republicans or Democrats, an increasing number of U.S. citizens are defining themselves as Independent.

_____ 4. There's no better way to teach responsibility to children than giving them daily chores to complete.

_____ 5. Without a doubt, the islands of the Caribbean are the most beautiful in the world.

### EXERCISE 9-12 . . . DETECTING BIAS

*Read the following passages and underline words and/or phrases that reveal the author's bias.*

#### Issue: Advertising and Ethics

The only essential ingredient in shampoo is a detergent of some sort. What, then, is all the advertising about? You can buy shampoos that are fruit or herb scented, protein enriched, and pH balanced or made especially for oily or dry hair. Shampoos for oily, normal, and dry hair seem to differ primarily in the concentration of the detergent. Shampoo for oily hair is more concentrated; shampoo for dry hair is more dilute.

—Hill, McCreary, and Kolb, *Chemistry for Changing Times*, p. 671

#### Issue: Environmental Issues

From its extraction to its various end uses, coal presents more environmental challenges than any other energy sources. Underground coal mining is a very hazardous occupation due to the potential for cave-ins, flooding, dust, and gas explosions. In 2010, mining accidents in the United States killed 48 coal miners, and accidents in China killed more than 2,400 miners. Even without accidents, thousands of underground coal miners suffer from respiratory diseases caused by inhaling coal dust.

Mining activities also have a direct effect on the environment. Mine tailings, the rock and debris from mining operations, often contain high concentrations of sulfide. When exposed to oxygen, these sulfides are transformed to sulfuric acid, which runs off into nearby streams, where it harms fish and other aquatic organisms.

Surface mining destroys the terrestrial ecosystems above the coal seams. The coal-mining industry in the United States has received especially harsh criticism for the environmental impact of mountaintop removal. In West Virginia and Kentucky, overburden from mountaintop removal has permanently buried more than 700 miles of mountain streams, thereby affecting wildlife, flooding nearby communities, and degrading water quality far downstream.

The exhaust and fly ash from coal fires contain a number of toxic chemicals that are harmful to many organisms, including humans. Fine particulate soot from coal fires can cause respiratory distress. In addition, coal usually contains mercury, which accumulated in the wetlands where it was formed. When coal is burned, this mercury is released into the atmosphere. Concentrations of mercury in streams and lakes near coal-fired power plants are often several times higher than normal. Eventually, this mercury accumulates in the tissues of animals, including humans, where it can cause a number of serious health problems, including neurological disorders. Fly ash also contains high concentrations of mercury, which makes it complicated to dispose of.

—adapted from Christensen, *The Environment and You*, pp. 463–464

## 9g    EVALUATING THE RELIABILITY OF DATA AND EVIDENCE

**LEARNING OBJECTIVE 7**
Evaluate data and evidence

Many writers who express opinions or state viewpoints provide readers with data or evidence to support their ideas. Your task as a critical reader is to weigh and evaluate the quality of this evidence. You must examine the evidence and assess its adequacy. You should be concerned with two factors: (1) the type of evidence being presented, and (2) the relevance of that evidence.

### Types of Evidence

Various types of evidence include

- personal experience or observation
- expert opinion
- research citation
- statistical data
- examples, descriptions of particular events, or illustrative situations
- analogies (comparisons with similar situations)
- historical documentation
- quotations
- description

Each type of evidence must be weighed in relation to the statement it supports. Acceptable evidence should directly, clearly, and indisputably support the case or issue in question.

### EXERCISE 9-13 . . . EVALUATING TYPES OF EVIDENCE

Refer to the article "Consequences of Social Class," on pages 6–9. For each of the following paragraphs, identify the type(s) of evidence the author provides.

1. Paragraph 2 _____

2. Paragraph 7 _____

3. Paragraph 11 _____

4. Paragraph 13 _____

## EXERCISE 9-14 . . . IDENTIFYING TYPES OF EVIDENCE

*For each of the following statements, discuss the type or types of evidence that you would need in order to support and evaluate the statement.*

1. Individuals must accept primary responsibility for the health and safety of their babies.
2. Apologizing is often seen as a sign of weakness, especially among men.
3. There has been a steady increase in illegal immigration over the past 50 years.
4. More college women than college men agree that marijuana should be legalized.
5. Car advertisements sell fantasy experiences, not the means of transportation.

## Evaluating Reliability

Three overall factors point to reliable, trustworthy writing:

- Quantity of information
- Relevance of the information
- Timeliness of the information

### Quantity of Information

As a general rule, the more evidence writers provide to support the thesis statement and main ideas of the selection, the more convincing their writing is likely to be. Suppose an article includes the following thesis statement:

> Married people lead healthier, happier lives than unmarried people.

Now suppose the writer includes just one fact to support this statement: "Research shows that most married people report higher levels of happiness than unmarried people do." Does this one piece of evidence provide full support for the thesis statement? Most likely, you would argue that it does not. You may know plenty of single people who are very happy and many married people who are miserable.

Now consider an article that supports the thesis statement with the following evidence:

- Married people have a larger support network that helps them stay healthy.
- Both married women and married men earn more money than their single co-workers.
- Research has shown that married people live longer.
- Married people report lower levels of stress and depression than single people do.

Each of these supporting pieces of evidence on its own may not be enough to help the writer prove his or her thesis statement, but as a whole they greatly strengthen the argument.

### Relevance of Information

Supporting evidence must be relevant to be convincing. That is, it must be closely connected to the thesis statement and to the subject under discussion. It is easy to be distracted by interesting pieces of information that are not relevant to the writer's thesis statement.

Consider the discussion of marriage and happiness above. For example, it is interesting that 48% of Americans are married, but this fact is not relevant to the thesis statement "Married people live healthier, happier lives than those who are single." When you encounter irrelevant information, ask yourself: "Why has the writer included this? Is it intended to steer my thinking in a specific direction, away from the topic at hand?"

### Timeliness of Information

When evaluating the information provided by the writer, check how recent the examples, statistics, data, and research are. In general, more current facts, figures, and research are better and more reliable. In the computer age, new information and knowledge are being generated at an astonishing rate, so articles published as recently as two years ago may be out of date, and the information they contain may be obsolete. Think about it this way: Look at how quickly technology becomes outdated. This year's smartphone will be replaced next year by an even faster, even better smartphone. In the same way, advances in many areas of study leave older information in the dust.

Keep in mind, though, that some things do not change. The components of the human body are the same today as they were 200 years ago. The principles of mathematics have not changed and are not likely to change. The U.S. Constitution, great works of literature, and other important documents remain the same today as when they were written.

---

### EXERCISE 9-15 . . . EVALUATING QUALITY AND RELEVANCE OF INFORMATION

*A magazine article has the following thesis statement: "It has been proven that animal companions, sometimes known as pets, have many benefits for their owners." A list of possible statements to support this thesis sentence follows. Place a check mark next to each statement that is relevant to the thesis statement.*

\_\_\_\_\_  1. The U.S. Centers for Disease Control, an important source of medical information in the United States, has stated that owning a pet can decrease your blood pressure and cholesterol levels.

\_\_\_\_\_  2. Men tend to prefer having dogs as pets, while women seem to prefer owning cats.

\_\_\_\_\_  3. Sadly, many animal shelters in the United States are underfunded and desperately in need of donations.

\_\_\_\_\_  4. The National Institute of Health has reported widespread benefits of pet ownership for older people.

\_\_\_\_\_  5. More than half of all U.S. households have a companion animal.

_____ 6. A growing number of studies have suggested that children who grow up in a home with a "furred animal" are less likely to develop allergies or asthma.

_____ 7. On the dating scene, many singles have reported that their pets have helped them strike up conversations with the opposite sex.

_____ 8. In general, people who own pets report less depression than people who do not own pets.

_____ 9. There are more than 51 million dogs, 56 million cats, and 45 million birds in U.S. households.

_____ 10. One study showed that stockbrokers with high blood pressure who adopted a cat or dog had lower blood pressure readings in stressful situations than people without pets.

### EXERCISE 9-16 . . . EVALUATING TIMELINESS OF INFORMATION

*Several types of information are provided below. Place a check mark next to each type of information that is not likely to change (that is, cases in which it is acceptable to use an older source of information).*

_____ 1. A mathematics textbook teaching students how to add and subtract

_____ 2. A manual teaching you how to use a computer

_____ 3. A diagram of the parts of the human brain

_____ 4. A history textbook explaining the pilgrims' reasons for leaving England

_____ 5. A medical book that suggests the use of leeches to reduce a fever

---

| SUMMARY OF LEARNING OBJECTIVES | **MySkillsLab**<br>Complete the mastery test for this chapter **in MySkillsLab.** |
|---|---|
| **1**  **Make inferences and draw conclusions.** *How can you make accurate inferences and draw conclusions?* | An **inference** is a reasoned guess about what you don't know based on what you do know from the facts and information presented in a text or image. **Combining inference and prior knowledge allows you to draw conclusions.** To make accurate inferences and conclusions, understand the literal meaning of the reading selection, pay attention to details (ask what is unusual or striking about them and why they have been included), add up the facts, be alert to clues, and consider the writer's purpose. Once you have made an inference, verify that it is accurate. |

| 2 | **Distinguish fact from opinion.** *How do you distinguish facts from opinions?* | A **fact** is a statement that can be verified (proven to be true or false). An **opinion** expresses feelings, attitudes, and beliefs, and it is neither true nor false. Look for evidence that supports an opinion and indicates that it is reasonable. By distinguishing statements of fact from opinions, you will know which ideas to accept and which to verify or question. |
|---|---|---|
| 3 | **Identify the author's purpose.** *Why should you identify an author's purpose?* | Writers have **different purposes for writing** (for example, to inform, to persuade, to entertain, or to provide an opinion). Recognizing a writer's purpose will help you grasp meaning more quickly and evaluate his or her work. |
| 4 | **Evaluate tone.** *How do you determine tone?* | **Tone** refers to the attitude or feeling a writer expresses about his or subject. To determine tone, pay particular attention to descriptive language and connotations (see Table 9-1, page 234, for a summary of tone words). Recognizing tone will help you evaluate what a writer is attempting to accomplish through his or her writing. |
| 5 | **Interpret figurative language.** *What is figurative language?* | **Figurative language** is a way of describing something that makes sense on an imaginative level but not a literal or factual level. Recognizing and understanding figurative language helps you better understand how a writer views his or her subject. **Similes** make comparisons by using the words *like* or *as*. **Metaphors** make a comparison without using the word *like* or *as*. **Personification** attributes human characteristics to ideas and objects. |
| 6 | **Identify bias.** *How do you identify bias?* | **Bias** refers to a writer's partiality, inclination toward or against a particular viewpoint, or prejudice. A writer is biased when he or she takes one side of a controversial issue and does not recognize opposing viewpoints. Sometimes bias is overt; other times, it is subtle. To identify bias, analyze connotations and notice descriptive language. Analyze tone and look for opposing viewpoints, especially in readings that discuss controversial issues. Recognizing tone will help you evaluate whether the author is providing objective, complete information or selectively presenting information that furthers his or her purpose. |
| 7 | **Evaluate data and evidence.** *How do you evaluate date and evidence?* | **Types of evidence** include personal experience or observation, expert opinion, research citations, statistical data, examples, particular events, illustrative situations, analogies, historical documentation, quotations, and descriptions. Acceptable evidence should directly, clearly, and indisputably support the case or issue in question. Three factors point to reliable, trustworthy writing: 1. The author provides sufficient support for his or her point. 2. The author provides relevant information. 3. The author provides timely information (recent examples, statistics, data, and research). By evaluating the quantity, relevance, and timeliness of information, you can determine how reliable a source is. |

# 10 Analyzing Issues and Arguments

### LEARNING OBJECTIVES

1 Understand the connection between contemporary issues and arguments
2 Define an argument
3 Explain the parts of an argument
4 Read arguments
5 Evaluate arguments
6 Recognize errors in logic
7 Write argument essays

Throughout your college studies you will read many source materials that take a stand on a specific question, such as "What is the best method of decreasing unemployment?" or "How does society go about lowering the crime rate and making the streets safer?" You will discuss these and many other issues in many of your academic courses. Even heavily scientific courses, such as biology, must deal with controversial problems, such as "Is it ethical to perform medical research on human beings?" and "What are the pros and cons of organ donation?"

The best discussions of these issues are based on specific arguments, opinions, and supporting evidence. In this chapter, you will learn the parts of an argument; strategies for reading, and evaluating, arguments, and how to recognize logical errors. You will also learn to write effective argument paragraphs and essays.

## 10a  CONTEMPORARY ISSUES AND ARGUMENTS

**LEARNING OBJECTIVE 1**
Understand the connection between contemporary issues and arguments

As discussed in Chapter 1, a **contemporary issue** is a current topic that is relevant to individuals, groups, and society today. Throughout this handbook and Part Two of this book, you will read selections about some of the most talked-about and controversial contemporary issues facing U.S.

society today: gun control, drugs and addiction, crime, animal rights, and cultural similarities and differences. This list of contemporary issues could go on for pages.

Most contemporary issues can be phrased in the form of a question, such as

- "Should cosmetics companies be allowed to use animals as test subjects?"

- "What exactly is sexual harassment, and how do we recognize it when we see it?"

- "Do racism and prejudice still exist in U.S. society?"

- "Should single people be allowed to adopt children?"

To answer these questions, writers conduct research, interview people, and read various source materials that help them formulate an opinion. Once their opinion has been formed, they can then write something (an article, a book, a blog, a contribution to a Web site) in which they state their opinion (often as a thesis sentence) and then provide support for their opinion.

### EXERCISE 10-1 . . . IDENTIFYING CONTEMPORARY ISSUES

*Place a check mark next to the questions that qualify as contemporary issues.*

_____ 1. Was the Great Pyramid at Giza one of the seven wonders of the ancient world?

_____ 2. Does the government have the right to draft young men and women into military service?

_____ 3. What should the legal drinking age be?

_____ 4. How many people gather in New York City's Times Square on a typical New Year's Eve?

_____ 5. Does a human heart have more chambers than a chimpanzee's heart?

_____ 6. Should the government deny health care and welfare benefits to undocumented immigrants?

_____ 7. Is it fair to tax people who don't have children in order to fund the school system?

_____ 8. Which Greek and Roman gods have months named after them?

_____ 9. Should infants be banned from flights intended for businesspeople?

_____ 10. What are three common types of sugars found in processed foods?

## 10b WHAT IS AN ARGUMENT?

**LEARNING OBJECTIVE 2**
Define an argument

Much of academic writing is based on **arguments**, which are civilized discussions in which people express different points of view about a topic. For example, in a government course you might read arguments for or against the freedom to burn the American flag; in a criminal justice course you might read arguments for or against parole for convicted criminals.

Note that the term *argument*, as used in academic reading and writing, does not have a negative connotation. In common language, an argument is often a heated, emotional, and unpleasant disagreement between two people. In college-level reading (and beyond), an argument is simply a well-thought-out, well-researched piece of writing that offers good reasons to support a particular viewpoint.

A single issue may have many questions and arguments associated with it, as in the following example:

### Issue: Terrorism

Question: How do we stop terrorism and prevent terrorist attacks?

- **Argument #1:** The United States must strongly secure the entire length of its borders with Canada and Mexico.

- **Argument #2:** While we must ensure air safety, conducting invasive body searches in airports is not the way to do it. These searches invade the American right to privacy.

- **Argument #3:** The United States must send more financial and military aid to countries that harbor terrorist groups as a way of helping those countries establish pro-democratic, pro-U.S. governments.

- **Argument #4:** The U.S. government should deport any immigrant who comes from a nation that is openly hostile to the United States.

Note that each argument is both an opinion and a thesis statement. Such arguments are likely to be found early in a reading selection, with the remainder of the reading offering various types of support and evidence. In the case of Argument #1, for example, a writer might prepare an essay arguing in favor of increased security at U.S. borders, pointing to the need to keep enemies off U.S. land and providing data showing that increased border controls would not only improve homeland security but also result in more jobs for Americans.

But another writer might disagree with Argument #1. That writer, who does not agree with the idea of spending large sums of money securing the borders, might argue that most terrorists have entered the United States through air travel rather than by crossing the Mexican or Canadian border. The writer might also argue that the money spent on patrolling the borders could be much better used to train bomb-sniffing dogs, develop sophisticated computer software to help identify terrorists, and increase security at major airports.

Here is a brief argument. As you read, notice that the argument offers reasons to support the viewpoint that U.S. society is subtly and overtly ageist.

**Issue: Ageism and Discrimination**

### Ageism: Creeping to the Forefront

We all know a little something about the "isms" in society: capitalism, communism, atheism, and so on. "Isms" represent systems of belief and usually encompass stereotypes as well. The time has come to discuss the next big "ism" creeping to the forefront of social stereotypes: ageism. Ageism—prejudice against and discrimination based solely on age—is likely to become more prevalent due in part to the growing population of older individuals in the United States.

Considering society's infatuation with the young and the beautiful, the media—especially TV—has a huge impact on the spread of ageism. In recent years, reality TV shows have flooded the market due to the fact that they are cheaper to produce than scripted shows. Offhand, you'd probably be able to list at least 10 different programs, but ask yourself this: How many participants over the age of 50 can you name? The cast of most shows is young. When the older generation is included in other TV shows, they're often depicted as hunched-over and wrinkled, with gray hair and liver spots. Such depictions reinforce stereotypes that lead to ageism and distort our perceptions of growing older. Recently I took my elderly father to the doctor. I noticed a distinct difference in the way in which we were treated. Often, nurses and the doctor would ask me questions about his health, rather than him. Since he has no impairment, I found this odd. But this subtle type of ageism is widely used when we assume the elderly to be senile, sick, or unable to function. In fact, sociologist Erdman Palmore suggests that medical professionals frequently engage in subtle ageism when they view the symptoms as simply a matter of being old.

—adapted from Carl, *Think Social Problems*, pp. 71–72

### EXERCISE 10-2 . . . IDENTIFYING AN ARGUMENT

*Answer the following questions based on "Ageism: Creeping to the Forefront."*

1. What might be another good title for this piece of writing? _____

   _____

2. What question does the author seek to answer in the passage? _____

   _____

3. What other "isms," not mentioned in the passage, are also contemporary issues that generate much controversy and debate? _____

   _____

## 10c    THE PARTS OF AN ARGUMENT

LEARNING OBJECTIVE 3
Explain the parts of
an argument

A good **argument** has three—sometimes four—parts: an issue, a claim about that issue, support for that claim, and, sometimes, a refutation of opposing arguments. Figure 10-1 illustrates the structure of an argument.

1. **An argument must address an issue—a problem or controversy about which people disagree.** As we've seen, these topics include energy conservation, the effects of social media on teenagers, and the right to privacy. Part Two of this text offers readings on a wide variety of contemporary issues.

2. **An argument must take a position on an issue.** This position is called a **claim**. You might think of the claim as a writer's specific viewpoint. For example, an argument may claim that handguns should be outlawed or that medical use of marijuana should be legalized.

   There are three common types of claims:

   • A **claim of fact** is a statement that can be proven or verified by observation or research.

   > Within our children's lifetimes, the average temperature of the planet will increase 2.5 to 10 degrees Fahrenheit.

### FIGURE 10-1 THE STRUCTURE OF AN ARGUMENT

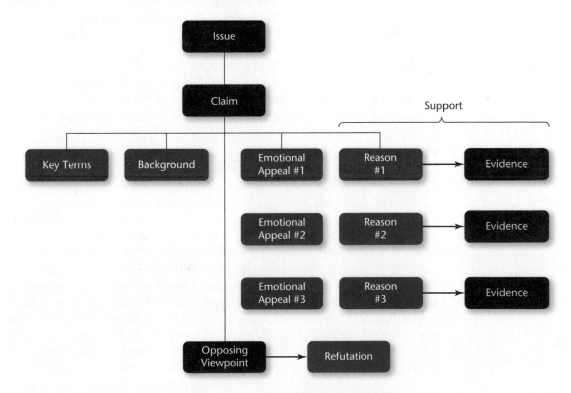

- A **claim of value** states that one thing or idea is better or more desirable than another. Issues of right versus wrong, or acceptable versus unacceptable, lead to claims of value. An argument against professional athletes' use of steroids is a claim of value. An author could argue that steroid use is unacceptable because it is harmful to athletes and unfair to competitors who do not use steroids. The following claim of value asserts that people convicted of drug use should take part in mandatory drug counseling.

> Requiring drug counseling and drug rehabilitation for convicted drug users increases the likelihood that these people will not return to using drugs.

- A **claim of policy** suggests what should or ought to be done to solve a problem. The following claim of policy states one writer's position on cyberbullying.

> To control bullying, schools should practice a zero-tolerance policy for any form of bullying, whether on the playground, in the classroom, or over the Internet or smartphones.

3. **The argument must offer support for the claim.** Support consists of reasons and evidence that the claim is reasonable and should be accepted. There are three common types of support:

- A **reason** is a general statement that supports a claim. It explains why the writer's viewpoint is reasonable and should be accepted. In "Ageism: Creeping to the Forefront" on page 248, the writer offers a good reason why we should be concerned about ageism: the population of older individuals in the United States is growing.

- **Evidence** consists of facts, statistics, experiences, comparisons, and examples that demonstrate why the claim is valid. The author of "Ageism: Creeping to the Forefront" offers a convincing example of the media's influence on society's perception of older people (reality TV).

- **Emotional appeals** are ideas that are targeted toward needs or values that readers are likely to care about. Needs include physiological needs (food, drink, shelter) and psychological needs (sense of belonging, sense of accomplishment, sense of self-worth, sense of competency). In "Ageism: Creeping to the Forefront," the author tells a story about his own elderly father in order to gain the reader's sympathy and agreement. Emotional appeals are often not fair or logical; for information on identifying and evaluating emotional appeals, see Section 10e (p. 254).

4. **Some arguments offer a refutation that considers opposing viewpoints and may attempt to disprove or discredit them.** Not all arguments include refutations, however. In "Ageism: Creeping to the Forefront," the author has not provided any refutation. However, the case might be made that reality TV is far from realistic and that we cannot measure society's approach to an entire group of people through TV shows like *Real Housewives* or *Jersey Shore*.

### EXERCISE 10-3 . . . IDENTIFYING CLAIMS

*Identify whether each of the following is a claim of fact (F), a claim of value (V), or claim of policy (P).*

_____ 1. Convicted criminals who cannot read and write should be required to enroll in literacy programs while serving their time in prison.

_____ 2. Many political scientists believe low voter turnout in elections is the result of voter cynicism and disgust with politics and politicians.

_____ 3. Texting while driving has become a problem of epidemic proportions.

_____ 4. All food-service workers should be required to wear hairnets and plastic gloves.

_____ 5. Testing cosmetics on rabbits and other innocent creatures is wrong.

### EXERCISE 10-4 . . . WRITING CLAIMS

*For two of the following contemporary issues, write two claims about the issue. For each issue, try to write two different types of claims.*

1. selling property in the United States to non-U.S. citizens

2. outsourcing of U.S. jobs abroad (to India, China, and elsewhere)

3. privacy concerns with Facebook

4. employers' electronic monitoring of employees

## 10d    STRATEGIES FOR READING AN ARGUMENT

**LEARNING OBJECTIVE 4**
**Read arguments**

Arguments need to be read slowly and carefully. Plan to read an argument more than once. The first time you read it, try to get an overview of its three essential elements: *issue*, *claim*, and *support*. Then reread it more carefully to closely follow the author's line of reasoning and to identify and evaluate the evidence provided.

### Thinking Before You Read

As you prepare to read an argument, ask yourself the following questions:

1. **What does the title suggest?** Before you read, preview following the guidelines in Section 1b and ask yourself what the title suggests about the issue, claim, and/or support.

2. **Who is the author, and what are his or her qualifications?** Check to see if you recognize the author or if any information about the author is included in a head note (or at the end of the book or article). Evaluate whether the author is qualified to write about the issue. The author's specific qualifications signal the credibility of the evidence provided.

3. **What is the date of publication?** Checking the date will prompt you to consider whether new, even possibly contradictory, evidence has recently developed.

4. **What do I already know about the issue or question being discussed?** Try brainstorming using a two-column pro/con list. By thinking about the issue on your own, before you read, you are less likely to be swayed by the writer's appeals and more likely to think about and evaluate the reasons and evidence objectively.

## Reading Actively

Use the following specific strategies as you begin reading an argument.

1. **Read once for an initial impression and the "big picture."** Identify the specific claim the writer is making and identify the reasons and evidence that support it.

2. **Reread the argument.** Read the argument again to examine whether the writer acknowledges or refutes opposing viewpoints. Evaluate the strength of the evidence and arguments as you read.

3. **Annotate while you read.** Record your thoughts; note ideas you agree with, those you disagree with, questions that come to mind, additional reasons or evidence overlooked by the author, and the counterarguments not addressed by the author. (For more information on annotation, see Section 8c, p. 205.)

4. **Highlight key terms and definitions.** Often, an argument depends on how certain terms are defined. In an argument on the destruction of Amazon rain forests, for example, what does "destruction" mean? Does it mean building homes within a forest, or does it refer to clearing the land for timber or to create fields for growing food crops like corn or wheat?

5. **Use a map or diagram to analyze structure.** Because many arguments are complex, you may find it helpful to map or diagram them (see Section 8f, p. 212), which may help you discover bias, claims for which evidence is not provided, or an imbalance between reasons and emotional appeals. You can use the format shown in Figure 10-1 (page 249) to help you analyze the structure of an argument.

### EXERCISE 10-5 . . . PREVIEWING AND READING AN ARGUMENT

*Preview but do <u>not</u> read the following argument. (For previewing guidelines, see Section 1b, p. 4.) Complete the activities that follow.*

**Issue: Welfare and Government Assistance**

## The Myth of the Ghetto Welfare Queen

Non-white stereotypes have long existed in American society—from cartoon images and television characters to iconic figures such as Aunt Jemima. One image that persists is that of the "ghetto welfare queen," typically portrayed as a lazy African American woman who uses her situation, and often her children, to cheat the welfare system. This image came to the forefront during Ronald Reagan's run for the Republican presidential nomination in 1976, when he used the example of an African American woman who had been arrested for welfare fraud. She allegedly used dozens of different names and Social Security cards and her children to collect numerous benefits, including welfare checks.

What is true about welfare recipients, contrary to the image of the welfare queen, is that the largest group of people receiving welfare benefits is children. According to data from a 2008 census, food-stamp recipients are 30 percent White, 22 percent Black, 15 percent Hispanic, 4 percent Native American, and 26 percent other. Furthermore, data from 1998 show that Black women accounted for only about 10 percent of total welfare recipients. So how did this image of a poor Black woman who abuses the welfare system come to be?

Historically, Blacks have not received a significant amount of public aid. A study conducted by the U.S. Department of Labor in 1931 showed that of families receiving mothers' pensions, 3 percent were Black, 93 percent were White, and 1 percent were of "other racial extractions." During this time, Blacks did not have the same access to public programs as Whites, particularly Blacks who lived in areas in which 19 percent to 45 percent of the families were Black. This was done through a "suitable home" clause that made Black women who lived in certain neighborhoods and who did not have husbands ineligible for public aid because their homes were considered "immoral." In the 1960s, politicians missed out on an opportunity to head off dependency on public aid by failing to pass a bill that would create a living wage for working families. This type of legislation had the opportunity to decrease poverty and reduce the need for many families, of all races, to accept public aid.

The media reinforces the false perception that connects Black women to welfare. In a 1999 experiment by a UCLA political scientist about race, gender, and welfare coverage in the news, viewers were shown a general news report that also contained a short segment on welfare. Respondents were grouped into four categories. One group was shown an image of a White woman, the second group was shown an image of a Black woman, the third group saw no image, and the fourth group (the control group) was not shown the news report at all. The results indicated that the overwhelming majority of viewers remembered the Black woman from the welfare segment and less than half remembered the White woman. The researchers suggest there is a cultural script of "Black woman on welfare" that is common knowledge in our society. Opposition to welfare spending increased in White viewers who saw the Black woman, compared to those who saw the report with no image. One surprising result was that people who identified as having liberal views and who saw the White woman showed the biggest increase in negative sentiments toward Blacks. The researchers suggest that the White liberal respondents blame Black women for their racial peers' plight.

—adapted from Scott, *Think Race and Ethnicity*, p. 165

1. What does the title suggest about the issue, claim, or evidence? _____

_____

2. What do you already know about the issue? Brainstorm a two-column "pro/con" list.

   *Now read the selection from start to finish and answer the following questions.*

3. What was your initial impression as you read? _____

_____

4. What is the writer's specific claim? _____

_____

5. Which key terms did you highlight? _____

## 10e   STRATEGIES FOR EVALUATING AN ARGUMENT

**LEARNING OBJECTIVE 5**
**Evaluate arguments**

Once you have understood an argument by identifying what is asserted and how it is asserted, you are ready to evaluate its soundness, correctness, and validity. The factors you need to consider in evaluating an argument are the accuracy of evidence and premises, the relevancy and sufficiency of evidence and premises, whether terms are clearly defined, the relationship between cause and effect, the presence of a stated or implied value system, whether opposing viewpoints are recognized and/or refuted, and the presence of unfair emotional appeals.

### Accuracy of Evidence and Premises

Evaluating an argument involves assessing the accuracy and correctness of the statements on which the argument is based. As a critical reader, your task is to assess whether the evidence or premises are sufficient to support the claim. Here are some questions to consider when evaluating evidence and premises:

### Questions to Ask When Evaluating Evidence and Premises

1. **Is the observer biased?** Did he or she exaggerate or incorrectly perceive a situation?

2. **Are the examples typical and representative?** That is, do the examples fairly represent the situation? Or has the writer used uncommon or rare examples, which weaken the argument?

3. **Are statistics used fairly and clearly?** Many people are impressed by statistics—the reporting of figures, percentages, averages, and so forth—and

assume they are irrefutable. Actually, statistics can be misused, misinterpreted, or used selectively to provide a biased or inaccurate view of the situation. Approach statistical evidence with a critical, questioning attitude.

4. **Are comparisons realistic and true?** The reliability of comparisons depends on how closely the comparison corresponds or how similar it is to the situation to which it is being compared. For example, Martin Luther King Jr. in his famous letter from the Birmingham jail, compared nonviolent protesters to a robbed man. To evaluate this comparison, you need to consider how the two are similar and how they are different.

## Relevancy and Sufficiency of Evidence

Once you have identified the evidence used to support an argument, you must determine whether the evidence provided directly supports the claim and whether sufficient evidence has been provided. This is always a matter of judgment; there are no easy rules to follow.

Suppose you are reading an article in your campus newspaper arguing that an introduction to literature course should not be required of all students at your college. As evidence, the writer includes the following statement:

> Studying literature does not prepare us for the job market. Nobody ever got a job based on his or her ability to analyze a poem or short story.

These statements provide neither adequate nor sufficient evidence. The writer does nothing to substantiate his statements about the irrelevancy of the course to the job market. For you to take the argument seriously, the writer would need to provide facts, statistics, expert opinion, and/or other forms of relevant, accurate documentation.

## Definition of Terms

A clear and effective argument carefully defines key terms and uses them consistently. For example, an essay arguing for or against animal rights should clearly define the term *animal rights*, describe or define those rights, and use that definition through the argument.

The following two paragraphs discuss the topic of illegal immigrants, sometimes called undocumented workers. In the first paragraph, the author defines the terms *undocumented workers* and *underground economy*, explaining how the two terms are related and how undocumented workers come to the United States and how they find work. In the second paragraph, the term *undocumented workers* is used, but the focus is on the controversies involved in preventing illegal immigration from Mexico. The terms *illegal migrant* and *undocumented worker* are not defined. Thus, someone reading the second paragraph might well ask, "But what exactly does *undocumented worker* mean?" Also note the differences in tone and purpose between the two paragraphs.

**Issue: Immigration**

### Paragraph 1—Specific Definitions

The million or so illegal immigrants who enter the United States each year are a part of the *underground economy*, the set of economic activities—whether legal or illegal—that people don't report to the government. Often called *undocumented workers* (referred to as *los sin documentos* in Mexico), they work for employers who either ignore their fake Social Security cards or pay them in cash. I asked a housekeeper from Mexico who had entered the United States illegally if she had a "green card" (the card given to immigrants who enter the country legally). She said that she did, adding, "They're sold on the street like candy."

—adapted from Henslin, *Sociology*, p. 403

### Paragraph 2—Discussion Without Definition

In 2005, the House of Representatives initiated legislation to reform U.S. immigration policy, particularly to stem a flow of undocumented workers now thought to have brought in 10 million people, more than half from Mexico. Opinions clashed, often along party lines, on proposals for amnesty programs, "guest worker" provisions, and the sanctioning and deportation of illegal migrants. One proposal proved especially divisive: a plan to construct a huge, high-tech, double-layered fence along the 2,000-mile U.S.–Mexico border, including powerful lighting, radar, cameras, and even unmanned aircraft. The Border Patrol would be augmented by 1,500 new troops.

—adapted from Faragher et al., *Out of Many*, p. 928

## Cause and Effect Relationships

Arguments are often built around the assumption of a cause and effect relationship. For example, an argument supporting gun-control legislation may claim that ready availability of guns contributes to an increased number of shootings. This argument implies that the easy availability of guns causes increased use of guns. If the writer provides no evidence that this cause and effect relationship exists, you should question the validity of the argument. (For more on cause and effect, see Section 6e, p. 160.)

## Implied or Stated Value System

An argument often implies or rests on a **value system** (a consistent set of ethical values regarding what is right, wrong, worthwhile, and important). Although our culture promotes many major common values (murder is wrong, human life is worthwhile, and so forth), there is ample room for disagreement. In addition, everyone possesses a personal value system that may sometimes clash with the larger social value system. For example, one person may think telling lies is always wrong; another person may say that the morality of lying depends on the circumstances. Some people have a value system based on religious beliefs; others may not share those same religious beliefs.

In evaluating an argument, look for value judgments and then decide whether the judgments are consistent with and acceptable to your personal value system. Here are a few examples of value judgments:

> Marriage should be defined as the union between one man and one woman.
>
> Torturing terrorists and enemy combatants until they provide information is a violation of basic human rights.
>
> People with disabilities should have access to the same opportunities and public locations that people without disabilities enjoy.

## Recognizing and Refuting Opposing Viewpoints

Many, but not all, arguments recognize opposing viewpoints. For example, a writer may argue against gun control, but he or she may recognize the opposing viewpoint that more guns means more shootings. Many arguments also attempt to refute opposing viewpoints (that is, explain why they are wrong, flawed, or unacceptable). To refute an opposing viewpoint, the author finds weaknesses in the opponent's argument. One way to do this is to question the accuracy, relevancy, or sufficiency of the opponent's evidence. Another way is to disagree with the opponent's reasons. A writer arguing against gun control may disagree with the statement "More guns means more shootings" by stating, "Guns don't kill people; people kill people."

When reading arguments that address opposing viewpoints, ask yourself the following questions:

- Does the writer address opposing viewpoints clearly and fairly?
- How many opposing viewpoints does the writer address? Have any opposing viewpoints been omitted?
- Does the writer refute the opposing viewpoint with logic and relevant evidence?

## Unfair Emotional Appeals

Emotional appeals attempt to involve or excite readers by appealing to their emotions, thereby shaping the reader's attitude toward the subject. Arguments often make use of the following emotional appeals. Because these arguments are based on emotion, they often do not stand up to close scrutiny.

1. **Emotionally charged or biased language.** By using words that create an emotional response, writers establish positive or negative feelings. For example, an advertisement for a new line of luxury automobiles promises to "indulge" and "pamper" the driver, using phrases such as "limousine comfort," "supple leather," and "animal sleekness" to interest drivers.

2. **False authority.** False authority involves using the opinion or action of a famous person or celebrity. We have all seen athletes endorsing sports drinks and movie stars selling shampoo and other consumer products. This type of appeal works on the notion that people admire celebrities, respect their opinions, and strive to be like them.

3. **Association.** A writer can make an emotional appeal by associating a product, idea, or position with others that are already accepted or highly regarded. Patriotism is valued in American society, so describing a product as "All-American" in an advertisement is an appeal to the emotions. An ad picturing a scenic waterfall and a person standing in front of an American flag are two more examples of association appeal.

4. **Appeal to "common folk."** Some people distrust those who are well educated, wealthy, highly artistic, or in other ways distinctly different from the average person. An emotional appeal can be made to this group by indicating that a product or idea originated from, is held by, or is bought by "ordinary citizens." For example, a commercial may advertise a product by showing its use in an average household. A politician may describe her background and education to suggest that she is like everyone else; a salesperson may dress in styles similar to his clients'. The next time you are watching a political debate, notice how many times the politicians use the word "folks" to imply that they are thinking about the interests of the average, or common, person.

5. **Ad hominem.** An argument that attacks the holder of an opposing viewpoint, rather than the viewpoint itself, is known as an *ad hominem*, or an attack on the man, argument. For example, the question, "How could a woman who does not even hold a college degree criticize a judicial decision?" attacks the woman and her level of education, not her viewpoint.

6. **"Join the crowd" appeal.** The appeal to do, believe, or buy what everyone else is doing, believing, or buying is known as *crowd appeal* or the *bandwagon effect*. Commercials that proclaim their product as the "#1 best-selling bottled water" use crowd appeal. Essays that cite opinion polls on a controversial issue in support of a position—"62 percent of Americans favor spending cuts to decrease the federal deficit"—also use this appeal.

## EXERCISE 10-6 . . . ANALYZING EVIDENCE

*Reread the argument "The Myth of the Ghetto Welfare Queen," on page 253, paying particular attention to the type(s) of evidence used. Then answer the questions that follow.*

1. What type(s) of evidence is/are used? _____

_____

_____

2. Is the evidence convincing? _____

3. Is there sufficient evidence? _____

4. What other types of evidence could have been used to strengthen the argument? _____

5. Is the term "ghetto welfare queen" adequately defined? _____

6. Which cause and effect relationships does the writer discuss? _____

_____

_____

7. What implied value system is found in the argument? _____

_____

8. Does the writer recognize and/or refute opposing viewpoints? _____

## EXERCISE 10-7 . . . ANALYZING EMOTIONAL APPEALS

*All of the following statements make use of an emotional appeal. Specify which emotional appeal on the line provided.*

_____  1. Now you, too, can have hair as beautiful as Jennifer Aniston's.

_____  2. Give your family the best by using Tide, America's best-selling laundry detergent.

_____  3. Does anyone really agree with fat, unattractive Rush Limbaugh's opinions on immigration?

_____  4. Vote for Jane Rodriguez. She knows what it's like to struggle to raise a family and pay the bills.

_____  5. Tolerance of polygamy can only lead to the death of the American family and the complete destruction of American morality.

## 10f   ERRORS IN LOGIC

**LEARNING OBJECTIVE 6**
Recognize errors in logic

Errors in reasoning, often called **logical fallacies**, are common in arguments. These errors invalidate the argument or render it flawed. This section describes several common errors in logic.

## Circular Reasoning

Also known as *begging the question*, **circular reasoning** involves using part of the conclusion as evidence to support that conclusion. Here are two examples.

> Female firefighters should not be sent to fight blazing fires because firefighting is a man's job.
>
> Cruel bullying of children is inhumane.

In an argument that uses circular reasoning, there is no reason to accept the conclusion because no evidence is given to support the claim.

## False Analogy

An analogy is an extended comparison between two otherwise unlike things. A sound analogy assumes that the two things are alike in some ways. A **false analogy** compares two things that do not share a likeness. A writer arguing against control may say,

> "Guns are not a major problem in this country. Fatal accidents on the road, in the workplace, and at home kill many more people than guns do."

Here the writer is suggesting that death by guns is similar to fatal accidents in the car, on the job, or at home. Yet, accidents and murder are not similar.

## Hasty Generalization

**Hasty generalization** occurs when a conclusion is derived from insufficient evidence. Here are two examples:

> A person listens to one piece of classical music and does not like it, so she concludes that she does not like classical music.
>
> By observing one performance of a musical group, a person concludes the group is unfit to perform.

## Non Sequitur ("It Does Not Follow")

The false establishment of cause and effect is a **non sequitur** (from Latin for "it does not follow"). For example, "Because my doctor is young, I'm sure she'll be a good doctor" is a non sequitur because youth does not ensure good medical practices. Here is another example of a non sequitur: "Arturo Alvarez is the best choice for state senator because he is an ordinary citizen." Being an ordinary citizen will not necessarily make someone an effective senator.

## False Cause

The **false cause** fallacy is the incorrect assumption that two events that follow each other in time are causally related. In other words, false cause implies that an event that happened later had to be caused by an event that happened earlier. Suppose you open an umbrella and then trip on an uneven sidewalk. If you said you tripped because you opened the umbrella, you would be committing the error of false cause. Or suppose you walk out of your house and it starts to rain. You would be committing the false-cause error if you suggest that it started to rain because you walked out of your house.

## Either–Or Fallacy

The **either–or fallacy** assumes that an issue has only two sides, or that there are only two choices or alternatives for a particular situation. In other words, there is no middle ground. Consider the issue of censoring TV violence. An either–or fallacy would assume that TV violence must be either permitted or banned. This fallacy does not recognize other alternatives such as limiting access through viewing hours, restricting certain types of violence, and so on.

## Abstract Concepts as Reality

Writers occasionally treat abstract concepts as absolute truths with a single acceptable position or outcome. For example, a writer may say, "Research proves that divorce is harmful to children." Actually, there are hundreds of pieces of research on the effects of divorce, and they offer diverse findings and conclusions. Some but not all research reports harmful effects. Here is another example: "Criminology shows us that prisons are seldom effective in controlling crime." Writers tend to use this device to make it seem as if all authorities are in agreement with their position. This device also allows writers to ignore contrary or contradictory evidence or opinions.

## Red Herring

A **red herring** is something added to an argument to divert attention from the issue at hand. It is introduced into an argument to throw readers off track. Think of a red herring as an argumentative tactic rather than an error in reasoning. Suppose you are reading an essay that argues against the death penalty. If the author suddenly starts reporting the horrific living conditions in death-row prisons and the unjust treatment of prisoners, the writer is introducing a red herring. The living conditions and treatment of prisoners on death row are valid issues, but they are not relevant to an argument that the death penalty is unjust.

### EXERCISE 10-8 . . . IDENTIFYING ERRORS IN LOGIC

*Identify the logical fallacy in each of the following statements.*

_____ 1. All Asian American students in my economics class earned A grades, so Asian Americans must excel in studying economics.

_____ 2. If you don't believe in global warming, then you clearly don't care about the earth.

_____    3. My sister cannot do mathematical computations or balance her checkbook because she suffers from depression.

_____    4. A well-known mayor, noting a decline in the crime rate in the four largest cities in his state, quickly announced that his new "get-tough on criminals" policy was successful and took credit for the decline.

_____    5. The instructor's apartment was robbed because she left her apartment without her cell phone.

## Supporting Your Position

As discussed on page 250, there are two primary types of support that can be used to explain why your position should be accepted: **reasons**—general statements that back up a position—and **evidence**, which includes facts and statistics, quotations from authorities, examples, and personal experience. Each is discussed in more detail in the section on writing argument essays.

## 10g    WRITE ARGUMENT ESSAYS

**LEARNING OBJECTIVE 7**
Write argument essays

The skills you learned for writing an argument paragraph apply to essay writing as well. See Chapter 11 for detailed coverage of essay-writing techniques. Use these guidelines to write an effective argument essay.

### Writing a Thesis Statement

Your thesis statement should identify the issue and state your claim about it. It may also suggest the primary reasons for accepting the claim. Place your thesis statement where it will be most effective. There are three common placements:

1. Thesis statement in the beginning
2. Thesis statement after responding to objections
3. Thesis statement at the end

In general, placing the thesis in the beginning is best when addressing an audience in agreement with your claim or one that is neutral about the topic under discussion. For an audience that does not agree with your argument, a later placement gives you the opportunity to respond to the audience's objections before you present your thesis.

### Providing Adequate Supporting Evidence

Here are five types of supporting evidence you can use to develop your thesis:

## Facts and Statistics

As in writing any other type of paragraph or essay, you must choose facts that directly support the position you express in your topic sentence. Here is an excerpt that uses facts and statistics as evidence to argue that the population of the United States is aging:

**Issue: Population Aging**

### Population Aging and the "Graying" of the Globe

The United Nations categorizes countries in which 7 percent or more of the population is over age 65 as "aged." Although many developing nations still have short life expectancies and young populations, the United States and most industrialized and postindustrial nations meet the criterion for "aged," and by 2020 almost all nations will (Novak, 2009). The United State is experiencing a "senior boom" due to the rapid growth of its elderly population. In 1900, people over age 65 made up only about 4 percent of the U.S. population (about 1 in 25 people); by 2010 over 14 percent, or more than 1 in 7 Americans (34.8 million), were over age 65. Today, that figure is approximately 44 million (U.S. Bureau of Census, 2009). Demographic projections indicate that by the year 2050, approximately 82 million Americans (over twice as many as today) will be over the age of 65. The 85 and older population in the United States stands at approximately 5.5 million and is also increasing dramatically. Currently, people over the age of 100 (centenarians) are the fastest-growing segment of the U.S. population, numbering over 72,000 (Huffington Post 4/26/11).

—Thompson and Hickey, *Society in Focus*, pp. 328–329

It is usually more effective to present more than one statistic. Suppose you are writing to convince taxpayers that state lotteries have become profitable businesses. You might state that more than 60 percent of the adult population now buy lottery tickets regularly. This statistic would have little meaning by itself. However, if you were to state that 60 percent of adults now purchase lottery tickets, whereas five years ago only 30 percent purchased them, the first statistic would become more meaningful.

In selecting statistics to support your position, be sure to consider the following:

1. **Obtain statistics from reliable print or online sources.** These include almanacs, encyclopedias, articles in reputable journals and magazines, or other trustworthy reference material from your library. Online sources include databases, online journals, and scholarly Web sites.

2. **Use up-to-date information, preferably from the past year or two.** Dated statistics may be incorrect or misleading.

3. **Make sure you define terms and units of measurement.** For example, if you say that 60 percent of adults regularly play the lottery, you should define what "regularly" means. Does it mean daily, weekly, or monthly?

4. **Verify that the statistics you obtain from more than one source are comparable.** For example, if you compare the crime rates in New York City and Los Angeles, be sure that each crime rate was computed the same way, that each represents the same types of crimes, and that report sources were similar.

### Quotations or Citations from Authorities

You can also support your claim by using expert or authoritative statements of opinion or conclusions. **Experts** or **authorities** are those who have studied a subject extensively, conducted research on it, or written widely about it. For example, if you are writing an essay calling for stricter preschool-monitoring requirements to prevent child abuse, the opinion of a psychiatrist who works extensively with abused children would provide convincing support.

### Examples

Refer to Chapter 5 for a review of how to use examples as supporting details. In an argument essay, your examples must represent your claim and should illustrate as many aspects of your claim as possible. Suppose your claim is that a particular movie should have been rated NC-17 because it contains excessive violence. The evidence you choose to support this claim should be clear, vivid examples of violent scenes.

The examples you choose should also, if possible, relate to your audience's experience. Familiar examples are more appealing, convincing, and understandable. Suppose you are taking a position on abortion. You're audience consists of career women between 30 and 40 years old. It would be most effective to use as examples women of the same age and occupational status.

### Personal Experience

If you are knowledgeable about a subject, your personal experiences can be convincing evidence. For example, if you were writing an essay supporting the position that physical separation from parents encourages a teenager or young adult to mature, you could discuss your own experiences with leaving home and assuming new responsibilities.

### Comparisons and Analogies

Comparison and analogies (extended comparisons) are useful, especially when writing for an audience that lacks background and experience with your subject. By comparing something unknown to something that is known and familiar, you can make your readers comfortable and nonthreatened. For example, you could explain a new dance step by likening it to dance steps that are traditional and familiar to most readers. Be sure to make it clear which characteristics or features are similar and which are not.

---

**EXERCISE 10-9 . . . SUPPORTING A TOPIC SENTENCE**

*Select a topic from the list below, generate ideas, and write a thesis statement. Then generate reasons and evidence to support your thesis.*

1. Advantages of nanotechnology
2. The right of insurance companies to deny medical coverage to certain individuals
3. Preventing teenage pregnancy
4. Disposing of toxic waste
5. Why people should be vegetarians
6. Buying American-made products
7. Wet land preservation
8. Prosecuting people who download music

## Researching Your Topic

An **argument essay** must provide specific and convincing evidence that supports the thesis statement. Often it is necessary to go beyond your own knowledge and experience. You may need to research your topic. For example, if you were writing to urge the creation of an environmentally protected wetland area, you would need to find out what types of wildlife live there, which are endangered, and how successful other protected wetland sites have been in protecting wildlife.

At other times, you may need to interview people who are experts on your topic or directly involved with it. Suppose you are writing a memo urging other employees in your department to participate in a walk-a-thon. It is being held to benefit a local shelter for homeless men and women. The director of the shelter or one of her employees could offer useful statistics, share personal experiences, and provide specific details about the clientele the shelter serves that would help you make a convincing case.

### EXERCISE 10-10 . . . EVALUATING EVIDENCE

*Evaluate the evidence you collected in Exercise 10-9, and research your topic further if needed. Write the first draft of the essay. Exchange essays with a classmate and critique each other's essays. Revise using your classmate's suggestion.*

Here is a sample argument written by one student. Note how he presents reasons and evidence for taking a specific action.

### Buckle Up

As a paramedic, I am the first to arrive at the scene of many grim and tragic accidents. One awful accident last month involved four women in one car. The front-seat passenger died instantly, another died during a mercy flight to the nearest hospital, one lost both legs, and one walked away from the accident without serious injury. Only one woman was wearing a seat belt. Guess which one? <u>Though many people protest and offer excuses, seat belts do save lives.</u>

Many people avoid wearing seat belts and say they would rather be thrown free from an accident. Yet they seldom realize that the rate at which they will be thrown is the same rate at which the car is moving. Others fear being trapped inside by their seat belt in case of a fire. However, if not ejected, those without a belt are likely to be stunned or knocked unconscious on impact and will not be alert enough to escape uninjured.

Seat belts save lives by protecting passengers from impact. During a crash, a body slams against the windshield or steering wheel with tremendous force if unbelted. The seat belt secures the passenger in place and protects vital organs from injury.

Recent statistics demonstrate that a passenger is five times more likely to survive a crash if a seat belt is worn. Life is a gamble, but those are good odds. Buckle up!

This writer introduces the topic with a startling example from his personal experience. The thesis statement occurs at the end of the first paragraph. The second and third paragraphs offer evidence that supports the writer's thesis. The last paragraph concludes the essay by offering a convincing statistic and reminding the reader of the thesis, "Buckle up." You can visualize this short argument as follows:

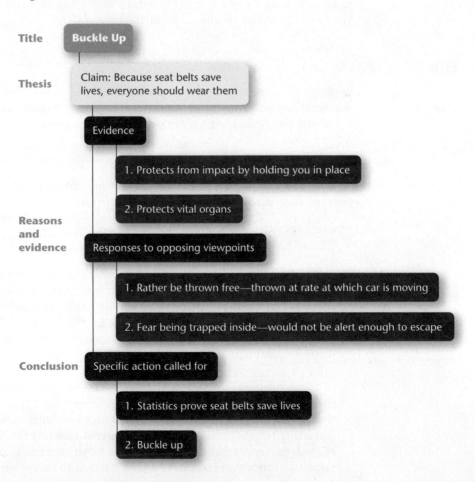

**Title**  Buckle Up

**Thesis**  Claim: Because seat belts save lives, everyone should wear them

Evidence

1. Protects from impact by holding you in place

2. Protects vital organs

**Reasons and evidence**  Responses to opposing viewpoints

1. Rather be thrown free—thrown at rate at which car is moving

2. Fear being trapped inside—would not be alert enough to escape

**Conclusion**  Specific action called for

1. Statistics prove seat belts save lives

2. Buckle up

## Responding to Opposing Ideas

It is helpful to respond to opposing ideas that do not support your claim. Your readers will regard you as fair and honest if you admit that there are ideas, opinions, and evidence that express opposite or differing viewpoints about your topic. There are three ways you can accomplish this.

1. **You can acknowledge the opposing viewpoint.** This means you admit that other viewpoints exist and that you have considered them. For example, if you are writing that voluntary community service should be a mandatory part of a college degree program, you can admit that college students are already stressed from studying and working.

2. **You can accommodate the opposing viewpoint by using part of it in your own argument.** For the argument about mandatory community service, you could write that although college students are already busy and stressed, community service would help relieve that pressure and stress by providing a hands-on, uplifting experience.

3. **You can refute the opposing viewpoint by explaining why it is wrong.** For the community service argument you could refute the opposing idea that college students cannot waste time with community service by arguing that it will give students new viewpoints and experiences that will help them in securing work after they graduate.

## Analyzing Your Audience

Analyzing your audience is a crucial step in planning a convincing argument. There are three types of audiences:

- **Audiences who agree with your claim.** These are the easiest to write for because they already accept most of what you will say. Audiences in agreement with you are likely to have positive feelings toward you because you think the way they do about the issue. For this audience, state your claim and explain why you think it is correct.

- **Neutral audiences.** These readers have not made up their minds or have not given much thought to the issue. They may have questions, they may misunderstand the issue, or they may have heard arguments supporting the opposing viewpoint. An essay written for a neutral audience should be direct and straightforward, like those written for an audience in agreement with your point of view. However, a fuller explanation of the issue is necessary to answer questions, clear up misunderstandings, and respond to opposing arguments.

- **Audiences who disagree with your claim.** These are the most difficult to address. Some members will have thought about the issue and taken a position that opposes yours. Others who disagree may not have examined the issue at all and may be making superficial judgments or may be relying on misinformation. Both types think their position is correct, so they will not be eager to change their minds. They may also distrust you because you think differently from them. For such an audience, your biggest challenge is to build trust and confidence. Before writing, carefully analyze this audience and try to answer these questions:

- **Why does your audience disagree with your claim?**
- **Is their position based on real facts and sound evidence, or on personal opinion?** If it is based on evidence, what type?
- **What type of arguments or reasons are most likely to appeal to your audience?** For example, will they be convinced by facts and statistics, or by statements made by authorities? Would personal anecdotes and examples work well?

Once you understand how your audience thinks, you can plan your essay more effectively.

Quinne Sember is a student at the State University of New York at Buffalo where she is a pre-medical student majoring in political science and biomedical science. Sember wrote this essay for a political science class. She was asked to choose an issue discussed in class and write an essay taking a position on the issue.

---

Sember 1

Quinne Sember

Dr. Thomas

ENG 112

18 March 2013

Marijuana: An Argument for Legalization

Marijuana is a commonly used drug in the United States. It is not as dangerous or addictive as alcohol or tobacco. Yet alcohol and tobacco are legal in the United States, while marijuana is not. It costs the United States millions of dollars to prosecute and detain people who possess marijuana when the government could be making money taxing the substance. The argument for the legalization of marijuana is a strong one and many people support a law that would take this action.

Sember 2

The economic effect of the criminalization of marijuana in the U.S. is astounding. We create a large number of criminals by sentencing people for non-violent acts, including possession of marijuana. The United States holds 25% of the world's prisoners, but has only 5% of its total population. We also spend $68 billion dollars just on corrections and one third of that money is spent on people serving time for drug crimes that are non-violent. In addition to that money, another $150 billion is spent on courts and police activity. The majority (47.5%) is spent on marijuana activity (Klein). For a nation that is in so much debt, that is a large amount of money that could be spent elsewhere. Shouldn't we improve the roads or healthcare before we spend so much money on people who are not committing violent crimes?

Legalization of marijuana, besides saving the country money, could also help us to make money. Taxation of the drug would produce considerable profits. In a report sent to the president, authored by Jeffrey Miron, it is estimated that the taxation of marijuana could produce $2.4 billion in revenue If it were taxed like most other consumer drugs. If it were taxed like alcohol, however, it could produce up to $6.2 billion per year (Moffatt). With the combined savings, the country could be over $200 billion richer with the legalization of marijuana. The government could make even more money if licenses were required to grow the plant. That is an astonishing amount of money that could be spent on healthcare, schools, or infrastructure. Miron's report was signed by over 500 economists who ensured its accuracy (Moffatt). Obviously, regulation and education about marijuana are more logical than the criminalization of its users.

Marijuana can have an effect on health and it is not always a negative one. Many people utilize the drug to assist them with medical conditions. Cannabis

Sember 3

can help to alleviate the symptoms of multiple sclerosis, Crohn's disease, and other inflammatory diseases. It can also increase appetite in people who are struggling with chemotherapy. In a handful of states, doctors can prescribe medical marijuana for these conditions. However, people in states where medical marijuana is illegal are out of luck. It is also very difficult for people without a specific disease who have other problems for which marijuana could be helpful to get medical marijuana. Nathan Seppa says "people smoke the drug to alleviate pain, sleep easier and deal with nausea, lack of appetite and mood disorders such as anxiety, stress and depression" (Seppa). The American Medical Association has recognized that marijuana can have a positive effect on nausea, glaucoma, extreme muscle tension, and pain (Cloud). With the legalization of marijuana, people could buy the drug on their own accord to treat whatever symptoms they may have without having to battle with a doctor to get a prescription.

Maybe the most convincing evidence for the legalization of marijuana is that people support it. A Gallup poll from 2009 shows that 44% of Americans favored legalizing the drug, while 54% opposed it. This was the highest rate since the poll started in 1970. The rate has continued to grow by one to two percent each year (Saad). Therefore, by 2012, the legalization of marijuana could be supported by a majority of the population. This was already the case in the West in 2009, where 53% of people favored legalization.

If this is not enough evidence, even the former U.S. Surgeon General, Joycelyn Elders, supports legalization. She told CNN, "What I think is horrible about all of this, is that we criminalize young people. And we use so many of our excellent resources . . . for things that aren't really causing any problems. It's not a toxic substance." Elders says that we have the "highest number of

Sember 4

people in the world being criminalized, many for non-violent crimes related to marijuana" (CNN). She strongly believes that our resources can be put to better use.

Marijuana legalization is opposed by some who claim it has a negative impact on health; however, marijuana is actually much healthier than tobacco or alcohol. No one has ever died of THC (the active chemical in the marijuana) poisoning or overdose (Cloud). People die every day from the effects of tobacco and alcohol and these drugs are legal. Tobacco is proven to cause cancer and while there has not been any evidence to show that smoking marijuana does cause cancer, there have not been any conclusive studies to show that it does not. Others argue that marijuana is an addictive substance. However, while one-third of tobacco users get hooked and fifteen percent of drinkers become addicted to alcohol, only nine percent of people using marijuana become addicted.

The legalization of marijuana would help a lot of people. It would directly help people who suffer from symptoms of illnesses that can be treated with the drug. It would also indirectly affect children who go to poor schools or people who cannot afford healthcare because of the amount of money that is tied up in the courts, prisons, and police activity regarding marijuana. This money could be used by the government for much more serious and useful things. Many people believe that the legalization and use of marijuana is risky. With education and regulation, this practice would not be any more risky (probably less risky, in fact) than the use of tobacco and alcohol, legal substances in our country.

Sember 5

Works Cited

Cloud, John. "Is Pot Good For You?" TIME. Time Inc., 4 Nov. 2002. Web. 15
   Apr. 2013.

"Former surgeon general calls for marijuana legalization." CNN. Turner Broadcasting System, Inc., 18 Oct. 2010. Web. 17 Apr. 2013.

Klein, Joe. "Why Legalizing Marijuana Makes Sense." TIME. Time Inc., 16 Apr.
   2009. Web. 15 Apr. 2013.

Moffatt, Mike. "Time to Legalize Marijuana?—500+ Economists Endorse
   Marijuana Legalization." About.com. New York Times Company, 2011.
   Web. 15 Apr. 2013.

Saad, Lydia. "U.S. Support for Legalizing Marijuana Reaches New High."
   Gallup. Gallup, Inc., 19 Oct. 2009. Web. 15 Apr. 2013.

Seppa, Nathan. "Not Just a High." Science News 177.13 (2010): 16–20.
   MasterFILE Premier. Web. 15 Apr. 2013.

### EXERCISE 10-11 . . . EXAMINING WRITING

*Analyze the student essay above and answer the following questions.*

1. For what type of audience does Sember seem to be writing—neutral, in agreement, or not in agreement?

2. Did you find her argument convincing? Why or why not?

3. What other reasons could Sember have included?

4. Does Sember rely too heavily on statistics? Why or why not? What other types of evidence could she have included?

## SUMMARY OF LEARNING OBJECTIVES

**MySkillsLab**
Complete the mastery test for this chapter in **MySkillsLab.**

**1** **Understand the connection between contemporary issues and arguments.** *How are contemporary issues and argument connected?*

A **contemporary issue** is a topic that is relevant to individuals, groups, and societies today. Writers often ask questions about aspects of these issues and then write an article, a book, or a blog post in which they state their opinion (often as a thesis sentence) and then provide support for their opinion.

**2** **Define an argument.** *What is an argument?*

An **argument** is a discussion in which a person expresses his or her point of view about a topic. A single issue may have many questions and arguments associated with it.

**3** **Explain the parts of an argument.** *What are the elements of an argument?*

A **good argument has three (sometimes four) parts**. *First*, it addresses an issue, problem or controversy about which people disagree. *Second,* it takes a position (called a claim) on the issue. *Third*, the argument offers support for the claim, usually in the form of reasons, evidence, and sometimes emotional appeals. *Fourth,* some arguments consider opposing viewpoints.

**4** **Read arguments.** *How do you read an argument effectively?*

**To read an argument, think before you read**. Ask yourself: What does the title suggest? Who is the author, and what are his or her qualifications? What is the date of publication? What do I already know about the topic? Then read actively, once for an initial impression, then for specific information. Annotate and highlight key terms. Draw a diagram or map to analyze the argument's structure.

**5** **Evaluate arguments.** *How do evaluate an argument?*

**To evaluate an argument**, consider the accuracy of evidence and premises. Next, examine the relevancy and sufficiency of evidence and whether terms have been clearly and fully defined. Finally, look for unfair emotional appeals (such as *emotionally charged language, false authority, association, appeal to common folk, ad hominem*, and *join the crowd appeal*) and evaluate the author's use of them.

**6** **Recognize errors in logic.** *What are errors and logic and how do you recognize them?*

**Errors in logic,** or *logical fallacies*, invalidate an argument or render it flawed. Be on the lookout for *circular reasoning, false analogies, hasty generalizations, non sequiturs, false causes, the either–or fallacy, abstract concepts presented as reality*, and *red herrings*.

**7** **Write argument essays.** *How do you structure an argument essay?*

To **write an argument essay**, create a thesis statement that identifies the issue and states your claim. Determine what type of audience you have and provide adequate support for your claim, using reasons, examples, facts, statistics, expert opinion, personal experience, and comparisons and analogies. Consider and refute opposing arguments.

# 11 Writing Essays and Documented Papers

## WRITING ESSAYS

## 11a    THE STRUCURE OF AN ESSAY

**LEARNING OBJECTIVE 1**
Structure an essay

An **essay** introduces an idea, states it, explains it, and draws a conclusion about it. Most essays begin with an **introductory paragraph** that states the subject of the essay. It also states the key point the essay will make in the **thesis statement.** **Supporting paragraphs** contain ideas that explain the when, where, and how of the key point. An essay usually has two or more of these paragraphs, which are linked by transition words and sentences. The **concluding paragraph** ties all the ideas in the essay together in relation to the thesis statement. See Chapter 2, page 35, for an idea map of an essay.

## 11b    PREWRITING: GENERATING AND ORGANIZING IDEAS AND PLANNING YOUR ESSAY

**LEARNING OBJECTIVE 2**
Generate and organize ideas and plan your essay

Writing an effective essay requires thought and planning. Use the following prewriting strategies to help you produce a well-written essay.

### Choosing Your Topic

When your instructor gives you an assignment, you might not like the topic, but at least a good part of topic selection and narrowing has been done for you. When your instructor allows you to choose your own topic, you have to brainstorm for ideas and explore possible topics using prewriting. Use the following suggestions to help you choose an appropriate, effective, and workable topic:

#### Tips for Choosing an Appropriate, Effective, and Workable Topic

- **Take time to think about your choice.** Don't grab the first topic you come upon. Instead, think it through and weigh its pros and cons. It is often helpful to think of several topics and then choose the one you feel you are best prepared to write about.
- **Choose a topic that interests you.** You will feel more like writing about it and will find you have more to say.
- **Write about something familiar.** Select a topic you know a fair amount about. Otherwise, you will have to research your topic in the library or online. Your experience and knowledge of a familiar topic will provide the content of your essay.
- **Use your writing journal as a source for ideas.**
- **Discuss possible topics with a friend or classmate.** These conversations may help you discover worthwhile topics.

Table 11-1 on page 276 lists additional sources of ideas for essay topics.

### EXERCISE 11-1 . . . BRAINSTORMING TOPICS

*Make a list of five possible topics you could use to write a two- to three-page, double-spaced essay.*

### Generating Ideas

Once you have chosen a working topic, the next step is to prewrite to generate ideas about it. This step will help you determine whether the topic you have selected is usable. It will also provide you with a list of ideas you can use in

## TABLE 11-1  SOURCES OF IDEAS FOR TOPICS

| SOURCES OF IDEAS | EXAMPLES |
| --- | --- |
| **Your daily life.** Pay attention to events you attend, activities you participate in, and routines you follow. | *Attending a sporting event may suggest topics about professional athletes' salaries, sports injuries, or violence in sports.* |
| **Your college classes.** Class lectures and discussions as well as reading assignments may give you ideas for topics. | *A class discussion in sociology about prejudice and discrimination may suggest you write about racial or ethnic identities, stereotypes, or types of discrimination (age, gender, weight, etc.).* |
| **Your job.** Your responsibilities, your boss, your co-workers, and your customers are all sources of ideas. | *Watching a family with wild, misbehaving children throwing food and annoying other customers in a restaurant may prompt you to write about restaurant policies, child rearing, or rude and annoying behavior.* |
| **The media.** Radio, television, movies, newspapers, magazines, and online sources all contain hundreds of ideas for a topic each day. | *A commercial for a weight-loss product may suggest an essay on society's emphasis on thinness or the unrealistic expectations for body image presented in commercials.* |

planning and developing your essay. If you have trouble generating ideas about a topic, consider changing topics. Here are four methods for generating ideas. (See page 29 in Chapter 2 for a detailed review of each.)

1. **Freewriting.** Write nonstop for a specified time, recording all the ideas that come to mind on the topic.
2. **Brainstorming.** Write a list of all ideas that come to mind about a specific topic.
3. **Questioning.** Write a list of questions about a given topic.
4. **Diagramming.** Draw a diagram showing possible subtopics into which your topic could be divided.

When a student, Ted Sawchuck, was assigned a two-page paper on a topic of his choice, he decided to write about online social networking sites. In this chapter, we will follow Ted as he works through the various stages of the writing process, and we will see his final essay on page 305. To generate ideas, Ted used brainstorming and wrote the following list of ideas:

### Sample Student Brainstorming

Social Networking Sites

Keep tabs on and connect with friends

Create your own profile—describe yourself as you like

Profiles aren't necessarily true or accurate

Receive requests from people who want to friend you

People date online

People cheat on spouses through online relationships

Employers check applicants' Facebook sites

Unless blocked, private information can be seen by strangers

High school students use them too

Facebook and Twitter are popular ones

What did people do before these sites were available?

### EXERCISE 11-2 . . . PREWRITING

*Select one of the topics you listed in Exercise 11-1. Use freewriting, brainstorming, questioning, or branching to generate ideas about the topic.*

## Narrowing Your Topic

Avoid working with a topic that is either too broad or too narrow. If your topic is *too narrow*, you will find you don't have enough to write about. If it is *too broad*, you will have too much to say, which will create several related problems:

- You will tend to write in generalities.
- You will not be able to explore each idea in detail.
- You will probably wander from topic to topic.
- You will become unfocused.

It is difficult to know if your topic is too broad, but here are a few warning signals:

- You feel overwhelmed when you try to think about the topic.
- You don't know where to start.
- You feel as if you are going in circles with ideas.
- You don't know where to stop.

You can use the ideas you generate during brainstorming, freewriting, questioning, or branching to help narrow your topic. Often, more than one round of narrowing is necessary. You may need to reduce a topic several times by dividing it into smaller and smaller subtopics using a prewriting technique or diagram to help you. After studying his brainstorming, Ted decided to write about online relationships. The following diagram shows how he further narrowed the topic of online relationships.

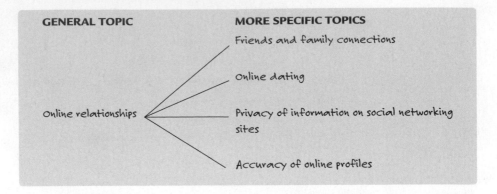

In this way, he wound up with several manageable topics related to online relationships to choose from and decided to write about online dating relationships.

A question many students ask is, "How do I know when to stop narrowing?" For an essay, you will need at least three or four main points to support your thesis. Make sure that you have at least this number and that you can support each one with adequate detail. If you cannot do this, you'll know you have narrowed too far.

---

**EXERCISE 11-3 . . . NARROWING TOPICS**

*Working with a classmate, generate ideas and then narrow one topic you chose for Exercises 11-1 and 11-2. Continue narrowing each one until you find a topic about which you could write a five- to seven-paragraph essay.*

---

## Grouping Ideas to Discover a Thesis Statement

A thesis statement very rarely just springs into a writer's mind: It evolves and, in fact, may change during the process of prewriting, grouping ideas, drafting, and revising. Once you know what you want to write about, the next step is to group or connect your ideas to form a thesis.

Ted discovered more ideas by first freewriting about his topic of online dating. As you can see, he wrote many ideas, far more than he needed, but that gave him choices.

### Sample Student Freewriting

I use Facebook, a popular social networking site, to keep tabs on what my friends do, buy, and feel. Facebook showed me when my friend who'd launched a Facebook crusade to get back his girlfriend left her for good, that my sociology of gender prof is still up at 3 a.m. and the journalism student I'm still interested in is also a fan of Kanye West. I upload videos and post links. It's become an essential part of my life and an essential part of my relationships.

Facebook owns the college crowd because from its September 2004 launch in a Harvard dorm room until September 2006, you needed a .edu address to join. College students made the site their own community, and there was a sense that this was our world even though there's no real way to prevent nonstudents with .edu addresses from joining. The first sign of nonstudents entering what was increasingly seen as a walled community occurred in May 2006 when employers were added as available networks, followed by Facebook opening to the public in September that year.

At the University of Maryland, the dating process goes like this:

1. Get someone's name.
2. Look the person up on Facebook.
3. Use that information to decide how to proceed.

A Facebook search is the first thing I do when I meet someone and she sets off those neurons that make me hum "Maybe it's love." A Facebook page will tell me age, indicate whether or not she's taken, and give me a decent idea (if the profile is not locked) of what image she's trying to present. Note that I don't trust Facebook to tell me who people are—merely who they want to show people they are. I look through photos and see what they value enough to show me. I check posted links, because what someone thinks is worth sharing is another window into who she is.

My first high school girlfriend couldn't even type when we started dating. She eventually got used to instant messaging, but was really slow for a year or two. After that, every relationship I had was conducted at least partially over instant messaging and e-mail at first, and then via text message later.

I e-mailed and instant messaged with romantic interests, eventually meeting a girl named Sunshine in a public chat room, which then were full of actual people instead of the ad-bots that populate them today. We talked via instant messaging for five years with the complete truthfulness you save for someone you're never going to meet in person, and fell in love. We tried to do distance, which is like feeding your heart a subsistence diet, and managed to hold it together with phone calls, instant messages, Skype and the occasional bus trip—17 hours one way. The relationship didn't work out, but technology made it possible. Although for most of our relationship Sunshine was pixels on a screen, she's still the standard by which I judge everyone I date.

I met Maggie at a campus newspaper meeting. After we took a liking to each other, we had a nice moment in her living room, sitting side-by-side in matching black armchairs with our laptops, as I updated my relationship status and she confirmed that we were in a relationship—although it was clear, there's something to be said for your partner being eager to share it with her friends. When we broke up, I defriended her on Facebook because I couldn't bear to read her status updates (or honestly, even realize she existed—the first week is tough), blocked her on my instant messenger, and took her e-mail address out of my contacts list. I deleted her LiveJournal from my bookmarks and finished by updating my relationship status to single. The next day, ten people asked how I was doing before I told anyone about it. Breaking up was hard to do before the Internet. Now my list after leaving someone includes blocking her on instant messaging, taking her e-mail address out of my quick contacts list and out of my e-mail's autocomplete list, avoiding her blog and LiveJournal, blocking her on Twitter, and defriending her on Facebook.

After freewriting, Ted reviewed what he had written and decided to limit his essay to one social network—Facebook. He highlighted usable ideas and tried to group or organize them logically: (1) finding someone to date, (2) dating, and (3) breaking up. Once he had grouped his ideas into these three categories, he wrote a working thesis statement:

| **Working Thesis Statement** | The dating process using Facebook involves screening, dating, and breaking up. |
|---|---|

This working thesis statement identifies his topic—dating online using Facebook—and suggests that he will examine how the dating process works. You can see that this thesis statement grew out of his idea groupings. Furthermore, this thesis statement gives readers clues as to how the essay will be organized; he will discuss the steps in the dating process.

How do you know which ideas to group? Look for connections and relationships among the ideas that you generate during prewriting. Here are some suggestions:

## Ways to Make Connections Between Ideas

1. **Look for categories.** Try to discover ways your ideas can be classified or subdivided. Think of categories as titles or slots in which ideas can be placed. Look for a general term that is broad enough to cover several of your ideas. For example, suppose you are writing a paper on where sexual discrimination occurs. You could break down the topic by location.

| **Sample Thesis Statement** | Sexual discrimination exists in the workplace, in social situations, and in politics. |
|---|---|

2. **Try organizing your ideas chronologically.** Group your ideas according to the clock or calendar. Ted organized the dating process in the order in which it happens, from start to finish.

| | |
|---|---|
| **Sample Thesis Statement** | Tracing metal working from its early be ginnings in history to modern times reveals certain social and economic patterns. |

3. **Look for similarities and differences.** When working with two or more topics, see if they can be approached by looking at how similar or different they are.

| | |
|---|---|
| **Sample Thesis Statement** | Wundt and James, influential founders of psy chology, advocated differing approaches to its study. |

4. **Separate your ideas into causes and effects or problems and solutions.** Events and issues can often be analyzed in this way.

| | |
|---|---|
| **Sample Thesis Statement** | Both employer and employees must work together to improve low morale in an office. |

5. **Divide your ideas into advantages and disadvantages or pros and cons.** When you are evaluating a proposal, product, or service, this approach may work.

| | |
|---|---|
| **Sample Thesis Statement** | Playing on a college sports team has many advantages but also several serious drawbacks. |

6. **Consider several different ways to approach your topic or organize and develop your ideas.** As you consider what your thesis statement is going to be, push yourself to see your topic from a number of different angles or a fresh perspective.

For example, Ted could have considered how online dating differs from traditional dating, or he could have examined his freewriting and decided to focus on his personal history using Facebook to date.

## Writing an Effective Thesis Statement

Think of your thesis statement as a promise; it promises your reader what your paper will deliver. Here are some guidelines to follow for writing an effective thesis statement:

### Guidelines for Writing an Effective Thesis Statement

1. **It should state the main point of your essay.** It should not focus on details; it should give an overview of your approach to your topic.

| Too Detailed | A well-written business letter has no errors in spelling. |
| Revised | To write a grammatically correct business letter, follow three simple rules. |

2. **It should assert an idea about your topic.** Your thesis should express a viewpoint or state an approach to the topic.

| Lacks an Assertion | Advertising contains images of both men and women. |
| Revised | In general, advertising presents men more favorably than women. |

3. **It should be as specific and detailed as possible.** For this reason, it is important to review and rework your thesis *after* you have written and revised drafts.

| Too General | Advertisers can influence readers' attitudes toward competing products. |
| Revised | Athletic-shoe advertisers focus more on attitude and image than on the actual physical differences between their product and those of their competitors. |

4. **It may suggest the organization of your essay.** Mentioning key points that will be discussed in the essay is one way to do this. The order in which you mention them should be the order in which you discuss them in your essay.

| Does Not Suggest Organization | Public-school budget cuts will negatively affect education. |
| Revised | Public-school budget cuts will negatively affect academic achievement, student motivation, and the drop-out rate. |

5. **It should not be a direct announcement.** Do not begin with phrases such as "In this paper I will" or "My assignment was to discuss."

| Direct Announcement | The purpose of my paper is to show that businesses lose money due to inefficiency, competition, and inflated labor costs. |
| Revised | Businesses lose money due to inefficiency, competition, and inflated labor costs. |

6. **It should offer a fresh, interesting, and original perspective on the topic.** A thesis statement can follow the guidelines above, but if it seems dull or predictable, it needs more work.

| Predictable | Circus acts fall into three categories: animal, clown, and acrobatic. |
| Revised | Each of the three categories of circus acts—animal, clown, and acrobatic—is exciting because of the risks it involves. |

## EXERCISE 11-4 . . . WRITING A WORKING THESIS STATEMENT

*For the topic you narrowed in Exercise 11-3, write a working thesis statement.*

## Audience, Purpose, Point of View, and Tone

Before you begin a draft, there are four important factors to consider: *audience, purpose, point of view,* and *tone.*

### Considering Your Audience

Analyzing your audience is always a first step when writing any essay. It will help you decide what to say and what type of detail to include. Here are some key questions to begin your analysis:

- **Is my reader familiar with the topic?**
- **How much background or history does my reader need to understand the information?**
- **Do I need to define any unfamiliar terms?**
- **Do I need to explain any unfamiliar people, places, events, parts, or processes?**

Suppose you are writing an essay on how to find an apartment to rent, and you need to decide how much information to present. This decision involves analyzing both your audience and your purpose. First, consider how much your audience already knows about the topic. If you think your readers know a lot about renting apartments, briefly review in your essay what they already know and then move on to a more detailed explanation of new information. However, if your topic is brand new to your readers, capture their interest without intimidating them. Relate the topic to their own experiences. Show them how renting an apartment resembles something they already know how to do, for example, by comparing renting an apartment to other types of shopping for something with certain desired features and an established price range.

If you are uncertain about your audience's background, it is safer to include information they may already know rather than to assume that they know it. Readers can skim or skip over information they know, but they cannot fill in gaps in their understanding without your help. Once you have identified your audience and decided what they will need to know, you will want to identify your purpose for writing.

### Considering Your Purpose

A well-written essay should have a **purpose**, or goal. There are three main purposes for writing:

- **To express yourself.** In expressive essays, you focus on your feelings and experiences. You might, for example, write an expressive essay about the value of friendship.

- **To inform.** Informative essays are written to present information. An essay on how to cook chili is an informative essay.
- **To persuade.** Persuasive essays attempt to convince readers to accept a particular viewpoint or take a particular action. A persuasive essay might attempt to convince you that zoos are inhumane.

When planning your essay, decide what you want it to accomplish, and focus on how to meet that goal.

### Considering Point of View

**Point of view** refers to the perspective you take on your topic. Your point of view may be expressed using first, second or third person. If you write in the first person (using words like *I* and *me*), then you are speaking personally to your reader. If you write in the second person (using words like *you* and *your*), you address your reader directly. If you write in the third person, you use nouns or pronouns to refer to a person or thing spoken about (using words like *he*, *she*, *Jody*, or *children*).

Your choice of person determines how formal or informal your essay becomes and also creates closeness or distance between the reader and writer. Most academic writing uses the third person. The second person is rarely used. Whatever person you choose to use, stay with it throughout your essay.

---

**EXERCISE 11-5 . . . DEFINING AUDIENCE AND PURPOSE AND GENERATING IDEAS**

*For two of the following topics, define your audience and purpose and generate a list of ideas to include in an essay.*

1. The lack of privacy in our society
2. The value of sports
3. Balancing job and school
4. Choosing a career
5. How to make new friends

---

### Considering Tone

**Tone** means how you sound to your readers and how you feel about your topic. An essay can have a serious, argumentative, humorous, informative or other tone, for example. Your tone should reflect your relationship to your audience: the less familiar you are with your audience, the more formal your tone should be. (For more about tone, see Chapter 2, page 26 and Chapter 9, page 232.)

Here are a few examples of sentences in which the tone is inappropriate for most academic and career writing, and how they could be revised to be appropriate for an academic audience.

| Inappropriate | That dude's swag. He's all swole up from lifting at the gym. |
| Revised | That man has style. He has a well-defined physical appearance from using weights at the gym. |
| Inappropriate | OMG, that jacket's dope! |
| Revised | I think that jacket is original and really well made. |

### Ways to Keep Your Tone Appropriate

Follow these suggestions to help keep your tone appropriate:

1. Avoid slang expressions.
2. Use first-person pronouns (*I, me*) sparingly.
3. Make your writing sound more formal than casual conversation or a letter to a close friend.
4. To achieve a more formal tone, avoid informal or everyday words. For example:

   Use *met* instead of *ran into*.
   Use *children* instead of *kids*.
   Use *annoying* instead of *bugging*.

### EXERCISE 11–6 . . . REVISING TONES

*Revise each of the following statements to give it a more formal tone.*

1. I used to be a dork in high school, but now I'm awesome in college.
2. Sam is the kind of guy every woman would like to sink her claws into.
3. Because Marco is one of those easygoing types, people think they can walk all over him.
4. In my talk to the group, I riffed on why scanners are a big money saver.
5. Emily Dickinson is a boring poet; some of her poems are really lame.

### EXERCISE 11–7 . . . DEFINING AUDIENCE, PURPOSE, POINT OF VIEW, AND TONE

*For the topic you chose in Exercise 11-3, define your purpose and audience and select a point of view. Also decide how you want to "sound" to your reader.*

## Organizing Ideas Using Outlining and Mapping

Outlining is one good way to organize your ideas, discover the relationships and connections between them, and show their relative importance. The most important ideas are placed closer to the left margin. Less important ideas are indented toward the middle of the page. A quick glance at an outline shows what is most important, what is less important, and how ideas support or explain one another (see Chapter 8, page 210, for more details).

### How to Use an Outline Format

Here are a few suggestions for using the outline format:

- **Do not be overly concerned with following the outline format exactly.** As long as your outline shows the organization of your ideas, it will work for you.

- **Write complete sentences whenever possible.** Complete sentences allow for fuller expression of ideas.

- **Pay attention to headings.** Be sure that all the information you place underneath a heading explains or supports that heading. Every heading indented the same amount on the page should be of equal importance.

Another way to write a solid, effective essay is to plan its development using an idea map, a list of the ideas you will discuss in the order in which you will present them. Here is a sample idea map for Ted's essay on online dating.

### Map of Ted's Essay on Online Dating

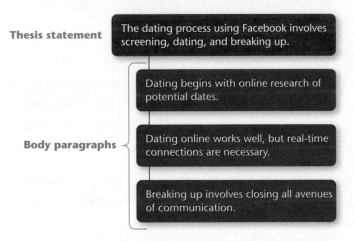

Thesis statement — The dating process using Facebook involves screening, dating, and breaking up.

Body paragraphs:
- Dating begins with online research of potential dates.
- Dating online works well, but real-time connections are necessary.
- Breaking up involves closing all avenues of communication.

---

**EXERCISE 11-8 . . . DRAWING A MAP OR OUTLINE**

*For the topic you chose in Exercise 11-3, draw a map or outline of your ideas.*

---

## Choosing a Method of Development

Analyzing your audience and purpose will also help you choose which method or methods of development to use—*illustration, process, definition, classification, cause and effect,* or *comparison and contrast* (see Chapter 6 for details). You can select the one that suits your audience and purpose best. See Table 11-2 for a few examples.

## TABLE 11-2  CHOOSING A METHOD OF DEVELOPMENT

| IF YOUR PURPOSE IS TO . . . | USE . . . |
| --- | --- |
| Explain how something works or how to perform a specific task | Process |
| Explain a topic, using specific examples | Example |
| Explain what something is | Definition |
| Emphasize similarities or differences between two topics or explain something by comparing it to something already familiar | Comparison and Contrast |
| Explain why something happened | Cause and Effect |

You may also use more than one of these methods of development. You might define a behavior and then offer examples to explain it. Or you might explain how a group of people are classified and argue that the classification is unfair and discriminatory.

### EXERCISE 11-9 . . . CHOOSING A METHOD OF DEVELOPMENT

*For the topic you chose in Exercise 11-3, choose a method of development that will best present your point.*

## 11c  DRAFTING AN ESSAY

**LEARNING OBJECTIVE 3**
Draft an essay

A **draft** is a tentative or preliminary version of an essay. Drafting involves adding, deleting and reorganizing content to be sure your essay has a narrow focus, a clear main idea, and adequate supporting details. You should plan to write several drafts before you end up with an essay you are satisfied with. Use the following general suggestions for getting started; then work on drafting each paragraph.

### Tips for Writing Essay Drafts

Here are some tips for writing essay drafts:

- **Leave time between your drafts.** If you try to write too many drafts in one sitting, you may find it difficult to sort them all out and see the strengths and weaknesses of each one.

- **Think of drafting as a chance to experiment.** Find out what works and what does not. You might want to write your essay several different ways, trying out different approaches, different content, and different ways of organizing the information.

- **Focus on ideas, not correctness.** Especially for the first few drafts, concentrate on recording your ideas. Do not worry yet about grammatical errors or sentence structure, for example.
- **Be prepared to make major changes.** Often as your essay develops, you may realize that you want to change direction or that you should further limit your topic. Do not hesitate to do so.
- **Have a friend or classmate read your drafts.** Ask your reviewer to identify and evaluate your thesis statement. Also ask him or her to evaluate how clearly and effectively your essay supports your thesis statement.

## Drafting Body Paragraphs

There are a number of different ways you can begin drafting the body paragraphs for your essay. Some students write an outline; others draw a map; still others write a list of topic sentences that support the thesis. Don't worry too much about the order of the items in your draft. At this point, it is more important to get your ideas down in writing. In later drafts, you can rearrange your ideas.

Once you have identified topics or topic sentences that support your thesis, you are ready to write first-draft paragraphs. These, too, may change, so concentrate primarily on making sure that each topic sentence supports the thesis and that each paragraph has a clear topic sentence, supporting details, and transitions (see Chapter 5).

### Sample Topic Sentences for an Essay

Here is a list of topic sentences Ted wrote for his online dating essay.

> Facebook owns the college crowd and is widely popular for dating.
>
> Here's how the dating process works at the U. of Maryland.
>
> On Facebook everyone is reduced to a set of bullets.
>
> I use Facebook to evaluate a potential date.
>
> When dating begins it is nice to change our status on Facebook together.
>
> Facebook can encourage infidelity.
>
> Breaking up was hard to do before the Internet.

You will see that he changed, added, and expanded these topic sentences as he wrote his first draft, which appears on page 291.

## Evaluating and Revising Your Thesis Statement

At various stages in the drafting process, you may decide to rewrite, revise, or completely change your thesis statement. Remember, a thesis statement should explain what your essay is about and also give your readers clues about its organization. You may not know, for example, how your essay will be organized until you have written one or more drafts. Use the following suggestions for making sure your thesis statement is clear and effective.

### How to Revise Your Thesis Statement

The best time to evaluate and, if necessary, revise your thesis statement is after you have written a first draft. When evaluating your thesis statement, ask the following questions:

1. **Does my essay develop and explain my thesis statement?** As you write an essay, its focus and direction may change. Revise your thesis statement to reflect any changes. If you discover that you drifted away from your original thesis and want to maintain it, work on revising so that your paper delivers what your thesis promises.

2. **Is my thesis statement broad enough to cover all the points made in the essay?** As you develop your first draft, you may find that one idea leads naturally to another. Both must be covered by the thesis statement. For example, suppose your thesis statement is "Media coverage of national political events shapes public attitudes toward politicians." If, in your essay, you discuss media coverage of international events as well as national ones, then you need to broaden your thesis statement.

3. **Does my thesis statement use vague or unclear words that do not clearly focus the topic?** For example, in the thesis statement "The possibility of animal-organ transplants for humans is interesting," the word *interesting* is vague and does not suggest how your essay will approach the topic. Instead, if your paper discusses both the risks and benefits of these transplants, this approach should be reflected in your thesis: "Animal-organ transplants for humans offer both risks and potential benefits."

### EXERCISE 11–10 . . . EVALUATING THESIS STATEMENTS

*Working with a classmate, identify what is wrong with the following thesis statements, and revise each one to make it more effective:*

1. Jogging has a lot of benefits.

2. Counseling can help people with problems.

3. Getting involved in campus activities has really helped me.

4. Budgeting your time is important.

5. Commuting to college presents problems.

6. The movie is about parenting.

7. Violence on television must be brought to an end.

8. Divorce laws are unfair and favor women.

9. Fad diets are losing their appeal.

10. Automobile air bags save lives.

**EXERCISE 11-11 . . . DRAFTING A THESIS STATEMENT**

*For the topic you chose in Exercise 11-3, draft a thesis statement.*

## Supporting Your Thesis with Substantial Evidence

Every essay you write should offer substantial evidence to support the thesis statement. **Evidence** can consist of personal experience, anecdotes (stories that illustrate a point), examples, reasons, descriptions, facts, statistics, and quotations (taken from sources).

Many students have trouble locating concrete, specific evidence to support their thesis. Though prewriting yields plenty of good ideas and helps you focus your thesis, prewriting ideas may not always provide sufficient evidence. Often you need to brainstorm again for additional ideas. At other times, you may need to consult one or more sources to obtain further information on your topic (see Section 11f, p. 308).

Ted realized that he did not have enough ideas for his essay on online dating. Table 11-3 lists ways to explain a thesis statement and gives an example of how Ted could use each in his essay. He would not need to use all of them, just those appropriate for his audience and purpose. He could also combine different types of evidence, *telling a story* that illustrates the *effects* of misleading online profiles, for instance.

Use the following guidelines in selecting evidence to support your thesis:

### TABLE 11-3  WAYS TO ADD EVIDENCE

TOPIC: ONLINE DATING

| EXPLAIN YOUR THESIS BY . . . | EXAMPLE |
| --- | --- |
| Telling a story | *Relate a story about an online dating experience.* |
| Adding descriptive detail | *Add a description of a social network profile.* |
| Explaining how something works | *Explain how a person can change his or her relationship status on Facebook.* |
| Giving an example | *Discuss specific instances of prescreening a potential date using Google.* |
| Giving a definition | *Explain the meaning of terms such as profile, friend, or timeline.* |
| Making distinctions | *Contrast prescreening a date online and without the use of a computer.* |
| Making comparisons | *Compare two social networking sites.* |
| Giving reasons | *Explain why breaking up is difficult when so many online connections exist.* |
| Analyzing effects | *Explain how online profiles can be misleading.* |

### Guidelines for Selecting Evidence

1. **Be sure your evidence is relevant.** That is, it must directly support or explain your thesis.
2. **Make your evidence as specific as possible.** Help your readers see the point you are making by offering detailed, concrete information. For example, if you are explaining the effects of right-to-privacy violations on individuals, include details that make the situation come alive: names of people and places, types of violations, and so forth.
3. **Be sure your information is accurate.** It may be necessary to check facts, verify stories you have heard, and ask questions of individuals who have provided information.
4. **Locate sources that provide evidence.** Because you may not know enough about your topic and lack personal experience, you may be unable to provide strong evidence. When this happens, locate several sources on your topic.
5. **Be sure to document any information that you borrow from other sources.** See Section 11f (p. 308), for further information on crediting sources.

Now let's take a look at how Ted developed his essay on online dating. As you read, notice, in particular, the types of evidence he uses and how his thesis statement promises what his essay delivers. In this first draft, he uses his free-writing from page 278 and his list of topic sentences on page 288.

### Sample First Draft Essay

Facebook is a social networking Internet site. It allows a user to connect with people, make friends, and join interest groups using the convenience of their own computer. It also allows a user to learn more information about said friends, as well as post text, photos, video, links, and information.

Facebook owns the college crowd, because from its September 2004 launch in a Harvard dorm room until September 2006, a user needed a .edu e-mail address to join. College students made the site their own community, and there was a sense that this was our world even though there's no real way to prevent non-students with .edu addresses from joining. The first sign of non-students entering what was our walled community occurred in May 2006 when employers were admitted, followed by Facebook opening to the public in September of that year.

Facebook has become widely popular. Much has been written about it in my student newspaper, but no one has yet dug into what the site has done to change our relationships, and specifically the dating process. The dating process has changed dramatically since Facebook came on the scene. Not all the changes have been positive.

I know when Facebook friends break up, fail tests, and hate their parents, but I don't really know them as people, just infobits on an LCD. The dating process works well initially over this medium, but real connections are only formed with substantial time-spending, preferably in person. Online talks, even via Skype or webcam, are still only a fraction of the experience and do not convey as high a percentage of the information one can glean during an in-person encounter.

At the University of Maryland, the dating process begins like this: get someone's name; look him or her up on Facebook; use that information to decide how to proceed. When I meet someone and she sets off those neurons that make me hum "Maybe it's love," I do a Facebook search. A profile page will tell me her age, indicate whether or not she's taken, and give me a decent idea (if the profile is not privacy protected) of what image she's trying to present. Note that I don't trust Facebook to tell me who people are—merely who they want to show people they are. I look through photos and see what they value enough to show me. I check posted links because what someone thinks is worth sharing is another window into who she is.

On Facebook, everyone seems reduced to a set of bullet points—"goth, tall, cat person"—that we rely on before even meeting someone. In real life, careful observation can reveal truths about people they won't discuss, especially things they don't want known.

However, a fidgety, nervous guy who sweats when he sees a pretty girl may have a better chance sending a Facebook message, which can be drafted and redrafted and edited and rewritten and shown to friends before sending, than approaching her in real life, so it does have its benefits.

After using Facebook to research the person, I have a decent idea of whether she's a probable friend or romantic interest. Next I hit Google—first searching with her e-mail address, then with her name, then with her nickname if I have reason to believe the person I'm into uses the Internet for more than e-mail. This turns up message boards, possibly her blog, and maybe even a Flickr site, all worth plumbing for details about my new fascination.

I have serious doubts as to whether being able to download someone's self with a little searching on Facebook and Google is actually a good thing for beginning relationships. For one, online searches result in tons of information with absolutely no context. Judging what you learn without cross-referencing it with the person him- or herself is a recipe for misinterpretative disaster, yet checking means admitting you've been snooping. I snoop anyway.

When I start dating someone new, it's usually a nice moment to change our relationship status on Facebook. After the last time I did that, we communicated more via messages on Facebook, posted on each other's walls, and even updated our statuses at the same time. I'm glad we never committed the ultimate act of Facebook couplehood, however.

I knew my housemate was in deep when her profile picture changed from just her to her being held by her girlfriend. I knew it was even worse when her girlfriend's photo changed the same way. The face they'd chosen to show couldn't be just theirs—it was sweet but creeped me out.

Internet access means access to your romantic interest, even during work in many cases. E-mail replaces IM for quick messages because many jobs require e-mail use. The Internet lets you do couples things like play Scrabble or check up on each other regardless of distance.

Time spent communicating with someone, especially just one person, can build connections that lead to relationships or strengthen current ones. Although Skyping someone without video is about as emotionally satisfying as being courteously deferential, you still get to hear his or her voice. Tone, pauses, nuance, and volume are all stripped from instant messages—at least Skype gives you those back. Human laughter beats "LOL" in pixels any day, but holding her while she tells you about her day wins whenever possible.

Facebook can also provoke new frontiers of infidelity. One way is through chatting online. It's very poor form to chat up someone else's girlfriend in a bar, but when chatting online there's no boyfriend looming over you to enforce her morality. Combine that freedom with the very personal qualities of online relationships and the large amount of time most people spend online and you've got a formula anyone who's dating anyone who gets online should worry about.

Breaking up is hard to do, but the Internet makes it easier. You don't want to get a continually updated feed of information about that person. Knowing someone's getting over you and trying to date is one thing; knowing they're doing it at seven-thirty at Club Kozmo with someone they met last weekend is another.

After I leave someone, he or she disappears from instant messaging, my e-mail contacts, Facebook friends, Twitter followers, and my web bookmarks. Forget one step and the "getting over her" process becomes that much harder. There's a measure of comfort to be found in thinking someone's fallen off the face of the earth romantically, especially if your return to dating hasn't been as successful. After the relationship ends, I like the flood of data the Internet provides much less than in my prescreening stage.

That level of cutting someone off requires an amount of effort commonly reserved for reporters on deadline or college students who fell asleep before they got to the all-nighter. You become like a recovering alcoholic, not just avoiding them in person. Certain sites take on new meaning. Any bit of forgotten information is another barb, another pang, another realization. Invariably, you'll miss something and see a status update or a text message or a voice mail. It helps at times, when missing someone so badly means wishing the person were dead. Once you get over it, refriend the person if you can do it without going crazy. Sometimes a little bit of ignorance can be blissful indeed, but most connections are worth preserving.

### EXERCISE 11-12 . . . WRITING A FIRST DRAFT

*Write a first draft of an essay for the working thesis statement you wrote in Exercise 11-4 (page 283). Support your thesis statement with at least three types of evidence.*

## Using Transitions to Make Connections Among Your Ideas Clear

To produce a well-written essay, be sure to make it clear how your ideas relate to one another. There are several ways to do this:

1. **Use transitional words and phrases.** Transitional words and phrases are helpful for making your essay flow smoothly and communicate clearly. Table 11-4 lists useful transitional words for each method of organization. Notice the use of these signal words and phrases in Ted's first draft: *however, next, for one, although, another, after.*

2. **Write a transitional sentence.** This sentence is usually the first sentence in the paragraph. It might come before the topic sentence or it might *be* the topic sentence. Its purpose is to link the paragraph in which it appears with the paragraph before it.

## TABLE 11-4  USEFUL TRANSITIONAL WORDS AND PHRASES

| TYPE OF CONNECTION | TRANSITIONAL WORDS AND PHRASES |
| --- | --- |
| Importance | *most important, above all, especially, particularly important* |
| Spatial relationships | *above, below, behind, beside, next to, inside, outside, to the west (north, etc.), beneath, near, nearby, next to, under, over* |
| Time sequences | *first, next, now, before, during, after, eventually, finally, at last, later, meanwhile, soon, then, suddenly, currently, after, afterward, after a while, as soon as, until* |
| Recounting events or steps | *first, second, then, later, in the beginning, when, while, after, following, next, during, again, after that, at last, finally* |
| Examples | *for example, for instance, to illustrate, in one case* |
| Types | *one, another, second, third* |
| Definitions | *means, can be defined as, refers to, is* |
| Similarities | *likewise, similarly, in the same way, too, also* |
| Differences | *however, on the contrary, unlike, on the other hand, although, even though, but, in contrast, yet* |
| Causes or results | *because, consequently, since, as a result, for this reason, therefore, thus* |
| Restatement | *in other words, that is* |
| Summary or conclusion | *finally, to sum up, all in all, evidently, in conclusion* |

3. **Repeat key words.** Repeating key words also enables your reader to stay on track. Key words often appear in your thesis statement, and, by repeating some of them, you remind your reader of your thesis and how each new idea is connected to it. You need not repeat the word or phrase exactly as long as the meaning stays the same. You could substitute "keeps your audience on target" for "enables your reader to stay on track," for example.

## EXERCISE 11-13 . . . ANALYZING A DRAFT

*Review the draft you wrote for Exercise 11-12. Analyze how effectively you have connected your ideas. Add key words or transitional words, phrases, or sentences, as needed.*

## Writing the Introduction, Conclusion, and Title

The introduction, conclusion, and title each serve a specific function. Each strengthens your essay and helps your reader understand your ideas.

### Writing the Introduction

An **introductory paragraph** has three main purposes:

- It presents your thesis statement.
- It interests your reader in your topic.
- It provides any necessary background information.

Although your introductory paragraph appears first in your essay, it does *not* need to be written first. In fact, it is sometimes best to write it last, after you have developed your ideas, written your thesis statement, and drafted your essay. Here are some suggestions on how to first interest your readers in your topic.

### TECHNIQUES FOR WRITING INTRODUCTIONS

| TECHNIQUE | EXAMPLE |
|---|---|
| Ask a provocative or controversial question. | *What would you do if you were sound asleep and woke to find a burglar in your bedroom?* |
| State a startling fact or statistic. | *Did you know that the federal government recently spent $687,000 on a research project that studied the influence of Valium on monkeys?* |
| Begin with a story or an anecdote. | *Mark Brown, a social worker, has spent several evenings riding in a police cruiser to learn about neighborhood problems.* |
| Use a quotation. | *As Junot Díaz wrote in The Brief Wondrous Life of Oscar Wao, "It's never the changes we want that change everything."* |
| State a little-known fact, a myth, or a misconception. | *It's hard to lose weight and even harder to keep it off. Right? Wrong! A sensible eating program will help you lose weight.* |

A straightforward, dramatic thesis statement can also capture your reader's interest, as in the following example:

The dream job that I'd wanted all my life turned out to be a complete disaster.

An introduction should also provide the reader with any necessary background information. You may, for example, need to define the term *genetic engineering* for a paper on that topic. At other times, you might need to provide a brief history or give an overview of a controversial issue.

*Write or revise your introduction to the essay you drafted in Exercise 11-12.*

## Writing the Conclusion

The final, **concluding paragraph** of your essay has two functions: it should reemphasize your thesis statement and draw the essay to a close. It should not be a direct announcement, such as "This essay has been about" or "In this paper, I hoped to show that." It's usually best to revise your essay *at least once before* working on the conclusion. During your first or second revision, you often make numerous changes in both content and organization, which may, in turn, affect your conclusion.

## Ways to Write an Effective Conclusion

Here are a few effective ways to write a conclusion. Choose one that will work for your essay:

1. **Suggest a direction for further thought.** Raise a related issue that you did not address in your essay, or ask a series of questions.
2. **Look ahead.** Project into the future and consider outcomes or effects.
3. **Return to your thesis.** If your essay is written to prove a point or convince your reader of the need for action, it may be effective to end with a sentence that recalls your main point or calls for action. If you choose this way to conclude, don't merely repeat your first paragraph. Be sure to reflect on the thoughts you developed in the body of your essay.
4. **Summarize key points.** Especially for longer essays, briefly review your key-supporting ideas. In shorter essays, this tends to be unnecessary.
5. **Make sure your conclusion does not contain new supporting details.** If you have trouble writing your conclusion, you may need to work further on your thesis or organization.

*Write or revise a conclusion for the essay you wrote for Exercise 11-12.*

## Selecting a Title

Although the title appears first in your essay, it is often the last thing you should write. The **title** should identify the topic in an interesting way, and it may also suggest the focus of the paper. To select a title, reread your final draft, paying particular attention to your thesis statement and your overall method of development. Here are a few examples of effective titles:

"Surprise in the Vegetable Bin" (for an essay on vegetables and their effects on cholesterol and cancer)

"Denim Goes High Fashion" (for an essay describing the uses of denim for clothing other than jeans)

"Babies Go to Work" (for an essay on corporate-sponsored day-care centers)

### Tips for Writing Accurate and Interesting Titles

To write accurate and interesting titles, try the following tips:

1. **Write a question that your essay answers.** For example: "Why Change the Minimum Wage?"
2. **Use key words that appear in your thesis statement.** If your thesis statement is "The new international trade ruling threatens the safety of the dolphin, one of our most intelligent mammals," your title could be "New Threat to Dolphins."
3. **Use brainstorming techniques to generate options.** Don't necessarily use the first title that pops into your mind. If in doubt, try out some options on friends to see which is most effective.

**EXERCISE 11–16 . . . SELECTING A TITLE**

*Come up with a good title for the essay you wrote for Exercise 11-12.*

## 11d    REVISING: EXAMINING YOUR IDEAS

**LEARNING OBJECTIVE 4**
Revise your ideas

**Revising** is a process of closely evaluating your draft to determine that it says what you want it to say and that it does so in a clear and effective way. Once you have revised your essay, you can move to editing to correct errors.

### General Essay Revision Strategies

Here are some general suggestions for revising your final essay draft. Also refer to the tips for revising (page 36) and the Paragraph Revision Checklist presented in Chapter 2 (page 37).

- **Allow time between finishing your last draft and revising, until the next day, if possible.** When you return to the draft, you will have a clear mind and a new perspective.
- **Look for common problems.** If you usually have trouble, for example, with writing thesis statements or with using transitions, then evaluate these features closely each time you revise.

- **Read the draft aloud.** You may hear ideas that are unclear or realize they are not fully explained.

- **Ask a friend to read your paper aloud to you.** If the person hesitates or seems confused or misreads, the person may be having trouble grasping your ideas. Reread and revise any trouble spots.

- **Read a print copy.** Although you may be used to writing on a computer, your essay may read differently when you see a paper copy.

## Using Revision Maps to Revise

A revision map will help you evaluate the overall flow of ideas as well as the effectiveness of individual paragraphs. To draw an essay revision map, work through each paragraph, recording your ideas in abbreviated form. Then write the key words of your conclusion. If you find details that do not support the topic sentences, or topic sentences that do not support the thesis, record those details to the right of the map (see Chapter 5, page 122 for more details).

When you've completed your revision map, conduct the following tests:

1. **Read your thesis statement along with your first topic sentence.** Does the topic sentence clearly support your thesis? If not, revise to make the relationship clearer. Repeat this step for each topic sentence.
2. **Read your topic sentences, one after the other, without corresponding details.** Is there a logical connection between them? Are they arranged in the most effective way? If not, revise to make the connection clearer or to improve your organization.
3. **Examine each individual paragraph.** Are there enough relevant, specific details to support the topic sentence?
4. **Read your introduction and then look at your topic sentences.** Does the essay deliver what the introduction promises?
5. **Read your thesis statement and then your conclusion.** Are they compatible and consistent? Does the conclusion agree with and support the thesis statement?

### EXERCISE 11-17 . . . DRAWING A REVISION MAP

*Draw a revision map of the essay you wrote in Exercise 11-12 and make necessary revisions.*

## Revising Essay Content and Structure

When you have completed your revision map, you are ready to evaluate your essay's content and organization. If you do not ask yourself the right questions when evaluating your draft, you won't discover how to improve it. Each of the following questions and corresponding revision strategies will guide you in producing a clear and effective final essay.

1. **Does your essay accomplish your purpose?**
   *If you are writing in response to an assignment, reread it and make sure you have covered all aspects of it.* Delete any sentences or paragraphs that do not fulfill your assignment or stated purpose. Do you have enough ideas left? If not, do additional freewriting to discover new ideas.

2. **Is your essay appropriate for your audience?**
   *Visualize your audience reading your essay.* How will they respond? If you are not sure, ask a classmate or a person who is part of your audience to read your essay. Then revise your essay with your audience in mind. Add examples that may appeal to them; delete those that would not. Examine your word choice. Have you used language that is understandable and will not either confuse them or create a negative impression?

3. **Is your thesis statement clearly expressed?**
   *Highlight your thesis statement.* Does it state the main point of your essay and make an assertion about your topic? If not, write one sentence stating what your essay is intended to explain or show. Use this sentence to help you revise your thesis statement. If you revise your thesis statement, be sure to revise the remainder of your essay to reflect your changes.

4. **Does each paragraph support your thesis?**
   *Reread each topic sentence.* Does each clearly and specifically explain some aspect of your thesis statement? If not, revise or drop the paragraph. Does the essay contain enough information to fully explain your thesis and make it under-standable to your reader? If not, do additional prewriting to help you discover more ideas. If you are stuck, your thesis statement may be too narrow or you may need to read more about your topic. Be sure to give credit for any ideas you borrow from print or online sources. (Refer to Section 11h, p. 315.)

5. **Is your essay logically organized?**
   *Examine your revision map to be sure your paragraphs are in the right order.* If not, rearrange them. Be sure to add sentences or transitions to connect your ideas and show your new organization. Use Table 11-2, "Choosing a Method of Development" (page 287) to consider different ways you might rearrange your ideas.

6. **Have you used transitions to connect your ideas?**
   *Circle all transitional words, phrases, and sentences.* Do you use transitions to move from each main point to another? If, not, add transitions, referring to Table 11-3 (page 290) as needed.

7. **Are your introduction, conclusion, and title effective?**
   *Reread your introduction.* If it does not lead your reader into the essay and/or does not offer needed background information, revise it by assuming your reader knows little about the topic and has shown little interest. Decide what to add to help this uninterested reader get involved with your essay. *Next, reread your conclusion.* Does it draw the essay to a close and remind the reader of your thesis statement? If not, revise it using the suggestions on page XX. *Finally, reconsider your title.* Is it an appropriate label for your essay? If it does not draw your reader into the essay, try to think of a snappier, more interesting title.

## Revising Paragraphs

Once you are satisfied with the overall content and structure of your essay, next evaluate each paragraph. Ask yourself the following questions about each paragraph. For any items for which you answer *no*, refer to the pages in Chapter 5 listed below .

- Is the topic of the paragraph specific enough so that it can be adequately covered in a single paragraph? (page 106)
- Does the topic sentence clearly identify the topic and express a point of view about it? (page 109)
- Are there enough relevant details to support the topic sentence? (page 110)
- Are the details arranged in a logical order? (page 114)
- Have I used signal words and phrases to connect my ideas? (page 117)

## Revising Sentences and Words

Once you are satisfied with your paragraphs, examine each sentence by asking the following questions:

- **Are your sentences wordy?** Do they express your meaning in as few words as possible? Here is an example of a wordy sentence, along with a possible revision. Notice that the first sentence contains empty words that do not contribute to its meaning.

| | |
|---|---|
| **Wordy** | *In light of the fact* that cell phone technology changes *every year or so*, upgrading *your cell phone is what everybody has to do.* |
| **Revised** | Cell phone technology changes yearly, so regular upgrades are necessary. |

- **Do your sentences repeat the same idea in slightly different words?** Here is an example of a sentence that says the same thing twice and a revised, more concise version of it.

| | |
|---|---|
| **Redundant** | *My decision to choose* to attend college was the best *decision I have made in a long time.* |
| **Revised** | Choosing to attend college was one of my best decisions. |

- **Do all of your sentences follow the same pattern?** That is, are they all short, or do they all start the same way? Do they seem choppy or monotonous? Sentences that are too similar make your writing seem mechanical and uninteresting.
- **Do you use strong active verbs?** These make your writing seem lively and interesting. Which of the following sentences is more interesting?

> The puppy was afraid of a laundry basket.
>
> The puppy *whimpered, quivered,* and *scampered* away when my sister carried a laundry basket into the room.

The second sentence helps you visualize the situation, while the first is simply factual. Reread your essay, looking for verbs that seem dull or convey very little meaning. Replace them, using a dictionary or thesaurus, as needed.

- **Have you used concrete, specific language?** Your words should convey as much meaning as possible. Which phrase in each of the following pairs provides more meaning?

| | |
|---|---|
| a fun vacation | *white-water rafting trip* |
| many flowers | *lavender petunias and white begonias* |

Reread your essay and highlight words that seem dull and ordinary. Use a dictionary or thesaurus to help you find more concrete and specific replacements.

- **Have you used words with appropriate connotations?** A word's connotative meaning is the collection of feelings and attitudes that come along with it. The words *strolled, swaggered,* and *lumbered* all mean walking in a forward direction, but only *swaggered* would be appropriate when describing someone walking in a bold and arrogant manner. To be sure you have used words with appropriate connotations, check any you are unsure of in a dictionary.

- **Have you avoided clichés?** A cliché is a tired, overused expression that carries little meaning. Here are a few examples.

| | |
|---|---|
| better late than never | shoulder to cry on |
| ladder of success | hard as a rock |
| green with envy | bite the bullet |

Reread your essay and replace clichés with more exact and descriptive information. You could, for example, replace *shoulder to cry on* with *sympathetic and understanding best friend* or *bite the bullet* with *accept responsibility.*

- **Have you avoided sexist language?** Sexist language expresses narrow or unfair assumptions about men's and women's roles, positions, or value. Here are a few examples of sexist language:

| | |
|---|---|
| **Sexist** | A compassionate *nurse* reassures *her* patients before surgery. |
| **Revised** | Compassionate *nurses* reassure *their* patients before surgery. |

> **Sexist**    Many *policemen* hold college degrees.
>
> **Revised**    Many *police officers* hold college degrees.

- **Have you used Standard American English and avoided using nonstandard dialect?** While dialects such as Black English, Spanglish, and Creole are acceptable in many situations, they are not acceptable when writing essays for college classes. If you speak a dialect of English in addition to Standard American English, be sure to reread your essay and replace any dialect words or expressions.

---

### EXERCISE 11-18 . . . EVALUATING AND REVISING A DRAFT

*Evaluate the draft of the essay you revised in Exercise 11-17, using the questions in the preceding section. Make revisions as needed.*

---

## 11e    EDITING AND PROOFREADING: FOCUSING ON CLARITY AND CORRECTNESS

**LEARNING OBJECTIVE 5**
Edit and proofread for clarity and correctness

Once you are satisfied that your essay expresses your ideas as you intended and is organized in a logical way, you are ready to make sure your essay is clear, error free, and presented in acceptable manuscript form. At this stage, you should try to correct errors in spelling, punctuation, and grammar, as well as typographical errors. Here are some general editing and proofreading suggestions:

### General Suggestions for Editing and Proofreading

- **Work with a double-spaced print copy of your essay.** You are likely to see more errors when working with a print copy than you do with an electronic version.

- **Create a log of common errors.** Read your paper once looking for each type of error and note them in your log.

- **Read your essay backward, starting with the last sentence and working toward the first.** Reading this way will help you focus on errors without the distraction of the flow of ideas.

- **Read your essay aloud.** You may catch errors in agreement, use of dialect, or punctuation.

- **Ask a classmate to proofread your paper.**

## Using a Proofreading Checklist

Use the following proofreading checklist to remind you of the types of errors to look for when proofreading.

### Proofreading Checklist

1. Does each sentence end with an appropriate punctuation mark (period, question mark, exclamation point, or quotation mark)?
2. Is all punctuation within each sentence correct (commas, colons, semicolons, apostrophes, dashes, and quotation marks)?
3. Is each word spelled correctly?
4. Have you used capital letters where needed?
5. Are numbers and abbreviations used correctly?
6. Are any words left out?
7. Have you corrected all typographical errors?
8. Are your pages in the correct order and numbered?

## Presenting Your Essay

Before your instructor even begins to read your essay, he or she forms a first impression of it. A paper that is carelessly assembled, rumpled, or has hand-written corrections creates a negative first impression. Always carefully follow any guidelines or requests that your instructor makes on format, method of submission, and so forth. Many instructors require you to use MLA format. See Section 11h, p. 315, for more about MLA format. Use the following suggestions to present your paper positively.

### Tips for Presenting Your Essay

- Make sure your name, the course and section number, and the date appear at the top of your essay (unless otherwise specified by your instructor).
- Type and double-space your essay.
- Number the pages and staple or paperclip them together.
- Present a neat, clean copy. (Carry it in a manila folder or envelope until you turn it in so it does not get rumpled or dirty.)
- If you need to make last-minute corrections, reprint your essay; do not make handwritten corrections.
- Avoid adjusting the margins to meet a page-length limit.
- If submitting your paper online, be sure to use an appropriate subject line identifying the submission.

In order to prepare his essay for publication, Ted made extensive revisions to his first draft (shown on page 291) and produced the final version shown next.

**Sample Final Essay**

Ted Sawchuck

Professor Marley

English 090

29 May 2013

Relationships 2.0: Dating and Relating in the Internet Age

Ted Sawchuck

Facebook is a social networking Internet site. It allows a user to conveniently connect online with people, make friends, and join interest groups via his or her computer. It also allows a user to learn more about his or her friends, as well as post text, photos, video links, and information. Facebook has become widely popular. Much has been written about it in my student newspaper, but no one has yet dug into how the site affects relationships on our campus, and specifically the dating process. Each stage of the dating process is influenced by Facebook; on our campus, not all the changes have been positive.

At the University of Maryland, the dating process begins like this: get someone's name; look him or her up on Facebook; then use that information to decide how to proceed. When I meet someone and she sets off those neurons that make me hum "Maybe it's love," I do a Facebook search. A profile page will tell me her age, indicate whether or not she is taken, and give me a decent idea (if the profile is not privacy protected) of what image she is trying to present. Note that I do not trust Facebook to tell me who people are—merely who they want to show other people they are. I look through photos and see what the person values enough to show me. I check posted links because what someone thinks is worth sharing is another window into who she is.

After using Facebook to check out someone, I have a decent idea of whether she is a probable friend or possible romantic interest. Next I hit Google— searching first with her e-mail address, then with her name, and next with her nickname. This search turns up message boards, possibly her blog, and maybe even a Flickr site, all worth plumbing for details about my new fascination.

I have serious doubts as to whether being able to download someone's self with a little searching on Facebook and Google is actually a good thing for beginning a relationship. For one thing, online searches result in tons of information with absolutely no context. Judging what you learn without cross-referencing it with the person is a recipe for misinterpretative disaster, yet checking means admitting you have been snooping. I snoop anyway.

Also, on Facebook, everyone seems reduced to a set of bullet points— "goth, tall, cat person"—that you rely on before even meeting the person. In real life, careful observation can reveal truths about people they will not discuss online, especially things they do not want generally known. However, a fidgety, nervous guy who sweats when he sees a pretty girl may have a better chance sending a Facebook message, which can be drafted and redrafted and edited and rewritten and shown to friends before sending, than approaching her in real life, so it does have its benefits.

The dating process works well online initially, but real connections are only formed by spending substantial time together in person. Online talks, even via Skype or webcam, are still only a fraction of the real experience and convey only a fraction of the information one can glean during an in-person encounter. Time spent online communicating with someone can build connections that lead to a relationship or strengthen a current one. However, tone, pauses, nuance, and volume are all stripped from instant messages. Human laughter beats "LOL" any day, and holding her while she tells you about her day wins whenever possible.

Facebook can also provide new avenues for infidelity. One way is through chatting online. It is very poor form to chat up someone else's girlfriend in a bar, but when chatting online there is no boyfriend looming over you to enforce boundaries. Combine that freedom with the very personal qualities of online relationships and the large amount of time most people spend online and you have a situation that anyone who's dating anyone who goes online a lot should worry about.

Breaking up is hard to do but the Internet makes it easier. Once a relationship ends, you do not want to get a continually updated feed of information about the other person from any source. Knowing someone is getting over you and trying to date is one thing; knowing she is doing it at seven-thirty at Club Kozmo with someone she met last weekend is another. So now my list for after leaving someone includes blocking her on instant messaging, taking her e-mail address out of my quick contacts list and out of my e-mail's autocomplete list, avoiding her blog, blocking her on Twitter, and defriending her on Facebook. Forget one step and the "getting over her" process becomes that much harder. There is a measure of comfort to be found in thinking someone has fallen off the face of the earth romantically, especially if your return to dating has not been as successful as hers.

Cutting someone off requires effort. Any bit of forgotten information is another barb, another pang, another realization of what you have lost.

Sawchuck 4

Invariably, you will miss something and see a status update or a text message or a voice mail. It helps at times, when missing someone so badly means wishing she were dead. Once you get over it yourself, refriend the person if you can do it without going crazy. Sometimes a little bit of ignorance can be blissful indeed, but most connections are worth preserving.

## EXERCISE 11-19 . . . PROOFREADING AND PRESENTING YOUR PAPER

*For the draft you have revised in Exercise 11-17, use the checklist on page 304 to prepare your essay for final presentation.*

# WRITING DOCUMENTED PAPERS

## 11f  USING SOURCES AND AVOIDING PLAGIARISM

**LEARNING OBJECTIVE 6**
Avoid plagiarizing sources

Using sources in an essay involves building the information into your paper correctly so as to give credit to the authors from whom you borrowed the ideas. You can incorporate researched information into your paper in one of two ways: (1) summarize or paraphrase the information or (2) quote directly from it. In both cases, you must give credit to the authors from whom you borrowed the information by documenting your sources in a list of references so your reader can locate it easily. Failure to provide documentation of a source is called plagiarism.

### What Is Plagiarism and How Can You Avoid It?

**Plagiarism** entails borrowing someone else's ideas or exact words *without giving that person credit*. Plagiarism can be intentional (submitting an essay written by someone else) or unintentional (failing to enclose another writer's words in quotation marks). Either way, it is considered a serious offense. If you plagiarize, you can fail the assignment or even the course.

**Cyberplagiarism** is a specific type of plagiarism. It takes two forms: (1) using information from the Internet without giving credit to the Web site that posted it, or (2) buying prewritten papers from the Internet and submitting them as your own work. For example: If you take information about Frank Lloyd Wright's architecture from a reference source (such as an encyclopedia or Web site) but do not specifically indicate where you found it, you have plagiarized. If you take the eleven-word phrase "Kelley, the lead government investigator, a fiery, temperamental and demanding man" from a news article on the war on terrorism, you have plagiarized.

Here are some guidelines to help you understand exactly what constitutes plagiarism:

## Guidelines for Understanding Plagiarism

*Plagiarism occurs when you . . .*

- use another person's words without crediting that person.
- use another person's theory, opinion, or idea without listing the source of that information.
- do not place another person's exact words in quotation marks.
- do not provide a citation (reference) to the original source that you are quoting.
- paraphrase (reword) another person's ideas or words without credit.
- use facts, data, graphs, and charts without stating their source(s).

Using commonly known facts or information is not plagiarism, and you need not provide a source for such information. For example, the fact that Neil Armstrong set foot on the moon in 1969 is widely known and does not require documentation.

### *To avoid plagiarism, do the following:*

- When you take notes from any published or Internet source, place anything you copy directly in quotation marks.
- As you read and take notes, separate your ideas from ideas taken from the sources you are consulting. You might use different colors of ink or different sections of a notebook page for each.
- Keep track of all the sources you use, clearly identifying where each idea comes from.
- When paraphrasing someone else's words, change as many words as possible and try to organize them differently. Credit the original source of the information.
- Write paraphrases without looking at the original text so that you rephrase information in your own words. (For more information on writing a paraphrase, see Section 8d, p. 207.)
- Use citations to indicate the source of quotations and all information and ideas that are not your own. A citation is a notation, set off in parentheses, referring to a complete list of sources provided at the end of the essay. (For more information on citation, see page 310).

As you start researching new areas, you may ask yourself, "How can I possibly write a paper without using someone else's ideas? I don't know enough about the subject!" The good news is that it is *perfectly acceptable* to use other people's ideas in your research and writing. The key things to remember are (1) you must credit all information taken from any published or Internet sources, and (2) you must provide specific information regarding the publication from which the information is taken, as described in the following sections.

### EXERCISE 11-20 . . . IDENTIFYING PLAGIARISM

*Read the following passage. Place a check mark next to each statement in the list that follows that is an example of plagiarism.*

### Issue: Ethnic minorities

**Mexican Americans.** Currently, Mexican Americans are the second-largest racial or ethnic minority group in the United States, but within two decades they will be the largest group. Their numbers will swell as a result of continual immigration from Mexico and the relatively high Mexican birth rate. Mexican Americans are one of the oldest racial-ethnic groups in the United States. Under the terms of the treaty ending the Mexican-American War in 1848, Mexicans living in territories acquired by the United States could remain there and be treated as American citizens. Those who did stay became known as "Californios," "Tejanos," or "Hispanos."

—Curry, Jiobu, and Schwirian, *Sociology for the Twenty-First Century,* p. 207

_____ 1. Mexican Americans are the second-largest minority in the United States. Their number grows as more people immigrate from Mexico.

_____ 2. After the Mexican-American War, those Mexicans living in territories owned by the United States became American citizens and were known as Californios, Tejanos, or Hispanos (Curry, Jiobu, and Schwirian, 207).

_____ 3. "Mexican Americans are one of the oldest racial-ethnic groups in the United States."

_____ 4. The Mexican-American War ended in 1848.

## Recording Information from Sources

As you use sources to research a topic, you will need to record usable information that you find. One option is to photocopy the pages from print sources and download and print information from print sources. This is useful if you plan to directly quote the source. Remember, you will need complete source information so you can cite your sources (see page xx). However, a good essay does not string together a series of quotations. Instead it uses and combines information to come up with new ideas, perspectives, and responses to what is found in the sources. There are several options for keeping track of information—annotating, paraphrasing, and summarizing. Each of these important skills is covered in Chapter 8.

### EXERCISE 11-21 . . . WRITING A FIRST DRAFT

*Write a first draft of a paper on a topic of your choice. To support your ideas, locate and use three sources. If any of these sources are dated or not focused enough for your thesis, you may need to locate additional ones.*

## 11g    SYNTHESIZING SOURCES

**LEARNING OBJECTIVE 7**
Synthesize sources

In daily life, we often consult several sources before drawing a conclusion or making a decision. For example, you might talk with several students who have taken the course American Labor History before deciding whether you want to register for it. You might talk to several friends who own pickup trucks before buying one. Suppose you are debating whether or not to see a particular film. You talk with three friends who have seen it. Each liked the movie and describes different scenes. However, from their various descriptions, you may conclude that the film contains too much violence and that you do not want to see it.

In each case, you draw together several sources of information and come to your own conclusion: the course is good; the Ford pickup is best; the film is too violent for you. In these situations, you are synthesizing information. **Synthesis** is a process of using information from two or more sources in order to develop new ideas about a topic or to draw conclusions about it.

Many college assignments require you to synthesize material—that is, to locate and read several sources on a topic and use them to produce a paper. Synthesizing in the college setting, then, is a process of putting ideas together to create new ideas or insights based on what you have learned from the sources you consulted. For example, in a sociology course, you may be asked to consult several sources on the topic of organized crime and then write a paper describing the relationship between organized crime and illegal-drug sales. In a marketing class, your instructor may direct you to consult several sources on advertising strategies and on the gullibility of young children, and write a paper weighing the effects of television commercials on young children. Both of these assignments involve synthesizing ideas from sources.

Did you notice that, in each of the above examples, you were asked to come up with a new idea, one that did not appear in any of the sources but was *based* on *all* the sources? Creating something new from what you read is one of the most basic, important, and satisfying skills you will learn in college.

Synthesis is also often required in the workplace:

- As a sales executive for an Internet service provider company, you may be asked to synthesize what you have learned about customer hardware problems.

- As a medical office assistant, you have extensive problems with a new computer system. The office manager asks you to write a memo to the company that installed the system, categorizing the types of problems you have experienced.

- As an environmental engineer, you must synthesize years of research in order to make a proposal for local river and stream cleanup.

## How to Compare Sources to Synthesize

Comparing sources is part of synthesizing. Comparing involves placing them side by side and examining how they are the same and how they are different. However, before you begin to compare two or more sources, be sure you understand each fully. Depending on how detailed and difficult each source is, use annotating, paraphrasing, and summarizing or underline, outline, or draw idea maps to make sure that you have a good grasp of your source material.

Let's assume you are taking a speech course in which you are studying nonverbal communication, or body language. You have chosen to study one aspect of body language: eye contact. Among your sources are the following excerpts:

### Issue: Nonverbal Communication

### Source A

Eye contact, or *gaze*, is also a common form of nonverbal communication. Eyes have been called the "windows of the soul." In many cultures, people tend to assume that someone who avoids eye contact is evasive, cold, fearful, shy, or indifferent; that frequent gazing signals intimacy, sincerity, self-confidence, and respect; and that the person who stares is tense, angry, and unfriendly. Typically, however, eye contact is interpreted in light of a pre-existing relationship. If a relationship is friendly, frequent eye contact elicits a positive impression. If a relationship is not friendly, eye contact is seen in negative terms. It has been said that if two people lock eyes for more than a few seconds, they are either going to make love or kill each other (Kleinke, 1986; Patterson, 1983).

—Brehm and Kassin, *Social Psychology*

### Source B

Eye contact often indicates the nature of the relationship between two people. One research study showed that eye contact is moderate when one is addressing a very high-status person, maximized when addressing a moderately high-status person, and only minimal when talking to a low-status person. There are also predictable differences in eye contact when one person likes another or when there may be rewards involved.

> Increased eye contact is also associated with increased liking between the people who are communicating. In an interview, for example, you are likely to make judgments about the interviewer's friendliness according to the amount of eye contact shown. The less eye contact, the less friendliness. In a courtship relationship, more eye contact can be observed among those seeking to develop a more intimate relationship. One research study (Saperston, 2003) suggests that the intimacy is a function of the amount of eye gazing, physical proximity, intimacy of topic, and amount of smiling. This model best relates to established relationships.
>
> —Weaver, *Understanding Interpersonal Communication*, p. 131

To compare these sources, ask the following questions:

1. **On what do the sources agree?** Sources A and B recognize eye contact as an important communication tool. Both agree that there is a connection between eye contact and the relationship between the people involved. Both also agree that more frequent eye contact occurs among people who are friendly or intimate.
2. **On what do the sources disagree?** Sources A and B do not disagree, though they do present different information about eye contact (see the next item).
3. **How do they differ?** Sources A and B differ in the information they present. Source A states that in some cultures the frequency of eye contact suggests certain personality traits (someone who avoids eye contact is considered to be cold, for example), but Source B does not discuss cultural interpretations. Source B discusses how eye contact is related to status—the level of importance of the person being addressed—while Source A does not.
4. **Are the viewpoints toward the subject similar or different?** Both Sources A and B take a serious approach to the subject of eye contact.
5. **Does each source provide supporting evidence for major points?** Source A cites two references. Source B cites a research study.

After comparing your sources, the next step is to form your own ideas based on what you have discovered.

## EXERCISE 11–22 . . . SYNTHESIZING SOURCES

*Read each of the following excerpts from sources on the topic of lost and endangered species. Synthesize these two sources, using the steps listed above, and develop a thesis statement about the causes of the decline and loss of plant and animal species.*

### Source A

#### Issue: Species Extinction

#### What Causes Extinction?

Every living organism must eventually die, and the same is true of species. Just like individuals, species are "born" (through the process of speciation), persist for some period of time, and then perish. The ultimate fate of any species is extinction, the death of the last of its members. In fact, at least 99.9% of all the species that have ever existed are now extinct. The natural course of evolution, as revealed by fossils, is continual turnover of species as new ones arise and old ones become extinct.

The immediate cause of extinction is probably always environmental change, in either the living or the nonliving parts of the environment. Two major environmental factors that may drive a species to extinction are competition among species and habitat destruction.

### Interactions with Other Species May Drive a Species to Extinction

Interactions such as competition and predation serve as agents of natural selection. In some cases, these same interactions can lead to extinction rather than to adaptation. Organisms compete for limited resources in all environments. If a species' competitors evolve superior adaptations and the species doesn't evolve fast enough to keep up, it may become extinct.

### Habitat Change and Destruction Are the Leading Causes of Extinction

Habitat change, both contemporary and prehistoric, is the single greatest cause of extinctions. Present-day habitat destruction due to human activities is proceeding at a rapid pace. Many biologists believe that we are presently in the midst of the fastest-paced and most widespread episode of species extinction in the history of life on Earth. Loss of tropical forests is especially devastating to species diversity. As many as half the species presently on Earth may be lost during the next 50 years as the tropical forests that contain them are cut for timber and to clear land for cattle and crops.

Audesirk, Audesirk, and Byers, Life on Earth, pp. 249–251

### Source B

The driving force behind today's alarming decline in species is the destruction, degradation and fragmentation of habitat due to our increasing human population and wasteful consumption of resources. Human populations virtually all around the globe are on the rise. . . . Because Americans consume so much more energy, food and raw material than our counterparts in other developed countries, our impact on our environment is proportionally much greater. As a result, wildlife and wild places in the United States are being pushed to the brink of extinction.

While the United States does not currently face as significant an increase in population as other countries, the movement of our population to new areas and the ensuing development has resulted in the destruction of species and their habitat. Thus, not surprisingly, there is a high correlation between human population and economic development trends in the United States and species decline and ecosystem destruction.

Sierra Club

### EXERCISE 11-23 . . . RECORDING SOURCES

*List source information for the paper you revised in Exercise 11-17 in your Works Cited or References List. See pages 317–321 for tips on what information to include.*

## 11h    DOCUMENTING SOURCES USING MLA

LEARNING OBJECTIVE 8
Document sources
using MLA style

There are a number of different documentation formats (these are often called *styles*) that are used by scholars and researchers. Members of a particular academic discipline usually use the same format. For example, biologists follow a format described in *Scientific Style and Format: A Manual for Authors, Editors, and Publishers*.

Two of the most common methods of documenting and citing sources are those used by the Modern Language Association (MLA) and the American Psychological Association (APA). Both use a system of in-text citation: a brief note in the body of the text that refers to a source that is fully described in the Works Cited list (MLA) or References (APA) at the end of the paper, where sources are listed in alphabetical order.

The MLA format is typically used in English and humanities papers, while the APA format is commonly used in social science papers. Use the following guidelines for providing correct in-text citations using the MLA and APA documentation styles.

For a comprehensive review of MLA style, consult the *MLA Handbook for Writers of Research Papers*, 7th edition, by Joseph Gibaldi or go to the MLA Web site.

### MLA In-Text Citations

When you refer to, summarize, paraphrase, quote, or in any other way use another author's words or ideas, you must indicate the source from which you took them by inserting an **in-text citation** that refers your reader to your "Works Cited" list. Place your citation at the end of the sentence in which you refer to, summarize, paraphrase, or quote a source. It should follow a quotation mark, but come before punctuation that ends the sentence. If a question mark ends the sentence, place the question mark before the citation and a period after the citation.

Here are some guidelines about what to include in your in-text citations and how to incorporate quotations into your paper:

1. **If the source is introduced by a phrase that names the author, the citation need only include the page number.**

   Miller poses the idea that if a good story is supposed to be a condensed version of life, then life should be lived like a good story in the first place (311).

2. **If the author is not named in the sentence, then include both the author's name and the page number in the citation.**

   If a good story is supposed to be a condensed version of life, then life should be lived like a good story in the first place (Miller 311).

3. **If there are two or three authors, include the last names of all of them.**

> Business ethics are important: "Many companies also have codes of ethics that guide buyers and sellers" (Lamb, Hair, and McDaniel 115).

4. **If there are four or more, include only the first author's last name and follow it with "et al.," which means "and others."**

> Therefore, impalas "illustrate the connections between animal behavior, evolution, and ecology" (Campbell et al. 703).

5. **If you have used two or more works by the same author, either include the relevant title in your sentence or include the title, if brief, or an abbreviated version in your citation.**

> In *Stealing MySpace: The Battle to Control the Most Popular Website in America*, Angwin concludes . . . (126).
>
> Or
>
> Angwin concludes . . . (*Stealing MySpace* 120).

6. **When you include a quotation in your paper, you should signal your reader that one is to follow.** For example, use such introductory phrases as the following:

> According to Miller, "[quotation]."
> As Miller notes, "[quotation]."
> In the words of Miller, "[quotation]."

7. **To use a direct quotation, copy the author's words exactly and put them in quotation marks.** You do not always have to quote the full sentences; you can borrow phrases or clauses as long as they fit into your sentence, both logically and grammatically.

> Miller comments that he "wondered whether a person could plan a story for his life and live it intentionally" (311).

8. **If the quotation is lengthy (four sentences or longer), set it apart from the rest of your paper.** Indent the entire quotation one inch from the margin, double-space the lines, and do not use quotation marks. Include an in-text citation after the final punctuation mark at the end of the quotation.

> When discussing adapting a screenplay from his memoir, Miller noted the following:
>
> > It didn't occur to me at the time, but it's obvious now that in creating the fictional Don, I was creating the person I wanted to be, the person worth telling

> stories about. It never occurred to me that I could re-create my own story, my real life story, but in an evolution. I had moved toward a better me. I was creating someone I could live through, the person I'd be if I redrew the world, a character that was me but flesh and soul other. And flesh and soul better too. (211)

## MLA Works Cited List

Your list of works cited should include all the sources you referred to, summarized, paraphrased, or quoted in your paper. Start the list on a separate page at the end of your paper and title it "Works Cited." Arrange these entries alphabetically by each author's last name. If an author is not named (as in an editorial), then alphabetize the item by title. Double-space between and within entries. Start entries flush left, and if they run more than one line, indent subsequent lines half an inch.

1. **The basic format for a book can be illustrated as follows:**

|  |  | Place of |  |  |  |
|---|---|---|---|---|---|
| Author | Title | Publication | Publisher | Date | Medium of Publication |

Lin, Marvin. *Kid A*. New York: Continuum, 2011. Print.

Special cases are handled as follows:

a. **Two or more authors.** If there are two or three authors, include all their names in the order in which they appear in the source. Only reverse the name of the first author, providing last name first. If there are four or more, give the first author's name only and follow it with "et al."

| Authors |  | Article Title |
|---|---|---|

Spicer, Mark S., and John R. Covach. *Sounding Out Pop: Analytical Essays in Popular Music.* Ann Arbor; Michigan UP, 2011. Print.

Place of Publication   Publisher   Date   Medium of Publication

b. **Two or more works by the same author.** If your list contains two or more works by the same author, list the author's name only once. For additional entries, substitute three hyphens followed by a period in place of the name.

Miller, Donald. *A Million Miles in a Thousand Years: What I Learned While Editing My Life*. Nashville: Nelson, 2009 Print.
---. *Searching for God Knows What*. Nashville: Nelson, 2004. Print.

c. **Editor.** If the book has an editor instead of an author, list the editor's name at the beginning of the entry and follow it with "ed."

> McDannell, Colleen, ed. *Catholics in the Movies*. Oxford: Oxford UP, 2008. Print.

d. **Edition.** If the book has an edition number, include it after the title.

> DeVito, Joseph A. *Human Communication: The Basic Course*. 11th ed. Boston: Pearson, 2011. Print.

e. **Publisher.** The entire name of the publisher is not used. For example, the Houghton Mifflin Company is listed as "Houghton."

2. **What format is used for articles?** The basic format for a periodical can be illustrated as follows:

Author     Article Title     Name of Periodical Volume/Issue No.

Wilentz, Sean. "Bob Dylan in America." *The New York Review of Books* 57.18 (2011): 34. Print.

Date   Page No.   Medium of Publication

Special cases are handled as follows:

a. **Newspaper articles.** Include the author, article title, name of the newspaper, date, section letter or number, page(s), and medium of publication. Abbreviate all months except May, June, and July, and place the day before the month.

> Weiner, Jonah. "Shaggy, Yes, but Finessed Just So." *New York Times* 25 Oct. 2009, New York ed.: AR20. Print.

b. **An article in a weekly magazine.** List the author, article title, name of the magazine, date, page(s), and medium of publication. Abbreviate months as indicated above.

> Lilla, Mark. "The President and the Passions." *New York Times Magazine* Dec. 2011: MM13. Print.

### Internet Sources

Information on the Internet comes from a wide variety of sources. For example, there are journals that are online versions of print publications, but there are also journals that are published only online. There are online books, articles from online databases, government publications, government Web sites, and more. Therefore, it is not sufficient merely to state that you got something from the Web. Citations for Internet resources must adequately reflect the exact type of document or publication that was used.

Include enough information to allow your readers to locate your sources. For some Internet sources, it may not be possible to locate all the required information; provide the information that is available. For sources that appear only online, include the following information: the name(s) of the author, editor, translator, narrator, compiler, performer, or producer of the material; the title of the work; the title of the Web site (if different); the version or edition used; the publisher or sponsor of the site (if unknown write n.p.); the date of publication (day, month, year), write n.d. if not known; the medium of publication (Web); and the date of access (day, month, year). *Do not* include the URL unless the site cannot be found without using it.

1. **The basic format for an Internet source is as follows:**

> Breihan, Tom. "My Morning Jacket Ready New Album." *Pitchfork*. Pitchfork Media Inc., 3 Mar. 2011. Web. 11 Oct. 2013.

2. **The basic format for an Internet source that originally appeared in print is as follows:** Start your entry with the same information you would for a print source. Then add the title of the Web site or database (in italics) followed by a period, the medium of publication (Web) followed by a period, and the date you accessed the source (day, month, year) followed by a period. DO NOT include the URL unless the site cannot be found without using it.

> Wald, Mathew L. "Study Details How U. S. Could Cut 28% of Greenhouse Gases." *New York Times,* 30 Nov. 2007: Business. nytimes.com. Web. 12 Aug. 2013

a. **Online book**—If you consulted an entire online book, use this format:

> Woolf, Virginia. *Monday or Tuesday*. New York: Harcourt, 1921. Bartleby.com. Web. 6 Aug. 2013.

b. **Online book**—If you consulted part of an online book, use this format:

> Seifert, Kelvin, and David Zinger. "Effective Nonverbal Communication." *Educational Psychology*. Boston: Houghton, 2011. *The Online Books Page*. Web. 6 Feb. 2013.

c. **Article from an online periodical**—If you accessed the article *directly* from an online journal, magazine, or newspaper, use this format:

> Sommers, Jeffrey. "Historical Arabesques: Patterns of History." *World History Connected* 5.3. University of Illinois at Urbana-Champaign, June 2008. Web. 15 May 2013.

d. **Article from an online database**—If you accessed an article using an online database, and a Digital Object Identifier (DOI) was provided for the article, include it. If not, include the name of the database and the document number, if available.

> Barnard, Neal D., et al. "Vegetarian and Vegan Diets in Type 2 Diabetes Management." *Nutrition Reviews*, 67(5), 255–263. Web. 21 Apr. 2011. doi:10.1111/j.1753-4887.2009.00198.x
>
> Bivins, Corey. "A Soy-free, Nut-free Vegan Meal Plan." *Vegetarian Journal*, 30(1), 14-17. *AltHealth Watch*. Web. 21 Apr. 2013. (20111118153)

e. **Online government publication**—If you consulted a document published by a government entity:

> United States. Financial Crisis Inquiry Commission. *The Financial Crisis Inquiry Report: Final Report of the National Commission on the Causes of the Financial and Economic Crisis in the United States*. Washington: Financial Crisis Inquiry Commission, 2011. *FDLP Desktop*. Web. 20 Mar. 2013.

## Other Electronic Sources

1. **CD-ROM nonperiodical publication**

> Beck, Mark. F. *Theory & Practice of Therapeutic Massage: Student CD-ROM*. Clifton Park, NY: Milady, 2011. CD-ROM.

2. **Interview from a radio Web site**

> Merritt, Stephin. Interview. *The Strange Powers of Stephin Merritt & the Magnetic Fields*. KEXP 11 Dec. 2011. Web. 13 Apr. 2013.

3. **Television documentary viewed on the Internet**

> Lacy, Susan, prod. "Troubadours." *American Masters*. PBS, 2 Mar. 2011. Web. 16 Apr. 2013.

4. **Photograph viewed on the Internet**

> Warhol, Andy. *Self-Portrait*. 1963–1964. Photograph. *The Warhol*. The Andy Warhol Museum. Web. 17 Aug. 2013.

---

**EXERCISE 11-24 . . . WRITING A WORKS CITED LIST**

*Using MLA style, add two quotations to the paper you revised in Exercise 11-17. Add in-text citations and write a Works Cited list for your paper including entries for all your sources.*

**Sample Documented Paper**

Adam Simmons

Professor Garcia

Sociology 111

20 February 2013

Weighing the Consequences of Censorship in Media

There are different opinions about censorship in the media. Each side has good intentions; one side is saying censorship is protecting people or the country and the other is saying censorship limits the Constitutional right to freedom of speech.

People in favor of censorship of the media often talk about the morality of the content. A common argument is that some media contain inappropriate material that could unintentionally be seen by young children. In this case, inappropriate material is defined as pornographic, violent, vulgar, or sexual in any way. The argument is that it could lead kids to try and repeat what they are seeing on the television or what they are hearing about in music (Pillai). By censoring such materials, children would hypothetically be less likely to repeat the behavior and would not be exposed to things that might not be appropriate for their age, so censorship would protect children.

Some people also believe that censorship is important when it is used to protect military information and "helps preserve the secrets of a nation being revealed" ("Pros of Censorship"). With the government monitoring what information the media offers, it is less likely that information the government does not want leaked out will be made public. This could mean keeping troops safe and protecting domestic and foreign policy, especially in wartime when enemies can track news sources to find out about U.S. strategy. It can also help keep dangerous information, such as details about weaponry, from getting into the wrong hands.

Censorship has some dangers though. It can be viewed as directly violating the First Amendment of the Constitution and taking away freedom of speech. The amendment states "Congress shall make no law . . . abridging the freedom of speech, or of the press . . ." There are some who say the First Amendment acts as a "complete barrier to government censorship" (Pember 43); since the Constitution creates this ban, censorship is in effect unlawful. However, there are Supreme Court cases that have modified the interpretation of this amendment, such as the Smith Act which makes it "a crime to advocate the violent overthrow of the government" (Pember 52).

There are other reasons that people object to censorship. Some people argue that censorship can also be abused by the government and in the wrong hands it can lead to a loss of freedom of speech and halt a flow of ideas in a society, as seen under various dictatorships (Neuharth). It can also be said that censorship stifles creativity. Saying that some works are immoral or unsuitable is making a legal statement that some art is good and some art is bad ("What Is Censorship?"). Art, in itself, is subjective and cannot really be labeled that way. If art has to be made to meet the requirements of the censors, then it will never be able to be completely creative and free.

Both viewpoints about censorship approach the topic with the hope of doing what is best for society, but come at it from completely different angles. One hopes to make things better by removing immoral or dangerous speech and the other seeks to let every person have the ability to say what they want regardless of whether it is seen moral by others.

Simmons 3

Works Cited

Neuharth, Al. "Google Is Gutsy to Spit in China's Eye." *USA Today* 26 Mar. 2011:

15a. Print.

Pember, Don R., and Clay Calvert. *Mass Media Law*. Boston: McGraw-Hill, 20011.

Print.

Pillai, Prabhakar. "Pros and Cons of Censorship." *Buzzle Web Portal: Intelligent Life

on the Web*. Buzzle.com, n.d. Web. 8 Apr. 2011.

"Pros of Censorship." *Laws.com*. n.d. Web. 8 Apr. 2011.

"What Is Censorship?" American Civil Liberties Union. 30 Aug. 2006. Web. 08

Apr. 2011.

## SUMMARY OF LEARNING OBJECTIVES

**MySkillsLab**
Complete the mastery test for this chapter **in MySkillsLab.**

**1   Structure an essay.**
*How are essays structured?*

An **essay** is a group of paragraphs about one subject. It contains three parts—an introductory paragraph that includes the thesis statement, supporting paragraphs (body), and conclusion.

**2   Generate and organize ideas and plan your essay.**
*How do you prepare to write an essay?*

Prepare to write an essay by **prewriting**, which involves choosing and narrowing your topic; generating ideas; grouping ideas to discover a thesis; writing a preliminary thesis; considering audience, purpose, and point of view; organizing ideas; choosing an appropriate tone; and choosing a method of development.

**3   Draft an essay.**
*What is involved in drafting?*

**Drafting** involves writing and rewriting your essay. It includes evaluating and revising your thesis statement; supporting your thesis with substantial evidence; using transitions to connect your ideas; drafting body paragraphs and writing an introduction, conclusion, title.

**4   Revise your ideas.**
*How do you revise a essay?*

**Revision** involves examining your ideas and how effectively you have expressed them. Use revision idea maps to revise and evaluate your essay's content and structure, paragraphs, sentences, and words.

**5   Edit and proofread for clarity and correctness.**
*How do you edit and proofread?*

**Editing and proofreading** involve making certain your essay is clear, error free, and presented in acceptable manuscript form. Correct errors in spelling, punctuation, and grammar, as well as typographical errors.

**6   Avoid plagiarizing sources.**
*How can you avoid plagiarism?*

Writing a paper **using sources** involves properly crediting sources to avoid plagiarism, recording information from sources, and using and synthesizing sources.

**7   Synthesize sources.**
*What does it mean to synthesize sources?*

Many college assignments require you to synthesize material from several sources on a topic and use them to produce a paper. **Synthesizing** means locating several sources on a topic, comparing how they are similar and different, and putting together the ideas you discover to create new ideas and insights about the topic.

**8   Document sources using MLA style.**
*What is MLA documentation style?*

The **Modern Language Association** *(MLA)* style is typically used for documenting sources in English and the humanities and consists of in-text citations that refer readers to a Works Cited list of all sources used in a paper that is organized alphabetically by authors' last names.

# Reading and Writing About Contemporary Issues

## MySkillsLab

The readings and activities in this part of the book can also be found in MySkillsLab. Some of the activities have been reformatted slightly to work online. However, by completing the activities in MySkillsLab, you will receive additional benefits, such as instant feedback on some of your answer choices.

# 12 Defining Ourselves: Our Multiple Identities

*Who are you?*

Some people might answer that question by stating their name. But many people would pause because they can't give a simple answer. Consider Pang Xu, a student at San Francisco City College. Thinking about the many roles she plays, Pang might see herself in many ways. She might say:

- I am a woman
- I am a daughter
- I am the mother of a two-year-old boy
- I am a wife
- I am an immigrant
- I am Chinese American
- I am a student
- I am an employee at The Gap
- I am a lover of animals

And the list could go on and on.

The readings in this chapter focus on *identity*: How we define ourselves, not only in our own heads but also in relationship to other people, groups, and society. Each reading in this chapter focuses on at least one type of identity, but sometimes multiple identities.

## WHY IS IDENTITY SUCH AN IMPORTANT CONTEMPORARY ISSUE?

Much of what you read in the contemporary press revolves around identity politics—groups' definitions of themselves and how others perceive them. These perceptions color individuals' experiences, expectations, and even the set of choices they face or the challenges they encounter. For example, government policies may offer assistance to people belonging to certain groups (e. g., people with disabilities, elderly people, sick people). But to offer help, the government must clearly define these terms. What exactly does *disabled* mean? At what age does a person become *elderly*? Should people with the flu be considered as sick as those with cancer?

## How does the Concept of Identity Tie in to My College Courses?

Identity is a core theme running through most humanities and social science courses. In a sociology course, for example, you might study ethnic groups in the United States and how some of them came to be considered ethnic minorities. Literature often focuses on self-expression and the quest for identity. In history and government courses, you will learn about the U.S. Census, which in recent years has struggled with defining racial and ethnic groups due to the huge diversity of the U.S. population. Abraham Maslow, a famous psychologist, defined a strong sense of self-identity as the ultimate achievement for any human being.

**TIPS FOR READING ABOUT IDENTITY**

Here are some tips for reading not only the selections in this chapter, but any reading about identity.

- **Consider the author's background.** Check the "Source and Context" section before each reading to learn more about the author. Doing so may give you perspective on his or her viewpoints. (Outside this text, check for any biographical information provided about the author.)

- **Keep an open mind.** Some of these readings may challenge your ideas or preconceptions about a topic. You may have an emotional response because some of the readings discuss difficult topics like obesity. Once you have experienced the emotion, reread the article more objectively, with a more critical eye, to better analyze and evaluate the author's thesis.

- **Look for similarities to your own life.** As you read, ask yourself whether the author's perceptions match yours. Have you had personal experiences with the topic; if so, do your opinions match the author's? Why or why not?

**SELECTION 1**
MySkillsLab

# The Space In-Between
## Santiago Quintana

## SOURCE AND CONTEXT

PERSONAL
ESSAY

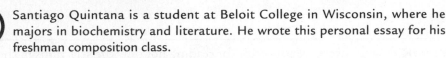

Santiago Quintana is a student at Beloit College in Wisconsin, where he majors in biochemistry and literature. He wrote this personal essay for his freshman composition class.

## A NOTE ON THE READING

Read the selection to understand how one young man grapples with his multiple identities and his interactions with others who've had similar experiences.

## PREVIEWING THE READING

*Using the steps listed on page 4, preview the reading selection. When you have finished, complete the following items.*

1. In what city and country was the author born? _____

2. In what city and state does the author live now? _____

3. Determine whether each statement is true (T) or false (F).

    _____ a. The author is likely to mention issues of race, gender, and nationality.

    _____ b. The author is unhappy with his current life.

 **MAKING CONNECTIONS**

*Most people feel that they are part of at least one minority group. What exactly is a minority group? To which minority group(s) do you belong, if any?*

## READING TIP

*Although this selection is fairly short, it contains some abstract language and sophisticated concepts. Adjust your reading rate to ensure you are achieving full comprehension. Read the selection several times if necessary.*

# The Space In-Between

## Santiago Quintana

1    There are around twenty million people living in Mexico City, and this number is constantly increasing. Mexico is where I was born and grew up, before I moved to Beloit, Wisconsin to attend Beloit College. The town of Beloit has roughly thirty thousand people. This means that about seven hundred towns the size of Beloit would fit inside Mexico City. In Mexico City, I was no more than a speck of dust in a dirty room. In Beloit, if I go have breakfast in one of three downtown cafés, I can be sure that there will be at least one person I know, probably around five or more. Beloit and Mexico City are two completely different worlds that I have come to call home.

2    I am Mexican. I should probably have beautiful cinnamon skin, hair black as night and falling straight like a waterfall to frame two glowing brown eyes. Many people think this is what a "true Mexican" looks like. Drawing a line between what is a true Mexican and what isn't based on looks is not a simple task. I myself think it is impossible. This stereotype has played a role in my life both in Mexico and Beloit. I have white skin, the only blue eyes in my family of brown eyes and curly light brown hair. In Mexico City, when I went to the market to buy vegetables for the week, people didn't bother to ask my name. They called me *güerito*, blond. I got asked if I am from the United States or from another country. I was never completely a part of the nation I was born and grew up in. In Beloit though, people are fascinated by my cultural background and ask about my customs and daily life back home. Inevitably, at some point in the conversation they tell me that I don't look Mexican. I live between two worlds: being racially "foreign" in Mexico, and being culturally "foreign" in Beloit.

3    Living a life in between two worlds, never completely a part of either, is a very complicated and extremely interesting place to be. Living in-between encourages growth and maturity. As a teenager, I struggled with feelings of not belonging and wanting to be a part of a group. I did not play soccer, or the guitar, and I suffered from bullying. The impact this had on my life was emotionally wrecking. Often when people find themselves in similar situations, they turn to familiar things for comfort. Things like a group they belong to, like a culture, or a race, or a religious group. This was not accessible to me in the same way as it was to others. On the other hand, though, standing on no man's land let me observe the effects of the culture I grew up with on my way of thinking, and has greatly influenced my area of focus in my college studies. Standing in this middle ground was a vantage point from which I could analyze the opinions I held and the habits I developed and see my virtues and faults through different eyes. The hardiest weeds live where the pavement meets the prairie. I live where outsider meets insider.

4        What happens in this middle ground is that concepts such as gender, race, nationality, and other identities seem held up by pins. They are extremely volatile and impermanent, constantly changing and molding. This knowledge is present with me every time I say "I am Mexican" or "I am white." I had thought that people who fit snugly into a stereotype would never experience being an outsider. But I soon found out otherwise.

5        The first time I touched on this subject with a friend of mine, he said that he saw what I meant. I was convinced he didn't. He was the perfect example of the "Mexican" racial stereotype. He explained that he couldn't know about my situation, but that he was having a similar problem with his family. His mom had recently mentioned that he should be going to church more, instead of hanging out with his friends on Sunday mornings. That was his middle place. He identified with these two seemingly separate identities that he had created: his Catholic self, and his social self. He was having trouble negotiating between the two. He stood in a place in the middle, where his church community was not understanding about his absences, and his friends made fun of his religious background. At the edges of these groups, he had thought about these two in much greater depth than I ever had, and he shared some incredible insights about the baggage associated with both identities, and how they weren't as solid as he thought; they had blurry edges and a lot of holes subject to interpretation.

6        It is the places in-between where the most potential for growth lives. All people have a place where they feel like outsiders, or not completely insiders. Realizing that this is where you are standing, and that it is perfectly fine to have one foot inside and one foot outside, will let the unique reveal itself through you. Being in-between can be difficult, but it is there that the most unexpected and wonderful things happen.

# UNDERSTANDING AND ANALYZING THE READING

## A. BUILDING VOCABULARY

### Context

*Using context and a dictionary if necessary, determine the meaning of each word as it is used in the selection.*

_____ 1. stereotype (paragraph 2)

    a. racial background

    b. ethnic group

    c. dual identity

    d. oversimplified idea

_____ 2. vantage point (paragraph 3)

    a. advantage

    b. intermediate location

    c. high score

    d. position

_____ 3. hardiest (paragraph 3)

    a.  most difficult

    b.  strongest

    c.  most stubborn

    d.  most beautiful

_____ 4. volatile (paragraph 4)

    a.  hot

    b.  unpredictable

    c.  weak

    d.  personal

_____ 5. baggage (paragraph 5)

    a.  emotional issues

    b.  suitcases

    c.  happiness

    d.  reasons

## Word Parts

### A REVIEW OF PREFIXES AND SUFFIXES

**IM-**  means *not*.
**-ER**  means *one who*.

*Use your knowledge of word parts and the review above to fill in the blanks in the following sentences.*

1. *Impermanent* (paragraph 4) means _____ permanent or _____ lasting.

2. An *outsider* (paragraph 4) is _____ sits outside the mainstream of a society or culture.

## B. UNDERSTANDING THE THESIS AND OTHER MAIN IDEAS

*Select the best answer.*

_____ 1. The statement that best expresses the thesis or central thought of this reading is

    a.  Outsiders face serious challenges in almost all aspects of their lives.

    b.  People of Mexican origin generally have difficulty adjusting to life as immigrants in the United States.

    c.  Not fully belonging to specific groups can be difficult, but it offers many opportunities for growth.

    d.  Most adolescents have difficulty "fitting in" when they go to college or take their first full-time job.

_____ 2. The topic of paragraph 2 is
    a. the differences between Mexico City and Beloit.
    b. Mexican stereotypes of Americans.
    c. the author's personal appearance.
    d. differences in ethnic groups in North America and South America.

_____ 3. The main idea of paragraph 5 can be found in the
    a. first sentence.
    b. third sentence.
    c. sixth sentence.
    d. last sentence.

## C. IDENTIFYING DETAILS

*Select the best answer.*

_____ 1. Which type of identity does the author *not* discuss in "The Space In-Between"?
    a. religious identity
    b. racial identity
    c. sexual identity
    d. national identity

_____ 2. The word that Mexicans use to describe the author's hair color is
    a. *güerito.*
    b. *rubio.*
    c. *peloso.*
    d. *rojo.*

_____ 3. The author's friend is struggling with two sides of himself: his _____ self and his __self.
    a. old, new
    b. social, Catholic
    c. angry, friendly
    d. American, Latino

_____ 4. Which of the following physical features is not described as typical of Mexicans?
    a. brown eyes
    b. black, straight hair
    c. cinnamon skin
    d. a prominent nose

## D. RECOGNIZING METHODS OF ORGANIZATION AND TRANSITIONS

*Select the best answer.*

_____ 1. The organizational pattern of paragraph 1 is
   a. chronological order.
   b. comparison and contrast.
   c. summary.
   d. order of importance.

_____ 2. The transitional word or phrase in paragraph 1 that signals its pattern of organization is
   a. born.
   b. no more than.
   c. speck of dust.
   d. different.

_____ 3. The organizational pattern of paragraph 3 is
   a. process.
   b. classification.
   c. cause and effect.
   d. definition.

## E. READING AND THINKING VISUALLY

*Select the best answer.*

_____ 1. A photo of the author appears on page 329. Suppose the author wished to include a second image with the reading. Which of the following would best help readers visualize his main ideas in paragraphs 1–3?
   a. a map showing the relative locations of Mexico City and Beloit
   b. a photo of a young man with traditionally or stereotypically Mexican features
   c. a photo of the author's brothers and sisters
   d. a photo of the Mexico City market in which he purchased the week's supply of vegetables

## F. FIGURING OUT IMPLIED MEANINGS

*Indicate whether each statement is true (T) or false (F).*

_____ 1. The author is an illegal immigrant in the United States.

_____ 2. The author implies that the definitions of race, gender, and nationality are quite complicated.

_____ 3. The author has not yet accepted his position as an "outsider" in America.

_____ 4. The author implies that most Americans hold racist views of Mexicans.

_____ 5. The author feels more popular and well known in Beloit than he ever did in Mexico City.

_____ 6. The author was probably a "loner" as a younger man.

## G. THINKING CRITICALLY: ANALYZING THE AUTHOR'S TECHNIQUE

*Select the best answer.*

_____ 1. The author's tone in "The Space In-Between" can best be described as
   a. nostalgic.
   b. angry.
   c. introspective.
   d. depressed.

_____ 2. Which of the following phrases is a metaphor for the way the author perceived himself when he lived in Mexico City?
   a. "a speck of dust in a dirty room" (paragraph 1)
   b. "people didn't bother to ask my name" (paragraph 2)
   c. "standing on no man's land" (paragraph 3)
   d. "perfect example of the 'Mexican' racial stereotype" (paragraph 5)

_____ 3. When the author says that identities have "blurry edges and a lot of holes" (paragraph 5), he means that identities
   a. are primarily dictated by one's country of birth.
   b. can be clearly defined.
   c. is purely an academic term used by sociology instructors and nobody else.
   d. have many sides that don't always fit together easily.

_____ 4. To support his argument, the author uses primarily
   a. personal experience.
   b. statistics.
   c. quotations from experts.
   d. academic research.

## H. THINKING CRITICALLY: ANALYZING THE AUTHOR'S MESSAGE

*Select the best answer.*

_____ 1. According to the author, all of the following can help those people standing in-between different groups to grow and mature, *except*

    a. recognizing and admitting that they are outsiders.

    b. understanding that it is perfectly fine to exist between two groups.

    c. viewing personal opinions and habits with a critical eye.

    d. choosing one primary group with which to identify themselves.

_____ 2. The author summarizes his *current* outsider status in one sentence when he says

    a. "There are around twenty million people living in Mexico City, and this number is constantly increasing." (paragraph 1)

    b. "Inevitably, at some point in the conversation, they tell me I don't look Mexican." (paragraph 2)

    c. "I live between two worlds: being racially 'foreign' in Mexico, and being culturally 'foreign' in Beloit.'" (paragraph 2)

    d. "As a teenager, I struggled with feelings of not belonging and wanting to be a part of a group." (paragraph 3)

_____ 3. When the author says, "The hardiest weeds live where the pavement meets the prairie." (paragraph 3), he means that

    a. he considers himself as worthless as a weed.

    b. it is easier to be an outsider in an urban setting than in a rural setting.

    c. his outsider status has given him great strength.

    d. he is succeeding in overcoming the discrimination he faces every day.

# WRITING IN RESPONSE TO THE READING

## I. WRITING A PARAPHRASE

*Complete the following paraphrase of paragraph 2 by filling in the missing words or phrases. Remember that a paraphrase substitutes your words for the author's.*

The author comes from the country of _____. Both Mexicans and non-Mexicans think he should have _____ skin, _____, and _____, _____. But, the author realizes, it's very difficult to define being Mexican by ————————————. Unlike the conventional image of Mexican people, the author has ——————— skin, ——————— eyes, and curly brown hair. All of these ——————— made people in Mexico City ask him if he was ——————— ———————. For this reason, he never truly felt like part of the country he was born in. At ——————— in Wisconsin, people ask him about life in Mexico and usually mention that he doesn't look like a "typical" Mexican. As a result, he doesn't feel quite at home in either place. He feels that his ——————— doesn't match that of the majority of the Mexican people, and that his ——————— doesn't match that of the people in ———————.

## J. ANALYZING THE ISSUE AND ARGUMENT

1. What question is the author trying to answer in this personal essay?
2. Write a brief statement summarizing the author's argument. Is this argument inductive or deductive?
3. "The Space In-Between" is relatively short. What other types of evidence could the author have provided to support his argument/thesis?
4. What is the author's background, and is he qualified to write about the topic? Why or why not?
5. Does the essay contain any appeals to emotion? If so, are they effective and fair to the reader?

## K. WRITING PARAGRAPHS AND ESSAYS

*Write a paragraph or essay in response to the following writing prompts.*

1. In paragraph 3, the author says that standing on no man's land "has greatly influenced my area of focus in my college studies." Write a paragraph in which you explore one factor that influenced your choice of major and or your approach to college.
2. Write a paragraph in which you summarize the author's feelings about Mexico City.
3. "The Space In-Between" is an emotional exploration of one man's feelings of being an outsider. Write a paragraph in which you suggest a few images that could effectively convey a visual sense of an outsider standing out from the crowd. For example, one image might be a punk rocker at a classical music concert.

4. This essay talks about the way a person is composed of multiple identities. What are your identities? How do they complement one another, or how do they conflict? Is one of your identities dominant over all the others? Write an essay exploring these questions.

5. Have you ever felt like an outsider looking in? Write an essay about your experience. Do you feel that you learned anything from the experience, or matured as a result of it?

6. Santiago Quintana refers to the places in-between as the places "where the most potential for growth lives" (paragraph 6). However, he does not provide many specific examples of the ways he has grown or of what he has learned. Assume that you can step out of yourself and observe yourself for a day, just like you would observe another person. Write an essay about what you'd learn about yourself and the conclusions you might reach.

# SELECTION 2

MySkillsLab

# Enhancing Your Body Image

Rebecca J. Donatelle

### SOURCE AND CONTEXT

TEXTBOOK
EXCERPT

The following reading was taken from the textbook *Access to Health*, by Rebecca J. Donatelle. Professor Donatelle teaches at Oregon State University in the College of Public Health and Human Sciences. In the introduction to her textbook, the author says her goal is "to empower students to identify their health risks, create plans for change, and make healthy lifestyle changes part of their daily routines." She also states that her book is based on scientifically valid information in order to help students "be smarter in their health decision making, more involved in their personal health, and more active as [advocates] for healthy changes in their community."

### A NOTE ON THE READING

Read the selection to understand how people perceive their own bodies, as well as their varying levels of acceptance of their physical appearance. Ask yourself: How much control does a person have over his or her physical appearance? Is there an ideal balance between being healthy and being overly concerned with physical appearance?

### PREVIEWING THE READING

*Using the steps listed on page 4, preview the reading selection. When you have finished, complete the following items.*

1. The topic of the reading is _____.
2. List three factors that influence body image.

   a. _____

   b. _____

   c. _____

3. Indicate whether each statement is true (T) or false (F).

   _____ a. Extreme dieting is an effective weight-loss strategy.

   _____ b. Some people cannot become slender no matter how hard they try.

 MAKING
CONNECTIONS

*Based on the magazines you read, the TV shows and movies you watch, and the advertisements you see all around you, what is the "ideal" body type for the American woman? For the American man?*

*As you read, highlight the author's main points.*

# Enhancing Your Body Image

Rebecca J. Donatelle

1    As he began his arm curls, Ali checked his form in the full-length mirror on the weight-room wall. His biceps were bulking up, but after 6 months of regular weight training, he expected more. His pecs, too, still lacked definition, and his abdomen wasn't the washboard he envisioned. So after a 45-minute upper-body workout, he added 200 sit-ups. Then he left the gym to shower back at his apartment: No way was he going to risk any of the gym regulars seeing his flabby torso unclothed. But by the time Ali got home and looked in the mirror, frustration had turned to anger. He was just too fat! To punish himself for his slow progress, instead of taking a shower, he put on his Nikes and went for a 4-mile run.

2    When you look in the mirror, do you like what you see? If you feel disappointed, frustrated, or even angry like Ali, you're not alone. A spate of recent studies is revealing that a majority of adults are dissatisfied with their bodies. For instance, a study of men in the United States, Austria, and France found that the ideal bodies they envisioned for themselves were an average of 28 pounds more muscular than their actual bodies. Most adult women—80 percent in one study—are also dissatisfied with their appearance, but for a different reason: Most want to lose weight. Tragically, negative feelings about one's body can contribute to disordered eating, excessive exercise, and other behaviors that can threaten your health—and your life. Having a healthy body image is a key indicator of self-esteem, and can contribute to reduced stress, an increased sense of personal empowerment, and more joyful living.

## What Is Body Image?

3    Body image is fundamental to our sense of who we are. Consider the fact that mirrors made from polished stone have been found at archaeological sites dating from before 6000 **BCE**; humans have been viewing themselves for **millennia**.

**BCE**
"Before the Common Era"; a synonym for B.C. (as opposed to A.D.)
**millennia**
thousands of years

Dissatisfaction with one's appearance and shape is an all-too-common feeling in today's society that can foster unhealthy attitudes and thought patterns, as well as disordered eating and exercising patterns.

But the term *body image* refers to more than just what you see when you look in a mirror. The National Eating Disorders Association (NEDA) identifies several additional components of body image:

- How you see yourself in your mind
- What you believe about your own appearance (including your memories, assumptions, and generalizations)
- How you feel about your body, including your height, shape, and weight
- How you sense and control your body as you move

4    NEDA identifies a *negative body image* as either a distorted perception of your shape, or feelings of discomfort, shame, or anxiety about your body. You may be convinced that only other people are attractive, whereas your own body is a sign of personal failure. Does this attitude remind you of Ali? It should, because he clearly exhibits signs of a negative body image. In contrast, NEDA describes a *positive body image* as a true perception of your appearance: You see yourself as you really are. You understand that everyone is different, and you celebrate your uniqueness—including your "flaws," which you know have nothing to do with your value as a person.

5    Is your body image negative or positive—or is it somewhere in between? Researchers at the University of Arizona have developed a body image continuum that may help you decide (see Figure 1, below). Like a **spectrum** of light, a continuum represents a series of stages that aren't entirely distinct. Notice that the continuum identifies behaviors associated with particular states, from total dissociation with one's body to body acceptance and body ownership.

**spectrum**
band of colors

## Many Factors Influence Body Image

6    You're not born with a body image, but you do begin to develop one at an early age as you compare yourself against images you see in the world around you, and interpret the responses of family members and peers to your appearance. Let's look more closely at the factors that probably played a role in the development of your body image.

### The Media and Popular Culture

7    Today images of six-pack loaded actors such as Taylor Lautner send young women to the movies in hoards and snapshots of emaciated celebrities such as Lindsay Lohan and Paris Hilton dominate the tabloids and sell magazines. The images and celebrities in the media set the standard for what we find attractive, leading some people to go to dangerous extremes to have the biggest biceps or fit into size 2 jeans. Most of us think of this obsession with appearance as a recent phenomenon. The truth is, it has long been part of American culture. During the early twentieth century, while men idolized the hearty outdoorsman President Teddy Roosevelt, women pulled their corsets ever tighter to achieve unrealistically tiny waists. In the 1920s and 1930s, men emulated the burly cops and robbers in gangster films, while women dieted and bound their breasts to achieve the boyish "flapper" look. After World War II, both men and women strove for a healthy, wholesome appearance, but by the 1960s, tough-guys like Clint Eastwood and Marlon Brando were the male ideal, whereas rail-thin supermodel Twiggy embodied the nation's standard of female beauty.

## FIGURE 1  BODY IMAGE CONTINUUM

This is part of a two-part continuum. Individuals whose responses fall to the far left side of the continuum have a highly negative body image, whereas responses to the right indicate a positive body image.

| BODY HATE/ DISSOCIATION | DISTORTED BODY IMAGE | BODY PREOCCUPIED/ OBSESSED | BODY ACCEPTANCE | BODY OWNERSHIP |
|---|---|---|---|---|
| I often feel separated and distant from my body—as if it belongs to someone else. | I spend a significant amount of time exercising and dieting to change my body. | I spend a significant amount of time viewing my body in the mirror. | I base my body image equally on social norms and my own self-concept. | My body is beautiful to me. |
| I don't see anything positive or even neutral about my body shape and size. | My body shape and size keep me from dating or finding someone who will treat me the way I want to be treated. | I spend a significant amount of time comparing my body to others. | I pay attention to my body and my appearance because it is important to me, but it only occupies a small part of my day. | My feelings about my body are not influenced by society's concept of an ideal body shape. |
| I don't believe others when they tell me I look ok. | I have considered changing or have changed my body shape and size through surgical means so I can accept myself. | I have days when I feel fat. | I nourish my body so it has strength and energy to achieve my physical goals. | I know that the significant others in my life will always find me attractive. |
| I hate the way I look in the mirror and often isolate myself from others. | | I am preoccupied with my body. | | |
| | | I accept society's ideal body shape and size as the best body shape and size. | | |

*Source: Smiley, King, and Avey, "Eating Issues and Body Image Continuum."*

8   Today, more than 66 percent of Americans are overweight or obese; thus, a significant disconnect exists between the media's idealized images of male and female bodies and the typical American body. At the same time, the media—in the form of television, the Internet, movies, and print publications—is a more powerful and pervasive presence than ever before. In fact, one study of more than 4,000 television commercials revealed that approximately one out of every four sends some sort of "attractiveness message." Thus, Americans are **bombarded** daily with messages telling us that we just don't measure up.

**bombarded**
continually
exposed to

### Family, Community, and Cultural Groups

9   The members of society with whom we most often interact—our family members, friends, and others—strongly influence the way we see ourselves. Parents are especially influential in body image development. For instance, it's common and natural for fathers of adolescent girls to experience feelings of discomfort related to their daughters' changing bodies. If they are able to navigate these feelings successfully, and validate the acceptability of their daughters' appearance throughout **puberty**, it's likely that they'll help their daughters maintain a positive body image. In contrast, if they verbalize or indicate even subtle judgments about their daughters' changing bodies, girls may begin to question how members of the opposite sex view their bodies in general. In addition, mothers who model body acceptance or body ownership may be more likely to foster a similar positive body image in their daughters, whereas mothers who are frustrated with or ashamed of their bodies may have a greater chance of fostering these attitudes in their daughters.

**puberty**
the period during
which adolescents
become capable of
reproduction

10   Interactions with siblings and other relatives, peers, teachers, coworkers, and other community members can also influence body image development. For instance, peer harassment (teasing and bullying) is widely acknowledged to contribute to a negative body image. Moreover, associations within one's cultural group appear to influence body image. For example, studies have found that European American females experience the highest rates of body dissatisfaction, and as a minority group becomes more **acculturated** into the mainstream, the body dissatisfaction levels of women in that group increase.

**acculturated**
becomes a part of
mainstream culture

11   Body image also reflects the larger culture in which you live. In parts of Africa, for example, obesity has been associated with abundance, erotic desirability, and fertility. Girls in Mauritania traditionally were force-fed to increase their body size in order to signal a family's wealth, although the practice has become much less common in recent years.

### Physiological and Psychological Factors

12   Recent neurological research has suggested that people who have been diagnosed with a body image disorder show differences in the brain's ability to regulate chemicals called *neurotransmitters*, which are linked to mood. Poor regulation of neurotransmitters is also involved in depression and in anxiety disorders, including obsessive-compulsive disorder. One study linked distortions in body image to a malfunctioning in the brain's visual processing region that was revealed by **MRI scanning**.

**MRI scanning**
magnetic resonance
imaging; technology
that creates images
of the interior of
the body, often for
medical diagnosis

## IS THE MEDIA'S OBSESSION WITH APPEARANCE A NEW PHENOMENON?

Although the exact nature of the "in" look may change from generation to generation, unrealistic images of both male and female celebrities are nothing new. For example, in the 1960s, images of brawny film stars such as Clint Eastwood and ultrathin models such as Twiggy dominated the media.

### How Can I Build a More Positive Body Image?

13    If you want to develop a more positive body image, your first step might be to bust some toxic myths and challenge some commonly held attitudes in contemporary society. Have you been accepting these four myths?[10] How would you answer the questions that accompany them?

14    **Myth 1: How you look is more important than who you are.**   Do you think your weight is important in defining who you are? How much does your weight matter to your success? How much does it matter to you to have friends who are thin and attractive? How important do you think being thin is in trying to attract your ideal partner?

15    **Myth 2: Anyone can be slender and attractive if they work at it.**   When you see someone who is extremely thin, what assumptions do you make about that person? When you see someone who is overweight or obese, what assumptions do you make? Have you ever berated yourself for not having the "willpower" to change some aspect of your body?

16    **Myth 3: Extreme dieting is an effective weight-loss strategy.**    Do you believe in trying fad diets or "quick-weight-loss" products? How far would you be willing to go to attain the "perfect" body?

17    **Myth 4: Appearance is more important than health.**    How do you evaluate whether a person is healthy? Do you believe it's possible for overweight people to be healthy? Is your desire to change some aspect of your body motivated by health reasons or by concerns about appearance?

# UNDERSTANDING AND ANALYZING THE READING

## A. BUILDING VOCABULARY

### Context

*Using context and a dictionary if necessary, determine the meaning of each word as it is used in the selection.*

_____ 1.  spate (paragraph 2)
   a.  large number in quick succession
   b.  type of malice
   c.  unscientific research study
   d.  set of possible answers

_____ 2.  continuum (paragraph 5)
   a.  ongoing process
   b.  sequence
   c.  natural light
   d.  questionnaire

_____ 3.  emaciated (paragraph 7)
   a.  attacked
   b.  world-famous
   c.  overpaid
   d.  extremely thin

_____ 4.  obese (paragraph 8)
   a.  slightly overweight
   b.  disproportionate
   c.  very heavy
   d.  unhealthy

_____ 5.  peers (paragraph 10)
   a.  close relatives
   b.  ancestors
   c.  people of the same age
   d.  English royalty

_____ 6.  toxic (paragraph 13)
   a.  poisonous
   b.  common
   c.  unrealistic
   d.  silly

## Word Parts

> ### A REVIEW OF PREFIXES AND ROOTS
>
> **DIS-**   means *apart, away,* or *not.*
>
> **NEURO**   means *nerve.*

*Use your knowledge of word parts and the review above to fill in the blanks in the following sentences.*

1. A person who is *dissatisfied* (paragraph 2) with his or her body is _____ satisfied with his or her appearance.

2. *Neurotransmitters* (paragraph 12) transmit electrical impulses between _____, while *neurology* is the study of _____ and _____.

### B. UNDERSTANDING THE THESIS AND OTHER MAIN IDEAS

*Select the best answer.*

_____ 1. Which of the following is the best statement of the selection's thesis or central thought?

    a. Understanding four common myths regarding weight loss can help people set more realistic goals when they begin a diet.

    b. Many people suffer from a negative body image that is reinforced by Hollywood celebrities, media, and companies that are trying to sell products.

    c. Body image is important to emotional well-being, and people vary greatly in their body acceptance, often subscribing to commonly held myths about physical appearance.

    d. Ideal body images change over time; women used to want voluptuous bodies but now want to be thin, while men used to prefer thinness but now want to be muscular.

_____ 2. Which of the following sentences states the main idea of paragraph 9?

    a. first sentence: "The members of society..."

    b. second sentence: "Parents are especially..."

    c. third sentence: "For instance, ..."

    d. sixth sentence: "In addition, mothers..."

_____ 3. The topic of paragraph 11 is
   a. the connection between body image and culture.
   b. body image in African countries.
   c. the connection between body image and fertility.
   d. the relationship between being wealthy and being overweight.

## C. IDENTIFYING DETAILS

*Select the best answer.*

_____ 1. Approximately what percentage of Americans are overweight or obese today?
   a. 25 percent
   b. 33 percent
   c. 50 percent
   d. 66 percent

_____ 2. On which continent has obesity been associated with desirability and fertility?
   a. North America
   b. Europe
   c. Africa
   d. Asia

_____ 3. Which of the following is *not* a result of having a healthy body image?
   a. an increased sense of personal empowerment
   b. increased self-esteem
   c. a lower level of stress
   d. a higher income level

_____ 4. Which of the following is *not* a component of your body image, as defined by the National Eating Disorders Association (NEDA)?
   a. how you feel about the shape and weight of your body
   b. how others perceive your physical appearance
   c. what you believe about your own appearance
   d. how you control your body as you move

## D. RECOGNIZING METHODS OF ORGANIZATION AND TRANSITIONS

*Select the best answer.*

_____ 1. The pattern of organization used in paragraph 3 is
   a. classification.              c. cause and effect.
   b. definition.                  d. process.

_____ 2. Which transitional word or phrase signals the organizational pattern of paragraph 3?
   a. fundamental to               c. refers to
   b. consider the fact that       d. what you believe

_____ 3. The overall pattern of organization used for paragraphs 6–12 (under the heading "Many Factors Influence Body Image") is
   a. classification.              c. chronological order
   b. order of importance.         d. definition.

## E. READING AND THINKING VISUALLY

*Select the best answer.*

_____ 1. The author likely chose to include the photos on page 343 to
   a. demonstrate the ideal body type for both women and men.
   b. illustrate how unrealistic images of both men and women have been used in the media for decades.
   c. provide role models for adolescents and young adults trying to develop a more positive body image.
   d. help readers understand the obesity crisis in America by picturing celebrities who have healthier body types.

_____ 2. Mariah looks in a mirror and thinks, "No matter how hard I exercise, my hips are too wide and I have too much belly flab. If I'm ever going to find anyone who's interested in dating me or marrying me, I'll need to have plastic surgery first." In which category of the body image continuum does Mariah fall?
   a. body preoccupied/obsessed
   b. distorted body image
   c. body hate/dissociation
   d. body acceptance

## F. FIGURING OUT IMPLIED MEANINGS

*Indicate whether each statement is true (T) or false (F).*

_____  1. Force-feeding girls to signify their families' wealth is common in Mauritania today.

_____  2. An older woman who thinks "My body is beautiful to me" has a sense of body ownership.

_____  3. Emphasis on body image in America is mostly a twenty-first-century phenomenon.

_____  4. A person who is bullied is more likely to develop a negative body image than one who is not bullied.

_____  5. Almost all people fit perfectly into one of the five categories of the body image continuum.

## G. THINKING CRITICALLY: ANALYZING THE AUTHOR'S TECHNIQUE

*Select the best answer.*

_____  1. The author begins the selection with Ali's story in order to

    a. criticize people who are obsessed with their bodies.

    b. imply that Ali needs to change his diet to achieve his fitness goals.

    c. provide a common example of a person with a negative body image.

    d. offer a role model for those who are trying to "bulk up."

_____  2. The author's primary purpose in "Enhancing Your Body Image" is to

    a. motivate overweight readers to begin a stricter exercise regimen and a healthier diet.

    b. challenge the "perfect body" stereotypes that are perpetuated by advertising agencies and the media.

    c. make readers aware of the importance of a healthy body image and the factors that affect it.

    d. emphasize the role of body chemistry and personal physiology in determining a person's weight and overall health.

_____ 3. To support her thesis, the author cites all of the following statistics, *except*

    a.  10 percent of college students suffer from body hatred.

    b.  66 percent of Americans are overweight or obese.

    c.  80 percent of adult women report dissatisfaction with their appearance.

    d.  25 percent of television commercials send messages about personal attractiveness.

_____ 4. The author's tone is best described as

    a.  informative.

    b.  irreverent.

    c.  self-righteous.

    d.  abstract.

_____ 5. Three of the following sentences from the reading are facts. One is an opinion. Which one is the opinion?

    a.  "A spate of recent studies is revealing that a majority of adults are dissatisfied with their bodies." (paragraph 2)

    b.  "Consider the fact that mirrors made from polished stone have been found at archaeological sites dating from before 6000 BCE; humans have been viewing themselves for millennia." (paragraph 3)

    c.  "The images and celebrities in the media set the standard for what we find attractive, leading some people to go to dangerous extremes to have the biggest biceps or fit into size 2 jeans." (paragraph 7)

    d.  "Today, more than 66 percent of Americans are overweight or obese." (paragraph 8)

## H. THINKING CRITICALLY: ANALYZING THE AUTHOR'S MESSAGE

*Select the best answer.*

_____ 1. In which paragraph can you find the author's key assumption about the benefits of a healthy body image?

    a.  paragraph 1

    b.  paragraph 2

    c.  paragraph 5

    d.  paragraph 6

_____ 2. What does the phrase "attractiveness message" mean in paragraph 8?

a. a component of a TV commercial that implies what is attractive and what isn't

b. a TV commercial that features only young people

c. a hidden message that only younger, hipper people will understand

d. a product endorsement made by an attractive celebrity or popular sports figure

_____ 3. The author uses a series of questions in paragraphs 14–17 in order to

a. allow readers to determine the category of the body image continuum into which they fit.

b. help students prepare for likely exam questions about this reading.

c. aid readers in distinguishing weight problems caused by physiological issues from weight problems caused by psychological issues.

d. get readers to examine their own ideas and assumptions about body image and physical appearance.

_____ 4. The author puts quotation marks around "quick-weight-loss" and "perfect" in paragraph 16 in order to

a. use the same terminology that many dieters use.

b. imply her skepticism regarding those terms.

c. signal the reader that these are key concepts in the reading.

d. suggest that fad diets are sometimes the most effective means of weight loss.

## WRITING IN RESPONSE TO THE READING

### I. REVIEWING AND ORGANIZING IDEAS WITH A MAP

*Complete the following map of the reading selection by filling in the missing words or phrases.*

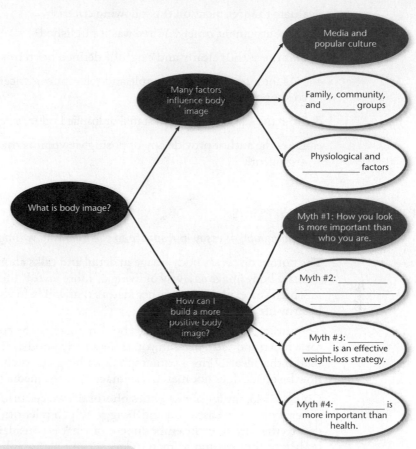

## J. ANALYZING THE ISSUE AND ARGUMENT

1. Identify at least three contemporary issues discussed in this reading. Then phrase each as a question that the author raises or answers.

**Example**

| Issue | Question |
| --- | --- |
| Obesity in America | Why are 66 percent of Americans obese? |

2. Write a statement that briefly summarizes the author's argument. Is the author's argument inductive or deductive?

3. Identify at least one claim of fact and one claim of value in the reading.

4. What is the author's background, and is she qualified to write about the topic? Why or why not? Do you find any bias in the selection?

5. Evaluate the argument on the following criteria:

   a. Is the argument timely? When was it published?

   b. Has the author clearly and carefully defined her terms?

   c. Has the author provided ample and relevant evidence? Provide examples to support your answer.

   d. Does the selection include a stated or implied value system? If so, describe it.

   e. Does the author provide any opposing viewpoints that would refute her argument?

## K. WRITING PARAGRAPHS AND ESSAYS

*Write a paragraph or essay in response to the following writing prompts.*

1. The author discusses body image in detail and talks about how to develop a positive body image as a way of living a "more joyful" life. Write a paragraph in which you explain some other factors that will help you lead a happy, healthy life.

2. The author mentions celebrities who demonstrate the current "body ideal" for women and men, but can you think of any popular figures who do not match this ideal? Write a paragraph describing one such figure, explaining how he or she does not match the image that the media portray as the ideal.

3. On page 343, the author provides photos of two celebrities of a previous generation: Clint Eastwood and Twiggy. Which celebrities would you suggest to the author as the embodiment of what is considered the "ideal" body type for men and women today? Write a paragraph outlining your recommendations to the author.

4. The author talks about obesity, but she doesn't explore the reasons why so many Americans are overweight. Write an essay in which you explore the reasons for Americans' obesity and outline some solutions to the problem.

5. Write an essay about someone you know (you do not have to provide his or her real name). Where do you think he or she falls on the body image continuum? Based on this reading, what recommendations would you give this person?

6. The author claims that the media send strong signals regarding what is attractive in our society. These signals are reinforced by advertisements. Write an essay exploring some ways you can affect or help change the practices of the media and advertisers who contribute to the high levels of negative body image in U.S. society.

# SELECTION
# 3
## MySkillsLab

# All Guts, No Glory

## Molly M. Ginty

## SOURCE AND CONTEXT

MAGAZINE
ARTICLE

A longer version of this article originally appeared in *Ms.* Magazine, a women's-rights magazine founded in 1971. According to its Web site, *Ms.* was the first U.S. magazine to explain and advocate for the ERA (equal rights amendment), rate presidential candidates on women's issues, put domestic violence and sexual harassment on the cover of a women's magazine, and blow the whistle on the influence of advertising on journalism. The author, Molly M. Ginty, has written not only for *Ms.*, but also for *On the Issues Magazine, Women's eNews,* and PBS.org.

## A NOTE ON THE READING

Read the selection to understand women's changing roles in the U.S. military. Ask yourself: How is it possible to be injured in wartime without serving on the battlefield? Should women fight alongside men in armed combat?

## PREVIEWING THE READING

*Using the steps listed on page 4, preview the reading selection. When you have finished, complete the following items.*

1. The topic of this reading is _____.

2. Indicate whether each statement is true (T) or false (F).

    _____ a. The article will discuss the problem of sexual assault on military women.

    _____ b. Women today compose almost one-sixth of the armed forces.

    _____ c. The U.S. approach to women in combat is similar to that of Canada and France.

**MAKING**
**CONNECTIONS**

*Have you ever served in the military, or do you know someone who has? If so, what roles have women played in the armed services? Do you know any women who have served in the military? Have you ever discussed their experiences with them?*

**READING TIP**

*As you read, keep track of the types of evidence the author uses to support her thesis and argument.*

## Military Women: All Guts, No Glory

### Molly M. Ginty

1    Captain Dawn Halfaker saw a flash of light and heard an explosion—then suffered shrapnel wounds, a 12-day coma, and the amputation of her right arm.

2    Sergeant Rebekah Havrilla collected the remains of a suicide bomber and his victims from a room where blood ran down the walls—then endured years of nightmares.

3    Private First Class Lori Piestewa was ambushed by insurgents, who killed three of the passengers in her Humvee—then was taken captive and died of her head wounds.

**belies**
contradicts

**emerita**
retired

**relegating**
consigning to an
inferior rank

4    If you ask the U.S. military, none of these women officially served in battle. That's because females in the armed forces don't technically fight in ground combat. But the Department of Defense (DOD) policy **belies** the reality of the conflicts in Iraq and Afghanistan, and its willful avoidance of the truth denies military women safety training, health care, and career advancement.

5    "It's time to give servicewomen the recognition they deserve," says Brigadier General Evelyn Foote, president **emerita** of the Alliance for National Defense in Alexandria, Virginia. "Let's join the 21st century and shed this exclusionary policy."

6    Military women today constitute almost one-sixth of the armed forces, but for most of its history, the U.S. military kept women out of battle, **relegating** them to support positions such as nursing. Although more than 80 percent of military jobs are now open to women, the DOD moved in 1994 to ban women from serving in "combat operations" such as the short-range field artillery, Special Forces, and infantry.

7    Is there a good reason for these bans? Not according to a 1997 report conducted by the Rand Corporation, which found that full gender integration in the armed services would have little effect on "readiness, cohesion, and morale." And both the Military Leadership Diversity Commission and the Defense Advisory Committee on Women in the Services have urged the DOD to lift the combat ban.

Military women today constitute almost one-sixth of the armed forces, yet their efforts are seldom recognized.

8    Modern military conflicts put every soldier, male or female, directly in the line of fire. For instance, according to Patricia Hayes, national director of women's health for the Veterans Health Administration, one of the most dangerous jobs in the military today is driving a truck—a position that many women hold.

9    "The issue of women in battle is coming to a head now because there's no demarcation between combat and non-combat in the Middle East," says former U.S. Representative Pat Schroeder (D-Colo.), who served on the U.S. House Armed Services Committee from 1973 to 1996. "As it stands, there no longer *is* an official front line."

10    Today, women represent 15 percent of the active military, 18 percent of the reserve, and 20 percent of all new recruits. With so many women in service (and with submarine assignments just opened to women in 2010), the DOD may no longer be able to keep arguing that it can legally bar women from certain jobs. "Everyone in uniform is in combat," says Representative Susan Davis (D-Calif.), ranking member of the House Subcommittee on Military Personnel. "Yet women in uniform are not afforded the proper training for combat since they are technically barred from engaging the enemy this way."

11    If they were officially allowed to serve in battle, military women could better protect themselves from injury and could get better care if they were hurt. Consider the bind of the military's "lioness" and "female engagement" teams of women soldiers who gather information from conservative Muslim women whose beliefs prevent them from talking directly to men.

12    "These female intelligence service members are 'attached' to units and not directly assigned to them," explains Greg Jacob, policy director for the New York City–based Servicewomen's Action Network. "And when their work is not documented by their parent command, their record doesn't always reflect their combat-related injuries."

13    Captain Barbara Wilson, creator of the website American Women in Uniform, says that when she served in the Air Force back in the 1950s, the men in her unit treated women recruits as "nothing more than secretaries in uniform." Even though Wilson could best them all at firing practice, the men claimed women couldn't operate machinery. "There was only one way to respond to this discrimination," says Wilson. "I tuned it out and just focused on my work."

14    When Wilson entered the service, critics also said women were too delicate to fight, or to pull fallen male soldiers to safety. They said the distraction of women batting their eyelashes would destroy military units' camaraderie. They predicted that if women and men served in battle together, they would be too busy flirting, or feuding, to effectively ward off the enemy. "None of these ridiculous prophecies came true," says Pat Schroeder.

15    "From the push-ups and drills of basic training onward, I busted my ass to keep up with the men so they had no reason to give me grief over my gender," says Sergeant Rebekah Havrilla, who spent a year in Afghanistan defusing bombs. "But I was the only female on my team and had to fend off sexual, emotional, and verbal abuse every day."

16    When it comes to rape, which Havrilla suffered in 2007 at the hands of a male colleague, the military's misogyny shows itself at its worst. Military women are twice as

likely as civilian women to be assaulted, often by the very men who are supposedly their comrades. One in three female vets reports rape or attempted rape. And if a soldier becomes pregnant as a result of sexual assault, military health benefits won't cover an abortion.

17    Women in the military say they are afraid to visit latrines at night because they could be assaulted. During recent congressional hearings (which keep racking up in number but do little to stem rampant rapes), one woman said she was reluctant to report being attacked because she feared she would be demoted for failing to carry a weapon when it happened.

18    "Opening more military jobs to women could help address the rampant problem of sexual assault," says Nancy Duff Campbell, copresident of the Washington-based National Women's Law Center. "We know from experience in other non-traditional employment environments—for example, with women police and firefighters—that when their members hit critical mass, incidents of sexual harassment declined."

19    While the U.S. government says women are not fit to serve in combat, the rest of the world doesn't agree—at least not Belgium, Canada, Denmark, France, Germany, Hungary, India, Israel, the Netherlands, New Zealand, Norway, Portugal, South Africa, South Korea, and Sweden.

20    In late September, Australia, which contributes the largest contingent of non-NATO soldiers to Afghanistan, was added to that list. "In the future," announced Australia's Defense Minister Stephen Smith, "your role in the defense force will be determined on your ability, not on the basis of your sex."

21    There's also no denying that U.S. women are already serving with valor in battle in Iraq and Afghanistan right now.

**convoy**
group of trucks
traveling together

22    Consider Nashville's Sergeant Leigh Ann Hester, who was awarded the Silver Star for saving members of her **convoy** when it was ambushed by 34 enemy soldiers. Or consider Lieutenant Tammy Duckworth, who lost both her legs and shattered her right arm when her helicopter was shot down in Iraq. Duckworth went on to serve as a high-ranking Veterans Affairs administrator, to race two Chicago Marathons on a hand-cranked bicycle, and to recently launch a vigorous campaign for Congress in Illinois. Oh yes, and she's still a member of the Illinois Army National Guard.

23    According to the iCasualties website, 126 servicewomen have died in Iraq and Afghanistan since 2001, and by the DOD's own admission, 60 percent of these deaths have stemmed from "hostile attacks." "The loss of life in battle can be the ultimate act of bravery," says retired Air Force pilot Brigadier General Wilma Vaught, president of the Women in Military Service for America Memorial Foundation in Arlington, Virginia. "There's nothing more frustrating than hearing it said that this sacrifice isn't happening, that somehow the loss of a servicewoman's life in battle isn't as noble or heroic or as meaningful."

*Molly M. Ginty is an award-winning reporter who has written for* Ms., On the Issues Magazine, Women's eNews, *PBS, Planned Parenthood, and RH Reality Check.*

# UNDERSTANDING AND ANALYZING THE READING

## A. BUILDING VOCABULARY

### Context

*Using context and a dictionary if necessary, determine the meaning of each word as it is used in the selection.*

_____  1. exclusionary (paragraph 5)

    a. leaving people out

    b. old-fashioned

    c. based on social class

    d. belonging to the special-forces unit

_____  2. artillery (paragraph 6)

    a. hand grenades

    b. fire bombs

    c. mounted projectile-firing guns

    d. nuclear weapons

_____  3. infantry (paragraph 6)

    a. hospital services

    b. rehabilitation centers

    c. soldiers who fight on foot

    d. the care of soldiers' children

_____  4. cohesion (paragraph 7)

    a. readiness for battle

    b. unity

    c. power

    d. preparation

_____  5. demarcation (paragraph 9)

    a. relationship

    b. connection

    c. prejudice

    d. distinction

_____  6. camaraderie (paragraph 14)

    a. friendship

    b. jealousy

    c. dislike

    d. anger

_____  7. latrine (paragraph 17)

    a. cafeteria

    b. toilet

    c. shower

    d. recreational center

_____  8. rampant (paragraph 18)

    a. widespread

    b. unacknowledged

    c. serious

    d. secretive

## Word Parts

> ### A REVIEW OF PREFIXES AND ROOTS
>
> **SUB-**   means *under* or *below*.
> **GYN**   means *woman*.

*Use your knowledge of word parts and the review above to fill in the blanks in the following sentences.*

1.   A *submarine* (paragraph 10) is a ship that sails _____ the water.

2.   *Misogyny* (paragraph 16) means the dislike or hatred of _____.

## B. UNDERSTANDING THE THESIS AND OTHER MAIN IDEAS

*Select the best answer.*

_____   1. Which of the following is the best statement of the selection's thesis or central thought?
   a.  The many women who have been injured or died in the wars in Iraq and Afghanistan have not received proper health care or an honorable burial by the military.
   b.  In most of the world's countries, men and women play equal roles in the military.
   c.  Women represent 20 percent of new recruits to the military and should therefore have special rights and living accommodations when they report for active duty.
   d.  Because women in the U.S. military perform essential roles in which they may be injured or killed, the U.S. military should classify them as having served in battle.

_____   2. The main idea of paragraph 10 can be found in the
   a.  first sentence.
   b.  second sentence.
   c.  third sentence.
   d.  fourth sentence.

_____   3. What is the implied main idea of paragraph 14?
   a.  Women lack the physical strength that men have.
   b.  Early predictions about women's ability to serve in the military have proven false.
   c.  On the battlefield, there is a real concern that men will find women a distraction from combat.
   d.  Most male–female relationships are based on either flirting or fighting.

_____ 4. What is the topic of paragraph 16?

    a. female veterans

    b. pregnancy

    c. sexual assault in the military

    d. health benefits

## C. IDENTIFYING DETAILS

*Select the best answer.*

_____ 1. On which type of military vessel were women not allowed to serve until 2010?

    a. submarines         c. tanks

    b. navy ships         d. airplanes

_____ 2. What is the role of the military's "lioness" and "female engagement teams"?

    a. to advocate for women's rights in the military

    b. to ensure that the families of women in the military receive proper care when a woman is deployed on a mission

    c. to gather information from Muslim women who will not talk to men

    d. to investigate alleged sexual assaults that have taken place on or off base

_____ 3. Which of the following women discussed in the article died as a result of military service?

    a. Barbara Wilson         c. Rebekah Havrilla

    b. Laurie Piestewa         d. Leigh Ann Hester

## D. RECOGNIZING METHODS OF ORGANIZATION AND TRANSITIONS

*Select the best answer.*

_____ 1. The pattern of organization used in paragraphs 11 and 12 is

    a. cause and effect.         c. definition.

    b. classification.         d. order of importance.

_____ 2. The pattern of organization used in paragraph 19 is

    a. chronology.         c. contrast.

    b. process.         d. definition.

_____ 3. Which paragraph serves as a summary of the entire article?

    a. paragraph 6        c. paragraph 19

    b. paragraph 10      d. paragraph 23

_____ 4. Which word or phrase used in paragraph 21 signals the addition pattern?

    a. also            c. valor

    b. already        d. right now

## E. READING AND THINKING VISUALLY

*Select the best answer.*

_____ 1. The author likely chose to include the illustration on page 354 to

    a. indicate that most of the U.S. soldiers who have died in battle were Christian.

    b. provide an abstract piece of art to provide relief from the heavy, emotional subject matter of the article.

    c. illustrate that both male and female military personnel die as a result of serving in the military.

    d. emphasize women's roles as the protectors of the family when their husbands die during military service.

_____ 2. Which of the following would be the *least* appropriate image to include with this selection?

    a. a photograph of Sergeant Leigh Ann Baxter

    b. a woman driving a military truck in Iraq

    c. an American female soldier talking with a Muslim woman who is wearing a burka

    d. a map of Afghanistan

## F. FIGURING OUT IMPLIED MEANINGS

*Indicate whether each statement is true (T) or false (F).*

_____ 1. Canada is the most recent country to allow women to serve in combat.

_____ 2. For most of U.S. history, women in the military served as nurses, secretaries, or in other non-combat roles.

_____ 3. Early opponents of women serving in combat argued that women were too weak to perform battlefield duties.

_____ 4. Both Israel and South Korea have a more progressive approach to women in the military than the United States does.

_____  5. Women constitute one quarter of the U.S. armed forces.

_____  6. The author believes the modern military conflicts are different from earlier military conflicts because modern conflicts endanger almost all military personnel, not just those on the front line.

_____  7. Only women are quoted in the reading.

## G. THINKING CRITICALLY: ANALYZING THE AUTHOR'S TECHNIQUE

*Select the best answer.*

_____  1. The author's primary purpose in "All Guts, No Glory" is to

a. provide inspirational stories regarding women in combat.

b. emphasize the bloody nature of warfare and the general population's ignorance of what happens on the battlefield.

c. call attention to the problems of sexual harassment in military organizations around the globe.

d. argue that U.S. servicewomen should receive the recognition and benefits they deserve.

_____  2. The author's tone in paragraph 22 could best be described as

a. worried.

b. cynical.

c. admiring.

d. nostalgic.

_____  3. To support her thesis, the author uses all of the following *except*

a. her own personal experience.

b. quotations from experts.

c. statistics.

d. historical examples.

_____  4. The author begins her article with three women's stories in order to

a. imply that women play a larger role in the military than men do.

b. emphasize that U.S. military women suffer serious physical and emotional damage on and off the battlefield.

c. contrast the experience of women who serve as officers in the U.S. military with the experience of women who fight on the front lines.

d. call attention to a few isolated cases to prove her larger point that military women rarely experience injuries.

## H. THINKING CRITICALLY: ANALYZING THE AUTHOR'S MESSAGE

*Select the best answer.*

_____ 1. Which of the following statements is an expression of an opinion?

a. "Captain Dawn Halfaker saw a flash of light and heard an explosion…" (paragraph 1)

b. "These female intelligence service members are 'attached" to units and not directly assigned to them…" (paragraph 12)

c. "They said the distraction of women batting their eyelashes would destroy military units' camaraderie." (paragraph 14)

d. "Women in the military say they are afraid to visit latrines at night…" (paragraph 17)

_____ 2. When Brigadier General Evelyn Foote says "Let's join the 21st century" (paragraph 5), she means

a. the leaders of the U.S. military should change policies that are based on outdated, disproven assumptions.

b. the United States should adopt the sophisticated, satellite-based methods of warfare used by other countries.

c. all the world's nations should band together to put an end to warfare once and for all.

d. the time has come to make men more aware of what constitutes sexual harassment and sexual assault—and that such practices must cease immediately.

_____ 3. Which paragraph outlines the assumptions made about female military personnel in the 1950s?

a. paragraph 10

b. paragraph 14

c. paragraph 16

d. paragraph 19

_____ 4. Which of the following is not a key component of the author's overall thesis and argument?

a. Most women enter the U.S. military specifically because they want to take part in combat.

b. The U.S. military's approach to women is outdated and unfair.

c. Reclassifying women as combatants will help them receive better medical care and benefits.

d. Recognizing that women have served or died in battle is an acknowledgment of their bravery and heroism.

# WRITING IN RESPONSE TO THE READING

## I. WRITING A SUMMARY

*Complete the following summary of the reading selection by filling in the missing words or phrases.*

According to official U.S. military rules, servicewomen who have been injured or ——————— on deployment have not officially served in battle. In the past, women in the U.S. military served mostly as ———————, ———————, or other support positions. This situation was based on outdated beliefs that women are not as ——————— as men and that allowing women to take part in combat would lessen soldiers' attention when they were fighting. But women today make up almost ——————— of the U.S. military, and more than ——————— percent of military assignments are now open to females. However, women are still not permitted to serve in what the military calls ———————, including infantry, artillery, and Special Forces. This ——————— persists even though several research studies have shown that allowing women to participate in combat would not affect troops' ———————, cohesion, or morale. And other countries, such as ———————, ———————, and ———————, have no such bans.

The author argues that the time has come to change these discriminatory policies against women. Modern military actions put every soldier in danger including ———————, ——————— and ———————, three positions held often or exclusively by women. If women were officially classified as taking part in ———————, they could better ——————— from harm and receive better care if they were injured. Some people also argue that opening more military jobs to women would help with the serious problems of ——————— and rape that many U.S. military women have reported. Ultimately, the author feels that recognizing women as active participants in combat would not only recognize the valor of women currently serving in ——————— and Afghanistan; it would also recognize the ——————— and nobility of all military women.

## J. ANALYZING THE ISSUE AND ARGUMENT

1. Write a one-sentence statement that summarizes the author's position on the issue.
2. What techniques does the author use to make her arguments? For example, does she speak about her own military service record, or does she allow experts to help her make those arguments?
3. Identify at least one claim of fact, one claim of value, and one claim of policy in the reading.

4. What is the author's background, and is she qualified is to write about the topic? Why or why not? Do you find any bias in the selection?

5. Evaluate the argument on the following criteria:

    a. Is the argument timely?

    b. Are the statistics used fairly and clearly?

    c. Has the author provided sufficient evidence to support her argument?

    d. Does the author offer any opposing viewpoints?

    e. Does the author quote only women, or does she also quote men?

    f. Does the article offer any emotional appeals? If so, identify them and evaluate their fairness.

## K. WRITING PARAGRAPHS AND ESSAYS

*Write a paragraph or essay in response to the following writing prompts.*

1. You might think of the question "Should women be allowed to participate in combat?" as an issue that can be considered in pro and con terms. "All Guts, No Glory" falls into the pro category. Write a paragraph in which you outline some of the cons.

2. How are the arguments from the 1950s against women serving in combat (discussed in paragraphs 13 and 14) similar to the arguments against gay people serving in the military? How are they different? Write a paragraph in which you discuss the similarities and differences.

3. Write a paragraph in which you describe your reaction to the illustration on page 344. You looked at the illustration during your preview of the selection. Do you feel differently about the illustration *after* reading the selection?

4. Do you think certain professions are better suited to men, while other professions are better suited to women? If so, which ones? If not, why not? Write an essay in which you explore this topic.

5. Gender issues have come to the forefront not only in the military, but also in other careers. For example, recent controversies have arisen over women as firefighters. Research this topic and write an essay in which you explain both sides of the argument—pro and con—for allowing women to serve as firefighters. Explain which side of the argument you agree with, and why. (You may also choose to examine a career other than firefighter, if you wish.)

6. If you have served in the military, write an essay about your experiences of working with the opposite sex. If you have not served, write about your experiences and opinions regarding your interactions with the opposite sex in another work-related situation. Do your experiences strengthen or weaken the argument in "All Guts, No Glory"?

# ACTIVITIES: EXPLORING IDENTITY

*On your own or with a group of classmates, complete two of the following four activities.*

1. List at least five aspects of your identity. Are any of these aspects in conflict with each other? If so, how do you negotiate the space in-between?

   _____

   _____

   _____

2. Collect at least five advertisements (from newspapers, magazines, Web sites, or any other source) that signal the "ideal" body type for men and women in the United States. What features do the women share? What features do the men share? How closely do these images reflect the faces and body types you see in your classroom?

   _____

   _____

   _____

3. Visit a U.S. military Web site (for example, the U.S. Army a or the U.S. Navy. What are the expectations for recruits (people who wish to join that branch of the military)? Would you make a good military officer? Why or why not? If you had to join a specific military branch, which one would you join and why?

   _____

   _____

   _____

4. The topic of identity is so broad that entire encyclopedias have been written about it. This chapter discussed just a few aspects of the topic. Other types of identity include (but are not limited to):

   - **family identity** (for example, being a mother, father, brother, sister, child, or grandchild)
   - **sexual and gender identity** (for example, being male, female, straight, gay, or transgendered)
   - **participation in a subculture** (for example, bikers, hip-hop, Goth, tattoo culture)
   - **religious identity** (for example, affiliation with a particular religion or style of worship)

   Write an essay or prepare a class presentation about an aspect of one these identities and how it affects other parts of a person's identity. You may, of course, draw on personal experience. For instance, you might think about the grandmother's role in Latino families. How does a woman's life change when she goes from being a mother to being both a mother and a grandmother? What social expectations does she face in her new role?

   This is a very broad assignment, so you should feel free to make it your own and write or present on any aspect of the topic that you find interesting.

# 13 Our Environment: Problems and Solutions

*What is the environment?*

You often hear people talking about "the environment." But what exactly is the environment, and why are so many people talking and writing about it? In general, the *environment* refers to nature and to the surroundings or conditions in which people, animals, and plants live. But you can think about the term in many different ways:

- You can think about your local environment as the conditions on your street, in your neighborhood, or in your city.
- You can think of the environments of larger regions (such as states) or entire parts of the country (such as the West Coast or the Midwest).
- You can think of the environmental issues facing entire continents, such as Asia or South America. (For example, China has become one of the most polluted places on Earth.)
- You can think about the environment as encompassing the entire Earth, including all its individual components, such as the land and the oceans.

The environment starts inside the Earth and continues up into the atmosphere. So, for example, oil companies drilling for oil deep inside the Earth can affect the environment on a local, regional, and even global scale. Factories that release pollution into the air or water can affect people half a world away. When a volcano explodes in Europe, weather in North America may reflect the effects.

All the readings in this chapter focus on *the environment*: how humans affect it, how it affects humans, debates about the effects of technology, and how and why natural disasters occur.

## WHY IS THE ENVIRONMENT SUCH AN IMPORTANT CONTEMPORARY ISSUE?

In recent decades, many scientists have sent up an alarm: Human beings, they argue, are burning too many fossil fuels (coal, oil, and gasoline), which is producing carbon dioxide and leading to global warming. Those who believe in global warming argue that the Earth cannot process all this pollution. Those who are more skeptical argue that Earth goes through many warming and cooling cycles over hundreds or thousands of years, and that we are simply now in a warmer period.

It is important to understand these debates because government policies (and even campus policies) are increasingly focused on human beings' roles as caretakers of the natural environment. You probably heard about these issues long before you started this chapter, but the readings here will help you understand some of these issues in greater detail.

### How Does the Concept of Environment Tie in to My College Courses?

Much of what you read, particularly in college science courses and even in general-interest newspapers and magazines, will discuss environmental issues. Courses in environmental science, geology, and ecology are concerned primarily with the environment. Because pollution often affects the poor more than the rich, you'll learn about the environment in sociology and political science courses as well. Business courses frequently examine companies and the roles they play in polluting the environment, as well as the steps they have taken and can take toward greater social responsibility.

---

**TIPS FOR READING ABOUT THE ENVIRONMENT**

Here are some tips for reading not only the selections in this chapter, but any reading about the environment.

- **Look for scientific reasoning and data.** Scientists collect data and perform numerous experiments to learn how people and the environment interact. You may need to decrease your reading speed so that you can fully understand scientific concepts with which you are not familiar.

- **Think about your life, how you affect the environment, and how the environment affects you.** For example, how does the car you drive (and the gas mileage it gets) affect you and your community? Do you take part in any recycling programs? Do you feel you have any control over environmental issues?

- **Familiarize yourself with some key concepts in environmental studies.** You will often encounter the following terms when reading about the environment. Make sure you understand these concepts before you undertake any of the readings in this chapter.

  - *Green* is a word used to describe a person, program, or policy that is intended to decrease humans' impact on the environment.

  - *Sustainable* refers to programs that seek to preserve the Earth for future generations by giving it time to renew its natural resources.

  - *Global warming* and *global climate change* refer to what some people see as the slow and steady increase in temperatures around the world. Some people also see global warming as the cause of the increased number of natural disasters, such as hurricanes and extreme winters, in recent years.

  - *Greenhouse gases* (water vapor, methane, nitrous oxide, carbon dioxide, and fluorinated gases) act to slow or prevent heat from leaving the atmosphere. Many scientists believe these gases, particularly carbon dioxide, are responsible for the warming of Earth's climate.

  - *Biodegradable* refers to a product that will break down over time into natural (organic) components through the action of living organisms.

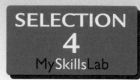

# SELECTION 4
MySkillsLab

# Wireless Interference:
# The Health Risks of RF-EMFs

## Christopher Ketcham

JOURNAL
ARTICLE

### SOURCE AND CONTEXT

The following article originally appeared in *Earth Island Journal*, a magazine whose goal is to "combine investigative journalism and thought-provoking essays that make the subtle but profound connections between the environment and other contemporary issues." The magazine has won six Project Censored Awards for uncovering stories not covered by other media outlets. The author of this article, Christopher Ketcham, has also written for *Harper's, The Nation, Salon, Mother Jones,* and *National Geographic*—all highly respected intellectual magazines.

### A NOTE ON THE READING

Read the selection to understand more about the technology used in cell phones and other wireless devices, as well as its possible effects on human health.

### PREVIEWING THE READING

*Using the steps listed on page 4, preview the reading selection. When you have finished, complete the following items.*

1.  This reading is about _____.

2.  Indicate whether each statement is true (T) or false (F).

    _____  a.  The author believes almost everyone lives within range of a cell tower.

    _____  b.  U.S. public health watchdogs have dismissed people's concerns about the health effects of wireless technology.

    _____  c.  A general principle of environmental science holds that technologies should be considered safe until proven otherwise.

MAKING
CONNECTIONS

*Do you use a cell phone? Do you have a wireless network connection in your home? How often do you use these devices, and have you ever heard about or considered any possible health risks?*

**READING TIP**

*Because this article is scientific, it contains a good deal of scientific/technical vocabulary in the form of abbreviations and acronyms, such as RF, EMF, and EHS. Be sure you fully understand what each abbreviation means, because you will encounter them several times throughout the reading.*

# Wireless Interference: The Health Risks of RF-EMFs

Christopher Ketcham

1    In January 1990, a cell tower goes up 800 feet from Alison Rall's dairy farm in Mansfield, Ohio. By fall, the cattle herd that pastures near the tower is sick, and Rall's three young children begin suffering bizarre skin rashes, raised red "hot spots." The kids are hit with waves of hyperactivity. The girls lose hair. Rall, when she becomes pregnant with a fourth child, can't gain weight.

2    Desperate to understand what is happening to her family and her farm, she contacts an Environmental Protection Agency scientist named Carl Blackman. He's an expert on the biological effects of radiation from electromagnetic fields (EMFs)—the kind of radiofrequency EMFs (RF-EMFs) by which all wireless technology operates, including not just cell towers and cell phones but also wi-fi hubs and wi-fi-capable computers, "smart" utility meters, and even cordless home phones. "With my government cap on, I'm supposed to tell you you're perfectly safe," Blackman tells her. "With my civilian cap on, I have to tell you to consider leaving."

3    When Rall contacts the cell phone company that operates the tower, she is told there is "no possibility whatsoever" that the tower is the source of her ills. But within weeks of abandoning the farm, the children recovered their health, and so did the herd.

4    We all live in range of cell towers now, and we are all wireless operators. As of October 2010 there were 5.2 billion cell phones operating on the planet. "Penetration," in the marketing-speak of the companies, often tops 100 percent in many countries, meaning there is more than one connection per person.

5    I don't have an Internet connection at my home in Brooklyn, and, like a dinosaur, I still keep a landline. Yet even though I have, in a fashion, opted out, I'm bathed in the radiation from cell phone panels on the parking garage next door. The waves are everywhere. We now live in a wireless-saturated normality that has never existed in the history of the human race, and the effects of EMFs on human beings are largely untested.

6    In May 2011, the International Agency for Research on Cancer (IARC) issued a statement that the electromagnetic frequencies from cell phones would henceforth be classified as "possibly carcinogenic to humans." The IARC decision followed multiple warnings, mostly from

European regulators, about the possible health risks of RF-EMFs. In September 2007, the **EU's** European Environment Agency suggested that widespread radiofrequency radiation "could lead to a health crisis similar to those caused by asbestos, smoking, and lead in petrol." Double-strand breaks in DNA—one of the undisputed causes of cancer—have been reported in tests with animal cells. Neuroscientists at Swinburne University of Technology in Australia discovered a "power boost" in brain waves when humans were exposed to cell phone radiofrequencies. The brain, one of the lead researchers speculated, was "concentrating to overcome the electrical interference."

**EU**
European Union, an alliance of 27 European countries

7    Yet the major public health watchdogs, in the United States and worldwide, have dismissed concerns. The American Cancer Society reports that "most studies published so far have not found a link between cell phone use and the development of tumors." The cell phone industry's lobbying organization assures the public that cell phone radiation is safe.

8    But according to a survey by Henry Lai of the University of Washington, although only 28 percent of studies funded by the wireless industry showed some type of biological effect from cell phone radiation, 67 percent of independently funded studies showed a bioeffect.

9    Despite the conflicting results, it is clear that some people are getting sick when they are heavily exposed to the new radiofrequencies. And we are not listening to their complaints.

10   Take the story of Michele Hertz. When a local utility company installed a wireless "smart" meter on her house in upstate New York in 2009, Hertz experienced "incredible memory loss," and, at the age of 51, feared she had Alzheimer's.

11   On a hunch, she told Con Edison of New York to remove the wireless meter. Within days, the worst symptoms disappeared. But her exposure to the meters has supersensitized Hertz to all kinds of other EMF sources. "Life," she says, "has dramatically changed."

12   In recent years, I've gotten to know dozens of "electrosensitives" like Hertz. To be sure, they constitute a tortured minority, often misunderstood and isolated. In Santa Fe, New Mexico, I met a woman who had taken to wearing an aluminum foil hat to kill wireless signals. I met a former world record marathoner who had lived at a house ringed by mountains that she said protected the place from cell frequencies. I met people who said they no longer wanted to live because of their condition.

13   The government of Sweden reports that the disorder known as electromagnetic hypersensitivity, or EHS, afflicts an estimated 3 percent of the population. Even the former prime minister of Norway, Gro Harlem Brundtland, has acknowledged that she suffers "strong discomfort" when she is exposed to cell phones.

14   Yet the World Health Organization reports that "there is no scientific basis to link EHS symptoms to EMF exposure." A study conducted in 2006 at the Mobile Phone Research Unit at King's College in London came to a similar conclusion.

15   "The scientific data so far just doesn't help the electrosensitives," says Louis Slesin, editor and publisher of *Microwave News*, a newsletter and website that cover the potential effects of RF-EMFs. "There is electrical signaling going on in your body all the time, and the idea that external electromagnetic fields can't affect us just doesn't make sense."

16   Maria Gonzalez, a nurse who lives in Queens, New York, took me to her daughter's school to see the cell phone masts, which were built in 2005. The operator of

the masts, Sprint Nextel, had built a wall of fake brick to hide them from view, but Gonzalez was skeptical. When she read a report published in 2002 about children in Spain who developed leukemia shortly after a cell phone tower was erected next to their school, she went into a quiet panic.

17    Sprint-Nextel was unsympathetic when she telephoned the company to express her concerns. A year later, Gonzalez sued the U.S. government, charging that the Federal Communications Commission had failed to fully evaluate the risks from cell phone frequencies. The suit was thrown out. The judge concluded that if regulators said the radiation was safe, it was safe. The message, as Gonzalez puts it, was that she was "crazy . . . and making a big to-do about nothing."

18    I'd venture, rather, that she was applying a commonsense principle in environmental science: the precautionary principle, which states that when something cannot be proven with certainty to be safe, then it should be assumed to be harmful. In a society thrilled with the magic of digital wireless, we have junked this principle. Because of our thoughtlessness, we have not demanded to know the full consequences of this technology. Perhaps the gadgets are slowly killing us—we do not know. What we do know, without a doubt, is that the electromagnetic fields are all around us, and that to live in modern civilization implies always and everywhere that we cannot escape their touch.

## UNDERSTANDING AND ANALYZING THE READING

### A. BUILDING VOCABULARY

#### Context

*Using context and a dictionary if necessary, determine the meaning of each word as it is used in the selection.*

_____ 1. bizarre (paragraph 1)
  a. carnival
  b. strange
  c. painful
  d. red

_____ 2. henceforth (paragraph 6)
  a. in the past
  b. accurately
  c. from now on
  d. never

_____ 3. carcinogenic (paragraph 6)
  a. causing cancer

  b. useful
  c. technological
  d. affecting the brain

_____ 4. tumor (paragraph 7)
  a. social network for teens
  b. abnormal uncontrolled growth of cells
  c. deafness caused by RF-EMFs
  d. paralysis caused by RF-EMFs

_____ 5. supersensitized (paragraph 11)
  a. burned by radiation
  b. caused painful swelling

c.  developed an allergy to

d.  highly allergic

_____ 6.  precautionary (paragraph 18)

a.  primary

b.  preventive

c.  scientific

d.  technological

## Word Parts

> ### A REVIEW OF PREFIXES, ROOTS, AND SUFFIXES
>
> **HYPER-** means *over* or *excessive*.
>
> **UN-** means *not*.
>
> **BIO** means *life*.
>
> **-ITY** refers to a *state*, *condition*, or *quality*.

*Use your knowledge of word parts and the review above to fill in the blanks in the following sentences.*

1.  Children suffering from *hyperactivity* (paragraph 2) are
    _____ active, often to the point where they
    cannot sit still or concentrate.

2.  *Normality* (paragraph 5) refers to the state or condition of being _____.

3.  *Undisputed* (paragraph 6) facts _____ be disputed or argued with.

4.  A *bioeffect* (paragraph 8) is an effect on a person's or organism's _____.

## B.  UNDERSTANDING THE THESIS AND OTHER MAIN IDEAS

*Select the best answer.*

_____ 1.  Which of the following best states the selection's thesis or central
          thought?

a.  All available evidence points to the conclusion that world
    governments should ban wireless technology.

b.  Although people love their cell phones and other electronic
    gadgets, they should not use them too often, thus protecting
    themselves from exposure to harmful radiation and radio waves
    that can have serious long-term effects.

c.  While some studies and governments have acknowledged the
    possible dangers of radio frequency technologies to humans and
    animals, the United States has not. In the meantime, we may be
    becoming addicted to technologies that are extremely harmful.

d.  Some people have become quite sick as a result of living near cell
    towers, but scientists are not sure whether this sickness is real or
    whether these people are suffering from psychological delusions.

_____ 2. What is the implied main idea of paragraph 1?

    a. Alison Rall is an unfit mother.

    b. Ohio has the highest cancer rate in the nation.

    c. The pastures were once used to dispose of nuclear waste.

    d. The cell tower caused serious illness in the Rall family and its dairy animals.

_____ 3. The topic of paragraph 6 is

    a. possible negative health effects of EMFs.

    b. Australian research into brain waves.

    c. asbestos and other cancer-causing materials.

    d. U.S. government attempts to suppress international scientific findings.

_____ 4. The main idea of paragraph 12 is found in

    a. the first sentence.

    b. the third sentence.

    c. the fourth sentence.

    d. the last sentence.

## C. IDENTIFYING DETAILS

*Match the abbreviation in Column 1 with its meaning in Column 2.*

| | Column 1: Abbreviation | Column 2: Meaning |
|---|---|---|
| _____ 1. | IARC | a. frequency on which radio signals are transmitted |
| _____ 2. | EMF | b. international agency that researches cancer |
| _____ 3. | EHS | c. a type of hypersensitivity to electromagnetism |
| _____ 4. | RF | d. a type of electrical/magnetic field on which wireless technology operates |

## D. RECOGNIZING METHODS OF ORGANIZATION AND TRANSITIONS

*Select the best answer.*

_____ 1. The primary organizational pattern used in paragraph 2 is

    a. definition.

    b. comparison and contrast.

    c. classification.

    d. order of importance.

_____ 2. The organizational pattern used in paragraph 3 is

    a. definition.

    b. process.

    c. enumeration.

    d. cause and effect.

_____ 3. The transitional word or phrase that signals the definition organizational pattern used in paragraph 4 is

    a. all.

    b. marketing-speak.

    c. often tops.

    d. meaning.

## E.  READING AND THINKING VISUALLY

*Select the best answer.*

_____ 1. Suppose the author wished to include a caption with the photo that appears on page 369. Which of the following captions *best* matches the author's purpose in "Wireless Interference: The Health Risks of RF-EMFs"?

    a. On planet Earth, there are now more cell phones in operation than there are people. Marketers refer to this situation as "100 percent penetration."

    b. While some people couldn't live without their smartphones, the author, Christopher Ketcham, doesn't even have an Internet connection in his home.

    c. In the United States, we're surrounded by technology and bathed in radiation everywhere we go, but we haven't seriously considered the possible health risks.

    d. Smart phones and other wireless technology cause serious health issues.

_____ 2. If the author wished to include a photo of a person who has suffered serious discomfort when exposed to cell phones, he would include a photo of

    a. Gro Harlem Brundtland.

    b. Michele Hertz.

    c. Louis Slesin.

    d. Henry Lai.

## F. FIGURING OUT IMPLIED MEANINGS

*Indicate whether each statement is true (T) or false (F).*

_____ 1. Carl Blackman believes that cell towers cause health-related problems.

_____ 2. The American Cancer Society does not see a link between the use of cell phones and the development of cancerous tumors.

_____ 3. Businesses use the term *penetration* to mean the percentage of the population that is using the product they sell.

_____ 4. Those who are highly sensitive to electromagnetism often feel alone and segregated from the world.

_____ 5. The human body is sensitive to EMFs because the body does not naturally make use of electrical signaling.

_____ 6. The precautionary principle holds that no technology should be used until it has been proven safe.

_____ 7. Cell phones are the only technological devices that use RF-EMF technology.

## G. THINKING CRITICALLY: ANALYZING THE AUTHOR'S TECHNIQUE

*Select the best answer.*

_____ 1. The author's primary purpose in "Wireless Interference: The Health Risks of RF-EMFs" is to

    a. argue for a total ban on technology that uses radio frequencies.

    b. provide a comprehensive summary of research results on the topic of RF-EMFs.

    c. sound a cautionary note about the possible dangers of RF-EMF technologies.

    d. imply that those who supposedly suffer from exposure to electromagnetism are simply seeking attention.

_____ 2. Throughout the selection, the author's tone could best be described as

    a. angry.

    b. concerned.

    c. impartial.

    d. cynical.

_____ 3. To support his thesis, the author uses all of the following *except*

    a. historical data from the 1980s.

    b. summaries of research studies.

    c. case studies of those made ill by RF-EMFs.

    d. data and expert opinions.

_____ 4. All of the following are statements of fact *except*

    a. "But within weeks of abandoning the farm, the children recovered their health, and so did the herd." (paragraph 3)

    b. "I don't have an Internet connection at my home in Brooklyn." (paragraph 5)

    c. "In September 2007, the EU's European Environment Agency suggested that widespread radiofrequency radiation 'could lead to a health crisis similar to those caused by asbestos, smoking, and lead in petrol.'" (paragraph 6)

    d. "A year later, Gonzalez sued the U.S. government, charging that the Federal Communications Commission had failed to fully evaluate the risks from cell phone frequencies." (paragraph 17)

## H. THINKING CRITICALLY: ANALYZING THE AUTHOR'S MESSAGE

*Select the best answer.*

_____ 1. In paragraph 2, Carl Blackman refers to his "government cap" and his "civilian cap." By using these terms, what is he implying?

    a. What he thinks is very different from what he must say as a representative of the government.

    b. The government is monitoring his conversation and reading his e-mail.

    c. He prefers working for the government to working for private enterprise.

    d. He believes the government is receiving payments from the providers of cell phone services and wireless Internet providers.

_____ 2. In paragraph 5, the author assumes that readers live where?

    a. developed areas such as the United States or Europe

    b. the southern hemisphere of the globe

    c. anywhere in the world

    d. a region that is not surrounded by mountains

_____ 3. Which paragraph outlines a chief underlying assumption of environmental science?

    a. paragraph 2

    b. paragraph 6

    c. paragraph 15

    d. paragraph 18

_____ 4. The author uses the phrase "tortured minority" in paragraph 12 to refer to

    a. those who have researched RF-EMFs and concluded they are harmless.

    b. public advocates for more research into the effects of cell phone technology.

    c. people who have taken extreme measures to avoid radio frequencies, which affect them negatively..

    d. small-scale Internet providers who are trying desperately to compete with massive mega-corporations.

## WRITING IN RESPONSE TO THE READING

### I. REVIEWING AND ORGANIZING IDEAS WITH A SUMMARY

*Complete the following summary of the reading selection by filling in the missing words or phrases.*

The case study of Alison Rall illustrates the possible _____ of living too close to a _____, because the health of Rall's family improved after they moved away. However, the cell company denies any _____ for the illness. The possibility that the radiofrequency electromagnetic fields (sometimes abbreviated _____) that power wireless technologies may cause serious harm is cause for concern because today most people are exposed to _____ from cell phone panels near their _____. In 2011, the _____ and the EU acknowledged the possibility that wireless technologies can harm people, but consumer advocates in _____ have not. Clearly, money is at stake here, because 67 percent of independent studies showed that RF-EMFs do have _____. Beyond the numbers, there are real people who are suffering, including a woman who suffered _____ when a utility company installed a _____ on her house, and a woman in Santa Fe who wears an _____ to stop _____ from affecting her. However, the research done to date doesn't support the assertions of people who consider themselves "electrosensitive," partially because electrical _____ is a natural occurrence in the human body. And judges have dismissed _____ brought by people who are concerned about locating cell towers near _____. The author of "Wireless Interference" believes that, as a society, we are ignoring an important principle of _____ science: that we should assume something is harmful until it is proven _____.

### J. ANALYZING THE ISSUE AND ARGUMENT

1. What specific question is the author addressing in "Wireless Interference: The Health Risks of RF-EMFs"?

2. Write a one-sentence summary of the author's argument.

3. In which paragraph are all of the author's underlying assumptions specifically stated?

4. Identify one claim of fact and one claim of value directly stated in the reading. What claim of policy is implied?

5. Identify two statements that the author provides as viewpoints that oppose his argument.

6. Evaluate the argument on the following criteria:

   a. Is the argument timely?

   b. Has the author provided ample evidence to support his thesis? Are the statistics used fairly and clearly?

   c. Has the author clearly defined the terms used in the reading?

   d. Are the examples of Alison Rall and Michele Hertz typical of most people's reactions to RF-EMFs?

   e. Does the article offer any emotional appeals? If so, identify them and evaluate their fairness.

## K. WRITING PARAGRAPHS AND ESSAYS

*Write a paragraph or essay in response to the following writing prompts.*

1. Technology often affects us physically. Write a paragraph in which you describe how your eyes feel if you've been staring at a computer screen too long, or how your fingers, wrists, and hands feel if you've been sending a high volume of text messages. (You may choose to write about other technology-induced side effects if you wish.)

2. The author begins his article with an attention-grabbing example. Write a different opening paragraph for the article that introduces the topic and the thesis.

3. Write a paragraph in which you offer advice to the person in the photograph on page 388 regarding the uses and misuses of personal technologies.

4. "Wireless Interference: The Health Risks of RF-EMFs" deals with the possible health dangers of radio frequencies and wireless technologies. However, the article deals only with internal effects on the body. Write an essay in which you explore some of the other dangers of wireless technologies. These dangers can be physical, social, or personal. (For example, what might happen when people text while they are driving or crossing the street? What could happen if one spends too much time on Facebook or Twitter?)

5. Suppose all wireless technology is banned tomorrow. That means you no longer have access to the Internet, to cell phones, and to cordless telephones. Write an essay in which you explore how this ban might affect society.

6. Conduct research into expert tips for making the best use of technology while not overdoing it. Write an essay in which you offer readers at least three tips. For example, you might consider *ergonomics* (the best way to sit at your computer) or the best ways to ensure that technology doesn't distract your attention from your studies or other important matters.

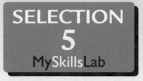

# Crisis Management:
# Why Climate Change Will Make
# You Love Big Government

## Christian Parenti

With for-profit insurance companies unable to address extreme weather and other implications of climate change, emergency assistance will need to come from government action.

### SOURCE AND CONTEXT

WEB
ARTICLE

This article originally appeared on TomDispatch.com, an online news source, in January, 2012. The Web site's mission statement says the site is "for anyone seeking a deeper understanding of our post-9/11 world and a clear sense of how our imperial globe actually works." The author, Christian Parenti, is the author of *Tropic of Chaos: Climate Change and the New Geography of Violence.* He is also a contributing editor at *The Nation* magazine, which has described itself as "the flagship of the [political] left." In other words, *The Nation* would be considered a liberal magazine with a liberal (rather than conservative) viewpoint.

### A NOTE ON THE READING

Recent years have seen many natural and weather-related disasters strike the United States and the rest of the world. Read the selection for one man's viewpoint on the role of government in helping society "pick up the pieces" and restore people's lives after weather disasters.

### PREVIEWING THE READING

*Using the steps listed on page 4, preview the reading selection. When you have finished, complete the following items.*

1. This topic of this reading is the need for _____
   following extreme weather events.

2. Three topics that you can expect the author to discuss are:
   a. _____
   b. _____
   c. _____

3. One natural disaster that affected New Orleans was _____.

**MAKING CONNECTIONS**

*Has your area experienced any natural disasters recently? To what types of natural hazards is your area most prone (for example, hurricanes, cyclones, wildfires, nor'easters, flooding)?*

**READING TIP**

*As you read, look for clues regarding the author's political viewpoint and possible biases. If your political views tend to be more liberal, ask yourself why you agree with the author. If your political views tend to be more conservative, read the selection with an open mind and annotate those sentences or sections you disagree with.*

## Crisis Management: Why Climate Change Will Make You Love Big Government

### Christian Parenti

1    Look back on 2011 and you'll notice a destructive trail of extreme weather slashing through the year. In Texas, it was the driest year ever recorded. An epic drought there killed half a billion trees, touched off wildfires that burned 4 million acres, and destroyed or damaged thousands of homes and buildings. The costs to agriculture, particularly the cotton and cattle businesses, are estimated at $5.2 billion—and keep in mind that, in a winter breaking all sorts of records for warmth, the Texas drought is not yet over. In August, the East Coast had a close brush with calamity in the form of Hurricane Irene, whose rains did at least $7 billion worth of damage.

2    Around the planet the story was similar. Wildfires consumed large swaths of Chile. Colombia suffered its second year of endless rain. In Brazil, the life-giving Amazon River was running low due to drought. Flooding in the Thai capital, Bangkok, killed more than 500 and displaced or damaged the property of millions. And that's just to start a 2011 extreme-weather list, not to end it.

3    Such calamities, devastating for those affected, have important implications for how we think about the role of government in our future. During natural

Only the government has the capital and the capacity to deal with the catastrophic implications of weather disasters (such as hurricanes) and climate change.

disasters, society regularly turns to the state for help, which means that such immediate crises are a much-needed reminder of just how important a functional big government turns out to be to our survival.

**the right**
those with more conservative political views (who are generally in favor of less government)

4    These days, big government gets big press attention—none of it anything but terrible. In the United States, especially in an election year, it's become fashionable to beat up on the public sector and all things governmental (except the military). **The right** does it nonstop in talking points that disparage the role of an oversized federal government.

5    By now, this viewpoint has taken on the aura of folk wisdom, as if the essence of democracy were to hate government. Even many on **the left** now regularly dismiss government as nothing but oversized, wasteful, bureaucratic, corrupt, and oppressive, without giving serious consideration to how essential it may be to our lives.

**the left**
those with more liberal political views (who are generally in favor of more government)

6    But don't expect the present "consensus" to last. Global warming and the freaky, increasingly extreme weather that will accompany it is going to change all that. After all, there is only one institution that actually has the capacity to deal with multibillion-dollar natural disasters on an increasingly routine basis. Private security firms won't help your flooded or tornado-struck town. Private insurance companies are systematically withdrawing coverage from vulnerable coastal areas. Voluntary community groups, churches, **anarchist** affinity groups—each may prove helpful in limited ways, but for better or worse, only government has the capital and the capacity to deal with the catastrophic implications of climate change.

**anarchist**
one who rejects government and authority in general

7    Consider Hurricane Irene: As it passed through the Northeast, states mobilized more than 100,000 National Guard troops. New York City opened 78 public emergency shelters prepared to house up to 70,000 people. In my home state, Vermont, where the storm devastated the landscape, destroying or damaging 200 bridges, more than 500 miles of road, and 200 miles of railroad, the National Guard airlifted in free food, water, diapers, baby formula, medicine, and tarps to thousands of desperate people.

8    The damage to Vermont was estimated at up to $1 billion. Yet the state has only 626,000 residents, so it could never have raised all the money needed to rebuild alone. Vermont businesses, individuals, and foundations have donated at least $4 million, possibly up to $6 million, in assistance, an impressive figure, but not a fraction of what was needed. The state government immediately released $24 million in funds, crucial to getting its system of roads rebuilt and functioning, but again that was a drop in the bucket, given the level of damage. Without federal money, which covered 80 percent to 100 percent of the costs of rebuilding many Vermont roads, the state would still be an economic basket case. Without aid from Washington, the transportation network might have taken years to recover.

**vaunted**
celebrated

9    As for flood insurance, the federal government is pretty much the only place to get it. The National Flood Insurance Program has written 5.5 million policies in more than 21,000 communities covering $1.2 trillion worth of property. As for the **vaunted** private market, for-profit insurance companies write between 180,000 and 200,000 policies in a given year. In other words, that is less than 5 percent of all flood insurance in the United States. This federally subsidized program underwrites the other 95 percent. Without such insurance, it's not complicated: Many of 2011's

waterlogged victims, whether from record Midwestern floods or from Hurricane Irene, would simply have no money to rebuild.

10    Or consider sweltering Texas. In 2011 firefighters responded to 23,519 fires. In all, 2,742 homes were destroyed by out-of-control wildfires. But government action saved 34,756 other homes. So you decide: Was this another case of wasteful government intervention in the marketplace, or an extremely efficient use of resources?

### Case Studies in Crisis Management

11    The early years of this century have already offered a number of examples of how disastrous too little government can be in the face of natural disaster, Katrina-inundated New Orleans in 2005 being perhaps the quintessential case.

12    There are, however, other less noted examples that nonetheless helped concentrate the minds of government planners. For example, in the early spring of 2011, a massive blizzard hit New York City. Dubbed "Snowmageddon" and "Snowpocalypse," the storm arrived in the midst of tense statewide budget negotiations, and a nationwide assault on state workers.

13    In New York [City], Mayor Mike Bloomberg was pushing for cuts to the sanitation department budget. As the snow piled up, the people tasked with removing it—sanitation workers—failed to appear in sufficient numbers. As the city ground to a halt, New Yorkers were left to fend for themselves. Chaos ensued. Though nowhere near as destructive as Katrina, the storm became a case study in too little governance and the all-too-distinct limits of "self-reliance" when nature runs amok. In the week that followed, even the rich were stranded amid the mounting heaps of snow and uncollected garbage.

14    More broadly, the question raised was: Can an individual, a town, a city, even a state really "go it alone" when the weather turns genuinely threatening? All the union bashing and attacks on the public sector that had marked that year's state-level budget debates began to sound unhinged.

15    In the Big Apple at least, when Irene came calling that August, Mayor Bloomberg was ready. He wasn't dissing or scolding unions. He wasn't whining about the cost of running a government. He embraced planning, the public sector, public workers, and coordinated collective action. His administration took unprecedented steps like shutting down the subway and moving its trains to higher ground. Good thing it did. Several low-lying subway yards flooded. Had trains been parked there, many millions in public capital might have been lost or damaged.

### The Necessity of Big Government During Natural Disasters

16    A slightly longer view of history is instructive in thinking about the forces of nature and the nature of infrastructure. And here's where to start: In the United States, despite its official pro-market myths, government has always been the main force behind the development of a national infrastructure, and so of the country's overall economic prosperity.

17    One can trace the origins of state participation in the economy back to at least the founding of the republic: from Alexander Hamilton's First Bank of the United States, which refloated the entire postrevolutionary economy when it bought

otherwise worthless colonial debts at face value; to Henry Clay's half-realized program of public investment and planning called the American System; to the New York state–funded Erie Canal, which made the future Big Apple the economic focus of the eastern seaboard; to the railroads, built on government land grants, that took the economy west and tied the nation together; to New Deal programs that helped pull the country out of the Great Depression and built much of the infrastructure we still use, like the Hoover Dam, scores of major bridges, hospitals, schools, and so on; to the government-funded and -sponsored interstate highway system launched in the late 1950s; to the similarly funded space race; and beyond.

18   It's simple enough: Big government investments (and thus big government) have been central to the remarkable economic dynamism of the country.

19   Government has created roads, highways, railways, ports, the postal system, inland waterways, universities, and telecommunications systems. Government-funded **R&D**, as well as the buying patterns of government agencies—(alas!) both often connected to war and war-making plans—have driven innovation in everything from textiles and shipbuilding to telecoms, medicine, and high-tech breakthroughs of all sorts. Individuals invent technology, but in the United States it is almost always public money that brings the technology to scale, be it in aeronautics, medicine, computers, or agriculture.

R&D
research and
development

20   Without constant government planning and subsidies, American capitalism simply could not have developed as it did, making ours the world's largest economy. It's not considered proper to discuss government planning in open, realistic, and mature terms, however, so we fail to talk about what government could—or rather, must—do to help us meet the future of climate change.

### The Future: Extreme Weather, Extreme Cooperation

21   The onset of ever more extreme and repeated weather events is likely to change how we think about the role of the state. But attitudes toward the Federal Emergency Management Agency, which stands behind state and local disaster responses, suggest that we're hardly at that moment yet. In late 2011, with Americans beleaguered by weather disasters, FEMA came under attack from congressional Republicans eager to starve it of funds. One look at FEMA explains why.

22   Yes, when George W. Bush put an unqualified playboy at its helm, the agency dealt disastrously with Hurricane Katrina back in 2005. Under better leadership, however, it is an eminently effective mechanism for planning focused on the public good, not private profit, a form of public insurance and public assistance for Americans struck by disaster. Every year FEMA gives hundreds of millions of dollars to local firefighters and first responders, as well as victims dealing with the aftershock of floods, fires, and the other calamities associated with extreme weather events.

23   FEMA's services include direct emergency assistance that ranges from psychological counseling and medical aid to emergency unemployment benefits. FEMA also subsidizes long-term rebuilding and planning in communities affected by disasters. In other words, it actually represents an excellent use of your tax dollars to provide services aimed at restoring local economic health and thus the tax base. The

**procurement**
the securing or
purchasing of
resources

**gross domestic
product (GDP)**
a measurement
of the total
market value of
all goods and
services produced
within a country
in a given period

**socialism**
a political
and economic
system in which
resources are
managed by the
government for
the maximum
benefit of all the
people in society

antigovernment right hates FEMA for the same reason that it hates Social Security—because it works!

24    As it happens, thanks in part to the congressional GOP's sabotage efforts, thousands of FEMA's long-term recovery projects are now on hold, even as the number of major disaster declarations by the federal government has been escalating sharply: only 12 in 1961, 17 in 1971, 15 in 1981, 43 in 1991, and in 2011—99!

25    Like it or not, government is a huge part of our economy. Altogether, federal, state, and local government activity—collecting fees, taxing, borrowing and then spending on wages, **procurement**, contracting, grant-making, subsidies and aid—constitutes about 35 percent of the **gross domestic product**. You could say that we already live in a somewhat "mixed economy": that is, an economy that fundamentally combines private and public economic activity.

26    The intensification of climate change means that we need to acknowledge the chaotic future we face and start planning for it. Think of what's coming, if you will, as a kind of storm **socialism.**

27    After all, climate scientists believe that atmospheric concentrations of carbon dioxide beyond 350 parts per million (ppm) could set off compounding feedback loops and so lock us into runaway climate change. We are already at 392 ppm. Even if we stopped burning all fossil fuels immediately, the disruptive effect of accumulated $CO_2$ in the atmosphere is guaranteed to hammer us for decades. In other words, according to the best-case scenario, we face decades of increasingly chaotic and violent weather.

28    In the face of an unraveling climate system, there is no way that private enterprise alone will meet the threat. To adapt to climate change will mean coming together on a large scale and mobilizing society's full range of resources. In other words, big storms require big government.

## UNDERSTANDING AND ANALYZING THE READING

### A. BUILDING VOCABULARY

## Context

*Using context and a dictionary if necessary, determine the meaning of each word as it is used in the selection.*

_____ 1. drought (paragraph 1)
    a. wildfire
    b. insect infestation
    c. tidal wave
    d. water shortage

_____ 2. calamity (paragraph 1)
    a. flooding
    b. disaster
    c. death
    d. lightning

_____ 3. implications (paragraph 3)
    a. effects on
    b. preventive measures
    c. government policies
    d. historical records

_____ 4. disparage (paragraph 4)
    a. play up
    b. request information about
    c. speak badly of
    d. continue the role of

_____ 5. oppressive (paragraph 5)
    a. creating jobs
    b. creating tax revenue
    c. creating life
    d. creating hardship

_____ 6. affinity (paragraph 6)
    a. liking for
    b. illegal activity
    c. prejudice against
    d. state of endlessness

_____ 7. sweltering (paragraph 10)
    a. very large
    b. holding conservative political beliefs
    c. economically developed
    d. extremely hot

_____ 8. ensued (paragraph 13)
    a. followed
    b. brought a lawsuit against
    c. stopped
    d. went on strike

_____ 9. collective (paragraph 15)
    a. military
    b. voluntary
    c. united
    d. hobby

_____ 10. beleaguered (paragraph 21)
    a. changed
    b. troubled
    c. cynical about
    d. unconcerned

## Word Parts

> ### A REVIEW OF PREFIXES AND ROOTS
>
> **ANTI-** means *against*.
>
> **POST-** means *after*.
>
> **AERO** means *air*.

*Use your knowledge of word parts and the review above to fill in the blanks in the following sentences.*

1. The *postrevolutionary* (paragraph 17) economy refers to the economy _____ the U.S. War of Independence from England.

2. *Aeronautics* (paragraph 19) refers to the science of traveling through the _____.

3. *Antigovernment* (paragraph 23) groups are _____ government interference in people's lives and business activities.

## B. UNDERSTANDING THE THESIS AND OTHER MAIN IDEAS

*Select the best answer.*

_____ 1.  The best statement of the author's thesis or central thought in "Crisis Management" can be found in

    a.  the article's subtitle and last paragraph.

    b.  the first paragraph.

    c.  the article's third subheading.

    d.  paragraph 27.

_____ 2.  The main idea of paragraph 8 can be found in

    a.  the first sentence.

    b.  the third sentence.

    c.  the fourth sentence.

    d.  the fifth sentence.

_____ 3.  The topic of paragraph 27 is

    a.  the causes of the greenhouse effect.

    b.  the likelihood of continued extreme weather due to carbon dioxide emissions.

    c.  government policies that can help counteract tendencies toward global climate change.

    d.  the science of compounding feedback loops.

## C. IDENTIFYING DETAILS

*Select the best answer.*

_____ 1.  The phrase used as a nickname for New York City in the reading is

    a.  The Windy City.

    b.  The Big Easy.

    c.  The Big Apple.

    d.  The City by the Bay.

_____ 2.  Government spending represents what percent of gross domestic product?

    a.  10 percent

    b.  25 percent

    c.  35 percent

    d.  50 percent

_____ 3.  The current concentration of carbon dioxide ($CO_2$) in the atmosphere is

    a.  350 ppm.

    b.  392 ppm.

    c.  423 ppm.

    d.  486 ppm.

_____ 4.  Hurricane Irene took place in

    a.  2005.

    b.  2007.

    c.  2009.

    d.  2011.

_____ 5.  The federal agency that supports state and local disaster relief is

    a.  FEMA.

    b.  GDP.

    c.  USGS.

    d.  $CO_2$.

## D. RECOGNIZING METHODS OF ORGANIZATION AND TRANSITIONS

*Select the best answer.*

_____ 1. The pattern of organization used in paragraph 2 is
a. definition.
b. generalization and example.
c. process.
d. comparison and contrast.

_____ 2. The organizational pattern used in paragraph 17 is
a. chronological order.
b. summary.
c. spatial order.
d. classification.

_____ 3. The transitional word or phrase that signals the use of the cause and effect pattern in paragraph 19 is
a. government-funded R&D.
b. alas!
c. have driven.
d. be it in aeronautics, medicine, computers, or agriculture.

_____ 4. Which paragraphs in the reading make use of summary?
a. paragraphs 6 and 25
b. paragraphs 9 and 10
c. paragraphs 21 and 27
d. paragraphs 18 and 28

## E. READING AND THINKING VISUALLY

*Select the best answer.*

_____ 1. The weather event shown in the photo on page 380 is most likely a
a. hurricane.
b. wildfire.
c. tsunami.
d. cyclone.

_____ 2. Which type of graphic would *best* summarize the contents of paragraph 17?
a. a process diagram
b. a time line
c. a map
d. a photo of Hoover Dam

## F. FIGURING OUT IMPLIED MEANINGS

*Indicate whether each statement is true (T) or false (F).*

_____ 1. The vast majority of flood insurance is provided by the U.S. government.

_____ 2. The author believes that most press coverage of the military is negative.

_____ 3. "Snowmageddon" did not affect the West Coast of the United States.

_____ 4. The author seems to regret that part of U.S. economic prosperity is the result of wars or preparation for war.

_____ 5. The number of official disaster declarations has risen every year since 1961.

## G. THINKING CRITICALLY: ANALYZING THE AUTHOR'S TECHNIQUE

*Select the best answer.*

_____ 1. The author's purpose for writing this selection is to

    a. convince readers that weather disasters and climate change require big government.

    b. provide a list of the pros and cons of disaster relief provided by the government.

    c. instruct readers regarding the sources of greenhouse gases and global warming.

    d. advocate for additional funding for rebuilding disaster areas in Vermont.

_____ 2. The author's tone in "Crisis Management" is best described as

    a. neutral.

    b. detached.

    c. polite.

    d. assertive.

_____ 3. All of the following phrases from the reading have a negative connotation *except*

    a. "catastrophic implications of climate change" (paragraph 6).

    b. "nationwide assault on state workers" (paragraph 12).

    c. "an unqualified playboy at its helm" (paragraph 22).

    d. "an excellent use of your tax dollars" (paragraph 23).

_____ 4. All of the following statements from the reading are opinions *except*

    a. "Wildfires consumed large swaths of Chile" (paragraph 2).

    b. "These days, big government gets big press attention—none of it anything but terrible" (paragraph 4).

    c. "All the union bashing and attacks on the public sector that had marked that year's state-level budget debates began to sound unhinged" (paragraph 14).

    d. "Without constant government planning and subsidies, American capitalism simply could not have developed as it did, making ours the world's largest economy" (paragraph 20).

## H. THINKING CRITICALLY: ANALYZING THE AUTHOR'S MESSAGE

*Select the best answer.*

_____ 1. In paragraph 8, the author uses the phrase "economic basket case" to imply that

a. Vermont is an excellent case study of FEMA's botched responses to natural disasters.

b. Vermont would not yet have recovered from the economic effects of Hurricane Irene without help from the U.S. federal government.

c. natural disasters have a much larger effect on local businesses than they do on local people and households.

d. businesses in states with smaller populations are simply unable to compete economically and therefore require government subsidies to survive.

_____ 2. The phrase "drop in the bucket" in paragraph 8 is an example of

a. a rhetorical question.

b. a simile.

c. a transitional phrase.

d. a metaphor.

_____ 3. What does the author mean when he says in paragraph 19 that public money "brings the technology to scale"?

a. Government money allows inventions and innovations to become widely used.

b. U.S. government funds are best invested in heavy machinery.

c. The scope of technology, as fueled by the computer revolution, is much larger than the scope of the nation's physical infrastructure.

d. Government investment should be limited to the four areas listed: aeronautics, medicine, computers, and agriculture.

_____ 4. Which of the following is not one of the author's stated or implied beliefs in "Crisis Management"?

a. The railroads were responsible for the westward expansion of the United States.

b. The U.S. government is responsible for the nation's wealth and prosperity.

c. The United States is a mixed economy that combines public and private economic activity.

d. Washington, DC, is the economic center of the U.S. East Coast.

# WRITING IN RESPONSE TO THE READING

## I. REVIEWING AND ORGANIZING IDEAS WITH A PARAPHRASE

*Complete the following paraphrase of paragraphs 16–18 by filling in the missing words or phrases.*

In the United States, the ——————— has been primarily responsible for building the nation's ——————— and contributing to the country's economic well-being. Government policies have a long history, beginning with the formation of the First Bank of the United States after the original colonies gained ——————— from Great Britain. In the decades following, ——————— created a partially implemented plan named the American System, and the state of New York funded the building of the ———————, which helped ——————— become the business center of the East Coast. The railway system was also put in place by the government, and it helped the country expand to the west while providing national ———————. When the Great Depression hit, a program called the ——————— sponsored many public works programs such as Nevada's ——————— Dam and built many other public buildings and structures. By the 1950s, the government was building the interstate ——————— system, and after that the U.S. government funded the ———————. In summary, large-scale ——————— by the U.S. national government are responsible for the country's economic success.

## J. ANALYZING THE ISSUE AND ARGUMENT

1. What contemporary issue is the author discussing in this reading? Phrase the issue as a question. Is the author arguing the "pro" side of this issue or the "con" side?

2. Write a one- or two-sentence summary of the author's argument.

3. Is the argument in "Crisis Management" inductive or deductive? Explain.

4. Is the author qualified to write on the topic? How do the author's political affiliations and beliefs affect his thesis?

5. Point to at least five specific examples of biased language in the reading and explain the connotations of each.

6. Evaluate the reading on the following criteria:

   a. Is the argument timely?

   b. Has the author provided sufficient evidence to support his argument? What types of evidence has he provided? What other types of evidence might he provide to strengthen the argument?

   c. Has the author defined his terms accurately and sufficiently?

d. Are the examples provided in the reading representative of government as a whole? In other words, is the author's position regarding "big government" valid for all areas of society, beyond disaster relief? Why or why not?

e. Does the author offer any opposing viewpoints? If so, what is his attitude toward them? Does he present them neutrally or fairly, or is he biased against them? How can you tell?

f. Does the reading offer any emotional appeals? If so, identify them and evaluate their fairness.

g. What explicit, overall claim of policy does the author make in this reading?

## K. WRITING PARAGRAPHS AND ESSAYS

*Write a paragraph or essay in response to the following prompts.*

1. As the Source and Context section notes (p. 379), Christian Parenti has written a book titled *Tropic of Chaos: Climate Change and the New Geography of Violence*. Look up the book on Amazon.com and write a brief (paragraph-length) summary of it. Read some of the Amazon reviews and indicate how interested you would be in reading this book.

2. Write a paragraph about any experience you may have had (direct or indirect) with a natural disaster. If you are fortunate enough not to have witnessed any natural disasters directly, feel free to write about a news report you saw or read about (in the United States or any other country).

3. This reading contains many examples of natural disasters. Search the Internet for relevant photos of three different types of natural disasters; print them out and write a caption for each, tying the photo to the content of the reading.

4. Visit the Web site on which this reading was originally published (see "Source and Context" before the reading, p. 379). Read an article of your choice and write an essay in response to it.

5. Write an essay in which you discuss one of the programs listed in paragraph 17. (You will likely need to do some additional research to complete this assignment.)

6. In 2011, a devastating earthquake and tsunami hit Japan, damaging several of its nuclear reactors and leaving thousands of people homeless. Do some additional research and, in an essay, provide an overview of what happened in Japan and the short- and long-term effects of the disaster. (Note that you will be writing an essay that makes strong use of the cause and effect organizational pattern.)

## SELECTION 6
MySkillsLab

# Sustainability on Campus
Jay Withgott and Scott Brennan

### SOURCE AND CONTEXT

This reading is taken from an environmental science textbook, *Environment: The Science Behind the Stories*. Environmental science is *multidisciplinary*, meaning it draws from many disciplines, including biology, economics, geography, chemistry, and earth science. In their preface, the authors write, "Environmental science helps show us how Earth's systems function and how we influence these systems. It gives us a big-picture understanding of the world and our place in it. Studying environmental science helps us comprehend the problems we create, and it can reveal ways to fix those problems. Environmental science is not just some subject you learn in college; it's something that relates to everything around you for your entire life!"

### A NOTE ON THE READING

Read the selection to learn how students and colleges are working together to do their part for the environment (and the future of Earth's natural resources).

### PREVIEWING THE READING

*Using the steps listed on page 4, preview the reading selection. When you have finished, complete the following items.*

1. This reading is about _____ on college campuses.

2. Indicate whether each statement is true (T) or false (F).

_____ a. Sustainability focuses on the past and the present, not on the future.

_____ b. Unfortunately, almost no recycling and waste-reduction efforts are in place on college campuses.

_____ c. Reducing greenhouse gas emissions has become a major priority in sustainability initiatives.

**MAKING
CONNECTIONS**    *Does your college campus take part in any environmentally friendly programs? You can usually find information about these programs on the school's Web site.*

*This scientific reading makes use of many vocabulary terms used in environmental science courses. Marginal definitions are provided to help you, but try to figure out the definitions of the words in bold before using the margin notes. Often, the examples and context that follow will provide clues to the definitions.*

# Sustainability on Campus

Jay Withgott and Scott Brennan

1   Whether on campus or around the world, *sustainability* means living in a way that can be lived far into the future. Sustainability involves conserving resources to prevent their depletion, protecting ecological processes, and eliminating waste and pollution, so as to ensure that our society's practices can continue and our civilization can endure.

2   A *sustainable solution* is one that results in truly renewable resource use, whereby whatever **natural capital** we take from Earth can be replenished by the planet's systems, so that resources are not depleted. A sustainable solution preserves ecosystem services so that they continue to function and provide us their many benefits. A sustainable solution eliminates pollution, being **carbon-neutral** and emitting no toxic substances. A sustainable solution enables us to reuse or recycle waste so as to truly close the loop in our processes of production. And a sustainable solution will satisfy all three pillars of sustainability: environmental quality, economic well-being, and social justice.

3   If we are to attain a sustainable civilization, we will need to make efforts at every level, from the individual to the household to the community to the nation to the world. Governments, corporations, and organizations must all encourage and pursue sustainable practices. Among the institutions that can contribute to sustainability efforts are colleges and universities.

**natural capital**
natural resources

**carbon–neutral**
having no impact on the emissions of carbon dioxide (a pollutant) into the atmosphere

## Why Strive for Campus Sustainability?

4   We tend to think of colleges and universities as enlightened and progressive institutions that benefit society. However, colleges and universities are also centers of lavish resource consumption. Institutions of higher education feature extensive infrastructure including classrooms, offices, research labs, and residential housing. Most have dining establishments, sports arenas, vehicle fleets, and road networks. The 4,300 campuses in the United States interact with thousands of businesses and spend nearly $400 billion each year on products and services. The **ecological footprint** of a typical college or university is substantial, and together these institutions generate perhaps 2% of U.S. carbon emissions.

5   Reducing the size of this footprint is challenging. Colleges and universities tend to be bastions of tradition, where institutional habits are deeply ingrained and where bureaucratic inertia can block the best intentions for positive change. Nonetheless,

**ecological footprint**
the total effect of human activities on the environment

faculty, staff, administrators, and students are progressing on a variety of fronts to make the operations of educational institutions more sustainable. Students are often the ones who initiate change, although support from faculty, staff, and administrators is crucial for success. Students often feel freest to express themselves. Students also arrive on campus with new ideas and perspectives, and they generally are less attached to traditional ways of doing things.

### An Audit is a Useful Way to Begin

6    Campus sustainability efforts often begin with a quantitative assessment of the institution's operations. An audit provides baseline information on what an institution is doing or how much it is consuming. Audits also help set priorities and goals. Students can conduct an audit themselves, as when University of Vermont graduate student Erika Swahn measured heating, transportation, electricity, waste, food, and water use to calculate her school's ecological footprint (it turned out to be 4.5 acres for each student, instructor, and staff member).

7    It is most useful in an audit to target items that can lead directly to specific recommendations. For instance, an audit should quantify the performance of individual appliances so that decision makers can identify particular ones to replace. Once changes are implemented, the institution can monitor progress by comparing future measurements to the audit's baseline data.

### Recycling and Waste Reduction are Common Campus Efforts

8    Campus sustainability efforts frequently involve waste reduction, recycling, or **composting**. According to the most recent comprehensive survey of campus sustainability efforts (Table 13-1), most schools recycle or compost at least some waste, and the average recycling rate reported was 29%. Waste management initiatives are relatively easy to start and maintain because they offer many opportunities for small-scale improvements and because people generally enjoy recycling and reducing waste.

**composting**
a process in which organic (once-alive) materials are piled up and allowed to decay; the decayed materials become rich natural soils and fertilizers

9    The best-known collegiate waste management event is *RecycleMania,* a 10-week competition among schools to see which can recycle the most. This annual competition, which was started by students, involved 607 schools in its 10th year in 2010, when California State University at San Marcos won the overall award, recycling 72% of its waste. Students at the United States Coast Guard Academy won the title for per capita recycling, with 37 kg (82 lb) of material recycled per student. In earlier years Colorado State University students had done so well in this event that they were recruited to run a recycling program at the 2008 Democratic National Convention in Denver and they succeeded in recycling 80% of the waste.

10    "Trash audits" or "landfill on the lawn" events involve tipping dumpsters onto a campus open space and sorting our recyclable items (Figure 13-1). When students at Ashlan University in Ohio audited their waste, they found that 70% was recyclable, and they used this data to press their administration to support recycling programs. Louisiana State University students initiated recycling efforts at home football games, and over three seasons they recycled 68 tons of refuse that otherwise would have gone to the landfill.

## TABLE 13-1    FREQUENCY OF CAMPUS SUSTAINABILITY EFFORTS

| ACTIVITY | PERCENTAGE OF CAMPUSES PERFORMING ACTIVITY* |
|---|---|
| **Waste Management** | |
| ▶ Recycling and composting | 50–89[†] |
| ▶ Diverting surplus materials from the waste stream through an exchange program | 77 |
| ▶ Reducing the need for paper | 68 |
| **Campus Buildings** | |
| ▶ Constructing or renovating green buildings with LEED certification | 35 |
| ▶ Creating green roofs | 13 |
| ▶ Water efficiency upgrades | 76 |
| **Energy Efficiency Upgrades** | |
| ▶ Upgrading lighting efficiency | 81 |
| ▶ Upgrading HVAC systems | 73 |
| ▶ Reducing energy load in IT systems | 66 |
| **Energy Use and Policy** | |
| ▶ Creating plans to reduce greenhouse gases | 27 |
| ▶ Purchasing carbon offsets | 8 |
| ▶ Generating clean renewable energy | 12 |
| ▶ Using clean renewable energy from off-campus | 32 |
| ▶ Sustainable purchasing policies | 61 |
| **Transportation** | |
| ▶ Offering free or discounted mass transit | 31 |
| ▶ Providing adequate and protected bike racks | 61 |
| ▶ Using alternative fuels in fleet vehicles | 27 |
| **Landscaping** | |
| ▶ Landscaping to help wildlife | 39 |
| ▶ Restoring habitat | 40 |
| ▶ Using integrated pest management | 61 |
| ▶ Removing invasive species | 38 |
| **Professional Development in Sustainability for Faculty** | 36 |
| **Staff Coordinator for Sustainability Issues** | 51 |

*Data are for 2008, based on voluntary responses from 1,086 schools. Most numbers are likely underestimates, as some campuses did not respond to some questions.

[†]50–89%, depending on type of material.

*Source:* McIntosh, M., et al., 2008. *Campus environment 2008; A national report card on sustainability in higher education.* National Wildlife Federation Campus Ecology; survey conducted by Princeton Survey Research Associates International.

11    Composting is becoming popular as well. Ball State University in Indiana composts bulky wood waste, shredding surplus furniture and wood pallets and making them into mulch to nourish campus plantings. At Ithaca College in New York, 44% of the food waste generated annually on campus is composted. Disposal fees at the local landfill are $60 per ton, so composting saves the college $11,500 each year. The compost is used on campus plantings, and experiments showed that the plantings grew better with the compost mix than with chemical soil amendments.

12    Reuse is more sustainable than recycling, so students at some campuses systematically collect unwanted items and donate them to charity or resell them to returning students in the fall. Students at the University of Texas at Austin run a "Trash to Treasure" program. Each May, they collect 40–50 tons of items that students discard as they leave and then resell them at low prices in August to arriving students. This keeps waste out of the landfill, provides arriving students with items they need at low cost, and raises $10,000–20,000 per year that gets plowed back into campus sustainability efforts.

## Green Building Design is a Key to Sustainable Campuses

13    Buildings are responsible for 70–90% of a campus's carbon emissions, so making them more efficient can make a big difference. Marry campuses now boast "green" buildings that are constructed from sustainable building materials and whose design and technologies reduce pollution, use renewable energy, and encourage efficiency in energy and water use. As with any type of ecolabeling, there need to be agreed-upon standards, and for sustainable buildings these are the *Leadership in Energy and Environmental Design (LEED)* standards. Developed and maintained by the nonprofit U.S. Green Building Council, LEED standards guide the design and certification of new construction and the renovation of existing structures.

14    One of the first green buildings on a college campus was the Adam Joseph Lewis Center for Environmental Studies at Oberlin College in Ohio: This building was constructed using materials that were recycled or reused, took little energy to produce, or were locally harvested, produced, or distributed. Carpeting materials are leased and then returned to the company for recycling when they wear out. The Lewis Center contains energy-efficient lighting, heating, and appliances, and it maximizes indoor air quality with a state-of-the-art ventilation system, as well as paints, adhesives, and carpeting that emit few **volatile** organic compounds. The structure is powered largely by solar energy from photovoltaic (PV) panels on the roof, active solar heating, and passive solar heating from south-facing walls of glass and a tiled slate floor that acts as a thermal mass. Over 150 sensors throughout the building monitor conditions such as temperature and air quality.

**volatile**
organic compounds organic (natural) substances that evaporate quickly and cause pollution

15    Sustainable architecture doesn't stop at a building's walls. Oberlin's Lewis Center is set among orchards, gardens, and a restored wetland that helps filter wastewater, and with urban agriculture and lawns of grass specially bred to require less chemical care. Careful design of campus landscaping can create livable spaces that promote social interaction and where plantings supply shade, prevent soil erosion, create attractive settings, and provide wildlife habitat. It has been said, in fact, that groundskeepers are more vital to colleges' recruiting efforts than are vice presidents!

## Water Conservation is Important

16   Conserving water is a key element of sustainable campuses—especially in arid regions, as students at the University of Arizona in Tucson know. Despite Tucson's dry desert climate, rain falls in torrents during the late-summer monsoon season, when water pours off paved surfaces and surges down riverbeds, causing erosion, carrying pollution, and flowing too swiftly to sink into the ground and recharge aquifers. So UA students sought to redirect these floodwaters and put them to use. With the help of a grant written by Dr. James Riley and student Chet Phillips, the group created an independent study course to design and implement a rainwater harvesting project on campus. Students surveyed sites, researched their hydrology, and worked with staff to design and engineer channels, dams, **berms**, and basins to slow the water down and direct it into **swales**, where it can nourish plants and sink in to recharge the aquifer.

17   Water conservation is just as important indoors. A student organization called Greeks Going Green pursues sustainable solutions for students in fraternities and sororities. In its water conservation program at the University of Washington, students installed 300 5-minute shower timers, 300 low-flow showerheads, and 500 low-flow **aerators** for sink faucets. Students at Reading Area Community College in Pennsylvania installed water-bottle fillers at drinking fountains in college buildings and mounted an information campaign urging their peers to fill used bottles with tap water instead of buying bottled water, which involves more environmental impacts.

**berms**
large deposits of soil or other materials used as barriers against erosion

**swale**
the place where two downward-sloping pieces of land meet

**aerator**
a device for pumping air into water

## Energy Efficiency is Easy to Improve

18   Students are finding many ways to conserve energy. At Colorado College, students launched a four-month public awareness campaign, using "eco-reps" in dorms to give advice on saving energy, as well as e-mails, murals, sculptures, and energy-saving equipment. In those four months, the college saved $100,000 in utility costs and reduced its greenhouse gas emissions by 10%. Students at SUNY-Purchase in New York saved their school $86,000 per year simply by turning down hot water temperatures by 5°F (2.8°C.)

19   Campuses can harness large energy savings simply by not powering unused buildings. Central Florida Community College booked its summer classes into a minimum number of efficient buildings so that other buildings could be shut down. Central Florida students also surveyed staff and then removed light bulbs the staff said they did not need. The college also installed motion detectors to turn off lights when people are not in rooms. At Augusta State University in Georgia, students studied lighting in the science building and concluded that installing automated sensors would save $1,200 per year in electricity bills and save 6.4 tons of $CO_2$ emissions. At this rate, the cost of the sensors would be recouped in just four years.

## Students are Promoting Renewable Energy

20   Campuses can reduce fossil fuel consumption and emissions by altering the type of energy they use. Middlebury College in Vermont is switching its central plant from fuel oil to carbon-neutral wood chips, which should reduce emissions by 40%.

FIGURE 13-1

A wind turbine at the University of Maine at Presque Isle saves $100,000 per year in electricity costs while reducing $CO_2$ emissions and serving as an educational resource for the campus.

21    Solar power plays a role on many campuses. Schools in sunny climates such as De Anza College are a natural fit for solar power, including solar thermal and photovoltaic (PV), systems. These applications provide a portion of De Anza's energy, and the Foothill–De Anza District plans to increase the PV-generated electricity to over 1 megawatt over the next few years. Butte College in California gets 28% of its electricity from its solar array. California State University, Long Beach, is installing a PV solar system that will decrease emissions equal to taking 50,000 cars off the road. Solar power also works in cooler and cloudier climes. At the University of Vermont, solar PV panels provide enough electricity for nine desktop computers or 95 energy-efficient light bulbs for 10 hours each day. William Paterson University in New Jersey is embarking on the installation of what could become the largest single campus PV solar installation in the nation, which could provide 14% of campus electricity needs and save $4.4 million over 15 years.

22    Middlebury College and Minnesota's Macalester College were pioneers in installing wind turbines to help meet their energy needs, but today more colleges are doing so. The University of Maine at Presque Isle installed a wind turbine that will save $100,000 each year in electricity expenses with a corresponding reduction in carbon emissions (Figure 13-2). St. Olaf College in Minnesota gets one-third of its electricity from its wind turbine. Massachusetts Maritime Academy is erecting a wind turbine expected to generate 25% of the school's electricity and save $300,000 per year.

## Carbon-Neutrality is a Major Goal

23    Now that global climate change has vaulted to the forefront of society's concerns, reducing greenhouse gas emissions from fossil fuel combustion has become a top priority for campus sustainability proponents. Today many campuses are aiming to become carbon-neutral.

24    Students at Lewis and Clark College in Oregon began the trend in 2002, when they made their school the first in the nation to comply with the **Kyoto Protocol.** After conducting a campus audit, student leaders reduced greenhouse emissions by the percentage required under the Protocol, largely by purchasing **carbon offsets** from a nonprofit that funds energy efficiency and revegetation projects. While U.S. leaders were citing economic expense in refusing to cut emissions at the national level,

**Kyoto Protocol** international agreement designed to fight global warming

**carbon offset** reduction in emission of greenhouse gases to compensate for an emission made elsewhere

Lewis and Clark students found that becoming Kyoto-compliant on their campus cost only $10 per student per year. Similarly, Western Washington University's carbon offset program costs Just $10.50 per student per year—an amount that students voted overwhelmingly to pay.

25    Today, student pressure and petitions at many campuses are nudging administrators and trustees to set targets for reducing greenhouse emissions. As of 2010, nearly 700 university presidents had signed onto the American College and University Presidents' Climate Commitment. Presidents taking this pledge commit to inventory emissions, set target dates and milestones for becoming carbon-neutral, and take immediate steps to lower emissions with short-term actions, while also integrating sustainability into the curriculum.

## Dining Services and Campus Farms Can Promote More Sustainable Food

26    Activism at landmark events is one way to promote sustainability concerns, but we all can make a difference three times a day, each time we eat. One way is by cutting down on waste, estimated at 25% of food that students take. Composting food scraps is an effective method of recycling waste once it is created, but trayless dining can reduce waste at its source. Coe College in Iowa is one of many schools where dining halls are eliminating trays and asking students to carry plates individually. Not having to wash trays saves on water, detergent, and energy, and Coe's dining manager calculated that the trayless system prevents 200–300 pounds of food waste per week.

27    Campus food services also can buy organic produce, purchase food in bulk or with less packaging, and buy locally grown or produced food. At Sterling College in Vermont, many foods are organic, grown by local farmers, or produced by Vermont-based companies. Some foods are grown and breads are baked on the Sterling campus, and food shipped in is purchased in bulk. Dish soap is biodegradable, and kitchen scraps are composted along with unbleached paper products. Some college campuses even have gardens or farms where students help to grow food that is eaten on campus. University of Montana students tend a 10-acre farm that produces 20,000 pounds of organic produce that is given to a local food bank.

28    Loyola University Chicago is going still further. Besides raising bees to produce honey on campus, Loyola students and staff are going into the community and tending community gardens to feed the homeless. They also are planting fruit- and nut-bearing trees in urban neighborhoods in Chicago to help establish homegrown food sources for working-class residents.

## Purchasing Decisions Wield Influence

29    The kinds of purchasing decisions made in dining halls favoring local food, organic food, and biodegradable products can be applied across the entire spectrum of a campus's needs. When campus purchasing departments buy recycled paper, certified sustainable wood, energy-efficient appliances, goods with less packaging, and other ecolabeled products, they send signals to manufacturers and increase the demand for such items.

30    At Chatham College in Pennsylvania, students chose to honor their school's best-known alumnus, Rachel Carson, by seeking to eliminate toxic chemicals on campus. Administrators agreed, provided that alternative products to replace the toxic ones

worked just as well and were not more expensive. Students brought in the CEO of a company that produces nontoxic cleaning products, who demonstrated to the janitorial staff that his company's products were superior. The university switched to the nontoxic products, which were also cheaper, and proceeded to save $10,000 per year.

### Transportation Alternatives are Many

31    Many campuses struggle with traffic congestion, parking shortages, commuting delays, and pollution from vehicle exhaust. Indeed, commuting to and from campuses in vehicles accounts for over half of the carbon emissions of the average college or university. Some are addressing these issues by establishing or expanding bus and shuttle systems; introducing alternative vehicles to university fleets; and encouraging walking, carpooling, and bicycling.

32    Juniata College in Pennsylvania runs a bike-sharing program in which students can borrow bikes from a fleet. University of Texas at Austin students refurbish donated bicycles and then provide them free to new students. Passing bikes from one generation to the next reduces traffic congestion, pollution, and parking costs while promoting a healthy mode of transportation.

33    Alternative vehicles and alternative fuels are playing larger and larger roles. Butte College in California operates three natural gas buses and 10 biodiesel buses that keep 1,100 cars off campus each day. These buses were funded through a student-approved fee. At University of California–Irvine, students pushed for the bus system to be converted to biodiesel, and the 20 converted buses today save 480 tons of carbon emissions per year. The State University of New York College of Environmental Science and Forestry in Syracuse acquired electric vehicles, a gas-electric hybrid car, and a delivery van that runs on compressed natural gas while also converting its buses to biodiesel. Middlebury College students began Project Bio Bus, which has crisscrossed North America each summer in a biodiesel bus spreading the gospel of this alternative fuel. Dartmouth College students are now taking their own Big Green Bus on the road in a similar effort. Meanwhile, students at Rice University, MIT, Loyola University Chicago, and the University of Central Florida are taking biodiesel initiatives to the next level—they are producing biodiesel. These students are collecting waste cooking oil from dining halls and restaurants, and brewing biodiesel for campus bus fleets.

The University of Washington is a leader in transportation efforts. Its transportation program provides unlimited mass transit access, discounts on bicycle equipment, rides

**FIGURE 13–2**

Bike-sharing at the University of Rhode Island

home in emergencies, merchant discounts, subsidies for carpooling, rentals of hybrid vehicles, and more. As a result, each day, three-quarters of the population commutes by some other means than driving alone in a car. The program has kept peak traffic below 1990 levels, despite 23% growth in the campus population."

## Campuses are Restoring Native Plants, Habitats, and Landscapes

34    No campus sustainability program would be complete without some effort to enhance the campus's natural environment. Such efforts remove invasive species, restore native plants and communities, improve habitat for wildlife, enhance soil and water quality, and create healthier, more attractive surroundings.

35    These efforts are diverse in their scale and methods. Seattle University in Washington landscapes its grounds with native plants and has not used pesticides since 1986. Its campus includes an ethno-botanical garden and areas for wildlife. At Warren Wilson College in North Carolina, students and the landscaping supervisor built a greenhouse, expanded an **arboretum**, and are propagating local grasses and wildflowers. Ohio State University and the New College of California in San Francisco have rooftop gardens.

**arboretum**
park in which many varieties of trees are grown

36    Some schools have embarked on ambitious projects of ecological restoration. The University of Central Florida manages 500 of its 1,400 acres for biodiversity conservation. It is using prescribed fire, and has so far restored 100 acres for fire-dependent species while protecting the campus against out-of-control wildfires.

At North Hennepin Community College in Minnesota, students have planted over 35,000 seedlings and are transforming 7 acres of lawn and channelized ponds into marsh, prairie/savanna, and native forest. Besides providing wildlife habitat, the restored area reduces erosion and maintenance costs and provides opportunities for biological and environmental education.

## Sustainability Efforts Include Curricular Changes

37    Along with this diversity of efforts to make campus operations more sustainable, colleges and universities have also been transforming their academic curricula and course offerings. As our society comes to appreciate the looming challenge of sustainability, colleges and universities are attempting to train students to confront this challenge more effectively. For instance, since 1992, De Anza College has been committed to institutionalizing Environmental Studies as a recognized department and discipline, along with Math, English, and other sciences and social sciences.

38    The percentage of schools that require all students to take at least one course related to environmental science or sustainability decreased from 8% in 2001 to just 4% in 2008. At most schools, fewer than half of students take even one course on the basic functions of Earth's natural systems, and still fewer take courses on the links between human activity and sustainability. As a result, students are slightly less likely to be environmentally literate when they graduate.

## Organizations Assist Campus Efforts

39    Many campus sustainability initiatives are supported by organizations such as the Association for the Advancement of Sustainability in Higher Education and the

Campus Ecology program of the National Wildlife Federation. These organizations act as information clearinghouses for campus sustainability efforts. Each year the Campus Ecology program recognizes the most successful campus sustainability initiatives with awards. In addition, national and international conferences are growing, such as the biennial Greening of the Campus conferences at Ball State University. With the assistance of these organizations and events, it is easier than ever to start sustainability efforts on your own campus and obtain the support to carry them through to completion."

### The Issues

#### Sustainability On Your Campus

40   Find out what sustainability efforts are being made on your campus. What results have these achieved so far? What further efforts would you like to see pursued on your campus? Do you foresee any obstacles to these efforts? How could these obstacles be overcome? How could you become involved?

# UNDERSTANDING AND ANALYZING THE READING

## A. BUILDING VOCABULARY

### Context

*Using context and a dictionary if necessary, determine the meaning of each word as it is used in the selection.*

_____ 1. depletion (paragraph 1)
   a. evaporation
   b. serious decrease
   c. waste
   d. use

_____ 2. replenished (paragraph 2)
   a. renewed
   b. recycled
   c. destroyed
   d. utilized

_____ 3. toxic (paragraph 2)
   a. poisonous
   b. oxygen-based
   c. carbon-based
   d. on fire

_____ 4. lavish (paragraph 4)
   a. wealthy
   b. unlimited
   c. extravagant
   d. careful

_____ 5. infrastructure (paragraph 4)
   a. tuition and fees
   b. steel girders and wood beams
   c. buildings and structures
   d. parking lots and parking decks

_____ 6. bastions (paragraph 5)
   a. unwanted children
   b. cities
   c. rumors
   d. defenders

_____ 7. quantitative (paragraph 6)
   a. impartial
   b. close
   c. accurate
   d. numbers-based

_____ 8. refuse (paragraph 10)
   a. disagree
   b. computer components
   c. garbage
   d. leftover food

_____ 9. arid (paragraph 16)
   a. western
   b. dry
   c. flowery
   d. bitter

_____ 10. vaulted (paragraph 23)
   a. screamed
   b. became controversial
   c. jumped
   d. pushed

## Word Parts

> ### A REVIEW OF PREFIXES, ROOTS, AND SUFFIXES
>
> **BI-** means *two*.
>
> **RE-** means *back* or *again*.
>
> **HYDRO** means *water*.
>
> **PHOTO** means *light*.
>
> **-LOGY** means *study* or *thought*.

1. *Photovoltaic* (paragraph 14) energy is electricity that is produced by
   _____ .

2. *Hydrology* (paragraph 16) is the study of _____.

3. The process of *revegetation* (paragraph 24) involves _____
   _____ to an area.

4. A *biennial* (paragraph 39) event happens every _____ years.

## B. UNDERSTANDING THE THESIS AND OTHER MAIN IDEAS

*Select the best answer.*

_____ 1. Which of the following is the best statement of the selection's thesis or main idea?

    a. In general, students on the East Coast tend to be more environmentally aware than students on the West Coast.

    b. The single best sustainability campaign involves the recycling of both organic and nonorganic products.

    c. The study of environmental science is growing, and that discipline's key insight is the need to reduce the release of volatile organic compounds and the emission of greenhouse gases.

    d. Across North America, colleges (which use tremendous amounts of natural resources) are taking part in a wide variety of sustainability initiatives.

_____ 2. The topic of paragraph 6 is

    a. the University of Vermont.

    b. conducting an energy audit.

    c. Erika Swahn.

    d. setting priorities and goals.

_____ 3. The main idea of paragraphs 12, 17, 21, and 33 is found in

    a. the first sentence.

    b. the second sentence.

    c. the third sentence.

    d. the last sentence.

_____ 4. Which of the following is the best statement of the implied main idea of paragraph 38?

    a. Although environmental awareness has increased greatly, many college students are not required to take an environmental science course.

    b. Environmental science courses are more common at four-year schools than they are at junior colleges or community colleges.

    c. Most students take an environmental science course grudgingly, and they do so only to fulfill their degree requirements.

    d. Courses that show the links between humanity and Earth's natural systems are the most important courses on any college campus.

_____ 5. Which aspect of sustainability is not discussed in the selection?

    a. alternative forms of transportation

    b. campus dining services and farms

    c. government incentives to develop geothermal energy

    d. the goal of carbon-neutrality

## C. IDENTIFYING DETAILS

*Match the school in Column 1 with its sustainability program in Column 2.*

| Column 1: School | Column 2: Sustainability Program |
|---|---|
| _____ 1. Oberlin College, Ohio | a. Students and staff tend community gardens to help feed the homeless |
| _____ 2. William Paterson University, New Jersey | b. Dining halls have gone "trayless" |
| _____ 3. Coe College, Iowa | c. Home to Adam Joseph Lewis Center, which is built from recycled, reused, or locally harvested materials |
| _____ 4. Loyola University, Chicago | d. Landscapes its grounds only with native plants and has not used pesticides since 1986 |
| _____ 5. Seattle University, Washington | e. Working on what could be the largest single-campus photovoltaic solar-power installation in the country |

## D. RECOGNIZING METHODS OF ORGANIZATION AND TRANSITIONS

*Select the best answer.*

_____ 1. The overall pattern of organization used in this reading is
   a. order of importance.
   b. process.
   c. comparison and contrast.
   d. listing.

_____ 2. The organizational pattern used in paragraph 2 is
   a. cause and effect.
   b. definition.
   c. classification.
   d. order of importance.

_____ 3. The organizational pattern used in paragraph 19 is
   a. cause and effect.
   b. process.
   c. definition.
   d. enumeration.

_____ 4. Which transitional word or phrase could be effectively used to introduce the second sentence in paragraph 21?
   a. On the other hand,
   b. However,
   c. Unlike houses,
   d. For example,

## E. READING AND THINKING VISUALLY

*Select the best answer.*

_____ 1. According to Table 13-1 (p. 395), the most common campus sustainability efforts involve _____, while the least common involve _____.

   a. water efficiency upgrades, restoring habitat

   b. waste management, purchasing carbon offsets

   c. providing bike racks, creating green roofs

   d. using integrated pest management, generating clean renewable energy

_____ 2. The caption to Figure 13-1, page 398, states that the wind turbine serves as "an educational resource for the campus." This means that the turbine

   a. was erected by the faculty and staff of the university.

   b. brings a nice level of profit to the university each year.

   c. is used to teach students and other interested parties about sustainability programs.

   d. was constructed by students as a final project for their engineering, geology, or environmental science course.

_____ 3. Why do you think the authors included the photo in Figure 13-2, page 400?

   a. to encourage students to take more exercise

   b. to advertise a new, more energy efficient bicycle

   c. to illustrate one way to cut down on traffic congestion, parking shortages, and pollution

   d. to show how well the University of Rhode Island maintains its bike fleet

## F. FIGURING OUT IMPLIED MEANINGS

*Indicate whether each statement is true (T) or false (F).*

_____ 1. The authors imply that most sustainability audits are based on flawed information and are therefore inaccurate or unreliable.

_____ 2. In general, sustainability initiatives focus on the present to ensure the availability of resources in the future.

_____ 3. The authors believe that a good way to get students interested in environmental issues is to sponsor contests in which students participate.

_____ 4. The authors imply that colleges and universities are only minor components in the economy, responsible mostly for small-scale purchases.

_____ 5. Often, college sustainability programs are aimed at making the campus better fit with its local environment.

_____ 6. The authors favor large, expensive sustainability programs over smaller, more local sustainability programs.

_____ 7. The authors believe that college campuses can be social leaders in the sustainability movement through their experiments with alternative energy sources, such as wind and solar power.

## G. THINKING CRITICALLY: ANALYZING THE AUTHOR'S TECHNIQUES

_Select the best answer._

_____ 1.  The authors' primary purpose in writing "Sustainability on Campus" is to
   a. provide a definition of sustainability and offer many examples of sustainability initiatives from college campuses.
   b. help a nonprofit organization lobby for funding to develop alternative energy sources.
   c. point the finger of shame at the many U.S. colleges who have not examined their energy-consumption and recycling practices.
   d. argue that recycling, composting, and the banning of pesticides are the three most common and effective sustainability programs used on today's college campuses.

_____ 2. The overall tone of the reading is
   a. optimistic.
   b. downbeat.
   c. skeptical.
   d. critical.

_____ 3. The tone of paragraph 38 is
   a. informative.
   b. unbiased.
   c. disapproving.
   d. neutral.

_____ 4. The type of evidence used most in "Sustainability on Campus" is
   a. the authors' personal experience.
   b. historical facts.
   c. quotations.
   d. examples.

_____ 5. All of the following are opinions *except*

    a. "If we are to attain a sustainable civilization, we will need to make efforts at every level, from the individual to the household to the community to the nation to the world." (paragraph 3)

    b. "We tend to think of colleges and universities as enlightened and progressive institutions that benefit society." (paragraph 4)

    c. "A student organization called Greeks Going Green pursues sustainable solutions for students in fraternities and sororities." (paragraph 17)

    d. "Activism at landmark events is one way to promote sustainability concerns, but we all can make a difference three times a day, each time we eat." (paragraph 26)

## H. THINKING CRITICALLY: ANALYZING THE AUTHOR'S MESSAGE

*Select the best answer.*

_____ 1. In paragraph 15, the authors state, "It has been said, in fact, that groundskeepers are more vital to colleges' recruiting efforts than are vice presidents." By this statement, they mean

    a. many students choose a college on the basis of what the campus looks like.

    b. most college vice presidents are drastically overpaid.

    c. groundskeepers are more in touch with the students, while college executives are removed from students' daily lives.

    d. on most college campuses, groundskeepers start and manage most sustainability efforts.

_____ 2. Which statement best summarizes the type of bias found in the reading selection?

    a. The authors are biased in favor of students over administrators.

    b. The authors are biased in favor of sustainability programs.

    c. The authors are biased against programs that have lower participation rates, such as purchasing carbon offsets.

    d. The authors are biased against community colleges and biased in favor of traditional four-year colleges and universities.

_____ 3. Which of the following is *not* one of the authors' underlying assumptions in paragraphs 1–3?

    a. Sustainability programs are valuable.

    b. Earth can renew itself, given enough time and the proper care.

    c. Governments must take the lead in establishing sustainability plans.

    d. Sustainability programs further many goals beyond environmental goals.

# WRITING IN RESPONSE TO THE READING

## I. REVIEWING AND ORGANIZING IDEAS WITH AN OUTLINE

*Complete the following outline of paragraphs 1–4 of the reading.*

### Sustainability on Campus

I. Introduction

   A. Sustainability involves:

      1. conserving _____

      2. preventing resource depletion

      3. protecting ecological processes

      4. _____

   B. Sustainable solution: results in replenishment of natural capital

      1. preserves ecosystem services so they continue to function

      2. eliminates _____ by being carbon-neutral and emitting _____

      3. reuses or recycles waste

   C. Three pillars of sustainability

      1. environmental quality

      2. _____

      3. _____

II. Why strive for campus sustainability?

   A. Campuses use many resources

   B. Reducing substantial _____ is a challenge

## J. ANALYZING THE ISSUE AND ARGUMENT

1. What contemporary issues are being discussed in this reading? Phrase each in the form of a question. Then write a one-sentence summary of the author's position on the issue.

2. What techniques do the authors use to make their arguments? For example, do they discuss their own experiences with global warming, or do they rely on the opinions, expertise, and experiences of others?

3. What are the authors' backgrounds, and are they qualified is to write about the topic? Why or why not? Does the source from which this reading is taken help you determine the authors' credibility? Do you find any bias in the selection?

4. Evaluate the reading's main argument on the following criteria:

    a. Is the argument timely?

    b. Are the statistics used fairly and clearly?

    c. Have the authors provided sufficient evidence to support their argument?

    d. Have the authors defined their terms sufficiently?

    e. Do the authors offer any opposing viewpoints? If not, what might some opposing arguments be?

    f. Does the article offer any emotional appeals? If so, identify them and evaluate their fairness.

## K. WRITING PARAGRAPHS AND ESSAYS

*Write a paragraph or essay in response to the following prompts.*

1. "Sustainability on Campus" includes three introductory paragraphs but no concluding paragraph. Write a concluding paragraph for the reading.

2. Examine your next two meals, including the dishes you eat on, the cups you drink from, and the napkins you use. Which parts of them could be recycled? Which could be composted? Write an essay outlining the most sustainable way to eat your next meal.

4. Write an essay about your campus's sustainability efforts. If your school does not currently participate in any sustainability programs, write an essay outlining your suggestions for making the campus a "greener," more energy-efficient place.

5. The reading talks about campus programs. How can you save energy and "go green" in your own life—from the house or apartment you live in, to the car you drive, to the other choices in your life? Write an essay in which you explore ways that you, personally, can contribute to sustainability.

## ACTIVITIES: EXPLORING ENVIRONMENTAL ISSUES

*On your own or with a group of classmates, complete two of the following four activities.*

1. List at least five ways you can have a positive effect the environment. These can be local/personal activities (for example, not using Styrofoam cups, which clog up landfills and do not break down into natural components) or community-based, national, or international activities (for example, volunteering for a committee that cleans up local parks).

   _____

   _____

   _____

   _____

   _____

2. Conduct a Web search for an organization that is devoted to preserving the environment, such as the World Wildlife Federation, Greenpeace, or the Sierra Club. What is the organization's mission? Read a couple of the articles on the organization's home page and summarize them. Would you consider joining one of these organizations? Why or why not?

3. As we mentioned at the start of this chapter, the environment is a very broad topic. This chapter discussed just a few aspects of the topic. Other environmental issues include

   - The development of alternative energy sources, such as biofuels
   - The effects of "fracking" (drilling for natural gas) on the land
   - *Environmental racism*, which refers to the fact that poor people are much more likely to live close to heavily polluted areas
   - *Carbon footprints* and how companies are trying to reduce their impact on the environment in an effort to be more socially conscious

   Write an essay or prepare a class presentation about any of these topics, or any other environmental topic you are interested in.

4. Perform an "energy audit" of your home or a part of your campus. Where do you see natural resources and utilities (such as gas, electricity, and lighting) being used in an environmentally friendly way? Where do you see waste? For the areas of waste, suggest improvements that might be made.

# 14 Relationships: Our Friends, Families, and Communities

*How many people do you interact with daily?*

If you're like most people, you don't keep track of the dozens, even hundreds, of people you see each day. Sociologists and psychologists often call humans "the social animal" because the vast majority of human beings seek the company of others. John Donne, the English poet, wrote a famous poem titled "No Man Is an Island," which begins:

> No man is an island,
>
> Entire of itself.
>
> Each is a piece of the continent,
>
> A part of the main.

But human relationships aren't necessarily easy. In fact, they often require a good deal of work, and they are at the center of many contemporary issues. Consider the following questions, which are often debated:

- Should gay people be allowed to marry? Is marriage a religious institution, or is it secular (nonreligious)?

- Is marriage the ideal situation for most people, or should society embrace looser definitions of what constitutes a "couple"?

- When should a relationship end? How do divorces and breakups affect not only the couple breaking up, but also their friends, family, and children?

The readings in this chapter look at just a few of the many issues surrounding interpersonal relationships today. Should two people have sex before they get married, or even on the first date? Almost everyone finds it difficult to find the perfect romantic match—might dating Web sites help you find your "soul mate"? How has the Internet changed the way we look at and define communities, and are online communities as "real" as physical communities in which people interact face-to-face?

## WHY ARE CONTEMPORARY ISSUES RELATED TO RELATIONSHIPS SO IMPORTANT?

Human beings are constantly redefining their relationships with other people, starting new relationships and sometimes ending other ones. Society's views of relationships affect people at the core of their being and influence their decisions. For example, it is often suggested that gay people tend to gather in liberal cities, where their relationships are more accepted. The legal system's laws regarding which relationships to recognize and which not to recognize can have major effects on spouses, ex-spouses, in-laws, and children.

## How Do Relationships Relate to My College Experience?

The phrase "college experience" connotes much more than simply taking courses and studying for exams. Rather, it refers to an entire constellation of experiences you will encounter in college—from having a roommate, to developing relationships with your instructors, to managing your life, to planning your career. Relationships are involved in almost every aspect of the college experience and in many college courses. For example, business courses often require teamwork, which requires getting along with others in a group setting. In science labs, you will often have a lab partner with whom you share the work, and entire disciplines (such as sociology and communications) focus on human interactions and relationships.

---

**TIPS FOR READING ABOUT RELATIONSHIPS**

Here are some tips for reading not only the selections in this chapter, but any reading about relationships.

- **Apply the reading to your own experiences and life.** Students often find readings about relationships to be fairly "easy" and immediately applicable to their lives. As you read, think about how the selection applies to you or to other people you know. This is an excellent way to learn the concepts and ideas discussed in the reading.

- **Distinguish between the writer's opinions and research presented as evidence to support a thesis or main idea.** Much of what you read about relationships will be based on the writer's personal experiences. Such readings can be illuminating, but they may not be representative of the way most people feel. They are therefore mostly opinion pieces. In contrast, scientific research presented in a reading is more fact-based. Most writers give credit to the person who conducted the research, either directly (by giving the person's name and affiliation) or indirectly, by using a parenthetical research citation. For example, (Smith, 2009) refers to a research study conducted by someone named Smith, who published his or her results in 2009. Complete sources for parenthetical citations are usually found in footnotes or endnotes.

- **Keep an open mind.** Some readings about relationships may make you uncomfortable if they challenge your beliefs or expectations. Read carefully, keeping an open mind, and engage in critical thinking. Annotate the reading to record your reactions, and then analyze your reactions, asking yourself why you reacted the way you did.

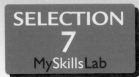

## SELECTION 7
MySkillsLab

# Hooking Up

## Jenifer Kunz

TEXTBOOK
SELECTION

### SOURCE AND CONTEXT

The following reading was taken from an introductory textbook, *Think Marriages and Families*, by Jenifer Kunz. This selection comes from a chapter titled "Friendship, Affection, Love, and Intimacy." The author is a professor of sociology at West Texas A&M University. According to her biography, Dr. Kunz's interest in studying the family grew out of her experiences of growing up in her own family. "We worked hard, played hard, and had fun together," she says. "I came to learn and understand that the family is the most important and most influential social institution in the world."

### A NOTE ON THE READING

How do college students begin to "experiment" with adulthood when they enter college? Read "Hooking Up" for a closer look at recent trends in the sexual behaviors of college students.

### PREVIEWING THE READING

*Using the steps listed on page 4, preview the reading selection. When you have finished, complete the following items.*

1. This reading is about _____.

2. Indicate whether each statement is true (T) or false (F).

_____    a. The reading will offer criticisms of hooking up, explaining why it has negative effects on those who hook up.

_____    b. The sexual double standard allows modern young men and women to enjoy healthy, active sex lives without guilt or negative effects on self-esteem.

 MAKING
CONNECTIONS    *How would you define "hooking up"? Who does it, and why?*

### READING TIP

*Readings about some contemporary issues may make you slightly uncomfortable, especially when they discuss sensitive topics like sex. As you read "Hooking Up," focus on the definitions and the research that attempts to shed light on the sexual behavior of college students. Pay close attention to the author's tone, purpose, and audience, and look for evidence of bias in the reading.*

# Hooking Up

### Jenifer Kunz

**norm**
normal, expected behavior

1    One day, dating might be considered an old-fashioned quirk of almost Victorian taste and prudery, as quaint as a woman dropping an embroidered handkerchief to encourage a man to approach her. On that day, "hooking up" will be the **norm**. This postmodern view of romance may just be one of the latest fashions of the some times alarmist media. Before losing all hope, we should ask ourselves, "What does 'hooking up' really mean?"

2    "Hooking up" is a term used to describe casual sexual activity with no strings attached between heterosexual college students who are strangers or brief acquaintances. When did people start to hook up? Although the term became common in the 1990s, its use with its modern meaning has been documented as early as the mid-1980s. Studies from the early 2000s show that hooking up was already a fairly common practice on U.S. campuses, practiced by as much as 40 percent of female college students. More recent studies have shed some light on the demographic and psychological **correlatives** of hooking up. In a 2007 study involving 832 college students, it emerged that hooking up is practiced less by African-American than Caucasian students. Hooking up is also associated with the use of alcohol and, interestingly, with higher parental income. Increased financial resources may give teens and young adults more opportunities to socialize and hook up. As far as personality traits, hookups seem to be more common for people displaying **extroversion**, although it is also common in neuroticism. Neuroticism is a personality trait characterized by negative emotions such as depression, anxiety, anger, embarrassment, vulnerability, and impulsiveness combined with emotional instability that may lead neurotics to hook up as a way to cope with fears and anxieties. The emotions stirred by hookups are varied, and women seem to be more likely than men to experience regret after a hookup, especially when sexual intercourse is involved.

**correlatives**
two or more factors working together

**extroversion**
outgoing personality type; the opposite is *introversion*, which refers to people who are more solitary

>>> A 2003 study of the phenomenon of "hooking up" among college students revealed that people thought their peers were more comfortable with hookups than they were. Based on these results, how do you think peer pressure affects sexual behavior in teenagers and young adults?

3    Not surprisingly, hooking up has received much criticism. Psychologists blame the hookup culture for young people's fear of commitment, saying that focusing only on sex does not teach people to respond to the emotional and romantic needs of the partner. In this sense, hookups are described as the worst possible preparation for long-term relationships and marriage. Other critics argue that the hookup culture has its risks, too, especially when it's strongly characterized by alcohol consumption. A 2007 study of 178 college students concluded that 23 percent of women and 7 percent of men had experienced unwanted sexual intercourse, including regretful or harmful sexual behavior such as assault and rape (although assault and rape were reported only by a small minority of interviewees). More significantly, 78 percent of unwanted sexual intercourse experienced by the interviewees took place during a hookup. Of course, unwanted sexual intercourse is not characteristic of hookups only, and dating is not exempt from it.

## Hookups and Dating

4    How does "hooking up" differ from dating? According to author Kathleen A. Bogle, the most significant difference lies in the timing of sex, where the term "sex" refers to any sexual activity from kissing to sexual intercourse. In dating, sex usually is postponed until the couple has gone on a few dates, whereas in a hookup, sex frequently happens on the first encounter. Second, when dating, two people get to know each other and possibly start a romantic relationship, which is not required in hooking up. Alcohol consumed in large quantities is also more characteristic of hookups than dating, since casual sex is more likely when **inhibitions** are lowered. Hooking up also differs from dating in terms of privacy: Dates tend to have a public nature (they take place in restaurants, movie theaters, etc.), whereas hookups are more spontaneous and often private. The private nature of the hookup culture has been facilitated by technology advancements in the last decades, such as mobile phones and the Internet. This new technology makes it much easier to get in touch with acquaintances through private channels.

**inhibitions**
feelings or beliefs that prevent people from behaving in certain ways

5    In a time of economic crisis, it might be tempting to hook up just to save money. Unlike dates, hookups do not require spending any money on nice dinners and flowers. It is also important to realize that hooking up is most common among college students, and that it is not necessarily representative of the entire single population. College years are often viewed as the last chance to have fun before settling down, so hookups may represent a chance to experiment sexually—something that dating does not provide.

**initiation**
action that makes something start

6    Hookups also show more gender equality in the **initiation** of the script, or sequence of automatic behaviors, although research shows that men still maintain more power in deciding whether the hookup will be a one night stand or lead to something more. In this regard, sexual exploitation is still very common both in the hookup and dating culture, meaning that men are often capable of keeping a partner just for sexual enjoyment regardless of the woman's true desires. This seems to stem from the fear that women have of being rejected if they don't perform to a man's standard. There is still a stigma attached to women with a more intense sexual life or those who have had many sexual partners. As liberating as the hookup script might seem, the sexual double standard that condemns women and praises men for the same level of sexual experience is still present today.

### Hooking Up versus Commitment

7   Kara is a sophomore in college. She hooked up a lot during her first year of school, but is now ready for a deeper relationship.

8   "When I first got to college, I was ready to have fun. Leaving home for the first time gave me a sense of adventure that carried over into my idea of relationships. I didn't want anything serious, but I wanted to see what was out there. During the first months of school I hooked up with a lot of guys, mostly people I met at parties. I loved not having the pressure of a relationship on top of school.

9   "Then I hooked up with Bill, a guy from my biology class. Since he wasn't a stranger, this encounter was slightly more intimate than what I'd been used to. I'd never thought about Bill romantically, but after we made out, I started to think that way.

10   "Bill and I didn't become a couple, but our relationship made me realize that hooking up can be fun for awhile, but ultimately I'd like to have someone to get close to. I want a guy who doesn't leave first thing in the morning and who calls me for something other than one passionate night."

## UNDERSTANDING AND ANALYZING THE READING

### A.  BUILDING VOCABULARY

#### Context

*Using context and a dictionary if necessary, determine the meaning of each word as it is used in the selection.*

_____ 1. quirk (paragraph 1)
   a. tradition
   b. habit
   c. law
   d. oddity

_____ 2. alarmist (paragraph 1)
   a. biased and untrustworthy
   b. loud and crass
   c. exaggerating dangers
   d. reporting on a specific topic

_____ 3. demographic (paragraph 2)
   a. having psychological issues
   b. enrolled in college
   c. specific part of the population
   d. inclined to bragging

_____ 4. exempt (paragraph 3)
   a. encouraged by
   b. freed from
   c. prohibited by
   d. unaware of

_____ 5. postponed (paragraph 4)
   a. anticipated
   b. put off
   c. experimented with
   d. not discussed

_____ 6. spontaneous (paragraph 4)
   a. unplanned
   b. frequent
   c. lighthearted
   d. enjoyable

_____ 7. facilitated (paragraph 4)
    a. exposed
    b. helped
    c. stopped
    d. affected

_____ 8. stigma (paragraph 6)
    a. mark of disgrace
    b. role of women
    c. signal of trust
    d. problem

### Word Parts

> **A REVIEW OF PREFIXES AND SUFFIXES**
>
> **HETERO-** means _different_ or _other_.
>
> **-FUL** refers to _the state_, _condition_, or _quality_; in this case, "full of."

_Use your knowledge of word parts and the review above to fill in the blanks in the following sentences._

1. A _heterosexual_ (paragraph 2) couple is composed of people of two
_____ sexes: male and female.

2. Someone who is _regretful_ (paragraph 3) about a particular situation is full
of _____ about what happened.

## B. UNDERSTANDING THE THESIS AND OTHER MAIN IDEAS

_Select the best answer._

_____ 1. The thesis or central thought of "Hooking Up" is best stated as
    a. In the modern world, hooking up is simply a rite of passage between adolescence and adulthood.
    b. Hooking up, a term used to refer to casual sexual activity between straight college students, is associated with specific demographic and psychological factors; it is fairly common but appears to have more drawbacks than benefits.
    c. Society has come a long way since Victorian days, when sexual prudery was the norm; now, casual sex is commonplace and it no longer carries any negative connotations for college-aged men and women.
    d. Research studies regarding the hooking-up phenomenon have been inconsistent in their findings, but for the most part they reveal that young, black, straight people hook up much more frequently than older, white, gay people.

_____ 2. The topic of paragraph 3 is
   a. relationships and marriage.
   b. criticisms of hooking up.
   c. unwanted sexual intercourse.
   d. women's emotional needs.

_____ 3. The main idea of paragraph 6 is found in the
   a. first sentence.
   b. second sentence.
   c. third sentence.
   d. last sentence.

## C. IDENTIFYING DETAILS

*Select the best answer.*

_____ 1. Hooking up is associated with all of the following *except*
   a. higher parental income.
   b. neuroticism.
   c. increased consumption of alcohol.
   d. religious affiliation.

_____ 2. According to Kathleen A. Bogle, what is the key difference between dating and hooking up?
   a. Two people who hook up tend to know each other longer than two people who go out on their first date.
   b. Two people who hook up tend to come from lower-income families than two people who go out on a first date.
   c. In a hookup, two people have sex on the first date; in dating, sex is usually postponed until the couple has gone out on a few dates.
   d. In a hookup, the two people usually have roommates; in dating, the two people usually have their own apartments or live independently.

_____ 3. Which of the following is not a trait of neuroticism?
   a. shyness
   b. impulsiveness
   c. anxiety
   d. anger

## D. RECOGNIZING METHODS OF ORGANIZATION AND TRANSITIONS

*Select the best answer.*

_____ 1. Which of the following organizational patterns is *not* used in paragraph 2?
  a. definition
  b. enumeration
  c. process
  d. cause and effect

_____ 2. The dominant pattern of organization in paragraph 3 is
  a. listing.
  b. classification.
  c. comparison and contrast.
  d. chronological order.

_____ 3. A transitional word or phrase used in paragraph 3 to signal its pattern of organization is
  a. not surprisingly.
  b. other critics.
  c. students concluded.
  d. of course.

_____ 4. The primary pattern of organization used in paragraph 4 is
  a. spatial order.
  b. cause and effect.
  c. comparison and contrast.
  d. process.

## E. READING AND THINKING VISUALLY

*Select the best answer.*

_____ 1. The author likely included the photo on page 415 in order to
  a. illustrate what typical college students look like.
  b. imply that attractive people are more likely to hook up than unattractive people.
  c. emphasize that homosexuals do not hook up.
  d. provide a visual reminder of the group of people who are most likely to hook up.

## F. FIGURING OUT IMPLIED MEANINGS

*Indicate whether each statement is true (T) or false (F).*

_____ 1. White students hook up more often than black students.

_____ 2. Poor people have more time on their hands and thus are more likely than rich people to hook up.

_____ 3. The authors see a connection between the rise of the Internet and the increase in hooking up.

_____ 4. In this reading, the term "hooking up" does not apply to college graduates or gay people.

_____ 5. Extroverts are more likely to hook up than introverts.

_____ 6. Neurotic people may hook up as a way of coping with their own anxieties and fears.

_____ 7. Hooking up did not become a common practice until 2010.

_____ 8. Hookups are often more private and spontaneous than dates are.

_____ 9. Men are more likely to express regret after a hookup than women are.

## G. THINKING CRITICALLY: ANALYZING THE AUTHOR'S TECHNIQUE

*Select the best answer.*

_____ 1. The author's overall purpose in "Hooking Up" is to
   a. define the term "hooking up" and explore the research surrounding the causes and effects of this common behavior.
   b. encourage young people to experiment with a variety of different lifestyles before choosing to settle down with one mate.
   c. make the case that young men, who have more power in romantic and sexual relationships, should engage in more responsible sexual behaviors.
   d. compare and contrast neurotic behaviors with other common behaviors that do not have psychological underpinnings.

_____ 2. The author's purpose for including Kara's story in the box titled "Hooking Up versus Commitment" (paragraphs 7–10) is to
   a. show that young college women are more likely to hook up than older women.
   b. indicate that hooking up is more common among freshmen and sophomores than among juniors and seniors.
   c. imply that romance and dating are more emotionally fulfilling than hooking up.
   d. provide a case study of one college student who holds very conservative views about dating and sex.

_____ 3. The overall tone of the reading selection is best described as
   a. emotional and angry.
   b. concerned and somewhat biased.
   c. neutral and inoffensive.
   d. light and insubstantial.

_____ 4. The key type of evidence the author uses to support her main ideas and her thesis is
   a. personal experience.
   b. research studies.
   c. historical information.
   d. reports from government-funded agencies.

## H. THINKING CRITICALLY: ANALYZING THE AUTHOR'S MESSAGE

*Select the best answer.*

_____ 1. With which of the following statements would the author of "Hooking Up" *not* agree?

a. Hooking up may be a way for college students to have fun before they settle down with a lifetime partner.

b. It usually costs more money to date than to hook up.

c. Overall, men have more power than women do in deciding whether a hookup will be a one-night stand or lead to something more.

d. The sexual double standard has led to greater equality between women and men.

_____ 2. The author of this reading selection, Jenifer Kunz, can best be described as

a. old-fashioned.

b. self-centered.

c. closed-minded.

d. feminist.

_____ 3. Which of the following statements best summarizes the "post-modern view of romance" to which the author refers in paragraph 1?

a. Hooking up is much harder work than dating.

b. Hooking up is normal, expected behavior.

c. Hooking up is necessary before a romance can get started.

d. Hooking up is the next logical step in women's liberation from outmoded ideas.

_____ 4. In paragraph 6, the author states that hookups "show more gender equality in the initiation of the script." She means that

a. while men and women are now socially equal, women still earn less money than men do.

b. men and women have about equal levels of power in any type of relationship, from a basic hookup to a more intense monogamous relationship.

c. men and women are almost equally likely to start behaving in ways that will lead to a hookup.

d. while both men and women are equally likely to initiate a hookup, more men will follow through on their desires than women will.

# WRITING IN RESPONSE TO THE READING

## I. REVIEWING AND ORGANIZING IDEAS WITH A PARAPHRASE

*Complete the following paraphrase of paragraphs 4–6 of the reading by filling in the missing words or phrases.*

Kathleen Bogle has written about the differences between hooking up and _____. The biggest difference lies in how long two people wait _____. In hooking up, they have sex on the _____ date. In _____, they usually wait a least a few dates before they have sex for the first time. In _____, two people make attempts to get to know each other, but in hooking up this does not happen. Dating usually doesn't require heavy drinking of _____, but hooking up often does (because drinking lowers _____). Hooking up is more _____ than dating, while dating is more _____ than hooking up. Often, hookups are spur-of-the-moment and aided by _____ devices such as _____. Dating requires one person _____, while hooking up usually does not. People of all ages date, but hooking up may be one way for _____ _____ to explore their options before they select someone for a long-term relationship.

Although both males and females seem _____ willing to start the process of hooking up with another person, men hold the _____ in terms of deciding whether to turn the hookup into something more meaningful. Women in our society still fear _____ from men, and there is a sexual _____ standard that looks down on women who enjoy sex or have had a number of sex partners.

## J. ANALYZING THE ISSUE AND ARGUMENT

1. What contemporary issue is the author discussing in this reading? Phrase the issue in the form of a question.

2. In "Hooking Up," is the author making an argument, or is she simply presenting information?

3. Describe the author's intended audience. How can you determine this information from the source of the reading?

4. Write a one- or two-sentence summary of the author's thesis or central idea.

5. Based on the source from which this reading is taken, do you think the information provided is reliable? Why or why not?

6. Do you perceive any bias in this reading? Explain your response.

7.  Evaluate the reading on the following criteria:

    a.  Is the information timely?

    b.  Has the author provided sufficient evidence to support her main ideas? What other types of evidence might she provide to make her main ideas stronger?

    c.  Has the author defined her terms accurately and sufficiently?

    d.  Does the author offer opposing viewpoints? If so, what is her attitude toward them, and does she discredit them fairly or unfairly?

    e.  Does the reading make any emotional appeals to readers? If so, identify them and evaluate their fairness.

## K. WRITING PARAGRAPHS AND ESSAYS

*Write a paragraph or essay in response to the following writing prompts.*

1.  Do you think hooking up is a common occurrence among the students on your campus? Write a paragraph explaining your answer.

2.  Do you think men and women would be equally likely to give an honest answer to the following question: "When was the last time you hooked up?" Write a paragraph in which you explain your opinion.

3.  Write a paragraph in which you explore the author's choice of the photo on page 415. Do you think this photo encourages hooking up, or is it meant simply as an illustration? Write a caption for the photo that summarizes the reading's key points.

4.  The boxed insert within the reading  (p. 415) begins "A 2003 study" and closes with the question "Based on these results and on personal experience, how do you think peer pressure affects sexual behavior in teenagers and young adults?" Write an essay in which you answer this question.

5.  "Hooking Up" discusses one common type of behavior among college students, suggesting that it is a form of experimentation. What other types of common experimental behaviors do you see among college students? Write an essay in which you explore some of these behaviors and the possible motivations behind them.

6.  In paragraph 1, the author refers to the "alarmist media." How would you describe today's media, from newspapers through TV newscasts through Web sites? Write an essay in which you explore the types of stories that receive the most press coverage. How newsworthy are these stories?

## SELECTION 8
MySkillsLab

# The High Art of Handling Problem People

### Hara Estroff Marano

MAGAZINE ARTICLE

### SOURCE AND CONTEXT

Hara Estroff Marano is the editor-at-large of a magazine titled *Psychology Today*. The selection that follows is an article from the May/June 2012 issue of the magazine.

### A NOTE ON THE READING

Read the selection to understand how difficult people present themselves and how you can develop the skills necessary to handle them artfully.

### PREVIEWING THE READING

*Using the steps listed on page 4, preview the reading selection. When you have finished, complete the following items.*

1. What word does the author use to describe a difficult situation at home? _____

2. What four types of problem people does the author present?

   a. _____

   b. _____

   c. _____

   d. _____

3. How many ways to diffuse a difficult encounter does the author present? ___

4. Determine whether each statement is true (T) or false (F).

   _____ a. It is a waste of time to try to talk a naysayer out of being negative.

   _____ b. Overpraised children do not present problems when they enter the workforce.

**MAKING CONNECTIONS**

*Difficult people are everywhere. Think of some people in your life who are difficult. How do they present themselves to you? What are your responses to their behavior? Do you wish you could respond to them in better ways?*

*As you read, think about the people in your life who are problem people. Read carefully the author's explanations of the different types of problem people, what motivates their behaviors, and suggestions for handling these people. Be sure to highlight and annotate as you read.*

# The High Art of Handling Problem People

Hara Estroff Marano

1    The walk-in medical clinic was about to close for the day when Susan Biali got a call from one of her longtime patients. Could the doctor please hang in a bit longer? The caller was feeling very ill and needed to see her immediately. An exhausted Biali extended her already burdensome day and waited for the patient to arrive. Some time later, the woman sauntered in; she was perfectly fine. She just needed a prescription refill.

2    "She totally lied to me," the Vancouver doctor recalls. "Afterwards, I was so upset that the degree of my reaction troubled me. I'm a general physician with some training in psychiatry. Yet I couldn't put my finger on exactly why I was so bothered. I thought it was a flaw in myself."

3    Eventually, she identified what set her off: "You think you're in an innocuous situation—a typical doctor-patient encounter. But the woman took complete advantage of my compassion. Then, not only wouldn't she acknowledge the lie, but she looked at me blankly and demanded, 'Can't you just move on and give me my prescription?' She made me feel that I was the problem."

4    Ever wonder how an encounter goes so quickly awry? Doubt your own perceptions? Feel thrown totally off balance by another person? Find yourself acting crazy when you're really a very nice person? Manipulation comes in many forms: There are whiners. There are bullies. There are the short-fused. Not to forget the highly judgmental. Or the out-and-out sociopath. But they often have one thing in common: Their MO is to provoke, then make you feel you have no reason to react—and it's all your fault to begin with! Feeling deeply discounted, even totally powerless, while having to jettison the original aim of an interaction is a distressing double whammy of social life—and a cardinal sign you're dealing with a difficult person. No, it's not you. It's them. And it's the emotional equivalent of being mowed down by a hit-and-run driver.

5    It doesn't take a sociopath; anyone can be difficult in a heartbeat. "To a great extent, the problem is in the eye of the beholder," says Topeka, Kansas, psychologist Harriet Lerner, author of the now-classic *Dance of Anger* and the just-released *Relationship Rules*. "We all come into relationships with hot-button issues from our own past. For one person what's difficult might be dealing with someone who's judgmental. For another it might be a person who treats you as if you're invisible." That said, she adds that there are certain qualities that make people persistently hard to handle—hair-trigger defensiveness that obliterates the ability to listen, meanness, and a sense of worthlessness that leads people to bulk up self-esteem by putting down others, just to name a few.

## IN THE HOTHOUSE AT HOME VS. TOUGH AT WORK

**In dealing with a difficult person, the setting is everything.**
Handling difficult people at work is not quite the same as coping with problem people in family life. The goal is to get the work done, and that requires great caution and considerable strategizing. "It's not like a marriage, where the dailiness of living will allow you to repair a lot of interactions gone wrong," Lerner observes.

In a marriage, she says, it's often advisable to exit a conversation. Of course, there are a variety of ways to do that. A common one is to scream "I hate you" and slam a door behind you. Better, she advises, to say something like: "I love you, I want to be here for you, I want to hear your criticisms, but I cannot listen when you throw them at me rat-a-tat-tat. I need you to approach me with respect. So let's set up a 15-minute meeting after breakfast and start over." The difference is clarifying a loving position versus escalating things further.

6     Experience motivates most of us to avoid or minimize interacting with such people. But sometimes that problem person is a sibling, a boss, a coworker. Even your mother. And managing the relationship by distancing yourself or cutting it off altogether is impossible or undesirable. The goal, in such cases, is to prepare in advance for an encounter, knowing it will take a special effort to hold onto your own sense of self, and to stay calm.

7     Although it is typically disturbing to be in the presence of such people, remaining composed in the face of unreasonableness helps you figure out exactly what species of difficulty you're dealing with. Therein lies your advantage. It allows you to predict the specific emotional trap being set for you, which is your passport to getting your own power back.

### THE HOSTILE

**Telltale signs:** High, sometimes explosive, reactivity. Frequently disagreeable. Cynical. Mistrustful. Does not like to be wrong.
**Where you'll find them:** Corner offices. The Internet, often under the cloak of anonymity.
**Call in the wild:** "I am going to come and burn the f**king house down."
**Notable Sightings:** Mel Gibson. Mike Tyson. Naomi Campbell. Chris Brown. Russell Crowe. Courtney Love.

8     People very low on the personality dimension of agreeableness typically express themselves with irritability, hostility, and noncooperativeness. They have a short fuse and are commonly cynical and mistrustful. They are not able to look at themselves, and they are hyper-quick to blame. Placating others is not a skill in their repertoire, nor do they endorse such a possibility.

9     The trouble is their responses run to the intense side, and their reactivity and intensity breed more of the same in those who must deal with them, says Lerner. And so, not only are these people angry but you may be suddenly on the receiving

It's futile to talk naysayers out of their misery. They are often immune to outside influence.

end of criticism that feels extremely unfair. The hostile person will not be thinking clearly and is probably not taking in anything you say. "It takes a great deal of emotional maturity to deal with someone who is very intense and angry," she notes. "The reactivity is contagious and you are likely to get reactive yourself."

10 One common manifestation of hostility, especially in the workplace, is the bully boss. Such people misuse power. They humiliate you in front of others. They are verbally abusive. They overcontrol and micromanage. They don't just differ with you, they do so contemptuously and lob unfair criticism at you. If bullies are technically competent at the jobs they do, they feel immune to punishment. As a result, there tend to be high rates of turnover among their underlings. In performance-oriented companies, getting rid of bullies may not be high on the agenda, no matter how much damage they do.

11 Like bully kids, bully bosses do not see themselves accurately. They often view themselves as better than others, and they are not sensitive to the feelings of staffers. They misuse power to deliberately hurt those of lesser status.

12 It is possible, and often necessary, to confront a bully directly. But do so calmly and professionally, and never in public; this is an activity for behind closed doors. The bully will never back down in front of an audience. You must declare the bully's behavior unacceptable, specify exactly what behaviors are at issue—"You may not demean me in front of my staff or others"—and instruct the bully, succinctly, on how you wish to be treated. "I need you to support me in the presence of others. Any issues you have with my work we can discuss civilly in private."

13 An all-too-common variant of hostility is passive aggression, in which the hostility is covert, expressed in nonobvious, underhanded ways—dragging one's heels on a project, failing to respond to a meaningful request. It's often difficult to pin down the hostility, but the effects are usually clear—your goals and dreams are sabotaged. A colleague briefs you on events but leaves out critical information you need for getting your job done. Your spouse belittles you in front of others—and then insists he was "just kidding" as you seethe with rage and humiliation.

14 Sarcasm is a common tool of passive aggression. And frustration is a common response: You may find yourself getting upset and angry but can't be entirely sure it is justified. Over time, it becomes difficult if not impossible to trust anything offered by a passive-aggressive person.

## THE NEUROTIC

**Telltale signs:** Anxiety. Pessimism. Obstructionism. Naysaying. Shooting down the ideas of others.

**Where you'll find them:** Online medical chat rooms. Political blogs. Doctors' offices.

**Call in the wild:** "Yes, but..."

**Notable Sightings:** Larry David. Woody Allen. Harold Camping. Chicken Little.

15     What you might experience as a minor frustration is, for the neurotic, a hopeless difficulty. Neuroticism is typically displayed as unhappiness, anxiety, and ease of emotional arousal. "These people don't realize they're being difficult," says Duke University psychologist Mark Leary. "But they quickly get on other people's nerves. They are demanding, and they worry about everything. They think they're only trying to be helpful and not creating problems."

16     What makes them especially difficult in work environments, he explains, is that they tend to be obstructionists. "They're so worried about something going wrong that they disagree with others' ideas. They are naysayers." And in dredging up so much negativity, they stir up residual doubts in others and erode confidence in novel ideas and projects.

17     A hallmark of this type of difficult person is a pessimistic thinking style, a concern with "what's going to go wrong next in my life?" Although these people are innocently difficult, says Leary, it's still hard to deal with them because they are always going to say "Yes, but..." They'll find the cloud in any silver lining, discourage you from taking that solo cross-country trip or starting a new business.

18     It's futile to talk naysayers out of their misery. They are often immune to outside influence. The best you can aim for is to understand their perspective without endorsing it: "My experience has been totally different," for example.

19     The basic challenge in dealing with difficult people of any stripe is to remain a calm presence in a highly charged emotional field. "You have to get your own reactivity down, even if it means deep-breathing to calm yourself," says Harriet Lerner. "That enables you to listen well and understand what the other person is saying, and to respond with clarity, rather than participate in a downward-spiraling conversation." There's a temptation to write someone off as a difficult person. Resist it. "Once you label someone as impossible, you are likely to miss all the good points the person might be making," Lerner observes.

## THE REJECTION-SENSITIVE

**Telltale signs:** Constantly scanning for slights real and imagined. All slights deemed intentional. Becoming unglued at the hint of disapproval. In extremis, stalking (primarily by males).

**Where you'll find them:** Your inbox (most likely in an email demanding to know why you failed to respond to a note, overture, etc.). Backstage. Poetry readings.

**Call in the wild:** "Are you annoyed with me for some reason?"

**Notable sightings:** Marilyn Monroe. Princess Diana. Michael Carrier. Liza Minnelli.

20    With a hair-trigger reaction to any indication that you don't like them or, in fact, disagree with them or didn't do what they asked, the rejection-sensitive walk around with what seems like a perpetual chip on their shoulder. They interpret everything through the lens "You somehow disrespect or dislike me." That's difficult, says Leary, because you have to walk on eggshells around them and make sure that everything you say or do doesn't push the imaginary button where they feel they're being devalued by you.

21    Threats lurk everywhere for these people, who are constantly scanning their environment for signs of being excluded. You didn't call or send an email right away because you were bogged down in deadlines, and then your eldest was sent home sick from school? The resulting drop in self-esteem experienced by the rejection-sensitive begets an overwrought response to slights real and imagined—all of which are presumed intentional.

22    They will dredge up evidence, citing lapses in your actions that defy memory. The irony is that, over time, the irritability, negativity, and self-doubt of the rejection-sensitive do in fact drive others to avoid them. And the rejection-sensitive don't act irrationally only in response to perceived slights; they expect rejection and anticipate it, and react automatically when reflective and strategic behavior would be in their better interests.

23    Rejection or the expectation of it makes them hostile. Their reactive aggression is more likely to manifest in passive rather than overt aggression, although stalking behavior is a form of aggression thought to result from rejection-sensitivity.

24    Unfortunately, the rejection-sensitive are present in increasing numbers. Many observers find that the psychological fragility that underlies rejection-sensitivity is on the rise. Common mood disorders such as depression are typically accompanied by hypersensitivity to rejection, and a whole generation of overpraised children, preoccupied with evaluation, has grown up and brought its overtuned rejection radar into the workplace as well as into personal relationships.

25    Fear of rejection tends to paralyze the afflicted. In the workplace, it can keep people from taking on new tasks or new assignments of any kind; instead they offer a host of irrational explanations for why each new project or new hire is a bad idea. Such a colleague may be unwilling to ask for needed help or direction for fear of rejection—and then fault you for not providing it. Competitive environments bring out the worst in them.

## THE EGOIST

**Telltale signs:** Own interests come first, last, and always. Takes everything personally. Unable to compromise, ever. Insists on being seen as right by everyone
**Where you'll find them:** Reality TV shows. Congress. Art school.
**Call in the wild:** "It's my way or the highway."
**Notable sightings:** Donald Trump. Kanye West. Chris Christie. Paris Hilton.

26    Our culture devalues stoicism and rewards overreacting to every little thing, especially on reality TV.

27    This is a group of people—Leary sees their numbers increasing—whose ego is far too involved in anything that happens. As a result they take everything personally.

**7 WAYS TO DEFUSE A DIFFICULT ENCOUNTER**

- **Minimize time with problem people. Keep interactions as short as possible.**
- **Keep it logical.** Communications should be fact-based with minimal details. Don't try to connect and reason with difficult people. Their response will often only make you more upset.
- **Focus on *them* in conversation.** One way to avoid being the target of demeaning comments, manipulation, or having your words twisted is to say as little as possible. They are a far safer subject of conversation than you are.
- **Give up the dream that they will one day be the person you wish them to be.** There are people in our lives who have moments when they seem to be the parent/partner/spouse/friend/whatever we've always wanted. Yet they end up disappointing or hurting us. Accepting the person as is can be a remarkable relief.
- **Avoid topics that get you into trouble.** Before any interaction with a difficult person, mentally review the topics that invite attack and make an effort to avoid them. If your in-laws always demean your choice of career, change the topic immediately if they ask how your work is going.
- **Don't try to get them to see your point of view.** Don't try to explain yourself or get them to empathize with you. They won't. And you'll just feel worse for trying.
- **Create a distraction. Play with a pet if there is one handy.** Plan the interaction around some kind of recreational activity or entertainment. Or get the other person to do something that absorbs their attention (taking it off you). Just don't use alcohol as your distraction of choice. It will only make you more likely to say or do something that will set you up as a target or make you feel bad later.

What makes them difficult is their fierce demands coupled with their inability to compromise. They frequently "lose it." Mention a problem to them and they immediately assume you are blaming them. "On top of the tangible problem, they add a layer of symbolism that makes everything about them," says Leary. "They live their life according to the symbolic meaning as opposed to solving the problem."

28    Leary argues that both egoic and egocentric individuals view the world through a self-centered lens, but the egoic are especially inclined to respond strongly when their desires are not satisfied. (Egotism, by contrast, refers to an inflated sense of one's positive qualities.)

29    Leary, who has long identified problems of the self, says, "This type hit me when I saw Congress discussing the debt ceiling. There was so much posturing—'I have to show everybody I'm right'—rather than movement toward solving the problem." The egoic person is convinced his ideas are 100 percent right—and must be seen as right. Further, he feels entitled to have things happen his way. "A person who is convinced his perspectives, beliefs, and values are right cannot tolerate any conciliatory

conversations. It's 'my way or no way.'" Politics is not the only home of the egoic. "These people wreck relationships, work, even societies," observes Leary.

30    There are times, he adds, when anyone can be egoic. "Something pushes a button and we get ego-involved and lose perspective." But with the truly egoic, such a response is independent of the stimulus.

31    With his Duke colleagues, Leary is currently investigating individual differences in how egoic and hyperegoic people tend to act. "The more egoic, the more difficult a person becomes."

32    It's thoroughly natural for people to put their own interests first, Leary observes. No animal can survive unless it does. "People have always been egoic about personal well-being," he explains. Today, however, he sees egoism on the rise because many traditional restraints on behavior have been removed.

33    "It used to be that anger was viewed as a character defect. People now fly off the handle at the slightest provocation when others disagree with them. We no longer value the stoicism by which we tried to keep anger in check." Leary thinks reality TV shows of the past decade have helped breed egoism "because they are based on people overreacting to things that have no or minor consequences for them."

## UNDERSTANDING AND ANALYZING THE READING

### A. BUILDING VOCABULARY

### Context

*Using context and a dictionary if necessary, determine the meaning of each word as it is used in the selection.*

_____ 1. innocuous (paragraph 3)
    a. healthy
    b. dangerous
    c. risky
    d. harmless

_____ 2. obliterates (paragraph 5)
    a. blocks
    b. destroys
    c. replaces
    d. disturbs

_____ 3. cynical (paragraph 8)
    a. optimistic
    b. worried
    c. distrustful
    d. sad

_____ 4. placating (paragraph 8)
    a. loving
    b. serving
    c. appeasing
    d. denying

_____ 5. demean (paragraph 12)
    a. embarrass
    b. criticize
    c. correct
    d. shame

_____ 6. succinctly (paragraph 12)
    a. politely
    b. rudely
    c. quickly
    d. concisely

_____ 7. futile (paragraph 18)

    a. useless

    b. helpless

    c. crazy

    d. difficult

_____ 8. stoicism (paragraph 26)

    a. honesty in all things

    b. indifference to pleasure or pain

    c. moderation in food and drink

    d. justice for all

_____ 9. conciliatory (paragraph 29)

    a. agreeable

    b. soothing

    c. opposing

    d. hostile

_____ 10. provocation (paragraph 33)

    a. suggestion

    b. situation

    c. annoyance

    d. difficulty

## Word Parts

> ### A REVIEW OF PREFIXES AND SUFFIXES
>
> **IM-** means *not*.
>
> **INTER-** means *between*.
>
> **-NESS** means *quality* or *state of*.
>
> **-ITY** means *state* or *condition of*.

*Use your knowledge of word parts and the review above to fill in the blanks in the following sentences.*

1. To minimize *interaction* (paragraph 6) with someone is to minimize the action _____ yourself and the other person.

2. An *impossible* (paragraph 6) task is one that is _____ possible to complete.

3. People who lack *agreeableness* (paragraph 8) lack the quality of being _____, and they express themselves with *irritability* (paragraph 8) or the state of being _____.

## B. UNDERSTANDING THE THESIS AND OTHER MAIN IDEAS

*Select the best answer.*

_____ 1. Which of the following best states the thesis or central thought of the reading?

    a. Difficult people are master manipulators.

    b. The key to dealing with difficult people is to avoid interacting with them if at all possible.

    c. Dealing with the different types of difficult people takes understanding and skill.

    d. People who create trouble for others do so for one reason only: they want to build up their feeling of self-worth.

_____ 2. The topic of paragraph 12 is
   a. the hidden danger associated with confronting a bully.
   b. the triggers of bully behavior.
   c. the unacceptable behavior of a bully.
   d. how to confront a bully.

_____ 3. The main idea of paragraph 25 is found in the
   a. first sentence.
   b. second sentence.
   c. fourth sentence.
   d. last sentence.

_____ 4. What is the implied main idea of paragraph 33?
   a. Flying off the handle is a natural outgrowth of egoicism.
   b. Expressing anger publicly has become commonplace and acceptable in our society.
   c. Reality TV is largely responsible for the ever-increasing number of problem people.
   d. In most cases, people generally fly off the handle over issues of great consequence.

## C. IDENTIFYING DETAILS

*Select the best answer.*

_____ 1. According to the author, there are certain qualities that make people hard to handle. The author cites all of the following *except*
   a. meanness.
   b. defensiveness.
   c. a sense of worthlessness.
   d. insecurity.

_____ 2. Which type of difficult person exhibits anxiety?
   a. the hostile
   b. the rejection-sensitive
   c. the neurotic
   d. the egoist

_____ 3. According to the reading, what question would the rejection-sensitive person be most likely to ask?
   a. "Have I done something to make you mad?"
   b. "Why can't we all just get along?"
   c. "Why are you being so sensitive?"
   d. "Why do you reject every idea I suggest?"

## D. RECOGNIZING METHODS OF ORGANIZATION AND TRANSITIONS

*Select the best answer.*

_____ 1. The pattern of organization used in paragraph 13 is
   a. classification.
   b. illustration.
   c. comparison and contrast.
   d. process.

_____ 2. The organizational pattern used in paragraph 33 is
   a. chronological order.
   b. listing.
   c. cause and effect.
   d. comparison and contrast.

_____ 3. The transitional word or phrase that provides a clue to the organizational pattern used in paragraph 10 is
   a. one common manifestation.
   b. if bullies are technically competent.
   c. such people.
   d. they don't just differ.

## E. READING AND THINKING VISUALLY

*Select the best answer.*

_____ 1. The author likely included the photo on page 428 (woman with signs on her face) in order to
   a. stress the importance of being able to pick up on the often-subtle signs that naysayers present.
   b. show the effects the outside world has on the naysayer.
   c. help the reader understand the split personality of the naysayer.
   d. illustrate the difficulty of dealing with a neurotic person and the roadblocks he or she presents.

## F. FIGURING OUT IMPLIED MEANINGS

*Indicate whether each statement is true (T) or false (F).*

_____ 1. The author believes that the best way to deal with a problem person at home is to allow the person to calm down before addressing a problem.

_____ 2. The author believes that problem people are good at shifting the blame.

_____ 3. The author implies that schools share some of the blame for the increasing numbers of rejection-sensitive people.

_____ 4. According to the author, there is an art to handling difficult people.

_____ 5. The author thinks that all members of Congress are egoic people.

_____ 6. The author implies that movie stars and important national figures all fall into one of the four categories of difficult people.

## G. THINKING CRITICALLY: ANALYZING THE AUTHOR'S TECHNIQUE

*Select the best answer.*

_____ 1. The author's primary purpose in "The High Art of Handling Problem People" is to

    a. discuss the mental health concerns of problem people.

    b. educate people about the problems that Hollywood stars present to others who have to deal with them.

    c. help people to understand problem people so that they can better deal with them.

    d. expose difficult people so that others can avoid them.

_____ 2. Overall, the author's tone in this selection can best be described as

    a. sarcastic.

    b. sympathetic.

    c. instructive.

    d. persuasive.

_____ 3. Which of the following is a fact, not an opinion?

    a. "She made me feel that I was the problem." (paragraph 3)

    b. "It's futile to talk naysayers out of their misery." (paragraph 18)

    c. "With his Duke colleagues, Leary is currently investigating individual differences in how egoic and hyperegoic people tend to act." (paragraph 31)

    d. "Leary thinks reality TV shows of the past decade have helped breed egoicism . . ." (paragraph 33)

_____ 4. Which of the following is not a piece of evidence used by the author to support her thesis or central thought?

    a. statistics that explain the growth in number of difficult people

    b. examples of the behavior of each of the four types of difficult people

    c. quotes from psychologists

    d. a description of each of the four types of difficult people

_____ 5. Throughout the reading, the author uses *rhetorical questions*—questions addressed directly to readers. Which of the following is *not* a rhetorical question found in the reading?

    a. Find yourself acting crazy when you are really a nice person?

    b. Do bully bosses see themselves inaccurately?

    c. Feel thrown totally off balance by another person?

    d. Ever wonder how an encounter goes so quickly awry?

_____ 6. Select the sentence that best explains the figurative expression "They'll (neurotic people) find the cloud in any silver lining . . ." (paragraph 17).

    a. Neurotic people walk around with a dark cloud hanging over them.

    b. Neurotic people will always find something negative even in something good.

    c. Even when silver is involved, neurotic people cannot be happy.

    d. Neurotic people often find a silver lining even in difficult situations.

## H. THINKING CRITICALLY: ANALYZING THE AUTHOR'S MESSAGE

*Select the best answer.*

_____ 1. Which of the following is an accurate statement?

    a. The author believes that the risks involved with dealing with a difficult person at home are equal to the risks involved with dealing with a difficult person at work.

    b. The author believes that dealing with a difficult person at home is easier than dealing with a difficult person at work.

    c. The author believes that considerable strategizing is necessary in dealing with difficult people both at home and at work.

    d. The author believes that repairing a relationship at work is more important than repairing a relationship at home.

_____ 2. In paragraph 5, the author states that "we all come into relationships with hot-button issues from our own past." What does she mean?

    a. Old habits die hard. It is difficult to let go of a grudge.

    b. Some people are very good at reading others, and they delight in "pushing their buttons."

    c. We all have certain things that annoy us, and we carry a dislike for these annoyances into our relationships with others.

    d. The qualities that we most dislike in others are the very ones that we see in ourselves.

_____ 3. In paragraph 24, what does the author mean when she writes of a "generation of overpraised children, preoccupied with evaluation . . ."?

   a. Children will not do their best on any task unless they know they are being evaluated.

   b. The emphasis that schools put on evaluation has carried over to the home, and children now expect to be evaluated on their performance at home.

   c. Children have been praised even when they fail.

   d. Because children have been given exceptional praise for completing tasks that really deserve little praise at all, they expect praise for almost everything they do.

_____ 4. "The High Art of Handling Problem People" can be interpreted as

   a. biased.

   b. false information.

   c. name calling.

   d. objective.

_____ 5. The intended audience for this article is

   a. a general audience of all people.

   b. those who work with a difficult boss.

   c. those who are difficult people.

   d. counselors who work to help others deal with difficult people.

# WRITING IN RESPONSE TO THE READING

## I. REVIEWING AND ORGANIZING IDEAS WITH A SUMMARY

*Complete the following summary of paragraphs 15–19 of the reading selection by filling in the missing words or phrases.*

Neurotics worry about everything. They are typically unhappy, anxious, and cannot handle frustration. They tend to be obstructionists because they _____ with other people's ideas and create _____ in others. They are pessimists, who always try to think of what could go _____. Neurotics cannot be talked out of their feelings; it is best to just _____ _____. It is best to keep _____ when dealing with neurotics; do not get involved in their _____. Also, avoid labeling someone as impossible because you will miss their _____.

## J. ANALYZING THE ISSUE AND ARGUMENT

1. What contemporary issue is the author discussing in this reading? Phrase the issue as a question. Is the author arguing the "pro" side of this issue or the "con" side?

2. What is the author's background? Is she qualified to write about the topic? Why or why not?

3. Does the source from which this reading is taken help you determine the credibility of the information presented? Do you find any bias in the selection? Please explain both of your answers.

4. Evaluate the reading on the following criteria:

    a. Is the reading timely?

    b. Has the author provided sufficient evidence to support her main ideas? What other types of evidence might she provide to strengthen her claims?

    c. Does the author offer opposing viewpoints? Overall, how would you summarize the author's viewpoints on the issues discussed in the reading?

    d. What assumptions (either stated or implied) do you find in the reading?

    e. Does the article offer any emotional appeals? If so, identify them and evaluate their fairness.

## K. WRITING PARAGRAPHS AND ESSAYS

*Write paragraph or essay in response to one of the following writing prompts.*

1. Do you agree with the author's assertion that "some types of troublemakers are on the rise"? Why or why not? Write a paragraph or essay expressing your opinion.

2. In many ways, television mirrors our society. Think of a TV character that you "know" well. Determine the type of troublemaker that he or she is, and then write a paragraph or essay explaining how this person fits into one of the four categories of difficult people. Be sure to use specific examples to support your thesis.

3. Who is the most difficult person you know? Write a paragraph or essay analyzing this person's behavior. In your writing, you should focus on the reasons for the person's difficult behavior and use examples to support your reasons.

4. Difficult people tend to be difficult everywhere they go. Sometimes, the most outrageous behaviors we witness are in public places, like the doctor's office, the grocery store, the post office, etc. Think of some outrageous incidents that you have witnessed in public. To what category would you assign each of the difficult people? In a paragraph or essay, describe the incidents and analyze the behavior of the participants. To what category would you assign each of the difficult people?

5. "The High Art of Handling Problem People" presents information that should help you deal with the difficult people in your life. Choose one difficult person from either your public or your private life and write a paragraph or essay in which you explain how you will handle this person the next time a difficult situation arises.

**SELECTION
9**
MySkillsLab

# The Many Ways Virtual Communities Impact Our World Offline

Jessica Lee

WEB
ARTICLE

## SOURCE AND CONTEXT

This reading originally appeared on a blog for Bruce Clay Inc., a company that provides advertising services for businesses and people who want to advertise on the Web. The author, Jessica Lee, formerly Bruce Clay, Inc.'s content and media manager, is an online content marketing consultant; her career is focused on what she calls "the Web marketing space." She holds her bachelor's degree in communications from San Diego State University and Tweets about her experiences on Twitter at @BzzContent.

## A NOTE ON THE READING

What exactly is a "community"? How do communities in the real world differ from those online? Read the selection for some answers to these questions.

## PREVIEWING THE READING

*Using the steps listed on page 4, preview the reading selection. When you have finished, complete the following items.*

1. This reading is about the ways ————————— affect the real world and vice versa.

2. List three topics you expect the author to discuss in the reading.

   a. _____

   b. _____

   c. _____

 **MAKING CONNECTIONS**

*Do you participate in any online communities or virtual reality simulations like Second Life? How are the relationships you form in these online networks similar to your relationships in the real world? How are they different?*

READING TIP

*As you read, keep the following groups of terms in mind:*

- *Virtual, online, avatar,* and *connectivity* all refer to interaction on the Internet.
- *Physical* and *offline* refer to interaction and relationships in the real world.

# The Many Ways Virtual Communities Impact Our World Offline

Jessica Lee

1 Technology has sufficiently crept into every nook and cranny of our lives. From the way we brush our teeth to the way we move about town to the way we interact with people, it's a part of who we are.

**SEO**
search engine optimization; the work involved in trying to make certain listings appear on the first page of an Internet search

2 I recently led a discussion along with Jen Lopez, community manager of **SEO**moz and author Becky Carroll at the Emerging Media Conference in San Francisco. The three of us, along with the audience, talked about how social media and virtual communities impact our lives in ways we could not have imagined prior. It was an exciting and engaging conversation that allowed us to explore social media and virtual worlds outside the realm of marketing.

3 And, since the topic is fresh in my mind, I thought I'd share some of those concepts with you today. Let's dive into some of the research on the virtual world's impact on the physical world, and explore how these virtual communities have impacted our relationships and what we should do with these discoveries.

## The Virtual World's Impact on the Physical World

4 We've reached a time where there's certainly no shortage of people studying the impact that virtual worlds are having on us as individuals and as a society. According to research by professor Jeremy Bailenson of Stanford University, half a billion people spend about 20 hours a week "wearing" avatars.

5 Avatars are the virtual representation of a person in a virtual world, and these virtual worlds include everything from massive multiplayer online games like World of Warcraft and Second Life to Farmville. You could even go so far to say that people wear avatars in their various social communities as well—representations of their physical selves in the virtual world.

6 Now, the term "wearing" is an important nuance, because reports from the same professor show that people tend to essentially act different than their true selves depending on how different their avatars look from them. For example, if a person's avatar is better looking than that person, the person's avatar tends to be more outgoing in the virtual world than this person might be in the physical world.

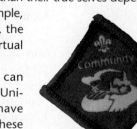

7 To take it a step further, these behaviors online can actually impact a person's behavior offline. Stanford University conducted tests where participants would have avatars created to resemble them. They would hook these participants up to special equipment and have them

move about the room while the avatars mimicked their body movements in the virtual world that was projected before their eyes.

8    What the study revealed was this: positive behavior can be reinforced in the physical world if the participant could visualize and experience a particular scenario in the virtual world. Let me explain:

- **Scenario one:** Participant mimics jogging and sees the avatar of him or herself jogging and losing weight at the rate of one pound for every four knees lifted.
- **Scenario two:** Participant eats junk food and participant experiences the avatar's body expanding.

9    The result? In the weeks following this experiment, participants ate healthier and exercised more in the physical world as a result of being able to visualize the consequences on themselves of that behavior. The same worked for retirement funds, where the participants would begin to save money for the future if they could make a connection with their future selves by seeing a computerized aging process on the avatars that resembled them.

10    This is one very inspirational example of how we could find new ways of using these types of virtual realities to impact personal growth in our everyday lives. The Nintendo Wii and Microsoft Kinect are examples of games created for this very purpose.

11    But, for every positive, there's a potential downside. Spending loads of time in these virtual worlds and being more connected to people than ever before has some consequences.

12    I think perhaps one of the most powerful demonstrations of how accessibility and connectivity in this new era of social networks can affect us negatively is the following story of a young woman (and several others) whose course in life was completely altered in less than three hours following a short video that was innocently posted to YouTube. An ex-boyfriend posted the young woman's address, and people began showing up at her apartment building in London to ask her to sing. The crowd continued growing into a "flash mob" that began dancing outside the building. What started out as a spontaneous party somehow turned into a riot, with 23 people ending up dead (including the young woman, Jacqueline May).

13    So the question here is not *if* virtual worlds and communities impact our lives, but *how* can we capitalize on the positive and seek solutions to some of the most negative impacts? Just like many of us are deeply involved in making our communities a better place, we should take these lessons and try to figure out how can we make these virtual communities better, improve our lives, and minimize the harmful risks.

## How Relationships Are Different Since the Advent of Online Social Communities

14    So we know that how people choose to spend their time in these virtual worlds and online communities can impact lives, but let's take a look at the relationships forged in those online communities—are they any less real? There's not a simple answer for that. These are real people, making real connections, but—and there is a "but" here—the depth of how far they go, I believe, is limited.

15    You can't always make a genuine connection with someone online. In person, you see how a person behaves and interacts with you and others; you can look into each other's eyes, share a smile, an emotion, an experience, camaraderie. Sure, you

can feel connected to someone online, but how connected? And do these online relationships strengthen or weaken our relationships in the physical world?

## How Virtual Communities Impact Offline Relationships

16    Being connected to these virtual worlds and communities impacts our experiences in the present time. Look around you next time you're at an event, at dinner, or just taking a walk. People are buried in their phones, in their virtual worlds. Sure, we've learned how to become more social online, but at what cost? Are we socializing less when we are together as a group? Are we missing out on the world around us?

17    Now, it would be a stretch for me to attribute the decline in social skills with the rising of technology, but I can tell you that when I see all those people sitting across from each other at dinner, with their heads buried in their phone updating their Facebook status or texting, it disappoints me. We lose out on the present when we let the virtual community win.

18    But, with the aid of these virtual communities, we've also been able to have richer experiences. Take this example: You're in Las Vegas for a weekend vacation. You decide to check-in to a location-based service like Facebook Places or Foursquare to let everyone know where you're at. To your surprise, you see that a friend of yours is in the hotel next door because of his check-in. And you and your group and he and his are now able to connect and spend time together that night, which would not have happened without this technology.

19    These kinds of stories happen all the time because of the luxuries our virtual communities afford us. And beyond just letting us find and connect with the people we know in the physical world, they give added layers of relevance to our experiences. We can unlock the best-kept secrets of the places we visit, score relevant deals, and get to know other regulars of our local hangouts—all of which would not be possible without these virtual communities.

20    In the business world, virtual meetings have made it possible for companies to cut down costs on travel and save time; in the field of mental health, many with depression or anxiety disorders have been positively affected by becoming a part of a larger narrative in the online multiplayer games; in the world of news and information, social media has made it possible to transmit information faster and further than ever been before, changing the way journalists do their jobs; and social media has totally changed the way politicians campaign, with Barack Obama leading the charge in this area.

## The Differences Between Virtual Communities and Offline Communities

21    It's really fascinating to see how virtual communities force us to behave in ways we perhaps would not have done before; on the flipside, virtual communities tend to take on characteristics of the way we behave in the physical world as they progress. Take Facebook for example. You post an update, everyone sees it, no matter who is in your friends list—whether it's Aunt Bee or the person you're casually dating. And while Facebook continues to make tweaks to its network's rules for a better experience, you still have to conform to the social norms of that virtual community—even if it's not how you're used to acting in the physical world. This is an example of the virtual community impacting how we would normally behave.

22    But what's interesting is that data show the average number of friends on Facebook is 120—this is just 30 less than Dunbar's number, a theory by British anthropologist Robin Dunbar, which states that there is a cognitive limit to the number of

23    people with whom one can maintain stable social relationships. So, this is an example of our social norms impacting virtual communities.

Then along comes Google+, which understands that we don't communicate the same way with Aunt Bee as we communicate with the person we're casually dating, and allows us to create virtual social circles that mimic how we interact in our daily lives. This is a great example of how the virtual community can develop to comply with our social norms.

24    But no matter how you slice it, participating in virtual communities makes our interactions more public than ever before. Social media researcher Danah Boyd once said that our interactions in the physical world seem more private by default (although there are a lot of factors involved in whether or not that's actually true), but in the online world, that sense of privacy is immediately dissolved and makes anything said potentially very public and immortalized. It's taken time for many people to come to terms with that. So the way we behave in our virtual communities may never fully coincide with the way we behave in our everyday lives.

25    But what does seem to be happening is this: Virtual communities as a whole first impose their rules on us, and as time goes on, we begin to impose our will on them, making the experience more fluid between our relationships in our virtual communities and our relationships in our physical communities.

### So, Where to Next?

26    We know that more and more time is being spent in these virtual worlds. And we know that this time spent has the ability to either negatively impact or positively impact us in our daily lives. Communities are communities, whether online or offline. And virtual worlds are proving to be very real.

27    So, my question is, how can we better spend our time in those communities? How can we use social communities online as an extension of our communities here in the physical world? How will we, as a society, use these virtual worlds to make a difference?

It's all still very new and these worlds are still developing. But, as the creators of these virtual worlds, we have a choice in how we shape them. How will you make a difference?

## UNDERSTANDING AND ANALYZING THE READING

### A. BUILDING VOCABULARY

### Context

*Using context and a dictionary if necessary, determine the meaning of each word as it is used in the selection.*

_____ 1. impact (paragraph 2)
   a. ruin
   b. expand
   c. pretend
   d. affect

_____ 2. realm (paragraph 2)
   a. history
   b. challenge
   c. domain
   d. time

_____ 3. nuance (paragraph 6)
    a. word
    b. concept
    c. subtlety
    d. activity

_____ 4. mimics (paragraph 8)
    a. considers
    b. imitates
    c. refuses
    d. lies

_____ 5. capitalize on (paragraph 13)
    a. make the most of
    b. turn into profit
    c. invest in
    d. become private

_____ 6. genuine (paragraph 15)
    a. online
    b. pleasant
    c. passionate
    d. real

_____ 7. camaraderie (paragraph 15)
    a. job experience
    b. trip outside the country
    c. political belief
    d. friendship among a group

_____ 8. norms (paragraph 21)
    a. characteristics
    b. Internet connections
    c. quirks
    d. accepted behaviors

_____ 9. coincide (paragraph 24)
    a. match
    b. affect
    c. meet expectations
    d. help

## Word Parts

> ### A REVIEW OF PREFIXES, ROOTS, AND SUFFIXES
>
> **IM-** means *not*.
>
> **MORT** means *death*.
>
> **-AL** means *referring to*.
>
> **-TION** means *the act of*.

*Use your knowledge of word parts and the review above to fill in the blanks in the following sentences.*

1. An *inspirational* (paragraph 10) example is one that provides _____ or motivation.

2. An act that is *immortalized* (paragraph 24) is prevented from _____; in other words, it lives on forever.

## B. UNDERSTANDING THE THESIS AND OTHER MAIN IDEAS

*Select the best answer.*

_____ 1. The thesis or central thought of this reading can be found in

   a. paragraph 1.

   b. paragraph 3.

   c. paragraph 4.

   d. paragraph 27.

_____ 2. The topic of paragraphs 7–9 is

   a. the creation of online avatars that better represent physical reality.

   b. the effects of computers on the aging process.

   c. the ways in which online behaviors can affect offline behaviors.

   d. the role played by the Internet in society's attitudes toward exercise and obesity.

_____ 3. The main idea of paragraph 18 is found in the

   a. first sentence.

   b. second sentence.

   c. fourth sentence.

   d. last sentence.

_____ 4. Which of the following is the best statement of the implied main idea of paragraph 24?

   a. By definition, participation in a virtual community causes people to lose their inhibitions.

   b. The existence of a virtual world makes the physical world seem somehow more private in comparison.

   c. It seems likely that people's behaviors in online communities will never fully match their expected behaviors in private (offline) life.

   d. According to Danah Boyd, the mere existence of the Internet prevents people from keeping matters private or secret.

## C. IDENTIFYING DETAILS

*Select the best answer.*

_____ 1. According to anthropologist Robin Dunbar, the maximum number of people with whom one can maintain a stable social relationship is

   a. 30.

   b. 90.

   c. 120.

   d. 150.

_____ 2. The reading mentions all of the following "massive multiplayer online games" *except*

   a. Farmville.

   b. Second Life.

   c. Mafia Wars.

   d. World of Warcraft.

_____ 3. The person who died after posting a short video to YouTube was:

    a. Jacqueline May.

    b. Danah Boyd.

    c. Jeremy Bailenson.

    d. Becky Carroll.

_____ 4. With which of the following statements would the author of this reading *disagree*?

    a. Technology now affects almost every area of our lives.

    b. The Internet has helped companies trim costs and save time.

    c. Virtual reality is almost always preferable to true reality.

    d. The Internet is a two-way street: It imposes its rules on people, and people impose their rules on it.

## D. RECOGNIZING METHODS OF ORGANIZATION AND TRANSITIONS

*Select the best answer.*

_____ 1. The organizational pattern used in paragraph 5 is

    a. process.

    b. spatial order.

    c. cause and effect.

    d. definition.

_____ 2. Which organizational pattern is used in paragraphs 8 and 9?

    a. classification

    b. chronological order

    c. cause and effect

    d. comparison and contrast

_____ 3. Which transitional word or phrase points to the use of cause and effect in paragraph 19?

    a. because

    b. beyond

    c. connect

    d. added layers

## E. READING AND THINKING VISUALLY

*Select the best answer.*

_____ 1. Which of the following is the best description of the connotation of the image shown on page 441?

    a. a traditional, homey sense of community

    b. a call to volunteerism

    c. an edgy, Web-oriented approach to society

    d. a city/urban feeling of communities and subcultures

## F. FIGURING OUT IMPLIED MEANINGS

*Indicate whether each statement is true (T) or false (F).*

_____ 1. The author implies that Google+ permits more customized social circles than Facebook does.

_____ 2. The author believes that applications like Facebook Places and Foursquare are more worthy than personal platforms like MySpace or Twitter.

_____ 3. The author does not approve of someone who takes part in online communities (for example, checking Facebook) while in the physical company of others.

_____ 4. The author shows an overwhelming bias toward physical communities over online communities.

_____ 5. The author believes that it can be difficult or impossible to forge a genuine connection with another person online.

_____ 6. The author praises social media for the speed with which it transmits information.

_____ 7. The author is clearly opposed to games like the Nintendo Wii and Microsoft Kinect.

## G. THINKING CRITICALLY: ANALYZING THE AUTHOR'S TECHNIQUE

*Select the best answer.*

_____ 1. The author's purpose in writing "The Many Ways Virtual Communities Impact Our World Offline" is to
  a. convince skeptics to take part in at least one virtual community in order to experience an important twenty-first-century phenomenon.
  b. explore the connections between the virtual world and the physical world and to raise some questions about how each affects the other.
  c. outline some key research studies that demonstrate how socially isolated and/or handicapped people can use the Internet to join virtual communities.
  d. criticize the people who spend too much time online instead of taking part in community or volunteer activities.

_____ 2. The tone of the reading can best be described as
  a. curious and open-minded.
  b. humorous and witty.
  c. bitter and cutting.
  d. skeptical and questioning.

_____ 3. The author uses all of the following to support her main ideas *except*
  a. research studies.
  b. direct quotations from university professors.
  c. conversations with colleagues.
  d. examples from the virtual world.

_____ 4. Which of the following excerpts from the reading is a fact?

   a. "What the study revealed is this: positive behavior can be rein-
      forced in the physical world if the participant could visualize and
      experience a particular scenario in the virtual world." (paragraph 8)

   b. "I think perhaps one of the most powerful demonstrations of
      how accessibility and connectivity in this new era of social net-
      works can affect us negatively is the following story of a young
      woman." (paragraph 12)

   c. "The depth of how far they go, I believe, is limited." (paragraph 14)

   d. "I can tell you that when I see all those people sitting across from
      each other at dinner, with their heads buried in their phone updating
      their Facebook status or texting, it disappoints me." (paragraph 17)

## H. THINKING CRITICALLY: ANALYZING THE AUTHOR'S MESSAGE

*Select the best answer.*

_____ 1. The best way to describe the author's approach in this reading is

   a. a "pro" approach to the question "Should people join online
      communities?"

   b. a "con" approach to the question "Should people take part in
      virtual societies?"

   c. a balanced approach that looks at the pros and the cons of
      virtual/online life.

   d. a "pro" approach to the question "Should we disconnect from social
      networks and spend more time developing in-person relationships?"

_____ 2. What does the author mean when she says "We lose out on the
      present when we let the virtual community win" (paragraph 17)?

   a. Because the Internet is the technology of the future, time spent
      online is an investment in the future rather than an investment
      in the present.

   b. The Internet is perpetually at war with physical reality, and at
      this point it appears that physical reality is losing.

   c. In-person relationships that allow for face-to-face, person-
      to-person interactions suffer when people choose the virtual
      world over the people who are physically close to them.

   d. Spending a good deal of time online has a number of costs
      involved, and not all of them can be measured in terms of money.

_____ 3. Which of the following questions does the author ask but *not*
      provide at least a partial answer to?

   a. "Let's take a look at the relationships forged in those online
      communities—are they any less real?" (paragraph 14)

   b. "Sure, we've learned how to become more social online, but at
      what cost?" (paragraph 16)

   c. "Are we missing out on the world around us?" (paragraph 16)

   d. "How will you make a difference?" (paragraph 27)

# WRITING IN RESPONSE TO THE READING

## I. REVIEWING AND ORGANIZING IDEAS WITH A MAP

*Complete the following map of the reading selection by filling in the missing words or phrases.*

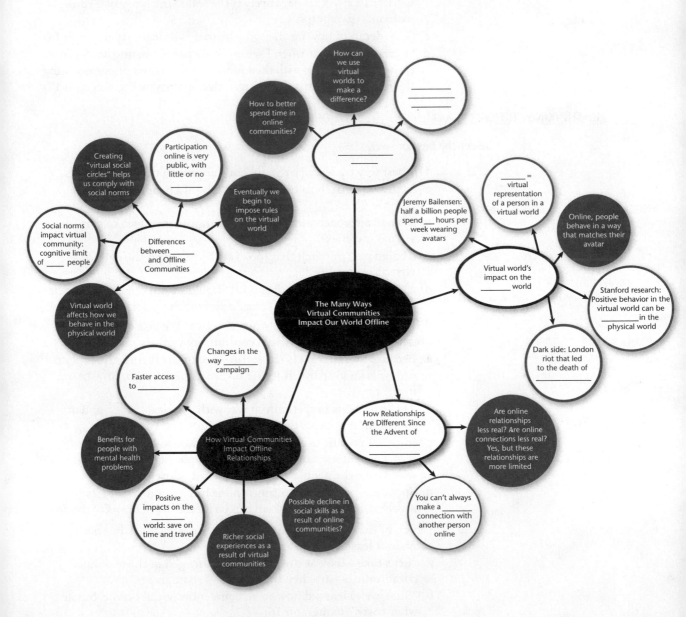

How can we use virtual worlds to make a difference?

_____

How to better spend time in online communities?

Participation online is very public, with little or no _____

Creating "virtual social circles" helps us comply with social norms

Eventually we begin to impose rules on the virtual world

_____

Social norms impact virtual community: cognitive limit of _____ people

Differences between _____ and Offline Communities

Jeremy Bailensen: half a billion people spend ___ hours per week wearing avatars

_____ = virtual representation of a person in a virtual world

Online, people behave in a way that matches their avatar

Virtual world's impact on the _____ world

Virtual world affects how we behave in the physical world

**The Many Ways Virtual Communities Impact Our World Offline**

Stanford research: Positive behavior in the virtual world can be _____ in the physical world

Dark side: London riot that led to the death of _____

Changes in the way _____ campaign

Faster access to _____

How Relationships Are Different Since the Advent of _____

Are online relationships less real? Are online connections less real? Yes, but these relationships are more limited

Benefits for people with mental health problems

How Virtual Communities Impact Offline Relationships

Positive impacts on the _____ world: save on time and travel

Richer social experiences as a result of virtual communities

Possible decline in social skills as a result of online communities?

You can't always make a _____ connection with another person online

## J. ANALYZING THE ISSUE AND ARGUMENT

1. What contemporary issue is the author discussing in this reading? Phrase the issue as a question. What "pro" sides of the argument does she list? Which "con" sides?

2. Write a one- or two-sentence summary of the author's overall argument regarding community, whether online or physical.

3. Is the author qualified to write on the topic? Does her affiliation with/ employment by a particular business affect the conclusions she reaches?

4. List at least three of the author's underlying assumptions.

5. Evaluate the reading on the following criteria:

   a. Is the reading timely?

   b. Has the author provided sufficient evidence to support her argument? What types of evidence has she provided? What other types of evidence might she provide to strengthen her main ideas?

   c. Has the author defined her terms accurately and sufficiently? Does she assume that readers are familiar with the basics of online communities?

   d. Does the author offer multiple viewpoints on any topics? If so, which topics and which viewpoints does she discuss? Does she present them neutrally or fairly, or do you detect any bias?

   e. Does the reading offer any emotional appeals? If so, identify them and evaluate their fairness.

## K. WRITING PARAGRAPHS AND ESSAYS

*Write a paragraph or essay in response to the following writing prompts.*

1. Write a paragraph about one aspect of an online community to which you belong. For example, you might talk about following a certain person on Twitter, why you do so, and what benefits you receive from taking part.

2. In paragraph 21, the author refers to "the social norms" of a virtual community. What are some of Facebook's "norms"—that is, what are the general rules (written or unwritten) for taking part? To what types of activities on Facebook do people respond well or poorly? Write a paragraph explaining your response.

3. Most social communities allow people to upload a photo of themselves or to create an avatar (defined in paragraph 5). Do you think people should try to upload actual images of themselves that reflect who they really are, or do you think it is acceptable to use enhanced images? Write a paragraph answering these questions, taking into account some of the research discussed in the reading.

4. What exactly is search engine optimization (SEO, referred to in paragraph 2)? Conduct some research and write an essay about the SEO business and why so many businesses have become focused on SEO.

5. Many companies have attempted to use social media to sell their products. Write an essay in which you explore the pro or con side of this practice. (Or you can choose to write about both the pros and cons.) Include some examples you have seen of people or companies trying to sell products or services through online communities.

6. Do you have a set of personal guidelines for how and when to take part in online communities? For example, do you set aside an hour a day to go online, do you log on and check your communities constantly, or something in between? Write an essay about the positive and/or negative effects of your participation in virtual communities. What benefits have you experienced? Have you experienced any negative effects of participating in an online community?

## ACTIVITIES: EXPLORING RELATIONSHIPS

*On your own or with a group of classmates, complete two of the following four activities.*

1. Compile a list of ten people with whom you have a relationship. Then define your relationship. For example, is the relationship a close friendship? A casual romantic relationship? A classmate whom you like but probably won't stay in touch with after the term ends?

2. Take a poll among ten friends, acquaintances, co-workers, or classmates. How many of them have used a dating Web site to meet other people? How many met current or ex- boyfriends or girlfriends through social media like Facebook or Twitter? Write an essay or give a presentation to the class about their experiences. Overall, how do they think online dating compares to old-fashioned dating? Do they prefer one or the other, and why?

3. The three readings in this chapter address only a few of the issues surrounding relationships today. Some other often-discussed questions include the following:

   • Are "friends" on Facebook real friends? How do online friendships differ from offline friendships?

   • Are portable technologies, such as cell phones and smartphones, taking the place of personal relationships? What are the benefits and dangers of conducing relationships in the "virtual" world?

- How are gender roles changing in the modern world, and how are these changes affecting relationships? (For example, more than ever before, women are acting as the main breadwinners in a relationship, while men stay home and care for the children.)
- Should romantic relationships be prohibited in the workplace? Why or why not?

Write an essay or prepare a class presentation about any of these topics, or any other relationship issue in which you are interested.

4. The readings in this chapter focused on different aspects of relationships: hooking up, using online dating services, and taking part in online communities. One topic not discussed is friendship. How exactly would you define a friend? Are there different types of friends for different situations? Write an essay about friendship, choosing the best organizational pattern to suit your purpose. For example, you might write a definition essay in which you define friendship, or you might write a classification essay in which you describe different types of friends.

# 15 Science and Ethics: Where Do We Draw the Line?

*How many of the things you use in your daily life were available five or ten years ago?*

If you want to see progress, just look around you. Science lies at the heart of most advances, whether in technology, medicine, communications, or any other field. At the heart of science is the *experimental method*, which offers a specific structure to help scientists formulate theories and test them. In the past, research was a long-term process. Today, ultrafast computers help scientists test their theories much more quickly.

But science itself is controversial. Consider the following questions, which are often debated:

- Is it acceptable for cosmetics companies to experiment on animals to ensure that their products are safe for human beings?
- Are humans interfering with natural processes by genetically engineering seeds that will produce large amounts of grains, fruits, or vegetables?
- What role do a person's religious beliefs play in the type of medical care he or she can receive? For instance, some religions will not allow people to accept a blood transfusion.

These are all complicated questions. Science may be able to provide solutions, but it almost always encounters questions of ethics at the same time. *Ethics* are moral principles. They guide people's behavior by telling them what is right and what is wrong. But ethical codes can come into conflict.

The readings in this chapter look at just a few of the many scientific/ethical issues facing society today. How do people and societies attempt to reconcile science with ethics? For example, should people be permitted to take "brain boosting" drugs? Is it right to grow organs solely for transplanting (which involves killing the donor)? How does the fertility industry work, and does it take advantage of desperate couples and underprivileged young women?

## WHY ARE SCIENCE AND ETHICS SUCH IMPORTANT CONTEMPORARY ISSUES?

A society tries to establish a basic moral code that most people can agree on. For example, in almost all societies, almost everyone agrees that murder is wrong. But on many other issues, there is a wide range of beliefs that are formed by a person's family background, age, religious affiliation, and other factors. Understanding these multiple perspectives helps the larger society agree on what is allowed and what isn't—what is lawful and what is unlawful. All of these decisions are the results of many decades of debate and argument. Ultimately, the question becomes: Where do we draw the line between what is right and what is wrong?

### How Do Science and Ethics Relate to My College Experience?

At one level, the honor code on your campus is an ethical system—it clearly states the rules regarding campus behavior, plagiarism, cheating, individual responsibility, and other aspects of campus life. In individual courses, though, you will learn about the ethics of scientific research and examine whether experiments are ethical or unethical. Psychology and sociology courses are filled with examples of famous studies that would be considered unethical today. Business courses discuss the ethical issues that companies face (you may have heard about the many scandals in the banking and investment industries, which were based on serious ethical lapses). Thinking about ethical issues expands your critical-thinking abilities and gets you considering a wide variety of topics in depth.

---

**TIPS FOR READING ABOUT SCIENCE AND ETHICS**

Here are some tips for reading not only the selections in this chapter but any reading about science and ethics.

- **Carefully distinguish between facts and opinions.** Ethical codes are often based on personal opinions and experiences. As you read, check to see if any opinions are stated as facts.

- **Look for bias in the selection.** Many articles concerning scientific ethics have an agenda. For example, the written results of a new drug's effectiveness may be very different depending on whether the report was written by the drug company or by a neutral researcher.

- **Weigh the process against the results.** In scientific readings, the assumption is sometimes made that "the ends justify the means." In other words, some people argue that (for example) it would be quite acceptable to perform gruesome experiments on monkeys if those experiments led to a cure for cancer. Ask yourself if this assumption underlies what you are reading, and whether you agree with it or not.

**SELECTION
10**
MySkillsLab

# Cosmetic Neurology:
# Tinkering with the Brain

### Carole Wade and Carol Tavris

TEXTBOOK
EXCERPT

## SOURCE AND CONTEXT

This reading is taken from an introductory psychology textbook, *Invitation to Psychology*. The selection is taken from Chapter 9, which is titled "Neurons, Hormones, and the Brain." In the preface to their textbook, the authors write, "These are especially exciting times for psychology teachers and students, because the field is bubbling over with many new ideas, possibilities, and controversies inspired by the biomedical revolution in science and society."

## A NOTE ON THE READING

What ethical issues are involved with the use of "brain boosting" drugs? Read the selection to explore some of the debates.

## PREVIEWING THE READING

*Using the steps listed on page 4, preview the reading selection. When you have finished, complete the following items.*

1. This reading is about _____, or attempts to make improvements to the brain with brain boosting drugs or "neuroenhancers."

2. Indicate whether each statement is true (T) or false (F).

   _____ a. The authors advocate a critical-thinking approach to cosmetic neurology.

   _____ b. Caffeine is a common choice for people who want to stimulate their brains.

   _____ c. Provigil is used to treat attention deficit disorder.

MAKING
CONNECTIONS

*Do you ever drink coffee, tea, cola, or other caffeinated drinks the night before an exam to keep you awake or alert? What are the positive effects of caffeine? The negative effects?*

READING TIP

*The root* neuro, *which means "related to the nerves or nervous system," is key to understanding this reading. All of the following terms are used in the reading:* neuroenhancers, neurology, neuroethics, neurologists, neuroscientists. *What does each term mean?*

# Cosmetic Neurology: Tinkering with the Brain

Carole Wade and Carol Tavris

## Cosmetic Neurology: Tinkering with the Brain

1   Should healthy people be permitted, even encouraged, to take "brain boosters" or "neuroenhancers"—drugs that will sharpen concentration and memory? What about a pill that could erase a traumatic memory? If having cosmetic surgery can change parts of your body that you don't like, what's wrong with allowing cosmetic neurology to tinker with parts of your brain that you don't like?

2   For centuries, people have been seeking ways to stimulate their brains to work more efficiently, with caffeine being an especially popular drug of choice. No one objects to research showing that diet and exercise can improve learning and memory. No one has a problem with the finding that **omega-3s** found in some kinds of fish, may help protect against age-related mental decline (Beydoun et al., 2007; van Gelder et al., 2007). But when it comes to medications that increase alertness or appear to enhance memory and other cognitive functions, it's another kettle of fish oil, so to speak.

3   What questions should critical thinkers ask, and what kind of evidence would be needed, to make wise decisions about using such medications? A new interdisciplinary specialty, *neuroethics,* has been formed to address the many legal, ethical, and scientific questions raised by brain research, including those raised by the development of neuroenhancing drugs (Gazzaniga, 2005).

4   Much of the buzz has focused on Provigil (modafinil), a drug approved for treating **narcolepsy** and other sleep disorders, and Ritalin and Adderall, approved for attention deficit disorders. Many students, pilots, business people, and jet-lagged travelers are taking one or another of these drugs, either obtaining them illegally from friends or the Internet or getting their own prescriptions. Naturally, most of these users claim the drugs help them, and one review of the literature concluded that Provigil does improve memory and may have other cognitive benefits (Minzenberg & Carter, 2008).

5   Yet, as is unfortunately true of just about all medications, there is a down side that rarely makes news, especially with new drugs that promise easy fixes to old human problems and have not yet been tested over many years. Adderall, like all **amphetamines,** can cause nervousness, headaches, sleeplessness, allergic rashes, and loss of appetite, and, as the label says, it has "a high potential for abuse." Provigil, too, is habit-forming. Another memory-enhancing drug being studied targets a

**omega-3s**
fatty acids with potential health benefits (such as controlling heart disease or lowering cholesterol)

**narcolepsy**
a sleep disorder characterized by unexpected and uncontrollable bouts of deep sleep

**amphetamines**
drugs that stimulate the central nervous system

**glutamate receptor**
an area in the brain that is activated by a glutamate, which is a type of amino acid found in the body

6    type of **glutamate receptor** in the brain. The drug apparently improves short-term memory nicely—at the price of detracting from long-term memories (Talbot, 2009).

Even when a drug is benign for most of its users, it may have some surprising and unexpected consequences. For example, cognitive psychologists have found that the better able people are to focus and concentrate on a task—the reason for taking stimulants in the first place—the less *creative* they often are. Creativity, after all, comes from being able to let our minds roam freely, at leisure. One neurologist therefore worries that the routine use of mind-enhancing drugs among students could create "a generation of very focused accountants." (quoted in Talbot, 2009).

7    Some bioethicists and neuroscientists feel that cognitive enhancement is perfectly fine, because it is human nature for people to try to improve themselves and society will benefit when people learn faster and remember more. After all, we use eyeglasses to improve vision and hearing aids to improve hearing; why not use pills to improve our memories and other mental skills? One team of scientists has argued that improving brain function with pills is no more objectionable than eating right or getting a good night's sleep. They wrote, "In a world in which human workspans and life spans are increasing, cognitive enhancement tools . . . will be increasingly useful for improved quality of life and extended work productivity, as well as to stave off normal and pathological age-related cognitive declines." (Greely et al., 2008).

**steroids**
performance-enhancing drugs used (often illegally) by athletes

8    Other scientists and social critics, however, consider cosmetic neurology to be a form of cheating that will give those who can afford the drugs an unfair advantage and increase socioeconomic inequalities. They think the issue is no different from the (prohibited) use of performance-enhancing **steroids** in athletics. Yes, people wear glasses and hearing aids, but glasses and hearing aids do not have side effects or interact negatively with other treatments. Many neuroethicists also worry that ambitious parents will start giving these medications to their children to try to boost the child's academic performance, despite possible hazards for the child's developing brain. One reporter covering the pros and cons of neuroenhancers concluded, "All this may be leading to the kind of society I'm not sure I want to live in: a society where we're even more overworked and driven by technology than we already are, and where we have to take drugs to keep up." (Talbot, 2009).

The prescription drugs Ritalin and Adderall have helped many children concentrate better. But what are the long-term effects of these drugs, and might they have unintended consequences?

9    How about using drugs not to enhance memory but to erase it, especially memories of sorrowful and traumatic events? By altering the biochemistry of the brain in mice or rats, or using a toxin to kill targeted cells,

researchers have been able to wipe out the animals' memories of a learned shock, their ability to recall a learned fear, or their memory of an object previously seen, while leaving other memories intact (Cao et al., 2008; Han et al., 2009; Serrano et al., 2008). If these results eventually apply to human beings, what, again, are the implications?

10      Some victims of sexual or physical abuse, wartime atrocities, or a sudden horrifying disaster might welcome the chance to be rid of their disturbing memories. But could a "delete" button for the brain be used too often, changing the storehouse of memories that make us who we are? Could memory erasure be misused by unscrupulous governments to eliminate dissent, as George Orwell famously predicted it would in his great novel *1984*? Should we wish to erase memories that evoke embarrassment or guilt, emotions that are unpleasant yet enable us to develop and retain a sense of morality and learn from our mistakes? And would we come to regret the **obliteration** of a part of our lives that contributed to creating the person we are now? Such concerns may be the reason that most people, when asked if they would take a pill to eradicate a painful memory, respond loudly and clearly: No, thanks (Berkowitz et al., 2008).

**obliteration**
complete
destruction

11      In contrast, many people might say "Yes, please" to brain-enhancing drugs. But before they do, they will need to think critically—by separating anecdotes from data, real dangers from false alarms, and immediate benefits from long-term risks. What is to be gained from neuroenhancers, and what might be lost?

# UNDERSTANDING AND ANALYZING THE READING

## A. BUILDING VOCABULARY

### Context

*Using context and a dictionary if necessary, determine the meaning of each word as it is used in the selection.*

_____ 1. tinker (paragraph 1)
   a. tamper
   b. break
   c. x-ray
   d. remove

_____ 2. deficit (paragraph 4)
   a. hyperactivity
   b. anger
   c. lack of
   d. pain

_____ 3. detracting (paragraph 5)
   a. enhancing
   b. lessening
   c. creating
   d. avoiding

_____ 4. benign (paragraph 6)
   a. experimental
   b. harmless
   c. effective
   d. addictive

_____ 5. roam (paragraph 6)

    a. wander

    b. deprive

    c. run

    d. hallucinate

_____ 6. stave off (paragraph 7)

    a. add to

    b. have an effect on

    c. hold back

    d. lead to

_____ 7. hazard (paragraph 8)

    a. addiction

    b. stimulus

    c. effect

    d. danger

_____ 8. atrocities (paragraph 10)

    a. shocking cruelties

    b. bombing attacks

    c. terrible wounds

    d. activities of war

_____ 9. unscrupulous (paragraph 10)

    a. sloppy

    b. democratic

    c. immoral

    d. federal

_____ 10. dissent (paragraph 10)

    a. social class

    b. income taxes

    c. interpersonal communication

    d. opposition or disagreement

## Word Parts

> ### A REVIEW OF PREFIXES, ROOTS, AND SUFFIXES
>
> **INTER-** means *between*.
>
> **PATH** or **PATHO** means *suffering, disease,* or *feeling*.
>
> **-LOGY** means *the study of*.

*Use your knowledge of word parts and the review above to fill in the blanks in the following sentences.*

1. Peace studies is an *interdisciplinary* (paragraph 3) course of college study. This means it combines or goes _____ at least two academic disciplines, such as philosophy, sociology, history, and political science.

2. A *pathological* (paragraph 7) study examines the causes of physical or mental _____.

## B. UNDERSTANDING THE THESIS AND OTHER MAIN IDEAS

*Select the best answer.*

_____ 1. Which statement best summarizes the thesis or central thought of "Cosmetic Neurology: Tinkering with the Brain"?

   a. Neuroenhancers show great promise for helping humans achieve their full potential while also helping them forget unpleasant or damaging experiences from their past.

   b. While it is quite common and acceptable for human beings to use eyeglasses, hearing aids, and legal drugs like caffeine to improve their lives or help them concentrate, many ethical questions have been raised by the idea of cosmetic neurology, which allows people to "enhance" their brains through drugs and procedures whose long-term effects are unknown.

   c. Brain researchers point to the importance of both concentration and creativity as key skills for success in school and the work-place, but given the number of people suffering from attention deficit disorder, concentration is somewhat more important than creativity.

   d. Although drugs like Adderall and Provigil have helped many people lead more fulfilling lives, critics charge that the U.S. government has illegally used these two drugs on political prisoners (especially those accused of terrorism or war crimes).

_____ 2. The topic of paragraph 4 is

   a. commonly prescribed drugs.

   b. narcolepsy.

   c. illegal drug use.

   d. Internet pharmacies.

_____ 3. The main ideas of paragraphs 5, 6, 7, and 8 are all found in the _____ of each paragraph.

   a. first sentence

   b. second sentence

   c. third sentence

   d. last sentence

_____ 4. Which of the following is the best statement of the implied main idea in paragraph 10?

   a. Drugs can be tremendously helpful to those who are battling painful memories.

   b. Government dissent can likely be controlled with the help of cosmetic neurology, but more research must be done before such programs are put into place.

   c. Unpleasant experiences can help humans become stronger people with a heightened sense of self.

   d. When asked if they would be willing to take a drug that will eliminate unpleasant memories of the past, most people indicate that they would not.

## C. IDENTIFYING DETAILS

*Select the best answer.*

_____ 1. Which drugs are often prescribed for attention deficit disorder?

   a. Provigil and Modafinil

   b. Celexa and Cymbalta

   c. Adderall and Ritalin

   d. Klonopin and Valium

_____ 2. The relatively new field of study that has been formed to address the scientific, legal, and ethical issues raised by brain research is

   a. neuroethics.

   b. brain pathology.

   c. cognitive psychology.

   d. behavior modification.

_____ 3. The authors make all of the following arguments against cosmetic neurology *except*

   a. Neuroenhancers can give an unfair advantage to the rich people who can afford them.

   b. Interfering with people's memories, even painful ones, can rob them of the experiences that have made them who they are.

   c. Even drugs that have positive effects in the short run may have unexpected consequences in the long run.

   d. Drugs that affect cognitive performance are more likely to increase creativity than they are to increase concentration.

## D. RECOGNIZING METHODS OF ORGANIZATION AND TRANSITIONS

*Select the best answer.*

_____ 1. The overall pattern of organization used in "Cosmetic Neurology: Tinkering with the Brain" is
   a. process.
   b. classification.
   c. listing/enumeration.
   d. chronological order.

_____ 2. One transitional word or phrase that provides a clue to the organizational pattern used in paragraph 5 is
   a. over many years.
   b. can cause.
   c. as the label says.
   d. a type of.

_____ 3. The pattern of organization used in individual paragraphs 6, 7, and 8 is
   a. spatial order.
   b. generalization and example.
   c. summary.
   d. comparison and contrast.

## E. READING AND THINKING VISUALLY

*Select the best answer.*

_____ 1. The author likely included the photo and caption on page 458 to
   a. encourage parents to consider Ritalin as an option for their children who are doing poorly in school.
   b. imply that neuroenhancers affect children much more strongly than they affect adults.
   c. summarize their thesis/central thought with one photo and one accompanying caption.
   d. make readers aware of a commonly prescribed drug and raise questions about its long-term effects.

## F. FIGURING OUT IMPLIED MEANINGS

*Indicate whether each statement is true (T) or false (F).*

_____ 1. The authors do not think that Provigil helps improve memory.

_____ 2. The authors consider caffeine a drug.

_____ 3. Adderall is an amphetamine.

_____ 4. Drugs that have been proven to eliminate rats' unpleasant memories are now being tested on humans.

_____ 5. The novel *1984* by George Orwell is about the ways a government can erase memories as a way of controlling its people.

_____ 6. The authors imply that intense concentration may lead to lower creativity.

_____ 7. Fish oil may help protect people from the mental decline sometimes associated with aging.

## G. THINKING CRITICALLY: ANALYZING THE AUTHOR'S TECHNIQUES

*Select the best answer.*

_____ 1. The authors' purpose in writing "Cosmetic Neurology: Tinkering with the Brain" is to

    a. list and explain all the arguments against using neuroenhancing drugs.

    b. compare and contrast the results of studies on animals with the results of studies on humans.

    c. present both sides of the debate regarding drugs that affect the brain and nervous system.

    d. warn readers about the side effects of drugs commonly prescribed for childhood disorders.

_____ 2. The tone of this selection is best described as

    a. dismissive but warm.

    b. formal and highly academic.

    c. awestruck, impressed, and slightly intimidated.

    d. mostly objective but slightly skeptical.

_____ 3. Throughout the selection, the authors place information in parentheses, including the following: (Gazzaniga, 2005) in paragraph 3, (Minzenberg & Carter, 2008) in paragraph 4, (Talbot, 2009) in paragraph 5. To what does the information in parentheses refer?

    a. personal anecdotes

    b. case studies of people who have used the drugs discussed in the reading

    c. published research studies

    d. names of international drug/pharmaceutical companies

_____ 4. Which statement best describes the approach to facts and opinions in this reading?

    a. The authors provide a series of facts that have been absolutely verified by large amounts of research.

    b. The reading is dominated by the authors' personal opinions on cosmetic neurology.

    c. The authors have examined both sides of a question mostly by providing expert opinions from professional psychologists.

    d. While the authors present the opinions of adults, they are equally concerned with presenting children's opinions regarding the medications they have taken.

## H. THINKING CRITICALLY: ANALYZING THE AUTHOR'S MESSAGE

*Select the best answer.*

_____ 1. The "kettle of fish oil" in paragraph 2 refers to

    a. free radicals.

    b. oxygenated substances.

    c. omega-3s.

    d. vitamins and minerals.

_____ 2. In paragraph 5, the authors state that Adderall has a "high potential for abuse" and that Provigil is "habit-forming." The authors mean that

    a. these two drugs can be addictive.

    b. these two drugs are often sold illegally.

    c. doctors tend to overprescribe these drugs.

    d. everyone who takes these drugs increases their risk of heart failure.

_____ 3. A neurologist in paragraph 6 is quoted as worrying that mind-enhancing drugs might create "a generation of very focused accountants." What is the neurologist implying?

    a. Accountants must be highly organized in order to be successful in their careers.

    b. The accounting profession requires much more concentration than creativity.

    c. Prescription drugs like Ritalin can help accounting students do better on exams.

    d. Many accountants would benefit from taking amphetamines like Adderall.

# WRITING IN RESPONSE TO THE READING

## I. REVIEWING AND ORGANIZING IDEAS WITH A SUMMARY

*Complete the following summary of the reading by filling in the missing words or phrases.*

In "Cosmetic Neurology: Tinkering with the Brain," Carole Wade and _____ explore the question of whether otherwise healthy people should take _____, which they define as drugs that will improve focus or memory or erase an unpleasant memory. _____ is the new field that addresses the many questions that arise as brain-enhancing drugs become available. People have been trying to improve their performance for a long time, often turning to _____, a popular and legal drug. But newer drugs are making their mark on a generation that is showing its willingness to take them. These drugs include _____, _____ and _____.

Most users say that these drugs have _____ effects on them, but there are concerns. First, some of these drugs are _____. Second, long-term use of the drug may have _____ effects.

Some argue that taking the new brain-enhancing drugs is totally acceptable because people naturally want to do whatever they can to _____ their lives. Others who are more skeptical think that these drugs can give well-off people even greater _____, and that some parents might start giving these drugs to their children just to help them _____ their grades in school.

Another controversial area surrounds the possibility of taking a drug to eliminate bad memories or _____. Scientists have created a drug that has this effect on rats, and it is possible that such a drug could help humans forget terrible events such as wartime horrors. But many neuroethicists believe that removing a person's _____ would be like taking away a part of what makes that person _____.

## J. ANALYZING THE ISSUE AND ARGUMENT

1. What contemporary issue is discussed in this reading? Phrase this issue in the form of a question.

2. Prepare a summary of the "pro" and "con" sides of the issue discussed in the reading. Can you think of any other pros or cons to add to this list?

3. Identify at least four rhetorical questions in the reading. A *rhetorical question* is a question that is posed as a starting point for discussion. (Many authors find rhetorical questions an effective method of introducing controversies or information.) For example, the first sentence of the reading is a rhetorical question ("Should healthy people be permitted, even encouraged, to take 'brain boosters' or 'neuroenhancers'—drugs that will sharpen concentration and memory?").

4. What are the authors' backgrounds, and are they qualified to write about the topic? Why or why not? Does the source from which this reading is taken help you determine the credibility of the information presented? Do you find any bias in the selection?

5. Evaluate the reading on the following criteria:

   a. Is the reading timely?

   b. Have the authors provided sufficient evidence to support their main ideas? What other types of evidence might they provide to strengthen their arguments?

   c. Are key terms well defined?

   d. Do the authors offer opposing viewpoints? Overall, how would you summarize the authors' viewpoint on this particular issue?

   e. What assumptions (either stated or implied) do you find in the reading?

   f. Does the article offer any emotional appeals? If so, identify them and evaluate their fairness.

## K. WRITING PARAGRAPHS AND ESSAYS

*Write a paragraph or essay in response to the following prompts.*

1. In "Cosmetic Neurology: Tinkering with the Brain," the authors discuss the use of drugs to help improve concentration. Write a paragraph in which you offer several suggestions to help improve concentration that do not require taking any drugs.

2. If you could swallow a pill that would help eliminate an unpleasant memory, would you take the pill? Why or why not? Write a paragraph in which you explain your answer.

3. Write at least three alternative captions for the photograph on page 458.

4. In this reading, the authors discuss one of the questions that neuroethicists have begun analyzing. Write an essay in which you explore another question that neuroethicists might ask such as "Do people have the right to assisted suicide?"

5. One reporter quoted in the reading states, "All this may be leading to the kind of society I'm not sure I want to live in: a society where we're even more overworked and driven by technology than we already are, and where we have to take drugs to keep up." Write an essay in which you assess this statement. Do you think society is moving in this direction? Why or why not? Provide specific examples to support your thesis and main ideas. If you think we are becoming an overworked, technology-driven society, do you think this is a good thing? What recommendations would you make for slowing society down and returning to a more "human" pace?

**SELECTION
11**
MySkillsLab

# Eggs for Sale

## M. A. Garcia

PERSONAL
ESSAY

### SOURCE AND CONTEXT

The following personal essay was written for a college composition course at Moorpark College in California. To protect her privacy, the author has chosen to use a *pseudonym*, or false name.

### A NOTE ON THE READING

Personal essays cover a wide range of topics, from small and humorous to serious and profound. Read "Eggs for Sale" to learn about one young woman's experiences serving as an egg donor for couples who are unable to have children of their own.

### PREVIEWING THE READING

*Using the steps listed on page 4, preview the reading selection. When you have finished, complete the following items.*

1. This reading is about a woman who sells her _____ and discovers that she has given an infertile couple the best possible gift.

2. The screening process consisted of three phases: a psychological examination, a _____, and a legal consultation.

MAKING
CONNECTIONS

*Do you know any couples who have experienced problems with fertility? What other options are available to people who cannot conceive children of their own?*

### READING TIP

*As you read the essay, trace the narrator's/author's state of mind. How does she feel at the beginning of the process? How does she feel at the end of the process? How did donating her eggs change her outlook on life?*

# Eggs for Sale

M. A. Garcia

1    Two months later, the long awaited day was finally here. The night before I had self administered what fertility doctors call a trigger shot and I was told to shower and not use any products on my hair or skin. This moment was the reason I had been injected with what seemed like hundreds of needles. I was going to be put under and cut open and my eggs were going to be aspirated as though they had a little sign that read, "Fertile Eggs for Sale." I clearly remember the last ten minutes before I underwent the procedure. I lay in a cold operating room, staring at the brightly lit ceiling. I had goose bumps all over my body and I wasn't sure if it was because of how cold I was or simply because reality was in full effect. My emotions started running all over the place. Immediately I felt a sense of satisfaction and knew that I had made the correct decision in donating my eggs to an infertile couple. In about nine months if everything went as planned, there would be a start of a child's life. As the anesthesiologist depressed the syringe into my IV a last thought jumped into my head right before I was knocked out. I was giving this couple something I had never given anyone before: "the gift of life." This day was a turning point in my life because after going through an extensive and thorough screening, a painful stimulating egg production cycle, and the actual egg retrieval procedure, I learned to value life and fertility for everything they are worth. This newfound feeling of giving for a lifetime of happiness was the culmination of my current journey through egg donation.

2    When I first decided to fill out a donor application at Donor Source, I did it in hopes that I would get picked only because of the monetary compensation. After I filled it out, it was processed and approved within a week. I then created an online profile where infertile couples could select a donor based on their particular needs. Only two weeks had gone by when I received a call from Donor Source. They told me a couple in Phoenix, Arizona, was interested in purchasing my eggs and wanted to immediately start the screening process. I hadn't hung the phone up and I was already thinking of things to do with the money I was getting. Everything happened so quickly; I agreed to becoming a donor as easily as I would have agreed to my sister borrowing my shoes.

3    The screening process consisted of a psychological and medical examination and a legal consultation. During my psychological screening I remember thinking what would happen if the psychologist found out that at this point I was only interested in the money and couldn't care less where my eggs went. In fear of rejection I lied and told her I had always considered egg donation. I definitely didn't tell her I already had a list of things I wanted to buy but had never thought about what it actually meant to donate my eggs. Even after I cleared the psychological screening and moved onto medical screening, my mind was still focused on the materialistic aspect of things. The medical screening was quick. I went in, had blood drawn and underwent an **ultrasound probe**. The probe was used to look as my ovaries, uterus, and other pelvic organs. Once the doctors determined I was 100% disease-free and healthy, I received a phone call from the agency's lawyer. During this two-hour conversation he went into detail about my legal rights and my responsibilities. In thinking back, this is one of those moments that made this process seem so real and life-changing

**ultrasound probe**
a medical device that uses sound waves to perform a medical examination

for me. I felt like at this point nothing was going to be as easy as I thought. I couldn't just hand over my eggs to this couple and pretend they were never a part of me. And I couldn't pretend it never happened because I had just agreed to be contacted in case the child had an illness in which either my organs or blood would help him or her live. I also agreed that if after his or her eighteenth birthday the child wanted to know who I was he or she was allowed to contact me. This no longer was something I could brush off. I thought about how I would react if years from now a young man or woman knocked on my door. Would he be thankful? Upset? Or tell me he had a crappy life? This made me ask myself if what I was doing was the right thing for all parties, not just myself. I didn't have an answer, and all I did was hope that the intended parents would give their soon-to-be child a life full of love and happiness.

4    After the consultation with the lawyer, I was constantly asking "What if?" What if the parents are awful? What if the child gets cancer? What if? What if? At this time I was also put on birth control in order to synchronize my menstrual cycle with the intending mother's. At this point I knew what I was doing, but I had not come to terms with reality. Reality slowly started seeping in the day I came home from work and saw a large FedEx box sitting right at my door. I stared at the box for a couple minutes. I knew what was inside because the nurses had previously told me, and the mailing address indicated the package had come from a fertility clinic. What I didn't know was that once I opened it how real everything was going to be and how my life for the next two months was all put into this single box. This box contained a large number of needles, vials, and what looked like a chunky blue pen. I carefully inspected each and found out the chunky pen was actually a Follistim pen and the vials contained Follistim (follicle stimulating hormone). The vials also held Lupron (used to suppress the pituitary gland and prevent premature ovulation) and HCG (used to induce final maturation of the eggs). It was here that I knew there was no turning back.

5    All of these medications were going to be used to activate my ovaries, to get them to create multiple eggs in a single cycle. The first medication I used was the Follistim. For my first application I got everything ready, and I thought I was going to do it quickly and be over with it, but I was wrong. I sat in front of the mirror for an hour and realized injecting myself wasn't going to be easy. I watched several videos on YouTube before I got over my fear and finally just did it. After a couple of days, this procedure became routine, but it didn't stop it from being uncomfortable. Little bruises formed around the injection sites, and my stomach would sting if I went near or on top of a previous site. During this time I also paid multiple visits to a monitoring clinic to make sure the Follistim was working. The clinic reviewed my progress by withdrawing what seemed like quarts and quarts of blood. It got to the point where I couldn't go out in public wearing a short-sleeve shirt because I looked like a heroin addict with bruised arms and needle trails everywhere. The pain and discomfort from the blood work are what made me question if this was worth it. At times I hated it and wanted it all to end, and other times I felt good about what I was doing but I never was 100% sure of what I felt. So I was relived when the doctor told me the next visit was going to be my last in California. On my last visit to the clinic, the doctor verified everything was going as planned and authorized me to fly to Phoenix.

6    The day I flew into Phoenix I went straight to the fertility clinic at which the retrieval would be performed. The nurse told me step by step what was going to happen that week. I didn't take much into consideration because by this time the

Follistim made me feel tired, moody, and hungry. All I wanted was to go to my hotel room and sleep. In Phoenix I was scheduled to get blood work daily. During this time the fertility clinic wanted to make sure it estimated the time correctly to retrieve my eggs at their most fertile state.

7       On the fourth day of going through this routine, I was ordered to take the trigger shot. I had seen the needle before, but I guess I never paid attention to the size because I was in shock when I picked it up. This needle was almost as thick as a toothpick. I found myself feeling the same way I did when I first attempted to inject the Follistim. I did not want to inject myself with this toothpick, so I sat on the hotel bed thinking of 101 ways to avoid it. But there was no avoiding it; this was something I had to do. I didn't come this far along to give up now. This was literally the step before the last, and I felt guilty for even thinking about not doing it. A couple was counting on me, and I couldn't let them down, so I finally summoned enough guts to inject myself. This shot sent a message to my ovaries to begin ovulation, which was needed for the retrieval to be successful.

8       The egg retrieval process took about 25 minutes, if that. The worst pain I felt through this process was when the nurse inserted an IV in my wrist so that the anesthesia could be administered; funny how I had to feel pain in order not to feel pain during surgery. I remember feeling cold, and I started realizing that I was 100% certain that this was all worth it. I was sure of what I was doing, and I couldn't be any happier. It had been weeks and weeks since I had given the monetary compensation thought. I was content and can't remember another time in my life when I felt better about myself. From the eggs they were retrieving, a new life would be born, and that life was going to give an infertile couple a chance that without me they would've never had—to be parents. I thought about how many of us don't value life or even the fact that we are fertile. And before I knew it I was asleep.

9       While I was pain-free and sedated, the doctors performed the ultrasound aspiration. They attached a tube to the ultrasound probe, and using that they guided a suctioning needle to remove mature eggs from each of my ovaries. The actual procedure I do not remember at all. I woke up still sleepy and crampy, and my stomach was beyond bloated. But none of this mattered because I felt like I had experienced a wake-up call. At the beginning of the process, I did not expect to feel this way, and all I cared about was how I was going to be compensated. But throughout the process I came to understand that my eggs aren't just eggs and that from them a living and breathing being would result and that is the best compensation of all. Egg donation has made me appreciate and value everything in life, life itself and fertility more now than I ever have before.

## UNDERSTANDING AND ANALYZING THE READING

### A.  BUILDING VOCABULARY

### Context

*Using context and a dictionary if necessary, determine the meaning of each word as it is used in the selection.*

_____ 1. syringe (paragraph 1)
    a. drug
    b. air bubble
    c. dose
    d. needle

_____ 2. extensive (paragraph 1)
    a. painful
    b. medical
    c. thorough
    d. inexpensive

_____ 3. culmination (paragraph 1)
    a. climax
    b. beginning
    c. middle
    d. temptation

_____ 4. compensation (paragraph 2)
    a. commitment
    b. answer
    c. payment
    d. option

_____ 5. materialistic (paragraph 3)
    a. related to material
    b. related to acquiring things
    c. related to fabric
    d. related to being a mother

_____ 6. seeping (paragraph 4)
    a. hitting
    b. oozing
    c. breaking
    d. cracking

_____ 7. vials (paragraph 4)
    a. small containers
    b. arguments
    c. syringes
    d. writing implements

_____ 8. maturation (paragraph 4)
    a. decomposition
    b. fattening
    c. tightening
    d. development

## Word Parts

### A REVIEW OF PREFIXES AND SUFFIXES

**IN-** means *not*.

**-OR** means *one who*.

*Use your knowledge of word parts and the review above to fill in the blanks in the following sentences.*

1. A woman who is *infertile* (paragraph 1) is _____ fertile. That is, she is unable to conceive a child.

2. A *donor* (paragraph 2) is one who gives or _____.

## B. UNDERSTANDING THE THESIS AND OTHER MAIN IDEAS

*Select the best answer.*

_____ 1. Which of the following statements is the best statement of the thesis or central thought of the author of "Eggs for Sale"?
    a. "Egg donation is only available to women who are in excellent physical and emotional health."

    b. "While I first chose to be an egg donor for the money, I came to see it as the most rewarding experience of my life."

    c. "Those who donate eggs need to prepare themselves for all the emotional and physical hardship that the process will put them through."

    d. "There are many reasons that women cannot conceive a child, and for these women, receiving a donated egg is the best possible way of coping with that situation."

_____ 2. The topic of paragraph 3 is

    a. the reasons for donating eggs to infertile couples.

    b. the unreasonable demands made on the author by Donor Source.

    c. the psychological, medical, and legal screening process for potential egg donors.

    d. the author's serious concerns about the child who might someday contact her.

_____ 3. The main idea of paragraph 9 can be found in the

    a. first sentence.

    b. second sentence.

    c. sixth sentence.

    d. last sentence.

## C. IDENTIFYING DETAILS

*Select the best answer.*

_____ 1. According to the author, approximately how long did the full egg-donation process take, from application through egg donation?

    a. 5 days

    b. 2 weeks

    c. 2 months

    d. 3 months

_____ 2. Which of the following drugs did the author *not* take as preparation for donating her eggs?

    a. Lisinopril

    b. HCG

    c. Follistim

    d. Lupron

_____ 3. The author lives in _____, while the couple to whom she is donating her eggs lives in _____.

    a. New York, Colorado

    b. Florida, Illinois

    c. Michigan, Texas

    d. California, Arizona

## D. RECOGNIZING METHODS OF ORGANIZATION AND TRANSITIONS

*Select the best answer.*

_____ 1. The *overall* primary pattern of organization used in "Eggs for Sale" is
   a. classification.
   b. process.
   c. order of importance.
   d. comparison and contrast.

_____ 2. A minor pattern of organization in the essay contrasts which two elements?
   a. the author's life and the lives of adopted children
   b. the experiences of infertile men and infertile women
   c. the author's feelings before egg donation and after egg donation
   d. the experience of being on drugs and the experience of being drug free

_____ 3. In paragraph 4, which type of punctuation is used to indicate the definition of Follistim?
   a. parentheses
   b. semicolon
   c. comma
   d. colon

_____ 4. Which transitional word or phrase in paragraphs 6–8 provides a clue regarding the reading's overall organizational pattern?
   a. step by step (paragraph 6)
   b. consideration (paragraph 6)
   c. counting on me (paragraph 7)
   d. I remember (paragraph 8)

## E. READING AND THINKING VISUALLY

*Select the best answer.*

_____ 1. This personal essay does not include any visual aids. Suppose the author of a sociology textbook decided to reprint this essay and add a graphic. Which of the following would be the *most* appropriate type of visual aid to include in the textbook?
   a. a diagram summarizing the ovulation process
   b. a diagram showing the steps involved in becoming an egg donor
   c. a photo of the types of syringes used to help a woman prepare for egg donation
   d. a diagram showing the best (least painful) way to inject yourself with a syringe

## F. FIGURING OUT IMPLIED MEANINGS

*Indicate whether each statement is true (T) or false (F).*

_____ 1. The author of "Eggs for Sale" is probably an unwed mother.

_____ 2. After donating her eggs, M. A. Merriweather will be unable to conceive a child of her own.

_____ 3. If the author had not been completely healthy and free of diseases, she would likely have been rejected as an egg donor.

_____ 4. The author sees egg donation as primarily a financial transaction that will help young women support themselves and pay their bills.

_____ 5. Donor Source matches potential eggs donors with infertile couples who wish to purchase eggs.

_____ 6. The author gives almost no thought to the child who will be conceived from one of her eggs.

_____ 7. The author finds the blood work and internal examinations she must undergo to be quite uncomfortable.

## G. THINKING CRITICALLY: ANALYZING THE AUTHOR'S TECHNIQUES

*Select the best answer.*

_____ 1. The author's overall purpose in "Eggs for Sale" is to
   a. lobby the government for better legal oversight of the egg-donation process and the possible problems that can result.
   b. advertise her willingness to serve as a surrogate mother for childless couples.
   c. describe the effects of fertility drugs on a woman's body and mind.
   d. explain how her feelings about egg donation changed after she became an egg donor.

_____ 2. The overall tone of *most* of the selection can best be described as
   a. angry.
   b. uncertain.
   c. ashamed.
   d. weak.

_____ 3. The tone of paragraph 9 is best described as
   a. greedy.
   b. cynical.
   c. proud.
   d. guilty.

_____ 4. To support her thesis, the author uses primarily
   a. her personal experiences.
   b. quotations from experts.
   c. references from medical journals.
   d. statistics about fertility.

## H. THINKING CRITICALLY: ANALYZING THE AUTHOR'S MESSAGE

*Select the best answer.*

_____ 1. What is the "trigger shot" to which the author refers?
   a. the shot of hormones that will synchronize the author's menstrual cycle with that of the woman to whom she is donating her eggs
   b. the final hormone shot before she undergoes a medical procedure to remove the eggs from her body
   c. the genetic-defect screening injection that will identify possible birth defects that might result from her eggs
   d. the moment at which she legally signs over her eggs to Donor Source

_____ 2. Which piece of advice do you think the author would be *most* likely to give young women?
   a. "Don't donate your eggs. The money is not worth the time, the pain, and the hassle."
   b. "Before you donate eggs, make sure you have very carefully investigated the people who will be buying them."
   c. "The decision to donate your eggs may seem easy, but it's actually very emotionally complicated and ultimately very rewarding."
   d. "The best way to get in touch with yourself, and to determine what kind of mother you will be, is to go through the process of egg donation, which really makes you think about your attitude toward children."

_____ 3. In paragraph 8, the author says, "funny how I had to feel pain in order not to feel pain during surgery." By "funny how I had to feel pain," the author is referring to
   a. the IV for anesthesia.
   b. emotional pain.
   c. the Follistim injections.
   d. the clinic's uncaring attitude toward her.

_____ 4. Throughout the emotional journey of making the decision to donate her eggs and then actually donating them, the author feels all of the following *except*

   a. materialistic.

   b. reluctant.

   c. depressed.

   d. appreciative of life.

# WRITING IN RESPONSE TO THE READING

## I. REVIEWING AND ORGANIZING IDEAS WITH A MAP

*Complete the following map of the reading selection by filling in the missing words or phrases.*

> The process of egg donation
>
> Woman considers the idea of donating eggs
>
> Woman fills out an _____ with _____
>
> When approved, woman creates an _____ profile
>
> Screening process begins with _____ medical, and _____ consultations
>
> Donor starts birth control to _____ with intended mother's menstrual cycle
>
> Donor begins _____ to activate her ovaries and create multiple eggs
>
> Donor pays multiple visits to a clinic, where her _____ is repeatedly tested
>
> Woman goes to _____ located near the purchaser of the eggs
>
> Clinic determines the best time to retrieve the donor's eggs
>
> Donor takes the _____ shot, the last step before her eggs are removed
>
> Donor undergoes surgery during which her _____ are removed

## J. ANALYZING THE ISSUE AND ARGUMENT

1. What contemporary issue or issues is the author discussing in this reading? List at least three issues.

2. Write a one-sentence summary of the author's experience and argument.

3. What are the author's qualifications? In other words, what makes her qualified to write on the topic?

4. What stated or implied value system do you find in the selection?

5. Evaluate the reading's argument on the following criteria:

   a. Is the argument timely?

   b. Has the author provided sufficient evidence to support her argument?

   c. Has the author defined her terms sufficiently?

   d. Does the author offer any opposing viewpoints? If not, what might some opposing arguments be?

   e. Does the reading offer any emotional appeals? If so, identify them and evaluate their fairness.

   f. Does the reading contain any possible errors in logic? If so, identify and discuss them.

## K. WRITING PARAGRAPHS AND ESSAYS

*Write a paragraph or essay in response to the following writing prompts.*

1. The title of this essay is provocative. Write an essay in which you examine or dissect the title. Do you think the title reflects the author's state of mind more at the beginning of the process, or more at the end of the process?

2. The author talks about the pain of the injections she had to give herself. Write a paragraph in which you describe the worst physical pain you ever felt. What caused it?

3. As you read "Eggs for Sale," you may have found yourself hoping to see some sort of image to accompany it. Write a paragraph in which you describe the types of images you would like to see with the reading, explaining your reasoning.

4. "Eggs for Sale" might be considered the "pro" side of the question "Should women donate their eggs to infertile couples?" Write an essay in which you explore the "con" side, offering several reasons why donating eggs might not be a good idea.

5. This reading focuses on one avenue that infertile couples can pursue to bring a child into their lives. Write an essay in which you explore several other options they might pursue, including some of the pros and cons of each.

6. Suppose you are part of an infertile couple. How would you feel about purchasing eggs from a donor? Are you comfortable with the idea? Do you have reservations—and if so, what are they? How does your background influence your thinking on this subject? Write an essay in which you explore your position on the subject.

**SELECTION
12**
MySkillsLab

# Xeno-Transplantation:
# The Ultimate Organ Factory

*Trends* E-magazine

WEB
ARTICLE

## SOURCE AND CONTEXT

The following reading was taken from *Trends*, an online magazine designed to help business executives track social changes. According to its Web site, *Trends* is "a solid source, an informed source, that will tell you what trends to expect—and how you can profit from them. It will give you 'inside' information so you'll have a terrific jump on others who don't have access to red-hot trend-developments." Note that this reading does not have a specific author; it is credited to the magazine's editorial staff.

## A NOTE ON THE READING

Are any solutions on the horizon for sick people who need organ transplants? Read "Xeno-Transplantation: The Ultimate Organ Factory" for some of the latest developments—and controversies—in the field.

## PREVIEWING THE READING

*Using the steps listed on page 4, preview the reading selection. When you have finished, complete the following items.*

1. This reading is about _____.

2. What is the key problem regarding the demand for organ transplants?

   _____

   _____.

3. The article lists three forecasts regarding the xeno-transplantation trend:

   a. Overall health-care costs will go _____.

   b. _____ issues will be raised about breeding animals as a source of human organs.

   c. In many countries, the usage of xeno-transplantation will be delayed by

      _____.

**MAKING
CONNECTIONS**

*Do you know anyone who has received an organ transplant? Or do you know anyone who needs a replacement organ, such as a lung or a kidney? What have their experiences been?*

*Because this reading focuses on a medical issue, it uses a good deal of medical vocabulary. Use word parts to determine the meanings of unfamiliar words. For example, an important root in this selection is* xeno, *which means "foreign." When in doubt, use the marginal glossary or consult a dictionary.*

## Xeno-Transplantation: The Ultimate Organ Factory

*Trends* E-magazine

### Xeno-Transplantation: The Ultimate Organ Factory

1    Some of the biggest and most important medical success stories from the second half of the 20th century involve organ transplants. However, the quantity of organs needed still outpaces the quantity supplied by a wide margin and, as the population ages, the gap will get wider still. Just consider these statistics:

- Currently, the United Network for Organ Sharing shows nearly 112,000 U.S. candidates on a waiting list for transplants. But, less than 30,000 will receive transplants this year.
- According to the National Institutes of Health, 3,000 Americans are now waiting for fewer than 2,000 hearts that will become available this year. Moreover, there is no effective market mechanism for the allocation of the limited supply of organs.

2    One approach suggested for addressing this shortage is to increase awareness of, and participation in, organ donor programs. Unfortunately, it is estimated that this would still not provide anywhere near the number of organs needed today or the much larger number needed in the future. Evidence seems to indicate that China is executing prisoners at an accelerated pace in order to meet the organ demands of the Chinese elite, as well affluent foreigners.

3    One more humane avenue that's been talked about for decades is so-called *xeno-transplantation*. This is the transplantation of organs and tissue from one species to another. For humans, the most likely animal donors are pigs, due to their comparable size, their rapid growth, and the physiological similarity of their organs to ours.

4    A major hurdle with any transplantation, but particularly xeno-transplantation, is the rejection of organs as the result of antibodies in the recipient's immune system, which attack the donated tissue. Strides have been made to overcome this problem, but other serious roadblocks remain, including

**anti-coagulation mechanisms**
bodily processes that prevent blood from clotting

**pathogens**
bacteria or viruses that cause disease

**stem cells**
cells that are capable of reproducing infinitely more cells of the same type

**dialysis**
a medical procedure in which a person is hooked up to a machine that purifies the blood because the patient's own kidneys are unable to

**net drop**
overall decrease

5

6

7

8

9

10

11

12

13

14

15

16

incompatibilities between human and pig **anti-coagulation mechanisms**, and the potential presence of **pathogens** that can be deadly to humans, such as those that lead to mad cow disease.

Now, however, a novel new approach has been developed that would eliminate all of these problems. What is this "game-changing" new approach? It's a futuristic idea called "blastocyst complementation."

Put simply, it's a technique in which the organs of one species are grown in a different, yet similar, species by injecting **stem cells** into embryos of the second species. Thanks to the efforts of researchers in Japan, this technique is no longer just theoretical.

Recently, scientists at the Center for Stem Cell Biology and Regenerative Medicine at the University of Tokyo have successfully engineered mice to grow rat organs. The mice had been genetically altered so they could not produce their own pancreases.

When stem cells from rats were injected into the mice embryos, they grew rat pancreases. The Japanese team believes this technique can be used to grow any type of organ in a compatible species. Professor Hiromitsu Nakauchi, director of the center, is confident we'll soon be able to apply this technique to produce *human* organs in other species.

Currently, the center is seeking permission to use human stem cells, but in the meantime, they have been able to generate human blood in pigs by injecting human blood stem cells into pig fetuses.

Understandably, this possible breakthrough is getting a lot of attention. Professor Chris Mason, Chair of Regenerative Medicine at University College London, paints an exciting scenario when he states, "For something like a kidney transplant where it is not urgent, it would be highly attractive to be able to take cells from a patient, grow them in this way, and deliver a personalized kidney."

Similarly, to treat people suffering from diabetes, human stem cells could be injected into a pig to grow a replacement pancreas.

However, as Mason adds. "There is [still] a long way to go before it could result in usable transplants, but it is an exciting vision." Undoubtedly, Mason is right, but for many patients, waiting for this vision to become reality is their only option.

In light of this trend, we offer the following three forecasts for your consideration:

*First, the overall cost of healthcare will be positively impacted when blastocyst complementation becomes commercially available.* Although raising donor animals will not be cheap, and this approach will involve surgical costs comparable to conventional transplants, there will be a greater savings when the costs of long-term care and treatment are reduced. Removing patients from **dialysis** and freeing people from the on-going costs and complications of diabetes and other maladies should yield a **net drop** in overall medical costs.

*Second, ethical issues are certain to be raised about breeding animals simply to be used as a source of human organs.* Animal rights activists will surely go into full swing, even attempting to block research and development through the courts.

Although they have succeeded in discouraging many people from wearing fur, they will face a steeper uphill battle arguing against a program that promises to extend the length and quality of life for ailing humans. One obvious counter-argument is that we already raise animals for life-sustaining food, so it is logical to raise them for life-sustaining and life-enhancing organs.

17    *Third, in many countries, adoption will undoubtedly be delayed by government regulations.* It will start from safety concerns, which are legitimate, since well-established procedures will need to be followed. This oversight will make procedures burdensome and costly, meaning that fewer people will benefit. This promises to open up another lucrative market for medical tourism.

### AUGUST 2011 TREND #4 RESOURCE LIST:

1. *For more information about the transplant waiting list in the U.S., visit the United Network for Organ Sharing website at* http://www.unos.org

2. *To access information regarding heart transplants, visit the National Heart Lung and Blood Institute web site,* http://www.nhlbi.nih.gov/health/dci/Diseases/ht/htbefore.html

3. THE GUARDIAN, August 26, 2009. "Executed Prisoners Are Main Source of Chinese Organ Donations," by Tania Branigan. © Copyright 2009 by Guardian News and Media Limited. All rights reserved. http://www.guardian.co.uk/world/2009/aug/26/china-organ donation prisoners

4. *The Telegraph,* June 19, 2011, "Pigs Could Grow Human Organs in Stem Cell Breakthrough," by Richard Gray. © Copyright 2011 by Telegraph Media Group Limited. All rights reserved. http://www.telegraph.co.uk/science/science-news/8584443/Pigs-could-grow-human-organs-in-stem-cell-breakthrough.html

5. Ibid.

## UNDERSTANDING AND ANALYZING THE READING

### A. BUILDING VOCABULARY

#### Context

*Using context and a dictionary if necessary, determine the meaning of each word as it is used in the selection.*

_____ 1. outpaces (paragraph 1)

a. exceeds

b. prevents

c. replaces

d. transplants

_____ 2. allocation (paragraph 1)

a. purchase

b. distribution

c. theft

d. donation

_____ 3.  affluent (paragraph 2)
   a.  greedy
   b.  Asian
   c.  rich
   d.  sick

_____ 4.  humane (paragraph 3)
   a.  experimental
   b.  theoretical
   c.  cost-effective
   d.  compassionate

_____ 5.  breakthrough (paragraph 10)
   a.  investment
   b.  discovery
   c.  technique
   d.  weapon

_____ 6.  forecasts (paragraph 13)
   a.  predictions
   b.  summaries
   c.  trends
   d.  conclusions

_____ 7.  maladies (paragraph 14)
   a.  infusions
   b.  illnesses
   c.  medications
   d.  operations

_____ 8.  lucrative (paragraph 17)
   a.  international
   b.  expensive
   c.  unethical
   d.  profitable

## Word Parts

> ### A REVIEW OF PREFIXES AND ROOTS
>
> **ANTI-** and **COUNTER-** mean *against*.
>
> **GEN** means *to create*.
>
> **RE-** means *again*.

*Use your knowledge of word parts and the review above to fill in the blanks in the following sentences.*

1. *Antibodies* (paragraph 4) are part of the human immune system. They work by acting _____ bacteria, viruses, and foreign substances in the body.

2. *Regenerative* (paragraph 7) organ medicine seeks to _____ _____ organs.

3. A *counter-argument* (paragraph 16) is an argument made _____, and usually in response to, another argument.

## B. UNDERSTANDING THE THESIS AND OTHER MAIN IDEAS

*Select the best answer.*

_____ 1. Which of the following is the best statement of the selection's thesis or central thought?

    a. Xeno-transplantation, which is being pioneered in Tokyo and London, will likely become the next large source of organ transplants throughout the world.

    b. The current organ donor system means that many people who need organs won't get them, but xeno-transplantation and blastocyst complementation offer possibly bright (but controversial) solutions.

    c. Human stem cells can be injected into other animals to help grow organs that can then be transplanted back into original human donor.

    d. The animals that show the greatest chances for successful blastocyst complementation are rats, mice, and pigs.

_____ 2. The main idea of paragraph 1 is stated in the

    a. first sentence.

    b. second sentence.

    c. first bulleted point.

    d. last sentence.

_____ 3. The topic of paragraph 2 is

    a. Chinese executions.

    b. organ donor programs.

    c. the organ demands of the wealthy.

    d. the number of organs needed today and in the future.

_____ 4. The overall topic of paragraphs 14–17 is

    a. the predicted results of increased interest in blastocyst complementation.

    b. the ethical issues involved in xeno-transplantation.

    c. government regulations of stem cell research.

    d. quality and safety concerns regarding blastocyst complementation.

## C.  IDENTIFYING DETAILS

*Select the best answer.*

_____  1. There is evidence that prisoners are being executed for their organs in
   a.  England.
   b.  Canada.
   c.  India.
   d.  China.

_____  2. Which two animals were used in stem cell experiments at the
      University of Tokyo?
   a.  dogs and wolves
   b.  rats and mice
   c.  fruit flies and mosquitoes
   d.  cats and lions

_____  3. The animal with the closest physiological similarity to humans, and
      therefore the best candidate to donate its organs to humans, is the
   a.  chimpanzee.
   b.  gorilla.
   c.  pig.
   d.  baboon.

_____  4. A key concern with xeno-transplantation is that
   a.  the human immune system will reject the donated organ.
   b.  it is still theoretical, with no research yet conducted.
   c.  the transplants will cause pancreas failure.
   d.  stem cells will not be able to grow key organs like kidneys and lungs.

## D.  RECOGNIZING METHODS OF ORGANIZATION AND TRANSITIONS

*Select the best answer.*

_____  1. The pattern of organization used in paragraph 1 is
   a.  classification.
   b.  generalization and example.
   c.  summary.
   d.  process.

_____  2. The organizational pattern used in paragraph 3 is
   a.  cause and effect.
   b.  comparison and contrast.
   c.  definition.
   d.  chronological order.

_____ 3. The transitional word or phrase used to signal the organizational pattern of paragraph 3 is

    a. this is.

    b. for decades.

    c. the most likely.

    d. due to.

## E. READING AND THINKING VISUALLY

*Select the best answer.*

_____ 1. The author likely chose to include the photo on page 480 in order to

    a. inject some humor into an otherwise serious article.

    b. advocate for experimentation on animals.

    c. imply (with the doctor's face mask) that pigs are unclean animals.

    d. illustrate the role that pigs play in the medicine of modern organ transplants.

_____ 2. Suppose the author wished to include an anatomical illustration of the organ most affected by diabetes. Which organ should be illustrated?

    a. liver

    b. kidneys

    c. pancreas

    d. lungs

## F. FIGURING OUT IMPLIED MEANINGS

*Indicate whether each statement is true (T) or false (F).*

_____ 1. The international community has come together to agree on a specific set of guidelines for organ donations and organ recipients.

_____ 2. The authors imply that kidney transplants may not be as urgent as other organ transplants.

_____ 3. It is likely that widespread blastocyst complementation will become a reality within the next couple of years.

_____ 4. The number of people who need organs currently exceeds the number of available organs.

_____ 5. It is possible for a transplanted organ to infect a human being with a disease.

_____ 6. The surgical costs of transplanting an organ will be much lower when animal donors are used than when human donors are used.

_____ 7. The authors believe that animal-rights activists will find it easier to argue against blastocyst complementation than it was to argue against the wearing of fur.

## G. THINKING CRITICALLY: ANALYZING THE AUTHOR'S TECHNIQUE

*Select the best answer.*

_____ 1. The evidence used to support the main idea of paragraph 1 is composed mainly of
  a. personal experience.
  b. statistical data.
  c. quotations.
  d. research citations.

_____ 2. All of the following are statements of opinion *except*
  a. "Thanks to the efforts of researchers in Japan, this technique is no longer just theoretical." (paragraph 6)
  b. "There is still a long way to go before it could result in usable transplants, but it is an exciting vision." (paragraph 12)
  c. "Animal rights activists will surely go into full swing, even attempting to block research and development through the courts." (paragraph 15)
  d. "Third, in many countries, adoption will undoubtedly be delayed by government regulations." (paragraph 17)

_____ 3. The author's approach to the topics of xeno-transplantation and blastocyst complementation can best be described as
  a. skeptical.
  b. cynical.
  c. uninformed.
  d. optimistic.

## H. THINKING CRITICALLY: ANALYZING THE AUTHOR'S MESSAGE

*Select the best answer.*

_____ 1. The author's purpose in writing this selection is to
  a. convey information about medical advances that may help solve the organ shortage.
  b. warn readers of the religious implications of using animal organs in the human body.
  c. build support for the idea that stem cell research should be banned.
  d. encourage those who need organ donations to explore alternative medical options.

_____ 2. paragraph 1 states, "there is no effective market mechanism for the allocation of the limited supply of organs." What does this mean?

    a. There are more people who need organs than people who are willing to donate them.

    b. Most bodily organs cannot be shipped across international borders.

    c. There is no agreed-upon business system in place to determine who receives the fairly small number of donated organs.

    d. Electronic devices and mechanisms can be used as organ substitutes.

_____ 3. What does the term "medical tourism" mean in paragraph 17?

    a. travel by retired people to other parts of the world

    b. the comparison of different countries' health-care plans

    c. the search for alternative, non-Western forms of medicine on other continents

    d. unhealthy people traveling to other countries to seek health care

_____ 4. Which of the following is *not* a stated or unstated assumption made within the reading?

    a. Stem cell research is very promising.

    b. The number of organs donated will always be lower than the number of organs needed.

    c. While blastocyst complementation is exciting, it should be conducted without experimentation on animals.

    d. Xeno-transplantation offers the opportunity to save human lives and improve human life.

## WRITING IN RESPONSE TO THE READING

### I. REVIEWING AND ORGANIZING IDEAS WITH A PARAPHRASE

*Write a paraphrase of paragraphs 1–5. The first sentence has been written for you.*

One of the greatest medical advances of the period 1950–2000 was human organ transplants.

_____

_____

_____

_____

_____

## J. ANALYZING THE ISSUE AND ARGUMENT

1. What contemporary issue is being discussed in this article? Phrase the issue as a question. Does the article argue the "pro" side or the "con" side of this question?

2. What is the reading's attitude toward animal rights?

3. Evaluate the argument on the following criteria:

   a. Are the terms used in the article carefully defined and explained?

   b. Is ample and relevant evidence provided to support the thesis or central thought? Give examples to support your answer. What other types of evidence could be used to support the selection's main ideas?

   c. Provide a summary of the reading's stated or implied value system.

   d. Identify at least one claim of value in the reading.

   e. Does the author commit any logical fallacies?

   f. Is there any bias in the article? Explain.

   g. Does the reading offer any appeals to the emotions? If so, are these appeals fair or unfair?

## K. WRITING PARAGRAPHS AND ESSAYS

*Write a paragraph or essay in response to the following writing prompts*

1. If you drive, have you checked the "organ donation" box on your driver's license? Why or why not? Write a paragraph explaining your reasons.

2. Suppose it becomes possible for people to buy donated organs. Who do you think would end up with those organs? Write a paragraph explaining what might happen if organs could be sold to the highest bidder.

3. Does the photo on page 480 seem to match the approach to animal rights put forth in the article? Why or why not? Write a paragraph explaining your answer.

4. Do you agree or disagree with the article's approach to animal experimentation in paragraph 16? Write an essay explaining your viewpoint.

5. Write an essay in which you explore the pros and cons of allowing pig organs to be transplanted into the human body.

6. The article ends with three predictions about blastocyst complementation. Write an essay in which you predict what will happen if this technique becomes the norm and doctors are able to grow as many organs as they need. Some questions you might consider include: What will happen to medical costs? Will people live much longer lives? What are the social and monetary costs of having such an elderly population?

## ACTIVITIES: EXPLORING SCIENCE AND ETHICS

*On your own or with a group of classmates, complete two of the following four activities.*

1. Many companies and scientists advertise on the radio for volunteers to take part in experiments, often to test new drugs. Participants receive the drug for free, and they are usually paid for their time and participation. In an essay or as part of a group discussion, come up with a list of rules for conducting this type of experiment ethically. What should the researchers do? What should they *not* do?

2. Selection 10, "Cosmetic Neurology," discusses the possibility of taking drugs to improve your mental performance. In your opinion, how is cosmetic neurology *similar* to cosmetic surgery (in which people alter their physical appearance, usually to look better or feel better about themselves)? In what ways are the two different? Make a list of typical cosmetic surgeries and discuss the controversies surrounding them.

   Here is one example you might discuss, but there are many others: A "lap band" is a type of flexible band placed around the stomach (inside the body) to help obese people lose a lot of weight. The technique is effective but can be dangerous. Is the lap band a good alternative, or is it chosen by people who do not want to diet and exercise?

3. The three readings in this chapter only scratch the surface of the many ethical issues facing scientists today. Other hotly debated questions include the following:

   - When an organ is donated, who should receive it? There are long waiting lists for all organs, and never enough organs available for transplant.
   - Do doctors "play God" when they help infertile couples become pregnant through the use of scientific technologies?
   - Should people eat meat, or should they eat an exclusively vegetarian diet? What ethical issues are involved in raising animals for meat?
   - Is it ethical to prolong the life of someone who is brain-dead? Who gets to make the decisions regarding whether a person should continue living or not?

   Write an essay or prepare a class presentation about any of these topics, or any other ethical issue in which you are interested.

4. In 1961, a Yale researcher named Stanley Milgram conducted what has become a famous experiment regarding obedience to authority. The results of the study are somewhat disturbing, but also disturbing are the ethical issues raised by the way the study was conducted. Conduct research into the "Milgram experiment," outline its results, and explain the ethical issues involved in it.

# 16 Communication and Technology: Life Online and Offline

*Are you wired?*

If you are like most people, you use technology every day, from the technologies that provide electricity to your home, to desktop or laptop computers, to handheld gadgets like smartphones. The strict denotation (dictionary meaning) of *technology* is "the application of scientific knowledge for practical purposes." By its very definition, then, the term applies to a wide variety of products and services that are intended to make life easier.

For most of human history, technological advance occurred slowly, as the result of many years of research and trial and error. But the last decade has seen an explosion in technology as a result of the computer revolution. It is not an exaggeration to say that technology now saturates every aspect of our lives.

The most visible and popular technologies today are those that facilitate communication—between people, between businesses, between groups. And these technologies are creating major changes in society. Consider just a few examples:

- Ten years ago, before everyone had an Internet connection, you had to go to stores to buy what you wanted or needed. Now you can order just about anything over the Internet. As a result, retail stores across the nation are going out of business.

- Before the explosion in popularity of Facebook and smartphones, people stayed in touch with friends by calling them on the telephone or getting together in person. Now people are increasingly communicating in very short sentences through text messages and spending time in front of a computer (often on Facebook) instead of spending "real time" in the company of friends.

All the readings in this chapter focus on communications technology and how it affects people. For example, how do criminals use the Internet and what types of scams should you be aware of? Do wireless communications technologies (such as cell phones) pose threats to human health? Do new types of mass entertainment made possible by satellite and cable technology, such as reality TV, somehow dehumanize those who are entertained by it?

## WHY IS COMMUNICATION TECHNOLOGY SUCH AN IMPORTANT CONTEMPORARY ISSUE?

Some might argue that technology is *the* key factor affecting people and businesses today. Advances in technology, which are aimed at increasing efficiency and productivity, often have the effect of eliminating jobs. What becomes of people who aren't trained on the latest technologies—do they remain unemployed?

And what of the Internet? Are we becoming too reliant on it? What happens when the power goes down or technology stops working? Just as important, does the rise of the Internet mean fundamental changes in the way we conduct our friendships and relationships? Are these changes positive or negative (or both)?

## How Does Technology Tie in to My College Courses?

Almost all of your college courses will require you to use technology. Because most books, journals, newspapers, and magazines are now online, you will likely conduct research on your computer without ever going to the library. Each discipline has its own specialized software packages that are an important part of working in that field. For example, accountants use Microsoft Excel (a spreadsheet program), while social scientists such as sociologists and psychologists use SPSS, which helps them collect and analyze data. Business courses are increasingly focusing on how companies are using social media, such as Twitter and Facebook, to promote their products, and of course you'll compose many of your college papers on a computer (which may have software that will correctly format all your references for you). But beware! Instructors also have access to software that will tell them if you have plagiarized any materials from Internet sources.

**TIPS FOR READING ABOUT COMMUNICATIONS TECHNOLOGY**

Here are some tips for reading not only the selections in this chapter, but any reading about communications technology.

- **Look for the pros and the cons.** Most technology is developed with a specific purpose, and it often helps people greatly improve their efficiency. Many of the current controversies over technology come from the *unexpected* effects of technology use. So, as you read, keep track of the pros as well as the cons of the subject under discussion.

- **Analyze your use of technology.** For example, how has your life changed since you bought a smartphone? Do you feel more connected to friends and family? How is technology helping you in your college studies? For example, as a result of technological advances, many students can now take courses exclusively online. What are the benefits of online courses? What are the drawbacks?

- **Think critically about technologies and their large-scale effects.** Because technology is developing so rapidly, you can witness changes as they happen. Think critically about these changes. Are they good for people? Are they good for society as a whole? How do all these technologies make the world both "smaller" and "larger"? What types of job opportunities are becoming available as a result of the computer revolution, and how will technological change affect the job market and the career you wish to pursue?

# SELECTION 13
## MySkillsLab

# Meet the Attackers

### Catherine LaBerta

**SOURCE AND CONTEXT**

TEXTBOOK SELECTION

The following reading was taken from an introductory computer textbook, *Computers Are Your Future*, 12th edition, by Catherine LaBerta. In the textbook, the material appeared in a chapter titled "Privacy, Crime, and Security." Note that the textbook has gone through many editions (it is now in its twelfth edition). Why do you think computer textbooks need to be revised on a regular basis?

**A NOTE ON THE READING**

How can someone attack your computer from the other side of the world? Who exactly breaks into computer systems, and why? Read "Meet the Attackers" for answers to these questions.

**PREVIEWING THE READING**

*Using the steps listed on page 4, preview the reading selection. When you have finished, complete the following items.*

1. This reading is about _____.

2. The general term for someone who illegally accesses a computer system is _____.

3. List at least five types of "attackers" that the reading will discuss.

   _____

   _____

   _____

**MAKING CONNECTIONS**

*Have you ever been the victim of an online scam, such as eBay fraud or phishing attempts to steal your passwords or identity?*

**READING TIP**

*As you read, think about the crimes discussed by the author. Are some worse than others? Why? What pattern of organization does the author use to organize her ideas?*

# Meet the Attackers

Catherine LaBerta

1    A surprising variety of people can cause computer security problems, ranging from pranksters to hardened criminals. Motives vary too. Some attackers are out for ego gratification and don't intend any harm. Others are out for money or are on a misguided crusade; some are just plain malicious.

## Hackers, Crackers, Cybergangs, and Virus Authors

2    To the general public, a hacker is a criminal who illegally accesses computer systems. Within the computing community, several terms are used to describe various types of hacking. However, it is important to note that accessing someone's computer without authorization is illegal, no matter what the motivation might be. The most celebrated intruders are computer hobbyists and computer experts for whom unauthorized access is something of an irresistible intellectual game. Hackers are computer hobbyists who enjoy pushing computer systems (and themselves) to their limits. They experiment with programs to try to discover capabilities that aren't mentioned in the software manuals. They modify systems to obtain the maximum possible performance. And sometimes they try to track down all of the weaknesses and loopholes in a system's security with the goal of improving security and closing the gaps. When hackers attempt unauthorized access, they rarely damage data or steal assets. Hackers generally subscribe to an unwritten code of conduct, called the hacker ethic, which forbids the destruction of data. Cybergangs are groups of hackers or crackers working together to coordinate attacks, post online graffiti, or engage in other malicious conduct. IP spoofing, one activity usually associated with hackers, is done by sending a message with an **IP address** disguised as an incoming message from a trusted source to a computer. The hacker must first locate and modify the **message packet headers** of a trusted source (called a port) and then manipulate the hacker's own communication so that it appears to come from the trusted port. IP spoofing deceives the message recipient into believing that the sender is a trusted source, and lures that person into responding to a false Web site.

3    Hacking goes beyond public sites. A few years ago, a 23-year-old hacker known as "RaFa" downloaded about 43 MB of data from a top-security **NASA** server, including a 15-slide PowerPoint presentation of a future shuttle design. He then sent the plans to a Computerworld reporter as proof that the NASA system was not secure. Although NASA didn't experience any direct financial loss from RaFa's activities, many companies do lose money because of hacker attacks—as much as $1 million can be lost from a single security incident.

4    However, a lot more is at stake than just money. What if terrorists or foreign agents could hack the U.S. government's computers and read, change, or steal sensitive documents? What if hackers could disrupt the networks that support vital national infrastructures such as finance, energy, and transportation? Recognizing the danger, the federal government, through The United States Computer Emergency Readiness Team (US-CERT), has emergency-response teams ready to fend off attacks on critical systems. Internationally, a group of security specialists is using honeypots—computers baited with fake data and purposely left vulnerable—to study how intruders operate in order to prepare stronger defenses.

**IP address**
the "Internet Protocol" address that identifies the computer from which a Web site originates or the source of an e-mail

**message packet headers**
packet of information included with an e-mail message that identifies the sender and computer of origin

**NASA**
the National Aeronautics and Space Administration, responsible for the U.S. space program

5   Crackers (also called black hats) are hackers who become obsessed (often uncontrollably) with gaining entry to highly secure computer systems. Their intent, however, is to destroy data, steal information, or perform other malicious acts. The frequency and sophistication of their attacks can cause major headaches for system administrators. Many U.S. government sites are constant targets for crackers and hackers, but they are usually able to divert them. However, in June 2007, Chinese crackers were able to breach an unclassified e-mail system in the Department of Defense, affecting more than 1,500 users and shutting down the network for more than a week. An attack on the Epilepsy Foundation's forums caused actual headaches, and much worse, for their viewers. Crackers posted hundreds of pictures and links to flashing animations that caused severe **migraines** and seizures in some visitors.

**migraine**
an extremely
painful type of
headache

6   Like hackers, crackers are often obsessed with their reputations in the hacking and cracking communities. To document their feats, they often leave calling cards, such as a prank message, on the systems they penetrate. Sometimes these traces enable law enforcement personnel to track them down.

7   Keep in mind that anyone who tries to gain unauthorized access to a computer system is probably breaking one or more laws. However, more than a few hackers and crackers have turned pro, offering their services to companies hoping to use hacker expertise to shore up their computer systems' defenses. Those who undertake this type of hacking are called ethical hackers, or white hats.

8   Computer virus authors create viruses and other types of malware to vandalize computer systems. Originally, authors were usually teenage boys interested in pushing the boundaries of antivirus software and seeking to prove their authoring skills over those of their competitors. These days, virus authoring has become big business, and many authors are involved with organized crime. If caught and convicted, virus authors face prison and heavy fines. David L. Smith, the 33-year-old programmer who created the Melissa virus, was sentenced to 20 months in jail and a $5,000 fine in 2002, and in 2004 a 19-year-old female cracker known as Gigabyte faced up to three years in jail and almost $200,000 in fines. More recently, Li Jun, the 25-year-old creator of the Fujacks, or Panda, worm, was sentenced by a Chinese court to four years in prison. Hackers and other cybercriminals can no longer be stereotyped—their members include all ages, both sexes, and many nationalities. With a 26.8 percent increase in infected computers around the world, and based on a total of 327,598,028 hacking attempts in the first quarter of 2010, knowing all you can about the current infections and how to prevent them seems essential.

## ETHICS

Several medical device security researchers recently hacked a combination pacemaker and heart defibrillator, causing it to stop. They accessed the device wirelessly, obtained patient information stored on it, and were able to reprogram it to shock the person on command. They published their exploits and how to fix the device on their Web site. How do you feel about this type of research? What are the advantages? What are the disadvantages? Should this type of information be freely distributed on the Internet?

### Swindlers

9    Swindlers typically perpetuate bogus work-at-home opportunities, illegal pyramid schemes, chain letters, risky business opportunities, bogus franchises, phony goods that won't be delivered, overpriced scholarship searches, and get-rich-quick scams. Today, the distribution media of choice include e-mail, Internet chat rooms, and Web sites. Estimates of the scope of the problem vary, especially because many cases of fraud are never reported. According to the 2008 Internet Crime Report, consumers reported losses of more than $265 million on a variety of Internet scams, that is 25 million more than in 2007—and the figure is growing by leaps and bounds (Figure 16-1).

### Cyberstalkers, Sexual Predators, and Cyberbullying

**cyberstalking** using the Internet or other electronic media to track and intimidate somebody

10    One of the newest and fastest growing of all crimes is **cyberstalking**, or using the Internet, social networking sites, e-mail, or other electronic communications to repeatedly harass or threaten a person. Cyberstalking, like real-world stalking, is a repeated, unwanted, and disruptive break into the life-world of the victim.

11    For example, one San Diego university student terrorized five female classmates for more than a year, sending them hundreds of violent and threatening e-mail messages. In another situation, Kathy Sierra was a well-known technology blogger and author who began receiving offensive comments on her blog, Creating Passionate Users. These comments included disturbingly edited images of Sierra and violent, sexual threats that finally escalated to death threats from several sources. The posts also appeared on other blogs. Because of their seriousness, Sierra cancelled plans to make a presentation at a technology conference, claiming she feared for her life, and she eventually suspended her blog. Although several people were linked to the comments, no one was ever prosecuted.

12    Cyberstalking has one thing in common with traditional stalking: Most perpetrators are men, and most victims are women, particularly women in college. One in every 12 women and one in every 45 men will be stalked, including being watched, phoned, written, or e-mailed in obsessive and frightening ways, during their lifetime.

FIGURE 16-1  COMPLAINTS CONCERNING ONLINE CRIME IN 2008 INCREASED BY 33.1 PERCENT OVER 2007.

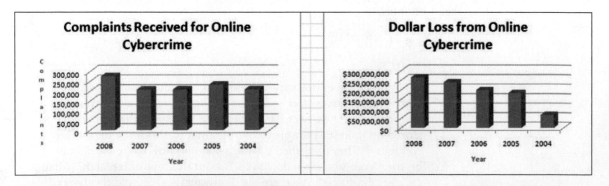

13    Concerns about online sexual predators and the risk they pose to children have continued to grow. The Crimes Against Children Research Center (CCRC) reports:

- Approximately 14 percent of 10- to 17-year-olds received some sort of sexual solicitation over the Internet.

- Just over one-third have been exposed to unwanted visually explicit sexual material.

- Four percent received a sexual solicitation in which they were asked to meet an individual or where the individual called them on the telephone or sent them money or gifts.

- Of the youth who encountered unwanted sexual material, approximately 1 out of 4 told a parent or guardian, and 4 out of 10 told a parent or guardian if the encounter was defined as distressing or made them feel upset or afraid.

**predator**
one who preys
on another

14    Some online **predators** may pose as children, but the CCRC reports that many predators admit that they are older and manipulate their victims by appealing to them in other ways. They attempt to develop friendships and often flatter or seduce their victims. Although there have been situations that have ended in kidnapping or murder, violence has occurred in only 5 percent of reported cases. In the majority of cases, the victims have gone with the predator willingly, expected to have a sexual relationship, and often met with the predator on multiple occasions.

**cyberidentity**
online identity

15    Online predators also look for new victims on cyberdating sites. Most cyberdating sites use profiling to match potential mates. The downside is that it is difficult to check someone's **cyberidentity** against his or her actual identity. Although some sites indicate that they perform background checks, it's doubtful that they are as comprehensive as necessary. Most are based on user-provided information—usually a credit card and birth date. An effective background check would require more detailed information, such as a Social Security number, home address, and possibly fingerprints. And this information would apply only to paying customers—it would not apply to free social networking sites.

16    Cyberbullying involves situations in which one or more individuals harass or threaten another individual less capable of defending himself or herself, using the Internet or other forms of digital technology. Cyberbullying can include sending threatening e-mail or text messages or assuming someone else's online identity for the purpose of humiliating or misrepresenting him or her. In a weird twist of fate, the woman who created a fake My-Space profile of a 16-year-old boy to start an Internet relationship with Megan Meier, the Missouri teen who hanged herself after receiving hurtful messages, is now believed to be the victim of a cyberbullying impersonator herself. The online harassment laws that were passed after Meier's death last year now may be used to help the middle-aged woman, who many believe was responsible for the 13-year-old girl's suicide. This isn't an isolated example. The Cyberbullying Research Center noted that 20 percent of the students they surveyed experienced cyberbullying in their lifetime.

17    Preventing cyberbullying can be just as difficult as preventing real-time bullying. In cases that involve school-age children, both the parents and schools need to make students aware of the dangers and provide them with the knowledge and confidence they need to stand up to bullies.

# UNDERSTANDING AND ANALYZING THE READING

## A. BUILDING VOCABULARY

### Context

*Using context and a dictionary if necessary, determine the meaning of each word as it is used in the selection.*

_____ 1. hardened (paragraph 1)
    a. accused
    b. elderly
    c. pitiless
    d. imprisoned

_____ 2. malicious (paragraph 1)
    a. mean and spiteful
    b. small and tasty
    c. old and experienced
    d. tired and worn-out

_____ 3. loopholes (paragraph 2)
    a. gaps
    b. strengths
    c. alarms
    d. viruses

_____ 4. vital (paragraph 4)
    a. outdated
    b. metallic
    c. technological
    d. essential

_____ 5. critical (paragraph 4)
    a. compromised
    b. essential
    c. modern
    d. expanded

_____ 6. breach (paragraph 5)
    a. destroy
    b. secure
    c. break into
    d. steal

_____ 7. bogus (paragraph 9)
    a. fake
    b. low-paying
    c. corporate
    d. Internet-based

_____ 8. solicitation (paragraph 13)
    a. ticket
    b. text message
    c. request
    d. adolescent

### Word Parts

> **A REVIEW OF PREFIXES AND SUFFIXES**
>
> **ANTI-** means *against*.
>
> **IR-** and **UN-** mean *not*.
>
> **MAL-** means *poorly* or *wrongly*.
>
> **-IBLE** refers to a *state*, *condition*, or *quality*.

*Use your knowledge of word parts and the review above to fill in the blanks in the following sentences.*

1. An *irresistible* (paragraph 2) snack is one that cannot be _____.

2. An *unclassified* (paragraph 5) document is _____ classified or secret.

3. *Malware* (paragraph 8) is a type of _____
software added to your computer without your knowledge.

4. An *antivirus* (paragraph 8) program helps protect your computer
_____ harmful viruses and other cyber-threats.

## B. UNDERSTANDING THE THESIS AND OTHER MAIN IDEAS

*Select the best answer.*

_____ 1. Which of the following best states the thesis or central idea of
"Meet the Attackers"?

a. The best defense against the damaging work of the black hats
is the constant hard work of the white hats who work for the
U.S. Computer Emergency Readiness Team.

b. In a world of cyberbullies and sexual predators, it is more
important than ever that parents take the proper precautions
and monitor their children's online activities.

c. If you receive an offer through the Internet that seems "too
good to be true," it is probably a scam that is trying to cheat
you out of money.

d. The criminals of the cyber-world fall into several categories:
those who hack into others' systems, those who swindle others,
and those who use the Internet to bully or stalk others.

_____ 2. The main idea of paragraph 1 is found in the

a. first sentence.

b. second sentence.

c. third sentence.

d. last sentence.

_____ 3. The topic of paragraphs 5 and 6 is

a. hackers.

b. e-mail systems.

c. crackers.

d. migraines and seizures.

_____ 4. The implied main idea of paragraph 9 can be stated as:

a. Many scams now use the Internet to cheat people.

b. The U.S. government is cracking down on those who gain illegal
access to others' computers.

c. Strong antivirus programs are required to defeat swindlers.

d. Swindlers deserve prison time.

## C. IDENTIFYING DETAILS

*Match each term in Column 1 with the correct definition in Column 2.*

|  | **Column 1: Term** | **Column 2: Definition** |
|---|---|---|
| _____ | 1. hacker | a. Group of hackers working together to coordinate attacks, post online graffiti, or engage in malicious conduct. |
| _____ | 2. honeypot | b. One who becomes obsessed with gaining entry into highly secure systems. Also called a black hat. |
| _____ | 3. white hat | c. A criminal who illegally accesses computer systems or a computer hobbyist who enjoys pushing computer systems to their limits. |
| _____ | 4. swindler | d. Team of government emergency-response workers who stand ready to fend off cyberattacks on important government computer systems. |
| _____ | 5. cybergang | e. One who perpetuates bogus opportunities, phony goods, or fake business propositions. |
| _____ | 6. cracker | f. A professional hacker who has turned pro, offering services to companies to help them improve the security of their computer systems. Also called an ethical hacker. |
| _____ | 7. US-CERT | g. A computer loaded with false data and purposely left vulnerable to hacking. |

## D. RECOGNIZING METHODS OF ORGANIZATION AND TRANSITIONS

*Select the best answer.*

_____ 1. The overall pattern of organization used in "Meet the Attackers" is
a. process.
b. classification.
c. order of importance.
d. cause and effect.

_____ 2. The organizational pattern used in paragraph 10 is
a. chronological order.
b. definition.
c. classification.
d. spatial order.

_____ 3. The transitional word or phrase that signals the listing/enumeration pattern in paragraph 11 is
a. more than a year.
b. another.
c. included.
d. because of their seriousness.

## E. READING AND THINKING VISUALLY

*Select the best answer.*

_____ 1. According to Figure 16-1 on page 496, in which year were the complaints about and the dollar loss from cybercrime highest?

    a. 2005

    b. 2006

    c. 2007

    d. 2008

## F. FIGURING OUT IMPLIED MEANINGS

*Indicate whether each statement is true (T) or false (F).*

_____ 1. All hackers have malicious intentions.

_____ 2. Most victims of online fraud report the crime to the authorities.

_____ 3. Organized crime has become involved in hacking schemes.

_____ 4. The majority of young people who receive unwanted sexual material through their computers tell a parent or guardian about it.

_____ 5. Companies always lose money as a result of hacker attacks.

_____ 6. Today's hackers are primarily young, male, and white.

_____ 7. The victims of cyberstalking are primarily female.

## G. THINKING CRITICALLY: ANALYZING THE AUTHOR'S TECHNIQUE

*Select the best answer.*

_____ 1. The author's primary purpose in "Meet the Attackers" is to

    a. encourage students to purchase antivirus software, such as AdAware, to protect their computers from hackers' activities.

    b. make readers aware of the existing, and growing, issues of cyberstalking and cyberbullying on the Internet.

    c. introduce readers to and define the various types of criminal activities that take place on the Internet.

    d. provide examples of successful hacking attempts that have had large-scale effects on U.S. and international businesses.

_____ 2. The overall tone of this reading can best be described as

    a. impassioned.

    b. informational.

    c. flippant.

    d. detached.

_____ 3. The author uses all of the following to support her thesis *except*
   a. examples.
   b. statistics.
   c. legal cases.
   d. personal experience.

_____ 4. All of the following sentences from the selection are facts *except*
   a. "When hackers attempt unauthorized access, they rarely damage data or steal assets." (paragraph 2)
   b. "Their intent, however, is to destroy data, steal information, or perform other malicious acts." (paragraph 5)
   c. "If caught and convicted, virus authors face prison and heavy fines." (paragraph 8)
   d. "Although some sites indicate that they perform background checks, it's doubtful that they are as comprehensive as necessary." (paragraph 15)

## H.  THINKING CRITICALLY: ANALYZING THE AUTHOR'S MESSAGE

*Select the best answer.*

_____ 1. All of the following phrases as used in the reading have a negative connotation *except*
   a. "ego gratification." (paragraph 1)
   b. "hacker ethic." (paragraph 2)
   c. "obsessed (often uncontrollably) with gaining entry." (paragraph 5)
   d. "overpriced scholarship searches and get-rich-quick scams." (paragraph 9)

_____ 2. According to the reading, all of the following should be part of an effective background check *except*
   a. user ID and password.
   b. home address.
   c. fingerprints.
   d. Social Security number.

_____ 3. According to the reading, which of the following is *not* a threat to people and businesses?
   a. cyberbullies
   b. crackers
   c. ethical hackers
   d. IP spoofers

# WRITING IN RESPONSE TO THE READING

## I. REVIEWING AND ORGANIZING IDEAS WITH A MAP

*Complete the following map of the reading by filling in the missing words or phrases.*

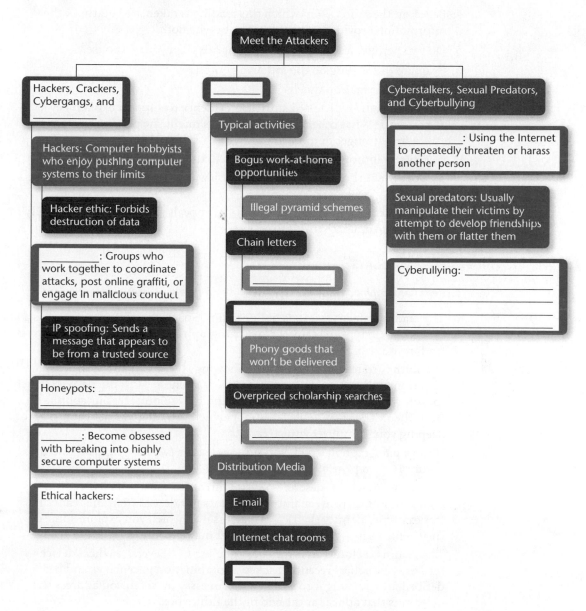

Meet the Attackers

**Hackers, Crackers, Cybergangs, and _____**

- Hackers: Computer hobbyists who enjoy pushing computer systems to their limits
- Hacker ethic: Forbids destruction of data
- _____: Groups who work together to coordinate attacks, post online graffiti, or engage in malicious conduct
- IP spoofing: Sends a message that appears to be from a trusted source
- Honeypots: _____
- _____: Become obsessed with breaking into highly secure computer systems
- Ethical hackers: _____

**_____**

- Typical activities
  - Bogus work-at-home opportunities
  - Illegal pyramid schemes
  - Chain letters
  - _____
  - Phony goods that won't be delivered
  - Overpriced scholarship searches
  - _____
- Distribution Media
  - E-mail
  - Internet chat rooms
  - _____

**Cyberstalkers, Sexual Predators, and Cyberbullying**

- _____: Using the Internet to repeatedly threaten or harass another person
- Sexual predators: Usually manipulate their victims by attempt to develop friendships with them or flatter them
- Cyberullying: _____

## J. ANALYZING THE ISSUE AND ARGUMENT

1. What contemporary issue is the author discussing in this reading? Is the author making an argument, or is she simply presenting information?

2. Describe the author's intended audience.

3. Write a one- or two-sentence summary of the author's thesis or central idea.

4. Based on the source from which this reading is taken, do you think the information provided is reliable? Why or why not?

5. Do you perceive any bias in this reading? Explain your response.

6. Evaluate the reading on the following criteria:

   a. Is the information timely?

   b. Has the author provided sufficient evidence to support explain key concepts? What other types of examples might she provide to make the reading stronger or more engaging?

   c. Has the author defined her terms accurately and sufficiently?

   d. Does the author offer any opposing viewpoints? If not, what might some opposing viewpoints be?

   e. Does the reading make any emotional appeals to readers? If so, identify them and evaluate their fairness.

## K. WRITING PARAGRAPHS AND ESSAYS

*Write a paragraph or essay in response to the following writing prompts.*

1. The reading refers to various online scams. Spam, or unwanted e-mail, is a very common type of scam. Write a paragraph about the kinds of spam you find in your e-mail in-box.

2. The author states in paragraph 8, "Knowing all you can about the current infections and how to prevent them seems essential." Conduct a Web search for information about current viruses and how to protect your computer from them. Then write a paragraph in which you offer at least three tips for keeping your computer virus free.

3. Write a paragraph in which you summarize the two bar graphs found in Figure 16-1 on page 496.

4. "Meet the Attackers" describes several threats to those who use computers regularly. But there are many other threats not described in the reading (for example, identity theft). Write an essay in which you explore some of the problems heavy users of the Internet may encounter.

5. The reading includes an Ethics box that begins, "Several medical device security researchers recently hacked a combination pacemaker and heart defibrillator, causing it to stop." Write an essay in which you address the questions that appear at the end of the Ethics box.

6. Stuxnet is a type of computer virus called a *worm*. Many people believe this virus was created by certain governments to disable Iran's ability to create fuel to power nuclear weapons. Conduct an Internet research on the topic and write an essay describing how Stuxnet works and the effects it has had.

# Technology and Social Media

Shelley D. Lane, Ruth Anna Abigail,
and John Casey Gooch

### SOURCE AND CONTEXT

TEXTBOOK
READING

This reading was taken from *Communication in a Civil Society*, a communications textbook published by Pearson. The author of the book, Dr. Shelley D. Lane is an associate professor of communications and an associate dean at the University of Texas in Dallas. Her co-authors are Dr. Ruth Anna Abigail and Dr. John Casey Gooch. Dr. Abigail has a PhD. in communication arts and sciences, and she serves as a professor and curriculum specialist for the School of Adult and Professional Studies at Azusa Pacific University in Azusa, California. Dr. John Case Gooch, an assistant professor in the School of Arts and Humanities, has a PhD. in technical communication. He is a colleague of Dr. Lane at the University of Texas in Dallas.

### A NOTE ON THE READING

The Internet, social media sites, and mobile technology have revolutionized the way we connect and keep in touch with the people in our lives. Although these tools help us to stay connected and re-connect with people, they also pose a threat to personal relationships. Read "Technology and Social Media" to help you think critically about the impact that technology and social media have on our relationships, our "friends," our language, and our public speaking.

### PREVIEWING THE READING

*Using the steps listed on page 4, preview the reading selection. When you have finished, complete the following items.*

1. This reading selection is about _____.

2. The areas of life that are discussed in this article are _____
   _____.

3. One of the dangers of YouTube videos is _____
   _____.

4. The key question the authors are asking is _____

**MAKING CONNECTIONS**

*Do you have a Facebook account or watch YouTube videos? Do you surf the Web, send text messages, or tweet? How do these social media tools affect your life? If you do not use any of the new media, think about why you do not use them.*

**READING TIP**

*This reading selection is relatively short, but it contains a lot of information about the various technology and social media tools available to users today. As you read, consider the background of the authors and their knowledge of and experiences with communication in a technology rich society. Think critically about the authors' opinions and whether you agree with them or not.*

## Technology and Social Media

1      The dramatic increase in the use of the Internet, social networking sites, and mobile technology has been hailed as a way for us to connect with more people and create stronger relationships. At the same time, new media have been criticized for creating communication that is increasingly shallow and for threatening personal relationships. Both viewpoints underscore the idea that new media are somehow changing our social connections.

### New Media and Relationships

2      Many studies about the effect of new media ask what new media do to us and whether the results are good or bad. Interestingly, research results are mixed and/or inconclusive. For example, while earlier studies of social interaction and the Internet suggested that time online caused people to feel lonely, recent studies dispute that conclusion. One study of high school students found that the amount of time communicating online and the total time spent online failed to correlate with increased loneliness. The same result was also found in a study of university students. In fact, research illustrates that loneliness is diminished when older adults use social networking cites to support existing friendships. While more time browsing and communicating online may be correlated with more loneliness, we can't conclude that time online *causes* loneliness. It may be that increased loneliness may actually encourage people to spend more time online.

**Yahoo! News**
an integrated
Internet news
site

3      Do new media allow us to avoid opinions and beliefs contrary to our own? New media allow us to personalize the news so we can see only the stories that interest us and visit websites that confirm our prejudices. However, research reveals that most Internet users spend their time on large integrated sites, such as **Yahoo! News**, which is accessed by a varied audience. When users leave integrated websites, they actually visit sites read by users who are not like themselves (e.g., people who spend time on liberal sites are also likely to visit **foxnews.com**). Of course, viewing a particular website says nothing about how we evaluate and use the information presented to

**Foxnews.com**
an integrated
Internet news
site

us, but those on the Internet typically seek out opposing information and don't stay within their communities. This research suggests that if there is increased polarization, it is not caused by the Internet.

4    Throughout history, new forms of media have been disruptive and have led to social reflection. "When they are new, technologies affect how we see the world, our communities, our relationships, and ourselves" (Baym, 2008). In truth, new media are tools that people can use to connect with others—tools that cannot be understood without taking into consideration who we are and our personal, social, cultural and historical background. We typically come to new media with our identity and world-views in place, and we replicate and enact them via technology. Therefore, to ask questions regarding how new media affect us and our relationships misses the point. This is because we bring who we are and our relationships to new media. "Digital media aren't saving us or ruining us. They aren't reinventing us. But they are changing the ways we relate to others and ourselves in countless, pervasive ways" (Baym, 2008).

## Facebook and Friendship

5    Among adults 18 and over, Facebook is the social networking site of choice, with almost three-fourths of young adults "friending" others and sharing information on this site. But what is friendship, and what are "friends" in the age of Facebook? Have we simply reduced friendship to a Wall post or a distraction?

6    Communication scholars have found that the meanings of *Internet friends* and *friendship* are personally subjective, ranging from a personal and positive acquain-tance to an indiscriminate addition designed to increase the sheer number of "friends" listed on one's profile. While Facebook makes it easy to collect virtual friends who we don't know well (weak ties), it also has the ability to extend these virtual friendships to those for whom we feel responsible and whom we trust (strong ties).

7    And what about the concern that users spend more time online with Facebook friends than they do face-to-face with friends? A number of studies illustrate that the majority of Facebook friends are those whom users have met and with whom they've interacted in person. According to a PEW Internet and American Life Project report, the primary motivation for social networking site users is to stay in touch with current friends and family members and to reconnect with friends with whom they've lost contact.

8    Overall, people who communicate via social networking sites are less likely to be socially isolated than those who do not, and "people on Facebook typically have a larger number of strong ties; this means that rather than undermine intimacy, Facebook supports it" (Hampton, 2011).

## Social Media and Language

9    Technology has dramatically changed our vocabulary, and the more technology evolves, the more our language changes. Some researchers contend that the Internet allows language users to be inventive and adaptive because it is a new medium that blends speaking and writing. Internet-mediated language is different from writing because of its immediacy and changeability, and it's different from speech because of the absence of nonverbal cues such as pitch, rhythm, and loudness. "Net lingo"

blends aspects of speech and writing and yet is not completely either one. The same is true of communication produced by text messaging. Users regard this form of textual communication as something other than writing. Texting lingo is described as a hybrid of speech and writing in which people try to speak with their fingers. People who are interrupted while text messaging don't say, "Hold on, I'm writing." Instead, they say, "Hold on, I'm talking to someone."

10    YouTube has become a place where you can view everything from "how to" videos to commercial movies. And in many ways, YouTube has changed the way we think about public speaking. Search for "public speaking how to" on YouTube, and you'll get more than 200,000 results. Want tips on how to control your public speaking anxiety? There are more than 2,500 videos. You can view examples of great speeches, and you can view examples of not-so-great speeches. And whereas public speaking once required an audience, it now requires just a video camera and a way to upload the result.

*SocialTimes* 11    An article by Megan O'Neill in ***SocialTimes*** argues that one of the ways YouTube
a comprehensive    has changed the world is that it has given people a place to speak out and spark
online source for    change through what they broadcast. YouTube allows people to raise awareness of
all types of social    issues that might have gone unnoticed in the past.
media

12    It would be difficult to argue that YouTube has not changed the world. But as with other social media, there are few checks and balances on information that is conveyed via YouTube. Given its open social nature, people may upload information that is not true, and there may be no way to refute it adequately.

# UNDERSTANDING AND ANALYZING THE READING

## A. BUILDING VOCABULARY

### Context

*Using context and a dictionary if necessary, determine the meaning of each word as it is used in the selection.*

_____ 1. hailed (paragraph 1)
    a. criticized
    b. acclaimed
    c. extracted
    d. derived

_____ 2. prejudices (paragraph 3)
    a. preferences
    b. preconceptions
    c. dislikes
    d. suspicions

_____ 3. integrated (paragraph 3)
    a. combined
    b. approved
    c. preferred
    d. conservative

_____ 4. polarization (paragraph 3)
    a. division
    b. distrust
    c. personalization
    d. related to the North and South pole

_____ 5. replicate (paragraph 4)
    a. modify
    b. demonstrate
    c. duplicate
    d. divide

_____ 6. pervasive (paragraph 4)
    a. random
    b. fulfilling
    c. widespread
    d. mutually agreed upon

_____ 7. indiscriminate (paragraph 6)
    a. prejudicial
    b. haphazard
    c. calculated
    d. intentional

_____ 8. inventive (paragraph 9)
    a. preventive
    b. creative
    c. secretive
    d. communicative

_____ 9. immediacy (paragraph 9)
    a. informality
    b. timeliness
    c. difference
    d. usage

_____ 10. lingo (paragraph 9)
    a. language
    b. habit
    c. mannerism
    d. message

## Word Parts

> ### A REVIEW OF PREFIXES AND SUFFIXES
>
> **IN-** means *not*
>
> **RE-** means *again*
>
> **-IBLE** refers to *a state, condition,* or *quality*
>
> **-IZE** means *to make or become*

*Use your knowledge of word parts and the review above to fill in the blanks in the following sentences.*

1. *Inconclusive* (paragraph 2) results are those that are _____ conclusive.

2. News that is *personalized* (paragraph 3) is news that is _____ personal.

3. Digital media aren't *reinventing* (paragraph 4) us or inventing us _____; they are changing the way we relate to others.

4. If we are *responsible* (paragraph 6), we possess the _____ of responsibility.

## B. UNDERSTANDING THE THESIS AND OTHER MAIN IDEAS

*Select the best answer.*

_____ 1. Which of the following best states the thesis or central thought of the reading?

a. Digital media has changed the nature of our social connections.

b. The decline in civility is due, in part, to the rapid growth of new media.

c. It has been proven conclusively that social media sites have contributed to the increasing isolation and loneliness of people in society.

d. Technology has impacted social relationships negatively.

_____ 2. The topic of paragraph 10 is

a. the types of videos on YouTube.

b. how to control your public speaking anxiety.

c. how YouTube has changed the way we think about public speaking.

d. the overall popularity of YouTube.

_____ 3. The main idea of paragraph 9 is found in the

a. first sentence.

b. second sentence.

c. fourth sentence.

d. last sentence.

_____ 4. What is the implied main idea of paragraph 12?

a. The Internet, by definition, lends itself to lies and the misrepresentation of reality.

b. As various court cases have proved, YouTube can be dangerous social media tool.

c. People may view and enjoy YouTube videos, but they must be aware that the validity of the information presented has not been confirmed.

d. The producers of YouTube videos should band together to create a more honest atmosphere for sharing information.

## C. IDENTIFYING DETAILS

*Select the best answer.*

_____ 1. According to the authors, most Internet users spend their time on

a. personal Web sites.

b. online shopping sites.

c. integrated sites.

d. news sites.

_____ 2. The selection discusses of all of the following social media tools *except*

    a. Facebook.

    b. Google.

    c. texting.

    d. YouTube.

_____ 3. According to the reading, the primary motivation for social networking site users is all of the following *except*

    a. to stay in touch with current friends.

    b. to stay in touch with family members.

    c. to share pictures with friends and family who do not live nearby.

    d. to reconnect with friends with whom they have lost contact.

## D. RECOGNIZING METHODS OF ORGANIZATION AND TRANSITIONS

*Select the best answer.*

_____ 1. The pattern of organization used in paragraph 2 is

    a. classification.

    b. illustration.

    c. comparison/contrast.

    d. process.

_____ 2. The organizational pattern used in paragraphs 3 is

    a. chronological order.

    b. listing.

    c. cause and effect.

    d. spatial order.

_____ 3. The transitional word or phrase that provides a clue to the organizational pattern used in paragraph 2 is

    a. for example.

    b. in fact.

    c. the same result.

    d. while more time.

## E. READING AND THINKING VISUALLY

*Select the best answer.*

_____ 1. If the authors were to decide to revise the selection and add a visual to support the thesis, what type of visual would be best to include?

    a. a photo of a television and a computer

    b. a photo of a lonely and isolated person

    c. a shot of a Facebook page

    d. a photo of a cell phone

## F. FIGURING OUT IMPLIED MEANINGS

*Indicate whether each statement is true (T) or false (F).*

_____ 1. The authors believe that Facebook can have a positive impact on social relationships .

_____ 2. The authors do not believe that new forms of media allow people to keep their own identities intact.

_____ 3. The authors believe that it is okay for users of texting to use a language different from what they speak or write.

_____ 4. According to the authors, the anxiety associated with public speaking has been diminished by the use of all social media tools.

_____ 5. The authors think that people need to be careful about posting, tweeting, or videoing personally incriminating information.

_____ 6. The authors imply that the change in the way we relate to others is not necessarily bad.

## G. THINKING CRITICALLY: ANALYZING THE AUTHOR'S TECHNIQUE

*Select the best answer.*

_____ 1. The authors' primary purpose in "Technology and Social Media" is to
   a. convince the reader of the dangers of digital media.
   b. examine how technology and social media have changed the way people relate to each other.
   c. offer a close analysis of the effects of social media on the public.
   d. describe the negative experiences of those who have lost their identity and become withdrawn and lonely as a result of time spent using digital media.

_____ 2. Overall, the authors' tone in this selection can best be described as
   a. skeptical and bitter.
   b. amused and slightly surprised.
   c. objective and informative.
   d. offhand and irreverent.

_____ 3. Which of the following is not a piece of evidence used by the authors to support their thesis or central thought?
   a. a set of statistics showing the makeup of Facebook "friends"
   b. a quotation from Yahoo! News
   c. evidence from research conducted on technology and social media
   d. a short synopsis of an article on YouTube

_____ 4. Throughout the reading, the authors use *rhetorical questions*—that is, questions addressed directly to readers. Rhetorical questions are used as starting-off points for a discussion or explanation. Which of the following is *not* a rhetorical question found in the reading?

a. Do new media allow us to avoid opinions and beliefs contrary to our own?

b. Want tips on how to control your public speaking anxiety?

c. Have we simply reduced friendship to a Wall post or a distraction?

d. What do you think accounts for the popularity of Facebook and other social networking sites?

## H. THINKING CRITICALLY: ANALYZING THE AUTHOR'S MESSAGE

*Select the best answer.*

_____ 1. Which of the following would not be an example of an indiscriminate addition to a Facebook friends' list?

a. a friend of a friend

b. a stranger who sends you a friend request

c. a relative who has been estranged from the family for a long time

d. some people in one of your classes who you only know by name

_____ 2. In paragraph 12, the authors write that "there are few checks and balances on information that is conveyed via YouTube." What do they mean?

a. YouTube offers its services free of charge to all users.

b. There is little in place to make sure that people post appropriate and true information online.

c. YouTube does not do a good job of balancing the types of videos they allow to be published.

d. The appropriate videos on YouTube far outweigh the inappropriate ones.

_____ 3. In paragraph 6, the authors state that "the meanings of Internet friends and friendship are personally subjective." Which of the following statement best describes the meaning of this statement?

a. Most of the information shared with friends on the Internet is of a personal nature.

b. The subject of most Internet interactions with friends is about family and friends.

c. Many Internet users subject themselves to online relationships that they later regret.

d. The terms *friends* and *friendship* mean different things to different people in an online environment.

_____ 4. In paragraph 3, what do the authors mean by "integrated sites"?

    a. Internet sites that appeal to a specific type of audience

    b. large Internet sites that are composed of many smaller sites

    c. Internet sites that attract liberal users

    d. Internet sites that feature controversial issues

# WRITING IN RESPONSE TO THE READING

## I. REVIEWING AND ORGANIZING IDEAS WITH A PARAPHRASE

*Write a paraphrase of the subheading "Facebook and Friendship," paragraphs 5–8 of the reading. The first two sentences are provided to get you started.*

A majority of young people use Facebook as their social media outlet. The popularity of this site brings up the question of what friends and friendship really are on Facebook.

_____

_____

_____

_____

## J. ANALYZING THE ISSUE AND ARGUMENT

1. What contemporary issue are the authors discussing in this reading? Phrase the issue as a question. Are the authors arguing the "pro" side of this issue or the "con" side?

2. Write a one- or two-sentence summary of the authors' argument.

3. Are the authors qualified to write on the topic? Why or why not? Is the source from which this reading is taken (see "Source and Context" before the reading) reliable? Why or why not?

4. Point to specific sentences and/or paragraphs in which the authors state their value system.

5. Evaluate the reading's argument on the following criteria:

  a. Is the argument timely?

  b. Have the authors provided sufficient evidence to support their argument? What other types of evidence might be provided to strengthen the argument?

  c. Have the authors defined their terms accurately and sufficiently?

  d. Are the examples provided in the reading representative of reality social media? Why or why not?

  e. Are the authors biased? If so, how?

  f. Do the authors offer any opposing viewpoints? If not, what might some opposing arguments be?

  g. Does the reading offer any emotional appeals? If so, identify them and evaluate their fairness.

  h. Do the authors state or imply any claims of policy?

## K. WRITING PARAGRAPHS AND ESSAYS

*Write a paragraph or essay in response to the following writing prompts.*

1. Write a paragraph about how technology and social media have impacted your life.

2. Do you agree with the authors' assertion that the dramatic increase in the use of the Internet, social networking sites, and mobile technology has been hailed as a way for people to create stronger relationships? Why or why not? Write a paragraph expressing your opinion.

3. If you had to choose between using Facebook, Twitter, or texting, which one would it be and why would you choose it? Write a paragraph explaining your choice.

4. In the reading, the authors ask the important question, "What is friendship, and what are 'friends' in the age of Facebook?" Write an essay in which you compare and contrast the two types of friendship.

5. The authors assert that "YouTube has changed the way we think about public speaking." Write an essay in which you discuss both the challenges and the advantages of using YouTube as a substitute for speaking in an organized public space

6. According to the authors, "Technology has dramatically changed our vocabulary, and the more technology evolves, the more our language changes." Write an essay in which you discuss the effects that technology has had on our language.

SELECTION
15
MySkillsLab

# Blogs and Democratization

## John Vivian

**SOURCE AND CONTEXT**

TEXTBOOK
EXCERPT

John Vivian is the author of a textbook titled *The Media of Mass Communication*. The selection that follows is an excerpt from a chapter in Vivian's book.

**A NOTE ON THE READING**

Read the selection to understand how blogs are providing mass audiences with easy access to unedited and often controversial information.

**PREVIEWING THE READING**

*Using the steps listed on page 4, preview the reading selection. When you have finished, answer the following questions.*

1. What word does the author use to indicate the promise that blogs hold for the masses? _____.

2. What do critics consider the polluting element of blogs?

    _____

3. Determine whether each statement is true (T) or false (F).

    _____ a. Accuracy and truth are issues associated with blogs.

    _____ b. Newsrooms across the country have chosen not to print any information that has its origin in blogs.

**MAKING
CONNECTIONS**

*Blogs have become a popular tool of mass communication. There are blogs on almost any subject you can imagine, from cooking to politics. There are even Web sites that provide instructions on how to create and maintain a blog. What exactly is a blog? What blogs do you follow?*

**READING TIP**

*Although this selection is fairly short, it contains some abstract language and sophisticated concepts. Adjust your reading rate to ensure you are achieving full comprehension. Highlight and annotate key information as you read.*

# Blogs and Democratization

## John Vivian

1    Blogs hold promise for democratizing mass communication with affordable and technologically easy access. Critics note, however, that there is a polluting element. Blogging has no codes of conduct that require readers to be on guard against irresponsible postings. There are no **gatekeepers**.

**gatekeepers**
people who
monitor activities

2    As a mass communication tool, the Internet has outpaced older media in democratizing mass communication. This has become an era in which the price of entry to media ownership precludes most mortals. But the Internet, although young as a mass medium, is already democratizing mass communication. The rules are new. The most powerful member of the U.S. Senate, Trent Lott, never figured that his career would be sidelined under pressure created by a pip-squeak citizen in the **hinterlands**. It happened.

**hinterlands**
remote areas

### People Power

3    Joshua Marshall, creator of his own Web site, talkingpointsmemo.com, picked up on a speech by Lott that, depending on your view, was either racist or racially insensitive. Lott uttered his comment at the 100th birthday party of Senator Strom Thurmond, once a strong segregationist. Mainstream news media missed the possible implications of Lott's comments. Not Joshua Marshall. In his blog on talkingpointsmemo.com, he hammered away at Lott day after day. Other bloggers, also outraged, joined in. Three days later the story hit NBC. Four days later Lott apologized. Two weeks later his Senate colleagues voted him out as majority leader.

4    As a blogger who made a difference, Joshua Marshall is hardly alone. Best known is Matt Drudge, whose revelations propelled the Bill Clinton–Monica Lewinsky dalliances in the Oval Office into a national scandal. Another blogger, college student Russ Kirk, at his computer in Arizona, looked for information on government refusals to release photographs of caskets of fallen U.S. soldiers in Iraq and Afghanistan, which he regarded as documents to which the public, himself included, had legal access. Kirk filed a request for the documents under the Freedom of Information Act. Then on his Web site thememoryhole.org, he posted the photographs of the flag-draped coffins and also of the astronauts who had died in the Columbia disaster. The photos became front-page news. At one point Kirk's blog was receiving 4 million hits a day—almost twice the circulation of *USA Today*.

### Accuracy, Truth

5    Both the beauty and the bane of blogs is their free-for-all nature. On the upside, the Web gives ordinary citizens access to mass audiences. It can be a loud and effective megaphone that is outside traditional news media, which have resulted from institutionalized practices and traditions. Joshua Marshall's work on Trent Lott is an example of outside-the-box news reporting.

6    The easy access that bloggers have to mass audiences is also a problem. Most bloggers are amateurs at news, and their lack of experience with journalistic traditions has a downside. It was bloggers, for example, who kept alive a story that presidential candidate John Kerry and an office intern had carried on an affair.

## MEDIA PEOPLE

Glenn Reynolds
blogger whose
Instapundit.com
has attracted a
large audience

**mogul**
an influential
person

**lark**
a carefree
adventure

### Glenn Reynolds

Never had Glenn Reynolds thought of himself as a media **mogul**. Although a young man of strong views, he saw his future as a college prof, not a media star. As a side line **lark** in 2001, he set up a Web site, Instapundit .com, and tapped out libertarian opinions for anybody who might be interested. At first nobody was.

Then, a month later, came the September 11 terrorism. People by the thousands turned to the Internet, found Reynolds' impassioned commentaries from Knoxville, Tennessee, and made Instapundit a daily routine. *Wired* magazine has declared Reynolds' site the world's most popular blog—a shortened word for "Web log" or diary.

At 120,000 visits a day, Reynolds has a larger audience than the average U.S. daily newspaper and more than most cable television pundits. He's prolific, writing 20 to 30 opinion items a day, some fairly long, mostly political. He's also gotten the attention of the traditional media. Fox News has posted his stuff on its site. MSNBC gave him a separate blog on its site.

Reynolds' blog is not alone in its success. Thousands exist, created by individuals who have something to say. Blogs fulfill a promise of the Internet to give people of ordinary means a printing press to reach the world, enriching the dialogue in a free society to an extent once possible only to media moguls and those relatively few whom they chose to print and air.

The Internet is transforming the structure of mass communication.

**Blogmeister.** He never aspired to a major media career, but his blog site Instapundit attracts more hits a day than the average U.S. newspaper's circulation.

### What Do You Think?

- How are blogs democratizing mass communication?
- What does this democratization mean for existing mass media industries?
- What does this democratization mean for society as a whole?

So persistent were the bloggers that neither the mainstream news media nor Kerry could ignore it, although Kerry and the intern denied the allegations and there was no evidence that there was anything to it. Kevin Drum, of calpundit.com, calls himself "unedited and unplugged." Although Drum never touched the Kerry intern story and is respected by his followers, his point that bloggers are "unedited and unplugged" is both the good news and the bad news about the democratizing impact of the Internet.

### New Gatekeeping

7    So-called mainstream media are introducing an element of old fashioned, journalistically valued gatekeeping into blogging. *The New York Times,* for example, picks up news generated by bloggers when it meets the paper's standards for what's worth reporting. The **imprimatur** of being cited in the *Times,* which involves fact-checking and news judgment, lends credibility to a blogger. When mainstream media are silent on blog content, their silence speaks volumes.

**imprimatur**
permission or approval

8    Increasingly common are mainstream-media summaries of blog content as a barometer of what's on the minds of participants in this emerging forum. Several times daily, CNN, as an example, reports what's new from the blogs.

9    Newsrooms everywhere keep an eye on YouTube and other self-post sites. Oddities worth reporting such as man-bites-dog items are picked up every day. YouTube attained a special status in the 2008 presidential elections when people were invited to upload questions for candidates. Questions were put to the candidates in CNN-hosted debates. Real issues by real people on video was undeniable as a new kind of vehicle for voters to assess candidates. The videos cut through carefully manipulated campaign tactics that had come to mark U.S. elections—staged photo-ops, town-hall meetings with only prescreened participants, and politically calibrated 30-second spots. Not all YouTube-posted questions made the debates, though. As a gatekeeper, CNN used journalistic standards to **winnow** the **chaff**.

**winnow**
to sift

**chaff**
unusable material

### Learning Check

● Has blogging added a common person's voice to public dialogue on important issues?
● How is blogging being integrated into mainstream-media news reporting?

## UNDERSTANDING AND ANALYZING THE READING

### A. BUILDING VOCABULARY

#### Context

*Using context and a dictionary if necessary, determine the meaning of each word as it is used in the selection.*

_____ 1. precludes (paragraph 2)
    a. comes after
    b. rules out
    c. copies
    d. adds to

_____ 2. propelled (paragraph 4)
    a. prevented
    b. revealed
    c. refused
    d. moved

_____ 3. bane (paragraph 5)

    a.  beauty

    b.  curse

    c.  benefit

    d.  argument

_____ 4. allegations (paragraph 6)

    a.  claims or assertions

    b.  illegal statements

    c.  conversations

    d.  demands

_____ 5. barometer (paragraph 8)

    a.  a summary

    b.  an introduction

    c.  a measuring device

    d.  an important announcement

## Word Parts

> ### A REVIEW OF PREFIXES AND SUFFIXES
>
> **IN-** means *not*.
>
> **-ER** means *one who*.

*Use your knowledge of word parts and the review above to fill in the blanks in the following sentences.*

1. A person who is *insensitive* (paragraph 3) is not _____ does not care about the feelings of others.

2. A *blogger* (paragraph 4) is someone who _____.

## B. UNDERSTANDING MAIN IDEAS

*Select the best answer.*

_____ 1. Which of the following best states the main idea of the entire piece of writing?

    a.  The government should do more to enforce journalistic standards on the Internet.

    b.  The type of information typically found on blogs is unreliable and misleading.

    c.  Mainstream media must start adapting its standards to compete with the Internet.

    d.  Blogs offer easy access to mass audiences but they lack codes of conduct or standards of quality.

_____ 2. The topic of paragraph 3 is

    a.  racially insensitive blogs.

    b.  the blog that negatively affected Senator Trent Lott.

    c.  the creation of the Web site talkingpointsmemo.com.

    d.  Senator Strom Thurmond's reaction to an insulting blog.

_____ 3. The main idea of paragraph 7 is that bloggers

    a. rely on mainstream media for fact-checking.

    b. gain credibility when they are cited by mainstream media.

    c. influence the quality of mainstream news reporting.

    d. have high standards for what is considered newsworthy.

## C. IDENTIFYING DETAILS

*Select the best answer.*

_____ 1. In this selection, the term *democratization* refers to how the Internet has made mass communication

    a. politically oriented.

    b. more modern.

    c. accessible to many.

    d. free from censorship.

_____ 2. The blogger who made public the Clinton–Lewinsky scandal was

    a. Matt Drudge.

    b. Joshua Marshall.

    c. Russ Kirk.

    d. Kevin Drum.

_____ 3. Which of the following Web sites is considered by *Wired* magazine to be the world's most popular blog?

    a. talkingpointsmemo.com

    b. thememoryhole.com

    c. calpundit.com

    d. instapundit.com

_____ 4. Which of the following is *not* an issue associated with blogs?

    a. accuracy of information

    b. easy access of bloggers to mass audiences

    c. truthfulness of information

    d. entertainment value of information

## D. RECOGNIZING METHODS OF ORGANIZATION AND SIGNAL WORDS

*Select the best answer.*

_____ 1. The organizational pattern of paragraph 3 is

    a. chronological order.

    b. comparison and contrast.

    c. summary.

    d. order of importance.

_____ 2. A transitional word or phrase in paragraph 3 that signals its
         pattern of organization is
         a. in his blog.
         b. three days later.
         c. also.
         d. other bloggers.

_____ 3. The organizational pattern of paragraph 6 is
         a. process.
         b. classification.
         c. definition.
         d. illustration.

## E. READING AND THINKING VISUALLY

_____ 1. The boxed feature about Glenn Reynolds deepens our under-
         standing of
         a. what it takes to become famous writing a blog.
         b. how blogging allows for the democratization of the news media.
         c. the amount of time it takes to write a blog each day.
         d. how easy it is to spread inaccurate stories with a blog.

## F. FIGURING OUT IMPLIED MEANING

*Indicate whether each statement is true (T) or false (F).*

_____ 1. The author suggests that bloggers have the capability of ruining a
         person's reputation.

_____ 2. The author is a well respected blogger.

_____ 3. The author believes that blogs have both good and bad qualities.

_____ 4. The author suggests that the mainstream media sees some value in
         blog content.

_____ 5. The author believes that the ordinary citizen does not have the
         capability to judge the truth of most blogs.

## G. THINKING CRITICALLY: ANALYZING THE AUTHOR'S TECHNIQUE

*Select the best answer*

_____ 1. When Kevin Drum calls himself "unedited and unplugged"
         (paragraph 6), he means that he is
         a. not in touch with the mainstream opinion.
         b. refusing to let others use his blogging material.
         c. not copyrighting his blogging material.
         d. freely writing whatever he wants to write without censorship.

_____ 2. To support his points, the author uses primarily

    a. academic research about popular blogs and bloggers.

    b. examples of popular blogs and bloggers.

    c. quotations from bloggers.

    d. statistics related to blog readership.

_____ 3. The author's purpose in writing "Blogs and Democratization" is to describe

    a. different modes of communication on the Internet.

    b. the effects of the widespread use of blogs.

    c. advertising and marketing on the Internet.

    d. the latest technology for wireless networks.

_____ 4. Which of the following is a fact, not an opinion?

    a. "Both the beauty and the bane of blogs is their free-for-all nature." (paragraph 5)

    b. "his (Drum) point that bloggers are 'unedited and unplugged' is both the good news and the bad news about the democratizing impact of the Internet." (paragraph 6)

    c. "The easy access that bloggers have to mass audiences is also a problem." (paragraph 6)

    d. "Several times daily, CNN, as an example, reports what's new from the blogs." (paragraph 8)

## H. THINKING CRITICALLY: ANALYZING THE AUTHOR'S MESSAGE

_Select the best answer._

_____ 1. According to the author, all of the following are positive effects of blogs, _except_

    a. removing a Congressman from a position of power because of his racially insensitive remarks.

    b. propelling an Oval Office affair into a national scandal.

    c. keeping alive a story that presidential candidate John Kerry and an office intern had carried on an affair.

    d. bringing to light the government's refusal to release photos of caskets of fallen U.S. soldiers in Iraq and Afghanistan.

_____ 2. When the author says that blogs can be "a loud and effective megaphone" (paragraph 5), he means that

    a. the messages that bloggers send tend to create a lot of noise.

    b. blogs have a widespread audience.

    c. blogs are intended for a diverse audience.

    d. blogs are very effective in getting the attention of the general public.

_____ 3. The author suggests that blogging is being integrated into mainstream-media news reporting in all of the following ways, *except*

    a. newsrooms reading blogs and watching YouTube videos for newsworthy subject matter.

    b. nationwide newspapers relying on blogs for most of their human interest stories.

    c. most newspapers carefully screening blogs before repeating information from them to make sure that they meet the required standards of news that is worth reporting.

    d. mainstream media sending a clear message about the credibility of a blog by refusing to comment on it or print it.

## WRITING IN RESPONSE TO THE READING

### I. REVIEWING AND ORGANIZING IDEAS WITH A SUMMARY

*Complete the following summary of paragraph 3 by filling in the missing words and phrases. Remember that a summary should cover all of the author's main points.*

Joshua Marshall is the _____ of the Web site named _____. He heard about a speech by _____ that was given at the 100<sup>th</sup> birthday celebration of Senator _____. Some people thought the speech was racially _____. For several days, _____ made this speech the subject of his _____, and then his comments got the attention of _____, a major news network. Although Lott _____, his colleagues in the _____ removed him from his position as _____.

### J. ANALYZING THE ISSUE

1. What contemporary issue is discussed in the reading? Is the author making an argument or simply presenting information?

2. Write a one- or two-sentence summary of the author's thesis or main point.

3. Based on the source information provided, do you think the information provided is reliable?

4. Evaluate the reading on the following criteria:

   a. Is the information timely?

   b. Does the author provide sufficient evidence to support key concepts? What other types of evidence could have been provided?

   c. Has the author defined terms accurately and sufficiently?

   d. Do you sense any bias in the reading? If so, explain.

   e. Does the reading offer any emotional appeals? If so, identify them and evaluate their fairness.

## K. WRITING PARAGRAPHS AND ESSAYS

*Write a paragraph or essay in response to one of the following writing prompts.*

1. Write a paragraph in which you discuss the effects of blogging on society as a whole.

2. In one of the aforementioned blogs, find an entry that expresses a view contrary to yours. Write a well-developed paragraph that contrasts your view with that of the blogger.

3. Write a paragraph in which you discuss the "beauty and the bane of blogs." (paragraph 5)

4. Read some of Joshua Marshall's blog entries and Russ Kirk's entries by locating them using a search engine. After reading some of the entries, decide on a controversial issue that you would like to address. Then write an essay-length blog entry of your own on the issue you have chosen. You may use any issue that you have strong feelings about. You do not necessarily have to use one of Marshall's or Kirk's issues.

5. Have you ever had something written about you that was not true? Write an essay in which you describe what happened and how it made you feel.

## ACTIVITIES: EXPLORING TECHNOLOGICAL ISSUES

*On your own or with a group of classmates, complete two of the following four activities.*

1. It is likely that you own a smartphone and that you use it to send text messages and/or post to Facebook or some other type of social media. List at least three ways that using a smartphone or social media site has improved your life. Then list at least three ways in which you see smartphones and/or social media being misused (for example, people who send text messages while driving create extremely dangerous road conditions that can lead to people getting killed).

_____

_____

_____

_____

_____

2. Conduct a Web search for an organization that is devoted to educating people about and preventing cyberbullying. Read about the organization's mission, as well as a couple of the articles on the organization's Web site. Summarize these articles in a paragraph, essay, or classroom presentation. Provide at least three tips for preventing or stamping out cyberbullying.

3. As we mentioned at the start of this chapter, technology has become pervasive in almost all areas of our lives. This chapter discussed just a few aspects of the topic. Other technological issues include the following:

   - The threat of identity theft through technological means
   - Brain research that suggests the addictive quality of technology
   - Serious privacy concerns as Web browsers track your movements online and then sell that information to companies who want to advertise their products to you
   - The effects of technology on the well-being of young children who spend a lot of time playing on computers
   - Technology's role in the theft of intellectual property such as music and books. (If you have ever downloaded a book or a song from a "share" site, you have most likely stolen intellectual property.)
   - The role technology plays in political campaigns and social unrest (for example, the Occupy Wall Street movement)

   Write an essay or prepare a class presentation about any of these topics, or any other technological topic in which you are interested.

4. Suppose you are the creator of reality TV programming and your boss gives you the following assignment: "Come up with a reality TV show that portrays people in a positive way, showing their innate goodness and generosity." Write an essay in which you explain the type of show you would create. What would the setting be? Who would the characters be? What sorts of events would drive the story and make TV viewers want to watch the show?

# 17 Society: Changes Big and Small

*How does society change from year to year, and from generation to generation? How does social change affect your life and the decisions you make?*

The technical definition of *society* is "a community of people living in a particular country or region and having shared customs, laws, and organizations." But this definition does not do justice to the richness and complexity of society and the changes it undergoes.

Sometimes social changes are gradual; other times they are rapid. For example, over the last five or six decades, people from minority groups have changed the face of America. What was once predominantly a white, European population has become extremely diverse, with people migrating to the United States from all over the planet. This process has been slow but steady. In contrast, it seems that smartphones and texting have achieved dominance over a period of just a few years. People who happily lived without smartphones just a few years ago now cannot imagine life without them.

At issue in society are some strong opinions regarding whether social change is desirable or not. Many elements of society—government, religion, politics, education—come together to debate many questions, including the following:

- *How do we define "marriage"?* Is marriage a legal status, or should it be something done within the boundaries of a particular religious faith? How do these questions help us determine who is permitted to get married, and under what conditions?

- *Is "cultural diversity" more of an advantage for society or more of a drawback?* How does a country benefit from having all kinds of people living in it? What challenges does it face from having so many people with widely divergent ideas, traditions, backgrounds, and languages?

- *What are the ideal living conditions for people?* Is it more environmentally friendly for people to live in large cities that provide public transportation? If so, should government policies provide incentives for people to live and work in cities?

The readings in this chapter look at several aspects of society and social change. The topics under discussion are residential segregation (housing patterns for the rich and the poor), the benefits of being bilingual (speaking two languages) in a multicultural society, and a serious social problem that has received much attention in recent years, bullying in schools.

## WHY IS SOCIETY SUCH AN IMPORTANT CONTEMPORARY ISSUE?

In a country like the United States, many important questions are debated on the basis of whether or not the proposed changes will be good for society. In this case, "society" means the majority of the people. Matters get tricky when many people would benefit, but some people would not. For example, higher taxes on the wealthy would benefit almost everyone by making more tax dollars available for education and other programs. However, the wealthy would not benefit from paying higher taxes—they would end up with less money each year. Societies are constantly weighing one concern against another and trying to determine what is best for most people. Understanding how social changes affect different people is essential to taking part in the debates.

### How Does the Concept of Society Tie in to My College Courses?

Of course, the study of society is the key goal of any sociology course you might take. Within psychology, the subfield of social psychology is concerned with people's interactions in society. Government and history courses are also concerned with societies and how they are governed. Society generally creates the need for businesses to develop and market products and services, so business courses in marketing and advertising teach future businesspeople how to reach different types of customers. Much scientific research is about finding ways to improve society—whether by creating new sources of energy or developing new pharmaceuticals and treatments for diseases like cancer or diabetes.

Overall, the study of society is the study of *you*—because society could not exist without you.

| | |
|---|---|
| **TIPS FOR READING ABOUT SOCIETY** | Here are some tips for reading not only the selections in this chapter, but any reading about society. |

- **Look closely at the organizational patterns used.** Many readings about society use the definition pattern (to explain a specific phenomenon), cause and effect (to show how certain events or laws affect people), and classification (to categorize people or social activities). You will also find the listing/enumeration and process patterns used quite frequently.

- **Consider the author's purpose.** Readings about society can have different purposes. Is the reading mostly definitional? If so, the author's goal is probably to inform the reader. Or is the author arguing a particular viewpoint? In this case, you should read critically and be alert for signs of bias.

- **Evaluate the examples and evidence provided.** Readings about society may talk about groups of people or about individuals. If you are reading about one person's experiences, are that person's experiences representative of the whole? Is it safe to generalize on the basis of that person's experiences? What other sources has the author used to support the thesis and main ideas, and are these sources reliable and trustworthy?

- **Tie the reading to your own life.** Annotate the reading with your responses and any questions you may have. These annotations can form the basis for excellent class or group discussion.

# SELECTION 16
MySkillsLab

# Bullying 2.0 Is More Like a Drama Class

### Emma Teitel

## SOURCE AND CONTEXT

The source of this article is *Maclean's*, Canada's only weekly current-affairs magazine. (Similar publications in the United States include *Time* and *The Week*.) According to the magazine's Web site, *Maclean's* "enlightens, engages, and entertains 2.4 million readers with strong investigative reporting and exclusive stories from leading journalists in the fields of international affairs, social issues, national politics, business, and culture."

## A NOTE ON THE READING

Do teenagers and adults view bullying in the same way? Read "Bullying 2.0 Is More Like a Drama Class" for one journalist's answer to this question.

## PREVIEWING THE READING

*Using the steps listed on page 4, preview the reading selection. When you have finished, complete the following items.*

1. This article is about _____.

2. Determine whether each statement is true (T) or false (F).

_____ a. Canada's legal code does not use the word *bullying*.

_____ b. The use of the word *drama* instead of *bullying* minimizes the effects of a dangerous and painful behavior.

MAKING CONNECTIONS

*Have you ever witnessed any bullying incidents? What do you think are the consequences of bullying for both the bully and the victim?*

## READING TIP

*This article is mostly concerned with Canadian (not U.S.) legislation. As you read, ask yourself how the concepts and research findings might (or might not) apply to the United States as well as Canada.*

# Bullying 2.0 Is More Like a Drama Class

Emma Teitel

MP
Member of
Parliament

1      What is likely the only thing Lady Gaga and Conservative **MP** Mike Allen have in common? Both believe that bullying should be a criminal offense. Following the suicide of 14-year-old Jamey Rodemeyer in Buffalo, New York (the teen was bullied mercilessly for being gay), Lady Gaga expressed via Twitter that "Bullying must become illegal," and underscored her position by pressing President Barack Obama about bullying while towering in heels (Obama has since described the encounter at a fundraiser as "intimidating"). New Brunswick's Mike Allen, for his part, has been working with BullyingCanada.ca to make bullying an illegal act. Despite their efforts, however, neither the pop star nor the politician has been successful. While various behaviors that fall under the bullying umbrella—assault, uttering threats, harassment, unauthorized use of a computer—are included in the Criminal Code of Canada, the term bullying itself is not. The young offender who last year allegedly attacked Mitchell Wilson—the 11-year-old Pickering, Ontario, boy who recently committed suicide after being bullied relentlessly for his **muscular dystrophy** symptoms—was charged with assault, not bullying. And maybe that's a good thing; because the divergent languages of bullying—what adults call it and what its younger victims do—may be more problematic than its pending legal status.

**muscular
dystrophy**
a disease
characterized
by progressive
weakening and
wasting of the
muscles

2      Recent research confirms what I—someone not far removed from adolescence—have suspected for a while. "Bullying" may be the accepted term for kid-on-kid brutality, but it's seldom used among kids themselves. "They view the term as adult-driven," says Wendy Craig, a Queen's University psychology professor and researcher at the Bully Lab. "Teens especially don't generally refer to the term." Craig echoes recent research by Danah Boyd and Alice Marwick, whose innovative paper on bullying in the United States found that young people don't use the word "bullying" in the same way and/or nearly as frequently as parents and educators do; not only is the term practically unused, it's considered painfully passé. In fact, when most teens hear about bullying they automatically assume a "grade school problem" that doesn't apply. On GritTV last year, actor John Fugelsang argued that the verb bullying should be retired for good. "Bullying is a **flaccid**, outdated, archaic, **Archie comic** term," he said. "It's quaint, it's useless, it's toothless."

**flaccid**
lacking force or
effectiveness

**Archie comic**
a comic book series,
first published in
1941, that focuses
on a group of high
school friends

3      So how, then, do young people label the humiliating and infuriating abuse of power adults call bullying? In classic teenager style, ironically and maybe even more insidiously, they call it "drama." Why drama? "The **emic** use of 'drama,'" wrote Boyd and Marwick, "allows teens to distance themselves from practices which adults may conceptualize as bullying. As such, they can retain agency—and save face—rather than positioning themselves in a victim narrative."

**emic**
related to the
description of
language in
terms of its
internal elements
and their
functions

4      In plain English, Jessica sends a mass email to everyone in her high school slandering Rachel, in order to win over Rachel's boyfriend, and the entire cyberbullying incident (as it might be referred to on the part of the school's principal) is chalked up (on the kids' part) to a whole lot of drama. "Why are you starting all this drama?" Rachel the Victim might ask Jessica the Perpetrator, from whom she'd likely hear: "God, Rachel, stop being so dramatic." Catch the poisonous and understated collusion in that exchange? The term drama minimizes the seriousness of the incident and the pain it causes, which only makes it twice as serious and painful.

5    There you have it: Bullying 2.0—a different beast than the kind concerned officials are currently battling. The problem is that the majority of adults who'd like to see bullying outlawed aren't familiar with the social nuances of the wholly social problem they want to eradicate. And this disconnect, if Boyd and Marwick are correct, could turn the "war on bullying" into the war on drugs, or the war on terror—other misnomers whose relative failures are bound up in the fact that advocates aren't even sure what they're fighting. Until that changes, bullying probably won't, either.

6    But Craig remains ever hopeful and—in the face of the optimism surrounding the issue, that bullying is some kind of new epidemic we're on the brink of curing—realistic. "People will always want power," she says, acknowledging that kid-on-kid conflict, by any name, will exist forever. "It's how we teach them to use that power that makes the difference . . . taking them out of school and putting people in jail doesn't help them change." It's a good point: isolating bullies—and especially putting them together—isn't ideal for the rehabilitation process. But more importantly, it doesn't teach us anything new about the problem we're trying to solve.

**semantics**
the meaning of a
word or phrase

7    Language does. That youth may shirk the term ("bullying") but not the act itself is more important than the legal **semantics** of something officials are only beginning to understand. It's also profoundly telling: the way teens use "drama" doesn't represent a mere generational shift in lingo, but rather an attempt to minimize the effects of a dangerous and painful behavior. And it's hard to confront that behavior—legally or otherwise—when both victim and perpetrator are reluctant to do so themselves. **George Carlin** was right. His Website says, "Language is a tool for concealing the truth," but if anti-bullying activists spend more time listening in than speaking out, they'll learn it has the power to reveal as well.

**George Carlin**
an American
stand-up
comedian

## UNDERSTANDING AND ANALYZING THE READING

### A. BUILDING VOCABULARY

#### Context

*Match each vocabulary term in Column A with its definition in Column B.*

|  | Column A: Vocabulary Term | Column B: Definition |
|---|---|---|
| _____ | 1. underscored (paragraph 1) | a. differing |
| _____ | 2. umbrella (paragraph 1) | b. sneakily |
| _____ | 3. divergent (paragraph 1) | c. secret agreement |
| _____ | 4. passé (paragraph 2) | d. emphasized |
| _____ | 5. insidiously (paragraph 3) | e. eliminate |
| _____ | 6. slandering (paragraph 4) | f. outdated |
| _____ | 7. collusion (paragraph 4) | g. gossiping maliciously |
| _____ | 8. nuances (paragraph 5) | h. subtle differences |
| _____ | 9. eradicate (paragraph 5) | i. avoid |
| _____ | 10. shirk (paragraph 7) | j. category |

## Word Parts

> ### A REVIEW OF PREFIXES AND ROOTS
>
> **CYBER-** means *related to computers or the Internet.*
>
> **MIS-** means *wrongly.*
>
> **NOM** means *name.*

*Use your knowledge of word parts and the review above to fill in the blanks in the following sentences.*

1. *Cyberbullying* (paragraph 4) refers to bullying that takes place _____
   _____.

2. A *misnomer* (paragraph 5) is a _____ that is wrongly or falsely given.

## B. UNDERSTANDING THE THESIS AND OTHER MAIN IDEAS

*Select the best answer.*

_____ 1. The thesis or central thought of "Bullying 2.0 Is More Like a Drama Class" is best stated as

   a. Countries should be more aggressive about enacting and enforcing anti-bullying laws.

   b. The term *bullying* is outdated and should be replaced with another term that better defines the behaviors that constitute bullying.

   c. Adults and teens use different words to describe the concept of bullying; adults use the term *bullying* to call attention to the issue, while teens use the word *drama* to minimize or deny the issue.

   d. Anti-bullying laws and programs are generally more effective when they are supported by high-profile celebrities such as Lady Gaga.

_____ 2. The topic of paragraph 2 is
   a. use of the term *bullying*.
   b. the Bully Lab.
   c. John Fugelsang.
   d. U.S.-Canadian differences.

_____ 3. The implied main idea of paragraph 3 is that
   a. adults consider bullying to be an abuse of power.
   b. teenagers use the term *drama* instead of *bullying* as way of pretending they are not victims and are in control of the situation.
   c. bullying can never be accurately defined because people of different generations view it in different ways.
   d. adults generally make a bigger deal out of trivial matters than teenagers do.

_____ 4. The main idea of paragraph 4 is found in the
   a. first sentence.
   b. second sentence.
   c. third sentence.
   d. last sentence.

## C. IDENTIFYING DETAILS

*Select the best answer.*

_____ 1. All of the following are academic researchers *except*
   a. John Fugelsang.
   b. Alice Marwick.
   c. Wendy Craig.
   d. Danah Boyd.

_____ 2. Mitchell Wilson was bullied over his
   a. weight.
   b. sexuality.
   c. height.
   d. medical problems.

_____ 3. The term the author uses to identify a more modern understanding of the dynamics of bullying, and the language issues surrounding it, is
   a. agency.
   b. saving face.
   c. bullying 2.0.
   d. semantics.

## D.  RECOGNIZING METHODS OF ORGANIZATION AND TRANSITIONS

*Select the best answer.*

_____ 1. The overall pattern of organization used in "Bullying 2.0 Is More Like a Drama Class" is
   a.  process.
   b.  definition.
   c.  order of importance.
   d.  classification.

_____ 2. Paragraph 4 uses two patterns of organization. The first is chronological order. The second is
   a.  spatial order.
   b.  cause and effect.
   c.  comparison and contrast.
   d.  classification.

_____ 3. The transitional words or phrases used to signal the addition pattern in paragraph 7 are
   a.  does, shirk.
   b.  only beginning, represent.
   c.  victim, perpetrator.
   d.  also, and.

## E.  READING AND THINKING VISUALLY

*Select the best answer.*

_____ 1. The photo on page 531 illustrates all of the following points from the article *except*
   a.  children and teenagers are the victims of bullying.
   b.  some bullying takes place in cyberspace or via electronics/computer equipment.
   c.  girls are more likely to be bullied than boys.
   d.  bullying does not necessarily involve physical violence.

## F.  FIGURING OUT IMPLIED MEANINGS

*Indicate whether each statement is true (T) or false (F).*

_____ 1. The author believes that isolating bullies from their classmates is the best way to end bullying.

_____ 2. George Carlin believed that words hide more than they reveal.

_____ 3. Teenagers tend to think of "bullying" as something that happens in grammar school, not high school.

_____ 4. Mike Allen has succeeded in making bullying illegal in Canada.

_____ 5. The author of "Bullying 2.0 Is More Like a Drama Class" is likely in her 20s.

_____ 6. The Bully Lab at Queen's University is a place where researchers study bullying and its effects.

_____ 7. The author believes that the term *drama* is more accurate and descriptive than the term *bullying*.

## G. THINKING CRITICALLY: ANALYZING THE AUTHOR'S TECHNIQUE

*Select the best answer.*

_____ 1. The author's primary purpose for writing "Bullying 2.0 Is More Like a Drama Class" is to

a. explore the phenomenon of cyberbullying and how it differs from in-person bullying or physical assaults and intimidation.

b. provide several examples of celebrities and politicians working together to outlaw bullying in the United States and Canada.

c. help parents understand whether or not their children are bullies or are being bullied at school.

d. call attention to intergenerational differences in the way teens and adults describe bullying, and to suggest that a better understanding of these differences will help in the fight against bullying.

_____ 2. The tone of the reading is best described as

a. puzzled.

b. distressed.

c. malicious.

d. sensational.

_____ 3. All of the following words from paragraph 2 have a negative connotation *except*

a. passé.

b. innovative.

c. useless.

d. toothless.

_____ 4. To support her thesis and main ideas, the author uses all of the following types of evidence *except*

a. examples of children who have been bullied to the point of suicide.

b. research studies.

c. a comparison of bullying today versus bullying 100 years ago.

d. quotations from experts.

_____ 5. All of the following statements from the reading are opinions,
*except*

a. "Both [Lady Gaga and Mike Allen] believe that bullying should
be a criminal offense." (paragraph 1)

b. "The divergent languages of bullying—what adults call it and
what its younger victims do—may be more problematic than its
pending legal status." (paragraph 1)

c. "Bullying is a flaccid, outdated, archaic, Archie comic term."
(paragraph 2)

d. "Until that changes, bullying probably won't, either." (paragraph 5)

## H. THINKING CRITICALLY: ANALYZING THE AUTHOR'S MESSAGE

*Select the best answer.*

_____ 1. In paragraph 2, the author asserts that teenagers see the term
*bullying* as "adult-driven." This means that teenagers believe that
the term *bullying*

a. was created and is used by adults and does not reflect a true
understanding of the situation.

b. is used by parents to discipline their children.

c. allows adults to ignore certain aspects of a situation.

d. is rapidly becoming obsolete in the Internet age.

_____ 2. John Fugelsang, quoted in paragraph 2, refers to *bullying* as an
"Archie comic term." By this he means that the word *bullying*

a. represents a problem that has been occurring for a very long
time.

b. is best applied to victims who are in grammar school, not in
high school.

c. is as outdated a term as the Archie comics, which started in the
1940s; it is not relevant today.

d. was useful only before teenagers started using computers to
bully classmates.

_____ 3. According to the last sentence in paragraph 3, bullied teenagers
prefer to use the term *drama* in order to avoid defining themselves as

a. unattractive.

b. unpopular.

c. children.

d. victims.

—— 4. According to paragraph 5, what does the author fear?

    a. She fears that bullying will become more prevalent in Canada as a result of undefined words in Canadian laws.

    b. She fears that anti-bullying advocates do not have a full understanding of what they are fighting against.

    c. She fears that Danah Boyd and Alice Marwick have falsified their research.

    d. She fears that Bullying 2.0 will always find new and creative ways to engage in bullying against children and teenagers who have been identified as targets for bullying.

## WRITING IN RESPONSE TO THE READING

### I. REVIEWING AND ORGANIZING IDEAS WITH A SUMMARY

*Write a summary of the reading. Three sentences have been provided to guide you.*

According to Emma Teitel in "Bullying 2.0 Is More Like a Drama Class," none of the attempts to criminalize bullying in Canada have succeeded, despite the involvement of high-profile celebrities and politicians.

_____

_____

_____

_____

_____

_____

_____

_____

In summary, teenagers' use of the word *drama* does not truly reflect the pain and consequences of bullying on both bullies and their victims. Those who advocate for anti-bullying laws need to better understand teens' perceptions of bullying, and the language they use to describe it, in order to combat the problem.

## J.  ANALYZING THE ISSUE AND ARGUMENT

1. What contemporary issue is the author discussing in this reading? Phrase the issue in the form of a question.

2. List at least two arguments the author makes in "Bullying 2.0 Is More Like a Drama Class." Phrase each in the form of a one- or two-sentence summary of the author's argument.

3. Consider the article's title. Does it reflect the article's content accurately? Why or why not?

4. Closely examine the language in the reading. Do you perceive any bias? Explain your response.

5. Has the author provided sufficient evidence to support her thesis and main ideas? What other types of evidence might she provide to make her main ideas stronger?

6. Evaluate the reading on the following criteria:

   a. Is the information timely?

   b. Has the author defined her terms accurately and sufficiently?

   c. Does the author offer opposing viewpoints? If so, what is her attitude toward them, and does she discredit them fairly or unfairly? If not, what might some opposing viewpoints be? List and evaluate them.

   d. Does the reading make any emotional appeals to readers? If so, identify them and evaluate their fairness.

   e. Discuss the author's assumptions. Are these explicitly stated or implied? What claims of fact and value are stated or implied?

## K.  WRITING PARAGRAPHS AND ESSAYS

*Write a paragraph or essay in response to the following writing prompts.*

1. Write a paragraph in which you define *bullying* as you understand it.

2. In your opinion, who are the most likely targets of bullying, and why? Write a paragraph exploring your thoughts.

3. Write a caption for the photo on page 531, tying the photo to the key arguments made in the reading.

4. Paragraph 7 makes reference to *lingo,* or the vocabulary used by a group of people. *Lingo* is sometimes used interchangeably with *slang* to describe language used by a particular group of people. Write an essay in which you explore the meanings of three slang words or phrases used by you and your friends. For some ideas, consult Urban Dictionary on the Web.

5. What are the benefits to having a celebrity involved in a cause (such as anti-bullying or environmental awareness)? What are the drawbacks to celebrity involvement? Write an essay exploring the pros and cons.

6. As defined in this reading, *drama* has a specific definition and a set of connotations. How does this definition of *drama* differ from the way you understand the term? Write an essay in which you discuss some of the similarities and differences.

## SELECTION 17
MySkillsLab

# Ten Proven Brain Benefits of Being Bilingual

## Meredith Nudo

### SOURCE AND CONTEXT

WEB ARTICLE

This article originally appeared on BestCollegesOnline.com, a Web site designed for students who want to attend college almost exclusively online. Most of the articles on the site are written by two staff writers, Michael Keathley and Lauren Bailey.

### A NOTE ON THE READING

What are the benefits of speaking more than one language fluently? Read the selection for the answer to this question.

### PREVIEWING THE READING

*Using the steps listed on page 4, preview the reading selection. When you have finished, complete the following items.*

1. This article is about the _____ of speaking two languages.

2. Indicate whether each statement is true (T) or false (F).

_____ a. The University of Pompeu Fabra is located in Italy.

_____ b. Most of the brain consists of gray matter.

_____ c. A benefit of being bilingual is heightened creativity.

**MAKING CONNECTIONS**

*Do you speak more than one language? If so, which languages do you speak? Are you equally comfortable speaking and writing in both languages?*

### READING TIP

*As you read, keep in mind that many debates about language are currently active in the United States. For example, some argue that English should be the national, official language of the United States and that the government should print materials only in English and not in any other languages.*

# Ten Proven Brain Benefits of Being Bilingual

### Meredith Nudo

1    These days, attaining fluency in two or more languages looks fabulous on college and job applications and presents opportunities in numerous corners of life completely denied to the monolingual. Old or young, however, bilingual individuals enjoy some decidedly physiological rewards for their linguistic capabilities, which aren't always immediately noticeable. Come to find out, the human body's most important organ receives generous stimulation from soaking up multiple tongues as well. So before griping about that mandatory foreign language course, take a look at some of the most excellent things that could happen after mastering one.

## Staves Off Dementia

**Alzheimer's**
a disease that
leads to loss of
brain function

**demographics**
groups of people

2    Bilingual individuals with **Alzheimer's** take twice as long to develop symptoms as their monolingual counterparts, and scientists at St. Michael's Hospital believe a distinct correlation exists between language development and delayed dementia. However, the symptoms between both **demographics** remained equally destructive; the only difference lay in the amount of damage needed for them to materialize. The prevailing hypothesis regarding why this phenomenon occurs involves how the multilingual mind strengthens itself by switching between tongues, which bolsters brain function overall.

## Improved Cognitive Skills

3    In general, the bilingual tend to enjoy far sharper cognitive skills, keeping the brain constantly active and alert even when only one language prevails. Studies conducted on preschoolers revealed that those capable of speaking multiple languages performed far better on sorting puzzles, both in speed and success. Their ability to strike a balance and switch between different "modes," as it were, eased the transition between various tasks with swapped-out goals. Specifically, the bilingual were better able to categorize shapes by color and form, even if the form sports a different color than that of the bin.

## Heightened Creativity

4    Learning a new language as either a child or an adult greatly benefits those pursuing creative careers or hobbies. Even the more technical still get something amazing out of the bargain, however, as bilingualism still nurtures the "outside-the-box" thinking necessary for sharp problem solving and innovation. Numerous studies linking acumen in multiple languages and creativity exist, including one by Texas Women's University.

Hola – Hello
Por Favor – Please
Bienvenido – Welcome
Gracias – Thanks

### Easier Time Focusing on Tasks

5     When presented with distractions, the bilingual individuals studied by York University maneuvered them more adroitly and displayed [more] heightened concentration on their assignments than the monolingual. The specific languages spoken held no influence over this mental flexibility; anyone fluent in more than one tongue reaps these cognitive rewards. However, some evidence exists that knowing two or more languages with structural similarities to one another might offer up a slight advantage.

### Greater Control Over Literacy Skills

6     York University also noted improvements in literacy and literacy skill acquisition in bilingual children. "Metalinguistic" abilities, which promote a more intimate understanding of verbal and nonverbal communication, receive the biggest boost here. Such abilities do come at a cost on the front end, however, as language acquisition in multilingual individuals does progress at a slightly slower pace.

### Heightened Environmental Awareness

7     University of Pompeu Fabra [located in Barcelona, Spain] researchers noted that their subjects fluent in one or more languages seem to express a much higher degree of environmental awareness. Essentially, this means their ability to process and "monitor" external **stimuli** sharpens alongside their verbal abilities. Because they must toggle between tongues, the bilingual's brains come fine-tuned to pick up on subtleties and patterns both on and off the page.

**stimuli**
causes of a
bodily response

### Easier Time Switching Between Tasks

8     As many other studies have no doubt already proven, the bi- and multilingual out there can brag that their brains multitask like a dream. Obviously, this directly ties into their sharpened cognitive skills resulting from bouncing back and forth between languages, which they do even when they're using only one language daily. Being able to switch off distractions with greater aplomb than the monolingual certainly doesn't hurt the mental gear shifting, either.

### Denser Gray Matter

9     Most of the brain consists of gray matter, which is responsible for dictating intelligence, particularly when it comes to acquiring and processing language, dictating attention spans, and establishing and storing memories. The bilingual possess more gray matter at a higher density than monolingual counterparts.

### Faster Response Time

10     When learning more about bilingualism and the brain, York University researchers noted that individuals who spoke both English and **Tamil** answered questions faster than those fluent only in the former. Understandable, considering how multilingualism acts as a sort of cognitive steroid dialing up the brain's potential. Scientists tested the phenomenon using a series of nonverbal reasoning questions between groups of similarly-educated individuals from more or less homogenous backgrounds.

**Tamil**
a language
spoken in
South Asia

### Higher Scores on Intelligence Tests

11    Crush together the swelling creativity, greater multitasking, generous environmental awareness, and other hallmarks of bilingualism and it probably comes as little
surprise that the bilingual typically score higher on intelligence tests. Studies conducted in 1974 and 1986 dissected the phenomenon using both verbal and nonverbal measures. Everything seems to boil down to "greater intellectual flexibility" in
general, with the language centers of the brain receiving an all-around power-up the
more a thinker engages with different tongues.

## UNDERSTANDING AND ANALYZING THE READING

### A. BUILDING VOCABULARY

#### Context

*Using context and a dictionary if necessary, determine the meaning of each word
as it is used in the selection.*

_____ 1. monolingual (paragraph 1)
   a. unable to speak
   b. speaking English
   c. speaking one language
   d. speaking with an accent

_____ 2. physiological (paragraph 1)
   a. related to the study of the brain
   b. related to the study of personality
   c. related to the study of mental illness
   d. related to the study of the body's
      processes

_____ 3. mandatory (paragraph 1)
   a. college-level
   b. challenging
   c. freshman
   d. required

_____ 4. correlation (paragraph 2)
   a. opposite
   b. cause
   c. relationship
   d. disconnect

_____ 5. bolsters (paragraph 2)
   a. boosts
   b. softens
   c. interferes with
   d. prevents

_____ 6. acumen (paragraph 4)
   a. state of excitement
   b. college courses
   c. natural ability
   d. creativity

_____ 7. adroitly (paragraph 5)
   a. slowly
   b. skillfully
   c. strongly
   d. subtly

_____ 8. toggle (paragraph 7)
   a. choose
   b. shut down
   c. switch
   d. leap

_____ 9. aplomb (paragraph 8)

    a. composure

    b. anger

    c. confusion

    d. apathy

_____ 10. homogenous (paragraph 10)

    a. similar

    b. natural

    c. disadvantaged

    d. urban

### Word Parts

> **A REVIEW OF PREFIXES AND SUFFIXES**
>
> **MULTI-** means *many.*
>
> **-IZE** means *make* or *do.*

*Use your knowledge of word parts and the review above to fill in the blanks in the following sentences.*

1. To *categorize* (paragraph 3) tasks is to put them into several _____.

2. The ability to *multitask* (paragraph 8) is the ability to work on _____ tasks simultaneously.

## B. UNDERSTANDING THE THESIS AND OTHER MAIN IDEAS

*Select the best answer.*

_____ 1. Which of the following best states the thesis or central thought of "Ten Proven Benefits of Being Bilingual"?

    a. Those who learn a language later in life never speak that language quite as well as those who speak it from birth.

    b. Research has shown many benefits of speaking more than one language.

    c. The bilingual have an advantage in relationships but are at a disadvantage in the workplace.

    d. People who speak only one language are generally able to concentrate better than those who speak more than one language.

_____ 2. The main idea of paragraph 3 is found in the

    a. first sentence.

    b. second sentence.

    c. third sentence.

    d. last sentence.

_____  3. The topics of paragraphs 2–11 can all be found in

    a. the last sentence of each paragraph.

    b. the first sentence of each paragraph.

    c. the heading that precedes each paragraph.

    d. the summary paragraph that concludes the reading.

## C. IDENTIFYING DETAILS

*In the following list, place an X next to the benefits of being bilingual that are discussed in the reading.*

_____  Greater control over literacy skills

_____  Better relationships with parents

_____  Quicker response time

_____  Increased likelihood of working for a multinational corporation

_____  Better communication with neighbors and co-workers

_____  Better ability to focus on tasks

_____  Increased environmental awareness

_____  Stronger creativity

_____  Faster language acquisition

_____  Higher levels of self-awareness

_____  Better scores on IQ tests

_____  Getting better grades in mandatory college courses

_____  Slower onset of dementia

## D. RECOGNIZING METHODS OF ORGANIZATION AND TRANSITIONS

*Select the best answer.*

_____  1. The overall pattern of organization used in this reading is

    a. classification.

    b. comparison and contrast.

    c. order of importance.

    d. enumeration or listing.

_____  2. Paragraph 3 makes use of several organization patterns. One pattern is comparison and contrast. Another is

    a. cause and effect.

    b. process.

    c. chronological order.

    d. definition.

_____ 3. The transitional word or phrase used in paragraph 5 to show contrast is

   a. when presented with.

   b. adroitly.

   c. held no influence.

   d. however.

## E. READING AND THINKING VISUALLY

*Select the best answer.*

_____ 1. The photo on page 540 shows words and their translations between English and Spanish. In the context of the reading, what is this photo implying?

   a. Bilingual people go back and forth between two languages with ease.

   b. Spanish is one of the easiest languages for native English speakers to learn.

   c. English is one of the easiest languages for native Spanish speakers to learn.

   d. Any study of a foreign language should begin with the words and phrases of everyday communication.

## F. FIGURING OUT IMPLIED MEANINGS

*Indicate whether each statement is true (T) or false (F).*

_____ 1. Bilingual people tend to be more aware of, and more in tune with, their surroundings.

_____ 2. Younger people enjoy more benefits of bilingualism than older people do.

_____ 3. Those who speak more than one language are less likely to get Alzheimer's disease at a young age.

_____ 4. Many of the benefits of being bilingual come from the brain being "trained" to switch back and forth between languages.

_____ 5. Gray matter in the brain is largely responsible for a person's intelligence level.

_____ 6. The benefits of bilingualism are greater for those who are taught multiple languages from birth than they are for people who learn a second language in school.

_____ 7. If you had to summarize the benefits of bilingualism in one phrase, a good choice would be "greater intellectual and mental flexibility."

## G. THINKING CRITICALLY: ANALYZING THE AUTHOR'S TECHNIQUES

*Select the best answer.*

_____ 1. The overall purpose of "Ten Proven Brain Benefits of Being Bilingual" is to

a. help readers determine which second language it will be easiest for them to learn.

b. encourage colleges to offer courses in more languages, such as Mandarin Chinese, Japanese, and Tagalog.

c. warn students of the dangers of putting off their language requirement until their final semester of college.

d. educate readers about the general and specific advantages that bilingual people enjoy.

_____ 2. The overall tone of the reading can best be described as

a. tentative.

b. enthusiastic.

c. neutral.

d. offhand.

_____ 3. The author uses all of the following to support the reading's main ideas *except*

a. hospital studies.

b. personal experience.

c. research from universities.

d. historical studies from 1974 and 1986.

_____ 4. The selection is primarily

a. fact based.

b. opinion based.

c. speculative.

d. unreliable.

## H. THINKING CRITICALLY: ANALYZING THE AUTHOR'S MESSAGE

*Select the best answer.*

_____ 1. According to the reading, what is the "body's most important organ" (paragraph 1)?

a. the heart

b. the liver

c. the pancreas

d. the brain

_____ 2. Paragraph 4 discusses "outside-the-box" thinking. This is a type of thinking that

    a. is learned primarily from textbooks.

    b. pushes past conventional boundaries and into the realm of creative thinking.

    c. is encouraged in grammar, middle, and high schools in the United States.

    d. closely examines and evaluates just one side of an argument.

_____ 3. Which word or phrase does the reading use to describe a closer, more intimate understanding of verbal and nonverbal communication?

    a. structural similarities (paragraph 5)

    b. metalinguistic (paragraph 6)

    c. gray matter (paragraph 9)

    d. greater intellectual flexibility (paragraph 11)

_____ 4. The "cost on the front end" (paragraph 6) refers to the fact that

    a. the costs of funding research into the positive and negative effects of bilingualism are quite high.

    b. people learn more quickly earlier in life, and more slowly later in life.

    c. college is an investment that requires a good deal of money paid up front in the hopes of getting a good-paying job later on.

    d. children who are learning more than one language early in life tend to learn those languages more slowly than children who are learning only one language.

_____ 5. In paragraph 10, the article refers to multilingualism as a "cognitive steroid dialing up the brain's potential." What does this phrase mean?

    a. Multilingualism is a powerful brain booster.

    b. Multilingualism is all about unrealized potential in the brain.

    c. The more languages a person learns, the greater that person's intellectual flexibility.

    d. The developing brain is extremely complex, so no accurate generalizations can be drawn about the language-acquisition process.

## WRITING IN RESPONSE TO THE READING

### I. REVIEWING AND ORGANIZING IDEAS WITH A MAP

*Complete the map of the reading by filling in the blanks.*

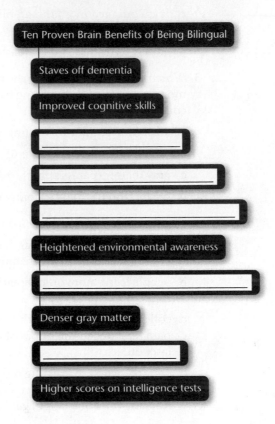

Ten Proven Brain Benefits of Being Bilingual

Staves off dementia

Improved cognitive skills

Heightened environmental awareness

Denser gray matter

Higher scores on intelligence tests

### J. ANALYZING THE ISSUE AND ARGUMENT

1. This reading discusses the benefits of bilingualism and multilingualism. How do these topics relate to other contemporary issues? List at least two contemporary issues about language that are currently being debated or discussed. Phrase each in the form of a question.

2. Prepare a one-sentence summary of the reading's thesis or central thought.

3. What kinds of typographical aids does the article use to help readers learn the material?

4. Examine the Web site from which this reading is taken. How credible do you find the site? Do you find any bias on the Web site or in the selection?

5. Evaluate the reading on the following criteria:

   a. Is the reading timely?

   b. Does the selection provide sufficient evidence to support its main ideas? Are specific details regarding the research studies provided? What other types of evidence might be provided to strengthen the arguments in the reading?

   c. Are key terms well defined?

   d. Does the article offer any opposing viewpoints? Can you think of any reasons why it would be better to be monolingual rather than bilingual?

   e. What assumptions (either stated or implied) do you find in the reading?

   f. Does the article offer any emotional appeals? If so, identify them and evaluate their fairness.

## K. WRITING PARAGRAPHS AND ESSAYS

*Write a paragraph or essay in response to the following writing prompts.*

1. What language would you like to learn? Write a paragraph explaining why you'd like to learn that language.

2. This reading points to the many benefits of being bilingual. Can you think of any drawbacks to being bilingual? Write a paragraph in which you explore this topic.

3. The selection includes a photo on page 540. Either write a caption to accompany this photo, or write a paragraph in which you describe another type of photo that could be used to effectively convey the information in the reading.

4. In some countries, students begin learning a second language as soon as they start school. Do you think the United States should institute this policy? Write an essay in which you argue this point, pro or con.

5. If you speak a language other than English, write an essay describing how the two languages are similar or different. (In other words, write a comparison and contrast essay.)

6. The reading discusses bilingualism's role in creativity. Write an essay in which you describe a creative person you know or admire. What do you admire about the person's creativity? What makes him or her so creative? In what areas do you feel you possess the most creativity?

# SELECTION 18
MySkillsLab

# What Is Residential Segregation?

## Mona Scott

TEXTBOOK
SELECTION

### SOURCE AND CONTEXT

The United States has always been a nation of immigrants, many voluntary (for example, the original Pilgrims) and many involuntary (slaves brought from Africa). It is estimated that within three decades, white people will become a minority group in the United States as the populations of current minority groups (such as Asian Americans and Latinos) continue to rise.

Within the United States, and in many other countries, immigrant minorities often live in segregated areas due to their lower socioeconomic status. Keep this background in mind as you read "What Is Residential Segregation?" The reading is taken from an introductory textbook, *THINK Race and Ethnicity*, by Mona Scott. The author is a professor of sociology at Mesa Community College in Arizona. For her research, Professor Scott draws on her observations growing up on the Navajo Indian Reservation, in South Central Los Angeles, and in the border town of Winslow, Arizona.

### A NOTE ON THE READING

How far has the United States come in terms of racial integration? Read "What Is Residential Segregation?" for a look at some of the effects of racial segregation by neighborhood.

### PREVIEWING THE READING

*Using the steps listed on page 4, preview the reading selection. When you have finished, complete the following items.*

1. This article will define and discuss the consequences of _____.

2. The author will discuss the consequences of residential segregation in relation to
   a. education
   b. _____.
   c. _____.
   d. _____.

MAKING
CONNECTIONS

*Can you divide up your town, county, or neighborhood based on the residents'*
*income levels, ethnic background, and/or race? Who lives where, and why?*

READING TIP

*As you read, note the tone of the selection. How does the author feel about her topic?*
*How does her use of language signal her approach to the subject?*

# What Is Residential Segregation?

Mona Scott

## Residential Segregation

1   When most people look for a house to buy or an apartment to rent, their principal concerns tend to be related to financial considerations, school districts, local services, and transportation. However, there are may be underlying and historic factors that lead people to live where they do. Cities all over the country have communities, suburbs, or neighborhoods that are defined by their predominant group: rich neighborhood, gay area, retirement community, Latino suburb, and so forth. This grouping of people in residential areas by a defining characteristic such as age, socioeconomic status, religion, race, or ethnicity is known as residential segregation.

2   One might be hard-pressed to think of anything wrong with a 70-year-old couple wanting to live in a retirement community. However, residential segregation does not always occur by choice; it may be driven by discrimination, both overt and covert. When residential segregation is drawn along racial lines, it is called racial residential segregation. As a major component of American society, racial residential segregation is responsible for the construction of the urban **underclass** and has had several consequences, particularly for African Americans, Latinos, and Native Americans. As a systemic problem, racial residential segregation diminishes the social and economic success of non-whites in the United States by sentencing them to a life in which poverty, joblessness, welfare, unwed motherhood, and lack of education are all a part of the standard social environment. This social environment is typically contained in segregated neighborhoods that concentrate poverty and reinforce and promote the decline of the non-white community.

> **underclass** group of people who are permanently consigned to poverty

3   We may think of residential segregation, particularly based on racial or ethnic discrimination, as a thing of the past. But a 2008 report to the United Nations Committee on the Elimination of Racial Discrimination shows that residential segregation by race is still prevalent in the United States. At the time of the report, U.S. Census data showed that the neighborhood of an average White American in a metropolitan area was 80 percent White and 7 percent Black. This differed greatly to the neighborhood of the average Black American, which was only 30 percent White and up to 51 percent Black. Daniel Lichter's study of racial segregation in rural areas and small

towns in the United States showed similar trends, with Blacks being the most highly segregated non-white group.

4      Additional studies have shown that residential segregation is not just between Blacks and Whites and that it extends beyond major metropolitan areas. Micropolitan areas, or communities with core urban populations between 10,000 and 50,000, are also settings for residential segregation, particularly for Latinos, whose populations have increased in these smaller communities due to the need for labor in rural industries. A recent study on this issue confirms that Latino-White segregation persists in micropolitan areas and reveals that it is the result of a growing Latino population and coinciding White **outmigration**. Latino concentration is especially strong in towns that border Mexico. In Southwest border towns such as Nogales, Arizona, and Rio Grande City, Texas, Latinos account for 81 percent and 98 percent of the population, respectively.

**outmigration**
the movement of people out of a specific area

## Consequences of Residential Segregation

5      There are many consequences of residential segregation. Housing inequality is just one issue, though important, as it can limit educational, career, and economic opportunities for those in highly segregated, high-poverty communities. If a family's housing options are limited, their choice of school district is limited as well—if you can't live in the area of your choice, your kids likely cannot go to the school of their choice either. This could conceivably affect future educational opportunities and earning potential. Furthermore, segregation concentrates poverty, which has obviously **knock-down** effects on available services, businesses, buildings, safety, as well as education and employment opportunities. However, these examples are only part of the story.

**knock-down**
additional

## Education

6      There seem to be several important effects of segregation on education that are unrelated to the quality of the schools in the area. Various studies show the effect of non-whites living in racially segregated areas or attending racially homogenous schools. A 2000 study revealed that families showed gains in education and employment opportunities when they moved out of segregated housing projects to predominately white suburbs. Similarly, another study showed that Blacks attending racially integrated schools were more likely to attend college than those who attended predominately black high schools.

7      Segregation can also affect academic performance. Latinos and Blacks who grew up segregated demonstrated lower academic performance. Factors such as socioeconomic status, differences in school quality, intellect, and social and psychological preparation were all controlled for in the study. Segregated students were also shown to have greater exposure to violence and to be more likely to have stressful life experiences and poorer heath, which further contributed to lower academic performance.

## Safety

8      Safety issues are another consequence of segregation. History shows that non-white neighborhoods have been the target of violent attacks and, in some cases, bombings as a hostile response to the non-whites' presence. The safety of racially segregated neighborhoods may be at further risk than other neighborhoods.

Do you think that segregation and discrimination are cyclical?

A 1988 study by the Los Angeles Police Department found that response times to 911 calls originating in non-white neighborhoods were significantly slower than in other neighborhoods. Although the Los Angeles Police Department denied any intentional bias, the difference still exists.

## Feeling Out of Place

9    Segregation can also have an impact on a non-white group's own perception of discrimination. That is, individuals residing in racially segregated areas may feel even more discriminated than others of the same race who do not live in racially segregated areas. A case study of Chinese immigrants in Toronto found that Chinese immigrants who lived in areas of high concentrations of other Chinese were more likely to feel discrimination against their ethnic group. Similarly, they also were more likely to report being victims of verbal abuse, such as racial slurs, compared to other Chinese immigrants who did not live in neighborhoods with high numbers of the same ethnicity. Living in segregated areas essentially puts non-white groups on their own island. When they enter exterior neighborhoods, they can feel like outsiders in their own city. This feeling is reflected in Roberto Gonzales's experiences growing up in one of the oldest Mexican neighborhoods in Los Angeles: "When I was growing up in East L.A. in the fifties, you knew where the Mexican areas were, and when you wandered out of those, you saw very few of us in places like Santa Monica and the west side . . . I would feel kind of funny . . . I felt out of place; I wouldn't see any other Mexicans at all." Because members of non-white groups who live in segregated areas often feel like outsiders, they may anticipate discrimination more than those who live in integrated areas.

## Physical Health

10    In addition to the psychological effects of racial residential segregation, there may even be physical effects, apart from the effect on one's heath due to the limited health care services of an area. The findings of one recent study looking at the relationship between the racial isolation of African Americans and body weight suggests that African Americans who live in more racially segregated areas are at higher risk for being overweight, whereas there seemed to be no similar correlation in the case of Whites. Other studies show that segregated Blacks have a higher mortality rate than Blacks in integrated neighborhoods, and that segregated non-whites are generally exposed to greater health risks. This may be one of the reasons why immigrants typically come to the United States healthier than the average American but over the course of one generation see that health decline.

**Homeownership Rates by Race and
Hispanic Origin, U.S. Census 2000**

| | |
|---|---|
| Total population | 66.2% |
| Non-Hispanic whites | 72.4% |
| Black only | 46.3% |
| Hispanic | 45.7% |
| Asian only | 53.4% |
| American Indian/Alaskan Native | 55.5% |
| Native Hawaiian/Pacific Islander | 45.0% |
| Other race | 40.5% |
| Two or more races | 46.3% |

This chart shows home ownership rates for the year 2000. How do
the home ownership rates compare to the total population, to
Whites, and across racial and ethnic groups?

**HUD**
the U.S. Department
of Housing and
Urban Development

**voucher
program**
government
program that
allows people
to move to new
neighborhoods
or their children
to attend schools
outside their
neighborhoods

**redlining**
an illegal
activity in
which banks
and other lenders
refuse to make
housing loans
to people who
want to buy
homes in what
are defined as
"undesirable"
neighborhoods

## Recommendations for Dismantling Racial Residential Segregation

11    The government and other public and private institutions have had a tremendous role in creating and perpetuating racial segregation. But what can and should they do to address the situation they have created? Scholars, researchers, and advocates have a lot to say about the role these institutions should take in rectifying the social and demographic circumstances that result from their own policies and practices.

12    In the 2008 U.N. report, U.S. housing scholars and research and advocacy organizations offered recommendations for dismantling racial residential segregation. They advocate changes in policy and practices in **HUD**, the Department of Justice, Congress, as well as state and local governments, and made recommendations for each of these institutions. The report suggests that HUD should take steps to facilitate the mobility of non-whites to integrated areas by promoting the development of public housing in nonsegregated areas. This can be done by creating a more inclusive **voucher program**, offering housing counseling for aid participants, and providing other services, such as job placement assistance. The Department of Justice should increase its resources and efforts to investigate and prosecute violations of housing and lending discrimination, such as racial steering and **redlining**. Subsequently, Congress should pass tougher laws against predatory lending practices, such as requiring that mortgage lenders adhere to uniform pricing standards, and should clarify fair housing standards in the Low-Income Housing Tax Credit (LIHTC). For all of these changes to take place, state and local governments need to be committed to finding new ways to integrate schools, which will have a future effect on integration of communities.

13    The report points out that studies have shown that students from integrated schools are more likely to have increased contact with other races later in life. States should require inclusionary zoning to promote integration by requiring that affordable housing be included in new developments.

14    While the government must create and rebuild programs and policies to combat segregation and promote integration, it is important to note that physical integration does not always equate to social integration. For example, Blacks, Whites, and Latinos, among other races, can all live in the same neighborhoods, have children who attend the same school, and work in similar industries. But this proximity does not necessarily mean their lives are integrated. Professor Leonard Steinhorn and Barbara Diggs-Brown explain, "Call it racial civility, decorous integration, or the politeness conspiracy—the bottom line is that our professed attitudes, symbols, and

public expression masquerade as integrated when our lives clearly are not. And what people say is less important than what they do." Furthermore, physical integration can be fleeting, Steinhorn and Diggs-Brown further state. "Integration exists only in the time span between the first black family moving in and the last white family moving out." That implies that integration will remain an illusion if all members of society do not recognize the realities of the problem.

# UNDERSTANDING AND ANALYZING THE READING

## A. BUILDING VOCABULARY

### Context

*Using context and a dictionary if necessary, determine the meaning of each word as it is used in the selection.*

_____ 1. covert (paragraph 2)
   a. hidden
   b. illegal
   c. social
   d. governmental

_____ 2. component (paragraph 2)
   a. drawback
   b. part
   c. type
   d. history

_____ 3. diminishes (paragraph 2)
   a. lessens
   b. affects
   c. divides
   d. prevents

_____ 4. consequences (paragraph 2)
   a. examples
   b. results
   c. patterns
   d. controversies

_____ 5. conceivably (paragraph 5)
   a. thoughtfully
   b. possibly
   c. negatively
   d. narrowly

_____ 6. impact (paragraph 9)
   a. strike
   b. meteor
   c. effect
   d. movement

_____ 7. correlation (paragraph 10)
   a. familiarity
   b. history
   c. relationship
   d. effect

_____ 8. mortality (paragraph 10)
   a. disease
   b. dropout
   c. immigration
   d. death

_____ 9. dismantling (paragraph 12)
   a. encouraging
   b. improving
   c. taking apart
   d. pushing

_____ 10. adhere (paragraph 12)
   a. conform
   b. institute
   c. disagree
   d. nullify

## Word Parts

> ### A REVIEW OF PREFIXES
>
> **MICRO-** means *small*.
>
> **HOMO-** means *same*.

*Use your knowledge of word parts and the review above to fill in the blanks in the following sentences.*

1. A *metropolitan* area refers to a large city; a *micropolitan* (paragraph 4) area refers to a _____ city.

2. A school with a *homogeneous* (paragraph 6) population refers to a school whose students come from the _____ background, ethnicity, or social class.

## B. UNDERSTANDING THE THESIS AND OTHER MAIN IDEAS

*Select the best answer.*

_____ 1. Which of the following best states the thesis or central thought of "What Is Residential Segregation?"

    a. Residential segregation occurs when people reside in neighborhoods based on age, socioeconomic status, religion, or ethnicity, while racial residential segregation refers to residential separation based on race (such as White, Black, or Latino).

    b. Those who live in racially segregated neighborhoods are subject to a wide variety of disadvantages that lower their chances of success in life but improve their chances of becoming a victim of a violent crime.

    c. We can put an end to residential segregation in two ways: by ensuring that government agencies make sure that banks obey the laws, and by sponsoring programs and policies that promote integration, such as voucher systems and "Big Brothers and Big Sisters"-type programs.

    d. Residential segregation based on race, which is quite common today, has numerous effects on people's lives (including their education, safety, health, and security); several recommendations have been made for ending residential racial segregation, which will be a very difficult goal to achieve.

_____ 2. The main idea of paragraph 2 is found in the

    a. first sentence.

    b. second sentence.

    c. third sentence.

    d. last sentence.

_____ 3. The topic of paragraph 10 is

    a. the presence of African Americans in inner-city neighborhoods.

    b. the causes and effects of obesity.

    c. physical effects of racial residential segregation.

    d. the health of immigrant parents and their children.

## C. IDENTIFYING DETAILS

*Select the best answer.*

_____ 1. Daniel Lichter studied racial segregation in

    a. the Southern United States.

    b. rural areas and small towns.

    c. New England.

    d. the United Kingdom.

_____ 2. In which U.S. city do Latinos account for 98 percent of the population?

    a. Brownsville

    b. Phoenix

    c. Nogales

    d. Rio Grande City

_____ 3. According to the reading, when looking to rent an apartment or buy a house, people tend to consider all of the following factors *except*

    a. money.

    b. school districts.

    c. transportation.

    d. proximity to family.

_____ 4. The ethnic group most commonly associated with unskilled rural labor is

    a. Blacks.

    b. Latinos.

    c. Native Americans.

    d. Asians.

_____ 5. One of the oldest Mexican neighborhoods in Los Angeles is

    a. La Cienega.

    b. Santa Monica.

    c. Compton.

    d. East Los Angeles.

## D. RECOGNIZING METHODS OF ORGANIZATION AND TRANSITIONS

*Select the best answer.*

_____ 1. The pattern of organization used in paragraph 1 is

    a. listing/enumeration.

    b. definition.

    c. process.

    d. classification.

_____ 2. All of the following transitional phrases points to the organizational pattern of paragraph 1 *except*

    a. principal concerns.

    b. are defined by.

    c. a defining characteristic.

    d. is known as.

_____ 3. The overall organizational pattern used in paragraphs 5–10 is

    a. chronological order.

    b. definition.

    c. listing/enumeration.

    d. comparison and contrast.

## E. READING AND THINKING VISUALLY

*Select the best answer.*

_____ 1. The author likely chose to include the photo and caption on page 553 in order to

    a. point to the growing Latino population in the United States.

    b. illustrate the way Latino immigrants are displacing African American residents of major U.S. cities.

    c. imply that racially segregated neighborhoods are often dangerous.

    d. provide a visual example of residential segregation by race.

_____ 2. According to the bar graph on page 553, which group has the second-highest rate of home ownership in the United States?

    a. Non-Hispanic Whites

    b. Asian only

    c. American Indian/Alaskan Native

    d. Black only

## F. FIGURING OUT IMPLIED MEANINGS

*Indicate whether each statement is true (T) or false (F).*

_____ 1. Residential segregation peaked in 1990 but has diminished since then.

_____ 2. Black students are more likely to attend college when they attend an integrated high school than when they attend a segregated high school.

_____ 3. The author believes that racial segregation is tied to the presence of a permanent underclass in the United States.

_____ 4. Children tend to do better in school when they move out of a racially segregated area and into a predominantly white suburb.

_____ 5. The children of immigrant parents tend to be less healthy than their parents.

_____ 6. Latinos are the most segregated non-White group.

_____ 7. Students who have attended segregated schools are more likely to have increased contact with other races later in life.

_____ 8. White neighborhoods tend to be safer than non-White neighborhoods.

## G. THINKING CRITICALLY: ANALYZING THE AUTHOR'S TECHNIQUE

*Select the best answer.*

_____ 1. The author's primary purpose in "What Is Residential Segregation?" is to

    a. provide an overview of racial residential segregation, discuss its effects on minority populations, and propose ways to end it.

    b. advocate for forced integration of schools in large metropolitan areas and in less populated rural areas within the United States.

    c. provide a critique of U.S. government policies over the past five decades, none of which have succeeded in ending racial segregation.

    d. analyze the effects of housing and neighborhood choice on the careers, incomes, and families of urban (city) dwellers in the United States.

_____ 2. The tone of the selection is best described as

    a. sympathetic toward minority groups.

    b. detached and unemotional.

    c. biased against white people.

    d. nostalgic and wistful.

_____ 3. Which of the following statements from the reading does *not* have a negative connotation?

    a. "As a systemic problem, racial segregation diminishes the social and economic success of non-whites in the United States by sentencing them to a life in which poverty, joblessness, welfare, unwed motherhood, and lack of education are all a part of the standard social environment." (paragraph 2)

    b. "This social environment is typically contained in segregated neighborhoods that concentrate poverty and reinforce and promote the decline of the non-white community." (paragraph 2)

    c. "Housing inequality is just one issue, though important, as it can limit educational, career, and economic opportunities for those in highly segregated, high-poverty communities." (paragraph 5)

    d. "The report points out that studies have shown that students from integrated schools are more likely to have increased contact with other races later in life." (paragraph 13)

_____ 4. To support her thesis and main ideas, the author uses primarily which type of evidence?

    a. personal experience

    b. research studies

    c. historical data from the nineteenth century

    d. analogies

_____ 5. Which of the following is a statement of opinion, not a statement of fact?

    a. "But a 2008 report to the United Nations Committee on the Elimination of Racial Discrimination shows that residential segregation by race is still prevalent in the United States." (paragraph 3)

    b. "In Southwest border towns such as Nogales, Arizona, and Rio Grande City, Texas, Latinos account for 81 percent and 98 percent of the population, respectively." (paragraph 4)

    c. "Although the Los Angeles Police Department denied any intentional bias, the difference still exists." (paragraph 8)

    d. "States should require inclusionary zoning to promote integration by requiring that affordable housing be included in new developments." (paragraph 13)

## H. THINKING CRITICALLY: ANALYZING THE AUTHOR'S MESSAGE

*Select the best answer.*

_____ 1. The term the author uses to refer to all minorities is
   a. non-white.
   b. ethnic groups.
   c. immigrants.
   d. gentiles.

_____ 2. The author suggests that the primary responsibility for eliminating residential segregation by race lies with
   a. landlords.
   b. government.
   c. employers.
   d. community leaders.

_____ 3. In which of the following situations does the author imply that residential segregation may be acceptable?
   a. when immigrants first move to the United States
   b. when most family members live in a particular neighborhood
   c. when people have other choices open to them but make a conscious choice to live in a segregated neighborhood
   d. when school districts require students to live in a particular neighborhood in order to attend specific schools

_____ 4. What does the author mean by the term "politeness conspiracy" (paragraph 14)?
   a. the tendency for most people to be polite rather than rude when interacting in a social setting
   b. the idea that most people who are polite on the surface are actually hiding their true feelings behind false smiles
   c. the disconnect between the *idea* that society is integrated and the *reality* that society is not integrated
   d. the desire of most white, non-minority people to live in more racially diverse neighborhoods

# WRITING IN RESPONSE TO THE READING

## I. REVIEWING AND ORGANIZING IDEAS WITH A PARAPHRASE

*Write a paraphrase of paragraphs 6–8 of the reading. Three sentences have been provided to help you get started.*

Residential segregation has several effects on education. These effects are not related to school quality. The Los Angeles police say that any bias is unintentional, but the difference cannot be denied.

_____

_____

_____

_____

_____

_____

## J. ANALYZING THE ISSUE AND ARGUMENT

1. What contemporary issue is the author discussing in this reading? Phrase the issue in the form of a question.

2. List at least two arguments the author makes in "What Is Residential Segregation?" Phrase each in the form of a one- or two-sentence summary of the author's argument.

3. Based on the source from which this reading is taken, do you think the information provided is reliable? Why or why not?

4. Closely examine the language in the reading. Do you perceive any bias? Explain your response.

5. Has the author provided sufficient evidence to support her main ideas? What other types of evidence might she provide to make her main ideas stronger?

6. Evaluate the reading on the following criteria:

   a. Is the information timely?

   b. Has the author defined her terms accurately and sufficiently?

   c. Does the author offer opposing viewpoints? If so, what is her attitude toward them, and does she discredit them fairly or unfairly? If not, what might some opposing viewpoints be? List and evaluate them.

   d. Does the reading make any emotional appeals to readers? If so, identify them and evaluate their fairness.

   e. Discuss the author's assumptions. Are these explicitly stated or implied? What claims of value are stated or implied?

   f. In which specific paragraph(s) does the author state her claim(s) of policy?

## K.  WRITING PARAGRAPHS AND ESSAYS

*Write a paragraph or essay in response to the following writing prompts.*

1.  The caption that accompanies the photo on page 553 asks, "Do you think that segregation and discrimination are cyclical?" In other words, "Do you think segregation and discrimination go in cycles, with different groups being discriminated against at different times?" Write a paragraph in which you respond to this question.

2.  In your city, county, or neighborhood, do you see a pattern of residential segregation? For example, do wealthy people live in one part of town, poor people in another part of town? Write a paragraph in which you examine the patterns you see.

3.  Write a paragraph in which you answer the questions raised in the caption to the figure titled "Homeownership Rates by Race and Hispanic Origin, U.S. Census 2000" (page 553).

4.  The word *segregation* refers to an enforced separation of groups. But, as the author points out, some people may choose to self-segregate based on their own wishes (for example, in a retirement community). Write an essay in which you explore the benefits and/or drawbacks of self-segregation.

5.  Some charter schools (schools that receive state or government funding to provide alternative educational options to those provided in public schools) have chosen to segregate their student population by allowing only male students or only female students. What is your opinion of schools that follow this policy? What might be the advantages of such a policy? The disadvantages? Write an essay exploring your thoughts.

6.  In paragraph 14, the author states, "Physical integration does not always equate to social integration." Write an essay in which you explore this argument. Do you agree? Use your own observations and evidence from your own life to support your thesis and main ideas.

## ACTIVITIES: EXPLORING SOCIAL ISSUES AND CONTROVERSIES

*On your own or with a group of classmates, complete two of the following four activities.*

1. Selection 18 focuses on bullying among teenagers (with a brief reference to bullying in grammar school). Make a list of at least five ways that bullying can happen among adults. (Consider the workplace and the college campus, for example.) What recommendations would you make for eliminating each type of bullying?

   *Example*: A salesperson bullies someone into buying an expensive extended warranty.

   * _____

   * _____

   * _____

   * _____

   * _____

2. An important part of any society is its traditions. Which traditions does society as a whole follow, and which traditions do you personally follow? List at least three of each.

   **Social Traditions**

   Example: Observe 4ᵗʰ of July as a holiday.

   1. _____

   2. _____

   3. _____

   **Personal Traditions**

   Example: Celebrate my birthday with a group of friends.

   1. _____

   2. _____

   3. _____

3. The readings in this chapter discussed just a few of the issues related to society. Other questions often or sometimes asked about society include:

   * Should polygamy (marriage to more than one spouse) be legal? Why or why not? This debate rages in certain U.S. states, such as Utah and Texas.

   * Do Hollywood celebrities receive special treatment from courts when they break the law?

   * Should society provide financial assistance and medical care to recent immigrants who have come to the country legally or illegally?

   * How should we punish those who bully others?

   Write an essay or prepare a class presentation about any of these topics, or any other topic regarding society.

4. Practice examining both sides of an argument (pro and con) by listing at least two "pros" and two "cons" for each of the following questions.

- Should American society try to equalize differences among the very rich and the very poor?
- Should we limit the number and types of weapons/guns that a person can buy?
- Should background checks be required before a person can purchase a gun?
- Have we lost the "War on Drugs"? Should we stop devoting so much money to this program and use the money more effectively on other social programs?
- Should we outlaw foods that we find unethical or unhealthy? (For example, some cities have outlawed *pate de fois gras*, which is a fatty goose liver, because they object to the cruelty that geese must undergo in order to fatten their livers.)

# 18 Conformity and Nonconformity: Following and Breaking the Rules

*Do you follow the rules, or do you break them? Do you do what's expected of you, or do you do your own thing?*

Every society is ruled by *norms*, which are spoken or unspoken rules of behavior. We grow up surrounded by these norms, and they become part of us. For example, even as a child, long before you have a driver's license, you learn that a red light means "stop." Many social scientists believe that without norms, society would not be able to function. Those who follow the norms are said to *conform* to social expectations.

Here are some examples of the norms that influence our lives:

- Most children in the United States are required to attend school until they are 16.
- People are expected to behave properly in public and wear clothes that are appropriate for the situation.
- Mothers and fathers are expected to care for their children, and family members are expected to help take care of the elderly and sick.

But not everyone conforms to expected norms. For example, while many people who want to be successful follow the norm of attending college and then looking for a full-time job, others drop out of school and start their own businesses (Bill Gates of Microsoft is a famous example). While many people live a 9-to-5 life of work, family, and home, some people become musicians, living their lives mostly at night and traveling around the country (or the world) for much of the year.

In addition, norms are always undergoing change. In some areas, the "rules" are evolving or have not been defined yet. For instance, what types of etiquette do portable technologies require? Is it acceptable to talk on a cell phone on a crowded bus and in other public places? Should people be allowed to text while driving, or should laws be passed to prevent this?

This chapter offers three readings about conformity and how our personal decisions affect our lives, from the purchases we make, through the people we marry, to the lifestyles we choose. Throughout the readings you'll find examples of people who are following society's rules, as well as examples of people who are breaking the rules.

# WHY ARE CONFORMITY AND NONCONFORMITY SUCH IMPORTANT CONTEMPORARY ISSUES?

American society has always been individualistic. The image of the tough, rugged American goes back to frontier days, when people built their own houses and farmed the land in order to survive. It's no surprise, then, that so many Americans struggle with the "rules" they feel are imposed on them. For example, feminism was a direct result of women's desire to have more choices in their lives, and the Civil Right Movement was a direct result of people's desire to see all Americans treated equally and fairly. Many of these struggles are ongoing. To understand the options available to you and others, it is important to understand social expectations. Only then can you think critically about the pros and cons of conformity and decide which decisions are right for you.

## How Do Conformity and Nonconformity Tie in to My College Courses?

Understanding the norms of the major social institutions (such as family, education, and religion) is a key goal of most sociology courses. A subfield of psychology, *social psychology*, examines group behavior and expectations, the ways people behave in social settings. Literature courses are filled with tales of people who break the rules and do things their own way, while history and political science courses talk about larger-than-life figures (such as conquerors, generals, and presidents) whose unorthodox or individualistic beliefs and behaviors affected millions of people and changed society. And, of course, business courses teach the "rules" of business, from accounting through management, and talk about the consequences of breaking those rules (from getting fired through ending up in jail).

---

**TIPS FOR READING ABOUT CONFORMITY AND NONCONFORMITY**

Here are some tips for reading not only the selections in this chapter, but any reading about conformity and nonconformity.

- **Consider context.** Different groups of people may be guided by very different sets of norms. For example, as a college student, you are expected to study and attend all your classes. At some colleges, however, student athletes follow a different set of "rules" from most other students. Their main focus may be the sport they play rather than their studies. As you read, ask yourself what specific *part* of society the author is writing about.

- **Pay close attention to the examples.** Readings about conformity and nonconformity often focus on individuals. What exactly are these people doing to follow or break society's rules? What are the consequences of their actions, for themselves and others? What guides their behaviors?

- **Link the reading to your life, experiences, and opinions.** If you are reading a personal essay, put yourself in the author's position. Would you make the same choices or different choices? How would the opinions of others affect (or not affect) your choices?

**SELECTION 19**
MySkillsLab

# A Brother Lost

## Ashley Womble

MAGAZINE ARTICLE

### SOURCE AND CONTEXT

Ashley Womble lives in New York City. In the following article, which first appeared in *Salon* magazine in July 2010, the author writes about Jay, her mentally ill brother who became homeless.

### A NOTE ON THE READING

We often make assumptions about a certain group of people until we meet a member of that group who challenges us to re-examine our preconceived ideas. Oftentimes, we miss out on opportunities to broaden our circle of friendship because we ignore or shun those folks whose lives do not conform to our societal norms. Read "A Brother Lost" to understand how the author's perception of homelessness changed after her own brother became homeless.

### PREVIEWING THE READING

*Using the steps listed on page 4, preview the reading selection. When you have finished, complete the following items.*

1. This reading is about _____.
2. Jay suffered from a mental illness called _____.
3. The tragic event that led to Jay's manic belief in "the Cahoots" was _____.

MAKING CONNECTIONS

_____

*What experience have you had with homeless people? How would you describe the homeless people you have seen in your city? Have you ever tried to help someone who did not want your help?*

### READING TIP

*As you read, note how the author's perception of homelessness changes.*

# A Brother Lost

## Ashley Womble

1    Like any New Yorker, I was no stranger to homeless people. I passed by them on my way to the shiny glass tower where I worked for a glossy women's magazine: the older lady perched atop a milk crate in the subway station, the man curled up in a dirty sleeping bag and clutching a stuffed animal. They were unfortunate ornaments of the city, unlucky in ways I never really considered.

2    Until one hot summer day in 2009 when my little brother Jay left his key on the coffee table and walked out of his house in West Texas to live on the streets. In the days that followed I spent hours on the phone with detectives, social workers, and even the FBI, frantically trying to track him down. A friend designed a "Missing" poster using the most recent picture I had of him; he was wearing a hoodie and a Modest Mouse T-shirt, a can of beer in his hand and a deer-in-headlights expression on his face. I created a Facebook group and contacted old acquaintances still living in our hometown of Lubbock, begging everyone I even remotely knew to help me find him. No luck. If it had been me, a pretty young white woman, chances are my face would have been all over the news—but the sudden disappearance of a 20-year-old guy with **paranoid schizophrenia** didn't exactly warrant an **Amber Alert**.

**Paranoid Schizophrenia** a chronic mental illness in which a person suffers from delusions and hallucinations

**Amber Alert** a public alert system that spreads information about a missing person through broadcast media and electronic billboards on highways

3    In the year and a half that mental illness had ravaged my brother's mind, I'd learned to lower my expectations of what his life would be like. The smart kid who followed politics in elementary school probably wouldn't become a lawyer after all. Instead of going to college after high school, Jay became obsessed with 9/11 conspiracy theories. What began as merely eccentric curdled into something manic and disturbing: He believed the planners of 9/11 were a group of people called "the Cahoots" who had created a 24-hour television network to monitor his actions and control his thoughts. Eventually, his story expanded until the Cahoots became one branch of the New World Order, a government whose purpose was to overturn Christianity, and he had been appointed by God to stop it.

4    This made it hard for him to act normal, even in public. He'd lost his job busing tables after yelling "Stop the filming and hand over the tapes" to everyone dining in the restaurant. Having friends or even a coherent conversation wouldn't be possible unless he took the antipsychotic medication he'd been prescribed while he was in the mental hospital. A legal adult, he was allowed to refuse treatment, and he did. Otherwise the Cahoots would win.

5    I counted each day he'd been missing until they became weeks, until the number was so high I wondered if he was even still alive. That number was about the only thing I continued to keep track of. Dirty clothes and dishes piled up at home, I missed deadlines at work, and I got out of bed only if it was absolutely necessary. I cried often, but

especially during thunderstorms, a reminder that wherever my brother was, he was unprotected. Eventually it became clear that I was losing it, too. So I did what my brother wouldn't allow himself to do: I started taking a pill that helped usher away my anxiety and depression.

6   Weeks after Jay disappeared, police in Maryland found him talking to a spider and had him hospitalized. He stayed for 72 hours. Then he went missing again.

7   September 11, 2009, was one of those drizzling mornings when I thought of my brother. There was the usual undertone of reverent sadness in the city, but for me, the date was a reminder of all that had gone wrong inside Jay's mind. And on that day my phone finally rang.

8   "Hello." Jay's Southern drawl was unmistakable. I sat straight up in my desk chair at work wondering what I should do. Record the call? Take notes?

9   "Where are you?" I asked, as images of him sitting in a jail cell or stranded alone in an alley flashed in my head.

10   "Manhattan," he said.

11   My heart filled with hope. Then he asked me if I'd gone to the witchcraft celebration at the World Trade Center, where the Sorcerers had ordered the wind and the rain to destroy the ceremony. Once again, I just felt like a helpless stranger.

12   I asked nervously if I could buy him dinner. To my surprise, he agreed. Twenty minutes later I met him near Penn Station; he was hunched under an awning next to a big blue tarp that covered his backpack and the paisley duffel he'd once borrowed. His pale skin had tanned and hair covered his face. He was staring at people as they walked by, but he didn't see me until I said his name. Standing face-to-face with him, I could see that he had lost a lot of weight. His cheekbones jutted out from his once-full face. If I had seen his picture I would have gasped. Instead, I just held out my arms.

**Zagat**
a guide to
restaurants in a
particular city

13   **Zagat** has no recommendations for where to take your homeless brother to dinner. We settled on the Mexican chain Chevys and sat in a booth near the back. He told me about hitchhiking to New York and sleeping in Central Park until the cops kicked him out. He grinned as he talked about sleeping on the steps of a downtown school, his smile still as charming as it had been when he was 7.

14   "Do you consider yourself homeless?" I asked.

15   "Oh, yes!" he answered proudly.

16   I wondered if the constant motion of wandering from town to town helped quiet the voices he heard. If it was his own kind of medication and, if so, could I really tell him that was the wrong way to live?

17   Earlier in the year I'd bribed him with a trip to visit me on the condition that he took his meds. Now he was sitting in front of me, and as much as I wanted to let him stay in my apartment, I knew I couldn't let him (my therapist discouraged it and my roommate rightly put her foot down). I approached the topic cautiously, my voice shaking as I asked, "Do you know why you can't stay with me?" His voice small and shamed, he answered, "Because I won't take my medication." He had always denied that he had schizophrenia, but his admission gave me hope that maybe some day that would change.

18   I tried to quiet my own inner voice, which told me Jay needed to be in the hospital where a team of psychiatrists could experiment with medications that

would fix his mind. I could do some things for my brother: I could give him a little money for cigarettes. I could buy him a new backpack, a sleeping bag, good walking shoes. But the more I pushed him to get help, the more my own sanity escaped me.

19    So I let him go. He went to New Jersey. Florida. Louisiana. To a place where he told me from a pay phone he wouldn't call anymore because he didn't want me to know his whereabouts. I can only imagine what he looks like after a year on the streets: His hair must be long, skin tan and hardened, and his rail-thin body caked in dirt. He probably doesn't look much different from the homeless people I pass by on the streets of New York City. Seeing them makes my heart ache, makes me think about those they may have left behind, people who long to dust them off and put them on the right path but who know, in the end, it's not their choice.

# UNDERSTANDING AND ANALYZING THE READING

## A. BUILDING VOCABULARY

### Context

*Using context and a dictionary if necessary, determine the meaning of each word as it is used in the selection.*

_____ 1. warrant (paragraph 2)
   a. cause
   b. justify
   c. offer
   d. document

_____ 2. ravaged (paragraph 3)
   a. starved to death
   b. invaded forcefully
   c. teased mercilessly
   d. caused terrible damage

_____ 3. eccentric (paragraph 3)
   a. inborn
   b. extreme
   c. odd
   d. challenging

_____ 4. curdled (paragraph 3)
   a. molded
   b. floated
   c. turned bad
   d. disappeared

_____ 5. coherent (paragraph 4)
   a. logical
   b. entertaining
   c. serious
   d. illogical

_____ 6. usher (paragraph 5)
   a. send
   b. escort
   c. throw
   d. challenge

_____  7. reverent (paragraph 7)
    a. respectful
    b. uncontrollable
    c. great
    d. approving

_____  8. admission (paragraph 17)
    a. confidence
    b. enlightenment
    c. confession
    d. humility

_____  9. sanity (paragraph 18)
    a. strong desire
    b. mental illness
    c. courage
    d. mental soundness

## Word Parts

---

### A REVIEW OF PREFIXES

**ANTI-** means *against*

**DIS-** means *not*, *apart*, or *away.*

---

*Use your knowledge of word parts and the review above to fill in the blanks in the following sentences.*

1. *Antipsychotic* medications (paragraph 4) are medications that work
_____ psychosis to improve a person's mental health.

2. The therapist who *discouraged* (paragraph 17) the author did
_____ encourage her to let her brother stay with her.

## B. UNDERSTANDING THE THESIS AND OTHER MAIN IDEAS

*Select the best answer.*

_____  1. The best statement of the thesis or central thought of "A Brother Lost" is
    a. people who suffer from mental illness are lost.
    b. one's preconceived notions about groups of people are oftentimes shattered after one gets to know and understand someone in the group.
    c. love for one's family member cannot be extinguished by the ravages of a mental illness.
    d. it is futile to try to help someone who does not want to be helped.

_____ 2. The topic of paragraph 4 is
   a. the Cahoots.
   b. busing tables.
   c. Jay's abnormal behavior.
   d. the antipsychotic medicine.

_____ 3. What is the implied main idea of paragraph 19?
   a. We cannot help someone who does not want to be helped.
   b. Everyone who is homeless has chosen to be homeless.
   c. Most homeless people have families who love them.
   d. Homeless people are dirty, thin, and sickly.

## C. IDENTIFYING DETAILS

_Select the best answer._

_____ 1. In which state did Jay live before he disappeared?
   a. Arizona
   b. New York
   c. Texas
   d. Florida

_____ 2. The purpose of the Jay's imagined New World Order was to
   a. control the thoughts of all people.
   b. monitor the actions of all people.
   c. overturn Christianity.
   d. abolish all government.

_____ 3. Jay lost his job because
   a. he couldn't carry on a coherent conversation with customers.
   b. he failed to show up for work regularly.
   c. he yelled out "Stop the filming and hand over the tapes" to customers in the dining room.
   d. he passed out literature and solicited members for the New World Order while at work.

_____ 4. What does Jay believe about 9/11?
   a. It was planned by terrorists who had been appointed by God.
   b. It was planned by the Cahoots.
   c. It was planned and carried out by mentally ill rebels.
   d. It was televised in an attempt to control the minds of Americans.

## D. RECOGNIZING METHODS OF ORGANIZATION AND TRANSITIONS

*Select the best answer.*

_____ 1. The organizational pattern used in paragraph 2 is
   a. listing/enumeration.
   b. classification.
   c. order of importance.
   d. chronological order.

_____ 2. What is the dominant organizational pattern of paragraph 3?
   a. comparison-contrast
   b. illustration
   c. cause-effect
   d. definition

_____ 3. Which transitional word or phrase is a clue to the dominant organizational pattern of paragraph 2?
   a. in the days that followed
   b. created and contacted
   c. even the FBI
   d. still living in our hometown

## E. READING AND THINKING VISUALLY

*Select the best answer.*

_____ 1. The author likely chose to include the photo on page 569 to
   a. illustrate the threat that a woman feels when she walks the streets of New York.
   b. illustrate the juxtaposition of good and evil.
   c. illustrate the differences between living in light and living in darkness.
   d. illustrate the indifference people have toward the homeless.

## F. FIGURING OUT IMPLIED MEANINGS

*Indicate whether each statement is true (T) or false (F).*

_____ 1. Before the encounter with her brother, the author ignored the homeless people that she passed each day.
_____ 2. The author implies that all homeless people are mentally ill.

_____ 3. The author believes that mentally ill people should be institutionalized and forced to take medication.

_____ 4. According to the author, mentally ill people are not able to hold down a job.

_____ 5. The author implies that the news media are not interested in the plight of the mentally ill.

_____ 6. The author believes that her brother's life would have been different if he had taken his medication.

_____ 7. The author suggests that her mother and father were not actively involved in her brother's life because of his mental illness.

## G. THINKING CRITICALLY: ANALYZING THE AUTHOR'S TECHNIQUES

*Select the best answer.*

_____ 1. The author's main purpose in "A Brother Lost" is to

  a. motivate others to volunteer with organizations that serve the mentally ill and the homeless.

  b. tell the story of her mentally ill and homeless brother in hopes that others will have a greater understanding of this segment of the population.

  c. provide a detailed psychological explanation of what happens to the mentally ill when they do not take their medication.

  d. tell the story of how she lost her brother to mental illness.

_____ 2. The intended audience for "A Lost Brother" is

  a. those who have a mentally ill family member.

  b. the mentally ill.

  c. the homeless.

  d. all people in society.

_____ 3. The tone of the reading selection can best be described as

  a. serious and introspective.

  b. comic and dismissive.

  c. nostalgic and critical.

  d. admiring and informative.

_____ 4. To support her thesis and main ideas, the author uses all of the following types of evidence except

  a. research citations.

  b. personal experience.

  c. examples of bizarre behavior.

  d. description.

_____ 5. Which one of the following sentences contains a metaphor?

    a. "Like any New Yorker, I was no stranger to homeless people." (paragraph 1)

    b. "They were unfortunate ornaments of the city, unlucky in ways I never considered." (paragraph 1)

    c. "Once again, I felt like a helpless stranger." (paragraph 11)

    d. "But the more I pushed him to get help, the more my own sanity escaped me." (paragraph 18)

## H. THINKING CRITICALLY: ANALYZING THE AUTHOR'S MESSAGE

*Select the best answer.*

_____ 1. With which of the following statements would the author of "A Lost Brother" be most likely to *disagree*?

    a. Homeless people are real people.

    b. Love transcends a body caked in dirt and a mind ravaged by mental illness.

    c. Homeless people are unfortunate ornaments of the city.

    d. No matter how difficult it may be, allowing a person to choose his own path is often the right thing to do.

_____ 2. What does the author mean in paragraph 18 when she writes that she "tried to quiet her own inner voice"?

    a. She is hinting that she, too, is a paranoid schizophrenic.

    b. She is implying that her conscience is speaking to her.

    c. She is suggesting that the ideas she has were spoken to her by her psychiatrist.

    d. She means that the voice she hears in her head is so loud that she cannot hear her brother speak.

_____ 3. In paragraph 15, the author states that her brother answered *proudly* when asked if he were homeless. Why does the author use this word to describe the manner in which he answered?

    a. She wants the reader to understand that all people have value.

    b. She is implying that her brother is too sick to realize what a dangerous lifestyle he has chosen to live.

    c. She wants to send the reader a message about the pride that comes from choosing one's own path in life.

    d. She wants to encourage others to be proud of their family members no matter what path in life they may choose.

_____ 4. In paragraph 1, the author describes her office building as a "shiny glass tower" and her job as working for a "glossy women's magazine." Why does she use these words?

    a. She wants to show the contrast between her life and the life of the homeless.

    b. She wants to let the reader know that she is a competent and respectable writer.

    c. She is implying that a good life awaits those who make wise choices in life.

    d. She is suggesting that her building and job are indicative of the glamour and glitz that characterizes New York City.

# WRITING IN RESPONSE TO THE READING

## I. WRITING A SUMMARY

_Write a summary of "A Lost Brother." (paragraphs 1-19)_

## J. ANALYZING THE ISSUE AND ARGUMENT

1. Is the purpose of this reading to convey information, to make an argument, or a combination of the two? Explain your answer.

2. Write a one- or two-sentence summary of the author's thesis or central thought.

3. Is the author qualified to write on the topic? Why or why not? How do her own experiences inform the article?

4. Identify at least three issues presented in this reading. Then phrase each issue as a question that the author raises, discusses, or answers.

5. Consider the author's choice of descriptive words such as _ravaged_ and _curdled_. What do these words connote? What is the author's reason for using these words?

6. Evaluate the reading on the following criteria:

    a. Is the reading timely?

    b. Has the author provided sufficient evidence to support his main ideas? What other types of evidence might he provide to strengthen the reading?

    c. Do you find any evidence of bias in the reading? Explain.

    d. Does the author offer any opposing viewpoints? If not, what might some opposing viewpoints be?

    e. Does the reading offer any emotional appeals? If so, identify them and evaluate their fairness.

7. The theme of Chapter 18 is "Conformity and Nonconformity: Following and Breaking the Rules." Analyze the reading by addressing the following questions:

   a. What examples of conformity has the author provided?

   b. What examples of nonconformity has the author provided?

   c. What rules does Jay, the nonconformist, break?

   d. How is he treated by those who encounter him?

   e. How does he feel about his nonconformist lifestyle?

   f. What does the author learn from her relationship with her brother, the nonconformist?

## K. WRITING PARAGRAPHS AND ESSAYS

*Write a paragraph or essay in response to the following prompts.*

1. Think of a situation in which you tried to help someone who was unwilling or unable to be helped. Write a paragraph describing that experience.

2. Do you agree with the author that the news media would have been more interested in her disappearance than that of her mentally ill brother? Write a paragraph explaining your answer.

3. Try to put yourself in the author's shoes and imagine what you would have done. Do you think you would have been able to let your loved one go? Write a paragraph explaining your answer.

4. Before her brother became homeless, the author viewed homeless people as "unfortunate ornaments of the city." Her experience shows that each homeless person is someone's brother, sister, daughter, or son. Write an essay explaining how you viewed homeless people before reading this article, and how you view them now, after reading the article.

5. The title of this piece, "A Brother Lost," has multiple meanings. Write an essay discussing at least three of these meanings.

6. In this article, the author must come to terms with letting her brother make his own choice about what is the "right path" for him. Write an essay about freedom of choice. You may focus on a difficult choice you made for yourself, or one that you believe represented the right path for another person. How did the choice work out in the end?

**SELECTION
20**
MySkillsLab

# Why My Mother Wants Me Dead

Sabatina James as told to Abigail Pesta

### SOURCE AND CONTEXT

MAGAZINE
ARTICLE

Sabatina James is the author of the autobiography *Condemned Without a Crime*. She is the founder of Sabatina, a foundation whose goal is to help Muslim women live "free, self-determined lives." The foundation's motto is "Freedom for women in chains," and its goal, as stated on the foundation's Web site, is to "provide assistance to Muslim women who—due to violence within the family, threatened, or already implemented forced marriage or honor killing threats—require the help of others." This article originally appeared in *Newsweek*, a weekly general-interest U.S. newsmagazine. Sabatina James is a *pseudonym*, a fake name used by the author to protect her privacy.

### A NOTE ON THE READING

Marriage customs vary widely from culture to culture. Read "Why My Mother Wants Me Dead" to learn about one family's expectations for their daughter and her arranged marriage.

### PREVIEWING THE READING

*Using the steps listed on page 4, preview the reading selection. When you have finished, complete the following items.*

1. The reading is about a woman's conflict with her _____.

2. Indicate whether each statement is true (T) or false (F).

    _____ a. The author's family is rooted in a tribal tradition.

    _____ b. The author believes she has paid a high price for her freedom.

**MAKING
CONNECTIONS**

*What are the expectations surrounding marriage in your family or among your friends? What are the common expectations regarding marriage in U.S. society?*

### READING TIP

*The content of this article is emotional and can be difficult to read, but it is fairly short. As you read, compare the role of women in the United States with the role women play in the tribal societies discussed by Ms. James.*

# Why My Mother Wants Me Dead

Sabatina James as told to Abigail Pesta

*When Sabatina James refused an arranged marriage, she sparked a violent war within her family—and a threat on her life.*

1    When I was 18, my parents threatened to kill me. And they meant it. If they had their way, I would probably be dead today.

2    The trouble started when I was 15. At the time, my family was living in the Austrian city of Linz, a world away from our native Pakistan, where I had grown up in a rural village in the shadow of the Kashmir mountains. I loved the freedoms of my new life in Europe—the T-shirts and jeans, the lipstick and eyeliner. My conservative parents didn't. We fought about swimming lessons and acting classes, which my father said were for prostitutes. Tampons were an issue, too—my mother thought they would ruin my virginity.

3    When my mother found my diary one day and learned that I had kissed a boy in the park after school, she cracked me across the cheek, slammed me against the wall, and kicked my legs, calling me a whore. When she herself was my age, she was settling into an arranged marriage. She thought it was time for me to do the same.

4    I disagreed. Thus began a violent three-year battle with my mother.

**tribal tradition**
way of life based
on the customs
of a tribe

5    In families like mine, rooted in **tribal tradition**, marriage is a daughter's fate. And fathers are not always the primary enforcers—sometimes it's the mothers. This is much worse, in my opinion. When you're becoming a mature young woman and your mother is beating you, it's very damaging. You have no anchor.

6    My mother began watching my every move. One day, when she found a T-shirt that she felt was too skimpy, she smacked me hard in the face with a shoe, splitting my lip. Still, I refused to submit. I didn't want to disappear into a forced marriage. I wanted my freedom.

7    To my parents, my rebellion was a source of deep shame. They felt embarrassed among their Pakistani peers in Austria. They became more determined than ever to marry me off and restore the family "honor."

8    When I was 16, my family visited Pakistan. I remember walking outside in an outfit I felt was perfectly modest—loose pants and a blouse. Others saw it differently. A crowd of men formed, hooting and catcalling. That day my mother beat me again, in front of a roomful of relatives.

9    And then she beat herself. I knew there were Pakistanis who flagellated themselves when they suffered, but I never expected to see my own mother doing it. I watched as she struck herself repeatedly in the chest with a rod, saying, "I have given birth to a whore!"

Sabatina James

Lahore    10
a city in Pakistan

Quran
the Koran, the
holy book of
Islam

the prophet
Muhammad, the    11
founder of Islam

mullah
in Islam, an    12
educated man
or a clergyman

underground    13
railroad
a network of
secret routes and    14
"safe houses"
that allow people
to escape from
persecution,    15
aided by
people who are
sympathetic to    16
their cause

My parents shipped me off to an Islamic school, or madrassa, in **Lahore**, to "get educated," as my mother said. I lived in a room with around 30 other girls—no chairs, no beds, no ventilation. In that room, we did nothing all day but study the **Quran**, pray, and listen to lectures on **the prophet** from a **mullah**, who stood behind a curtain. If a girl spoke out of turn, she would be publicly caned in the courtyard of the compound. Flies and vermin swarmed the washrooms. There were no sanitary napkins, just blood-stained towels. The toilet was a hole in the ground.

After three months, I stopped eating, and got expelled. Eventually, I agreed to marry a man my family had chosen, so I could return to Austria during the engagement. Later, when my parents realized I did not intend to go through with the wedding, my father told me, "The honor of this family is more important than my life or your life."

That was a direct threat on my life. It sounds extreme, but it happens. According to the United Nations, 5,000 women and girls are murdered around the world each year for "shaming" the family by acting in ways deemed disobedient or immodest.

I fled, surviving by sleeping in a shelter and working at a local café in Linz. My parents harassed me at both places, showing up and ordering me to wed. Every day they closed in, like possessed demons, until I lost my job. I was 18.

I escaped to Vienna with the help of friends. There I started a new life, changing my name and converting to Catholicism. I wrote a book about my experience, and my parents sued for defamation. The court ruled in my favor.

Today I'm trying to break the marry-or-die tradition. I run a foundation called Sabatina, in Germany, where I live. My group acts as an **underground railroad**, helping women escape their families by finding them shelter and jobs.

I rarely go out alone. I often wonder if someone is lurking around the corner. I have always loved my freedom—but I have paid a high price.

## UNDERSTANDING AND ANALYZING THE READING

### A. BUILDING VOCABULARY

#### Context

*Using context and a dictionary if necessary, determine the meaning of each word as it is used in the selection.*

_____ 1. rural (paragraph 2)
   a. out of touch with reality
   b. ringed by mountains
   c. located along a water route
   d. country

_____ 2. primary (paragraph 5)
   a. main
   b. masculine
   c. elementary
   d. related to voting

_____ 3. enforcers (paragraph 5)
   a. abusers
   b. persons of traditional upbringing
   c. persons who compel obedience
   d. family elders

_____ 4. skimpy (paragraph 6)
   a. tight
   b. thin
   c. insubstantial
   d. bright

_____ 5. modest (paragraph 8)

    a. newest

    b. decent

    c. perfect

    d. cutting-edge

_____ 6. flagellated (paragraph 9)

    a. screamed at

    b. committed suicide

    c. whipped

    d. went on a hunger strike

_____ 7. madrassa (paragraph 10)

    a. holy person

    b. convent

    c. house of worship

    d. Islamic school

_____ 8. vermin (paragraph 10)

    a. rodents

    b. bad odors

    c. dirty water

    d. spiders

## Word Parts

> ### A REVIEW OF PREFIXES AND SUFFIXES
>
> **IM-** means *not*.
>
> **-TION** means *the act of*.

1. A person who is *immodest* (paragraph 12) is _____ modest in his or her appearance or behavior.

2. *Defamation* (paragraph 14) is the _____ injuring another person's reputation.

## B. UNDERSTANDING THE THESIS AND OTHER MAIN IDEAS

*Select the best answer.*

_____ 1. Which of the following is the best statement of the author's thesis or central thought?

    a. "By refusing to abide by the traditional rules set by my family, I have become a disgrace to the family and I fear for my life, but I feel the sacrifice has been worth it."

    b. "Muslim women should obey their parents outwardly while holding strong to their own ideals within themselves."

    c. "While I have established a group to help young Muslim women flee their abusive families, I wish I had not made the choices I've made."

    d. "In general, European society is secular and a serious threat to the religious faith of Muslim women, which is why most Muslim girls should be educated in Muslim countries such as Pakistan and Bangladesh."

_____ 2. The implied main idea of paragraph 9 is

    a. Pakistan is a backward, conservative country.

    b. The young women of Pakistan are held to strict standards in dress and behavior.

    c. In general, Pakistani fathers are not involved in the raising of their children and are generally absent from family life.

    d. In traditional Pakistani families, mothers see themselves as responsible for their daughters' behaviors.

_____ 3. What is the topic of paragraph 10?

    a. the conditions in a madrassa

    b. the friendships among young women

    c. the roles of women and men in Islam

    d. sanitary conditions in Pakistan

## C. IDENTIFYING DETAILS

*Select the best answer.*

_____ 1. In which country has the author not lived?

    a. Pakistan

    b. Austria

    c. England

    d. Germany

_____ 2. The author argued with her parents over all of the following *except*

    a. her clothes.

    b. cosmetics.

    c. her pregnancy.

    d. forced marriage.

_____ 3. The Kashmir Mountains are located in

    a. Austria.

    b. Germany.

    c. Russia.

    d. Pakistan.

_____ 4. According to the United Nations, approximately how many women and girls are murdered each year for shaming their families?

    a. 1,000

    b. 5,000

    c. 10,000

    d. 25,000

## D. RECOGNIZING METHODS OF ORGANIZATION AND TRANSITIONS

*Select the best answer.*

_____ 1. The overall pattern of organization used in this reading is
   a. classification.
   b. process.
   c. chronological order.
   d. order of importance.

_____ 2. The pattern of organization in the very brief paragraph 4 is
   a. cause and effect.
   b. comparison and contrast.
   c. classification.
   d. definition.

_____ 3. The transitional word that signals the organizational pattern in paragraph 4 is
   a. disagreed.
   b. thus.
   c. began.
   d. battle.

## E. READING AND THINKING VISUALLY

*Select the best answer.*

_____ 1. The inclusion of the photograph of James is surprising within the context of the reading because
   a. in Islam, women are generally prohibited from having photographs taken of them.
   b. the author says she has changed her name and lives in hiding, so it seems unlikely she would want her photograph to appear in the article.
   c. Sabatina James does not look like a typical Muslim or Arabic woman; her features seem to be much more Italian or Mediterranean.
   d. it does not seem to truly represent the content of the reading, "Why My Mother Wants Me Dead."

## F. FIGURING OUT IMPLIED MEANINGS

*Indicate whether each statement is true (T) or false (F).*

_____ 1. The author currently lives in Europe.

_____ 2. Sabatina James's parents saw her as a threat to the family's honor.

_____ 3. In general, the author's parents saw her as a possession and believed they had the right to rule her life.

_____ 4. The author went on a hunger strike so that she would get expelled from the madrassa.

_____ 5. The author is generally in favor of arranged marriages.

_____ 6. Despite all of her experiences, the author is still a devout Muslim woman.

_____ 7. The author believes that "reputation" and "honor" are a family's two most prized possessions in traditional tribal societies.

## G. THINKING CRITICALLY: ANALYZING THE AUTHOR'S TECHNIQUES

*Select the best answer.*

_____ 1. The author's purpose in "Why My Mother Wants Me Dead" is to

a. encourage young Muslim women to become more modern and to desert their abusive families.

b. tell the story of her battle against her parents and her society.

c. argue for anti-Muslim legislation in Europe and the United States.

d. put an end to the Pakistani madrassas that mistreat young Muslim women.

_____ 2. The author's tone in this reading could accurately be described by all of the following terms *except*

a. courageous.

b. nostalgic.

c. angry.

d. stubborn.

_____ 3. All of the following are statements of fact *except*

a. "When she herself was my age, she was settling into an arranged marriage." (paragraph 3)

b. "When you're becoming a mature young woman and your mother is beating you, it's very damaging." (paragraph 5)

c. "That day my mother beat me again, in front of a roomful of relatives." (paragraph 8)

d. "The court ruled in my favor." (paragraph 14)

_____ 4. The main type of evidence used in the reading selection is
   a. statistics.
   b. quotations from experts.
   c. research citations.
   d. personal experience.

## H.  THINKING CRITICALLY: ANALYZING THE AUTHOR'S MESSAGE

*Select the best answer.*

_____ 1. In paragraph 5, the author states "You have no anchor." She means
that
   a. women without a formal education have no way to support
      themselves financially.
   b. people who move from country to country often do not feel at
      home anywhere.
   c. a young woman needs a supportive mother to help her become
      a mature woman.
   d. the lack of a male role model in Muslim families leads to
      mothers having too much power in the family.

_____ 2. Why does the author use quotation marks around the word
"honor" in paragraph 7?
   a. to imply irony, because honor should be something that one
      feels proud of, not something outmoded, sexist, and abusive
   b. to emphasize honor as a key term that readers should highlight/
      annotate
   c. to underscore the importance of honor as the key concept that rules
      all traditional, rural, tribal families
   d. to suggest that the Muslim code of honor is always based on the
      subjugation of women

_____ 3. What is the most likely reason that the mullah stands behind a
curtain? (paragraph 10)
   a. The mullah wishes to be perceived as a mysterious figure to be
      worshipped.
   b. The mullah is likely blind and does not want the students to
      see him.
   c. The school is trying to prevent flirtation between the teacher
      and his students.
   d. Traditional Islam requires men to be separated from women.

_____ 4. The word or phrase that *best* summarizes the authors' attitude toward her parents is

    a. "conservative" (paragraph 2).

    b. "primary enforcers" (paragraph 5).

    c. "possessed demons" (paragraph 13).

    d. "lurking around the corner" (paragraph 16).

_____ 5. All of the following are the author's underlying assumptions in this article *except*

    a. fundamentalist Islam values women's contributions to society.

    b. young women have a right to personal freedom.

    c. a mother is a key figure in a young woman's development.

    d. women should not be abused in public for their choices.

# WRITING IN RESPONSE TO THE READING

## I. REVIEWING AND ORGANIZING WITH A PARAPHRASE

*Complete the following paraphrase of paragraphs 8–10 by filling in the missing words or phrases.*

At age 16, the author, Sabatina James, visited _____ with her family. Wearing a modest _____ and loose pants, she went outdoors. A group of men gathered near her and began _____ her. That same night, she was beaten by her mother in front of her relatives. Then her mother beat her own chest with a _____, calling her daughter a _____. Ms. James was then sent to an Islamic _____, where she lived in one room with 30 other girls. She spent all day studying the _____, _____, and listening to the teachings of a mullah. Girls who spoke out of turn were punished by a public _____, and the _____ was filthy, filled with flies and _____, and had no working sanitation system to dispose of human waste.

## J. ANALYZING THE ISSUE AND ARGUMENT

1. What contemporary issue or issues is the author discussing in this reading? List at least two issues.

2. Write a one-sentence summary of the author's experience and argument.

3. What are the author's qualifications? In other words, what makes her qualified to write on the topic?

4. What stated or implied value system do you find in the selection?

5. Evaluate the reading's argument on the following criteria:

    a. Is the argument timely?

    b. Has the author provided sufficient evidence to support her argument? What other types of evidence might she provide to strengthen her argument?

    c. Has the authors defined her terms sufficiently?

    d. Is the author's experience representative? How can you find more information to help you answer this question?

    e. Is the author biased? If so, how?

    f. Does the author offer any opposing viewpoints? If not, what might some opposing arguments be?

    g. Does the reading offer any emotional appeals? If so, identify them and evaluate their fairness.

## K. WRITING PARAGRAPHS OR ESSAYS

*Write a paragraph or essay in response to the following writing prompts.*

1. Write a paragraph summarizing Sabatina James's life and mission.

2. Sabatina James's case is an extreme one, but social rejection comes in many forms, from not being invited to a party to being bullied on Facebook. Have you ever witnessed a social rejection? Write a paragraph explaining what happened and why.

3. The reading selection includes a photo of the author. What other types of photos or visual aids might be helpful to readers? Write a paragraph discussing your recommendations.

4. Visit Sabatina's Web site (conduct a Google search to find it). Write an essay in which you discuss the various components of the Web site.

5. Nobody denies the important roles that parents play in a child's life. Write an essay in which you explore what the ideal parent would do, and would *not* do, in order to raise a healthy, happy child who becomes a healthy, happy adult.

6. In her article, the author discusses the "underground railroad" (paragraph 15) she runs for women who are trying to escape their families. There have been many famous underground railroads in history, including one in the United States to help escaped slaves get to Canada, as well as one designed to help protect Jews in Hitler's Nazi Germany. Conduct research into one of these underground railroads (or another one of your choice) and write an essay explaining the underground railroad's purpose, locations, and results.

# SELECTION 21
MySkillsLab

# Groups and Conformity
Michael R. Solomon

TEXTBOOK
SELECTION

## SOURCE AND CONTEXT

The following reading is taken from a business textbook, *Consumer Behavior: Buying, Having, and Being*. Consumer behavior is often considered a subfield of psychology, and it is the study of how, when, and why people buy (or do not buy) products and services. The author, Michael R. Solomon, is professor of marketing and Director of the Center for Consumer Research at Saint Joseph's University.

## A NOTE ON THE READING

How do other people influence your decisions regarding what to buy? Read "Groups and Conformity" for some insight into this question.

## PREVIEWING THE READING

*Using the steps listed on page 4, preview the reading selection. When you have finished, complete the following items.*

1. This reading is about _____.

2. Indicate whether each statement is true (T) or false (F).

_____ a. The term *reference group* is generally used to describe any external influence that provides social cues.

_____ b. We are acquainted with the people in aspirational reference groups.

_____ c. We tend to get away with less in a group setting.

MAKING CONNECTIONS

*How do you go about making decisions regarding what to buy? Does your process differ if you are buying something cheap (for example, gum) versus something more expensive (for example, a car)? If so, how?*

## READING TIP

*As you read, pay attention to the boldfaced terms, which indicate important concepts in the field of consumer behavior. Annotate while you read and note how each of these terms relates to your own life and experiences.*

# Groups and Conformity

### Michael R. Solomon

1    Zachary leads a secret life. During the week, he is a straitlaced stock analyst for a major investment firm. He spends a big chunk of the week worrying about whether he'll have a job, so work is pretty stressful these days. However, his day job only pays his bills to finance his real passion: cruising on his Harley-Davidson Road Glide Custom. His Facebook posts are filled with lunchtime laments about how much he'd rather be out on the road (hopefully his boss won't try to friend him). Actually, Zach feels it's worth the risk: He's participating in Harley's free country social media promotion that encourages riders to post their stories ("freedom statements") on Facebook and Twitter to see if they'll include one of his posts on a Harley banner ad. His girlfriend worries a bit about his getting totaled in an accident, but Zach knows if he stays alert the only way that will probably happen is if he can't kick his habit of texting her while he's driving the bike.

2    Come Friday evening, it's off with the Brooks Brothers suit and on with the black leather, as he trades his Lexus for his treasured Harley. A dedicated member of the HOG (Harley Owners Group), Zachary belongs to the "RUBs" (rich urban bikers) faction of Harley riders. Everyone in his group wears expensive leather vests with Harley insignias and owns custom "**low riders.**" Just this week, Zach finally got his new Harley perforated black leather jacket at the company's Motorclothes Merchandise web page. As one of the Harley web pages observed, "it's one thing to have people buy your products. It's another thing to have them tattoo your name on their bodies." Zach had to restrain himself from buying more Harley stuff; there were vests, eyewear, belts, buckles, scarves, watches, jewelry, even housewares ("home is the road") for sale. He settled for a set of Harley salt-and-pepper shakers that would be perfect for his buddy Dan's new **crib.**

**low rider**
a type of motorcycle in which the rider sits low in the seat, closer to the ground than on a typical motorcycle

**crib**
house or apartment

**foursquare**
a social media Web site

3    Zachary's experiences on social media platforms make him realize the lengths to which some of his fellow enthusiasts go to make sure others know they are hog riders. Two of his riding buddies are in a lively competition to be "mayor" of the local Harley dealership on **foursquare**, while many others tweet to inform people about a group ride that will occur later in the day—kind of a flashmob on wheels.

4    Zach spends a lot of money to outfit himself to be like the rest of the group, but it's worth it. He feels a real sense of brotherhood with his fellow RUBs. The group rides

together in two-column formation to bike rallies that sometimes attract up to 300,000 cycle enthusiasts. What a sense of power he feels when they all cruise together—it's them against the world!

5      Of course, an added benefit is the business networking he's accomplished during his jaunts with his fellow professionals who also wait for the weekend to "ride on the wild side—these days it would be professional suicide to let your contacts get cold, and you can't just count on LinkedIn to stay in the loop" (Schouten and Alexander, 1992).

### Reference Groups

6      Humans are social animals. We belong to groups, try to please others, and look to others' behavior for clues about what we should do in public settings. In fact, our desire to "fit in" or to identify with desirable individuals or groups is the primary motivation for many of our consumption behaviors. We may go to great lengths to please the members of a group whose acceptance we covet.

7      Zachary's biker group is an important part of his identity, and this membership influences many of his buying decisions. He has spent many thousands of dollars on parts and accessories since he became a RUB. His fellow riders bond via their consumption choices, so total strangers feel an immediate connection with one another when they meet. The publisher of *American Iron*, an industry magazine, observed, "You don't buy a Harley because it's a superior bike, you buy a Harley to be a part of a family" (Machan, 1997).

8      Zachary doesn't model himself after just *any* biker—only the people with whom he really identifies can exert that kind of influence on him. For example, Zachary's group doesn't have much to do with outlaw clubs whose blue-collar riders sport big Harley tattoos. The members of his group also have only polite contact with "Ma and Pa" bikers, whose rides are the epitome of comfort and feature such niceties as radios, heated handgrips, and floorboards. Essentially, only the RUBs comprise Zachary's *reference group*.

9      A reference group is "an actual or imaginary individual or group conceived of [as] having significant relevance upon an individual's evaluations, aspirations, or behavior" (Park and Lessig, 1977, pp. 102–110). Reference groups influence us in three ways: *informational, utilitarian,* and *value-expressive.* Table 18.1 describes these influences. Other people, whether fellow bikers, coworkers, friends, family, or simply casual acquaintances, influence our purchase decisions. We'll consider how our group memberships shape our preferences because we want others to accept us or even because we mimic the actions of famous people we've never met.

### When Are Reference Groups Important?

10      Recent research on smoking cessation programs powerfully illustrates the impact of reference groups. The study found that smokers tend to quit in groups: When one person quits, this creates a ripple effect that motivates others in his or her social network to give up the death sticks also. The researchers followed thousands of smokers and nonsmokers for more than 30 years, and they also tracked their networks of relatives, coworkers, and friends. They discovered that over the years, the smokers tended to cluster together (on average in groups of three). As the overall U.S. smoking rate declined dramatically during this period, the number of clusters

## TABLE 18.1  THREE FORMS OF REFERENCE GROUP INFLUENCE

**Informational Influence**

- The individual seeks information about various brands from an association of professionals or independent group of experts.
- The individual seeks information from those who work with the product as a profession.
- The individual seeks brand-related knowledge and experience (such as how Brand A's performance compares to Brand B's) from those friends, neighbors, relatives, or work associates who have reliable information about the brands.
- The brand the individual selects is influenced by observing a seal of approval of an independent testing agency (such as Good Housekeeping).
- The individual's observation of what experts do (such as observing the type of car that police drive or the brand of television that repairmen buy) influences his or her choice of a brand.

**Utilitarian Influence**

- So that he or she satisfies the expectations of fellow work associates, the individual's decision to purchase a particular brand is influenced by their preferences.
- The individual's decision to purchase a particular brand is influenced by the preferences of people with whom he or she has social interaction.
- The individual's decision to purchase a particular brand is influenced by the preferences of family members.
- The desire to satisfy the expectations that others have of him or her has an impact on the individual's brand choice.

**Value-Expressive Influence**

- The individual feels that the purchase or use of a particular brand will enhance the image others have of him or her.
- The individual feels that those who purchase or use a particular brand possess the characteristics that he or she would like to have.
- The individual sometimes feels that it would be nice to be like the type of person that advertisements show using a particular brand.
- The individual feels that the people who purchase a particular brand are admired or respected by others.
- The individual feels that the purchase of a particular brand would help show others what he or she is or would like to be (such as an athlete, successful business person, good parent, etc.).

*Source:* Adapted from C. Whan Park and V. Parker Lessig, "Students and Housewives: Differences in Susceptibility to Reference Group Influence," *Journal of Consumer Research* (4 September 1977): 102. © 1977 Journal of Consumer Research, Inc. Reprinted with permission of The University of Chicago Press.

in the sample decreased, but the remaining clusters stayed the same size; this indicated that people quit in groups rather than as individuals. Not surprisingly, some social connections were more powerful than others. A spouse who quit had a bigger impact than did a friend, whereas friends had more influence than siblings. Coworkers had an influence only in small firms where everyone knew one another.

11      Reference group influences don't work the same way for all types of products and consumption activities. For example, we're not as likely to take others' preferences into account when we choose products that are not very complex, that are low in perceived risk, or that we can try before we buy. In addition, knowing what others prefer may influence us at a general level (e.g., owning or not owning a computer, eating junk food versus health food), whereas at other times this knowledge guides the specific brands we desire within a product category (e.g., if we wear Levi's jeans versus Diesel jeans, or smoke Marlboro cigarettes rather than Virginia Slims).

## Types of Reference Groups

12      Although two or more people normally form a group, we often use the term reference group a bit more loosely to describe any external influence that provides social cues. The referent may be a cultural figure who has an impact on many people (e.g., Michelle Obama) or a person or group whose influence operates only in the consumer's immediate environment (e.g., Zachary's biker club). Reference groups that affect consumption can include parents, fellow motorcycle enthusiasts, the Tea Party, or even the Chicago Bears, the Dave Matthews Band, or Spike Lee.

13      Some people influence us simply because we feel similar to them. Have you ever experienced a warm feeling when you pull up at a light next to someone who drives the exact car as yours? One reason that we feel a bond with fellow brand users may be that many of us are a bit narcissistic (not you, of course); we feel an attraction to people and products that remind us of ourselves. That may explain why we feel a connection to others who happen to share our name. Research on the name-letter effect finds that, all things being equal, we like others who share our names or even initials better than those who don't. When researchers look at large databases like Internet phone directories or Social Security records, they find that Johnsons are more likely to wed Johnsons, women named Virginia are more likely to live in (and move to) Virginia, and people whose surname is Lane tend to have addresses that include the word lane, not street. During the 2000 presidential campaign, people whose surnames began with B were more likely to contribute to George Bush, whereas those whose surnames began with G were more likely to contribute to Al Gore.

14      Obviously, some groups and individuals are more powerful than others and affect a broader range of our consumption decisions. For example, our parents may play a pivotal role as we form our values on many important issues, such as attitudes about marriage or where to go to college. We call this normative influence—that is, the reference group helps to set and enforce fundamental standards of conduct. In contrast, a Harley-Davidson club exerts comparative influence because it affects members' decisions about specific motorcycle purchases.

## Membership versus Aspirational Reference Groups

15    A **membership reference group** consists of people we actually know, whereas we don't know those in an aspirational reference group, but we admire them anyway. These people are likely to be successful businesspeople, athletes, performers, or whoever rocks our world. Not surprisingly, many marketing efforts that specifically adopt a reference group appeal concentrate on highly visible, widely admired figures (such as well-known athletes or performers); they link these people to brands so that the products they use or endorse also take on this aspirational quality. For example, an amateur basketball player who idolizes Miami Heat star Dwayne Wade might drool over a pair of Air Jordan 12 Dwayne Wade PE shoes. One study of business students who aspired to the "executive" role found a strong relationship between products they associated with their *ideal selves* and those they assumed that real executives own. Of course, it's worth noting that as social media usage increases, the line between those we "know" and those we "friend" gets blurrier. Still, whether offline or online, we tend to seek out others who are similar. Indeed, one study even found that people on Twitter tend to follow others who share their mood: People who are happy tend to re-tweet or reply to others who are happy, while those who are sad or lonely tend to do the same with others who also post negative sentiments.

## Positive versus Negative Reference Groups

16    Reference groups impact our buying decisions both positively and negatively. In most cases, we model our behavior to be in line with what we think the group expects us to do. Sometimes, however, we also deliberately do the opposite if we want to distance ourselves from avoidance groups. You may carefully study the dress or mannerisms of a group you dislike (e.g., "nerds," "druggies," or "preppies") and scrupulously avoid buying anything that might identify you with that group. For example, rebellious adolescents do the opposite of what their parents desire to make a statement about their independence. In one study, college freshman reported consuming less alcohol and restaurant patrons selected less fattening food when drinking alcohol and eating junk food linked to members of avoidance groups.

17    Your motivation to distance yourself from a negative reference group can be as powerful or more powerful than your desire to please a positive group. That's why advertisements occasionally show an undesirable person who uses a competitor's product. This kind of execution subtly makes the point that you can avoid winding up like that kind of person if you just stay away from the products he buys. As a once-popular book reminded us, "Real men don't eat quiche!"

## We Like to Do It in Groups

18    We get away with more when we do it in a group. One simple reason: The more people who are together, the less likely it is that any one member will get singled out for attention. That helps to explain why people in larger groups have fewer restraints on their behavior. For example, we sometimes behave more wildly at costume parties or on Halloween than we do when others can easily identify us. We call this phenomenon deindividuation—a process whereby individual identities become submerged within a group.

19    Even shopping behavior changes when people do it in groups. For example, people who shop with at least one other person tend to make more unplanned purchases, buy more, and cover more areas of a store than do those who browse solo. Both normative and informational social influence explains this. A group member may buy something to gain the approval of the others, or the group may simply expose her to more products and stores. Either way, retailers are well advised to encourage group-shopping activities.

20    The famous Tupperware party is a successful example of a home shopping party that capitalizes on group pressures to boost sales. In this format a company representative makes a sales presentation to a group of people who gather at the home of a friend or acquaintance. The shopping party works due to informational social influence: Participants model the behavior of others who provide them with information about how to use certain products, especially because a relatively homogeneous group (e.g., neighborhood homemakers) attends the party. Normative social influence also operates because others can easily observe our actions. Pressures to conform may be particularly intense and may escalate as more and more group members "cave in" (we call this process the *bandwagon effect*).

## Conformity

21    The early Bohemians who lived in Paris around 1830 made a point of behaving, well, differently from others. One flamboyant figure of the time earned notoriety because he walked a lobster on a leash through the gardens of the Royal Palace. His friends drank wine from human skulls, cut their beards in strange shapes, and slept in tents on the floors of their **garrets**. Sounds a bit like some frats we've visited.

**garrets**
top-floor or attic rooms

22    Although in every age there certainly are those who "march to their own drummers," most people tend to follow society's expectations regarding how they should act and look (with a little improvisation here and there, of course). Conformity is a change in beliefs or actions as a reaction to real or imagined group pressure. In order for a society to function, its members develop norms, or informal rules that govern behavior. Without these rules, we would have chaos. Imagine the confusion if a simple norm such as stopping for a red traffic light did not exist.

23    We conform in many small ways every day, even though we don't always realize it. Unspoken rules govern many aspects of consumption. In addition to norms regarding appropriate use of clothing and other personal items, we conform to rules that include gift-giving (we expect birthday presents from loved ones and get upset if they don't materialize), sex roles (men often pick up the check on a first date), and personal hygiene (our friends expect us to shower regularly). We also observe conformity in the online world; research supports the idea that consumers are more likely to show interest in a product if they see that it is already very popular.

24    One study analyzed how millions of Facebook users adopted apps to personalize their pages. Researchers tracked, on an hourly basis, the rate at which 2,700 apps were installed by 50 million Facebook users. They discovered that once an app had reached a rate of about 55 installations a day, its popularity started to soar. Facebook friends were notified when one of their online buddies adopted a new app, and they could also see a list of the most popular ones. Apparently this popularity feedback was the key driver that determined whether still more users would download the software.

25    Still, we don't mimic others' behaviors all the time, so what makes it more likely that we'll conform? These are some common culprits:

- **Cultural pressures**—Different cultures encourage conformity to a greater or lesser degree. The American slogan "Do your own thing" in the 1960s reflected a movement away from conformity and toward individualism. In contrast, Japanese society emphasizes collective well-being and group loyalty over individuals' needs.

- **Fear of deviance**—The individual may have reason to believe that the group will apply *sanctions* to punish nonconforming behaviors. It's not unusual to observe adolescents shunning a peer who is "different" or a corporation or university passing over a person for promotion because she is not a "team player."

- **Commitment**—The more people are dedicated to a group and value their membership in it, the greater their motivation to conform to the group's wishes. Rock groupies and followers of TV **evangelists** may do anything their idols ask of them, and terrorists willingly die for their cause. According to the **principle of least interest**, the person who is least committed to staying in a relationship has the most power because that party doesn't care as much if the other person rejects him. Remember that on your next date.

- **Group unanimity, size, and expertise**—As groups gain in power, compliance increases. It is often harder to resist the demands of a large number of people than only a few, especially when a "mob mentality" rules.

- **Susceptibility to interpersonal influence**—This trait refers to an individual's need to have others think highly of him or her. Consumers who don't possess this trait are role-relaxed; they tend to be older, affluent, and to have high self-confidence. Subaru created a communications strategy to reach role-relaxed consumers. In one of its commercials, a man proclaims, "I want a car. . . . Don't tell me about wood paneling, about winning the respect of my neighbors. They're my neighbors. They're not my heroes."

**evangelists**
zealous advocates of religious causes

**unanimity**
total (100 percent) agreement

# UNDERSTANDING AND ANALYZING THE READING

## A. BUILDING VOCABULARY

### Context

*Using context and a dictionary if necessary, determine the meaning of each word as it is used in the selection.*

_____ 1. straitlaced (paragraph 1)

a. well-dressed

b. wealthy

c. successful

d. conservative

_____ 2. faction (paragraph 2)

a. percentage

b. role model

c. group within a larger group

d. extreme enthusiast

_____ 3. jaunts (paragraph 5)
    a. concerts
    b. conversations
    c. trips
    d. company meetings

_____ 4. covet (paragraph 6)
    a. desire
    b. dislike
    c. need
    d. refuse

_____ 5. epitome (paragraph 8)
    a. symbol
    b. metaphor
    c. center
    d. embodiment

_____ 6. niceties (paragraph 8)
    a. stolen goods
    b. accessories
    c. attachments
    d. unnecessary items

_____ 7. narcissistic (paragraph 13)
    a. self-conscious
    b. impatient
    c. self-centered
    d. aging

_____ 8. pivotal (paragraph 14)
    a. central
    b. secondary
    c. unimportant
    d. parental

_____ 9. flamboyant (paragraph 21)
    a. modest
    b. dashing
    c. flammable
    d. floating

_____ 10. notoriety (paragraph 21)
    a. significant income
    b. jail time for bad behavior
    c. admiration for bad behavior
    d. being widely and unfavorably well-known

## Word Parts

> ### A REVIEW OF PREFIXES AND SUFFIXES
>
> **HOMO-** means *same*.
>
> **-TION** means *the act of*.

*Use your knowledge of word parts and the review above to fill in the blanks in the following sentences.*

1. In a relatively *homogeneous* (paragraph 20) group, many of the people are _____.

2. *Improvisation* (paragraph 22) is the _____ improvising, or responding without preparation.

## B. UNDERSTANDING THE THESIS AND OTHER MAIN IDEAS

*Select the best answer.*

_____ 1. The thesis or central thought of "Groups and Conformity" is best stated as

    a. Conformity is the result of several factors, including cultural pressures, fear of deviance, commitment, group unanimity, and susceptibility to interpersonal influence.

    b. Because human beings are inherently social, they often look to different types of reference groups as they make purchase decisions; and in many these decisions, the desire to conform to social norms plays an important role.

    c. While most reference groups are based on membership or aspiration, a completely different type of reference group, called an avoidance group, reflects an individual's desire not to be like the members of a group that the individual dislikes or disdains.

    d. While groups are an important determinant of consumer behavior in the United States, the influence of social groups (such as friends and coworkers) is much smaller in other countries, where the dominant culture focuses more on individuality than on group conformity.

_____ 2. The main idea of paragraph 13 is found in the

    a. first sentence.

    b. second sentence.

    c. fifth sentence.

    d. last sentence.

_____ 3. The topic of paragraph 20 is

    a. the bandwagon effect.

    b. group pressures.

    c. Tupperware.

    d. home shopping parties.

*For questions 4–8, match the term in column A with its definition in column B.*

| Column A: Term | Column B: Definition |
|---|---|
| _____ 4. aspirational reference group | a. A change in actions or beliefs in reaction to imagined or real group pressures. |
| _____ 5. deindividuation | b. The idea that the person who is least committed to being in a relationship holds the most power in that relationship. |

| Column A: Term | Column B: Definition |
|---|---|
| ——— 6. principle of least interest | c. A process by which individual people, and their identities and personalities, become submerged within a group identity. |
| ——— 7. normative influence | d. A group of people, usually composed of highly visible, widely admired athletes or performers, whose success people wish to associate themselves with (or whose behaviors they seek to emulate). |
| ——— 8. conformity | e. The process by which a reference group helps establish and enforce basic standards of conduct for its group members. |

## C. IDENTIFYING DETAILS

*Select the best answer.*

——— 1. To which group do wealthy Harley-Davidson owners often belong?

    a. WYSIWIGs

    b. RUBs

    c. DOAs

    d. HOGs

——— 2. The motorcycle group most likely to have extremely comfortable motorcycles are

    a. Ma and Pa bikers.

    b. wealthy bikers.

    c. RUBs.

    d. subscribers to *American Iron*.

——— 3. The average number of smokers in a "smoking cluster" is

    a. three.

    b. five.

    c. six.

    d. eight.

——— 4. According to the reading, what is the most likely address for a man named Brian Court?

    a. 14 Main Street

    b. 2605 Adriana Road

    c. 173 Phoenix Court

    d. 42689 Palisade Avenue

_____ 5. Suppose you have an aversion to punk rockers. For you, punk rockers are a(n)

    a. aspirational reference group.

    b. utilitarian reference group.

    c. normative group.

    d. avoidance group.

## D. RECOGNIZING METHODS OF ORGANIZATION AND TRANSITIONS

*For questions 1–4, match the paragraph in column A with its organizational pattern in column B.*

| Column A: Paragraph | Column B: Organizational Pattern |
|---|---|
| _____ 1. paragraph 9 | a. generalization and example |
| _____ 2. paragraph 11 | b. addition |
| _____ 3. paragraph 23 | c. definition |
| _____ 4. paragraph 25 | d. listing/enumeration |

*Select the best answer.*

_____ 5. The transitional word or phrase that points to the cause and effect pattern in paragraph 24 is

    a. analyzed.

    b. personalize.

    c. popularity.

    d. driver.

## E. READING AND THINKING VISUALLY

*Based on Table 18.1 on page 592, indicate whether each item is a type of informational influence, utilitarian influence, or value-expressive influence.*

_____ 1. An aspiring young athlete purchases basketball shoes that are advertised by a professional basketball player such as Michael Jordan or Kobe Bryant.

_____ 2. A female employee at a local flower shop decides to wear the same brand of perfume favored by the shop's other female employees.

_____ 3. A recent college graduate buys a car that is recommended as a "Best Buy" by *Consumer Reports*, an unbiased consumer-advocacy magazine.

## F. FIGURING OUT IMPLIED MEANINGS

*Indicate whether each statement is true (T) or false (F).*

_____ 1. In both the real world and the online world, we tend to seek people who are similar to us.

_____ 2. In Japan, people are more likely to focus on individualistic efforts rather than group needs.

_____ 3. In the decision to quit smoking, spouses have a stronger influence than friends.

_____ 4. Consumers are more likely to take other people's preferences into account when they are buying products with a low perceived value.

_____ 5. A role-relaxed woman does not care much about what people think of her.

_____ 6. Parents are more likely to exert comparative influence than normative influence.

_____ 7. In general, people in larger groups have fewer restraints on their behavior.

_____ 8. A person named Sara Thompson is more likely to like someone named Sally Tremont than someone named Barbara Michaels.

_____ 9. The early Bohemians were known for their strict adherence to social norms.

## G. THINKING CRITICALLY: ANALYZING THE AUTHOR'S TECHNIQUES

*Select the best answer.*

_____ 1. The author's purpose in "Groups and Conformity" is to

a. provide an overview of the influence of reference groups and conformity on consumers' buying decisions, while providing key definitions, examples, and research findings.

b. make students aware of the unseen forces at work in advertising, on the Internet, and in public gathering places like malls and coffeehouses.

c. explain the differences between specific reference groups and specific conformist groups, while showing readers how to make better purchasing decisions.

d. expose the unethical practices of companies like Harley-Davidson and Tupperware, which take advantage of people's desires to be part of a group or community.

_____ 2. In "Groups and Conformity," the author often uses informal language. Which of the following is *not* an example of informal language?

   a. "perfect for his buddy Dan's new crib" (paragraph 2)

   b. "they link these people to brands" (paragraph 15)

   c. "sounds a bit like some frats we've visited" (paragraph 21)

   d. "remember that on your next date" (paragraph 25)

_____ 3. In paragraph 10, "death sticks" is figurative language whose literal meaning is

   a. baseball bats.

   b. falling branches.

   c. swords.

   d. cigarettes.

_____ 4. The type of evidence used to support the main ideas in paragraphs 10 and 24 is

   a. the author's personal experience.

   b. quotes from experts.

   c. research studies.

   d. analogies.

## H. THINKING CRITICALLY: ANALYZING THE AUTHOR'S MESSAGE

*Select the best answer.*

_____ 1. What is the connotation of the phrase "freedom statements" that is used on Harley-Davidson's social media? (paragraph 1)

   a. important business documents, such as spreadsheets and corporate mission statements

   b. historical records of freed slaves, such as Harriet Tubman

   c. sense of freedom from responsibilities and the demands of one's job

   d. Twitter updates by political prisoners in countries like Russia and China

_____ 2. According to the reading, what is the best definition of a "ripple effect" (paragraph 10)?

   a. a pattern that is not easily explained

   b. the likelihood that people will give up smoking in groups instead of individually

   c. the overall decrease in sales of a particular product (such as cigars and cigarettes)

   d. the continuing and spreading results of an event or action

_____ 3. paragraph 24 uses the term "popularity feedback." Which of the following is the best example of popularity feedback?

    a. A singer's CD is #1 on the charts, so more people buy a copy of that CD.

    b. The most attractive people tend to be the most popular in social situations.

    c. A college freshman from out of state attempts to make as many friends as possible during his first year on campus.

    d. A young woman who works for a political action committee avoids buying goods in stores that make use of underpaid overseas child labor.

_____ 4. The term "mob mentality" in paragraph 25 refers to

    a. people who see the Mafia as an aspirational reference group.

    b. the tendency for large groups of people to exert powerful influence over the individuals in that group.

    c. the belief that most people prefer the company of others rather than being alone.

    d. the large number of psychological or mental disorders in urban areas with large populations.

## WRITING IN RESPONSE TO THE READING

### I. REVIEWING AND ORGANIZING IDEAS WITH AN OUTLINE

*Complete the following outline of the reading by filling in the missing words or phrases.*

I. Introduction: Story of _____, proud owner of a Harley-Davidson motorcycle

II. Reference Group: _____

    _____

    A. When Are Reference Groups Important?

        1. Recent research on smoking _____: Powerful impact of reference groups

        2. Not all reference groups influence work the same way

B. Types of Reference Groups

    1. Name-letter effect: _____

    _____

    2. _____

    _____

    3. _____

    _____

C. Membership versus Aspirational Reference Groups

    1. _____

    2. _____

D. _____

    1. _____: People we want to distance ourselves from

E. We Like to Do It in Groups

    1. _____

    _____

    2. Group shopping behavior and _____ parties: People more likely to buy more when shopping in a group, where pressure to conform may be intense (bandwagon effect)

III. Conformity

A. _____: change in beliefs or actions as a reaction to real or imagined group pressure

B. Norms: _____

C. Factors that influence conformity

    1. Cultural pressures

    2. _____

    3. _____

    4. _____

    5. _____

## J. ANALYZING THE ISSUE AND ARGUMENT

1. List at least three arguments the author makes in "Groups and Conformity."

2. Is the author qualified to write on the topic? Why or why not? How does the source of the reading provide a hint regarding its overall reliability?

3. Does the author provide sufficient evidence to support his main ideas? What other types of evidence might he provide to strengthen his arguments?

4. Which terms does the author define clearly and directly? Which terms are defined indirectly or not at all? What are the definitions of the latter terms?

5. What assumptions does the author make about his readers?

6. Evaluate the reading on the following criteria:

    a. Is the reading timely?

    b. Do you find any evidence of bias in the reading? Explain.

    c. Does the author offer any opposing viewpoints? If so, does he refute them, and how? If not, what might some opposing viewpoints be?

    d. Does the reading offer any emotional appeals? If so, identify them and evaluate their fairness.

## K. WRITING PARAGRAPHS AND ESSAYS

*Write a paragraph or essay in response to the following writing prompts.*

1. The reading begins with the example of Zachary, who uses his motorcycle as a way of getting away from his everyday life. What hobby do you engage in when you want to forget about your problems or have a sense of freedom? (For example, do you surf the Web or rent movies?) Write a paragraph about your favorite get-away-from-it-all pastime.

2. The reading discusses the way people can influence one another to quit smoking. Write a paragraph in which you explore some of the ways people can help friends or family members achieve a goal (for instance, getting more exercise, losing weight, or getting a good grade on an exam).

3. Write a one-paragraph summary of the information included in Table 18.1 on page 592.

4. Write an essay in which you explore three groups to which you aspire (that is, three groups you would like to belong to).

5. Think about a celebrity who endorses a particular product. Why do you think the company chose that spokesperson? To whom is the company trying to appeal? Do you think that celebrity endorsements help sell products? Do such techniques work on you? Why or why not? Write an essay in which you explore these questions.

6. What are the norms for behavior in the college classroom and on campus? Write an essay in which you explore these norms. What are the sanctions for deviating from these norms?

## ACTIVITIES: EXPLORING CONFORMITY AND NONCONFORMITY

*On your own or with a group of classmates, complete two of the following four activities.*

1. In Reading Selection 20, Sabatina James talks about arranged marriages. Her underlying assumption is that an arranged marriage is not based on love. Think about the factors that help create a good marriage and the factors that lead to a bad marriage. Compile a list of at least five in each category. One in each category is provided to get you started.

   **Factors in a Happy Marriage**

   Similar desires to have children

   1. _____
   2. _____
   3. _____
   4. _____
   5. _____

   **Factors in an Unhappy Marriage**

   Disagreements about money

   1. _____
   2. _____
   3. _____
   4. _____
   5. _____

2. Celebrity magazines (like *Us* and *People*) are filled with photos of glamorous Hollywood stars and musicians. What norms are dominant in Hollywood? How do you think the lives of celebrities are fundamentally different from those of the typical American? Provide at least three examples of the ways in which celebrities' lives differ from that of the "average" person. For instance, some celebrities have hundreds of thousands of followers on their Twitter accounts. Does the average person have that many followers? Why would so many people choose to follow a celebrity's "tweets"?

3. The readings in this chapter discussed just a few aspects of conformity and nonconformity. Other issues related to this topic include:

   - **Dress codes:** What is appropriate to wear in different situations? Do men's dress codes differ from women's? If so, how and why? How have dress codes changed over the years?

   - **Hairstyles:** If you are going for a job interview, what are the expectations for how you should wear your hair? What are the "do's" and the "don'ts" for both women and men?

   - **Body adornment:** How does society view piercings, tattoos, and other body adornments? How have these perceptions changed over the years? For example, what did a tattoo signal in 1950, and what does it signal today?

   - **Political protest:** The United States protects freedoms of speech and demonstration. How is political protest a form of nonconformity, and what types of new tools for political protest or political change are now available (that were not available 20 years ago)?

- **Life on and off the grid:** "The grid" refers to the system by which companies and the government track you and your activities: your Social Security number, your address, your place of employment, and so forth. Some people, the ultimate nonconformists, choose to live "off the grid." What motivates these people, and why?

Write an essay or prepare a class presentation about any of these topics, or any other topic regarding conformity or nonconformity.

4. As mentioned in the introduction to this chapter, different sets of norms apply to different groups of people. Write an essay or prepare a presentation in which you compare and contrast two sets of norms. Choose from the list below, or choose two other groups you find particularly interesting.

- Team athletes (for example, baseball and football players) versus individual athletes (for example, gymnasts and ice skaters)
- Upperclassmen (juniors and seniors) versus underclassmen (freshmen and sophomores)
- Students in introductory courses (for example, introduction to psychology) versus students in a discipline's upper-level courses (for example, psychological statistics or abnormal psychology)
- Adolescents/teenagers versus senior citizens

# 19 Personal Freedoms and Limitations: Lifestyle Choices

*How do you define the word* freedom?

When you hear the word, do you think about societal freedoms, like freedom of speech and freedom of the press? Or do you think about more personal freedoms, such as the freedom to make the right choices for your life and your family?

People in the United States enjoy some of the greatest personal freedoms in the world, and Americans have become used to living in a free society. But such freedoms are not found around the world. In some Middle Eastern countries, for example, women may not drive cars or leave the house without a male escort. Some countries, such as China and Russia, try to control information by censoring the Internet and throwing journalists into jail. Here are some examples of the personal decisions most Americans are free to make:

- They can decide to remain single (rather than get married) and to remain childless (instead of having children).
- They can choose to join groups and organizations that reflect their beliefs and values. For example, the NRA (National Rifle Association) has a very strong membership composed of people who believe that Americans have the right to bear arms. However, the millions of Americans who believe in gun control would never join the NRA.
- They can decide how much education to get (college or trade school?), where to live (city, suburb, or rural area?), and where to work.

But even the freest of societies place some limitations on their people. Laws prevent people from hurting others or society, and illnesses or other factors can limit a person's choices. All the readings in this chapter focus on personal freedoms and/or limitations. For example, why do people choose to join (or remain a member of) a particular religious group, and what are the benefits of that religious affiliation? Why do some people choose not to have children, and how does society view such people? How does a mental illness, such as bipolar disorder, limit a person's choices, activities, and relationships?

## WHY IS FREEDOM SUCH AN IMPORTANT CONTEMPORARY ISSUE?

The United States was founded on the principle of freedom—specifically, freedom of worship. The Puritans who first came to North America were fleeing religious persecution in England. Key documents in the history of the United States, such as the Bill of Rights written by the Founding Fathers, are very specific about the freedoms permitted to citizens. As a country, we have always been concerned with our freedoms, and these concerns become more pressing in the twenty-first century, when Americans are having more limitations placed on them. For example, air travel now requires personal searches and body X-rays. Many see these searches as an invasion of privacy, while others argue that such rules are required to prevent terrorist attacks. Recent news reports have also pointed to other limitations that are being proposed or put into place. For example, in 2012 the mayor of New York City proposed banning sugary soft drinks of more than 16 ounces as a way of combating the health problems that go with obesity. Does the government really have the right to tell us how much soda and juice we can drink? This is a question that many people are asking.

### How do Personal Freedoms and Limitations Tie in to My College Courses?

History and political science courses almost always trace the history of groups who are looking for freedom. Psychology courses often discuss decision making and offer tips for analyzing a situation and choosing the best course of action. Sociology courses look at the freedoms and limitations placed on people around the world. And, of course, simply by attending college and choosing a major, you have made personal choices about your education and the path you want your life to take.

---

**TIPS FOR READING ABOUT PERSONAL FREEDOMS AND LIMITATIONS**

Here are some tips for reading not only the selections in this chapter, but any reading about personal freedoms and limitations.

- **Look for and analyze opposing viewpoints.** Many of today's most controversial issues regarding personal freedoms revolve around a "benefit analysis." That is, do laws that restrict personal freedoms do more good for society as a whole than they do harm to individuals? Try to understand both sides of the argument to develop a deeper understanding of the topic you are reading about. For example, those who believe in the right to bear arms see this right as essential to defending themselves and their families against people who would hurt them. Meanwhile, those who believe in gun control believe that the murder rate would decrease drastically if guns were not available.

- **Look for indications of bias.** Closely consider the author's thesis and look for signs of bias. Remember that bias is not necessarily negative; a writer may be biased *in favor of* something or *against* something. Understanding the sources of bias will help you better evaluate the reading and its main ideas.

- **Tie the reading to your life and experiences.** Put yourself in the author's position. How would you feel? Would you make the same choices or different choices? How would you react to having limitations placed on your choices?

# Bipolar Disorder: The Agony and the Ecstasy

## Thomas Wheaton

PERSONAL
ESSAY

### SOURCE AND CONTEXT

The author of "Bipolar Disorder: The Agony and the Ecstasy" is a freelance journalist who chose to publish this personal essay under a pseudonym (a false name) to protect her/his privacy.

### A NOTE ON THE READING

More than one-quarter of the adult U.S. population suffers from some form of mental illness, from mild depression through severe disorders like schizophrenia. Read "Bipolar Disorder: The Agony and the Ecstasy" to understand one person's experience with mental illness.

### PREVIEWING THE READING

*Using the steps listed on page 4, preview the reading selection. When you have finished, complete the following items.*

1. This reading is about _____.
2. Determine whether each statement is true (T) or false (F).

   _____  a. Bipolar disorder affects nearly 7.5 million Americans.

   _____  b. Bipolar disorder is not a medical condition.

 **MAKING CONNECTIONS**

*Have you ever experienced a period of depression? How long has it lasted?*

### READING TIP

*Understanding word parts can help you better understand the author's definition of bipolar disorder. Bi- means "two," and bipolar disease means alternating between two "poles": depression and euphoria. In the past, people who suffered with bipolar disorder were called "manic-depressives," but psychologists no longer use that term.*

# Bipolar Disorder: The Agony and the Ecstasy

## Thomas Wheaton

1    Bipolar disorder (BP) is a mental health condition typified by mood swings between gushing euphoria and draining depression. Out of the 26.2 percent of Americans over age 18 with a form of mental illness, BP affects 5.7 million (NIMH 2012). Bipolar disorder is a medical condition like heart disease or arthritis. It doesn't have anything to do with someone being weak or lazy. Living with bipolar disorder requires more personal strength and hard work than the non-bipolar can imagine.

2    There are three types of bipolar disorder, as defined in the *Diagnostic and Statistical Manual: IV*, the current reference manual for psychiatric diagnosis. Bipolar 1 requires at least one episode of **mania** or a mixed episode in a person's lifetime. (A mixed episode is an epic freak-out where mania and depression coexist. They're awful.) Bipolar 2 describes patients who alternate mood states between severe depression and a milder form of mania. Bipolar 2 often looks like high functionality. The intense mood intervals, or cycles, last a few days each. Cyclothymic disorder is very much like BP, but with less severe mood swings happening more frequently (NIMH 2008).

> **mania**
> a period of intense, robust activity accompanied by euphoria

3    Bipolar disorder requires multidisciplinary treatment. Medication alone isn't enough. In addition to writing in my journal daily, I have biweekly appointments with my therapist to talk about feelings and bimonthly appointments with my psychiatrist to make sure the meds are working. I'm prescribed 1500 mg of Depakote daily, 100 mg of Zoloft, and the occasional Xanax for panic attacks. 50 mg of Trazodone makes sure I sleep all night. If I take my meds exactly on time every day, stability's easier. If I'm off a few hours one day, I can feel the difference. If I miss a dose, I'm not suitable for the general public. I need them for stability, but the meds have side effects.

4    Dealing with the side effects requires more than just taking medication on time. Because pills are broken down in the stomach and intestines before being filtered through the liver and kidneys, I must drink uncomfortable amounts of water to avoid organ damage. The medications make me heat-sensitive. My mouth is always dry. Sometimes my head buzzes when I stand up. Everything I take has a warning label for dizziness. Being without medication, though, is far worse than taking it. That's because my specific type of bipolar disorder is unusually challenging.

5    Based on the current definitions, my diagnosis is "Bipolar-Not Otherwise Specified, with ultra-ultra rapid cycling." That means I experience significant mood swings from mania to depression more than once daily, but my symptoms don't meet the strict criteria for Bipolar 1, 2, or cyclothymic disorder (NAMI). Cycles this short are rare and very challenging, because I have to deal with both depression and mania, sometimes less than minutes apart. What are those states like? Here's a brief primer for those not lucky enough to know firsthand.

> **inpatient facility**
> a medical building in which patients stay for a period of time (often several days or weeks) to help get their illness under control

6    Depression is soul-wrenchingly awful. If you've never been depressed, imagine being sad, except the saddest you've ever been and all the time. When my meds are working, I get an occasional horrible thought, but it goes no further. Before doctors got my medications balanced, thinking about suicide to the point of holding a knife to my wrist was familiar territory. I tried to kill myself twice, at age six and early freshman year. I finally got the help I needed in an **inpatient facility** where trained

professionals could watch and medicate me. Not everyone with BP needs that level of help, but I did. I was lucky to have access to inpatient care—the number of available beds has been shrinking nationwide (Daviss). Unfortunately, depression is only half of the bipolar experience.

7     Manic mood states lead to impulsivity, hypersexuality, and rash decisions. Untreated bipolar disorder is the reason I bought 29 pairs of sneakers and nearly had to buy a friend an $80 drinking glass from a Web site. (I'm glad they were out of stock.) Manic or elevated moods can also involve high energy, rapid speech, and the ability to take care of what's been neglected while depressed. As long as I'm not overly agitated, manic focus rivals the feelings described by students who utilize **amphetamines** as study drugs. Mania is an elevated state of mood that, for me, feels very much like being "in the zone." I enjoy being manic. Previously, that led me away from taking my meds.

**amphetamines** drugs that stimulate the central nervous system, such as caffeine; "uppers"

8     Going on and off meds can wreak havoc on a class schedule. I barely showed up to college classes, but when I did I was annoyingly attentive. I didn't have my diagnosis yet, so professors thought I was high all the time. This did not go over well. Bipolar disorder usually develops in one's twenties—having mental health care available on campus is crucial. Waiting only means things get worse.

9     Bipolar has a "kindling effect"—it gets worse the longer it's not dealt with (Purse). My symptoms appeared early—I can remember BP moments in preschool. Later in life, it manifested itself in spending a large percentage of my income on recreational drugs. I was the guy who'd do and say the stuff you wanted to but knew societal rules meant you shouldn't. Every day without mood stabilizers was another twig thrown on the growing fire of my instability. Every day I regret not getting a diagnosis and proper medication sooner.

**confounding** causing surprise or confusion in someone, often by acting against their expectations

10     There's speculation that the kindling effect can increase the cycling speed of mood swings, one of the most **confounding** aspects of bipolar disorder. It's like being *both* Dr. Jekyll and Mr. Hyde, but without the ability to choose when. I'd drive girlfriends to tears, and then switch moods and try to cuddle. It's harder to fix tears you brought on. I've learned to recognize when I'm not in control of my mood by the reactions of others—and how to give myself a minute outside. These skills help keep my actions from getting too much in the way of relationships, but at the cost of having to constantly watch everything I do, everything I say, and everyone's reaction to it.

**electrolytes** chemicals in the body that regulate nerves, muscles, blood pressure, and other important functions

11     Having to pay constant attention is a theme for anyone with BP who wants to thrive, not just survive. Sleeping enough, eating healthy, and managing my **electrolyte** levels can buy me enough time not to yell at the police. Nutrition and self-care aren't fixes any more than meds are, though. I can eat and sleep and take meds and rehydrate perfectly but still be talking a mile a minute or be totally uninterested in playing with kittens. Times like that are when I rely on my safety net or learn how strong I really am.

12     Family and friends make the bipolar life much, much easier. When you're all wrapped up in your own head, calm outside input can make all the difference. I can always depend on my mom to focus on the actual problem instead of my emotional response. My girlfriend knows that occasionally I need to hide under a blanket in the dark until the depression fades. If it weren't for Nikki gently reminding me that I'm talking a little too fast, I might not notice. She's good at spotting when I need alone

time. Her and others' perception is very helpful. But I still can't let my guard down. This constant internal struggle is one of my least favorite parts of living with BP.

13    Being bipolar doesn't just suck on the inside. The world thinks it's acceptable to insult people by calling them crazy. That word hurts a lot more when you have a diagnosis. When I leave my therapist's office, I make sure to fold the yellow full-page receipt and get it out of view so people won't treat me differently. As much as I've wanted to write this essay, I wouldn't dare do it under my real name.

14    Living with bipolar disorder requires a terribly intimate knowledge of yourself. Maintaining stability requires maintaining all aspects of regular health plus the ability to find strength when moods cycle anyway. I need a thick skin to deal with the challenges BP brings, especially taking meds on time. It'd be much harder without my safety net of family, friends, and doctors. I must fight every single frustrating day to be good to and for myself. Living with bipolar, however, is far better than the alternative.

### Works Cited

Daviss, Steven R., MD, DFAPA. "Running Out of Psychiatric Beds." *Psychology Today*. Psychology Today, 8 Mar. 2011. Web. 01 Aug. 2012.

Purse, Marcia. "The 'Kindling' Model in Bipolar Disorder." *About.com*. About.com, 15 May 2012. Web. 31 July 2012.

"The Numbers Count: Mental Disorders in America." *NIMH: National Institute of Mental Health*. NIH: National Institutes of Health, n.d. 2 Aug. 2012. Web. 03 Aug. 2012.

"What Is Bipolar Disorder?" *NAMI: National Alliance on Mental Illness*. NAMI, n.d. Web. 31 July 2012.

"What is Bipolar Disorder?" *NIMH: National Institute of Mental Health*. NIH: National Institutes of Health, n.d. Web. 03 Aug. 2012.

## UNDERSTANDING AND ANALYZING THE READING

### A. BUILDING VOCABULARY

### Context

*Using context and a dictionary if necessary, determine the meaning of each word as it is used in the selection.*

_____  1. epic (paragraph 2)

a. classic

b. expensive

c. large-scale

d. wonderful

_____  2. interval (paragraph 2)

a. emotion

b. cycle

c. variable

d. avoidance

_____ 3. criteria (paragraph 5)

    a. effects

    b. lags

    c. medications

    d. standards

_____ 4. primer (paragraph 5)

    a. first in a series

    b. liquid used to prepare wood for finishing

    c. instruction in the basics

    d. most exciting event of a lifetime

_____ 5. rash (paragraph 7)

    a. impulsive and hasty

    b. red and irritated

    c. expensive and unnecessary

    d. emotionally draining

_____ 6. utilize (paragraph 7)

    a. depend on

    b. use

    c. sell

    d. advocate for

_____ 7. havoc (paragraph 8)

    a. unpredictability

    b. swing made from cloth

    c. complete destruction

    d. attendance problem

_____ 8. manifested (paragraph 9)

    a. showed

    b. prepared

    c. energized

    d. created

_____ 9. speculation (paragraph 10)

    a. disagreement

    b. anger

    c. guessing

    d. research

_____ 10. thrive (paragraph 11)

    a. save money

    b. graduate

    c. flourish

    d. live

## Word Parts

---

### A REVIEW OF PREFIXES, ROOTS, AND SUFFIXES

**CO-** means *joint, mutual,* or *together.*

**HYDRO-** means *water.*

**HYPER-** means *over* or *excessive.*

**-ITY** refers to a *state, condition,* or *quality.*

**MULTI-** means *many.*

**RE-** means *back* or *again.*

---

*Use your knowledge of word parts and the review above to fill in the blanks in the following sentences.*

1. When two groups of people *coexist* (paragraph 2), they live _____, or side by side, in peace.

2. When used to describe college studies, *multidisciplinary* refers to courses that use information from _____ different disciplines. As used in paragraph 3, *multidisciplinary* refers to _____ different methods of treatment.

3. Someone who engages in a period of *hypersexuality* (paragraph 7) has an _____ amount of sex.

4. To *rehydrate* (paragraph 11) means to add _____ back into the body.

## B. UNDERSTANDING THE THESIS AND OTHER MAIN IDEAS

*Select the best answer.*

_____ 1. The thesis statement for "Bipolar Disorder: The Agony and the Ecstasy" is
   a. the first sentence of paragraph 2.
   b. the last sentence of paragraph 1.
   c. the first sentence of paragraph 5.
   d. the third sentence of paragraph 14.

_____ 2. The topic of paragraph 6 is
   a. suicide.
   b. medication.
   c. inpatient care.
   d. depression.

_____ 3. The main idea of paragraph 9 is found in the
   a. first sentence.
   b. second sentence.
   c. fourth sentence.
   d. fifth sentence.

_____ 4. The main idea of paragraph 14 is found in the
   a. first sentence.
   b. second sentence.
   c. fifth sentence.
   d. sixth sentence.

## C. IDENTIFYING DETAILS

*Select the best answer.*

_____ 1. The author lists all of the following as side effects of his medications *except*

    a. dry mouth.

    b. a buzzing head.

    c. stupor.

    d. dizziness.

_____ 2. Which of the following does *not* characterize the manic state?

    a. paranoia

    b. impulsiveness

    c. rapid speech

    d. high energy

_____ 3. When the author refers to his "safety net," he means

    a. the medications prescribed for him.

    b. his doctors, friends, and family.

    c. the college counseling center.

    d. his own feelings of self-esteem and worthiness.

## D. RECOGNIZING METHODS OF ORGANIZATION AND TRANSITIONS

*Select the best answer.*

_____ 1. Which paragraph makes use of the definition pattern of organization?

    a. paragraph 5

    b. paragraph 8

    c. paragraph 11

    d. paragraph 13

_____ 2. Which paragraph makes use of the classification organizational pattern?

    a. paragraph 2

    b. paragraph 4

    c. paragraph 7

    d. paragraph 9

_____ 3. The sentences 5–8 of paragraph 3 all use the _____ pattern.

    a. comparison and contrast

    b. process

    c. cause and effect

    d. chronological order

_____ 4. Two transitional phrases that signal the cause and effect pattern in paragraph 7 are

    a. can also involve, the ability to.

    b. lead to, the reason.

    c. manic focus, elevated state.

    d. high energy, rapid speech.

## E. READING AND THINKING VISUALLY

*Select the best answer.*

_____ 1. Often, a photo of the author accompanies a personal essay. Why do you think no author photo is included with "Bipolar Disorder: The Agony and the Ecstasy"?

    a. The author is not young and handsome.

    b. The author does not want to imply that bipolar disorder affects only men.

    c. The author's girlfriend asked him not to include a photo of himself.

    d. The author wishes to remain anonymous.

## F. FIGURING OUT IMPLIED MEANINGS

*Indicate whether each statement is true (T) or false (F).*

_____ 1. Medications are broken down in the stomach and intestines.

_____ 2. The amount of inpatient care for those suffering from BP is increasing in the United States.

_____ 3. Cyclothymic disorder is a type of bipolar disorder.

_____ 4. Trazodone functions as a type of sleeping pill.

_____ 5. The author attempted to commit suicide three times.

_____ 6. The author's BP diagnosis clearly falls into the "Bipolar 2" category.

_____ 7. Those who suffer from BP enjoy their manic periods much more than they enjoy their depressive periods.

_____ 8. Nikki is the author's mother.

## G. THINKING CRITICALLY: ANALYZING THE AUTHOR'S TECHNIQUES

*Select the best answer.*

_____ 1. The author's purpose in "Bipolar Disorder: The Agony and the Ecstasy" is to
   a. encourage readers to engage in self-reflection and self-evaluation.
   b. distinguish among the different types of bipolar disorder.
   c. describe his experiences and struggles with bipolar disorder.
   d. criticize the medical system for its tendency to overprescribe drugs.

_____ 2. The tone of the selection can accurately be described as all of the following *except*
   a. personal.
   b. removed.
   c. revealing.
   d. informative.

_____ 3. In paragraph 9, "twig thrown on the growing fire of my instability" is an example of _____, while in paragraph 10 "It's like being both Dr. Jekyll and Mr. Hyde" is an example of _____.
   a. classification, literary allusion
   b. personification, pathetic fallacy
   c. symbolism, apostrophe
   d. metaphor, simile

_____ 4. The author supports his thesis primarily with
   a. research, statistics, and personal experience.
   b. case studies of anonymous people who suffer from BP.
   c. an explanation of the different types of bipolar disorder.
   d. expert opinions and quotations from doctors.

_____ 5. What is the author's attitude toward the way society commonly uses the word *crazy*?
   a. He thinks the word has comedic overtones that create a humorous effect.
   b. He thinks the word applies to almost everyone who is diagnosed with bipolar disorder.
   c. He thinks the word is hurtful to people who are suffering from mental disorders.
   d. He thinks people with BP are not crazy, but those with schizophrenia are.

## H. THINKING CRITICALLY: ANALYZING THE AUTHOR'S MESSAGE

*Select the best answer.*

_____ 1. The phrase "high functionality" in paragraph 2 refers to

    a. a type of high brought on by large doses of medication.

    b. the positive effects of seeing a therapist and discussing one's personal issues.

    c. a state in which a person performs well in his or her personal life and at work.

    d. the mathematics and statistics required to understand psychological diagnoses.

_____ 2. When the author says "I'm not suitable for the general public" in paragraph 3, he means

    a. he has not washed his hair or taken a shower for several weeks.

    b. his BP makes it likely that he will behave inappropriately around other people.

    c. his employer has asked him to take sick leave to care for his illness.

    d. he avoids crowded areas, such as movie theaters, restaurants, and shopping malls.

_____ 3. In paragraph 14, the author states "Living with bipolar, however, is far better than the alternative." What does he mean?

    a. Medications have made living with bipolar disorder much easier on those who are affected by it.

    b. BP people generally prefer to have other BP people as roommates.

    c. Living with a mental illness is better than being dead.

    d. His girlfriend would rather have him (and his accompanying BP) than a different boyfriend who does not have a psychological illness.

_____ 4. In the title, "the agony" refers to _____, and "the ecstasy" refers to _____.

    a. school, sex

    b. depression, manic episodes

    c. mental illness, friends and family

    d. bipolar disease, medication

# WRITING IN RESPONSE TO THE READING

## I. REVIEWING AND ORGANIZING IDEAS WITH A PARAPHRASE

*Complete the following paraphrase of paragraphs 1–3 of the selection by filling in the missing words or phrases.*

Bipolar disorder, or _____, is a psychological illness characterized by two extreme emotional states: _____ (or mania) and _____. Twenty-two point six percent of American adults are diagnosed with BP, and living with this diagnosis requires great _____ and hard work. Psychological professionals identify _____ types of BP. The first is _____, which requires at least one manic episode or _____ episode (the simultaneous appearance of mania and depression) in a person's life. The second, _____, describes people who move back and forth between serious _____ and lesser states of mania. _____ disorder creates a higher number of mood swings, but these are less severe. Treatment for bipolar disorder usually requires a mixture of medication, therapy, and the services of a _____. Unfortunately, most medications have _____.

## J. ANALYZING THE ISSUE AND ARGUMENT

1. What contemporary issue is the author discussing in this reading? Write a one- or two-sentence paraphrase of the author's thesis statement.

2. Is the author making an argument in "Bipolar Disorder: The Agony and the Ecstasy," or is his primary goal to provide information? Explain your answer.

3. Is the author qualified to write on the topic? Why or why not? Are his experiences typical and representative of those who suffer from bipolar disorder?

4. Like many personal essays, this selection uses multiple patterns of organization. What is the overall pattern of organization for the entire essay? What other organizational patterns are used? Which transitional words or phrases signal these patterns? How does the use of multiple patterns make this reading richer and more informative?

5. Evaluate the reading on the following criteria:

   a. Is the reading timely?

   b. Has the author provided sufficient evidence to support his thesis? What other types of evidence might he provide to strengthen the reading's main ideas?

   c. Has the author defined terms accurately and sufficiently?

d. Do you find any evidence of bias in the reading? Explain.

e. Does the author offer any opposing viewpoints? If so, does he refute them, and how? If not, what might some opposing viewpoints be?

f. Does the reading offer any emotional appeals? If so, identify them and evaluate their fairness.

g. What does the author imply about society's assumptions regarding mental illness?

h. What claim(s) of policy does the author make?

## K. WRITING PARAGRAPHS AND ESSAYS

*Write a paragraph or essay in response to the following writing prompts.*

1. Write a paragraph summarizing the three major types of bipolar disorder.

2. Suppose a friend asks you, "What does a person with bipolar disorder typically experience?" Write a paragraph explaining the disorder to your friend.

3. What type of photo (or other visual aid) might the author use to illustrate the main points raised in his essay? Write a paragraph describing your recommendations.

4. The author says that manic moods lead to "impulsivity." Have you ever made an impulsive decision? What were the effects of that decision? Write an essay describing your experience.

5. What types of mental health care are available on your campus? Write an essay providing information about the available options.

6. People who are diagnosed with bipolar disorder are sometimes called crazy, according to the author. Write an essay in which you explore the differences between being "called crazy" and being diagnosed with "bipolar disorder."

## I Don't Want to Have Kids.
## Get Over It.

### Yashar Ali

### SOURCE AND CONTEXT

BLOG
ENTRY

This entry appeared on Yashar Ali's blog, "The Current Conscience." A blog is a personal Web site in which a person (sometimes an expert, sometimes an amateur) offers various opinions on which readers are free to comment. Yashar Ali lives in Los Angeles and has commented on state and national politics in *The Wall Street Journal, Time, The Huffington Post,* and *The San Francisco Chronicle.*

### A NOTE ON THE READING

Why do individuals and society feel they have the "right" to question a person's individual choices regarding parenthood? Read "I Don't Want to Have Kids. Get Over It" for one man's perspective on this question.

### PREVIEWING THE READING

*Using the steps listed on page 4, preview the reading selection. When you have finished, complete the following items.*

1.  This selection is about a man who does not want to have _____.

2.  Indicate whether each statement is true (T) or false (F).

_____ a.  The author believes society still sees women primarily as "baby makers."

_____ b.  The author is an early riser.

_____ c.  The author considers himself a feminist.

**MAKING CONNECTIONS**

*Do you have children, or have you thought about whether or not you'd like to have children in the future? How strongly do social pressures (such as friends or parents) influence your thinking?*

### READING TIP

*As you read, note that the author speaks from his perspective as a man but also explores women's experiences. How does this technique contribute to his argument and your willingness to listen to what he has to say?*

# I Don't Want to Have Kids. Get Over It.

### Yashar Ali

1   There is a script in my life that repeats itself over and over again: I tell someone, a friend, colleague, family member, that I don't want to have kids and with rare exception, I hear the following, "Oh no, you *have* to have kids, you'd be a great father! You're just saying that now, but you'll change your mind."

2   I have known from a young age that I wasn't meant to and didn't want to have kids–it's just not part of my life. I understand why people would have given me the advice that I might change my mind when I was 18 years old. But now that I'm 32, I wonder when are these people going to believe me and trust that I know what I want.

3   Why don't we trust people when they decide that they don't want to have kids? I'm making an assumption here, but the folks who argue that I would be a good dad are basing their idea on what they perceive as my ability to empathize with others and/or on the way I care for my friends—it's a big compliment. But being empathetic or caring with friends does not mean I would make a good parent. These friends of mine have no clue about my parental abilities; they are making assumptions based on seeing a few minutes of my interaction with kids, or worse yet, on my behavior towards adults.

4   Some have characterized a person's lack of interest in parenting as a problem of a missing gene or a chip, "Oh, you don't have the parental gene."

**social conditioning**
a set of expectations placed on individuals by society

5   The idea that people who choose NOT to have kids are somehow "missing a gene" or are abnormal is a deep part of our **social conditioning**. There exists this assumption that everyone must want to parent, and if someone doesn't have that desire, there's just something strange about this person—that he or she is somehow sad and solitary.

6   For me, this association between "missing gene" and people who choose not to have kids carries negative and problematic implications. I don't think anybody's decision to live a life without kids should register them as "normal" or not. I'm not "missing" anything, and referring to somebody as missing a gene or being abnormal suggests that having kids is and should be part of everyone's life.

7   This piece is not about judging people who do choose to have kids. I emphatically support anyone who chooses to have kids—all the parents I know believe that their children are the greatest gift they've been given in life. They wouldn't give them up for the world. And I think they are generally well-intentioned in pushing the parental role on those who aren't yet parents, since they hope their friends and family can experience the same joys they feel in having children in their lives.

8    It goes without saying that being a parent is a life-altering, monumental decision. In talking to others, what I find to be remarkable is the universal nature of the message for having kids, "You'll change your mind, you would be a great parent, you're crazy."

9    This is a major decision pushed on those who don't want to have children so casually.

10    It's almost as if our loved ones are pushing us to buy a piece of clothing at a department store, "You look so good in it, come on, you gotta get it."

11    What's also remarkable to me is the sadness that comes across the faces of my friends when I tell them I don't want to have kids. Shouldn't the answer be, "It's good to know what you want, especially when it comes to a major responsibility like parenting"?

12    But whenever I grow frustrated with these conversations, I remember that I have it easy compared to the women who make a definitive choice to refrain from having kids. Obviously, I don't have the ability to give birth to children, and as a man, I also don't have to deal with nearly as much societal pressure to have kids.

13    Despite whatever progress we've made, women are still seen as baby makers, and a woman who doesn't want to have a child is often identified as more than "missing a gene" or being an abnormality—she is seen as selfish, cold, lacking any empathy.

14    Why are people so uncomfortable if a woman is resolute in her decision not to have kids?

15    This is a question Amanda, 40, has been asking herself. For some time, she has known that having kids wasn't in the cards for her. A few years ago, Amanda told her sister about her choice, and her sister broke into tears and proclaimed, "That's the most selfish thing I've ever heard you say."

16    Her sister went on to explain how she thought Amanda would be a terrific mom and wondered why she would deny herself the unconditional love that comes with having children.

17    Amanda's friends, who had children, were equally as confused about her decision. They all worked to find ways to justify her decision, including the fact that she's been in a long-term relationship with an older man who already has kids of his own.

18    Amanda is up against a sea of people who are convinced that there must be a logical reason for someone to remain childless, beyond an internal desire to not want kids—and this is something that I have also faced.

19    People in our lives have to come up with a reason for why we wouldn't possibly want children. After all, just not wanting kids can't be enough of a justification. Folks who don't know me very well often say, "Well, you want to party, to have fun. You'll get it out of your system."

20    Since high school, I've been going to bed early and waking up around 5 am. But even if I did want to party into the wee hours of the morning, my decision not to have kids is my prerogative—I don't feel the need to justify it. Other friends, women, often hear, "You haven't met anyone yet. Once you find the person you love, you'll want kids."

21    And this need for detailed justification is especially pinned on women who reveal their decision to live their lives without children. There is a pattern in our culture where women are forced to publicly defend this decision, as if this choice must be somehow rendered legitimate with good reasons. When it comes to women and their decision to have children, why are they constantly forced to "defend" this life decision?

22    Ironically, women are always defending their professional and private moves: defending their choice to have kids, or not, defending their choice to enter into professional life, defending their choice to stay at home and raise kids.

23    This pattern of other people working to change the mind of someone who doesn't want children spills into familial relationships as well. Families of those who choose to remain childless also put on the pressure/guilt trip in attempts at altering reality.

24    Even for those folks who want to have kids eventually, the pressure exists to speed up the process. This isn't news to anyone reading this column—we have all seen the scenario portrayed in popular culture and in our own families. Our parents or parent beg for grandchildren or say, "When is it going to happen?"

25    It's usually seen as endearing and sweet. And I get it. Parents just want their children to be happy, and I think that with respect to the reality of life cycles, we are looking at an attempt by our parents to ensure that we are taken care of later in life. But, despite their best intentions, and how endearing people think it is, I think it's the opposite. This parental pressure is nonetheless a kind of pressure that pushes us to head towards a path that we may not feel comfortable about entering. I only think of the number of people who have had children simply because they feel pressured.

26    Some may read this and remark that because I'm a feminist writer, I must want all women to go childless (and let's be frank, become bra-less lesbians). That's simply wrong and a mis-characterization of what feminism means.

27    Feminism is about freedom and equality—it's all inclusive. So it means that a woman who chooses to have kids at 23 has made just as valid of a decision as a woman who never wants to have children. But feminism most definitively refers to the idea that all women (and men) are entitled to choose their life paths, whether that consists of having children (or not), and that these decisions are fully respected by the rest of society.

28    Despite the progress we've made as a culture, we still derive a great deal of comfort from women who fit into a prescribed, gender path. The negative responses women receive when they announce their choice not to have children is symptomatic of what we still expect women to do with their lives.

29    Why don't we see a woman who elects to live a life without kids as someone who has carefully made a decision about her future because she's weighed the import and responsibility of being a parent, with her desire to actually *be* a parent?

30    We would never see her as making a thoughtful choice . . .

31    Because as we see it, she's just being thoughtless.

## UNDERSTANDING AND ANALYZING THE READING

### A. BUILDING VOCABULARY

### Context

*Using context and a dictionary if necessary, determine the meaning of each word as it is used in the selection.*

_____ 1. empathize (paragraph 3)
  a. identify with someone's feelings
  b. become friends with
  c. enter into a romantic relationship with
  d. give advice to

_____ 2. abnormal (paragraph 5)
  a. selfish
  b. odd
  c. short-sighted
  d. insane

_____ 3. solitary (paragraph 5)
    a. unpredictable
    b. mighty
    c. alone
    d. depressed

_____ 4. emphatically (paragraph 7)
    a. grudgingly
    b. angrily
    c. forcefully
    d. spitefully

_____ 5. monumental (paragraph 8)
    a. expensive
    b. personal
    c. huge
    d. related

_____ 6. resolute (paragraph 14)
    a. firm
    b. bitter
    c. isolated
    d. unaffected

_____ 7. prerogative (paragraph 20)
    a. choice
    b. business
    c. life
    d. research project

_____ 8. frank (paragraph 26)
    a. honest and open
    b. critical and questioning
    c. condemning and disapproving
    d. loose and unstructured

## Word Parts

> ### A REVIEW OF PREFIXES AND SUFFIXES
>
> **UN-** means *not*.
>
> **MIS-** means *wrongly* or *incorrectly*.
>
> **-IAL** or **-AL** refer to *a state* or *condition*.

*Use your knowledge of word parts and the review above to fill in the blanks in the following sentences.*

1. *Unconditional* (paragraph 16) love is love that is given freely and _____ conditions attached to it.

2. *Familial* (paragraph 23) relationships refer to relationships within a _____.

3. A *mischaracterization* (paragraph 26) is a _____ characterization of a person.

## B. UNDERSTANDING THE THESIS AND OTHER MAIN IDEAS

*Select the best answer.*

_____ 1. Which of the following best states the thesis or central idea of "I Don't Want to Have Kids. Get Over It"?

    a. Those who do not have children save the taxpayers and the school system a great deal of money.

    b. As a result of people choosing not to have children, the U.S. population will begin shrinking by the year 2075.

    c. The decision to have children is an extremely personal choice that is often met with resistance, and women experience this resistance more strongly than men do.

    d. Society perceives those who do not want to have children as selfish and immature, but research has shown that people without children are happier than people who have children.

_____ 2. The topic of paragraph 5 is

    a. children.

    b. missing genes.

    c. abnormality.

    d. social conditioning.

_____ 3. Which of the following is true of the main idea in paragraph 27?

    a. The main idea is stated directly in the first sentence.

    b. The main idea is stated directly in the second sentence.

    c. The main idea is stated directly in the last sentence.

    d. The main idea of this paragraph must be inferred from context.

## C. IDENTIFYING DETAILS

*Select the best answer.*

_____ 1. The reading includes an example of a woman, Amanda, who has made the decision not to have children. How old is Amanda?

    a. 18

    b. 25

    c. 35

    d. 40

_____ 2. The author believes that his friends think he'll be a good parent because

    a. he is good-looking and carries good genes.

    b. he comes from a stable family.

    c. he cares about his friends.

    d. he gets along better with children than he does with adults.

_____ 3. According to the author, society sees women who do not want to have children as
   a. career-oriented.
   b. cold.
   c. lesbians.
   d. feminists.

## D. RECOGNIZING METHODS OF ORGANIZATION AND TRANSITIONS

*Select the best answer.*

_____ 1. The dominant organizational pattern in paragraph 25 is
   a. classification.
   b. cause and effect.
   c. definition.
   d. summary.

_____ 2. The dominant organizational pattern in paragraph 27 is
   a. definition.
   b. comparison and contrast.
   c. order of importance.
   d. spatial order.

_____ 3. The transitional word or phrase that signals the organizational pattern of paragraph 27 is
   a. inclusive.
   b. means.
   c. choose.
   d. respected by.

## E. READING AND THINKING VISUALLY

*Select the best answer.*

_____ 1. The author likely included the photo on page 623 to
   a. portray the author's feeling of isolation from people and society.
   b. illustrate how society in general feels about people who decide not to have children.
   c. encourage readers to reconsider their decision about having children.
   d. imply that those who have children are happier than those who do not have children.

## F. FIGURING OUT IMPLIED MEANINGS

*Indicate whether each statement is true (T) or false (F).*

_____ 1. The author does not support the people who decide to have children; he thinks they have not considered the consequences of their decision.

_____ 2. The author believes that having a child completely changes the parent's life.

_____ 3. The author asserts that feminism is mostly about a woman's decision to pursue a career.

_____ 4. The author thinks that men who decide not to have children have it easier than women who decide not to have children.

_____ 5. Most of the author's friends believe that he'll change his mind and that someday he will want to have children.

_____ 6. The author feels somewhat angry at all the people who won't accept his decision not to become a father.

## G. THINKING CRITICALLY: ANALYZING THE AUTHOR'S TECHNIQUES

*Select the best answer.*

_____ 1. The author's primary purpose in "I Don't Want to Have Kids. Get Over It" is to

   a. offer one man's perspective on his decision not to have children and society's reactions when men and women make that decision.

   b. compare and contrast his experience with that of his friend Amanda.

   c. explore cultural differences in attitudes toward child-rearing.

   d. convince those who do not want children to form support groups that will help them deal with the societal pressures they face.

_____ 2. The author's tone in this selection is best described as

   a. bemused.

   b. frustrated.

   c. confused.

   d. mocking.

_____ 3. What does the author see as society's underlying assumption regarding children?

    a. All women should have children, but having children is not a necessity for men.

    b. Each individual should be permitted to make his or her own choices regarding the decision to have children.

    c. It is the responsibility of all well-adjusted, happy men and women to have children.

    d. Often, the people who have children are the people who can least afford to take care of those children after they are born.

_____ 4. The selection is best described as based on

    a. facts.

    b. opinions.

    c. statistics.

    d. research.

## H. THINKING CRITICALLY: ANALYZING THE AUTHOR'S MESSAGE

*Select the best answer.*

_____ 1. When the author refers to the "script in my life" in paragraph 1, he is saying that

    a. a movie should be made of his life.

    b. he is taking several prescription medications to deal with depression.

    c. he believes the course of his life has been charted for him by a greater power in the universe.

    d. he has the same conversations over and over again.

_____ 2. With the phrase "missing a gene" (paragraph 5), the author is pointing to the societal assumption that people who don't want to have children

    a. are not normal.

    b. should not reproduce.

    c. have genetic abnormalities that can cause birth defects.

    d. are likely to become criminals or loners.

_____ 3. The author uses the phrase "sea of people" in paragraph 18 to imply that

    a. deep down inside, all people are the same.

    b. huge numbers of people do not support Amanda's decision.

    c. the world is facing overpopulation.

    d. more people live on the coasts (near the water) than in the center of the country.

# WRITING IN RESPONSE TO THE READING

## I. REVIEWING AND ORGANIZING IDEAS WITH A SUMMARY

*Write a summary of the reading selection. The first few sentences are provided to help you get started.*

Yashar Ali has the same conversation over and over. He tells people he doesn't want to have children, and they begin arguing with him. But he is firm in his decision and frustrated by society's unwillingness to accept his personal choices.

_____

_____

_____

_____

## J. ANALYZING THE ISSUE AND ARGUMENT

1. What contemporary issue is discussed in this reading? Phrase this issue in the form of a question.

2. Would you describe the author's approach to the issue as "pro" or "con"?

3. Identify at least three rhetorical questions in the reading. A *rhetorical question* is a question that is asked directly and then answered or discussed. (Many authors find rhetorical questions an effective method of introducing controversies or information.) For example, the first sentence of paragraph 3 is a rhetorical question: "Why don't we trust people when they decide that they don't want to have kids?"

4. What is the author's background, and is he qualified to write about the topic? Why or why not? (Take into account the nature of this reading: Is it meant to provide information, or is meant to be an essay about a very personal decision?)

5. Do you find any bias in the selection? Explain.

6. Does the author ever explain why he does not want to have children? Does this increase or decrease the effectiveness of the reading?

7. Evaluate the reading on the following criteria:

    a. Is the reading timely?

    b. Has the author provided sufficient evidence to support his argument? What other types of evidence might he provide to strengthen his main ideas?

    c. Are key terms well defined?

    d. Does the author offer any opposing viewpoints? If so, does he refute them? If not, what might some opposing viewpoints be?

    e. What assumptions (either stated or implied) do you find in the reading?

    f. Does the article offer any emotional appeals? If so, identify them and evaluate their fairness.

## K.  WRITING PARAGRAPHS AND ESSAYS

*Write a paragraph or essay in response to the following writing prompts.*

1. The author of this selection states that he doesn't want to have children and that he's tired of people questioning his decision. But he never states why he doesn't want to have children. Write a paragraph in which you speculate on the reasons why people might choose not to have children.

2. The author argues that the decision to have (or not to have) children is a highly personal one. Write a paragraph in which you discuss another type of highly personal decision (for example, the decision to move back home after graduation).

3. Write a caption to accompany the photo on page 623. Tie the caption to the reading's content.

4. In "I Don't Want to Have Kids. Get Over It" the author argues one side of a contemporary issue. Write an essay in which you explore the other side of the issue, listing some of the reasons people should have (or may want) children.

5. What do you think are the greatest joys of being a parent? What do you think are the greatest challenges of being a parent today? Write an essay exploring one of these questions.

6. The author discusses women's rights and suggests that feminism has not accomplished all it set out to do. In what ways do you think feminism has improved women's rights and position in society? What type of progress still needs to be made? Write an essay answering these questions.

# What Is Religion?

James M. Henslin

## SOURCE AND CONTEXT

TEXTBOOK
READING

This reading originally appeared in an introductory sociology textbook, *Sociology: A Down-to-Earth Approach*, by James M. Henslin. Sociology is the study of society and human behavior. "Welcome to sociology!" the author writes in his preface. "Many of us find that it holds the key to understanding social life. If you like to watch people and try to figure out why they do what they do, you will like sociology."

## A NOTE ON THE READING

Why is religion such a powerful force in society? Read "What Is Religion?" to understand the many roles religion plays in society and in people's personal lives.

## PREVIEWING THE READING

*Using the steps listed on page 4, preview the reading selection. When you have finished, complete the following items.*

1. This reading will define the term _____.
2. List at least three functions of religion that you expect the reading to discuss.

   _____

   _____

   _____

 **MAKING
CONNECTIONS**

_____

*Do you have strong religious faith or attend religious services on a regular basis? If so, what benefits do you receive from attending religious services?*

## READING TIP

*This reading offers a functionalist view of religion. Functionalism is a school of sociological thought that sees society as a complex set of structures that work together to promote social stability. The reading also reprints a common element found in textbooks, the "boxed insert." Boxed inserts (found here under the heading "Down-to-Earth Sociology/Religion and Health: What We Know and Don't Know," paragraphs 20–31) provide additional, more detailed information about a topic mentioned (but not discussed in detail) in the text.*

# What Is Religion?

James M. Henslin

## What Is Religion?

1      All human societies are organized by some form of the family, as well as by some kind of economic system and political order. These key social institutions touch on aspects of life that are essential to human welfare. Here we focus on religion, another universal social institution.

2      What does sociology have to do with something so personal and intimate as religion? As with the family, sociologists do two primary things: They analyze the relationship between society and religion, and they study the role that religion plays in people's lives.

3      It is also important to ask what sociologists do *not* do in their research on religion. Just as sociologists do not try to prove that one family form is better than another, so they do not try to prove that one religion is better than another. Sociologists don't even have tools for deciding that one course of action is more moral than another, much less that one religion is the "correct" one. Religion is a matter of faith—and sociologists deal with empirical matters, things they can observe or measure. Sociologists can study how religious beliefs and practices affect people's lives, but unlike **theologians**, they have nothing to say about the truth of a religion's teachings.

**theologians** those who study religion and religious theory

When I visited a Hindu temple in Chattisgargh, India, I was impressed by the colorful and expressive statues on its roof. Here is a close-up of some of those figures, which represent some of the millions of gods that Hindus worship. What three elements of religion did Durkheim identify? What are "sacred" and "profane"?

4      Religion was a major interest of Emile Durkheim, probably because he was reared in a mixed-religion family, by a Protestant mother and a Jewish father. Durkheim decided to find out what all religions have in common. After surveying religions around the world, he published his findings in *The Elementary Forms of the Religious Life.* This 1912 book is complicated, but let's summarize Durkheim's three main findings. The first is that the world's religions have no specific belief or practice in common. The second is that all religions develop a community centering on their beliefs and practices. The third is that all religions separate the sacred from the profane. By sacred, Durkheim referred to aspects of life having to do with the supernatural that inspire awe, reverence, deep respect, even fear. By profane, he meant the aspects of life that are not concerned with religion but, instead, are part of ordinary, everyday life.

5      Durkheim (1912/1965) summarized his conclusions by saying,

> *A religion is a unified system of beliefs and practices relative to sacred things, that is to say, things set apart and forbidden—beliefs and practices which unite into one single moral community called a Church, all those who adhere to them.*

6      Religion, then, has three elements:

1. **Beliefs** that some things are sacred (forbidden, set apart from the profane)
2. **Practices** (rituals) centering on the things considered sacred
3. **A moral community** (a church), which results from a group's beliefs and practices

7      Durkheim used the word *church* in an unusual sense, to refer to any "moral community" centered on beliefs and practices regarding the sacred. In Durkheim's sense, *church* refers to Buddhists bowing before a shrine, Hindus dipping in the Ganges River, and Confucians offering food to their ancestors. Similarly, the term *moral community* does not imply morality in the sense familiar to most of us—of ethical conduct. Rather, a moral community is simply a group of people who are united by their religious practices—and that would include sixteenth-century Aztec priests who each day gathered around an altar to pluck out the beating heart of a virgin.

## The Functionalist Perspective

8      Functionalists stress that religion is universal because it meets universal human needs. What are religion's key functions?

## Functions of Religion

9      **Questions about Ultimate Meaning.** Around the world, religions provide answers to perplexing questions about ultimate meaning. What is the purpose of life? Why do people suffer? Is there an afterlife? The answers to questions like these give followers a sense of purpose, a framework for living. Instead of seeing themselves buffeted by random events in an aimless existence, believers see their lives as fitting into a divine plan.

10     **Emotional Comfort.** The answers that religion provides about ultimate meaning bring comfort by assuring people that there is a purpose to life, even to suffering. The religious rituals that enshroud crucial events such as illness and death assure the individual that others care.

11     **Social Solidarity.** Religious teachings and practices unite believers into a community that shares values and perspectives ("we Jews," "we Christians," "we Muslims"). The religious rituals that surround marriage, for example, link the bride and groom with a broader community that wishes them well. So do other religious rituals, such as those that celebrate birth and mourn death.

12     **Guidelines for Everyday Life.** The teachings of religion are not all abstractions. They also provide practical guidelines for everyday life. For example, four of the ten commandments delivered by Moses to the Israelites concern God, but the other six contain instructions for getting along with others, from how to avoid problems with parents and neighbors to warnings about lying, stealing, and having affairs.

13     The consequences for people who follow these guidelines can be measured. For example, people who attend church are more likely to exercise and less likely to

abuse alcohol, nicotine, and illegal drugs than are people who don't go to church (Gillum 2005; Wallace et al. 2007; Gallup Poll 2010). In general, churchgoers follow a healthier lifestyle and live longer than people who don't go to church. How religion affects health is discussed in the Down-to-Earth Sociology box (p. 614).

14    **Social Control.** Although a religion's guidelines for everyday life usually apply only to its members, nonmembers feel a spillover. Religious teachings, for example, are incorporated into criminal law. In an earlier United States, people could be arrested for **blasphemy** and adultery. Some states still have laws that prohibit the sale of alcohol before noon on Sunday, laws whose purpose was to get people out of the saloons and into the churches.

**blasphemy**
disrespect for
God or religion

15    **Adaptation.** Religion can help people adapt to new environments. For example, it isn't easy for immigrants to adjust to the customs of a new land. By keeping their native language alive within a community of people who are going through similar experiences, religion serves as a bridge between the old and new: It provides both continuity with the immigrants' cultural past and encouragement to adapt to the new culture. This was the case for earlier U.S. immigrants from Europe, and it remains true today for immigrants from all over the globe. The many **mosques** and thousands of Spanish-speaking churches around the United States are an outstanding example.

**mosques**
Muslim houses
of worship

16    For their part, governments reciprocate by supporting God. Some governments sponsor a particular religion and ban or place a heavy hand on others. They provide financial support for building churches, **synagogues**, mosques, and **seminaries**, and even pay salaries to the clergy. These religions are known as state religions**.** During the sixteenth and seventeenth centuries in Sweden, the government sponsored Lutheranism; in Switzerland, Calvinism; and in Italy, Roman Catholicism. In some Arab countries today, this is the practice regarding Islam.

**synagogues**
Jewish houses
of worship

**seminaries**
schools to train
clergy

17    Even though a government sponsors no particular religion, religious beliefs can be embedded in a nation's life. This is called civil religion (Bellah 1970). For example, in their inaugural speeches, U.S. presidents—regardless of whether or not they are believers—invariably ask God to bless the nation. U.S. officials take office by swearing in the name of God that they will fulfill their duty. Similarly, Congress opens each session with a prayer led by its own chaplain. The Pledge of Allegiance includes the phrase "one nation under God," and coins bear the inscription "In God We Trust."

18    **Social Change.** Although religion is often so bound up with the prevailing social order that it resists social change, religious activists sometimes spearhead change. In the 1960s, for example, the civil rights movement, whose goals were to desegregate public facilities and abolish racial discrimination at southern polls, was led by religious leaders. African American churches served as centers at which demonstrators were trained and rallies were organized.

19    **Support for the Government.** Most religions provide support for the government. An obvious example is the way some churches prominently display the U.S. flag. Some fly it in front of the church building, and many display both the U.S. flag and a church flag on stands at the front of the worship center. Religions that become hostile to the government—or even seem strange—can run into trouble.

# DOWN-TO-EARTH SOCIOLOGY

## RELIGION AND HEALTH: WHAT WE KNOW AND DON'T KNOW

20 *"After seeing the data, I think I should go to church," said Lynda Powell, an epidemiologist at Rush University Medical Center in Chicago (Helliker 2005).*

21 This was the response of a non-churchgoing scientist when she saw the data on health and religion. Although scientists cannot determine the truth of any religion, they can study the effects of religion on people's lives. Health is one of those areas that can be measured, and the research is bringing some surprises.

22 Powell, along with two colleagues, evaluated the published research on the effects of religion on health. They evaluated only research that met rigid criteria. For example, they threw out studies that didn't **control for** age, gender, or race–ethnicity, significant variables in health (Powell et al. 2003). Their most outstanding finding? *People who attend religious services once a week or more have 25 percent fewer deaths in a given time period than people who don't go to church.* Think about it: For every hundred deaths of non-churchgoers, there are only 75 deaths of people who attend church weekly.

23 How could this possibly be? Perhaps the churchgoers were already healthier. This wasn't the reason, though, for the researchers compared people who were at the same levels of health.

24 How about healthier lifestyles? Churchgoers are less likely to smoke, to get drunk, and so on. Not this either. The researchers also controlled for lifestyle and social class. The weekly churchgoers actually had 30 percent less mortality, but when the researchers adjusted for lifestyle and social class, the difference was 25 percent (Powell et al. 2003).

25 What explanation could there be, then? Remember that the researchers are scientists, so they aren't going to say "God." But they do suggest three mechanisms that might account for the lower mortality of churchgoers: finding a sense of self-worth and purpose in life, learning calming ways of coping with crises, and experiencing positive emotions. Other researchers have documented the power of this last mechanism: People who have a positive world view and those who believe that God is loving have better health (Campbell et al. 2010).

26 What else might account for this remarkable reduction in mortality? Some researchers think they've put their finger on it: prayer. Prayer (or meditation) seems to change people's brain activity in a way that improves their immune response. Scientists are investigating this hypothesis (Kalb 2003).

27 One researcher points to something else about religion—the practice of forgiveness. It turns out that people who forgive easily are more likely to be in good psychological heath. They are especially less likely to be depressed (Krause and Ellison 2003; Newport et al. 2010). To forgive someone who has done you wrong apparently brings release from feelings of resentment, bitterness, and hatred—but holding on to grudges rips you apart inside.

28 What have researchers found about praying for people who are sick? So far, most researchers haven't found any difference between people who are prayed for and those who are not (Benson et al. 2006). But researchers have encountered

**control for**
take into account; in psychological studies, controlling for a variable means taking that variable into account when conducting research and analyzing results

a problem. How do they find a control group of people who are not being prayed for? There is so much prayer—from parents, siblings, aunts and uncles, friends, and neighbors—that some people don't even know they are being prayed for. I'm sure that researchers will solve this.

29 At this initial stage of research on religion and health, we have hardly any answers, but we do have this remarkable finding about mortality: People who go to religious services more than once a week live seven and a half years longer than those who don't attend religious services (Hummer et al. 1999; Hummer et al. 2004).

30 So, if you want to live longer . . .

**For Your Consideration**

31 If you attend a church, synagogue, or mosque, what difference do you think that your attendance makes in your life? How does your religion affect your lifestyle? What decisions would you have made differently if you did not practice your religion?

# UNDERSTANDING AND ANALYZING THE READING

## A. BUILDING VOCABULARY

### Context

*Using context and a dictionary if necessary, determine the meaning of each word as it is used in the selection.*

_____ 1. empirical (paragraph 3)
   a. religious
   b. concerned with morality
   c. based on facts and data
   d. theoretical

_____ 2. perplexing (paragraph 9)
   a. puzzling
   b. common
   c. unanswerable
   d. philosophical

_____ 3. buffeted (paragraph 9)
   a. eaten
   b. varied
   c. victimized by
   d. knocked around

_____ 4. enshroud (paragraph 10)
   a. kill
   b. embalm
   c. hide
   d. surround

_____ 5. reciprocate (paragraph 16)
   a. place a ban on
   b. give something in return
   c. provide tax benefits to
   d. placate the public

_____ 6. spearhead (paragraph 18)
   a. act as leader
   b. work against
   c. maintain at a specific level
   d. overwork

_____ 7. abolish (paragraph 18)

    a. diminish

    b. end

    c. research

    d. uncover

_____ 8. colleagues (paragraph 22)

    a. co-workers

    b. family members

    c. teachers

    d. scientists

_____ 9. hypothesis (paragraph 26)

    a. result

    b. theory

    c. lie

    d. likelihood

_____ 10. siblings (paragraph 28)

    a. aunts and uncles

    b. mother and father

    c. brothers and sisters

    d. in-laws

## Word Parts

> ### A REVIEW OF PREFIXES, ROOTS, AND SUFFIXES
>
> **DE-** means *away* or *from*.
>
> **MORT** means *death*.
>
> **-AL** means *pertaining to* or *referring to*.
>
> **-ITY** refers to *a condition* or *state*.

*Use your knowledge of word parts and the review above to fill in the blanks in the following sentences.*

1. To *desegregate* (paragraph 18) means to move away from _____ and toward a racially and ethnically integrated society.

2. *Mortality* (paragraph 24) refers to the state of being mortal, or subject to _____ .

## B. UNDERSTANDING THE THESIS AND OTHER MAIN IDEAS

*Select the best answer.*

_____ 1. The best statement of the thesis or central thought of "What Is Religion?" (paragraphs 1–19) is which of the following?

    a. The term *sacred* refers to aspects of life that concern the supernatural, while the term *profane* refers to ordinary, everyday life.

    b. Religion not only provides emotional comfort for adherents, it also provides social solidarity, guidelines for everyday life, and social control.

    c. Overall, religious belief helps people live longer, healthier lives.

    d. Religion has three key elements (beliefs, practices, and moral community) and meets many universal human needs.

_____ 2. The main idea of paragraph 15 is found in the
   a. first sentence.
   b. second sentence.
   c. last sentence.
   d. first and last sentences.

_____ 3. The topic of paragraph 17 is
   a. Calvinism.
   b. civil religion.
   c. state religions.
   d. church buildings.

_____ 4. The best statement of the thesis or central thought of "Religion and Health: What We Know and Don't Know" (paragraphs 20–31) is which of the following?
   a. While theologians are concerned primarily with spiritual matters, scientists can apply scientific methods to the study of religion.
   b. It is difficult to collect data and facts about religion and attendance at religious services, but scientists have begun the process of doing so.
   c. Several scientific studies have pointed to the health effects of religious attendance, including a lower death rate and a longer lifespan, which have been linked to stronger psychological health and happiness.
   d. While researchers have been able to determine the effects of religious attendance on a person's life expectancy, they have been unable to determine the effects of prayer on those who are prayed for.

## C. IDENTIFYING DETAILS

*Select the best answer.*

_____ 1. Which of the following is *not* one of Emile Durkheim's three main findings regarding religions?
   a. All religions believe in a heaven and a hell.
   b. All religions separate the sacred from the profane.
   c. The world's religions have no specific belief or practice in common.
   d. All religions develop a community centering on their beliefs and practices.

_____ 2. In the sixteenth and seventeenth centuries, the Italian government sponsored
   a. Judaism.
   b. Protestantism.
   c. Roman Catholicism.
   d. Islam.

_____ 3. People who attend religious services more than once a week live an average of _____ years longer than those who don't attend religious services.
   a. thee
   b. five
   c. seven and a half
   d. nine and a half

_____ 4. The original ten commandments given to Moses concern all of the following *except*
   a. God.
   b. treatment of animals.
   c. how to avoid problems with neighbors and parents.
   d. warnings against stealing, lying, and having extramarital affairs.

## D. RECOGNIZING METHODS OF ORGANIZATION AND TRANSITIONS

*Select the best answer.*

_____ 1. The overall pattern of organization used under the heading "Functions of Religion" (paragraphs 9–19) is
   a. chronological order.
   b. order of importance.
   c. process.
   d. listing/enumeration.

_____ 2. The organizational pattern used in paragraph 6 is
   a. generalization and example.
   b. summary.
   c. process.
   d. cause and effect.

_____ 3. All of the following transitional words and phrases point to the cause and effect pattern in paragraph 25 *except*
   a. explanation.
   b. mechanisms.
   c. account for.
   d. self-worth.

## E. READING AND THINKING VISUALLY

*Select the best answer.*

_____ 1. The figures in the photo on page 634 are sacred to
   a. Muslims.
   b. Protestants.
   c. Hindus.
   d. Buddhists.

## F. FIGURING OUT IMPLIED MEANINGS

*Indicate whether each statement is true (T) or false (F).*

_____ 1. In Emile Durkheim's definition, *moral community* does not imply ethical conduct.

_____ 2. The profane aspects of human life are a part of everyday, ordinary life.

_____ 3. Sociologists attempt to determine which religion's beliefs are the most accurate.

_____ 4. In any given week, those who attend church are less likely to die than those who do not attend church.

_____ 5. All of the world's major religions share a belief in one God.

_____ 6. Emile Durkheim used the term *church* to refer specifically to Christian faiths.

_____ 7. Those who attend church are less likely to drink alcohol and smoke than people who don't go to church.

## G. THINKING CRITICALLY: ANALYZING THE AUTHOR'S TECHNIQUES

*Select the best answer.*

_____ 1. The author's purpose in "What Is Religion?" is to

  a. define the term *religion*, explain the positive roles it plays in society, and look at the health effects of religious attendance.

  b. compare and contrast the world's major religions (Christianity, Islam, and Buddhism) to answer the question "Which religion best serves human needs?"

  c. examine both the benefits and drawbacks of religion as a social institution, not only in the United States but also around the world.

  d. persuade readers to attend religious services (no matter what their religious faith) more than once a week.

_____ 2. The tone of the selection is best defined as

  a. skeptical.

  b. positive.

  c. passionate.

  d. satirical.

_____ 3. The parenthetical expression in paragraph 13 (Gillum 2005; Wallace et al. 2007; Gallup Poll 2010) refers to which type of evidence?

  a. birth dates for the people listed

  b. a timeline of religious belief

  c. credible research studies

  d. various members of the clergy from different religions

_____ 4. All of the following sentences from the reading are facts *except*:

    a. "Religion was a major interest of Emile Durkheim, probably because he was reared in a mixed-religion family, by a Protestant mother and a Jewish father." (paragraph 4)

    b. "Rather, a moral community is simply a group of people who are united by their religious practices—and that would include sixteenth-century Aztec priests who each day gathered around an altar to pluck out the beating heart of a virgin." (paragraph 7)

    c. "Similarly, Congress opens each session with a prayer led by its own chaplain." (paragraph 17)

    d. "It turns out that people who forgive easily are more likely to be in good psychological health." (paragraph 27)

## H. THINKING CRITICALLY: ANALYZING THE AUTHOR'S MESSAGE

*Select the best answer.*

_____ 1. The author refers to "key social institutions" in paragraph 1. Which of the following would *not* fall into this category?

    a. the political system

    b. the economic system

    c. the sports recruitment system

    d. the educational system

_____ 2. The term "social control" in paragraph 14 refers to

    a. parents' discipline of their children within their own homes.

    b. the criminal justice system of police, detectives, and jailhouses.

    c. laws and customs that prevent people from behaving inappropriately.

    d. indoctrination of students into specific ways of thinking as part of their college education.

_____ 3. With which of the following statements would the author of "What Is Religion?" disagree?

    a. Sociologists are unconcerned with the ways religion affects people's lives.

    b. Civil religion is a part of U.S. society.

    c. Religion can provide both emotional comfort and guidelines for everyday living.

    d. People who attend religious services more than once a week live longer than those who do not attend religious services.

## WRITING IN RESPONSE TO THE READING

*Complete the following map of the reading selection by filling in the missing words or phrases.*

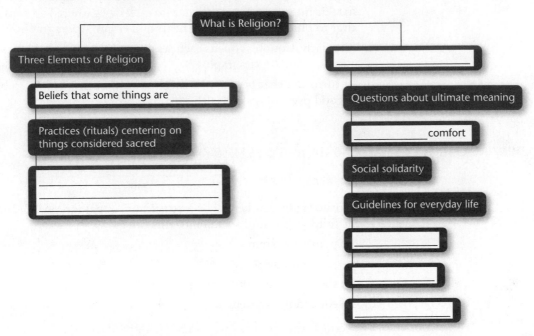

What is Religion?

Three Elements of Religion

Beliefs that some things are _____

Practices (rituals) centering on things considered sacred

_____

_____

Questions about ultimate meaning

_____ comfort

Social solidarity

Guidelines for everyday life

_____

_____

_____

## J. ANALYZING THE ISSUE AND ARGUMENT

1. What contemporary issue is the author discussing in this reading? Phrase the issue as a question. Is the author arguing the "pro" side of this issue or the "con" side?

2. Write a one- or two-sentence summary of the author's argument.

3. Is the author qualified to write on the topic? Why or why not? Is the source from which this reading is taken reliable? Why or why not?

4. Like many longer readings, this selection uses multiple patterns of organization. Point to at least four different organizational patterns used in the reading. Which transitional words or phrases are used to signal each? How does the use of multiple organizational patterns make this reading richer and more informative?

5. Evaluate the reading on the following criteria:

   a. Is the reading timely?

   b. Has the author provided sufficient evidence to support his argument? What other types of evidence might he provide to strengthen the argument?

   c. Notice the dates of the cited research. Some is quite old (1912) while some is much more recent (2010). Is the old research still valid and reliable? Why or why not? Must a research citation be extremely recent in order to be valid?

   d. Has the author defined terms accurately and sufficiently?

   e. Do you find any evidence of bias in the reading?

   f. Does the author offer any opposing viewpoints? If not, what might some opposing arguments be?

   g. Does the reading offer any emotional appeals? If so, identify them and evaluate their fairness.

   h. Does the author state or imply any claims of policy?

## K. WRITING PARAGRAPHS AND ESSAYS

*Write a paragraph or essay in response to the following writing prompts.*

1. Unlike many readings, this reading does not contain a concluding paragraph. Write a concluding paragraph for the selection.

2. What is the difference between a sociologist and a theologian? Write a paragraph explaining the difference.

3. The photo on page 611 ends with two questions. Write a paragraph answering these questions.

4. Write an essay in which you answer one of the questions found in paragraph 31 of the reading.

5. If you attend religious services, what benefits do you think this attendance has for your life? Write an essay in which you discuss these benefits.

6. The author defines the *sacred* as "the aspects of life having to do with the supernatural that inspire awe, reverence, deep respect, even fear" (paragraph 4). Write an essay in which you explore the idea of the sacred in your life, family, community, or city. Which ideas or elements inspire awe, deep respect, or fear? Why?

## ACTIVITIES: EXPLORING PERSONAL FREEDOMS AND LIMITATIONS

*On your own or with a group of classmates, complete two of the following four activities.*

1. Reading Selection 22, "Bipolar Disorder: The Agony and the Ecstasy" discusses one common type of mental disorder. Research another mental disorder and write an essay or prepare a class presentation explaining it. Choose from the following list:

   • antisocial personality disorder

   • paranoid personality disorder

   • borderline personality disorder

   • narcissistic personality disorder

   • dependent personality disorder

2. In Reading Selection 23, Yashar Ali talks about the most personal of decisions: the decision not to have children. A related topic is the decision to get married or to remain single. Prepare a list of the pros and cons of staying single versus getting married. Which do you think is the right choice for you?

3. Attending regular religious services seems to contribute to longevity. What other lifestyle choices do you think contribute. Choose one factor and write an essay explaining how and why it may improve longevity. Research your topic, if necessary.

4. The readings in this chapter discussed just a few aspects of the broad topic of personal freedoms and limitations. Other issues related to personal freedoms include:

- *Technological surveillance:* Is it acceptable to place video cameras at intersections to catch people who run red lights? Should stores be allowed to monitor the store, including dressing rooms, with video cameras?

- *Database compilation and sales:* Do companies have the right to sell your personal information to other companies who are looking to advertise their products to you?

- *Social media:* How do your posts on Facebook, or your tweets on Twitter, affect the way possible employers will view you?

- *"Gag rules":* Many companies prevent their employees from discussing company business with the media. Yet, at the same time, the United States has laws to protect "whistle blowers" who expose a company's dangerous practices. Do businesses have the right to tell employees how they should behave in their private lives?

- *Gender roles:* Today, there are more female firefighters than ever before, as well as more male nurses. Should both men and women have to pass the same physical tests to become firefighters and police officers? Why or why not?

- *Sports teams:* Some schools' sports teams have begun allowing girls to play on otherwise all-male teams, while other activities (such as cheerleading) have begun allowing boys to take part in otherwise all-female activities. What are the pros and cons of these developments?

Write an essay or prepare a class presentation about any of these topics, or any other topic concerning personal freedoms or limitations.

# MAKING CONNECTIONS: SYNTHESIZING WHAT YOU READ

*In many college courses, instructors will expect you to read and evaluate a wide variety of materials. These activities and assignments are designed to provide practice in pulling together ideas from a variety of sources.*

## THINKING WITHIN THE ISSUES

1. "The Space In-Between" (Selection #1, page 328) and "All Guts, No Glory" (Selection #2, page 353) both appear in the chapter titled "Defining Ourselves: Our Multiple Identities." "All Guts, No Glory" focuses on women in military service and combat, while "The Space In-Between" is one student's reflections on his experiences as an immigrant in the United States. Yet these descriptions oversimplify the concept of identity: Women soldiers are more than just members of the military, and Santiago Quintana is more than just a Mexican immigrant living in Wisconsin. What other aspects of their identities might the subjects of these readings identify? List three components of identity that are not directly considered in the readings. For example, the female soldiers in "All Guts, No Glory" may also be mothers.

2. Both "The High Art of Handling Problem People" (Selection #8, page 425) and ""The Many Ways Virtual Communities Impact Our World Offline" (Selection #9, page 440) examine human interactions. How many of the people that we interact with in our daily lives fit into the "problem people" category? Is it a small percentage, a medium percentage, or a large percentage? Do you think people seek membership in virtual communities because they perceive online relationships as somehow "easier" or less stressful than in-person relationships?

3. "Eggs for Sale" (Selection #11, page 468) and "Xeno-Transplantation: The Ultimate Organ Factory" (Selection #12, page 479) both focus on transplanting biological materials into the human body. The reading selections focus on the benefits of these transplantations, but arguments can be made against such activities. Thinking critically about the issues, list at least three arguments against transplanting eggs and organs into the human body.

4. "Technology and Social Media" (Selection #14, page 505) and "Blogs and Democratization" (Selection #15, page 516) both discuss ways in which the Internet and social media are changing society. Compile a list of at least five ways (not discussed in either selection) in which the Internet is changing society. What are the benefits and drawbacks of each?

5. "Groups and Conformity" (Selection #21, page 589) ends a chapter devoted to conformity and nonconformity, or people's decisions to follow or break society's rules. How do the parents in "Why My Mother Wants Me Dead" (Selection #20, page 579) conform to their society's rules? Do they conform to the "rules of parenting" that are more common in the United States?

## THINKING ACROSS THE ISSUES

6. "Eggs for Sale" (Selection #11, page 468) and "Bipolar Disorder: The Agony and the Ecstasy" (Selection #22, page 610) are both personal essays. What types of details do the authors provide to help readers understand their experiences? How are the authors' experiences fundamentally different? How are they similar? "Eggs for Sale" appears in the chapter titled "Science and Ethics: Where Do We Draw the Line?" Why would it also be appropriate to include this reading in Chapter 19, "Personal Freedoms and Limitations: Individual Rights and Controversies"? In which other chapters, or under what other issues, might "Bipolar Order: The Agony and the Ecstasy" appear? Explain your answers.

7. *Social justice* refers to the idea that society should be based on principles of fairness and equality, with all people having a reasonable standard of living and equal access to opportunities. For example, "Crisis Management: Why Climate Change Will Make You Love Big Government" (Selection #6, page 398) explores the idea that government must help mitigate the effects of environmental disasters brought about by climate change. Identify at least two other readings in this book that are concerned with social justice. In each reading, what is the key problem identified by the author(s)? How do the authors suggest these problems may be remedied?

8. Several readings in this book are focused on parents and children: "Eggs for Sale" (Selection #11, page 468), "Why My Mother Wants Me Dead" (Selection #20, page 579), "I Don't Want to Have Kids. Get Over It" (Selection #23, page 622). In the United States, what is the traditional role of the family? What are the expectations regarding marriage and family for young unmarried people? How are these expectations changing or evolving, and how does each of these readings either support or challenge traditional ideas of marriage and family?

9. Many college campuses are a microcosm of the larger society. In other words, the college campus often reflects what is happening in the larger society. In some cases, campus trends follow trends in society; in other cases, colleges are at the forefront of research, technology, and other movements that will later find their way into the surrounding communities (and the nation and the world). Identify three readings that are likely

to be of interest to college students. For example, you might choose "Sustainability on Campus" (Selection #4, page 368), "Hooking Up" (Reading #7, page 414), and "Ten Proven Brain Benefits of Being Bilingual" (Selection #17, page 539). Now suppose that you are counseling a high school senior about the college experience. Based on these readings, what five pieces of advice would you give him or her?

10. The goal of many textbook writers is to define key terms that will help students understand the world better. Each textbook chapter (or textbook section) usually offers further details about those key terms, providing richer information about them. Consider two readings that are primarily definitional: "What Is Residential Segregation?" (Selection #18, page 550) and "What is Religion?" (Selection #24, page 633). What do these two readings have in common? How are they different? For example, when does the author answer the question in the reading's title – at the beginning, in the middle, or at the end of the reading? Do the authors focus primarily on the United States, or do they discuss other countries as well? What are the authors' purposes for writing?

# Casebook for Critical Thinking: Global Warming and Climate Change

PART

THREE

# EXAMINING ONE ISSUE IN DEPTH

Throughout this text, you've read many selections that look at various aspects of contemporary issues. As you pursue your college studies, you will often be asked to study one topic in more depth, consulting multiple sources to gain a deeper understanding of it. In term papers and on written exams, you will need to synthesize all of these sources to demonstrate your mastery of the topic.

In this section, we take a closer look at a contemporary issue—global warming and climate change. Because the issue is so important, it is studied across different academic disciplines. You may think that students who take courses in the Earth science department study weather and climate, and you would be correct. But the topic is also a part of many other college courses. For example,

- **Sociology** courses may examine how climate change impacts society.
- **Geography** courses may look at the impact of climate change in different countries.
- **Environmental science** courses may examine the pollution and global warming caused by extracting and burning fossil fuels.
- **Business** courses may look at the effects of environmental laws on businesses.
- **Political science** courses may study the success or failure of political parties that run on a platform of environmental awareness.

To give you a taste of how different disciplines approach the same topic, the readings in this section will present different aspects of global warming and climate change. These readings come from different types of sources, including textbooks, Web sites, government agencies, and blogs.

## Tips for Reading About Global Warming and Climate Change

Here are some tips for reading not only the selections in this section, but any reading about global warming and climate change.

- **Know the difference between climate and weather.** Time is the key difference between weather and climate. **Weather** refers to atmospheric conditions over a relatively short period of time (such as a year or a decade). **Climate** refers to patterns in the atmosphere over relatively long periods of time, such as centuries, millennia, or longer. (A century is a period of 100 years, and a millennium is a period of 1,000 years.)
- **Understand the role of computer modeling in weather and climate studies.** It is impossible to predict weather and climate perfectly. The further into the future the prediction is, the more it must rely on computer simulations that use past history, as well as scientific observations, to predict what will happen in the future. But many argue that these computer models are wrong or unreliable.

- **Be aware of underlying concerns about financial considerations and lifestyle.** Resistance to laws that seek to limit global warming and climate change is often based on financial considerations. Many argue that it will be extremely expensive to change current methods of energy production, and many fear that such massive expenses will cause high levels of unemployment. Others believe that people should not change their traditions or lifestyles over an issue whose importance they believe is being exaggerated. And still others fear that the eventual costs will be overwhelming if climate change is not aggressively addressed now.

As you read any selection on the topic of global warming and climate change, it is essential that you examine the credibility of the source and look for indications of bias.

## Tips for Synthesizing Sources

As you consult many sources to learn more about a specific topic, you will need to *synthesize* this information into a coherent, useful whole. Here are some tips to help you work with and synthesize multiple sources.

1. **Choose sources that are trustworthy and reliable.** Carefully examine the results of your initial search for information. For example, suppose you conduct a Google search on the topic. Do not assume that the first ten "hits" are the best sources of information. Always examine the "About Us" section of a Web site for more information about its sponsor. Do not assume that nonprofit organizations (denoted by .org in their Web addresses) are unbiased.

2. **Read for the "big picture": Identify the thesis or central thought and main ideas.** As you set out to learn more about a particular topic, you should first establish a broad base of knowledge. The first time you read each source, look for the key ideas. What argument is the author making? What are the author's main points? You can go back and learn the details later.

3. **Use electronic search tools if you are working with electronic documents.** Suppose you are working with ten documents and you are researching the topic of extinction. Conduct a search for the word *extinction* to help you find information about that topic within the document. In printed books, consult the index.

4. **Look for areas of common agreement.** As you read multiple sources, you may encounter the same information several times. Make note of the facts on which most reliable, credible people agree. Having a solid understanding of these facts can help you evaluate an author's claims and determine whether the author is biased.

5. **Be suspicious of highly emotional language.** As you read multiple sources, you may find yourself favoring readings that are colorful and intense while paying less attention to sources that seem more "dry" or dull. Avoid this tendency and seek objective sources as you begin your research. As you learn more about the topic, you will be better able to evaluate and synthesize sources in which the author offers strong opinions or exhibits strong bias.

## Previewing

An important part of working with multiple sources is the ability to find the information you are looking for. Previewing can be extremely helpful in this regard.

**EXERCISE 1:** **Working Collaboratively to Activate Background Knowledge**

*Before you preview the following readings, work with a small group of your peers to activate your background knowledge by discussing the following questions and relating them to your own experiences. At the conclusion of your group discussion, you should be prepared to actively participate in a whole class discussion of the questions.*

1. What do you already know about global warming and climate change?
2. Do you think summers have felt hotter in recent years?
3. Have you, a friend, or a family member been affected by a weather-related natural disaster such as a hurricane, cyclone, or wildfire?
4. How much do you know about the reasons dinosaurs went extinct?
5. Do you have friends or family in other countries? What are their opinions about global warming and climate change?
6. Does the company you work for have any "green" (environmentally friendly) policies or programs?
7. Why are some people so skeptical of climate change? Why are others so convinced it is a reality?

**EXERCISE 2:** **Locating Information**

*Preview each of the eight readings on pages 656–675. Indicate the reading(s) in which you can find the type of information listed.*

| Information on Global Warming and Climate Change | Source 1 | Source 2 | Source 3 | Source 4 | Source 5 | Source 6 | Source 7 | Source 8 |
|---|---|---|---|---|---|---|---|---|
| 1. Rising temperatures in the United States | | | | | | | | |
| 2. An overview of the ways climate change may affect Earth | | | | | | | | |
| 3. The geologic time scale | | | | | | | | |

(Continued)

| Information on Global Warming and Climate Change | Source 1 | Source 2 | Source 3 | Source 4 | Source 5 | Source 6 | Source 7 | Source 8 |
|---|---|---|---|---|---|---|---|---|
| 4. The effects of climate change on countries around the world | | | | | | | | |
| 5. Effects of climate change on weather, sea level, and people | | | | | | | | |
| 6. The opinions of climate-change skeptics | | | | | | | | |
| 7. The government's role in managing the effects of climate change | | | | | | | | |
| 8. Details of Hurricane Sandy | | | | | | | | |
| 9. Corporate citizenship and the role of businesses in protecting the environment | | | | | | | | |
| 10. An argument for retreating from the ocean's edge in terms of human population and development | | | | | | | | |
| 11. The extinction of plants and animals | | | | | | | | |

## READING AND EVALUATING SOURCES

The following eight sources present a variety of perspectives on the issue of global warming and climate change. Your instructor may assign all of the readings or select among and assign specific sources. Each reading is followed by critical thinking questions specific to the reading. At the end of the casebook, you will find Synthesis and Integration questions that draw upon two or more of the sources contained here.

As you read the sources, use the tips provided above for reading about global warming and synthesizing sources. You might also want to highlight as you read and/or write a brief summary of each source.

**SOURCE 1**
NASA Web Site

# How Will Global Warming Change Earth?

*This reading is taken from the Web site of the National Aeronautics and Space Administration (NASA), the U.S. government agency responsible for the space program and space exploration. NASA satellites take images of the globe, and NASA makes these images available free on the Web.*

1   The impact of increased surface temperatures is significant in itself. But global warming will have additional, far-reaching effects on the planet. Warming modifies rainfall patterns, amplifies coastal erosion, lengthens the growing season in some regions, melts ice caps and glaciers, and alters the ranges of some infectious diseases. Some of these changes are already occurring.

Global warming will shift major climate patterns, possibly prolonging and intensifying the current drought in the U.S. Southwest. The white ring of bleached rock on the once-red cliffs that hold Lake Powell indicate the drop in water level over the past decade—the result of repeated winters with low snowfall.

## Changing Weather

2    For most places, global warming will result in more frequent hot days and fewer cool days, with the greatest warming occurring over land. Longer, more intense heat waves will become more common. Storms, floods, and droughts will generally be more severe as precipitation patterns change. Hurricanes may increase in intensity due to warmer ocean surface temperatures.

3    It is impossible to pin any single unusual weather event on global warming, but emerging evidence suggests that global warming is already influencing the weather. **Heat waves, droughts, and intense rain events have increased in frequency** during the last 50 years, and human-induced global warming more likely than not contributed to the trend.

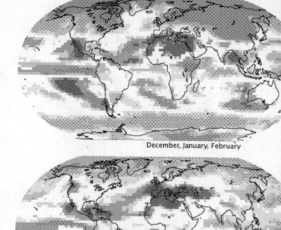

December, January, February

June, July, August

**Precipitation Change** (percent)

-20   -10   -5   0   +5   +10   +20

## Rising Sea Levels

4    The weather isn't the only thing global warming will impact: rising sea levels will erode coasts and cause more frequent coastal flooding. Some island nations will disappear. The problem is serious because up to 10 percent of the world's population lives in vulnerable areas less than 10 meters (about 30 feet) above sea level.

**stippled**
dotted

Apart from driving temperatures up, global warming is likely to cause bigger, more destructive storms, leading to an overall increase in precipitation. With some exceptions, the tropics will likely receive less rain (orange) as the planet warms, while the polar regions will receive more precipitation (green). White areas indicate that fewer than two thirds of the climate models agreed on how precipitation will change. **Stippled** areas reveal where more than 90 percent of the models agreed. (©2007 IPCC WG1 AR-4.)

5    Between 1870 and 2000, the sea level increased by 1.7 millimeters per year on average, for a total sea level rise of 221 millimeters (0.7 feet or 8.7 inches). **And the rate of sea level rise is accelerating.** Since 1993, NASA satellites have shown that sea levels are rising more quickly, about 3 millimeters per year, for a total sea level rise of 48 millimeters (0.16 feet or 1.89 inches) between 1993 and 2009.

6    The Intergovernmental Panel on Climate Change (IPCC) estimates that sea levels will rise between 0.18 and 0.59 meters (0.59 to 1.9 feet) by 2099 as warming sea water expands, and mountain and polar glaciers melt. These sea level change predictions may be underestimates, however, because they do not account for any increases in the rate at which the world's major ice sheets are melting. As temperatures rise, ice will melt more quickly. Satellite measurements reveal that the Greenland and West Antarctic ice sheets are shedding about 125 billion tons of ice per year—enough to raise sea levels by 0.35 millimeters (0.01 inches) per year. If the melting accelerates, the increase in sea level could be significantly higher.

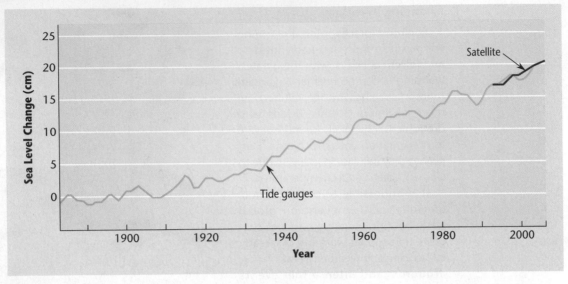

Sea levels crept up about 20 centimeters (7.9 inches) during the twentieth century. Sea levels are predicted to go up between 18 and 59 cm (7.1 and 23 inches) over the next century, though the increase could be greater if ice sheets in Greenland and Antarctica melt more quickly than predicted. Higher sea levels will erode coastlines and cause more frequent flooding.

### Impacting Ecosystems

7    More importantly, perhaps, global warming is already putting pressure on ecosystems, the plants and animals that co-exist in a particular climate zone, both on land and in the ocean. Warmer temperatures have already shifted the growing season in many parts of the globe. The growing season in parts of the Northern Hemisphere became two weeks longer in the second half of the 20th century. Spring is coming earlier in both hemispheres.

8    This change in the growing season affects the broader ecosystem. Migrating animals have to start seeking food sources earlier. The shift in seasons may already be causing the lifecycles of pollinators, like bees, to be out of synch with flowering plants and trees. This mismatch can limit the ability of both pollinators and plants to survive and reproduce, which would reduce food availability throughout the food chain.

9    Warmer temperatures also extend the growing season. This means that plants need more water to keep growing throughout the season or they will dry out, increasing the risk of failed crops and wildfires. Once the growing season ends, shorter, milder winters fail to kill **dormant** insects, increasing the risk of large, damaging infestations in subsequent seasons.

**dormant**
in a state of rest
or sleep

**indigenous**
native

10    In some ecosystems, maximum daily temperatures might climb beyond the tolerance of **indigenous** plants or animals. To survive the extreme temperatures, both marine and land-based plants and animals have started to migrate towards the poles. Those species, and in some cases, entire ecosystems, that cannot quickly migrate or adapt, face extinction. The IPCC estimates that 20–30 percent of plant and animal species will be at risk of extinction if temperatures climb more than 1.5° to 2.5°C.

## Impacting People

11   The changes to weather and ecosystems will also affect people more directly. Hardest hit will be those living in low-lying coastal areas, and residents of poorer countries who do not have the resources to adapt to changes in temperature extremes and water resources. As tropical temperature zones expand, the reach of some infectious diseases, such as malaria, will change. More intense rains and hurricanes and rising sea levels will lead to more severe flooding and potential loss of property and life.

12   Hotter summers and more frequent fires will lead to more cases of heat stroke and deaths, and to higher levels of near-surface ozone and smoke, which would cause more "code red" air quality days. Intense droughts can lead to an increase in malnutrition. On a longer time scale, fresh water will become scarcer, especially during the summer, as mountain glaciers disappear, particularly in Asia and parts of North America.

13   On the flip side, there could be "winners" in a few places. For example, as long as the rise in global average temperature stays below 3 degrees Celsius, some models predict that global food production could increase because of the longer growing season at mid-to-high latitudes, provided adequate water resources are available. The same small change in temperature, however, would reduce food production at lower latitudes, where many countries already face food shortages. On balance, most research suggests that the negative impacts of a changing climate far outweigh the positive impacts. Current civilization—agriculture and population distribution—has developed based on the current climate. The more the climate changes, and the more rapidly it changes, the greater the cost of adaptation.

14   Ultimately, global warming will impact life on Earth in many ways, but the extent of the change is largely up to us. Scientists have shown that human emissions of greenhouse gases are pushing global temperatures up, and many aspects of climate are responding to the warming in the way that scientists predicted they would.

One inevitable consequence of global warming is sea-level rise. In the face of higher sea levels and more intense storms, coastal communities face greater risk of rapid beach erosion from destructive storms like the intense nor'easter of April 2007 that caused this damage. (Photograph ©2007 metimbers2000.)

This offers hope. Since people are causing global warming, people can mitigate global warming, if they act in time. Greenhouse gases are long-lived, so the planet will continue to warm and changes will continue to happen far into the future, but the degree to which global warming changes life on Earth depends on our decisions now.

## CRITICAL THINKING QUESTIONS

1. What are some possible effects of longer, more intense heat waves? Think about the effects on individuals, on agriculture, and on energy usage.
2. Does this reading state conclusively that humans are responsible for creating the more intense weather events of the past 50 years?
3. All of the measurements in this reading are given first in the metric system, followed by a conversion into the U.S. system—for example, "0.18 and 0.59 meters (0.59 to 1.9 feet)."
   Why do the authors use metric measurements first? What does this tell you about the intended audience for the article?
4. Identify at least three statements of fact and three statements of opinion in the reading.
5. What do the authors mean by the following phrase in paragraph 8? "This mismatch can limit the ability of both pollinators and plants to survive and reproduce, which would reduce food availability throughout the food chain."
6. Do you perceive bias in this selection, or does the selection represent an attempt to present multiple sides of the issue? Explain.
7. Explain the meaning of the following sentence in paragraph 13: "The more the climate changes, and the more rapidly it changes, the greater the cost of adaptation."
8. Provide three words to describe the tone of this reading.

---

**EXERCISE 3:**   **Working Collaboratively**

*After answering the critical thinking questions on your own, pair up with a classmate and share your answers. As you discuss the questions, add to your answers the information you learn from your partner.*

---

**SOURCE 2**
Coastalcare.org
Web Site

# We Need to Retreat from the Beach

### Orrin Pilkey

*CoastalCare.org is an environmental organization. According to its Web site, two of its goals are to "raise awareness of the many unsustainable practices that are harming the world's beaches and coasts" and to "advocate for sensible, science-based policies and regulations that will protect and preserve coastlines and beaches around the world." The author, Orrin H. Pilkey, is James B. Duke Professor Emeritus of Geology at Duke University.*

1      As ocean waters warm, the Northeast is likely to face more Sandy-like storms. [Hurricane Sandy affected a large section of the East coast in November 2012.] And as sea levels continue to rise, the surges of these future storms will be higher and

North Carolina 12 is buckled from pounding surf leading into Mirlo Beach in Rodanthe, N.C. on Tuesday, Oct. 30, 2012, as a result of Hurricane Sandy.

even more deadly. We can't stop these powerful storms. But we can reduce the deaths and damage they cause.

2     Hurricane Sandy's immense power, which destroyed or damaged thousands of homes, actually pushed the footprints of the **barrier islands** along the South Shore of Long Island and the Jersey Shore landward as the storm carried precious beach sand out to deep waters or swept it across the islands. This process of barrier-island migration toward the mainland has gone on for 10,000 years.

**barrier islands**
narrow strips of land near the coast

3     Yet there is already a push to rebuild homes close to the beach and bring back the shorelines to where they were. The federal government encourages this: there will be billions available to replace roads, pipelines and other **infrastructure** and to clean up storm debris, provide security and emergency housing. Claims to the National Flood Insurance Program could reach $7 billion. And the Army Corps of Engineers will be ready to mobilize its sand-pumping dredges, dump trucks, and bulldozers to rebuild beaches washed away time and again.

**infrastructure**
system of buildings and transportation that helps society function

4     But this "let's come back stronger and better" attitude, though empowering, is the wrong approach to the increasing hazard of living close to the rising sea. Disaster will strike again. We should not simply replace all lost property and infrastructure. Instead,

we need to take account of rising sea levels, intensifying storms and continuing shore-line erosion.

5      I understand the temptation to rebuild. My parents' retirement home, built at 13 feet above sea level, five blocks from the shoreline in Waveland, Miss., was flooded to the ceiling during Hurricane Camille in 1969. They rebuilt it, but the house was completely destroyed by Hurricane Katrina in 2005. (They had died by then.) Even so, rebuilding continued in Waveland. A year after Katrina, one empty Waveland beachfront lot, on which successive houses had been wiped away by Hurricanes Camille and Katrina, was for sale for $800,000.

6      That is madness. We should strongly discourage the reconstruction of destroyed or badly damaged beachfront homes in New Jersey and New York. Some very valu-able property will have to be abandoned to make the community less vulnerable to storm surges. This is tough medicine, to be sure, and taxpayers may be forced to compensate homeowners. But it should save taxpayers money in the long run by ending this cycle of repairing or rebuilding properties in the path of future storms. Surviving buildings and new construction should be elevated on pilings at least two feet above the 100-year flood level to allow future storm overwash to flow under-neath. Some buildings should be moved back from the beach.

7      Respecting the power of these storms is not new. American Indians who occupied barrier islands during the warm months moved to the mainland during the winter storm season. In the early days of European settlement in North America, some com-munities restricted building to the bay sides of barrier islands to minimize damage. In Colombia and Nigeria, where some people choose to live next to beaches to reduce exposure to **malarial** mosquitoes, houses are routinely built to be easily moved.

**malarial**
carrying malaria  8      We should also understand that armoring the shoreline with sea walls will not be successful in holding back major storm surges. As experience in New Jersey and elsewhere has shown, sea walls eventually cause the loss of protective beaches. These beaches can be replaced, but only at enormous cost to taxpayers. The 21-mile stretch of beach between Sandy Hook and Barnegat Inlet in New Jersey was replen-ished between 1999 and 2001 at a cost of $273 million (in 2011 dollars). Future

**continental shelf**
the submerged,  9  replenishment will depend on finding suitable sand on the **continental shelf**, where it is hard to find.

shallow borders of a continent      And as sea levels rise, replenishment will be required more often. In Wrightsville Beach, N.C., the beach already has been replenished more than 20 times since 1965, at a cost of nearly $54.3 million (in 2011 dollars). Taxpayers in at least three North Carolina communities—Carteret and Dare Counties and North Topsail Beach—have voted down tax increases to pay for these projects in the last dozen years. The atti-tude was: we shouldn't have to pay for the beach. We weren't the ones irresponsible enough to build next to an eroding shoreline.

10     This is not the time for a solution based purely on engineering. The Army Corps undoubtedly will be heavily involved. But as New Jersey and New York move for-ward, officials should seek advice from oceanographers, coastal geologists, coastal and construction engineers and others who understand the future of rising seas and their impact on barrier islands.

11     We need more **resilient** development, to be sure. But we also need to begin to retreat from the ocean's edge.

## CRITICAL THINKING QUESTIONS

1. What is the thesis or central thought of this selection? What course of action is the author arguing for or against?
2. What does the author imply about the cost of waterfront property in the United States?
3. What evidence does the author provide to support his assertion that previous generations were more successful in protecting themselves (and their homes) from storm damage than current generations?
4. Identify at least three ways coastal communities could minimize damage from future storms.
5. What does the author imply about engineers' approaches to controlling the effects of hurricanes and other extreme weather events that affect coastal areas?
6. This article does not specifically mention climate change or global warming. How is this article's content related to the topics of climate change and global warming?

**EXERCISE 4:** **Working Collaboratively**

*After answering the critical thinking questions on your own, pair up with a classmate and share your answers. As you discuss the questions, add to your answers the information you learn from your partner.*

**SOURCE 3**
*Human Events*
Online Newspaper

# The Debunking of Global Warming Continues

### John Hayward

*The* Human Events *Web site offers what it calls "powerful conservative voices." According to the organization's mission statement,* Human Events *aims for accurate presentation of the facts but admits that its coverage is not unbiased. The "About Us" section of their Web site states, "We look at events through eyes that favor limited constitutional government, local self-government, private enterprise, and individual freedom. These were the principles that inspired the Founding Fathers. We believe that today the same principles will preserve freedom in America."*

1    The Cult of Global Warming still has a huge amount of money and political influence, so no landmark on the steady unraveling of their con job should go unremarked. A big one arrived in the form of a study conducted by Anthony Watts and an army of volunteer assistants: the data assembled by the National Oceanic and Atmospheric Administration, and commonly cited for years in support of the global warming scare, is wildly inaccurate. It literally doubled the amount of actual warming that took place over the past half-century.

**heat envelope**
an area of higher temperature found within cities; usually the result of heat produced by buildings and humans

2    This occurred because most of the climate stations in the United States are located within the **heat envelopes** of major cities. They weren't detecting any "global warming." They were, in essence, detecting engine heat. The readings from accurate weather stations were actually adjusted upwards to agree with the inaccurate readings.

**apocalyptic** 3
referring to the
end of the world

Global-warming skeptics couldn't be any more vindicated if the entire climate change establishment cried "Never mind!" in unison, then scurried back to their labs to conjure up a new **apocalyptic** man-made threat they could blame on capitalist success.

**Climategate** 4
refers to a
situation in
which several
scientists were
found to have
falsified data
about global
warming

"Is this a case of deliberate fraud by Warmist scientists hell bent on keeping their funding gravy train rolling?" asks highly vindicated skeptic James Delingpole. "Well, after what we saw in **Climategate** anything is possible. (I mean it's not like NOAA is run by hard-left eco activists, is it?) But I think more likely it is a case of confirmation bias. The Warmists who comprise the climate scientist establishment spend so much time communicating with other warmists and so little time paying attention to the views of dissenting scientists such as Henrik Svensmark—or Fred Singer or Richard Lindzen or indeed Anthony Watts—that it simply hasn't occurred to them that their temperature records need adjusting downwards, not upwards."

**arbitrary** 5
randomly chosen

**contention**
disagreement

**indoctrinated**
brainwashed

This is not an **arbitrary** point of **contention** between academics. Billions of dollars in wealth has been destroyed in the name of global warming. Americans still live under the dominion of laws passed on the basis of junk science. A generation of children has been aggressively **indoctrinated** in this garbage throughout their school years. The indoctrination remains useful to the Left, because it has taught kids to view the human race as a kind of cancer, which can be controlled only by a synchronized effort between politically correct scientists and government agencies.

6

Delingpole facetiously cautions against triumphalism in the wake of this NOAA analysis, because it would be "plain wrong" to dance on global warming's grave. He's kidding, of course. In truth, it is critical to make the shame and fraud of global warming part of our common knowledge. We must carefully document how this scam was perpetrated, and remember the techniques it employed—from corrupt "hockey stick graphs" to mountains of wildly inaccurate data—so that we never fall for anything like it again. Politicized pseudo-science comes at the expense of real science, and that is an expense we can never afford.

## CRITICAL THINKING QUESTIONS

1. Identify at least four examples of biased and/or emotional language in this selection.
2. Which single piece of evidence does the author use to argue that global warming is a hoax? Is enough evidence offered to support the thesis? Why or why not?
3. The author uses the terms *junk science* (paragraph 5) and *pseudo-science* (paragraph 6). What do these terms mean?
4. "Many people who argue in favor of global warming are actually pursuing a personal agenda against the wealthy and against businesses." Would the author agree or disagree with this statement? Why or why not? Cite direct support (or direct contradiction) of this statement within the reading.
5. Suppose a scientist believes that children who have only one parent grow up to have more emotional problems than children with two parents. The scientist communicates with other scientists who believe the same thing and may therefore be likely to dismiss evidence that refutes their belief. According to this article, what type of bias is affecting these scientists?

6.  Provide three words that describe the tone of this selection.

7.  How does the author's use of the word *critical* in paragraph 6 differ from the meaning of the word in the phrase "critical thinking"?

8.  Overall, what was the author's purpose for writing "The Debunking of Global Warming Continues"?

---

**EXERCISE 5:**  **Working Collaboratively**

*After answering the critical thinking questions on your own, pair up with a classmate and share your answers. As you discuss the questions, add to your answers the information you learn from your partner.*

---

**SOURCE 4**
Environmental
Textbook

# Climate Change and Extinction

### Jay Withgott and Scott Brennan

*The following selection is taken from an introductory environmental science textbook,* Environment: The Science Behind the Stories. *Both authors have taught environmental science to college students. In a letter to students, the authors write, "Within your lifetime, our global society must chart a promising course for a sustainable future—or it will risk peril. The stakes could not be higher, and the path we take will depend largely on how we choose to interact with our environment."*

**natural
selection**
the natural
process by
which stronger
individuals
survive and pass
their genes on to
their offspring,
which makes
the species more
likely to survive

**Monteverde**
a town in Costa
Rica

**cloud forest**
a type of tropical
or subtropical
forest characterized
by persistent cloud
cover

## Some Species Are More Vulnerable to Extinction than Others

1    In general, extinction occurs when environmental conditions change rapidly or severely enough that a species cannot adapt genetically to the change; the slow process of **natural selection** simply does not have enough time to work. All manner of events can cause extinction—climate change, the rise and fall of sea level, the arrival of new species, severe weather events, and more. In general, small populations are vulnerable to extinction because fluctuations in their size could easily, by chance, bring the population size to zero. Species narrowly specialized to some particular resource or way of life are also vulnerable, because environmental changes that make that resource or way of life unavailable can doom them.

2    The golden toad was a prime example of a vulnerable species. It was endemic to the **Monteverde cloud forest**, meaning that it occurred nowhere else on the planet. Endemic species face relatively high risks of extinction because all their members belong to a single and sometimes small population. At the time of its discovery, the golden toad was known from only a 4-km² (988-acre) area of Monteverde. It also required very specific conditions to breed successfully. During the spring at Monteverde, water collects in shallow pools within the network of roots that span the cloud forest's floor. The golden toad gathered to breed in these root-bound reservoirs, and it was here that Jay Savage and his companions collected their specimens in 1964. Monteverde provided ideal habitat for the golden toad, but the extent of

that habitat was minuscule—any environmental stresses that deprived the toad of the resources it needed to survive might doom the entire world population of the species.

**amphibian** 3
family of animals that includes frogs, toads, newts, and salamanders

In the United States, a number of **amphibians** are limited to very small ranges and thus are vulnerable to extinction. The Yosemite toad is restricted to a small region of the Sierra Nevada in California, the Houston toad occupies just a few areas of Texas woodland, and the Florida bog frog lives in a tiny region of Florida wetland. Fully 40 salamander species in the United States are restricted to areas the size of a typical county, and some of these live atop single mountains (Figure 4-1).

### Earth Has Seen Several Episodes of Mass Extinction

4
Most extinction occurs gradually, one species at a time. The rate at which this type of extinction occurs is referred to as the *background extinction rate.* However, Earth has seen five events of staggering proportions that killed off massive numbers of species at once. These episodes, called *massive extinction events,* have occurred at widely spaced intervals in Earth history and have wiped out 50–95% of our planet's species each time.

**paleontologist** 5
one who studies fossilized animals and plants

**hypotheses**
scientific guesses

**methane**
a colorless, odorless flammable gas

The best-known mass extinction occurred 65 million years ago and brought an end to the dinosaurs (although birds are modern representatives of dinosaurs). Evidence suggests that the impact of a gigantic asteroid caused this event, called the Cretaceous-Tertiary, or K-T, event. As massive as this extinction event was, however, it was moderate compared to the mass extinction at the end of the Permian period 250 million years ago. **Paleontologists** estimate that 75–95% of all species may have perished during this event, described by one researcher as the "mother of all mass extinctions." Scientists do not yet know what caused the end-Permian extinction event, although **hypotheses** include an asteroid impact, massive volcanism, **methane** releases and global warming, or some combination of factors.

**FIGURE 4-1**

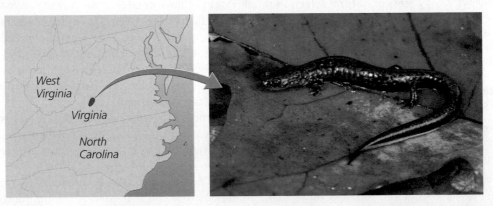

The Peaks of Otter salamander (*Plethodon hubrichti*) lives on only a few peaks in Virginia's Blue Ridge Mountains. About 40 other salamander species in the United States are restricted to similarly small ranges. Small range sizes leave these creatures vulnerable to extinction if severe changes occur in their local environment.

### The Sixth Mass Extinction Is upon Us

6    Many biologists have concluded that Earth is currently entering its sixth mass extinction event—and that we are the cause. Indeed, the Millennium Ecosystem Assessment estimated that today's extinction rate is 100–1,000 times higher than the background rate, and rising. Changes to Earth's natural systems set in motion by human population growth, development, and resource depletion have driven many species extinct and are threatening countless more. The alteration and outright destruction of natural **habitats**, the hunting and harvesting of species, and the introduction of species from one place to another where they can harm native species—these processes and more have combined to threaten Earth's **biodiversity**.

**habitat**
natural home of
a plant or animal

**biodiversity**
the variety of life
in the world

7    Amphibians such as the golden toad are disappearing faster than just about any other type of organism. According to the most recent scientific assessments, 40% of frog, toad, and salamander species are in decline, 30% are in danger of extinction, and nearly 170 species have vanished just within the last few years or decades. Some species are disappearing in remote and pristine areas, suggesting that chytrid fungus could be responsible. But researchers think a variety of causes are affecting amphibians in a "perfect storm" of impacts.

**geologic**
related to the
study of Earth

**speciation**
the evolution of
a new species

8    When we look around us, it may not appear as though a human version of an asteroid impact is taking place, but we cannot judge such things on our own timescale. On the **geologic** timescale, extinction over 100 years or even 10,000 years appears instantaneous. Moreover, **speciation** is a slow enough process that it will take life millions of years to recover—by which time our own species will most likely not be around.

—Withgott and Brennan, *Environment: The Science Behind the Stories*, pp. 58–61

## CRITICAL THINKING QUESTIONS

1.  How much did you know about extinction before you read this selection? How has the reading changed your ideas about extinction (if at all)?

2.  What role does climate change play in extinction? Does the author provide sufficient evidence to support his position?

3.  Suppose higher temperatures cause entire plant species to die. How might the extinction of plant species be related to the extinction of animal species?

4.  The reading discusses the golden toad of Monteverde. Can you think of other examples of endemic species—that is, plants or animals that are found in only one place on Earth? (Hint: Think about Australia.)

5.  In which mass extinction may global warming have played a role, the Cretaceous-Tertiary event or the extinction at the end of the Permian period? What was the likely cause of the other mass extinction event?

6.  In paragraph 8, which specific species do the authors imply will be extinct millions of years from now?

**EXERCISE 6:    Working Collaboratively**

*After answering the critical thinking questions on your own, pair up with a classmate and share your answers. As you discuss the questions, add to your answers the information you learn from your partner.*

**SOURCE 5**
Environmental
Defense Fund
Blog

# Hot Topic: Climate Change and Our Extreme Weather

### Steven Hamburg

*This reading is taken from the Web site of the Environmental Defense Fund, an organization whose stated mission is to "preserve the natural systems on which all life depends, focusing on the most critical environmental problems." It was posted July 13, 2012. Steven Hamburg, the author of this selection, writes and speaks about the organization's commitment to science-based advocacy and, according to the Web site, "is responsible for the scientific integrity of EDF's positions and programs."*

1      Americans have been griping all summer about the weather. It feels hotter than usual this year.

2      Turns out, that's because—it is.

3      The National Oceanic and Atmospheric Administration (NOAA) just confirmed that America is enduring the hottest weather in our recorded history.

4      In fact, the past 12 months have been **the warmest 12 months in the continental U.S. since record-keeping began back in 1895**.

5      It's not a coincidence either. NOAA says the odds of our record heat being a random event—rather than part of a global warming trend—are about **1 in 1.6 million**.

6      How hot is it, really? Consider these facts from NOAA:

- From June 1st through July 10th of this year, the U.S. broke **147 all-time high-temperature records**.
- In June of 2012, communities across the U.S. **broke 2,284 daily maximum temperature records**. In the week of July 1st through July 9th of this year, they **broke another 2,071**.
- The average temperature in the contiguous United States was 71.2 degrees Fahrenheit this June—**two full degrees** above the 20th-century average.

7      Those scary statistics are just for the past six weeks. But our miserable June followed the blistering heat from *last* year.

8      Take a look at this partial list of cities that broke records from June of 2011 through May of 2012:

- **Detroit—101 degrees** (daily record)
- **Syracuse—101 degrees** (daily record)
- **Mitchell, SD—102 degrees** (daily record)
- **Minneapolis—103 degrees** (daily record)
- **Bridgeport, CT—103 degrees** (all-time record)
- **Denver—105 degrees** (all-time record)

- **Newark—108 degrees** (all-time record)
- **Houston—109 degrees** (all-time record)
- **Miles City, MT—111 degrees** (all-time record)
- **Wichita—111 degrees** (daily record)
- **Little Rock—114 degrees** (all-time record)
- **Childress, TX—117 degrees** (all-time record)

9    We've included some of those temperatures in our newest EDF public service announcement, which is running on the jumbo screen in Times Square. The blazing temperatures have led to other problems as well:

- The U.S. Drought Monitor says more than **56 percent of the contiguous United States is now under drought conditions**—the highest level since record-keeping began in 2000.
- Wildfires destroyed 1.3 million acres in Colorado and across the U.S. last month.
- Wyoming recorded its driest June ever this year; Colorado and Utah recorded their second-driest Junes.

10    At the same time:

- **Florida recorded its wettest June ever**—thanks in part to Tropical Storm Debby, which dumped more than two feet of rain on some towns, and spawned flash floods and almost two dozen tornadoes.
- **Duluth, Minnesota, also had record floods** last month.
- Large parts of the East Coast got hit by a killer **Derecho storm** that killed more than two dozen people; more than three million lost electricity, some for more than a week.
- Washington, D.C., broke its record for worst heat wave ever, according to the *Washington Post*.

**Derecho storm**
a type of windstorm

**IPCC**
Intergovern-
mental Panel
on Climate
Change; created
by the United
Nations to study
climate change
worldwide

11    Unfortunately, these bad weather trends are not unexpected. For a long time now, the world's top climate researchers have told us about the strong evidence of links between dangerous weather and climate change.

12    Here at EDF, we've been talking—and blogging—about the issue for a long time. It was barely more than six months ago that we posted about the **IPCC** report on climate change and extreme weather. Sadly, looking back at the last round of weather disasters gives our current sweltering summer a sense of déjà vu.

13    Greenhouse gas pollution traps heat in our atmosphere, which interferes with normal weather patterns. That means we can expect more—and probably worse— weird weather in the future.

14    Climate change doesn't just mean higher heat. It means more severe and damaging weather events across the country—including more frequent and heavier rains in some areas, increased drought in others, a potential increase in the intensity of hurricanes, and more coastal erosion because of rising sea levels.

15    Changing weather patterns changes will affect our agriculture, water supplies, health and economy. They'll affect every American community and, ultimately, every American.

16    That's why EDF is dedicated to reducing carbon pollution.

17    After all the reports, and all the statistics, and all the bad weather—there's no excuse for not fighting climate change.

## CRITICAL THINKING QUESTIONS

1. What does the author see as the main cause of climate change? Do you think the author provides adequate evidence to support this position?
2. Which type of graphic or visual aid would best express the information found in paragraphs 8 and 10?
3. How has the author chosen to use boldface type in this reading? What purpose does it serve?
4. The author's biographical note discusses EDF's commitment to "science-based advocacy." What does this term mean, and what does it imply about the reading's possible level of bias?
5. The biographical note explains that the author, Steven Hamburg, is responsible for the "scientific integrity" of EDF's positions and programs. What does this mean?
6. This article refers to all temperatures in the Fahrenheit scale (which is used in the United States), not in the Celsius scale (which is used in many other parts of the world). What does this imply about the author's audience?

---

**EXERCISE 7:    Working Collaboratively**

> *After answering the critical thinking questions on your own, pair up with a classmate and share your answers. As you discuss the questions, add to your answers the information you learn from your partner.*

---

**SOURCE 6**
The Business
Ethics Blog

# Storms, Global Warming, and Corporate Citizenship

### Chris MacDonald

*Chris MacDonald, Ph.D., teaches at Ryerson University in Toronto, Canada, where he is Director of the Jim Pattison Ethical Leadership Education & Research Program. This selection is taken from his personal blog about business ethics.*

**Frankenstorm**
refers to
Hurricane Sandy,
which did billions
of dollars of
damage to the
U.S. east coast in
2012

**CFL**
compact
fluorescent light
bulb

1    Humans are (very likely) changing the earth's climate. And changes in climate are (very likely) making storms worse. And worse storms are (definitely) a bad thing. Granted, it's hard—in fact, foolish—to try to draw a straight line between any individual's or even any corporation's behavior and the **Frankenstorm** that just slammed New York and surrounding areas, but the fact remains that the devastation that storm wrought was not the effect of a mere freak of nature. As *Business Week* bluntly put it, "it's global warming, stupid."

2    But what matters more than the cause of global warming is what we can do about it. In particular, what can business do about it?

3    Large-scale problems tend to require large-scale solutions, and so there's a natural tendency to leave such issues to government. This is so for two reasons. First is simple scope: you driving a hybrid car or switching to **CFL** bulbs just isn't going to accomplish much. Second is the nature of collective action problems: each of us benefits from a wasteful, energy-intensive lifestyle, and it seems narrowly rational to let other people (or other companies) bear the costs of doing things differently. But

the fact that it's tempting, or even narrowly rational, to let others bear the burden, or to wait for government to act, doesn't make it the right thing, or even the minimally decent thing, to do.

4    So what can businesses do—what is it possible for them to do—in response to a trend in global warming that is clearly posing increased risks?

5    To begin, of course, they can work to avoid making things worse, by avoiding burning carbon and adding to the load of carbon dioxide in the atmosphere. This means looking at relatively small, obvious stuff like seeking energy efficiencies in their operations, promoting telecommuting, reducing air travel, and so on. Luckily, most such efforts are relatively painless, since they tend to reduce costs at the same time. Sometimes mere laziness or a focus on "how we've always done things" gets in the way of making such win-win changes. Don't be lazy. Innovate. Share best practices with your suppliers, with other companies in your sector, and if you're a **B2B** company, with your customers.

**B2B**
business-to-business

6    The second thing that businesses can do is to work with, rather than against, government efforts at making things better. In particular, it is a fundamental obligation of corporate citizenship not to block government action aimed at effective action at slowing climate change, and in particular action aimed at dealing effectively with the effects of climate change. If, for example, a government wants to pass rules forcing businesses to pay the full cost of their energy usage, or rules that impose industry-wide energy efficiency rules, business should welcome rather than oppose such changes. Energy inefficiencies impose costs on other people, and hence count as the kind of **externalities** that go against the fundamental principles of a market economy.

**externalities**
side effects

7    It's also worth noting that asking what business can do is not quite the same as asking what your business, or any particular business, can do. Business organizations and trade associations abound, and there's plenty they can do to a) help members share best practices and b) foster industry-wide standards that can help businesses live up to their social obligations while at the same time maintaining a level playing field.

**synergistic**
two or more
people or groups
working together
to achieve
more than they
could achieve
separately

8    Finally, business can do the things that business is supposed to be good at: efficient management, **synergistic** use of a range of kinds of **human capital**, and innovation. That stuff isn't just a good recipe for commercial success. It's an absolute obligation. And innovation is clearly the key among those three aptitudes. Efficiency—tightening our belts—will only get us so far. We desperately need a whole slew of truly brilliant new ideas for products, services, and productive processes over the next decade if we are to meet the collective challenge posed by changes in our environment. And it's foolish to expect government to provide those ideas. It's time for business to step up to the plate. There can be no better way to manifest a commitment to corporate citizenship than to be the kind of corporate citizen that sees a business model in trying to help us all cope with global warming.

**human capital**
the talents
and training of
individuals

## CRITICAL THINKING QUESTIONS

1.   The author uses the phrase "(very likely)" twice in the first paragraph. Why has he used parentheses to enclose this phrase?

2.   Why are the solutions to large-scale problems (such as global warming) often left to governments rather than individuals?

3.   What is the overall thesis or central idea of this article? What is the author arguing for or against? What types of evidence does the author offer to support this thesis?

4. What does the author mean by the phrase "win-win changes" in paragraph 5?
5. The author states that businesses should work to protect the environment because that is the right thing to do. But what other benefits do such practices have for businesses?
6. Based on paragraph 7, who is the intended audience for this blog post?
7. According to the author, which is the most important of a business's "three aptitudes"? What role can this aptitude play in fighting global warming?

### EXERCISE 8:    Working Collaboratively

*After answering the critical thinking questions on your own, pair up with a classmate and share your answers. As you discuss the questions, add to your answers the information you learn from your partner.*

SOURCE 7
*The Huffington Post*

# Climate Change: Countries That May Be Hit Hardest

### Jeremy Hsu

*This selection is taken from a widely read online newspaper,* The Huffington Post. *It was originally published in* InnovationNewsDaily, *which, according to its Web site, "reports on futuristic technologies, innovations, disruptive ideas, and cool gadgets that will shape the future, and explain why it all matters and how it will affect your life."*

1    Rising seas threaten to drown island countries such as the Maldives and Kiribati in the era of global warming—a dire scenario that has forced leaders to plan for floating cities or consider moving their entire populations to neighboring countries. Most countries won't need to take such drastic steps to simply survive, but many more will similarly experience the uglier side of climate change.

2    The countries potentially facing the worst fates may not necessarily experience the greatest climate change, but instead lack the resources to cushion their people against climate-related disasters such as hurricanes, floods, heat waves and droughts. That has historically made a huge difference in rates of death or displacement from such events—Hurricane Jeanne killed just three people in the U.S. in 2004, but resulted in the deaths of more than 1,500 people in Haiti and displaced about 200,000 Haitians.

3    "This of course is different than future likelihood to suffer, but I believe that those who suffered most in the past are probably most vulnerable to future disasters, because they are unable to prepare for, cope with, and recover from these kinds of disasters," said J. Timmons Roberts, a professor of environmental studies and sociology at Brown University.

4    The most fortunate countries could fortify themselves against the worst of climate change and possibly take in climate change refugees from other parts of the world. Both historical data and climate model predictions have given some idea of what to expect.

### Climate Change Hotspots

5    North America, Europe, and Asia can generally expect more severe heat waves and droughts alongside more intense storms related to flooding, said Michael

Wehner, a climate scientist at Lawrence Berkeley National Laboratory in California. On the other hand, cold snaps could become less severe.

6    Other regions could see even more radical changes in their normal climates.

7    "Central America, the Caribbean, and the Mediterranean are projected to experience what is now considered drought as a new normal condition," Wehner told InnovationNewsDaily. "The impacts on agriculture could be severe, especially on impoverished nations."

8    The melting Arctic is experiencing some of the greatest warming—often with devastating consequences for local wildlife and people—but climate change's greatest impact may take place in more densely populated regions. Jason Samson, a former Ph.D. candidate at McGill University in Canada, highlighted the relationship between climate conditions and population density in a 2011 paper published in the journal *Global Ecology and Biogeography*.

9    "Strongly negative impacts of climate change are predicted in Central America, central South America, the Arabian Peninsula, Southeast Asia, and much of Africa," wrote Samson and his colleagues.

10    That paper's findings echo the vulnerable regions identified by the Intergovernmental Panel on Climate Change (IPCC)—the Arctic, Africa, small islands (such as the Maldives and Kiribati), and the Asian and African **megadeltas** where huge cities filled with millions of people face rising seas, **storm surges**, and flooding rivers.

**biogeography**
the study of the distribution of plants and animals across the world

**megadelta**
a delta is the fertile region at the end of a river; a *megadelta* is a very large delta

**storm surges**
higher levels of water at coastlines following heavy rains or winds

## Countries in the Danger Zone

11    So what countries face the greatest danger from climate change? Maplecroft, a British consultancy, has created a "Climate Change and Environment Risk Atlas," a list of 193 countries ranked by those most vulnerable to climate change because of factors such as population density or state of development.

12    The 2012 edition of the risk atlas identified 30 countries as being at extreme risk. The top 10 most at risk include: Haiti, Bangladesh, Sierra Leone, Zimbabwe, Madagascar, Cambodia, Mozambique, Democratic Republic of Congo, Malawi, and the Philippines.

13    Some countries with lower risk ratings still have danger zones that face "extreme risk" from climate change. Maplecroft pointed to the southwest of Brazil and China's coastal regions as examples, even though both countries rate as "medium risk" overall. Six of the world's fastest-growing cities also received "extreme risk" ratings: Calcutta in India, Manila in the Philippines, Jakarta in Indonesia, Dhaka and Chittagong in Bangladesh, and Addis Ababa in Ethiopia.

14    The countries in the best position to adapt to climate change's challenges mostly include those in Northern Europe, such as Finland, Ireland, Sweden, and Norway, CNN reported. Iceland topped the list, but the United States also had a relatively low risk rating.

## Living with Climate Change

15    The climate risk assessments emphasized the wealth difference between the most and least vulnerable countries. That has proven historically true as well, Roberts said. He and a colleague, Bradley Parks, looked at 4,040 climate-related disasters from 1980 to 2003 in their book *A Climate of Injustice* (MIT Press, 2006).

16    "The rates [of people killed or made homeless], when adjusted for population, were 100 times higher in some African and Pacific islands than in the USA," Roberts explained.

17   But even developed countries such as the U.S. face risks when it comes to climate-related disasters—regardless of whatever future climate change may bring. Wehner suggested that climate change during his lifetime would be "manageable" as far as living in the U.S., but added that his grandchildren would face tougher choices.

18   Roberts, who lives in Rhode Island on top of a hill near Narragansett Bay, took an even more cautious approach about buying beachfront property even in the U.S.

19   "While I would love to look out over the water, I would think twice before buying land or property, and especially before putting my family right at sea level, in a place that may suffer storm surge," Roberts said.

## CRITICAL THINKING QUESTIONS

1.  What does the phrase "projected to experience" in paragraph 7 mean?
2.  What is a "new normal condition" (paragraph 7), and how does this phrase relate to global warming and climate change?
3.  What are some possible benefits of global warming?
4.  Which type of visual or graphic aid would best represent the information presented in paragraphs 12–14?
5.  Overall, what is the relationship between a country's level of wealth and its vulnerability to climate change? What is the overall relationship between a country's level of wealth and its ability to adapt to climate change?
6.  What does the phrase "developed countries" (paragraph 17) mean? Provide examples of three developed countries.
7.  Is climate change more likely to affect highly populated areas or lightly populated areas? Explain your answer.

> **EXERCISE 9:   Working Collaboratively**
>
> *After answering the critical thinking questions on your own, pair up with a classmate and share your answers. As you discuss the questions, add to your answers the information you learn from your partner.*

**SOURCE 8**
Infographic

# Global Warning?

*This infographic originally appeared on the Web site of Reusethisbag.com, a company that sells reusable shopping bags. On the "About Us" page of its Web site, the company quotes its president, Doug Lober: "We started the company as a way to give back and help the environment! We all grew up here in California and have seen plastic bags on the beach and in the water for years! Recently I was running on the beach and found 6 plastic bags during my mile and a half trip. Other than that, there isn't much one person alone can do to make a significant impact on this crazy world. But . . . if we spread the word about the importance of reusing our grocery bags, work together, and somehow this movement catches on, the resulting benefit is going to be huge!"*

# Global Warning?

Or a global-sized myth? We'll explore the two sides of the ever-growing debate on global warming and who's causing it.

**phytoplankton**
microscopic
plants floating
in water

The U.S.A. is home to 5.7% of the population and 25% of the Earth's $CO_2$ pollution.

70% of the Earth's oxygen is produced by ocean **phytoplankton**.

Ocean waters have warmed by a full degree Fahrenheit since 1970.

## Scientific Consensus

## The Climate Skeptics

I'm melting!

Arctic ice is rapidly disappearing, and the region may have its first completely ice-free summer by 2040 or earlier. Polar bears and **indigenous** cultures are already suffering from the sea-ice loss.

**indigenous**
native

"Most climate science is based on computer modeling. **The climate is too complex and unpredictable for us to model accurately.**"

## Scientific Consensus

**⬆ 70%**
Coral Bleaching

Coral reefs, which are highly sensitive to small changes in water temperature, suffered the worst bleaching—or die-off in response to stress—ever recorded in 1998, with some areas seeing bleach rates of 70 percent.

**Hottest in 400 years**

The rate of warming is increasing. The 20th century's last two decades were the hottest in 400 years and possibly the warmest for several millennia.

**2,500** Scientists From **130** Countries

Have concluded that **humans have caused** all or most of the current **planetary warming.**

## The Climate Skeptics

"Climate change assumes a man-made cause so most research is conducted under that assumption. **We need more studies to examine possible natural causes.**"

"Climate sensitivity to $CO_2$ is relatively unknown and based on many assumptions. Further research is needed before we take drastic steps that might hurt us economically."

"Climate change skepticism among US citizens has risen 14% from 1997."

## The Solution?

The future is still unclear. The amount by which the temperature will continue to rise depends at least in part on what actions are taken (or not taken) to limit the amount of **greenhouse gas** emissions globally.

**⬇ 50%**
**⬇ 80%**
(Greenhouse Gases)

Stabilizing GHG concentrations around 450-550 parts per million (ppm), or about twice pre-industrial levels. This is the point at which many believe the most damaging impacts of climate change can be avoided.

**Is the change worth it?** Is focusing on short term economic gain too risky in light of the state of Earth's precious **ecosystems?**

**How much do we have to change?** How much of a reduction in greenhouse gas emissions would be enough to have a significant effect?

### ANSWER?

Depending on our choices, scientists predict that the Earth could eventually warm by as little as 2.5 degrees or as much as 10 degrees Fahrenheit.

**2.5°**  **10°**
( By reacting)   (By not reacting)

**greenhouse gas**
includes water vapor, methane, nitrous oxide, carbon dioxide, and fluorinated gases that slow or prevent heat leaving the atmosphere

**ecosystem**
a biological community of organisms that interact

**Sources**
http://news.nationalgeographic.com/news/2004/12/1206_041206_global_warming.html
http://science.howstuffworks.com/environmental/green-science/climate-skeptic1.htm
http://www.acoolerclimate.com/making-sense-of-global-warming-debate/http://www.website.com
http://www.drroyspencer.com/global-warming-natural-or-manmade/

Designed by Shawn Murdock

Infographic Brought to you by:
BrowThisDay.com
Created by oBizMedia.com

## CRITICAL THINKING QUESTIONS

1. List three points with regard to global warming on which most scientists agree.
2. List three arguments made by people who are skeptical of the claim that climate change is a serious issue.
3. Why are the numbers cited in this infographic—"2500 scientists from 130 countries"—possibly misleading?
4. What does the infographic mean when it refers to "pre-industrial levels" of greenhouse gas (GHG) emissions?
5. Does this infographic imply that global warming is inevitable, or does it imply that global warming can be stopped?
6. According to this source, what is the single best way to combat global warming?

**EXERCISE 10:** **Working Collaboratively**

*After answering the critical thinking questions on your own, pair up with a classmate and share your answers. As you discuss the questions, add to your answers the information you learn from your partner.*

## SYNTHESIS AND INTEGRATION QUESTIONS AND ACTIVITIES

The following questions and activities ask you to synthesize information from two or more sources.

1. **Comparing Tone and Author's Purpose.** Compare the tone of Source 1 and Source 2. How does the writer's purpose in Source 1 differ from the writer's purpose in Source 2?

2. **Summarizing Sources.** Summarize what you have learned about the role of global warming in the extinction of species. Use information from Source 1 and Source 4.

3. **Examining Authors' Viewpoints.** Compare and contrast the author's view of time in Source 4 and Source 5. Why is the study of time so essential to an understanding of global warming and climate change?

4. **Comparing Sources.** How and why are some of the conclusions of Source 5 incompatible with the information provided in Source 1?

5. **Determining Agreement and Disagreement Between Sources.** Would Professor J. Timmons Roberts, who is quoted in Source 7, agree with the author's thesis in Source 2? Why or why not?

6. **Creating a Visual Summary.** Create a graphic or visual aid to summarize, the place-specific information found in Sources 5 and 7.

7. **Finding Agreement Among Sources.** Based on your reading of three or more of these sources, including Source 8, what facts do most people agree on with regard to climate change?

8. **Finding Disagreement Among Sources.** Based on your reading of three or more of these sources, including Source 8, what are the major areas of disagreement?

9. **Identifying Statements of Opinion.** Using three or more sources, underline at least five statements of opinion.

10. **Assessing Reliability.** Place the sources in order from most reliable/most unbiased to least reliable/most biased. Be prepared to explain your ranking.

11. **Preparing a Fact Sheet.** Prepare a list of ten facts regarding global warming and climate change that would be useful in writing a response paper on the issue of global warming.

# Credits

## Photo Credits

**Cover:** Richard T. Nowitz/Corbis; **1 (t):** Diego Cervo/Shutterstock; **(b):** Diego Cervo/Shutterstock; **8:** Bob Daemmrich/The Image Works; **89:** Chris Madden/Cartoon Stock; **91:** Samuel Acosta/Shutterstock; **193:** Felipe Rodriguez/VWPics/SuperStock; **221:** Ronald Sumners/Shutterstock; **224:** David Borchart/The New Yorker Collection/www.cartoonbank.com; **325:** Goodluz/Shutterstock; **329:** Santiago Quintana Garcia; **339:** Fuse/Getty Images, **341 (l).** Tedd Foxx/Alamy; **(r):** Dmitriy Shironosov/Alamy; **343 (l):** CBS Photo Archive/Getty Images; **(r):** Popperfoto/Getty Images; **354:** Pete Ryan; **369:** Peter Cade/Getty Images; **380:** NOAA; **398:** University of Maine at Presque Isle; **400:** Victoria Arocho/AP Images; **415:** Sam Edwards/Getty Images; **428:** Jeff Riedel/Getty Images; **441:** Keith Morris/Alamy; **458:** Sylvain Sonnet/Getty Images; **480:** Mediaphotos/iStock/Thinkstock; **518:** Christian Lange Photography; **531:** Chris Whitehead/Getty Images; **540:** Ivelin Radkov/Shutterstock; **553:** Eco Images/UIG/AGE Fotostock; **569:** Paul Colangelo/Corbis; **580:** Johannes Simon/WireImage/Getty Images; **590:** Ljupco Smokovski/Shutterstock; **623:** Angela Hampton Picture Library/Alamy; **634:** James Henslin; **651 (t):** Weston Colton/Getty Images; **(b):** Diego Cervo/Fotolia; **656:** A. Karnholz/Fotolia; **659:** epa european pressphoto agency b.v./Alamy; **661:** The Virginian-Pilot/Steve Earley/AP Images; **666:** Lynda Richardson/Corbis; **675:** ReuseThisBag.

## Text Credits

### Chapter 1

**p. 6:** James M. Henslin, *Sociology: A Down-to-Earth Approach*, 11th ed., pp. 261–264, © 2012. Printed and electronically reproduced by permission of Pearson Education, Inc., Upper Saddle River, New Jersey; **p. 10:** April Lynch, Barry Elmore, and Tanya Morgan, *Choosing Health*, 1st ed., pp. 77–78, © 2012. Adapted and electronically reproduced by permission of Pearson Education, Inc., Upper Saddle River, New Jersey; **p. 14:** Mary Ann Schwartz and BarBara Marliene Scott, *Marriages and Families: Diversity and Change*, 7th ed. Upper Saddle River, NJ: Pearson, 2012, p. 212, **p. 20:** John D. Carl, *Think Social Problems*, 2010 Census Update. Upper Saddle River, NJ: Pearson Prentice Hall, 2012, p. 189.

### Chapter 2

**p. 30:** Brainstorming list. Reprinted by permission of Santiago Quintana Garcia; **p. 32:** Sample outline. Reprinted by permission of Santiago Quintana Garcia; **p. 34:** Les Rowntree, Martin Lewis, Marie Price, and William Wyckoff, *Diversity Amid Globalization: World Regions, Environment, Development*, 5th ed. Upper Saddle River, NJ: Pearson, 2012, p. 326; **p. 41:** First Draft of Santiago's Essay. Reprinted by permission of Santiago Quintana Garcia; **p. 43:** Revisions of paragraphs 3 and 4. Reprinted by permission of Santiago Quintana Garcia.

### Chapter 3

**p. 53:** Warren J. Keegan and Mark C. Green, *Global Marketing*, 7th ed. Upper Saddle River, NJ: Pearson Prentice Hall, 2013, p. 104; **p. 54:** James M. Rubenstein, *Contemporary Human Geography*, 2nd ed. Upper Saddle River, NJ: Pearson, 2013, p. 190; **p. 55:** Mark C. Carnes and John A. Garraty, *The American Nation: A History of the United States*, 11th ed. New York: Longman, 2003, p. 267; **p. 55:** Warren J. Keegan and Mark C. Green, *Global Marketing*, 7th ed. Upper Saddle River, NJ: Pearson Prentice Hall, 2013, p. 105; **p. 60:** Saundra K. Ciccarelli and J. Noland White, *Psychology*, 3rd ed. Upper Saddle River, NJ: Pearson Prentice Hall, 2012, p. 547; **p. 62:** Rebecca J. Donatelle, *Health: The Basics*, Green Edition, 9th ed. San Francisco: Pearson Benjamin Cummings, 2011, pp. 329–330; **p. 65:** Ronald J. Ebert and Ricky W. Griffin, *Business Essentials*, 8th ed. Upper Saddle River, NJ: Pearson Prentice Hall, 2011, p. 21.

### Chapter 4

**p. 74:** Joseph A. DeVito, *Human Communication: The Basic Course*, 12th ed. Upper Saddle River, NJ: Pearson Allyn & Bacon, 2012, p. 182; **p. 76:** R. Glenn Hubbard and Anthony Patrick O'Brien, *Essentials of Economics*, 3rd ed. Upper Saddle River, NJ: Pearson, 2013, p. 408; **p. 77:** Mark Krause and Daniel Corts, *Psychological Science: Modeling Scientific Literacy*. Upper Saddle River, NJ: Pearson, 2012, p. 569; **p. 77:** Mary Ann Schwartz and BarBara Marliene Scott, *Marriages and Families: Diversity and Change*, 7th ed. Upper Saddle River, NJ: Pearson, 2012, p. 211; **p. 77:** Norm Christensen, *The Environment and You*. San Francisco: Pearson Benjamin Cummings, 2013, p. 336; **p. 78:** John J. Macionis, *Society: The Basics*, 12th ed. Upper Saddle River, NJ: Pearson, 2013, p. 376; **p. 79:** Joseph A. DeVito, *Human Communication: The Basic Course*, 12th ed. Upper Saddle River, NJ: Pearson Allyn & Bacon, 2012, pp. 127–128; **p. 80:** Saundra K. Ciccarelli and J. Noland White, *Psychology*, 3rd ed. Upper Saddle River, NJ: Pearson Prentice Hall, 2012, p. 191; **p. 80:** Richard T. Wright and Dorothy O. Boorse, *Environmental Science: Toward a Sustainable Future*, 11th ed. San Francisco: Pearson Benjamin Cummings, p. 150; **p. 81:** James N. Danzinger, *Understanding the Political World: A Comparative Introduction to Political Science*, 11th ed. Upper Saddle River, NJ: Pearson, 2013, p. 320; **p. 81:** John D. Carl, *Think Sociology*, 1st ed. Upper Saddle River, NJ: Pearson Prentice Hall, 2010, p. 122; **p. 82:** Thomas F. Goldman and Henry R. Cheeseman, *The Paralegal Professional*, 3rd ed. Upper Saddle River, NJ: Pearson Prentice Hall, 2011, p. 459; **p. 82:** Suzanne G. Marshall, Hazel O. Jackson, and M. Sue Stanley, *Individuality in Clothing Selection and Personal Appearance*, 7th ed. Upper Saddle River, NJ: Pearson Prentice Hall, 2012. p. 293; **p. 82:** Ronald J. Ebert and Ricky W. Griffin, *Business Essentials*, 7th ed. Upper Saddle River, NJ: Pearson, 2009, p. 161; **p. 83:** Michael R. Solomon, *Consumer Behavior*, 10th ed., p. 21, © 2013. Adapted and electronically reproduced by permission of Pearson Education, Inc., Upper Saddle River, New Jersey; **p. 83:** Joan Salge Blake, *Nutrition and You: My Plate Edition*, 2nd ed. San Francisco: Pearson Benjamin Cummings, 2012, pp. 66–67; **p. 88:** Rebecca J. Donatelle, *My Health: An Outcomes Approach*. Upper Saddle River, NJ: Pearson, 2013, p. 122; **p. 88:** Hugh D. Barlow, *Criminal Justice in America*. Upper Saddle River, NJ: Pearson Prentice Hall, 2000, p. 238; **p. 88:** John W. Hill, Terry W. McCreary, and Doris K. Kolb, *Chemistry for Changing Times*, 13th ed. Upper Saddle River, NJ: Pearson Prentice Hall, 2013, p. 663; **p. 93:** John W. Hill, Terry W. McCreary, and Doris K. Kolb, *Chemistry for Changing Times*, 13th ed. Upper Saddle River, NJ: Pearson Prentice Hall, 2013, p. 644; **p. 94:** Michael R. Solomon, *Consumer Behavior*, 5th ed. Upper Saddle River, NJ: Pearson Prentice Hall, 2002, p. 184; **p. 95:** Joseph A. DeVito, *Messages: Building Interpersonal Communication Skills*, 5th ed. Boston: Pearson Allyn & Bacon, 2002, p. 290; **p. 96:** William E. Thompson and Joseph V. Hickey, *Society in Focus*, 7th ed. Boston: Pearson Allyn & Bacon, 2011, p. 216; **p. 96:** Henry M. Sayre, *Discovering the Humanities*, 2nd ed. Upper Saddle River, NJ: Pearson, 2013, pp. 490–491; **p. 97:** Rebecca J. Donatelle, *Health: The Basics*, 10th ed.

Upper Saddle River, NJ: Pearson, 2013, pp. 92–93; **p. 97:** Ronald J. Ebert and Ricky W. Griffin, *Business Essentials*, 7th ed. Upper Saddle River, NJ: Pearson Prentice Hall, 2009, p. 188; **p. 98:** Warren J. Keegan and Mark C. Green, *Global Marketing*, 7th ed. Upper Saddle River, NJ: Pearson, 2013, p. 192; **p. 99:** Nancy Bonvillain, *Cultural Anthropology*, 3rd ed. Upper Saddle River, NJ: Pearson, 2013, pp. 186–187.

## Chapter 6

**p. 136:** Sydney B. Newell, *Chemistry: An Introduction*. Boston: Little, Brown, 1980, p. 11; **p. 142:** Joseph A. DeVito, *Human Communication: The Basic Course*, 12th ed. Boston: Pearson, 2012, p. 106; **p. 143:** Daniel Limmer and Michael F. O'Keefe, *Emergency Care*, 12th ed. Upper Saddle River, NJ: Pearson Brady, 2012, pp. 211–212; **p. 145:** Colleen Belk and Virginia Borden Maier, *Biology: Science for Life with Physiology*, 4th ed. San Francisco: Pearson Benjamin Cummings, 2013, pp. 435–436; **p. 151:** Les Rowntree, Martin Lewis, Marie Price, and William Wyckoff, *Diversity Amid Globalization: World Regions, Environment, Development*, 5th ed. Upper Saddle River, NJ: Pearson, 2012, p. 26; **p. 152:** Barbara Miller, *Cultural Anthropology in a Globalizing World*, 3rd ed. Upper Saddle River, NJ: Pearson, 2011, pp. 275–276; **p. 153:** Rebecca J. Donatelle, *Health: The Basics*, Green Edition, 9th ed. San Francisco: Pearson Benjamin Cummings, 2011, p. 68; **p. 154:** Paragraph reprinted by permission of Ted Sawchuck; **p. 157:** David Krogh, *Biology: A Guide to the Natural World*, 4th ed. San Francisco: Pearson Benjamin Cummings, 2009, p. 429; **p. 158:** Gerard R. Tortora, *Introduction to the Human Body: The Essentials of Anatomy and Physiology*, 2nd ed. New York: HarperCollins College Publishers, 1991, p. 56; **p. 158:** James M. Henslin, *Sociology: A Down-to-Earth Approach*, 10th ed., pp. 109, 111, © 2010. Adapted and electronically reproduced by permission of Pearson Education, Inc., Upper Saddle River, New Jersey; **p. 161:** Alex Thio, *Sociology: A Brief Introduction*, 7th ed. Upper Saddle River, NJ: Pearson, 2009, p. 409; **p. 162:** April Lynch, Barry Elmore, and Tanya Morgan, *Choosing Health*, 1st ed., p. 92, © 2012. Adapted and electronically reproduced by permission of Pearson Education, Inc., Upper Saddle River, New Jersey; **p. 163:** Rebecca J. Donatelle, *Access to Health*, 12th ed., pp. 646–647, © 2012. Printed and electronically reproduced by permission of Pearson Education, Inc., Upper Saddle River, New Jersey; **p. 168:** James A. Fagin, *CJ2012*. Upper Saddle River, NJ: Pearson, 2013, p. 43; **p. 169:** Gary Armstrong and Philip Kotler, *Marketing: An Introduction*, 11th ed. Upper Saddle River, NJ: Pearson Prentice Hall, 2013, pp. 327–328; **p. 170:** Norm Christensen, *The Environment and You*. Upper Saddle River, NJ: Pearson, 2013, p. 86.

## Chapter 7

**p. 185:** Molly M. Ginty, "All Guts, No Glory," *Ms.* magazine, Fall 2011; **p. 186:** Molly M. Ginty, "All Guts, No Glory," *Ms.* magazine, Fall 2011; **p. 186:** Bruce Watson, "Innocent Until Proven a Pet 'Owner'." © Bruce Watson. Reprinted with permission of the author; **p. 191:** James M. Henslin, *Sociology: A Down-to-Earth Approach*, 10th ed., p. 317, © 2010. Printed and electronically reproduced by permission of Pearson Education, Inc., Upper Saddle River, New Jersey; **p. 192:** James M. Henslin, *Sociology: A Down-to-Earth Approach*, 10th ed., p. 39, © 2010. Printed and electronically reproduced by permission of Pearson Education, Inc., Upper Saddle River, New Jersey; **p. 193:** James M. Henslin, *Sociology: A Down-to-Earth Approach*, 10th ed., p. 39, © 2010. Printed and electronically reproduced by permission of Pearson Education, Inc., Upper Saddle River, New Jersey.

## Chapter 8

**p. 202:** Mary Ann Stuppes and Carolyn Cressey Wells, *The Social Work Experience: An Introduction to Social Work and Social Welfare*, 6th ed. Upper Saddle River, NJ: Pearson, 2013, p. 148; **p. 203:** Sandra Moriarty, Nancy D. Mitchell, and William D. Wells, *Advertising & IMC: Principles and Practice*, 9th ed. Upper Saddle River, NJ: Pearson, 2012, p. 405; **p. 204:** R. Glenn Hubbard and Anthony Patrick O'Brien, *Essentials of Economics*, 3rd ed. Upper Saddle River, NJ: Pearson, 2013, p. 371; **p. 205:** Sharon S. Brehm, Saul Kassin, and Steven Fein, *Social Psychology*, 6th ed. Boston: Houghton Mifflin, 2005, p. 189; **p. 208:** Barbara Miller, *Cultural Anthropology*, 8th ed. Upper Saddle River, NJ: Pearson, 2013, p. 166; **p. 209:** William E. Thompson and Joseph V. Hickey, *Society in Focus*, 7th ed., 2010 Census Update. Boston: Pearson Allyn & Bacon, 2012, p. 383; **p. 211:** Warren

J. Keegan and Mark C. Green, *Global Marketing*, 7th ed. Upper Saddle River, NJ: Pearson, 2013, pp. 202, 204; **p. 213:** Alex Thio, *Sociology: A Brief Introduction*, 5th ed. Boston: Pearson Allyn and Bacon, 2003, pp. 35–36.

## Chapter 9

**p. 223:** David Batstone, excerpt from "Katja's Story: Human Trafficking Thrives in the New Global Economy," *Sojourners Magazine*, June 2006. © 2006 David Batstone. Reprinted by permission of the author; **p. 226:** William E. Thompson and Joseph V. Hickey, *Society in Focus*, 7th ed., 2010 Census Update. Boston: Pearson Allyn & Bacon, 2012, p. 239; **p. 226:** Mary Ann Schwartz and BarBara Marliene Scott, *Marriages and Families: Diversity and Change*, 7th ed. Upper Saddle River, NJ: Pearson, 2012, p. 255; **p. 227:** James A. Fagin, *Criminal Justice*, 2nd ed. Upper Saddle River, NJ: Pearson, 2007, pp. 245–246; **p. 228:** Michael R. Solomon, *Consumer Behavior*, 10th ed., p. 23, © 2013. Printed and electronically reproduced by permission of Pearson Education, Inc., Upper Saddle River, New Jersey; **p. 229:** Robert L. Lineberry and George C. Edwards III, *Government in America: People, Politics, and Policy*, 4th ed. Glenview, IL: Scott Foresman, 1989, p. 540; **p. 230:** Rebecca J. Donatelle, *Access to Health*, 12th ed., p. 386, © 2012. Printed and electronically reproduced by permission of Pearson Education, Inc., Upper Saddle River, New Jersey; **p. 231:** William E. Thompson and Joseph V. Hickey, *Society in Focus*, 7th ed., 2010 Census Update. Boston: Pearson Allyn & Bacon, 2012, p 383; **p. 238:** John W. Hill, Terry W. McCreary, and Doris K. Kolb, *Chemistry for Changing Times*, 13th ed. Upper Saddle River, NJ: Pearson Prentice Hall, 2013, p. 634; **p. 239:** John W. Hill, Terry W. McCreary, and Doris K. Kolb, *Chemistry for Changing Times*, 13th ed. Upper Saddle River, NJ: Pearson, 2013, p. 671; **p. 239:** Norm Christensen, *The Environment and You*. Upper Saddle River, NJ: Pearson, 2013, pp. 463–464.

## Chapter 10

**p. 248:** John D. Carl, *Think Social Problems*, 1st ed. Boston: Pearson, 2011, pp. 71–72; **p. 253:** Mona Scott, *Think Race and Ethnicity*, 1st ed., p. 165, © 2012. Adapted and electronically reproduced by permission of Pearson Education, Inc., Upper Saddle River, New Jersey; **p. 256:** James M. Henslin, *Sociology: A Down-to-Earth Approach*, 11th ed., p. 403, © 2012. Adapted and electronically reproduced by permission of Pearson Education, Inc., Upper Saddle River, New Jersey; **p. 256:** John Mack Faragher, Mari Jo Buhle, Daniel Czitrom, and Susan H. Armitage, *Out of Many: A History of the American People*, 7th ed. Upper Saddle River, NJ: Pearson, 2010, p. 928; **p. 263:** William E. Thompson and Joseph V. Hickey, *Society in Focus*, 7th ed. Boston: Pearson Allyn & Bacon, 2011, pp. 328–329; **p. 268:** Quinne Sember, "Marijuana: An Argument for Legalization." Reprinted by permission of the author.

## Chapter 11

**p. 276:** Sample Student Brainstorming. Reprinted by permission of Ted Sawchuck; **p. 278:** Diagram and Sample Student Freewriting. Reprinted by permission of Ted Sawchuck; **p. 288:** Sample Topic Sentences for an Essay. Reprinted by permission of Ted Sawchuck; **p. 291:** Sample First Draft Essay. Reprinted by permission of Ted Sawchuck; **p. 305:** Ted Sawchuck, "Relationships  2.0: Dating and Relating in the Internet Age." Reprinted by permission of Ted Sawchuck; **p. 310:** Tim Curry, Robert Jiobu, and Kent Schwirian, *Sociology for the Twenty-First Century*, 3rd ed. Upper Saddle River, NJ: Prentice Hall, 2002, p. 207; **p. 312:** Sharon S. Brehm, Saul Kassin, and Steven Fein, *Social Psychology*, 6th ed. Boston: Houghton Mifflin, 2005; **p. 312:** Richard L. Weaver II, *Understanding Interpersonal Communication*, 7th ed. New York: HarperCollins College Publishers, 1996, p. 131; **p. 313:** Gerald Audesirk, Teresa Audesirk, and Bruce E. Byers, *Life on Earth*, 5th ed. San Francisco: Pearson Benjamin Cummings, 2009, pp. 249–251; **p. 314:** Sierra Club Web site, August 16, 1999.

## Chapter 12

**p. 329:** Santiago Quintana, "The Space In-Between." Reprinted by permission of the author; **p. 339:** Rebecca J. Donatelle, *Access to Health*, 12th ed., pp. 280–283, © 2012. Printed and electronically reproduced by permission of Pearson Education, Inc., Upper Saddle River, New Jersey; **p. 341:** Smiley, King, and Avey, from "Eating Issues and Body Image Continuum," The University of Arizona Campus Health Service (1997). Copyright Arizona Board of Regents for the University of Arizona.

Reprinted with permission; **p. 354:** Molly M. Ginty, "Military Women: All Guts, No Glory," *Ms.* magazine, Fall 2011. As appeared in *Utne Reader*, March/April 2012. Reprinted by permission of *Ms.* magazine, © 2011.

## Chapter 13

**p. 369:** Christopher Ketcham, "Warning: High Frequency," *Earth Island Journal*, Winter 2012. As appeared in *Utne Reader*, May/June 2012, titled "Wireless Interference: The Health Risks of RF-EMFs." Reprinted by permission of Earth Island Journal. www.earthislandjournal.org; **p. 380:** Christian Parenti, "Crisis Management: Why Climate Change Will Make You Love Big Government," TomDispatch.com, January 26, 2012. © 2012 Christian Parenti. Reprinted by permission of the author; **p. 393:** Jay Withgott and Scott Brennan, *Environment: The Science Behind the Stories*, 4th ed., pp. 666–667, 669–677, © 2011. Adapted and electronically reproduced by permission of Pearson Education, Inc., Upper Saddle River, New Jersey.

## Chapter 14

**p. 415:** Jenifer Kunz, *Think Marriages and Families*, 1st ed., pp. 83–84, © 2011. Printed and electronically reproduced by permission of Pearson Education, Inc., Upper Saddle River, New Jersey; **p. 426:** Hara Estroff Marano, "The High Art of Handling Problem People." Reprinted with permission from *Psychology Today* Magazine, (Copyright © 2012 Sussex Publishers, LLC.); **p. 441:** Jessica Lee, "The Many Ways Virtual Communities Impact Our World Offline," BruceClay.com, February 7, 2012. © 2012 by Bruce Clay, Inc. Reprinted by permission.

## Chapter 15

**p. 457:** Carole Wade and Carol Tavris, *Invitation to Psychology*, 5th ed., pp. 139–140, © 2012. Adapted and electronically reproduced by permission of Pearson Education, Inc., Upper Saddle River, New Jersey; **p. 480:** "Xeno-Transplantation: The Ultimate Organ Factory," *Trends Magazine*, August 2011. Reprinted by permission of AudioTech, Inc.

## Chapter 16

**p. 494:** Catherine LeBerta, *Computers Are Your Future*, 12th ed., pp. 423–426, © 2012. Printed and electronically reproduced by permission of Pearson Education, Inc., Upper Saddle River, New Jersey; **p. 506:** Shelley D. Lane, Ruth Anna Abigail, and John Casey Gooch, *Communication in a Civil Society*, 1st ed., pp. 15, 117, 53, 238, © 2014. Printed and electronically reproduced by permission of Pearson Education, Inc., Upper Saddle River, New Jersey; **p. 517:** John Vivian, *The Media of Mass Communication*, 9th ed., pp. 246–250, © 2009. Printed and electronically reproduced by permission of Pearson Education, Inc., Upper Saddle River, New Jersey.

## Chapter 17

**p. 530:** Emma Teitel, "Bullying 2.0 Is More Like Drama Class," *Maclean's*, October 17, 2011, p. 13. © 2011 Rogers Media. Reprinted by permission of Maclean's; **p. 540:** Meredith Nudo, "Ten Proven Brain

Benefits of Being Bilingual," BestCollegesOnline.com, April 2, 2012. © 2012 BestCollegesOnline.com. Reprinted by permission; **p. 551:** Mona Scott, *Think Race and Ethnicity*, 1st ed., pp. 163–167, © 2012. Printed and electronically reproduced by permission of Pearson Education, Inc., Upper Saddle River, New Jersey.

## Chapter 18

**p. 569:** Ashley Womble, "A Brother Lost," as it appears in *Utne Reader*, excerpted from the original article "The Homeless Brother I Cannot Save," Salon.com, July 27, 2010. This article first appeared in Salon.com, at http://www.Salon.com. An online version remains in the Salon archives. Reprinted by permission; **p. 580:** Sabatina James, as told to Abigail Pesta, "Why My Mother Wants Me Dead." From *Newsweek*, March 5, 2012. © 2012 The Newsweek/Daily Beast Company LLC. All rights reserved. Used by permission and protected by the Copyright Laws of the United States. The printing, copying, redistribution, or retransmission of this Content without express written permission is prohibited. www.newsweek.com; **p. 590:** Michael R. Solomon, *Consumer Behavior*, 10th ed., pp. 405–407, 409–415, © 2013. Printed and electronically reproduced by permission of Pearson Education, Inc., Upper Saddle River, New Jersey.

## Chapter 19

**p. 623:** Yashar Ali, "I Don't Want to Have Kids. Get Over It," the current conscience, February 27, 2012. © 2012 the current conscience. Reprinted with permission; **p. 634:** James M. Henslin, *Sociology: A Down-to-Earth Approach*, 11th ed., pp. 502–505, © 2012. Adapted and electronically reproduced by permission of Pearson Education, Inc., Upper Saddle River, New Jersey.

## Part Three

**p. 660:** Orrin H. Pilkey, "We Need to Retreat from the Beach." From *The New York Times*, November 15, 2012, p. A35. © 2012 The New York Times. All rights reserved. Used by permission and protected by the Copyright Laws of the United States. The printing, copying, redistribution, or retransmission of this Content without express written permission is prohibited. www.nytimes.com; **p. 663:** John Hayward, "The Debunking of Global Warming Continues," *Human Events*, July 30, 2012. Reprinted by permission of Human Events; **p. 665:** Jay Withgott and Scott Brennan, *Environment: The Science Behind the Stories*, 4th ed., pp. 58–61. © 2011. Printed and electronically reproduced by permission of Pearson Education, Inc., Upper Saddle River, New Jersey; **p. 668:** Steven Hamburg, "Hot Topic: Climate Change and Our Extreme Weather," http://blogs.edf.org, July 13, 2012. Reprinted by permission of the Environmental Defense Fund; **p. 670:** Chris MacDonald, "Storms, Global Warming, and Corporate Citizenship," *The Business Ethics Blog*, November 2, 2012. Reprinted by permission of Chris MacDonald; **p. 672:** Jeremy Hsu, "Climate Change: Countries That May Be Hit Hardest." © 2012 InnovationNewsDaily, a TechMediaNetwork company. Published at HuffingtonPost.com, August 14, 2012. Reprinted by permission of TechMediaNetwork.

# Index